BUSINESS SERVICES AND INFORMATION

The Guide to the Federal Government

Management Information Exchange, Inc.

Editors

TIMOTHY C. WECKESSER

JOSEPH R. WHALEY

MIRIAM WHALEY

A WILEY-INTERSCIENCE PUBLICATION

JOHN WILEY & SONS, NEW YORK · CHICHESTER · BRISBANE · TORONTO

Library of Congress Catalog Card No. 78-65641
ISBN 0-471-05366-X

Although great care has been taken in the research, writing, editing, and production of this book, no liability is assumed by author or publisher for any error or omission. Prices and information stated are derived from information provided by research sources and are subject to change without notice.

Printed in U.S.A.

3 4 5 6 7 8 9 10

PREFACE

The United States Government is, to many business executives, a vast uncharted territory. As with the mariners' maps of old, much of it might as well be marked "here be dragons"—and, of course, there really are some fearsome (and expensive) dragons such as the Internal Revenue Service (IRS), Occupational Safety and Health Administration (OSHA), and a host of specialized regulatory agencies. It appears, however, that few businesses are aware of the many ways in which the Federal Government can help.

Once aware of them, businesses can profit from a vast array of government services, data sources, assistance programs, facilities, and publications. Every day the Federal Government gathers and disseminates information on a remarkably wide range of subjects important to business by using media ranging from newsletters to computerized data bases. Technical assistance programs, information and research centers, and counseling services can directly benefit business by increasing profitability and productivity. Financial aid is available to more firms than may realize it.

Business Services and Information: The Guide to the Federal Government (BSI) serves business executives by helping them to discover every potentially valuable resource, whether it be for solving problems or for generating new opportunities and money-making ideas. BSI should be useful to top management, marketing departments seeking data, research and development divisions that need the latest technical data and reports, business service groups, management consultants, new businesses and entrepreneurs, personnel managers, educators, and minority business executives.

BSI was designed to be easy to use. Each of the hundreds of annotations includes a clear description of the resource and full instructions on how to gain direct access to it. Included are nationwide addresses and direct-dial telephone numbers to call for immediate assistance from exactly the right office. BSI is organized by business topic or problem area rather than by agency. All resources relevant to a particular business topic are found in one place, regardless of the agencies from which they are available.

A new user of BSI should first take a moment to read the chapter titles and then browse through the Finder's Guide that begins on page 9. A concise introduction (pages 3 to 6) explains how to use BSI and how to obtain publications and services. It also includes advice from the editors. A table of addresses and telephone numbers begins on page 313 and the Index begins on page 375.

BSI is based on a comprehensive research effort. All standard government reference sources were consulted, and the entire output of the Government Printing Office was reviewed for relevant publications. All unclassified research centers were analyzed, and direct contacts were made with hundreds of offices. Although errors and omissions are inevitable in a project of this scope, a vigorous effort has been made to make BSI complete, accurate, and comprehensive. Readers are requested to advise of any errors, omissions, or suggestions by writing to Management Information Exchange, Inc., P.O. Box 1894, Rockville, MD 20850.

Laws and regulations are beyond the scope of BSI, but full coverage is given to assistance available in the vital areas of affirmative action, occupational safety and health, energy, and the environment. BSI concentrates on services relevant to business in general and does not attempt to cover the numerous specialized regulatory agencies.

BSI was researched, written, and edited by three individuals for Management Information Exchange, Inc. Timothy C. Weckesser has had extensive experience as a management consultant and is a Ph.D. candidate at the New School for Social Research in New York. Joseph R. Whaley holds a Juris Doctor degree from the Columbus School of Law, Catholic University of America in Washington D.C., and has had experience in the public and private sector both in the United States and abroad. Miriam Whaley has a B.A. in psychology from the University of Colorado and is a member of Phi Beta Kappa and Sigma Xi. BSI is published with the cooperation of John Wiley & Sons, Inc., and subsequent editions are planned.

Management Information Exchange, Inc.

TIMOTHY C. WECKESSER
JOSEPH R. WHALEY
MIRIAM WHALEY

Rockville, Maryland
September 1978

TABLE OF CONTENTS

PART A

Introduction

Understanding the Guide

A1.0 Purpose of the *Guide*

The purpose of this *Guide* is to provide business administrators and business service organizations of all kinds with easy access to the vast array of information and services offered to them by the federal government.

Every day, the government assembles and disseminates information on a remarkably wide range of subjects relevant to the world of business. Much of this information is available in low-cost or free publications; much of it is available on computerized data bases. Bulletins and newsletters describing the latest research and trends in areas relevant to business are published regularly. Special programs, information centers, and counseling services can directly benefit business by helping to cut costs and increase productivity. The *Guide* makes it possible for the manager or executive to identify, precisely and quickly, the exact resource which will be of the most value.

To accomplish this, the information has been organized by business subject area rather than by government agency; in general, the chapters correspond to developmental stages and various activities of business. Within the chapters, the descriptions of the various publications and services include a reference to an address and a direct-dial telephone number to call for immediate assistance.

No attempt has been made to treat every office that administers every law in government, or regulations dealing with a relatively small segment of the business population; that is beyond the scope of the *Guide*. Rather, the purpose is to deal with services useful to business in general.

A1.1 How to Use the *Guide*

Every distinct service or information source (item) has been assigned an item number. These numbers form the basic identification tool of the book.

The number preceding the decimal point indicates the chapter in which the item occurs. The number after the decimal point refers to the sequence number of the item within the chapter. Thus, 8.165 refers to Item No. 165 in Chapter 8.

The *Guide* has four parts. Part A is introductory. Part B contains all the annotations of items; no letter precedes these numbers, as it does in Parts A and C. Part C, the Appendix, contains agency addresses and telephone numbers (C1), and a discussion of the use of census data by business (C2). (A reference such as "see C1.150" means: Part C, first section, Item No. 150 in the sequence.) Part D is the Index.

If the service or information referred to in a given item is available from one primary source, the full address and, where possible, telephone number will appear at the end of the item. Otherwise, each item will close with a reference to the Appendix for national or field offices of the appropriate agency.

A1.2 Finder's Tools

There are two basic finder's tools in the *Guide:* (1) the Detailed Summary of Part B (the Finder's Guide), taken with the Table of Contents, and (2) the Index.

The Table of Contents allows the reader to gain a quick overview of the information available on the subject in question. Having determined which chapter is of interest, the reader can then look at the corresponding section of the Detailed Summary of Part B, the Finder's Guide. This constitutes a complete summary of what is in the *Guide*; every item is listed there by its number and title. In the text, the item numbers of items appearing on a given page are indicated prominently at the top of the page for the reader's easy reference.

To obtain help with a specific problem or to locate a specific service or source of information, the reader may consult the Index. A reader who knows the desired agency but not its address or telephone number may obtain that information in Appendix C1.

Dealing with the Government

A2.0 Access to Government Resources

According to the Small Business Administration (SBA) definition of small business, 97 percent of all businesses in the country fall into that category. Such businesses may range in size from one or two employees up to 1,500.

For both small and large businesses, the *Guide* is a versatile tool for taking advantage of the widespread and profitable services and information available from the federal government.

In addition, there are some further steps the enterprising business administrator can take to gain a sound orientation to the range and use of government resources:

—Peruse the publications displays at a GPO bookstore (see C1.0), a Department of Commerce district office (see C1.10), or an SBA field office (see C1.110).
—Become familiar with the major information storage systems, covering virtually every field imaginable, annotated in Chapter 9.
—Subscribe to the *GPO Monthly Catalog* and/or the *Selected United States Government Publications* (see 4.101).
—Visit an SBA or Department of Commerce district office and discuss specific questions or problems.

The federal bureaucracy is large, complicated, highly structured, and unwieldy. As a result, the government sometimes suffers from problems of communication. However, there are many highly dedicated, knowledgeable civil servants who are fully aware of their responsibility to the public and eager to be of help.

The information contained in this *Guide* was freely given in a spirit of cooperation. Usually, government departments and agencies are eager to let the public know of their missions and functions; however, most of them lack funds for widespread publicity. Hence, as a rule, the main obstacle for a business is to discover, first, that a given service exists, and then to find out how to obtain it. That is the function of this *Guide*.

However, if difficulty is encountered in obtaining information which is not otherwise restricted, the reader may consider filing a request pursuant to the Freedom of Information Act. The Act is designed to assure the release of information by the government, with certain narrow exceptions. Virtually all agencies of the executive branch of the federal government have issued regulations to implement the Freedom of Information Act and can give directions on how to proceed.

A2.1 How to Order Publications

Most of the publications annotated in the *Guide* are available either through the Government Printing Office (GPO) or the National Technical Information Service (NTIS).

To order from GPO:

While GPO has branch offices nationwide (see C1.0), orders are usually placed by writing one of the following addresses:

Superintendent of Documents
U.S. Government Printing Office
Washington, DC 20402

Public Documents Distribution Center
Pueblo, CO 81009

Including the proper order number will expedite the order. All publications are sold at cost, and prices are subject to change without notice. Return of publications for exchange or credit is not accepted unless an error was made by GPO. There is a minimum charge of $1.00 for each mail order. Checks or money orders should be made payable to the Superintendent of Documents. Payment in advance is required. A discount of 25 percent is allowed on purchases of 100 or more copies of a single publication. Foreign purchasers should add 25 percent to purchase prices.

To order from NTIS;

Because NTIS (see C1.17) must recover its costs from sales, it operates essentially as a business. For example, NTIS offers:

(1) *Rush Handling Service*. For a $10.00 charge per item, an order will be airmailed within 48 hours. 702-557-4700.

(2) *Telex*. 89-9405

(3) *Telecopier or 3-M Facsimile Service*. 703-321-8547, 202-724-3378.

(4) *Pick-Up Service*. For a $6.00 charge per item, an order may be picked up within 24 hours at the NTIS Washington Information Center and Bookstore, 425 13th Street N.W., Washington, DC 20003; 202-724-3382, 3383, 3509. Or it can be picked up at NTIS Operations Center, 5285 Port Royal Road, Springfield, VA 22161; 703-557-4650.

(5) *Information*. 202-724-3382, 3383, 3509.

(6) *Order Follow-up*. 703-557-4660.

(7) *Telephone Orders for Documents and Reports*. 703-557-4650.

(8) *Subscriptions*. 703-557-4630.

(9) *Selected Research in Microfiche (SRIM)*. 703-557-4630.

(10) *NTISearches and On-Line Searches*. 703-557-4642.

(11) *Customer Accounts*. 703-557-4770.

(12) *Airmail Delivery*. $2.00 surcharge per item ($3.00 for airmail delivery outside North America).

(13) *Computer Products*. 703-557-4763.

An NTIS Deposit Account is necessary for some services of NTIS, and very convenient for others. Repeat customers find it particularly useful. It can be set up with a minimum deposit of $25.00, although some special services require more. Details are available upon request, in a brochure, #NTIS-PR-33.

Prepayment helps to expedite orders and can be accomplished through the use of an NTIS Deposit Account, check, money order, or American Express account number. For ship and bill orders, NTIS charges $5.00 extra for each order (regardless of the number of items), $5.00 extra for each Published or On-Line NTISearch, and $2.50 for each subscription. NTIS does not ship and bill for magnetic tapes or for orders outside North America.

Checks should be made payable to the National Technical Information Service.

Foreign prices are usually higher; request current price information from NTIS.

All NTIS prices are subject to change without notice. A catalog of current publications and price code list is available upon request.

Editors' Highlights: Basic Services and Information

A3.0 Directories to Government Resources

United States Government Manual

The *Manual* is the official handbook of the federal government. It describes the organization, purpose, and programs of most government agencies and lists top personnel. Briefer statements are included for quasi-official agencies and certain international organizations.

#022-003-00917, $6.50; GPO (see C1.0).

Catalog of Federal Domestic Assistance (see 9.206)

Directory of Federal Technology Transfer (see 9.205)

A Directory of Information Resources in the United States: Federal Government (see 9.201)

A3.1 Key Services

Department of Commerce Business Counseling (see 7.200)

Trade Opportunities Program (see 7.100)

Economic Development Administration Technical and Financial Assistance (see 1.400, 1.401)

Employee Recruitment Services (see 5.500-5.505, 5.600)

Employee Testing Services (see 5.550-5.554)

Job Analysis Services (5.650-5.668)

Technical Data Center of Occupational Safety and Health Administration (see 6.557)

Educational Courses sponsored by National Institute for Occupational Safety and Health (NIOSH) (see 6.516)

NIOSH Current Intelligence Services (see 6.551)

NIOSH On-Site Assistance (see 6.450)

Small Business Administration and Department of Agriculture Loans (see 2.0-2.60

Crime, Flood, and Riot Insurance (see 2.202-2.204)

Small Business Institute Program (see 1.551)

Service Corps of Retired Executives/Active Corps of Executives (see 1.550)

General Services Administration Business Counseling (see 6.450)

Unsolicited Research and Development Proposals (see 3.302-3.304, 3.307)

Mineral Exploration Loans (see 1.53)

Mineral Lands Leasing (see 1.203)

Royalty-Free Patents (see 1.55-1.60)

Soil Surveys (see 1.354)

Water Resources Planning (see 1.351)

Energy Utilization in Site Location (see 1.357)

Technical Assistance from the Federal Mediation and Conciliation Service (see 5.155, 5.156)

A3.2 Key Information Centers

Government Printing Office (see A2.1, C1.0)

National Technical Information Service (see A2.1, 9.0-9.121)

Office of the Ombudsman for Business (see 4.61)

Federal Information Centers (see 9.122)

Industrial Applications Centers (see 9.20-9.21)

National Audio-Visual Center (see 4.500)

National Referral Center (see 9.40)

National Center for Productivity and Quality of Working Life (see 4.700)

National Energy Information Center (see 8.57)

United States International Environmental Referral Center (see 8.507)

A3.3 Basic Current Awareness Services

The Federal Register (see 9.100)
Selected United States Government Publications (see 4.101)
Monthly Catalog of United States Government Publications (see 4.101)
Business Service Checklist (see 4.101)
Data User News (see 3.53)
Commerce America (see 7.53)
Weekly Government Abstracts (see 9.11)
Commerce Business Daily (see 3.251)
Bureau of Labor Statistics Mailing Lists on Labor Relations (see 5.2)
Monthly Labor Review (see 5.0)
Government Reports Announcements and Index (see 9.13)

A3.4 Statistics

Bureau of the Census Catalog (see 3.54)
Bureau of the Census Guide to Programs and Publications (see 3.55)
Major Programs 1976, Bureau of Labor Statistics (see 3.62)
Directory of Federal Statistics for Local Areas (see 3.50)
Statistical Abstract of the United States (see 3.100)
U.S. Industrial Outlook (see 4.300)
Survey of Current Business (see 4.309)
County Business Patterns (see 3.101)
County and City Data Book (see 3.103)
Status, A Chartbook on Prices, Wages and Productivity (see 4.101)

A3.5 A Basic Business Library

Measuring Markets—A Guide to the Use of Federal and State Statistical Data (see 3.0)
Business Packaging (see 1.503)
Handbook for Analyzing Jobs (see 5.660)
Handbook for Job Restructuring (see 5.659)
Guide to Resources for Equal Employment Opportunity and Affirmative Action (see 6.1)
A Directory of Resources for Affirmative Recruitment (see 6.200)
United States Government Purchasing and Sales Directory (see 3.250)
Pensions and Pension Plans, Selected References (see 5.456)
Job Analysis for Human Resources Management—A Review of Selected Research and Development (see 5.651)
Occupational Safety and Health, A Bibliography (see 6.357)
A Basic Guide to Exporting (see 7.1)
A Guide to Voluntary Compliance (OSHA) (see 6.504)
Energy Conservation Program Guide for Industry and Commerce (see 8.0)
Franchise Opportunities Handbook (see 1.5)
Starting and Managing a Small Business of Your Own (see 1.502)
Handbook on Small Business Finance (see 1.750)
Tax Guide for Small Business (2.154)
A look at Business in 1990 (see 4.102)
Recent Initiatives in Labor-Management Cooperation (see 5.153)
Directory for Reaching Minority Groups (see 6.205)
Job Satisfaction: Is There a Trend? (see 5.653)
Improving Productivity, A Description of Selected Company Programs (see 5.703)
A Plant-Wide Productivity Plan in Action (see 5.704)
Occupational Alcoholism, Some Problems and Some Solutions (see 5.802)
Productivity and Technical Innovation, Selected Information Sources (see 5.702)
Publications for American Business from the Domestic and International Business Administration (see 7.5)
Occupational Outlook Handbook (see 5.59)

PART B

Government Services
and
Information for Business

DETAILED SUMMARY: FINDER'S GUIDE

Chapter 1

STARTING A BUSINESS: OPPORTUNITIES, SITE SELECTION, MANAGEMENT

Reference Guides to Demographic Data (1.250-(1.255)

1.250 *Bureau of the Census Catalog*
1.251 *Bureau of the Census Guide to Programs and Publications: Subjects and Areas*
1.252 *1970 Census Users' Guide*
1.253 *Mini-Guide to the 1972 Economic Census*
1.254 *Data User News*
1.255 *Major Programs 1976: Bureau of Labor Statistics*

Specific Location Data (1.300-1.307)

1.300 *Statistical Abstract of the United States*
1.301 *County Business Patterns*
1.302 *County and City Data Book*
1.303 Neighborhood Population and Housing Data
1.304 County-Level Socioeconomic Data Base
1.305 Census of Business
1.306 *National Travel, the 1972 Census of Transportation*
1.307 Census of Agriculture: Area Reports

Physical Resources and Energy Information (1.350-1.358)

1.350 Water Resources Studies
1.351 Water Resources Planning
1.352 Snow Survey and Water Supply Forecasting
1.353 Typographic Surveys and Mapping
1.354 Soil Surveys
1.355 Land Information and Analysis Office
1.356 *NASA Earth Resources Survey Program*
1.357 Energy Utilization Assistance in Site Selection
1.358 National Weather Service

Financial and Technical Assistance (1.400-1.405)

1.400 Financial Incentives in Site Selection
1.401 Office of Technical Assistance
1.402 Economic Injury Loans
1.403 *Loans to Local Development Companies*
1.404 Pool Loans for Facility Construction
1.405 Lease Guarantee Program

Management Assistance for New Business (1.500-1.661)

Starting a Business (1.500-1.505)

1.500 *Choosing a Form of Business Organization*
1.501 Free Publications on Business Start-Up
1.502 *Starting and Managing a Small Business of Your Own*
1.503 Business Planning
1.504 Free Publications on Management
1.505 Bibliography on Management

Comprehensive Advisory Services and Training (1.550-1.556)

1.550 Service Corps of Retired Executives and Active Corps of Executives
1.551 Small Business Institute Program
1.552 University Business Development Centers
1.553 Management Training, Seminars, and Workshops
1.554 Management Assistance through Professional and Trade Associations
1.555 Graduate School of the Department of Labor
1.556 Business Counseling Service

Management Aids (1.600-1.609)

1.600 Free Publications on Personnel Management
1.601 Bibliography on Personnel Management
1.602 Buying Surplus Government Property to Obtain Supplies
1.603 *How to Buy Surplus Personal Property from the Department of Defense*
1.604 *Arranging Transportation for Small Shipments*
1.605 Free Publications on Crime Prevention in Business
1.606 Free Publications on Environmental Protection
1.607 Small Business Administration *Annual Report*
1.608 Assistance to Private Forest Owners

1.609 Films on Business Management

Marketing and Sales Assistance (1.650-1.661)

1.650 *Measuring Markets—A Guide to the Use of Federal and State Statistical Data*
1.651 *Practical Business Use of Government Statistics*
1.652 *Selecting Advertising Media—A Guide for Small Business*
1.653 *Training Salesmen to Serve Industrial Markets*
1.654 Free Publications on Marketing and Sales
1.655 Free Publications on Government Procurement
1.656 Government Research and Development Opportunities for Small Firms
1.657 *Selling to the U.S. Government*
1.658 *Commerce Business Daily*
1.659 *Small Business Marketing to the Department of Defense*
1.660 Defense Contracting Emphasis in Labor Surplus Areas
1.661 *Small Business and Labor Surplus Area Specialists*

Financing, Taxes, and Insurance (1.700-1.761)

Grant, Loan, and Guarantee Programs (1.700-1.710)

1.700 Definition of Small Business for Small Business Administration (SBA) Loan Purposes
1.701 Grants to Help Develop Private Business
1.702 *SBA Business Loans*
1.703 Economic Injury Loans
1.704 Property Improvement Loans
1.705 Economic Opportunity Loan Program
1.706 Small Business Investment Company (SBIC) Financing
1.707 SBIC Management Assistance for Small Business
1.708 Minority Enterprise Small Business Inestment Company
1.709 Industrial and Commercial Property Lease Guarantee Program
1.710 Business Loans for Farmers

Financial Management Aids (1.750-1.761)

1.750 *Handbook of Small Business Finance*
1.751 *Financial Recordkeeping for Small Stores*
1.752 *Cash Planning in Small Manufacturing Companies*
1.753 *Financial Control by Time-Absorption Analysis*
1.754 *Insurance and Risk Management for Small Business*
1.755 *Cost Accounting for Small Manufacturers*
1.756 Free Publications on Financial Management
1.757 *Financing New Technological Enterprise*
1.758 Tax Information and Education
1.759 *Tax Guide for Small Business*
1.760 Business Tax Kit
1.761 Tax Publications List

Chapter 2

MONEY AND FINANCIAL MANAGEMENT

Chapter Abstract

Financial Assistance Programs (2.0-2.60)

Loan and Grant Programs and Financing Sources (2.0-2.19)

2.0 Definition of Small Business for Small Business Administration (SBA) Loan Purpose
2.1 *SBA Business Loans*
2.2 *SBA Disaster Loans*
2.3 Economic Injury Loans
2.4 Pool Loans for Business Development
2.5 Occupational Safety and Health Administration Compliance Loans
2.6 Loans and Guarantees from the Economic Development Administration
2.7 Housing Production Loans and Mortgage Insurance
2.8 Property Improvement Loans
2.9 Minerals Discovery Loan Program
2.10 Economic Opportunity Loan Program

Chapter 3

MARKET RESEARCH, MARKETING, GOVERNMENT PROCUREMENT

5.406 Statistical Studies in Wages and Industrial Relations
5.407 *A Directory of BLS Studies in Employee Compensation, 1960-1975*
5.408 *Publications on Equal Pay*
5.409 *Directory of Wage Chronologies, 1948-June 1975*

Pensions and Benefits (5.450-5.464)

5.450 Employee Retirement Income Security Act of 1974 (ERISA)
5.451 *ERISA Guidelines*
5.452 Introductory Publications on ERISA
5.453 ERISA Technical Information
5.454 ERISA Technical Releases and Interpretive Bulletins
5.455 *A Directory of BLS Studies in Employee Compensation, 1960-1975*
5.456 *Pensions and Pension Plans, Selected References 1971-1974*
5.457 Publications on Pension Administration
5.458 Employee Stock Ownershp Plan (ESOP)
5.459 *Broadening the Ownership of New Capital: ESOP's and Other Alternatives*
5.460 Advisory Opinions on Pension and Welfare Benefit Programs
5.461 *Benefit Series Service—Unemployment Insurance*
5.462 Technical Assistance in Unemployment Insurance
5.463 *Comparison of State Unemployment Insurance Laws*
5.464 Publications on Retirement

Equal Employment Opportunity Planning (5.500-5.608)

Recruitment (5.500-5.507)

5.500 A No-Fee Recruitment Source: State Employment Service
5.501 Staffing Services for New Plants
5.502 Tax Credit and Training Reimbursement: Work Incentive Program
5.503 *Directory for Reaching Minority Groups*
5.504 Recruitment of Veterans
5.505 Assistance from the National Alliance of Businessmen
5.506 Job Service Improvement Program
5.507 Demonstration Project to Create Jobs

Testing and Counseling (5.550-5.555)

5.550 Testing Tools Used by Employment Service Counselors
5.551 Research in Employment Service Testing Program
5.552 *Preemployment Inquiries and Equal Employment Opportunity Law*
5.553 Publications on Equal Employment Opportunity (EEO) Testing
5.554 *Questions and Answers on the OFCC Testing and Selection Order*
5.555 Publications on EEO Counseling

Training (5.600-5.608)

5.600 Comprehensive Employment and Training Act of 1973
5.601 National On-The-Job Training Program
5.602 Vocational Education and On-The-Job Training
5.603 Technical Assistance with Apprenticeship and Training
5.604 *Model for Training the Disadvantaged: TAT (Training and Technology) at Oak Ridge, Tennessee*
5.605 Publications on Training
5.606 Work Experience at Facilities of Energy Research and Development Administration
5.607 Graduate School of the Department of Agriculture
5.608 Cooperative Extension Service

Productivity and Human Resources Management (5.650-5.756)

Job Analysis and Restructuring (5.650-5.668)

5.650 Occupational Analysis Services
5.651 *Job Analysis for Human Resource Management: A Review of Selected Research and Development*
5.652 Publications on Job Analysis
5.653 *Job Satisfaction: Is There a Trend?*
5.654 *Developing Your Manpower*
5.655 *Dictionary of Occupational Titles*
5.656 *Selected Characteristics of Occupa-*

Chapter 6

AFFIRMATIVE ACTION, OSHA, AND PRODUCT SAFETY

6.452 On-Site Consultation Provided by State Agencies
6.453 OSHA National Emphasis Program
6.454 NIOSH Occupational Health Programs

Training (6.500-6.517)

6.500 Information on Training Programs
6.501 *Training Requirements of OSHA Standards*
6.502 *Directory of Training and Education Resources in Occupational Safety and Health*
6.503 *The Industrial Environment—Its Evaluation and Control*
6.504 *A Guide to Voluntary Compliance*
6.505 *Principles and Practices of Occupational Safety and Health*
6.506 *Employer-Employee Rights and Responsibilities*
6.507 *Safety and Health in Excavation and Trenching Operations*
6.508 *Construction Safety and Health Training*
6.509 *An Audio Aid on OSHA Recordkeeping*
6.510 *Sloping, Shoring, and Shielding*
6.511 *OSHA Safety and Health Training Guidelines for General Industry*
6.512 *OSHA Safety and Health Training Guidelines for Construction*
6.513 *OSHA Safety and Health Training Guidelines for Maritime Operations*
6.514 NIOSH Training for Small Business
6.515 OSHA Training Institute Instructor's Courses
6.516 NIOSH-Sponsored College and University Courses
6.517 Job Safety and Health Training Programs

Data Bases and Research Information Sources (6.550-6.560)

6.550 NIOSH Applied Research
6.551 Current Intelligence System
6.552 Illness and Injury Surveillance
6.553 Industry Hazard Trends
6.554 NIOSH Technical Information Services
6.555 National Technical Information Service (NTIS) Published Searches
6.556 *NIOSH Reports Available from NTIS*
6.557 OSHA Technical Data Center
6.558 Health Impact of Psychological Job Stress
6.559 Human Elements in Work Accidents
6.560 Center for Fire Research

Data on Specific Hazards (6.600-6.613)

6.600 Proficiency Analytical Testing Program of NIOSH
6.601 Product Criteria Documents
6.602 *Protection for Workers in Imminent Danger*
6.603 *Carbon Monoxide, Lead,* and *Carcinogens*
6.604 *Mercury, Vinyl Chloride*
6.605 *Women Workers and Job Health Hazards*
6.606 *New Hazards for Firefighters*
6.607 *Essentials of Machine Guarding*
6.608 MEDLINE, TOXLINE
6.609 *Toxicity Bibliography*
6.610 *Toxicology Research Projects Directory*
6.611 Toxicity Data Base and Carcinogens
6.612 *Standards on Noise Measurement, Rating Schemes, and Definitions: A Compilation*
6.613 Checklist of Publications on Specific Hazards

Audio-Visual Aids on Occupational Safety and Health (6.650-6.651)

6.650 Filmographies on Occupational Safety and Health:

Employer and Employee Rights and Responsibilities
Excavation and Trenching Operations
Guide to Voluntary Compliance
An Audio Aid on OSHA Recordkeeping
Access America
I Never Had an Accident in My...

6.651 Films on Occupational Safety and Health

Consumer Product Safety (6.700-6.708)

6.700 Consumer Product Safety Laws

6.701 *Handbook and Standard for Manufacturing Safer Consumer Products*
6.702 Technical Assistance for New Product Safety
6.703 Open Meetings of the Consumer Product Safety Commission
6.704 *Publications, Films, Fact Shows, Radio and TV Spots*
6.705 Center for Consumer Product Technology of the National Bureau of Standards
6.706 National Electronic Injury Surveillance System
6.707 National Injury Information Clearinghouse
6.708 Product Safety Indexed Document Collection

Chapter 7

EXPORTING

Chapter Abstract

Exporting Guides, Bibliographies, and Information Sources (7.0-7.12)

7.0 Organization of the Bureau of International Commerce
7.1 *A Basic Guide to Exporting*
7.2 *Export Marketing for Smaller Firms*
7.3 *How to Develop Export Markets for U.S. Foods and Agricultural Products*
7.4 *Services Available to HUD-Related Businesses in International Trade*
7.5 *Publications for American Business from the Domestic and International Business Administration*
7.6 *Foreign Investment and Licensing Checklist*
7.7 *Department of Commerce Publications Catalog and Index*
7.8 *Selected Publications Checklist*
7.9 *Fifteen Ways the U.S. Department of Commerce Can Help Make Your Business More Profitable*
7.10 *The Multinational Corporation: Studies on U.S. Foreign Investment*
7.11 Technology Applications for Less Developed Countries
7.12 National Technical Information Service

Current Awareness Services (7.50-7.54)

7.50 *Business Service Checklist*
7.51 *Export Briefs*
7.52 *International Marketing Newsmemo*
7.53 *Commerce America Newsletter* and *Magazine*
7.54 *Weekly Government Abstracts: Business and Economics*

Immediate Trade Opportunities (7.100-7.109)

7.100 Trade Opportunities Program
7.101 New Product Information Service
7.102 American International Traders Register
7.103 Foreign Traders Index
7.104 Foreign Investment Services Staff
7.105 Index to Trade Lists
7.106 Major Projects Programs
7.107 Target Industry Program
7.108 Overseas Product Sales Group
7.109 Trade Contact Survey

Overseas Promotional Assistance (7.150-7.171)

7.150 United States Trade Center Exhibitions
7.151 *U.S. Trade Promotion Facilities Abroad*
7.152 *International Marketing Events*
7.153 International Trade Fairs
7.154 *Overseas Trade Promotions Calendar*
7.155 Commercial Exhibitions
7.156 Joint Export Establishment Promotion
7.157 Catalog Exhibitions
7.158 In-Store Promotions
7.159 Between-Show Promotions
7.160 *How to Get the Most from Overseas Exhibitions*
7.161 Carnet: Customs Privileges for Promotional Purposes
7.162 Foreign Buyer Program
7.163 Product Marketing Service
7.164 U.S. Technical Sales Seminar
7.165 Trade Missions
7.166 Trade Announcement Service
7.167 World Traders Data Reports
7.168 *Key Officers in Foreign Posts, A Guide for Businessmen*

7.169 Agricultural Attaches
7.170 Foreign Agricultural Service
7.171 East-West Trade Assistance

Advisory and Technical Assistance (7.200-7.210)

7.200 Business Counseling Service
7.201 *Export Directory*
7.202 Domestic Seminars
7.203 District Export Councils
7.204 Agent Distributor Service
7.205 Market Development Cooperators
7.206 State Departments of Agriculture and State Export Agencies
7.207 Briefings on Foreign Commerce Affairs
7.208 Office of the Ombudsman
7.209 Telephone Directory of Country Marketing Managers
7.210 Department of Agriculture Export Specialists

Country and Commodity Intelligence (7.250-7.271)

7.250 *Global Market Surveys*
7.251 *Foreign Economic Trends and their Implications for the United States*
7.252 *Overseas Business Reports*
7.253 *Urban Institutions Abroad*
7.254 *HUD International Country Profile, Housing and Urban Development in (country)*
7.255 *Country Report Series, Housing in (country)*
7.256 *Market Potential for U.S. Agricultural Commodities in Select Mideastern and North African Countries*
7.257 *Sources of Information on American Firms for International Buyers*
7.258 *Engineers' Overseas Handbook*
7.259 *Country Market Sectoral Surveys*
7.260 *Producer Goods Research*
7.261 *Consumer Goods Research*
7.262 *Investment Handbooks*
7.263 *Markets Abroad for U.S. Consumer Goods*
7.264 *Foreign Market Reports*
7.265 *Special Report on Techniques of Aided Self-Help Housing, Some Examples of Overseas Experience*
7.266 *Industrialized Housing—Opportunities and Problems in the Developing Areas*
7.267 *Bibliography on Housing, Building, and Planning*
7.268 Bibliography on Agricultural Exporting
7.269 Daily Foreign Press and Radio Translations
7.270 *Trading with the USSR and Eastern Europe*
7.271 *Japan, The Government-Business Relationship*
7.272 Foreign Area Studies of the American University

Financing (7.300-7.311)

7.300 *Export Opportunities for American Business through the International Banks*
7.301 The Export Credit Sales Program
7.302 *A Guide to Financing Exports*
7.303 *Foreign Investment Organizations Assist U.S. Firms*
7.304 Export Management Companies
7.305 Private Export Funding Corporation
7.306 Domestic International Sales Corporation
7.307 Western Hemisphere Trading Corporation
7.308 Overseas Private Investment Corporation
7.309 Export-Import Bank of the United States
7.310 Foreign Credit Insurance Association
7.311 *Official U.S. and International Financing Institutions: A Guide for Exporters and Investors*

International Market Trend Information (7.350-7.357)

7.350 *Guide to Foreign Trade Statistics*
7.351 *International Economic Indicators and Competitive Trends*
7.352 Monthly Import and Export Data on World Commodities
7.353 *Market Share Reports*
7.354 *International Finance*
7.355 *Foreign Agricultural Trade of the United States*
7.356 Economic Research Service
7.357 *Foreign Trade Reports*

Chapter 8

ENERGY AND THE ENVIRONMENT

Chapter 9

TECHNICAL INFORMATION AND DATA BASES

Chapter Abstract

Sources of Technical Information (9.0-9.122)

National Technical Information Service (NTIS) (9.0-9.13)

- 9.0 Description of NTIS
- 9.1 NTISearch
- 9.2 NTISearch Published Searches
- 9.3 NTIS Bibliographic Data File
- 9.4 NTIS Key Word Title Index to Bibliographic Data File
- 9.5 NTIS Information Analysis Assistance
- 9.6 Selected Research in Microfiche
- 9.7 Engineering Index, Inc. Published Searches
- 9.8 *Data Item* of Engineering Sciences Data Unit
- 9.9 Special Technology Groups
- 9.10 Information Analysis Centers
- 9.11 *Weekly Government Abstracts*
- 9.12 *Subject Guide to the NTIS Information Collection*
- 9.13 *Government Reports Announcements and Index*

National Aeronautics and Space Administration (NASA) (9.20-9.21)

- 9.20 Industrial Applications Centers
- 9.21 NASA Field Centers

Smithsonian Science Information Exchange, Inc. (SSIE) (9.30)

- 9.30 Description of SSIE

Library of Congress (9.40-9.41)

- 9.40 National Referral Center for Science and Technology
- 9.41 Scientific and Technical Literature Searches

National Bureau of Standards (NBS) (9.50-9.52)

- 9.50 Institutes of NBS
- 9.51 National Standard Reference Data System
- 9.52 Standard Reference Materials Program

National Science Foundation (NSF) (9.60)

- 9.60 Description of NSF Programs

Department of Agriculture (9.70-9.75)

- 9.70 Economic Research Service (ERS)
- 9.71 Publications of ERS
- 9.72 Cooperative State Research Service
- 9.73 Agricultural Marketing Service
- 9.74 National Agricultural Library
- 9.75 Agricultural Research Information Data Base

Additional Sources of Technical Information (9.100-9.122)

- 9.100 *Federal Register*
- 9.101 Government-Industry Data Exchange Program
- 9.102 Water Resources Scientific Information Center
- 9.103 Geological Survey Land Information and Analysis Programs
- 9.104 Publications of the Geological Survey
- 9.105 Topographic Surveys and Mapping
- 9.106 National Archives and Records Service
- 9.107 Technology Clearinghouse to Aid Minority Business
- 9.108 Experimental Technology Incentives Program
- 9.109 Technology Transfer by Bureau of Mines
- 9.110 Mineralogical Services of Bureau of Mines
- 9.111 Federal Assistance Programs Retrieval System
- 9.112 Office of Weights and Measures of the National Bureau of Standards (NBS)
- 9.113 Calibration and Test Services of NBS
- 9.114 Center for Building Technology of NBS
- 9.115 Center for Consumer Product Technology of NBS
- 9.116 Research Associate Program of NBS

Chapter 10

MINORITIES AND THE DISADVANTAGED

	Occupational Change
10.6	*The Vital Majority, Small Business in the American Economy*
10.7	Publications on Crimes against Business
10.8	*Minority Enterprise Progress Report*
10.9	Small Business Administration *Annual Report*
10.10	*Manual on Business Opportunities for Small and Minority Businesses*

Technical Assistance (10.50-10.102)

Management Assistance (10.50-10.59)

10.50	Services for Minority Businesses
10.51	Service Corps of Retired Executives/Active Corps of Executives
10.52	Small Business Institute Program
10.53	University Business Development Centers
10.54	Management Training and Workshops
10.55	Management Assistance through Professional and Trade Associations
10.56	Contracted Management Consultation
10.57	Technical Assistance from the Economic Development Administration
10.58	Management Assistance from Small Business Investment Companies
10.59	Inter-Agency Council on Minority Enterprise

Technology Transfer (10.100-10.102)

10.100	Technology Assistance Program for Small Business
10.101	Experimental Technology Incentives Program
10.102	Technology Clearinghouse to Aid Minority Business

Marketing Assistance (10.150-10.159)

10.150	Minority Business Associations and Purchasing Councils
10.151	Minority Vendor Data Base System
10.152	*Small Business and Labor Surplus Area Specialists Designated to Assist Small, Minority, and LSA Businessmen*
10.153	Services to Small and Minority Businesses from National Aeronautics and Space Administration
10.154	Procurement by Department of Defense
10.155	Special Opportunities for Disadvantaged Contractors: The 8(a) Program
10.156	Research and Development Opportunities for Small Firms
10.157	Subcontracting Possibilities Published by Department of Defense
10.158	Certificates of Competency
10.159	Minority Business Resource Center, Federal Railroad Administration

Financial Assistance (10.200-10.215)

10.200	Definition of Small Business for Small Business Administration Loan Purposes
10.201	Small Business Investment Company
10.202	Minority Enterprise Small Business Investment Company
10.203	Economic Opportunity Loan Program
10.204	Pool Loans
10.205	Loans for Assistance to the Handicapped
10.206	*SBA Business Loans*
10.207	Small Business Administration Disaster Loans
10.208	Economic Injury Loans
10.209	Loans to Local Development Companies
10.210	Minority-Owned Financial Institutions
10.211	Revolving Line of Credit
10.212	Lease Guarantee Program
10.213	Surety Bond Guarantee Program
10.214	Federal Crime Insurance Program
10.215	Riot Insurance

Chapter 1

STARTING A BUSINESS: OPPORTUNITIES, SITE SELECTION, MANAGEMENT

CHAPTER ABSTRACT

Persons thinking of going into business, as well as those already in business but looking for a new business or product or a place in which to locate, relocate, or expand will find in this chapter an array of government services and information at their disposal.

"New Business and Product Opportunities" (1.0-1.156) itemizes information sources on buying a business, franchising, and using free government patents, and lists other ideas with business potential. The section entitled "Government Business Opportunities" (1.100-1.105) points out information sources which may suggest opportunities for starting or expanding a business around government procurement needs. (See also 3.250-3.259, "Selling to the Government.") "Technology for Product Development" (1.150-1.156) lists sources of information for researching the field of business and product planning and improvement.

"Site Location" (1.200-1.405) lists reference sources, including general aids, demographic data guides and specific data publications, information on energy and environmental matters, and sources on financial incentives and technical assistance.

"Management Assistance for New Business" (1.500-1.661) is generally oriented toward beginners; Chapters 2, 3, 4, and 5 are also relevant. Introductory reading materials are listed in "Starting a Business" (1.500-1.505). Programs which offer personal, specialized consultation at no cost are listed in "Comprehensive Advisory Services and Training" (1.550-1.556). "Marketing and Sales Assistance" (1.650-1.661) includes sources of information and help in such areas as market research, advertising, marketing, and selling to the United States government.

"Financing, Taxes, and Insurance" (1.700-1.761) offers clues to various sources of grants and loans for start-up, as well as information on financial management for business.

New Business and Product Opportunities (1.0-1.156)

New Business Ideas and Guides (1.0-1.13)

1.0 *Buying and Selling a Business*

Problems that confront buyers and sellers of business are discussed in this book. It covers such areas as the buy-sell process, sources of information for decision-making, use of financial statements in the buy-sell transaction, and determination of the market position of the company.

#SBA1.2:B98, 122 pp., $1.60; GPO (see C1.0).

1.1 Urban Business Profiles

These profiles provide a potential businessman with a better understanding of the opportunities, requirements, and problems associated with a specific business, and provide guidelines on types of information required for feasibility studies for plant location.

As priced; GPO (see C1.0).

Beauty Shops, #003-011-00056-9, 20 pp., 45¢
Bowling Alleys, #003-011-00065-8, 22 pp., 50¢
Building Service Contracting, #003-011-00068-2, 28 pp., 50¢
Children's and Infants' Wear, #003-011-00061-5, 14 pp., 45¢
Contract Construction, #003-011-00055-1, 26 pp., il., 50¢
Contract Dress Manufacturing, #003-011-00067-4, 16 pp., 45¢
Custom Plastics Industries, Warm Thermoforging, Cold Stamping, Casting, Foamed Plastics, Fabricating (Thermoforming), #003-011-00064, 30 pp., 60¢
Dry Cleaning, #003-011-00066-6, 16 pp., 45¢
Furniture Stores, #003-011-00054-2, 20 pp., 45¢
Industrial Launderers and Linen Supply, #003-011-00057-7, 22 pp., 50¢
Machine Shop Job Work, #003-011-00058-5, 23 pp., 45¢
Mobile Catering, #003-011-00060-7, 18 pp., 45¢
Pet Shops, #003-011-00071-2, 24 pp., 50¢
Photographic Studios, #003-011-00069-1, 15 pp., 45¢
Real Estate Brokerage, #003-011-00053-4, 18 pp., 45¢
Savings and Loan Associations, #003-011-00062-3, 24 pp., 50¢
Supermarkets, #003-011-00063-1, 27 pp., 50¢
Preparing a Business Profile, Supplement to the Urban Business Profiles Series, #003-011-00059-3, 12 pp., 40¢

1.2 Bibliography on Specific Businesses

These leaflets furnish sources of information for specific types of business.

Free; SBA (see C1.110).

Handicrafts, #1
Home Business, #2
Selling by Mail Order, #3
Retailing, #10
The Nursery Business, #14
Restaurants and Catering, #17
Basic Library Reference Sources, #18
Advertising—Retail Store, #20
Variety Stores, #21
Food Stores, #24
National Mailing List Houses, #29
Retail Credit and Collections, #31
Drugstores, #33
Mobile Homes and Parks, #41
Bookstores, #42
Men's and Boys' Wear Stores, #45
Woodworking Shops, #46
Soft-Frozen Dessert Stands, #47
Apparel and Accessories for Women, Misses, and Children, #50
Trucking and Cartage, #51
Hobby Shops, #53
Wholesaling, #55
Painting and Wall Decorating, #60
Photographic Dealers and Studios, #64
Motels, #66
Machine Shop—Job Type, #69
Tourism and Outdoor Recreation, #77

1.3 Books on Starting and Managing Specific Businesses

Designed to help the small entrepreneur understand the problems attendant on starting a new business, this series consists of twenty booklets. The first one deals with the subject in general; each of the others deals with one type of

business in detail.
As priced; GPO (see C1.0).

Starting and Managing a Small Business of Your Own, #SBA 1.15:1, 97 pp., $1.35
Starting and Managing a Service Station, #SBA 1.15:3, 80 pp., 70¢
Starting and Managing a Small Bookkeeping Service, #SBA 1.15:4, 64 pp., 90¢
Starting and Managing a Small Building Business, #SBA 1.15:5, 102 pp., $1.40
Starting and Managing a Small Restaurant, #SBA 1.15:9, 116 pp., $1.20
Starting and Managing a Small Retail Hardware Store, #SBA 1.15:10, 73 pp., $1.10
Starting and Managing a Small Retail Drugstore, #SBA 1.15:11, 103 pp., $1.25
Starting and Managing a Small Dry Cleaning Business, #SBA 1.15:12, 80 pp., 95¢
Starting and Managing a Small Automatic Vending Business, #SBA 1.15:13, 70 pp., 75¢
Starting and Managing a Carwash, #SBA 1.15:14, 76 pp., $1.10
Starting and Managing a Swap Shop or consignment Sale Shop, #SBA 1.15:15, 78 pp., 95¢
Starting and Managing a Swap Shop or Consignment Sale Shop, #SBA 1.15:15, 78 pp., 95¢
Starting and Managing a Small Shoe Service Shop, #SBA 1.15:16, 86 pp., $1.00
Starting and Managing a Small Retail Camera Shop, #SBA 1.15:17, 86 pp., 95¢
Starting and Managing a Retail Flower Shop, #SBA 1.15:18, 121 pp., $1.20
Starting and Managing a Pet Shop, #SBA 1.15:19, 40 pp., 60¢
Starting and Managing a Small Retail Music Store, #SBA 1.15:20, 81 pp., $1.30
Starting and Managing a Small Retail Jewelry Store, #SBA 1.15:21, 78 pp., 90¢
Starting and Managing an Employment Agency, #SBA 1.15:22, 118 pp., $1.30
Starting and Managing a Small Drive-In Restaurant, #SBA 1.15:23, 65 pp., 75¢
Starting and Managing a Small Shoestore, #SBA 1.15:24, 104 pp., $1.35

1.4 Starting a Small Business Investment Company (SBIC)

Details on the organization and regulation of small business investment companies for the benefit of investors interested in profit-sharing with smaller firms are given in the pamphlet, *Starting a Small Business Investment Company (SBIC).*

SBIC's are government-backed, flexible financing devices for furnishing equity capital and long-term loan funds to small businesses to operate, grow, and modernize. They are formed to operate under the regulations of the Small Business Investment Act once they have followed the simplified steps to obtain an SBIC license.

When SBIC's were developed, they were visualized as potential sources of capital and expertise for small firms previously limited to short-term financing. Since that time, they have proved to be adaptable to inner city as well as rural economic development by funneling investment capital into economically depressed communities, and to socially or economically disadvantaged small business entrepreneurs.

Free; SBA (see C1.110).

1.5 *Franchise Opportunities Handbook*

Franchisors are listed in this book, together with a brief summary of the terms, requirements, and conditions under which the franchises are available. Information on evaluating a franchise is also given.

$3.10; GPO (see C1.0).

1.6 Investigating Franchise Opportunities

An evaluation process that may be used to investigate franchise opportunities is presented in a booklet entitled *Franchise Index!Profile.* The index tells what to look for in a franchise; the profile is a worksheet for listing data relevant to a specific possibility.

#SBA 1.12:35, 56 pp., 65¢; GPO (see C1.0).

1.7 *Franchising in the Economy*

In this summary report of a special survey of franchisors, the products and services distributed through franchising are classified on the basis of major activity designated by the franchisor. Also, summary data on franchising grants between 1974 and 1976, data on sales distribution by franchising, and various other franchising statistics are given.

$2.00; GPO (see C1.0).

1.8 Franchising Instruction

Educators and businessmen who teach management courses will find in this publication, *Franchising*, a complete one or more session presentation, including a lesson plan, lecture, visual aids, case studies, study assignments, and selected bibliography and handout material.

Topic 18, #045-000-00088-5, 67 pp., $3.60; GPO (see C1.0).

1.9 *Franchise Business Risks*

Detailed information on how to evaluate a franchise opportunity and avoid a deceptive franchising scheme is given in this booklet.

#018-000-00140-3, 12 pp., 25¢; GPO (see C1.0).

1.10 *Are You Ready for Franchising*

This pamphlet is part of the Small Business Administration's Small Marketers Aids series.

#115, free; SBA (see C1.110).

1.11 *Manual on Business Opportunities for Small and Minority Businesses*

In this handbook, the roles of the housing development team are described: attorney, planner, architect, sponsor/developer, real estate appraiser/broker, contractor, consultant, mortgage banker, and management.

Information within each of the chapters regarding increased opportunities for minority participation in housing production encourages greater minority participation within the housing delivery system.

The tools and methods described in the text point the direction for improved cooperation between private enterprise and government and acceleration of participation by minorities in developing their environment.

The booklet serves as a resource for paraprofessionals and persons with limited experience who are interested in participating in the housing development process. It will also help minority professionals to become more familiar with their job and help them expand their participation in housing.

#023-000-00336-8, $2.15; GPO (see C1.0).

1.12 Agri-Business Program

The Agri-Business Program of the Agricultural Research Service helps plan and establish profit-making businesses in order to provide jobs for rural Americans. It seeks to achieve early commercialization of Department of Agriculture research developments in a variety of fields, and provides project planning that puts to work research findings and practical knowledge concerning manufacturing, raw materials, management, distribution, marketing, and financial requirements.

Agri-Business Program, Agricultural Research Service, Federal Center Building, Hyattsville, MD 20782; 301-436-8625.

1.13 Farmer Cooperatives

A cooperative is a business formed by a group of people to obtain certain services for themselves more effectively or more economically than they can obtain them individually. These people own, finance, and operate the business for their mutual benefit. Often by working together through such a cooperative business, member-owners obtain services not available to them otherwise.

Cooperatives perform one or more of three kinds of functions: marketing products; purchasing supplies; and providing such services as electricity, credit, irrigation and domestic water, and artificial insemination.

In certain respects, cooperatives are organized like other businesses and operate in the same way. They usually incorporate under the laws of the state in which they have their main office. They draw up bylaws and other necessary legal papers. Members elect a board of directors. The board hires a manager and makes general policies. The manager runs the day-to-day business.

In three important respects, however, cooperatives are unlike other businesses: (1) Their main purpose is to serve members—not to provide goods or services for others at a profit. (2) Savings over the cost of doing business are distributed to member-owners in proportion to their use of its services, not in proportion to their investment. Dividends, if any, on capital invested in the cooperative are limited. (3) Voting control of the business is based on membership, not amount of investment. Usually, each member has only one vote.

Cooperatives vary greatly in size and in the services they provide. They range from small local cooperatives with only a few members, to large regional cooperatives with thousands of members from several states. The regionals may have individuals, local cooperatives, or both, as members. Some cooperatives offer only one kind of service; some offer many. The trend today is toward multiple-service cooperatives. For example, a farmer may process and market several products through a cooperative, get some of his farm production supplies through the same cooperative, and even obtain such services as insurance, market news, and production advice there.

The Farmer Cooperative Service, Department of Agriculture, Washington, DC 20250; 202-447-6486.

New Product Ideas and Guides (1.50-1.64)

1.50 Publications on Developing New Products

Development of new products is the subject of two pamphlets in the Management Aids Series published by the Small Business Administration. They are: *Wishing Won't Get Profitable New Products* (#92) and *Finding a New Product for Your Company* (#216).

Free; SBA (see C1.110).

1.51 Foreign Firms Seeking United States Licensing

Over 200 countries have notified the Department of Commerce that they want their proprietary products made and sold in the United States, by United States companies, under licensing and, in some cases, joint venture arrangements. A list of the products offered and the countries of origin, as well as of names and addresses of the potential licensors/partners, and, in most cases, product literature, is available. However, staff limitations dictate that requests for information be restricted to no more than five file numbers at any one time.

Domestic Investment Services Staff, Office of Export Development, Bureau of International Commerce, Department of Commerce (see C1.10).

1.52 Technical Assistance on New Product Safety

Regional offices of the Consumer Product Safety Commission (CPSC) will offer informal opinions, on request, to businesses wishing to take preventive measures in advance of marketing new products.

CPSC (see C1.100).

1.53 Minerals Discovery Loan Program

To encourage exploration for specified minerals within the United States and its territories, the Geological Survey will contribute to the total allowable costs of exploration, to a maximum of 75 percent for nine specified mineral commodities, and to a maximum of 50 percent for 27 others. Funds must be used for the exploration of geologic targets considered to be favorable for the occurrence of deposits of ore of the specified commodities. Loans are paid back by means of royalties on mineral production if a discovery is certified by the government. In some cases, if no discovery is made, the loan need not be repaid.

Office of Minerals Exploration, National Center, Geological Survey (see C1.50); 703-860-6681.

1.54 Leasing of Mineral Lands

Citizens of the United States who are 21 years of age or older, associations of such citizens including partnerships, domestic corporations organized under the laws of the United States or any state thereof, and municipalities may lease federally owned mineral deposits in public lands. During the period of the lease, the leaseholder has the right to extract or remove the minerals for which the lease is issued. The purpose of the program is to assure orderly and timely development of the resource, obtain fair market value for it, and at the same time assure maximum environmental protection.

Division of Upland Minerals, Bureau of Land Management, Department of the Interior, Washington, DC 20240; 202-343-2718.

1.55 *Government Inventions for Licensing*

Chemistry, nuclear technology, biology, medicine, metallurgy, instruments, electrotechnology, and mechanical devices and equipment are among the subjects covered by the current awareness service entitled *Government Inventions for Licensing*. This is one of a series of 26 newsletters known as *Weekly Government Abstracts*. (For an annotation of the entire series, see 9.11.) Each newsletter contains summaries of government research performed by hundreds of organizations, including United States government agencies, private researchers, universities, and special technology groups. The research summaries are listed within two weeks of their receipt at the National Technical Information Service (NTIS). The last issue of each year is a subject index containing up to ten cross references for each research summary indexed.

$165.00 per year; NTIS (see C1.17).

1.56 Royalty-Free Patents

Patented inventions available for licensing from the government, often through royalty-free nonexclusive licenses, are listed in a four-volume compilation of about 16,000 inventions patented by the government between 1966 and 1974. The compilation, *U.S. Government Patent Portfolio*, is arranged by subject and is illustrated and indexed. The portfolio is described in PR #249, available from National Technical Information Service (NTIS).

$200.00; NTIS (see C1.17).

1.57 Technical and Financial Assistance with Energy-Related Inventions

To encourage innovation in developing nonnuclear energy technology, the Energy Research and Development Administration (ERDA) and the National Bureau of Standards (NBS) provide assistance to individual inventors and small business research and development companies. The assistance provided includes evaluation of energy-related inventions and ideas, advice concerning engineering, marketing, business planning, licensing and patents, and limited funding where appropriate.

Inventions to be evaluated should be submitted to the Office of Energy-Related Inventions, NBS, Washington, DC 20234. Ask for an Evaluation Request Form (NBS-1019).

For further information, write Office of Industry, State, and Local Relations, ERDA, Washington, DC 20545; 202-376-4119. See also field offices (see C1.150).

1.58 Granting of Energy Patent Licenses

Nonexclusive, royalty-free, revocable licenses are granted by the Energy Research and Development Administration (ERDA) upon request to United States citizens and corporations on over 4,600 ERDA-owned United States patents. Exclusive and limited-exclusive licenses may also be granted. Similar licenses on over 3,500 ERDA-owned foreign patents may be accorded to United States citizens and corporations, and to others under terms and conditions which depend upon particular facts. Copies of United States patents may be obtained from the Patent and Trademark Office, Department of Commerce, Washington, DC 20231, at 50c per copy.

Assistant General Counsel for Patents, ERDA, national office; see also field offices (C1.150).

1.59 Agricultural Patents

Patents resulting from agricultural research discoveries are available for licensing without charge.

Administrator, Agricultural Research Service, Department of Agriculture, Washington, DC 20250; 202-447-3656.

1.60 *NASA Patent Abstracts Bibliography*

Patented NASA inventions are available for exclusive or nonexclusive licenses, under a NASA policy to promote fast commercial use of space technology. *Patent Abstracts Bibliography* describes all available NASA patents twice a year.

800 pp., $9.00; GPO (see C1.0).

For technical assistance, write Technology Utilization Office, NASA Scientific and Technical Information Facility, P.O. Box 8756, Baltimore/Washington International Airport, MD 21240.

1.61 Searching for and Examining Patents

A search room is provided where the public

may search and examine United States patents granted since 1836. Patents are arranged according to a classification system with over 300 subject classes and 64,000 subclasses. By searching in these classified patents, it is possible to determine, before actually filing an application, whether an invention has been anticipated by another United States patent. It is also possible to obtain the information contained in patents relating to any field of endeavor.

Patent Office Search Room, 2021 Jefferson Davis Highway, Arlington, VA 22202.

1.62 Scientific Library of the Patent and Trademark Office

The Scientific Library of the Patent and Trademark Office has available for public use over 120,000 volumes of scientific and technical books in various languages, about 90,000 bound volumes of periodicals devoted to science and technology, the official journals of foreign patent offices, and over eight million foreign patents in bound volumes.

Patent Library, Crystal Plaza, 2021 Jefferson Davis Highway, Arlington, VA 22202.

1.63 Cooperating Libraries for Patent Searches

Those who cannot come to the Patent Office search room may order from the Patent Office copies of lists of original patents or of cross-referenced patents contained in the subclasses comprising the field of search, or may inspect printed copies of the patents, in a specially designated library which has a numerically arranged set of patents. A list of these libraries follows.

Albany, N.Y., University of the State of New York
Atlanta, Ga., Georgia Tech Library
Boston, Mass., Public Library
Buffalo, N.Y., Buffalo and Erie County Public Library
Chicago, Ill., Public Library
Cincinnati, Ohio, Public Library
Cleveland, Ohio, Public Library
Columbus, Ohio, Ohio State University Library
Detroit, Mich., Public Library
Kansas City, Mo., Linda Hall Library
Los Angeles, Calif., Public Library
Madison, Wisc., State Historical Society of Wisconsin
Milwaukee, Wisc., Public Library
Newark, N.J., Public Library
New York, N.Y., Public Library
Philadelphia, Pa., Franklin Institute
Pittsburgh, Pa., Carnegie Library
Providence, R.I., Public Library
St. Louis, Mo., Public Library
Stillwater, Okla., Oklahoma Agricultural and Mechanical College
Sunnyvale, Calif., Public Library
Toledo, Ohio, Public Library

1.64 Publications of the Patent and Trademark Office

Except where otherwise indicated, the following publications are available from GPO (see C1.0).

Patents

Over 3.8 million patents have been issued, and the specifications and drawings for each of them are available for sale to the public. Printed copies of any patent identified by its patent number may be purchased from the Patent and Trademark Office at a cost of 50¢ each, postage free, except design patents, which are 20¢ each. Future patents in subclasses of interest to particular individuals may be obtained by a subscription service.

Patent and Trademark Office, Department of Commerce, Washington, DC 20231.

Official Gazette of the United States Patent and Trademark Office

The *Official Gazette* is the official journal relating to patents and trademarks. It contains an abstract and a selected figure of the drawings of each patent granted on a given day; notices of patent and trademark suits; indexes of patents and patentees; lists of patents available for license or sale; and much more general information such as orders, notices, changes in rules, and changes in classification. Copies of the *Official Gazette* may be found in many libraries.

Weekly, $342.20 per year for first class mailing or $250.00 for fourth class, single copies $6.60 each.

The Trademark Section of the *Official Gazette*

Weekly, $88.40 per year, $1.70 for single copies.

Index of Patents

The *Index of Patents*, an annual index to the *Official Gazette*, is currently issued in two volumes, one an index of patentees and the other an index by subject matter of patents.

Index of Trademarks

This is an annual index of registrants of trademarks.

$7.90.

Manual of Classification

Contained in this loose-leaf book is a list of all the classes and subclasses of inventions in the Patent and Trademark Office classification system, a subject matter index, and other information relating to classification. Substitute pages are issued from time to time.

$44.00 per year, including the basic manual and substitute pages.

General Information Concerning Patents

An overview of the activities of the Patent and Trademark Office, this booklet attempts to answer many of the questions commonly asked of the Office and is useful to inventors and prospective applicants for patents.

75c.

General Information Concerning Trademarks

This publication serves the same purpose with respect to trademarks as does the above publication with respect to patents.

95¢.

Classification Definitions

Changes in classification of patents as well as definitions of new and revised classes and subclasses are contained in this volume.

Patent and Trademark Office, Department of Commerce. Washington, DC 20231.

Weekly Class Sheets

Classifications of patents as listed in the *Official Gazette* are summarized in this publication.

Patent and Trademark Office, Department of Commerce, Washington, DC 20231.

Patent Laws

Patent laws currently in force are compiled in this publication.

$2.10.

Trademark Rules of Practice of the Patent and Trademark Office

Rules governing procedures in the Patent Office in trademark matters, as well as a compilation of trademark laws currently in force, are contained in this brochure.

$5.00.

Patents and Inventions—An Information Aid for Inventors

The information in this booklet may help inventors decide whether to apply for patents, and aid them in obtaining patent protection and promoting their inventions.

45¢.

Directory of Registered Patent Attorneys and Agents by States and Countries

$3.40.

Manual of Patent Examining Procedures

A loose-leaf manual, this publication serves primarily as a detailed reference work on patent examining practice and procedure for the Patent Office's Examining Corps. Subscription service includes basic manual, quarterly revisions, and change notices.

$19.65 per year.

Guide for Patent Draftsmen

Requirements for patent drawings are explained in this publication.

65¢.

The Story of the United States Patent Office

The development of the United States Patent and Trademark Office and patent system, and of inventions which had unusual impact on the American economy and society, is set forth in this chronological account.

55¢.

Government Business Opportunities (1.100-1.105)

1.100 *Government Business Opportunities*

Counseling and technical assistance offered by Business Service Centers (BSC) of the General

Services Administration are described in this booklet. It also describes government procurement procedures and contains answers to many typical questions of potential sellers.

Free; BSC (see C1.105).

1.101 Research and Development Opportunities for Small Firms

The Small Business Administration (SBA) publishes, on a regional basis, directories identifying the names and major procurement installations for use in locating small business sources for R&D procurements. SBA also makes direct referrals to procuring installations for specific R&D solicitations.

SBA; (see C1.110).

1.102 Defense Subcontracting Possibilities

The Defense Supply Agency (DSA) of the Department of Defense, the largest government procurer of goods and services, publishes for each of its regions a listing of the companies which either have a contract currently or did at one time, and the product or service provided by the company. There is a separate publication for each region. A business can use this as a guide for contacting government contractors with whom there may be subcontracting possibilities. Minority contractors are listed separately in the volume. Although the volumes vary in size from region to region, they are usually well over 100 pages in length and are organized alphabetically.

DSA (see C1.21).

1.103 *Small Business and Government Research and Development*

Owners of small research and development firms seeking government contracts will find this introductory booklet useful. It includes a discussion of procedures necessary to locate and interest government markets.

#SBA 1.12:28, 41 pp., 75¢; GPO (see C1.0).

1.104 *United States Government Purchasing and Sales Directory*

Produced by the Small Business Administration (SBA), this volume is of general interest to businesses which wish to sell to the government. It includes descriptions of how the government buys, how to get on bidders' lists, how to prepare bids and proposals, and how the SBA can help a business sell to the government. It also includes listings of products purchased by military and civilian agencies and the location of purchasing offices. It describes the government's system of federal and military product specifications and indexes them. It includes a chapter on buying surplus property from the government. Finally, it provides sample forms and a list of field offices.

$2.00; GPO (see C1.0).

1.105 Submission of Unsolicited Proposals to Government Agencies

Many government agencies encourage the submission of unsolicited proposals for research and development activities in their areas of interest. A listing of the appropriate offices to contact in civilian and military agencies with major research and development activities can be found in *U.S. Government Purchasing and Sales Directory*.

#4500-00118, $2.35; GPO (see C1.0).

Technology for Product Development (1.150-1.156)

1.150 National Technical Information Service

The National Technical Information Service (NTIS) of the Department of Commerce emphasizes that searching before researching can save much effort, time, and money. Whether the research is intended to develop new technology or products or to provide data with which business decisions can be made, the resources available through NTIS may be useful.

NTIS is the central source for the public sale of government-sponsored research, development, and engineering reports and other analyses. Much of the material to which NTIS can give access is related to engineering and the hard sciences, but there is a growing array of data sources of potentially great value for business planners, market researchers, and others who may need statistics or other data about social, psychological, or demographic factors.

For a complete description of NTIS capability, including on-line literature and research searches, published searches, bibliographic services and more, see 9.0-9.13.

1.151 Industrial Applications Centers

Countless dollars and much effort are wasted in research and design facilities because technicians do not search existing literature before starting new programs. The six regional National Aeronautics and Space Agency (NASA) Industrial Applications Centers (IAC) answer this need both by searching the literature and by helping evaluate and apply the results. The centers maintain computerized access to about three-quarters of a million space-related reports, as well as to ten times that many reports and articles from private and nonspace governmental sources. The centers' resources cover the contents of more than 15,000 scientific and technical journals throughout the world, plus thousands of specialized governmental and industrial research reports. NASA believes that it is the world's largest technical data bank.

Major information sources accessible through IAC's now include:

Air Pollution Technical Information Center
Chemical Abstracts Condensates
Education Resources Information Center (ERIC)
Engineering Index (Ei)
Government Reports Announcements and Index (including data from all government agencies)
NASA International Aerospace Abstracts
NASA Tech Briefs
NASA Scientific and Technical Aerospace Reports
Nuclear Science Abstracts

The IAC's also utilize specialized data files dealing with food technology, textile technology, metallurgy, medicine, business, economics, social sciences, and physical sciences.

Other types of services provided include retrospective searches, current-awareness searches, and technical assistance, together with examples of industrial use of NASA technology and addresses and phone numbers of the nationwide facilities.

For more on IAC's, see 9.20.

1.152 *NASA Tech Briefs*

NASA research results in many innovations with potential for commercial application, and the monthly *NASA Tech Briefs* are one or two page reports on new products and devices,uriocesses and techniques, and materials. Briefs are issued in nine categories: electronic components and circuits, electronic systems, physical sciences, materials, life sciences, mechanics, machinery, fabrication technology, and mathematics and information sciences.

Subscription to all nine categories $40.00, single category $25.00, annual indexes under $10.00; NTIS (see C1.17).

Briefs are also collected and published quarterly by NASA. Free; Director, Technology Utilization Office, P.O. Box 8757, Baltimore/Washington International Airport, MD 21240. See also C1.107.

1.153 *Directory of Federal Technology Transfer*

An easty-to-use directory of federal technology transfer activities across a wide spectrum of federal government departments, agencies, and commissions, this report provides a tool for private industry to share more effectively the results of federal programs aimed at the development of knowledge and technologies. The report is a product of the Committee on Domestic Technology Transfer of the Federal Coordinating Council for Science, Engineering, and Technology.

Each section gives a description of an agency's program, including the agency's research base, its technology transfer policy and objectives, areas of responsibility, methods of implementation, accomplishments, and user organizations. Contact points through which a user can find the most pertinent elements of the agency are provided. There is an index to help users find activities or applications related to their areas of interest and also to determine whether activity areas are common to more than one federal agency.

$4.30; GPO (see C1.0).

1.154 Experimental Technology Incentives Program

The Experimental Technology Incentives Program is a new program which is a joint effort between the Small Business Administration (SBA) and the National Bureau of Standards to devise new means and methods of assisting the small business research and development community.

Regional offices of SBA will be informed when the program becomes operational.

SBA (see C1.110).

1.155 Technology Transfer Program for Small Business

In order to make the technological advances resulting from federally financed R&D available to small business concerns, the Technology Transfer Program for Small Business provides educational and technical assistance through workshops, consultation, and technical publications which identify technological advances from the federal government's stockpile of information.

SBA (see C1.110).

1.156 Technology Clearinghouse to Aid Minority Business

The Office of Minority Business Enterprise (OMBE) of the Department of Commerce has developed a program to provide minority-owned business firms with improved access to technical innovations developed under federal government contracts and by private corporations without federal aid.

The first phase of this new technology utilization program involved gaining support among a broad base of federal agencies and private businesses who conduct technology utilization programs.

Under the second phase, the Booker T. Washington Foundation of Washington, D.C. will design and test the operation of a clearinghouse which will offer access to information concerning (1) product identification, (2) feasibility analysis, (3) marketing, and (4) financing to minority firms in adapting new technology for the development of commercial products. The new center will begin providing services to minority firms nationally when the design has been fully tested.

OMBE (see C1.12).

Site Selection (1.200-1.405)

Information and Publications on Site Selection (1.200-1.205)

1.200 Free Publications on Site Location

The following publications on the subject of site selection are offered, free, by the Small Business Administration (SBA) (see C1.110).

Locating or Relocating Your Business, Management Aids Series #201
Factors in Considering a Shopping Center Location, Small Marketers Aids #143
Using a Traffic Study to Select a Retail Site, Small Marketers Aids #152
Using Census Data to Select a Store Site, Small Marketers Aids #154

1.201 Bibliography on Site Selection

Business Building Statistics, A Study of Physical and Economic Characteristics of Business Buildings, #048-000-00279-0, $1.15; GPO (see C1.0).

Small Business Location and Layout, #045-000-00082-6, 64pp., $3.55; GPO (see C1.0).

Included in this publication is a complete one or more session subject presentation, with a lesson plan, a lecture, visual aids, case studies, study assignments, and selected bibliography and handout material. It is useful for educators and businessmen who teach management courses.

Measuring Markets—A Guide to the Use of Federal and State Statistical Data

Some of the measurable characteristics and dimensions of a market, and the principal statistical series of interest, are described in this booklet. A series of cases illustrates how government statistics can aid in measuring markets and in planning plant location and sales territories. See C2 for examples.

$1.35; GPO (see C1.0).

Practical Business Use of Government Statistics

Government statistics and marketing are discussed in this publication. It gives real examples which apply to the three basic market analysis questions: How big is the market, where is it, and what are its characteristics?

28 pp., 1975, 35¢; GPO (see C1.0).

1.202 Sale of Isolated Public Lands

The Department of the Interior provides for the sale of isolated or disconnected tracts of public land, or public lands that are mountainous or too rough for cultivation, and which are more valuable under nonfederal ownership. The program is not applicable to the original thirteen states, Hawaii, Kentucky, Tennessee, Texas, or West Virginia. Transactions include sale, exchange, or donation of property and goods. The land is sold at auction, at not less than its fair market value.

Division of Lands and Realty, Bureau of Land Management, Department of the Interior, Washington, DC 20240; 202-343-3651.

1.203 Leasing of Mineral Lands

Citizens of the United States who are 21 years of age or older, associations of such citizens including partnerships, domestic corporations organized under the laws of the United States or any state thereof, and municipalities may lease federally-owned mineral deposits in public lands. During the period of the lease, the leaseholder has the right to extract or remove the minerals for which the lease is issued. The purpose of the program is to assure orderly and timely development of the resource, obtain fair market value for it, and at the same time assure maximum environmental protection.

Division of Upland Minerals, Bureau of Land Management, Department of the Interior, Washington, DC 20240; 202-343-2718.

1.204 Locating in New Towns

The New Communities Administration (NCA) of the Department of Housing and Urban Development assists new towns in their efforts to attract business and industry. The NCA encourages business to locate in new towns and take advantage of the unique opportunities available there.

New Communities Administration, Department of Housing and Urban Development, Room 7134, 451 7th St. S.W., Washington, DC 20410; 202-755-6174.

1.205 Films on Site Selection

The following films are available, as priced, from National Audio-Visual Center, General Services Administration, Attention: Order Section, NACDO, Washington, DC 20409.

The Right Location
The importance of the right location and some of the essential factors to consider in making a site selection study are dramatized in this film.

#007283, 16 min., 16 mm., sound, color; sale 16 mm., $72.75; rental 16 mm., $10.00.

It's Your Move
Small business owners faced with relocation problems because of urban renewal can find out about help available through Small Business Administration and urban renewal offices which will motivate them to take positive steps.

#441100, 13 min., 16 mm., sound, color; sale 16 mm., $59.00; rental 16 mm., $10.00.

Reference Guides to Demographic Data (1.250-1.255)

1.250 *Bureau of the Census Catalog*

The publications, computer tapes and punchcards, and related nonstatistical materials and services made available from January of each year are described in this catalog. Part I, *Publications*, is a classified, annotated bibliography of all publications issued by the Bureau of the Census during the period covered. Geographical and subject indexes are provided. Part II, *Data Files and Special Publications*, provides a listing of those materials which became available at the Bureau during the catalog period. Included are basic data files (on computer tape or punchcards), special tabulations (tapes, cards, and printed data) prepared for sponsors, and nonstatistical materials such as maps and computer programs.

A monthly supplement to the catalog lists major special publications, reports issued in a series at irregular intervals, and regular publications issued less frequently than quarterly.

Subscription price, including 4 quarterly issues and 12 monthly supplements, $14.40 per year; quarterly prices vary but generally stay between $2.00 and $4.00; GPO (see C1.0).

1.251 *Bureau of the Census Guide to Programs and Publications: Subjects and Areas*

A comprehensive review of the statistical programs of the Bureau of the Census and of the reports issued by the Bureau in the 1960's and early 1970's appears in this guide. It shows the geographic areas and principal subjects for most of the publications. For reports issued periodically, the areas covered in the latest issues are shown. Almost all statistical and geographic reports, including maps, published between 1968 and 1972 are covered.

$2.40; GPO (see C1.0).

1.252 *1970 Census Users' Guide*

Most of the information that data users will need for effective access and use of 1970 census data products is furnished in this two-part publication. Part I covers the decennial census program and related services. Part II is concerned exclusively with computer tape products.

Part I, $2.35; Part II, $4.40; GPO (see C1.0).

1.253 *Mini-Guide to the 1972 Economic Census*

Nine economic census programs are described in this publication. The programs are: census of wholesale trade, retail trade, selected service industries, manufactures, mineral industries, construction industries, transportation, enterprise statistics, and outlying areas. The publication provides useful information and references on data collected, publication programs, geographic areas, and Standard Industrial Classification Manual.

$1.00; GPO (see C1.0).

1.254 *Data User News*

This basic subscription service of the Bureau of the Census provides information on applications of census data and on new computer programs, news on user-oriented programs and products, announcements of workshops and seminars, a reader's exchange, and more. Eight or more pages each month bring news of activities, products, and publications in the field of small-area census data. A special section highlights the applications readers around the country have found for census data. Articles by Bureau specialists explain technical points, methodology, and processing techniques of the Bureau of the Census.

$4.00 per year; Subscriber Services Section, Bureau of the Census, Department of Commerce, Washington, DC 20233.

1.255 *Major Programs 1976: Bureau of Labor Statistics*

All the major surveys of the Bureau of Labor Statistics (BLS) and the publications that result from those surveys are described in this guide. Surveys useful in manpower planning include annual average employment levels for detailed occupational groups, worker characteristics and work-life expectancy, earnings by demographic groups, occupational mobility, job search methods, employment by industry for over 226 detailed areas, labor turnover in 215 manufacturing industries and 95 areas, insured unemployment statistics, state and area occupational projections, and much more. Uses for the data are suggested in the guide.

Free; BLS (see C1.70).

Specific Location Data (1.300-1.307)

1.300 *Statistical Abstract of the United States*

The *Statistical Abstract of the United States* constitutes a one-volume basic reference source. Issued annually since 1878, it is the standard summary of statistics on the social, political, and economic organization of the United States. It presents a comprehensive selection of statistics from the publications and records of government and private agencies.

This edition contains more than 1,400 tables and charts and an extensive guide to sources of additional data, as well as a two-page presentation of metric weights and measures. Although emphasis is given primarily to national data, many tables present data for regions and a smaller number for cities. Sections 33 and 34 present comprehensive data for states and for 157 standard metropolitan statistical areas having 200,000 or more inhabitants in 1970. Additional information for cities, counties, metropolitan areas,

Congressional districts, and other small units, as well as more historical data, is available in various supplements to the abstract.

There are 78 entirely new tables in this edition, covering health-related problems, crime, environmental concerns, federal government benefits and taxes, earnings, income shares of poorest and wealthiest, cost of living, big business, and oil and gas.

1976, $8.00 paperbound, $10.50 clothbound; GPO (see C1.0).

1.301 *County Business Patterns*

Social Security tax records and census data are source materials for this publication. It contains a series of separate reports for each state, and a United States summary with data on employment, number and employment size of reporting units, and taxable payrolls for various segments of the economy. It is especially useful for analyzing market potential, establishing sales territories and sales quotas, and locating facilities.

$5.45; GPO (see C1.0).

1.302 *County and City Data Book*

Demographic, social, and economic data for counties, cities, standard metropolitan statistical areas, and urbanized areas are presented from the most recent censuses as well as from other governmental and private sources. The topics include agriculture, bank deposits, births, marriages, climate, home equipment, hospitals, family income, migration, population characteristics, presidential vote, local government finances, retail trade, school enrollment, selected services, manufacturing, and others. The book also includes maps for each state, showing counties, standard metropolitan statistical areas, and large cities; explanatory notes and source citations; and appendixes that expand or explain the coverage of the tables. A unique feature of this book is the availability of its contents on compendia tape and punchcards.

$18.65; GPO (see C1.0).

1.303 Neighborhood Population and Housing Data

Census tract reports from the census of population and housing present information on both population and housing subjects for small areas within each of the standard metropolitan statistical areas in the country. Population subjects include household and family characteristics, voter participation, fertility, school enrollment, number of minorities, migration patterns, and many more population profile subjects. Housing subjects include tenure, number of rooms, plumbing facilities, year built, property value, and more. The reports can be extremely useful in many areas of business management, including locating or relocating a business, market research, and sales territory layout and evaluation.

Areas covered by census data and examples of data use in business are described in Appendix C2.

Department of Commerce (see C1.10); or Subscriber Services Section, Bureau of the Census, Washington, DC 20233. See also Bureau of the Census (see C1.13, C1.14).

1.304 County-Level Socioeconomic Data Base

Market forecasters, local governments, business planners, and demographers can use the National Technical Information Service (NTIS) county-level socioeconomic statistical data base to produce specialized reports. The data base, compiled by the Economic Development Administration, merges the first and fourth counts of the 1970 Census of Population and Housing with summary data from the 1960 census, *County and City Data Book, County Business Patterns*, and *Income Data Files.*

Help in formulation of a search request and an estimate of search costs and time is available through information specialists at NTIS.

NTIS (see C1.17).

1.305 Census of Business

The following censuses can guide businesses looking for locations by demonstrating precisely where the competition lies:

Retail Trade presents statistics by kinds of business for states, standard metropolitan statistical areas, counties, and cities of 2,500 or more. It includes data on the number of establishments, sales, payroll, and personnel.

Wholesale Trade gives data on number of establishments, sales, payroll, and personnel for kinds of business for states, standard metropolitan statistical areas, and counties.

Selected Services presents data on hotels, motels, barber shops, beauty parlors, and other retail organizations, including number of establishments, receipts, and payrolls for states, standard metropolitan statistical areas, counties, and cities.

Prices vary; GPO (see C1.0); see also Bureau of the Census (C1.13, C1.14).

1.306 *National Travel, 1972 Census of Transportation*

The volume and characteristics of travel by the civilian population of the United States are described in this publication. Included are such aspects of the subject as who went where, when, and for how long, by what means of transport and the primary reason for the trip, as well as related socioeconomic factors. The volume is in three sections: *Summer Travel, Spring Travel,* and the annual *Travel During (year).*

$2.45; GPO (see C1.0).

1.307 *Census of Agriculture: Area Reports*

In this series, which consists of a separate paperbound report for each state (two or more for larger states), data are presented by state and county on farms, land use, farm income and sales, machinery and equipment, and more.

Prices vary; GPO (see C1.0).

Physical Resources and Energy Information (1.350-1.358)

1.350 Water Resource Studies

The Water Resources Division of the Geological Survey is responsible for appraising the quantity and quality of the nation's water resources and for research on hydrologic problems related to the occurrence and distribution of both surface and ground water.

The Survey monitors and evaluates surface and ground water resources through a nationwide network of water stations and a series of resource investigations with the cooperation of state, federal, and public agencies. Each year, over 800 reports and maps are produced which help in the correlation of the available supply of man's water demands. To make the data more readily available, the Survey has transferred to computer tape about 245,000 station-years of records, and information on more than 40,000 ground water wells and 5,000 water-quality stations.

Water Resources Division, Geological Survey, Reston, VA 22092; 703-860-7444; see also field offices (see C1.50).

1.351 Water Resources Planning

Information regarding water availability, purity, and conservation can be obtained from the river basin commissions, associated with the United States Water Resources Council. Such information may be useful to industries in site selection, environmental protection, and energy conservation. Helpful information may also be gained in these matters from state water agencies, many of which have information specifically for business.

River Basin Commissions (see C1.152).

1.352 Snow Survey and Water Supply Forecasting

The Soil Conservation Service (SCS) makes and coordinates snow surveys in the western states and Alaska and prepares forecasts of seasonal water supplies in affected streams for the purpose of relating available water supply to agricultural, industrial, and municipal plans and operations.

SCS (see C1.3).

1.353 Topographic Surveys and Mapping

The National Mapping Program of the Geological Survey of the Department of the Interior makes graphic or digital cartographic data and services readily available for a multiplicity of uses. Cartographic products include:

Aerial photographs: low to high-altitude photographs which provide basic information on the character of the land surface for mapping and other purposes.

Geodetic data: positions, elevations, and descriptions of control points which are used in the preparation of the map base

Standard Topographic maps: the basic map series

from which smaller scale and special maps are usually derived

Orthophotoquads: rectified aerial photographs in standard quadrangle format and with map information superimposed

Smaller scale and special maps: standard series at scales ranging from 1:50,000 to 1:1,100,000 and National Park Service maps and special products such as slope maps at various scales

Digital map data: a numerical representation of the information normally shown on multipurpose topographic maps, to be used in planning and management activities as well as in map production and revision

The National Atlas: a bound collection of full-color maps and charts showing physical features such as land forms, geology, soil, vegetaion, and climate, as well as economic, social, and cultural data

$100.00; Geological Survey (see C1.50); selected *National Atlas* maps have been published in separate sales editions and can be purchased individually.

The National Cartographic Information Center of the Geological Survey provides a focal point for information on United States maps and charts, aerial photographs and space imagery, geodetic control, and related cartographic data. The center serves the user of cartographic data in three ways: It furnishes information on cartographic data available from federal, state, and private organizations; it furnishes information on the data-collection plans of these organizations; and it processes orders for cartographic data.

National Cartographic Information Center, United States Geological Survey, Reston, VA 22092; 703-860-7444.

Inquiries about map and report availability in a given area should be directed to a public inquiries office (see C1.50). Maps of areas east of the Mississippi, including Minnesota, Puerto Rico, and the Virgin Islands, may be ordered from Branch of Distribution, Geological Survey, 1200 South Eads St., Arlington, VA 22202; 703-557-2751. Maps of areas west of the Mississippi, including Alaska, Hawaii, Louisiana, Guam, and American Samoa, may be ordered from Branch of Distribution, Geological Survey, Box 25286, Stop 306, Denver Federal Center (Bldg. 41), Denver, CO 80225; 303-234-3832.

1.354 Soil Surveys

The Soil Conservation Service (SCS) gives technical assistance to individuals, groups, organizations, cities, and other units in reducing costly waste of land and water resources and in putting to good use these national assets. SCS's technical staff diagnoses resource problems and prescribes safe use and treatment. The technical staff includes soil scientists; economists; agricultural, irrigation, hydraulic, drainage, and cartographic engineers; and specialists in agronomy, biology, forestry, plant materials, range management, geology, and sedimentation.

These services may be particularly valuable in selecting a site for a factory or other building. The soil surveys are utilized by land use planners, developers and builders, construction engineers, and others. Such surveys can help avoid unnecessary complications that attend failure of foundations, soil slippage, flooded basements, and other structural breakdowns caused by adverse soil properties.

SCS publishes soil surveys of counties throughout the United States. The boundaries of each kind of soil in the county surveyed, gradated by soil hazard, are shown on detailed maps. Soil surveys describe important soil properties, such as flood hazard, natural drainage, depth to bedrock, depth to seasonal water table, permeability, shrinking and swelling potential, bearing capacity, and content of silt, sand, and clay. Soil surveys also provide interpretations of soil suitability and limitations for foundations of commercial buildings, for sanitary landfills, sewage lagoons, and septic tank absorption fields; for installation of underground pipelines; and for development of parks and other recreation areas. Since the manner in which tracts are subdivided is a major consideration in pricing units and estimating costs, soil surveys can help in planning lot size and layout of buildings, streets, and utilities in accordance with soil suitability and limitations.

Soil maps and supporting data provide information about flood hazard, wetness, erodability, bearing capacity, shrink-swell slippage, organic layers, and ease of excavation.

Interested parties may call the local office of the SCS to determine whether a soil survey of the area in question is available. If the survey has not yet been published, arrangements can be made to examine maps in their preliminary form.

SCS (see C1.3).

1.355 Land Information and Analysis Office

The Land Information and Analysis Offices manages five multidisciplinary programs which may be useful to business in selecting a site:

The *Earth Sciences Applications* program is responsible for integrating the earth-science information collected by the Geological Survey for use in analyzing land resource problems. The products, mainly thematic maps and reports, provide insight into the environmental consequences of land use decisions.

The *Resource and Land Investigations* program encompasses the multidisciplinary, multibureau efforts of the Department of the Interior. The national problems addressed include, for example, the delineation of environmentally endangered areas, the development and application of land use inventory systems, and the siting of onshore facilities associated with outer continental shelf energy resource development.

The *Geography* program calls for the application of geographic analysis techniques to land and resource problems. Land use data are systematically collected, revised, and analyzed on a nationwide basis, and basic geographic research is conducted.

The *Earth Resources Observation Systems* (EROS) program is the largest departmental program to be managed by this new office. Since 1966, numerous experiments have been conducted, applying remotely sensed data, primarily photographs and telecommunicated images obtained from satellites and high-altitude aircraft, to a wide variety of resource and environmental problems. The key facility of this program is the EROS Data Center in Sioux Falls, South Dakota, where the data are stored, reproduced, and distributed. The program includes research as well as user training in the interpretation and application of remotely sensed data and also includes the development of improved sensor and data processing systems.

The *Environmental Impact Analysis program* directs the preparation and review of the environmental impact statements required of the Geological Survey by the National Environmental Policy Act of 1969.

Land Information and Analysis Office, Geological Survey (see C1.50).

1.356 *NASA Earth Resources Survey Program*

Land use analysis, soil types and moisture levels, reflectance of vegetation, soil, and water, earth resources, and space benefits are among the subjects covered by the current-awareness service entitled *NASA Earth Resources Survey Program*. This is one of a series of 26 newsletters known as *Weekly Government Abstracts*. (For an annotation of the entire series, see Chapter 9.) Each newsletter contains summaries of government research performed by hundreds of organizations, including United States government agencies, private researchers, universities, and special technology groups. The research summaries are listed within two weeks of their receipt at the National Technical Information Service (NTIS). The last issue of each year is a subject index containing up to ten cross references for each research summary indexed.

$40.00 per year; NTIS (see C1.17).

1.357 Energy Utilization Assistance in Site Selection

Field installations of the Energy Research and Development Administration (ERDA) have technicians who can assist businesses in a variety of ways. For example, they can advise about appropriate energy systems for new facilities, or energy conversion in existing facilities. They can also advise about environmental pollution and energy conservation. ERDA supports a variety of research centers with specialized or general focus.

ERDA (see C1.150).

1.358 National Weather Service

The National Weather Service provides daily weather forecasts and warns the nation of impending natural disasters such as hurricanes and tornadoes. It provides information on weather patterns and tendencies in specific areas, which is useful to agriculturalists, environmentalists, and businesses looking for a suitable location.

National Weather Service, 8060 13th St., Room 401, Silver Spring, MD 20910.

Financial and Technical Assistance (1.400-1.405)

1.400 Financial Incentives in Site Selection

Business development assistance is offered by

the Economic Development Administration (EDA) to help businesses locate new facilities or expand in economically lagging areas of the nation, defined by EDA. The main purpose of such assistance is to help upgrade the area economically, primarily through the creation of permanent jobs and higher incomes for local residents. EDA financial assistance for projects takes the following forms: (1) direct loans or purchase of evidences of indebtedness to finance the cost of fixed assets; (2) direct loans to provide working capital; (3) guarantees of loans to private borrowers by private lending institutions to provide working capital; and (4) guarantees of rental payments of leases from qualified lessors for fixed assets; i.e., buildings (including the underlying land) and equipment.

EDA cannot help a business relocate from one area to another, nor can it help if there exists or is anticipated a long-range excess capacity situation. In addition, financial assistance must be unavailable from other sources on terms and conditions that would permit the accomplishment of the project. Finally, there must be reasonable assurance of ability to repay the loan.

EDA (see C1.11).

1.401 Office of Technical Assistance

The Office of Technical Assistance of the Economic Development Administration (EDA) can conduct feasibility, marketing, and other studies for firms on a repayment basis if the results of such work will likely result in increased jobs and economic upgrading. The project need not take place in an EDA-specially-designated area, although it is more likely to be approved if it is.

EDA (see C1.11).

1.402 Economic Injury Loans

Any small business is eligible for an economic injury loan if it suffers substantial economic injury as a result of its displacement by, or location in, adjacent to, or near a federally-aided urban renewal, highway, or other construction project.

A Small Business Administration (SBA) loan can help reestablish the business either in its existing location or in a satisfactory new location. The loan supplements funds the firm receives from the public agency involved as compensation for the taking of the property and other losses.

Therefore, SBA loans may be used to:

(1) remodel the firm's building in its existing location; or to purchase and, if necessary, remodel a building at another location; or to purchase land and construct a new building,

(2) provide working capital for any increased rental or other operating costs resulting from a new, rented location,

(3) make leasehold improvements on rented property,

(4) replace fixtures, machinery, and equipment, with reasonable upgrading permitted (but the trade-in value of the old equipment must be applied to the cost of the replacements),

(5) purchase a larger or different type of inventory that may be better suited to a new location, and

(6) pay moving expenses in excess of the amount provided by the public agency involved in the construction project.

SBA (see C1.110).

1.403 *Loans to Local Development Companies*

The Small Business Administration (SBA) is authorized to make loans to state and local development companies for use in assisting specific small businesses. SBA may lend up to $500,000 for each small business that is to be assisted. Thousands of loans have been made to such companies to enable them to help start, expand, or modernize small businesses.

In many areas, federal assistance is now being provided through privately-supported local development companies which are often organized by local chambers of commerce, committees of 100, or simply a group of public-spirited citizens who have a sincere interest in furthering the economic development of their community. This kind of organization has grown fastest in areas of limited commercial and industrial development where it is difficult to obtain sufficient funds from private sources to support an adequate program.

The loans may be used to finance construction, modernization, or conversion of plants, including purchase of land, and to purchase machinery and equipment. They may not be used for working capital or for debt repayment, except interim debt incurred for construction of the project involved.

A loan may not be made if the funds needed

are available from banks or other private lenders. To the extent that private sources do have funds, they may, and frequently do, participate with SBA in helping finance projects. A development company is usually required to provide from its own funds at least 20 percent of the cost of the project.

The SBA booklet, *Loans to Local Development Companies*, furnishes more information.

SBA (see C1.110).

1.404 Pool Loans for Facility Construction

Under Section 7(a)(5) of the Small Business Act, SBA is authorized to make loans to pools formed by several small business concerns. Formation of such pools must be cleared by the Department of Justice, and information must be furnished to the Federal Trade Commission. Loan proceeds must be used to obtain raw materials, equipment, inventories, supplies, or benefits of research and development, or to construct facilities for such purposes.

SBA (see C1.110).

1.405 Lease Guarantee Program

Under the lease guarantee program, small businesses can be provided with the credit required to compete on a more equal basis with large businesses for space on prime industrial and commercial property. Either through participating private insurance companies, or directly if no participation is available, the Small Business Administration (SBA) will guarantee the payment of the rent under leases entered into by small businesses which qualify.

SBA (see C1.110).

Management Assistance for New Business (1.500-1.661)

Starting a Business (1.500-1.505)

1.500 *Choosing a Form of Business Organization*

Part of the Small Business Administration's Management Development series, this is a complete subject presentation, including a lesson plan, a lecture, visual aids, case studies, study assignments, and selected bibliography and handout material, suitable for use by educators and businessmen who teach management courses.

#045-000-00080-0, 62 pp., $3.20; GPO (see C1.0).

1.501 Free Publications on Business Start-Up

The following publications on business start-up are available, free, from the Small Business Administration (see C1.110):

Incorporating a Business, Management Aids Series, #223

Business Plan for Small Construction Firms, Management Aids Series, #221

Checklist for Going into Business, Small Marketers Aids Series, #71

Business Plan for Retailers, Small Marketers Aids Series, #150

Business Plan for Small Service Firms, Small Marketers Aids Series, #153

1.502 *Starting and Managing a Small Business of Your Own*

A prospective businessman thinking of starting a new business should ask himself certain questions about his ability, resources, and knowledge. These things, and others which should be considered in choosing what business he is to go into, are discussed in clear and graphic form in *Starting and Managing a Small Business of Your Own.*

The pros and cons of buying a going business or investing in a franchise are discussed, as well as how to start a business from scratch. The basic aspects of managing a business (buying, pricing, selling, personnel, recordkeeping, and more) are explained in detail. Also, taxes, insurance, and laws and regulations a businessman is subject to are gone into in some detail.

The final pages of the booklet are devoted to a comprehensive checklist for starting a business and include the field offices of the Small Business Administration.

#045-000-00123-7, 95 pp., $1.35; GPO (see C1.0).

1.503 Business Planning

While designed and composed primarily for minority business development, a book called *Business Packaging* will be of general interest to any businessman. It discusses business development as an ongoing process of planning, financing, marketing, and resource utilization. It begins with a discussion of the characteristics generally required of an entrepreneur, and how to evaluate a business idea. It then discusses developing the business package, which includes market research, sales planning, a technical and operational plan, and financial planning. It points out both private and public-section recourses available to the entrepreneur, with a complete discussion of the Small Business Administration. Finally, it presents two case studies in detail. Each section includes not only narrative, but also sample forms and charts that can be used both to organize and to evaluate efforts at each stage.

Office of Community Development, Department of Housing and Urban Development national or regional offices (see C1.40).

1.504 Free Publications on Management

The following publications on management are available free, from SBA (see C1.110).

Order No.

Management Aids Series

169 *Designing Small Plants for Economy and Flexibility*
179 *Breaking the Barriers to Small Business Planning*
181 *Numerical Control for the Small Manufacturer*
189 *Should You Make or Buy Components?*
195 *Setting Pay for Management Jobs*
206 *Keep Pointed Toward Profit*
207 *Pointers on Scheduling Production*
208 *Problems in Managing a Family-Owned Business*
212 *The Equipment Replacement Decision*
214 *The Metric System for Small Business*
218 *Business Plan for Small Manufacturers*
221 *Business Plan for Small Construction Firms*
224 *Association Services for Small Business*

Technical Aids Series

73 *Pointers in In-Plant Trucking*
91 *A Tested System for Achieving Quality Control*

Small Marketers Aids Series

25 *Are You Kidding Yourself about Your Profits?*
105 *A Pricing Checklist for Managers*
114 *Pleasing Your Boss, the Customer*
116 *How to Select a Resident Buying Office*
118 *Legal Services for Small Retail and Service Firms*
123 *Stock Control for Small Stores*
124 *Knowing Your Image*
125 *Pointers on Display Lighting*
130 *Analyze Your Records to Reduce Costs*
132 *The Federal Wage-Hour Law in Small Firms*
133 *Can You Afford Delivery Service?*
135 *Arbitration: Peace-Maker in Small Business*
137 *Outwitting Bad Check Passers*
138 *Sweeping Profit Out the Back Door*
139 *Understanding Truth-in-Lending*
140 *Profit by Your Wholesalers' Services*
141 *Danger Signals in a Small Store*
145 *Personal Qualities Needed to Manage a Store*
149 *Computers for Small Business—Service Bureau or Time-Sharing?*
150 *Business Plan for Retailers*
153 *Business Plan for Small Service Firms*
155 *Keeping Records in Small Business*
157 *Efficient Lighting in Small Stores*

Small Business Bibliographies

10 *Retailing*
15 *Recordkeeping Systems—Small Store and Service Trades*
18 *Basic Library Reference Sources*
58 *Automation for Small Offices*
75 *Inventory Management*
85 *Purchasing for Owners of Small Plants*
86 *Training for Small Business*

1.505 Bibliography on Management

The following publications on management are available, as priced, from GPO (see C1.0).

Improving Material Handling in Small Business
The basics of material handling, the method of laying out workplaces, and other factors in

setting up an efficient system, are discussed.
#SBA 1.12:4, 42 pp., 60¢.

Ratio Analysis for Small Business
Ratio analysis is the process of determining relationships among certain financial or operating data of a business to provide a basis for managerial control. The purpose of this booklet is to help the owner/manager in detecting favorable or unfavorable trends in the business.
#SBA 1.12:20, 65 pp., 90¢.

Guides for Profit Planning
Guides for computing and using the break-even point, the levels of gross profit, and the rate of return on investment are contained in this booklet. It is designed for readers who have no specialized training in accounting or economics.
#SBA 1.12:25, 52 pp., 85¢.

Profitable Community Relations for Small Business
Practical information on how to build and maintain sound community relations by participation in community affairs is provided in this booklet.
#SBA 1.12:27, 36 pp., 70¢.

Management Audit for Small Manufacturers
A series of questions in this booklet will indicate whether the owner/manager is planning, organizing, directing, and coordinating business activities efficiently.
#SBA 1.12:29, 58 pp., 75¢.

Management Audit for Small Retailers
149 questions in this booklet guide the owner/manager of a small retail store in examining himself and his business.
#SBA 1.12:31, 72 pp., 80¢.

Small Store Planning for Growth
The nature of growth, the management skills needed, and some techniques for use in promoting growth are discussed in this booklet, as well as a consideration of merchandising, advertising and display, and checklists for increase in transactions and gross margins.
#SBA 1.12:33, 99 pp., $1.75.

Managing for Profits
Various aspects of small business management, such as marketing, management, and credit, are discussed in the ten chapters of this book.
#SBA 1.2:M31/11, 170 pp., $1.95.

Strengthening Small Business Management
This 21-chapter book reflects the experience which the author gained in a lifetime of work with the small business community.
#SBA 1.2:M31/14, 158 pp., $2.25.

Profitable Small Plant Layout
The small business owner whose costs on finished goods are rising may find that his decreasing net profits and his lowered production stem from lack of economical and orderly movement of production materials from one process to another throughout the shop.
#SBA 1.12:21, 48 pp., 80¢.

Comprehensive Advisory Services and Training (1.550-1.556)

1.550 Service Corps of Retired Executives and Active Corps of Executives

The Service Corps of Retired Executives (SCORE) is a group of public-spirited, knowledgeable, and experienced retired executives from every job sector. Many were owners of small businesses. SCORE has a present membership of 5,198, with 292 chapters.

The Active Corps of Executives (ACE) is an important auxiliary to SCORE. It augments SCORE and furnishes needed special talents which may not be represented among other volunteers.

Both SCORE and ACE members participate in conducting workshops and in offering a wide range of management and technical counseling to the small business community. The volunteers donate their time to present and potential small business owners. SBA reimburses them for out-of-pocket expenses. A counselor will meet with a client at a SCORE office or at the client's place of business; usually that will resolve the problem. At other times, counseling continues as long as necessary.

SBA (see C1.110).

1.551 Small Business Institute Program

The Small Business Institute program, a three-way cooperative between collegiate schools of business administration, members of the nation's small business community, and the Small Business Administration (SBA) is a new source of management assistance. Under the supervision of university faculty and SBA staff, senior and graduate students of business administration work directly with owners of small firms, providing vital management assistance to small businesses while undergoing meaningful learning experiences themselves.

The program began in the fall of 1972. In the first year of its life, 1,100 small firms received counseling, and 2,200 students were involved. In 1976, 385 schools participated, and 22,000 students and 8,800 small businesses were involved. Satisfaction rate among clinets was over 80 percent.

SBA (see C1.110).

1.552 University Business Development Centers

Growing out of the Small Business Institute concept (see 1.551), the University Business Development Center (UBDC) program is an experimental Small Business Administration concept being tested in eight universities. It is a university-based and administered program to interrelate the academic, professional, and technological resources of universities with all existing government programs designed to assist the business community. While each agency continues to administer its own programs, the university serves as a funnel or mixing device for them, so that the collection of programs will work as an integrated unit serving the whole community, rather than as an uncoordinated variety of programs.

A functioning UBDC can offer the following services to its business clients:

—Business and product evaluation and development
—Entrepreneur evaluation, recommendations, counseling, and training
—Analysis, correction, and follow-up of financial, marketing, technical, production, legal, and any other type of problem faced by small business owners
—Feasibility studies and development of business plans for present and future entrepreneurs
—Access to and application of technology, paid for by the taxpayers in over $350 billion worth of research and development projects since 1947
—Assistance not only in surviving (when 57% of new businesses fail in the first five years), but also in expanding on a solid basis

Universities currently involved are the Universities of Maine at Bangor, Missouri at St. Louis, Nebraska at Omaha, Georgia at Athens, and West Florida at Pensacola; and Rutgers University, New Brunswick, New Jersey; California State University at Chico; and California Polytechnic at Pomona.

1.553 Management Training, Seminars, and Workshops

Small Business Administration (SBA) field offices offer prebusiness workshops, conferences, and problem clinics on developing a business plan for small businesses or those thinking about starting a business. SBA makes special efforts to increase the number of minority and disadvantaged businesses included in such groups.

SBA (see C1.110).

1.554 Management Assistance through Professional and Trade Associations

The Small Business Administration is entering into agreements with ten to fifteen trade and professional associations to provide specialized management and technical assistance to small businesses that are socially or economically disadvantaged.

SBA (see C1.110).

1.555 Graduate School of the Department of Agriculture

Continuing education and training of managers, technicians, and employees can be accomplished at modest cost at the Graduate School of the Department of Agriculture, located in Washington, D.C. The Graduate School is open to the public and offers courses on a wide variety of subjects of value to business, but does not grant degrees.

Correspondence courses are available in such subjects as executive development, management, and supervision; accounting; engineering; English usage and writing; mathematics and statistics; and computer sciences.

For further information, contact the Office of Independent Study Programs, Room 6847, South Building, Department of Agriculture, Washington, DC 20250; 202-447-7123.

The Individual Learning Center offers individualized, programmed, and self-instructional courses which allow students to advance in easy step-by-step procedures through difficult material. Subjects available include grammar; punctuation; spelling; vocabulary; reading; metric system; fractions; decimals; algebra; calculus; statistics; accounting; management and supervision; computer programming; and office skills such as fililng, shorthand, and business letters.

Employers with affirmative action problems may wish to consult with the staff of the Career Planning and Development Programs. Upward mobility of employees can depend upon increased educational and skills-training opportunities, and the staff can help employers with the following services:

(1) Planning and developing upward mobility career development programs,

(2) Assessment services for determining training needs of employers,

(3) Vocational testing and counseling services for individuals or groups, and

(4) Development of special seminars and courses to meet specific needs.

Career Planning and Development Programs/Individual Learning Center, Room 6834, South Building, Department of Agriculture, Washington, DC 20250; 202-447-6693 or -6694.

For a copy of the current catalog of the Graduate School, write Information Office, Room 6847, South Building, Department of Agriculture, Washington, DC 20250; 202-447-4419.

1.556 Business Counseling Service

Counseling services, including assistance with market research, product promotion, and financing, are offered by the Department of Commerce district offices and by the Business Counseling Section of the Bureau of International Commerce in Washington, D.C. Designed to give businessmen a maximum amount of information in a minimum amount of time, the service helps him analyze his problems and determine answers. The service emphasizes exporting. (See C1.10.)

The Washington office also has country specialists (see C1.15) with whom an exporter can discuss specific marketing problems. Finally, the Department of State has country desk officers (see C1.90) who can brief businessmen on the political climate in specific countries.

Management Aids
(1.600-1.609)

1.600 Free Publications on Personnel Management

The following publications are available, free, from SBA (see C1.110).

Order No. Management Aids Series

185 *Matching the Applicant to the Job*
186 *Checklist for Developing a Training Program*
191 *Delegating Work and Responsibility*
195 *Setting Pay for Management Jobs*
197 *Pointers on Preparing an Employee Handbook*
198 *How to Find a Likely Successor*
205 *Pointers on Using Temporary Help Services*
209 *Preventing Employee Pilferage*

Small Marketers Aids Series

106 *Finding and Hiring the Right Employee*
136 *Hiring the Right Man*
132 *The Federal Wage-Hour Law in Small Firms*
135 *Arbitration: Peace-Maker in Small Business*

Small Business Bibliographies

72 *Personnel Management*

1.601 Bibliography on Personnel Management

The following publications on personnel management are available, as priced, from GPO (see C1.0):

An Employee Suggestion System for Small Companies

The basic principles for starting and operating a suggestion system are explained. The booklet also warns of various pitfalls and gives

examples of suggestions submitted by employees.
#SBA 1.12:1, 18 pp., 40¢.

Human Relations in Small Business
Finding and selecting employees, developing them, and motivating them is the subject of this book.
#SBA 1.12:3, 68 pp., 60¢.

Better Communications in Small Business
Smaller manufacturers can help themselves in winning cooperation by means of more skillful communications. The booklet discusses this and also seeks to explain how communications within the firm can improve operating efficiency and competitive strength.
#SBA 1.12:7, 37 pp., 65¢.

Personnel Management Guides for Small Business
Various aspects of personnel management in small firms are discussed.
#SBA 1.12:26, 79 pp., $1.10.

1.602 Buying Surplus Government Property to Obtain Supplies

A wide variety of personal property located throughout the country is continually being offered for sale by the federal government. Included are automobiles and other motor vehicles, aircraft, hardware, plumbing and heating equipment, paper products, typewriters and other office machines, furniture, medical items, textiles, and industrial equipment. The condition of the property offered ranges from good to poor. It may be used or unused, require minor or major repair, or even be offered as scrap. As items become available for sale, catalogs are distributed by the General Services Administration (GSA) and the Department of Defense (DOD) to those on their mailing lists who have expressed an interest in the types of property being offered. GSA and DOD, the principal sources of surplus personal property in government, have regional information and sales offices around the country (for DOD, see C1.21; for GSA, see C1.105).

To get on the GSA mailing list, ask for a free application from their regional office. To get on DOD's list, write to DOD Surplus Sales, P.O. Box 1370, Battle Creek, MI 49016.

1.603 *How to Buy Surplus Personal Property from the Department of Defense*

The mechanics of how to buy surplus personal property available for sale by the Department of Defense are explained in this booklet.
#008-007-02598-8, 26 pp., 40¢; GPO (see C1.0).

1.604 *Arranging Transportation for Small Shipments—Shipper Rights, Remedies, and Alternatives*

The services that small shippers and receivers of freight may legally expect from motor common carriers regulated by the Interstate Commerce Commission are summarized in this pamphlet.
#026-000-01036, 8 pp., 35¢; GPO (see C1.0).

1.605 Free Publications on Crime Prevention in Business

The following publications are available, free, from the Small Business Administration (see C1.110).

Order No.	Management Aids Series
209	*Preventing Employee Pilferage*
	Small Marketers Aids Series
119	*Preventing Retail Theft*
129	*Reducing Shoplifting Losses*
134	*Preventing Burglary and Robbery Loss*
151	*Preventing Embezzlement*

1.606 Free Publications on Environmental Protection

Environmental protection is the subject of two publications in the Small Business Administration's Management Aids Series. They are *Reducing Air Pollution in Industry* (#217) and *Solid Waste Management in Industry* (#219).
Free; SBA (see C1.110).

1.607 Small Business Administration *Annual Report*

The *Annual Report* of the Small Business

Administration (SBA) provides a description and performance analysis of each of the agency's financial and management assistance programs, demonstrating the breadth of SBA's activity.

$3.20; GPO (see C1.0).

1.608 Assistance to Private Forest Owners

The Forest Service of the Department of Agriculture cooperates with private forest owners and processors of forest products in seeking to increase job opportunities and raise the income of rural people. Assistance is provided to improve fire control and protection of forests from insects and disease; to broaden land use planning; to develop multiple-use management so as to obtain the maximum use potential from forest resources; and to improve practices in harvesting, processing, and marketing of forest products. Branches of the Forest Service can be found throughout the country.

Forest Service, Department of Agriculture, Washington, DC 20250.

1.609 Films on Business Management

The following films are available from the National Audio-Visual Center, General Services Administration, Attention: Order Section, NACDO, Washington, DC 20409; for sale or rent, except no rental of 8 mm.

Variations on a Theme

Many of the factors involved in implementing a successful sales event are pointed out in this film. Step-by-step preparations for an anniversary sale are illustrated.

13 min., 16 mm., sound, color, #780500; sale 16 mm., $59.00, rental 16 mm., $10.00; sale 8 mm., $40.50 (#009084).

The Business Plan—for Small Businessmen

In a dramatization concerning a failing business, discussion reveals that lack of planning has been a key factor in the decline. Reasons for planning and the main points in a business plan are then presented.

15 min., 16 mm., sound, color, 1972, #003510; sale 16 mm., $68.00, rental 16 mm., $10.00; sale 8 mm., $42.75 (#009088).

You and Your Customers

Situations which small retailers may encounter involving customer relations are presented. Audience involvement is stimulated by providing opportunity to stop the film for discussion following some of the more detailed situations, then offering possible solutions to the problems presented on the screen.

14 min., 16 mm., sound, color, 1970, #826720; sale 16 mm., $63.50, rental 16 mm., $10.00; sale 8 mm., $39.00 (#009076).

The Heartbeat of Business

The importance of financial management is emphasized in this film. Some examples of good and bad financial management show that good practices are critical to success.

15 min., 16 mm., sound, color, 1971, #001428; sale 16 mm., $68.00, rental 16 mm., $10.00; sale 8 mm., $43.25 (#009087).

Three Times Three

Through dramatization and narration, this film illustrates nine important keys to small business success: personal ability of the owner; use of outside assistance and informational understanding of insurance, regulations, and taxes; business opportunity; knowing sources of capital; maintenance and use of business records; understanding financial factors; effective organization and planning; and using good management techniques.

14 min., 16 mm., sound, color, 1969, #747425; sale 16 mm., $63.50, rental 16 mm., $10.00; sale 8 mm., $40.00 (#009080).

The Calendar Game

The need for advertising, planning, and budgeting by small retail and service businesses is the main point of emphasis in this film. Budgeting, timing, choice of media, and plans for specific promotions are all discussed.

14 min., 16 mm., sound, color, 1967, #194215; sale 16 mm., $63.50, rental 16 mm., $10.00; sale 8 mm., $40.75 (#009079).

The Follow-Up

The value of following up on advertisements and promotions becomes clear in this dramatization. Illustrations of following up on a radio commercial, soliciting customers' reactions to store layouts and point-of-sale ads, and getting business associates' opinions of ads used or planned bring out many of the factors to consider in advertising/sales promotion follow-up.

13 min., 16 mm., sound, color, 1967, #335459; sale 16 mm., $59.00, rental 16 mm., $10.00; sale 8 mm., $40.00 (#009072).

Marketing and Sales Assistance (1.650-1.661)

1.650 *Measuring Markets—A Guide to the Use of Federal and State Statistical Data*

Some of the measurable characteristics and dimensions of a market, and the principal statistical series of interest, are described in this booklet, along with a series of cases which illustrate how government statistics can aid in measuring markets. (See also Appendix C2, "Understanding and Using Census Data.")

$1.35; GPO (see C1.0).

1.651 *Practical Business Use of Government Statistics*

Government statistics and marketing are discussed in this publication. It gives real examples which apply to the three basic market analysis questions: How big is the market, where is it, and what are its characteristics?

28 pp., 1975, 35¢; GPO (see C1.0).

1.652 *Selecting Advertising Media? A Guide for Small Business*

Helping small businesses to decide which medium to use for making a product, a service, or a store known to potential customers and what is the best use of advertising money is the purpose of this book.

#SBA 1.12:35, 56 pp., 65¢; GPO (see C1.0).

1.653 *Training Salesmen to Serve Industrial Markets*

The role of sales in marketing programs of small manufacturers, suggestions for salesmen to use in servicing their customers, and materials useful in training programs are discussed in this book.

#SBA 1.12:36, 85 pp., $1.15; GPO (see C1.0).

1.654 Free Publications on Marketing and Sales

The following publications on the subject of marketing and sales are available, free, from SBA (see C1.110).

Order No.	Management Aids Series
85	*Analyzing Your Cost of Marketing*
178	*Effective Industrial Advertising for Small Plants*
187	*Using Census Data in Small Plant Marketing*
188	*Developing a List of Prospects*
190	*Measuring the Performance of Salesmen*
192	*Profile Your Customers to Expand Industrial Sales*
193	*What Is the Best Selling Price?*
194	*Marketing Planning Guidelines*
196	*Tips on Selecting Salesmen*
200	*Is the Independent Sales Agent for You?*
203	*Are Your Products and Channels Producing Sales?*
204	*Pointers on Negotiating DOD Contracts*
215	*How to Prepare for a Pre-Award Survey*
	Small Marketers Aids Series
109	*Stimulating Impulse Buying for Increased Sales*
111	*Interior Displays: A Way to Increase Sales*
113	*Quality and Taste as Sales Appeals*
121	*Measuring the Results of Advertising*
128	*Building Customer Confidence in Your Service Shop*
156	*Marketing Checklist for Small Retailers*
	Small Business Bibliographies
3	*Selling by Mail Order*
9	*Marketing Research Procedures*
12	*Statistics and Maps for National Market Analysis*
13	*National Directories for Use in Marketing*
20	*Advertising—Retail Stores*
29	*National Mailing-List Houses*
56	*Training Commercial Salesmen*
67	*Manufacturers Sales Representatives*

1.655 Free Publications on Government Procurement

The following publications on government

procurement are available, free, from SBA (see C1.110).

Order No.	Management Aids Series
211	*Termination of DOD Contracts for the Government's Convenience*
215	*How to Prepare for a Pre-Award Survey*
	Technical Aids Series
78	*Controlling Quality in Defense Production*
82	*Inspection on Defense Contracts in Small Firms*

1.656 Government Research and Development Opportunities for Small Firms

The Small Business Administration (SBA) publishes, on a regional basis, directories identifying the names and major capabilities of small R&D business firms. These are distributed to major procurement installations for use in locating small business sources for R&D procurements. SBA also makes direct referrals to procuring installations for specific R&D solicitations.

SBA (see C1.110).

1.657 *Selling to the United States Government*

Government buying methods, the process of locating government agencies and learning what they buy and how to bid on government contracts and orders, and preparation of bids and proposals are described in this publication.

Free; SBA (see C1.110).

1.658 *Commerce Business Daily*

Every business day, this publication lists hundreds of new specific business proposals for products and services wanted or offered by the United States government. It lists current information received daily from military and civilian procurement offices. It is of particular value to firms interested in bidding on United States government purchases or seeking subcontract opportunities from prime contractors.

Daily, $105.00 per year first class, $80.00 second class; GPO (see C1.0).

1.659 Small Business Marketing to the Department of Defense

The law and the Department of Defense (DOD) regulations provide that entire procurements, or parts of procurements, may be set aside exclusively for the competition of small business. A major portion of Defense Supply Agency (DSA) contracts goes to small business firms, as defined by the Small Business Administration (see 1.700). There is a small business and economic utilization specialist at each DSA buying office whose job is to help small businesses participate in DSA procurements. In addition, there are specialists available for consultation in each of the eleven Defense Contract Administration Services regional offices and several of the district offices. These specialists can also assist in obtaining subcontractors under large DOD prime contractors.

DOD (see C1.20, C1.21, C1.22).

1.660 Defense Contracting Emphasis in Labor Surplus Areas

It is the policy of the Department of Defense to aid firms in labor surplus (high unemployment) areas. In order to execute this policy, a part of a procurement may be set aside for negotiation with concerns which are certified to be eligible or which will perform a substantial portion of the contracts thus awarded. The small business and economic utilization specialist at each buying office and at each Defense Contract Administration Office can explain this preference program and help those who wish to participate in Defense Supply Agency (DSA) procurements.

DSA (see C1.21).

1.661 *Small Business and Labor Surplus Area Specialists*

Small Business and Labor Surplus Area Specialists Designated to Assist Small, Minority, and LSA Businessmen is a publication intended for potential small business suppliers to the Department of Defense. It lists the locations of military and Defense Supply Agency procurement offices and small business specialists throughout the United States.

#008-000-00223-1, 1976, 61 pp., $1.10; GPO (see C1.0).

Financing, Taxes, and Insurance (1.700-1.761)

Grant, Loan, and Guarantee Programs (1.700-1.710)

1.700 Definition of Small Business for Small Business Administration (SBA) Loan Purposes

For loan eligibility purposes, a small business is defined as one that is (1) independently owned and operated, (2) not dominant in its field of operations, and (3) is within the pertinent SBA size standards. A business may be considered small if it has 250 employees or less, and large if it employs 1,500 or more. A firm which falls in the range between 250 and 1,500 may be considered either small or large, depending on the SBA size standard worked out for that particular field of operations.

There is an alternative size standard. Regardless of the number of employees, a business, together with its affiliates, may qualify if its assets do not exceed $9 million; its net worth does not exceed $4 million; and its average net income for the preceding two years, after federal income taxes, did not exceed $400,000. Average net income must be computed without benefit of any carryover loss.

According to the SBA definition, 97 percent of United States businesses fall into the small business category, and they account for 48 percent of the gross national product.

1.701 Grants to Help Develop Private Business

The Farmers Home Administration (FmHA) makes grants to facilitate development of private business enterprises in rural areas or cities up to 50,000 population, with priority to applications for projects in open country, rural communities, and towns of 25,000 or smaller.

Eligibility is limited to public bodies, such as incorporated towns and villages, boroughs, townships, counties, states, authorities, and districts.

Funds may be used to finance industrial sites that will result in development of private business enterprises. Costs that may be paid from grant funds include the acquisition and development of land and the construction of buildings, plants, equipment, access streets and roads, parking areas, utility and service extensions, refinancing, and fees.

Grant funds may be used jointly with funds furnished by the applicant, including FmHA loan funds.

FmHA (see C1.2).

1.702 *SBA Business Loans*

The basics of Small Business Administration (SBA) loaning procedures and limitations are explained in this sixteen-page booklet, *SBA Business Loans*.

SBA can aid business directly or indirectly in a number of ways. When financing is not available otherwise on reasonable terms, SBA may guarantee up to 90 percent or $350,000, whichever is less, of a bank loan to a small firm. If an SBA-guaranteed loan is not available, SBA will then consider advancing funds on an immediate participation basis with a bank. SBA will consider making a direct loan only when these forms of financing are not obtainable. The agency's share of an immediate participation loan may not, at the present time, exceed $150,000. Direct loans may not exceed $100,000 and at times may not be available due to fiscal restraints.

SBA's specific lending objectives are to (1) stimulate small business in deprived areas, (2) promote minority enterprise opportunity, and (3) promote small business contribution to economic growth.

Loans may be for as long as ten years, except those portions of loans for new construction purposes, which may have a maturity of fifteen years. However, working capital loans are usually limited to six years. Interest rates on SBA's portion of immediate participations, as well as direct loans, may not exceed a rate set by a statutory formula relating to the cost of money to the government, usually between 6 percent and 7½ percent.

Ineligible applicants include nonprofit enterprises, newspapers, magazine and book publishers, and radio and TV broadcasting companies.

SBA (see C1.110).

1.703 Economic Injury Loans

Any small business is eligible for this type of loan if it suffers substantial economic injury as a result of its displacement by or location in, adjacent to, or near a federally-aided urban renewal, highway, or other construction project.

A small Business Administration (SBA) loan can help reestablish the business either in its existing location or in a satisfactory new location. The loan supplements funds the firm receives from the public agency involved as compensation for the taking of the property and other losses.

Therefore, SBA loans may be used to:

(1) remodel the firm's building in its existing location or to purchase, and, if necessary, remodel a building at another location; or to purchase land and construct a new building;

(2) provide working capital for any increased rental or other operating costs resulting from a new, rented location;

(3) make leasehold improvements on rented property;

(4) replace fixtures, machinery, and equipment, with reasonable upgrading permitted (but the trade-in value of the old equipment must be applied to the cost of the replacements);

(5) purchase a larger or different type of inventory that may be better suited to a new location; and

(6) pay moving expenses in excess of the amount provided by the public agency involved in the construction project.

SBA (see C1.110).

1.704 Property Improvement Loans

Property improvement loans may be made for the construction of small structures for commercial, industrial, or agricultural use, under the National Housing Act administered by the Department of Housing and Urban Development (HUD). The loans may be made for repairs, alterations, and improvements.

The customer must have a steady or determinable income adequate to permit repayment of the loan. The brochure, *Dealer and Contractor Guide to Property Improvement Loans,* clarifies the conditions under which loans may be made.

#HUD-30-F(3), free; HUD (see C1.40).

1.705 Economic Opportunity Loan Program

The Economic Opportunity Loan program (EOL) makes it possible for disadvantaged individuals who have the capability and desire to own their own businesses to borrow money for starting or expanding. It provides both financial and management assistance. The maximum amount of an EOL is $100,000 for up to fifteen years.

SBA (see C1.110).

1.706 Small Business Investment Company (SBIC) Financing

A Small Business Investment Company (SBIC) is a privately owned and privately operated small business investment company which has been licensed by the Small Business Administration (SBA) to provide equity capital and long-term loans to small firms. Often, an SBIC also provides management assistance to the companies it finances.

Small businesses generally have difficulty obtaining long-term capital to finance their growth. Prior to 1958, there were few places a small company could turn to for money once it had exhausted its secured line of credit from banks or SBA. To help close this financing gap, Congress passed the Small Business Investment Act of 1958, which authorized SBA to license, regulate, and help finance privately organized and privately operated SBIC's.

Today there are SBIC's located in all parts of the country. As an industry, the SBIC's have total assets of millions of dollars, and additional funds are available to them through borrowings from SBA and private sources.

Many SBIC's are owned by relatively small groups of local investors. An SBIC finances small firms in two general ways—by straight loans and by venture capital or equity investments. In some cases, these investments give the SBIC actual or potential ownership of a minority of a small business' stock. However, SBIC's are generally prohibited from taking a control position in a small concern. Generally, financing must be for at least five years, except that a borrower may elect to have a prepayment clause included in the financing agreement.

There are three free brochures put out by SBA which together given an overview of the SBIC: *SBIC Financing for Small Business; SBIC, Starting a Small Business Investment Company; and Section 301(d) SBIC's.*

Local attorneys, accountants, bankers, investment bankers, and business associates or advisers who have had dealings with SBIC's may be helpful. Also, SBA field offices will offer help. An agency information specialist will provide a list of licensed SBIC's and, while he is not permitted to recommend a specific company, he may be able to point out the types of investments various SBIC's in the area have been making.

Lists of licensed SBIC's may also be obtained from the SBA.

SBA (see C1.110).

1.707 SBIC Management Assistance for Small Business

Since the ultimate success of a Small Business Investment Company (SBIC) is linked to the growth and profitability of its so-called portfolio companies (that is, those it has helped to finance), many SBIC's offer management services as a supplement to financing. As a condition of financing, it may insist on certain improvements in the operations of a small business; for example, installation of better accounting methods or inventory controls. Similarly, as part of the financing agreement, the small business may be required to furnish the SBIC with regular financial statements or progress reports.

The extent of management services offered varies with the individual SBIC.

A large SBIC is usually staffed by an experienced and diversified management team. If desirable, a specialist from the SBIC may work with a portfolio company to iron out specific problems which arise during the company's growth. Other SBIC's have small staffs which divide their time between seeking new investments and working with portfolio companies. Many SBIC managers call in consultants to supplement their work with portfolio companies, while others draw on the talents of their own board members. Some SBIC's which concentrate on well-secured loans do not offer management assistance.

SBA (see C1.110).

1.708 Minority Enterprise Small Business Investment Companies

Under Section 301(d) of the Small Business Investment Act of 1958, special small business investment companies called Minority Enterprise Small Business Investment Companies (MESBIC) can be and have been established which concentrate on providing equity funds, long-term loans, and management assistance to small business concerns owned by socially or economically disadvantaged persons. The Small Business Administration (SBA) booklet entitled *Section 301 (d) SBIC's* reviews the procedure for setting up and operating a MESBIC. It is available at field offices of SBA (see C1.110).

A listing of MESBIC's can be found in Appendix C1.16.

1.709 Industrial and Commercial Property Lease Guarantee Program

This program is designed to provide small businesses with the credit required to compete on a more equal basis with large businesses for space on prime industrial and commercial property. Either through participating private insurance companies, or directly if no participation is available, the Small Business Administration (SBA) may guarantee the payment of the rent under leases entered into by small businesses which qualify.

The program has been suspended but may be reinstated in the future.

SBA (see C1.110).

1.710 Business Loans for Farmers

The Farmers Home Administration (FmHA) makes loans to family farmers and ranchers and gives technical and management assistance for development and operation of nonfarm enterprises to supplement farm income. If a real estate loan is to be made, the enterprise must be located on the borrower's farm. Each person applying for credit gets equal consideration without regard to race, creed, sex, or national origin. Applications of eligible veterans are given preferance. Veterans and nonveterans must meet the same requirements and qualifications for loans.

Enterprises for which loans can be made include repair shops, service stations, restaurants, grocery stores, welding shops, roadside stands, boarding animals, cabinet shops, riding stables, sporting goods stores, beauty shops, custom services, camping sites, and barber shops.

Applications are made at the local county office of the Farmers Home Administration.

FmHA state offices (see C1.2).

Financial Management Aids (1.750-1.761)

1.750 *Handbook of Small Business Finance*

Procedures for keeping accurate, well organized accounting records and for making regular financial reports are described in this handbook. Also, proper techniques to analyze the reports are explained. It discusses such topics as good bookkeeping methods, profit-and-loss statements, balance sheets, and techniques (such as ratio analysis) for measuring performance of a business.

#045-000-00139, 64 pp., 75¢; GPO (see C1.0).

1.751 *Financial Recordkeeping for Small Stores*

A basic recordkeeping system for small store owners whose businesses do not justify hiring a trained full-time bookkeeper is described in this book. It discusses accounts receivable, depreciation, taxes, maintaining records of transactions, and more.

#045-000-00142, 135 pp., $1.60; GPO (see C1.0).

1.752 *Cash Planning in Small Manufacturing Companies*

Designed for owners of small firms and the specialists who study them, this book reports on research on cash planning for small manufacturers.

#SBA 1.20:1, 276 pp., $2.70; GPO (see C1.0).

1.753 *Financial Control by Time-Absorption Analysis*

A profit-control technique that can be used by all kinds of business is described in this book. It includes a step-by-step approach which shows how to establish this method in a particular business.

#SBA 1.12:37, 138 pp., $1.40; GPO (see C1.0).

1.754 *Insurance and Risk Management for Small Business*

The definition of insurance, the necessity of obtaining professional advice on buying insurance, and the main types of insurance a small business may need are all discussed in this book.

#SBA 1.12:30, 72 pp., 95¢; GPO (see C1.0).

1.755 *Cost Accounting for Small Manufacturers*

The importance of determining and recording costs accurately is stressed in this book, designed for small manufacturers and their accountants. It includes diagrams, flow charts, and illustrations to make the material easier to understand.

#SBA 1.12:9, 163 pp., $1.60; GPO (see C1.0).

1.756 Free Publications on Financial Management

The following publications on financial management are available, free, from SBA (See C1.110).

Order No.	Management Aids Series
170	*The ABC's of Borrowing*
174	*Is Your Cash Supply Adequate?*
176	*Financial Audits: A Tool for Better Management*
220	*Basic Budgets for Profit Planning*
222	*Business Life Insurance*
	Small Marketers Aids Series
110	*Controlling Cash in Small Retail and Service Firms*
126	*Accounting Services for Small Service Firms*
142	*Steps in Meeting Your Tax Obligations*
144	*Getting the Facts for Income Tax Reporting*
146	*Budgeting in a Small Service Firm*
147	*Sound Cash Management and Borrowing*
148	*Insurance Checklist for Small Business*
	Small Business Bibliographies
20	*Retail Credit and Collections*
87	*Financial Management*

1.757 *Financing New Technological Enterprise*

Problems associated with the acquisition of venture capital, particularly those relating to new technologically oriented businesses, are examined in this report. Steps to be taken to improve capital flow are recommended.

50¢; GPO (see C1.0).

1.758 Tax Information and Education

Information and guidance on tax matters, including assistance in the preparation of returns, is available to individuals or groups interested in the tax system or having questions on his or their tax returns. Various types of tax courses can be arranged for groups of taxpayers with unusual circumstances such as those who have suffered property losses in natural disasters. Toll-free telephone services are available to any taxpayer in the nation.

IRS (see C1.95).

1.759 *Tax Guide for Small Business*

Tax Guide for Small Business contains information useful in starting, operating, or disposing of a business. It explains how the federal tax laws apply to sole proprietorships, partnerships, and small corporations. The latest edition reflects the provisions of the Tax Reform Act of 1976 which contains substantial changes in the tax laws affecting business.

If the *Tax Guide* does not answer all the questions a businessman might have, he may call an IRS area office for assistance.

IRS (see C1.95).

1.760 Business Tax Kit

The Internal Revénue Service (IRS) will assemble a tax information and forms kit tailored to an individual business. It usually consists of selected publications from their publications list. The kit can be obtained from the Public Affairs Division, Internal Revenue Service, Department of the Treausry, 1111 Constitution Avenue N.W., Washington, DC 20224; 202-964-4021. Area offices will also be able to provide the proper guides and forms.

IRS field offices (see C1.95).

1.761 Tax Publications List

The following publications are available, free, from IRS (see C1.195).

Order No.	
225	*Farmer's Tax Guide*
349	*Federal Highway Use Tax*
463	*Travel, Entertainment, and Gift Expenses*
505	*Tax Withholding and Declaration of Estimated Tax*
509	*Tax Calendar and Checklist for 1977*
510	*Information on Excise Taxes for 1977*
512	*Credit Sales by Dealers in Personal Property*
521	*Tax Information on Moving Expenses*
522	*Tax Information on Disability Payments*
529	*Miscellaneous Deductions and Credits*
533	*Information on Self-Employment Tax*
534	*Tax Information on Depreciation*
535	*Tax Information on Business Expenses*
537	*Tax Information on Installment and Deferred-Payment Sales*
538	*Tax Information on Accounting Periods and Methods*
539	*Withholding Taxes and Reporting Requirements*
541	*Tax Information on Partnership Income and Losses*
542	*Corporations and the Federal Income Tax*
544	*Sales and Other Dispositions of Assets*
545	*Income Tax Deduction for Interest Expense*
547	*Tax Information on Disasters, Casualty Losses, and Thefts*
548	*Tax Information on Deductions for Bad Debts*
549	*Condemnations of Private Property for Public Use*
550	*Tax Information on Investment Income and Expenses*
552	*Recordkeeping Requirements and a Guide to Tax Publications*
556	*Audit of Returns, Appeal Rights, and Claims for Refund*
557	*How to Apply for Recognition of Exemption for an Organization*
558	*Tax Information for Sponsors of Contests and Sporting Events*
564	*Tax Information on Mutual Fund Distributions*
572	*Tax Information on Investment Credit*
575	*Tax Information on Pension and Annuity Income*
578	*Tax Information for Private Foundations and Foundation Managers*

582 *Federal Use Tax on Civil Aircraft*
583 *Recordkeeping for a Small Business*
584 *Workbook for Determining Your Disaster Loss*
587 *Business Use of Your Home*
588 *Tax Information on Condominiums and Cooperative Apartments*
589 *Tax Information on Subchapter S Corporations*
590 *Tax Information on Individual Retirement Savings Programs*
595 *Tax Guide for Commercial Fishermen*
900 *Quick Index to Taxpayer Information Publications*

Chapter 2

MONEY AND FINANCIAL MANAGEMENT

CHAPTER ABSTRACT

All the major loan and grant programs of the federal government are listed in this chapter. Also listed are publications on financial management, programs and publications on taxes and insurance, and information on export financing.

Since many of the loan programs originate with the Small Business Administration (SBA), it is important to note the first item in this chapter, "Definition of Small Business for SBA Loan Purposes" (2.0). The definition is broad enough to include the bulk of United States business and industry.

"Rural Development Loans" (2.50-2.60) describes a variety of loan and grant programs which aim at increasing employment opportunities and living standards in rural areas. Frequently, the definition of rural includes towns of 10,000 to 50,000 population; the applicability of such loans is therefore quite extensive.

"Financial Management Assistance" (2.100-2.115) describes many useful management tools and broad-based sources of technical assistance.

The tax credit available under the Work Incentive Program is one of several tax credits described in "Tax Credits and Tax Planning" (2.150-2.157), along with other guides and aids to tax planning.

"Insurance" (2.200-2.204) describes crime, flood, and riot insurance available on excellent terms from the Department of Housing and Urban Development.

The section entitled "Export Financing" (2.250-2.260) describes organizations concerned with exporting, and the help they can give businesses who wish to explore this field. (See also Chapter 7, *Exporting*.)

Financial Assistance Programs (2.0-2.60)

Loan and Grant Programs and Financing Sources (2.0-2.19)

2.0 Definition of Small Business for Small Business Administration (SBA) Loan Purposes

For loan eligibility purposes, a small business is defined as one that is (1) independently owned and operated, (2) not dominant in its field of operations, and (3) within the pertinent SBA size standards. A business may be considered small if it has 250 employees or less, and large if it employs 1,500 or more. A firm which falls into the range between 250 and 1,500 may be considered either small or large, depending on the SBA size standard worked out for that particular field of operations.

There is an alternative size standard. Regardless of the number of employees, a business, together with its affiliates, may qualify if its assets do not exceed $9 million; its net worth does not exceed $4 million; and its average net income for the preceding two years, after federal income taxes, did not exceed $400,000. Average net income must be computed without benefit of any carry-over loss.

By this definition, 97 percent of United States businesses fall into the small business category, and they account for 48 percent of the gross national product.

2.1 *SBA Business Loans*

The basics of Small Business Administration (SBA) loaning procedures and limitations are explained in the booklet, *SBA Business Loans.*

SBA can aid business directly or indirectly in a number of ways. When financing is not available otherwise on reasonable terms, SBA may guarantee up to 90 percent or $350,000, whichever is less, of a bank loan to a small firm. If an SBA guaranteed loan is not available, SBA will then consider advancing funds on an immediate participation basis with a bank. SBA will consider making a direct loan only when these forms of financing are not obtainable. The agency's share of an immediate participation loan may not, at the present time, exceed $150,000. Direct loans may not exceed $100,000 and at times may not be available due to fiscal restraints.

SBA's specific lending objectives are (1) to stimulate small business in deprived areas, (2) to promote minority enterprise opportunity, and (3) to promote small business contribution to economic growth.

Loans may be for as long as ten years, except those portions of loans for new construction purposes, which may have a maturity of fifteen years. However, working capital loans are usually limited to six years. Interest rates on SBA's portion of immediate participations, as well as direct loans, may not exceed a rate set by a statutory formula relating to the cost of money to the government, usually between 6 and 7½ percent.

Ineligible applicants include nonprofit enterprises, newspapers, magazine and book publishers, and radio and television broadcasting companies.

SBA (see C1.110).

2.2 SBA Disaster Loans

SBA is authorized to make loans to small firms suffering from the effects of government actions and other situations not caused by the small firm:

Economic Injury Disaster Loans are made to small firms suffering economic injury as the result of physical disasters such as floods, hurricanes, and tornadoes. This is one of the largest SBA loan programs.

Product Disaster Loans may be approved to small firms suffering from the effects of diseased food products.

Coal Mine Health and Safety Loans are made to small coal mine operators to assist them in complying with the Federal Coal Mine and Safety Act of 1969.

Consumer Protection Loans are those offered to firms having to comply with standards set up under the Egg Products Act of 1970, the Wholesale Poultry and Poultry Products Act of 1968, or the Wholesale Meat Act of 1967.

Base Closing Economic Injury Loans may be made to businesses which suffer from the effects of the closing of major military installations.

Air Pollution Control Loans are authorized for firms having to comply with requirements of the Clean Air Act of 1970.

Water Pollution Control Loans are those made to small businesses having to comply with various water pollution controls.

Emergency Energy Shortage Economic Injury Loans are available to small businesses suffering economic injury caused by an energy shortage.

Strategic Arms Economic Injury Loans are made to small businesses directly or seriously affected by the significant reduction of the scope or amount of federal support for any project as a result of any international agreement limiting the development of strategic arms facilities.

SBA (see C1.110).

2.3 Economic Injury Loans

Any small business is eligible for this type of loan if it suffers substantial economic injury as a result of its displacement by or location in, adjacent to, or near a federally aided urban renewal, highway, or other construction project.

A Small Business Administration (SBA) loan can help reestablish the business either in its existing location or in a satisfactory new location. The loan supplements funds the firm receives from the public agency involved as compensation for the taking of the property and other losses.

Therefore, SBA loans may be used:

(1) to remodel the firm's building in its existing location; or to purchase and, if necessary, remodel a building at another location; or to purchase land and construct a new building;

(2) to provide working capital for any increased rental or other operating costs resulting from a new, rented location;

(3) to make leasehold improvements on rented property;

(4) to replace fixtures, machinery, and equipment, with reasonable upgrading permitted (but the trade-in value of the old equipment must be applied to the cost of the replacements);

(5) to purchase a larger or different type of inventory that may be better suited to a new location; and

(6) to pay moving expenses in excess of the amount provided by the public agency involved in the construction project.

SBA (See C1.110).

2.4 Pool Loans for Business Development

Under Section 7(a)(5) of the Small Business Act, SBA (Small Business Administration) is authorized to make loans to pools formed by several small business concerns. Formation of such pools must be cleared by the Department of Justice and information must be furnished to the Federal Trade Commission. The loan must be used to obtain raw materials, equipment, inventories, or supplies. It may also be used to gain access to benefits of research and development, or to construct facilities.

SBA (see C1.110).

2.5 Occupational Safety and Health Administration Compliance Loans

A booklet entitled *SBA Loans for OSHA Compliance* discusses how to get and use a loan before and after inspection by the Occupational Safety and Health Administration (OSHA).

Free; OSHA (see C1.79).

2.6 Loans and Guarantees from the Economic Development Administration

Business development assistance is offered by the Economic Development Administration (EDA) to help businesses locate new facilities or expand in economically lagging areas of the nation, defined by EDA. The main purpose of such assistance is to help upgrade the area economically, primarily through the creation of permanent jobs and higher incomes for local residents. EDA financial assistance for projects takes the following forms: (1) direct loans or purchase of evidences of indebtedness to finance the cost of fixed assets, (2) direct loans to provide working capital, (3) guarantees of loans to private borrowers by private lending institutions to provide working capital, and (4) guarantees of rental payments of leases from qualified lessors for fixed assets; i.e., buildings (including the underlying land) and equipment.

EDA cannot help a business relocate from one area to another; nor can it help if a labor surplus situation exists or is anticipated. In addition, financial assistance must be unavailable from other sources on terms and conditions that would permit the accomplishment of the project. Finally, there must be reasonable assurance of ability to repay the loan.

EDA (see C1.11).

2.7 Housing Production Loans and Mortgage Insurance

The Department of Housing and Urban Development (HUD) administers a wide variety of loans and mortgage insurance for private, profit-making firms; for example, Property Improvement Title I, Section 2, Class 2(a) loan insurance, which is available to insure the financing of commercial structures. In addition, mortgage insurance is available to private mortgagors involved in renewal, low and moderate income housing, and housing for the elderly.

HUD (see C1.40).

2.8 Property Improvement Loans

Property improvement loans may be made for the construction of small structures for commercial, industrial, or agricultural use, under the National Housing Act administered by the Department of Housing and Urban Development (HUD). The loans may be made for repairs, alterations, and improvements.

The customer must have a steady or determinable income adequate to permit repayment of the loan. The brochure, *Dealer and Contractor Guide to Property Improvement Loans*, clarifies the conditions under which loans may be made.

#HUD-30-F(3), free; HUD (see C1.40).

2.9 Minerals Discovery Loan Program

To encourage the exploration for specified minerals within the United States and its territories, the Geological Survey will contribute to the total allowable costs of exploration to a maximum of 75 percent for nine specified mineral commodities, and to a maximum of 50 percent for 27 others. Funds must be used for the exploration of geological targets considered to be favorable for the occurrence of deposits of ore of the specified commodities. Loans are paid back by means of royalties on mineral production if a discovery is certified by the government. In some cases, if no discovery is made, the loan need not be repaid.

Office of Minerals Exploration, National Center, Geological Survey (see C1.50); 703-860-6681. See also field offices (C1.50).

2.10 Economic Opportunity Loan Program

The Economic Opportunity Loan Program (EOL) makes it possible for disadvantaged individuals who have the capability and desire to own their own businesses to borrow money for starting or expanding. It provides both financial and management assistance. The maximum amount of an EOL is $100,000 for up to fifteen years. There are procedures to follow for both new and existing firms desiring to participate.

SBA (see C1.110).

2.11 Loans for Assistance to the Handicapped

Under legislation passed in 1973, the Small Business Administration (SBA) may make loans to small firms owned by handicapped persons as well as to nonprofit organizations where at least 75 percent of the manhours are performed by handicapped individuals.

SBA (see C1.110).

2.12 Loans to Local Development Companies

The Small Business Administration (SBA) is authorized to make loans to state and local development companies for use in assisting specific small businesses. SBA may lend up to $500,000 for each small business that is to be assisted. Thousands of loans have been made to such companies to enable them to help start, expand, or modernize their businesses.

The loans may be used to finance construction, modernization, or conversion of plants, including purchase of land, and to purchase machinery and equipment. They may not be used for working capital or for debt repayment, except interim debt incurred for construction of the project involved.

A loan may not be made if the funds needed are available from banks or other private lenders. To the extent that private sources do have funds, they may, and frequently do, participate with SBA in helping to finance projects. A development company is usually required to provide from its own funds at least 20 percent of the cost of the project.

The SBA booklet, *Loans to Local Development Companies,* furnishes more information.

SBA (see C1.110).

2.13 Water Pollution Control Loans

Direct loan funds are provided to qualified small businesses for use in purchasing and establishing such additions, alterations, or changes in method of operation as are necessary and adequate to comply with pollution control requirements established under the Federal Water Pollution Control Act, under a program sponsored by the Office of Water and Hazardous Materials of the Environmental Protection Agency and the Small Business Administration.

Water Planning Division, Office of Water and Hazardous Materials, Environmental Protection Agency, Washington, DC 20460; 202-755-6023. See also EPA regional offices (C1.151).

2.14 Surety Bond Guarantee Program

Small contractors who would not ordinarily be capable of securing bid, performance, and payment bonds through the established surety bond industry channels are provided surety bond assistance through this program. The SBA assistance for the required bonding consists of a 90 percent guarantee of the potential losses of private surety companies on a contract bond issued to the small contractor.

SBA (see C1.110).

2.15 Lease Guarantee Program

Under the lease guarantee program, small businesses can be provided with the credit required to compete on a more equal basis with large businesses for space on prime industrial and commercial property. Either through participating private insurance companies, or directly if no participation is available, the Small Business Administration (SBA) will guarantee the payment of the rent under leases entered into by small businesses which quality.

SBA (see C1.110).

2.16 Public Rulemaking Participation Assistance, Federal Trade Commission

Funds for the representation of certain interests in trade regulation rulemaking proceedings, when the expense of participation would otherwise make such representation impossible, are available through the Federal Trade Commission (FTC). Reasonable attorney fees, expert witness fees, and other costs of participating in trade regulation rulemaking proceedings may be included in the compensation.

Compensation is restricted to persons who have or represent an interest which would not otherwise be adequately represented in the proceeding, representation of which is necessary for a fair determination of proceedings taken as a while, and who cannot participate effectively because of inability to pay certain participation costs.

FTC (see C1.104).

2.17 *Starting a Small Business Investment Company (SBIC)*

Details on the organization and regulation of small business investment companies for the benefit of investors interested in profit-sharing with smaller firms are given in the pamphlet, *Starting a Small Business Investment Company (SBIC)*.

SBIC's are government-backed, flexible financing devices for furnishing equity capital and long-term loan funds to small businesses to operate, grow, and modernize. They are formed to operate under the regulations of the Small Business Investment Act once they have followed the simplified steps to obtain an SBIC license.

When SBIC's were developed, they were visualized as potential sources of capital and expertise for small firms previously limited to short-term financing. Since that time, they have proved to be adaptable to inner city as well as rural economic development by funneling much-needed investment capital into economically depressed communities, and to socially or economically disadvantaged small business entrepreneurs.

Free; SBA (see C1.110).

2.18 Minority Enterprise Small Business Investment Companies

Under Section 301 (d) of the Small Business Investment Act of 1958, special small business investment companies called Minority Enterprise Small Business Investment Companies (MESBIC) can be and have been established which concentrate on providing equity funds, long-term loans, and management assistance to small business concerns owned by socially or economically disadvantaged persons. The Small Business Administration (SBA) booklet entitled *Section 301 (d) SBIC's* reviews the procedure for setting up and operating a MESBIC. It is available at field offices of SBA (see C1.110).

A listing of MESBIC's can be found in Appendix C1.17.

2.19 New Community Development Corporation

The New Community Development Corporation of the Department of Housing and Urban Development (HUD) makes loan guarantees, grants, and technical assistance available to private developers of new community development projects approved by the Secretary of HUD. The program is set up to encourage the private sector to undertake the building of new towns.

New Community Development Corporation, HUD, Washington, DC 20410. See also HUD field offices (C1.40).

Rural Development Loans (2.50-2.60)

2.50 Business and Industrial Loans

The Farmers Home Administration is authorized to make loans to for-profit as well as to nonprofit organizations for the purpose of improving, developing, or financing business, industry, and employment and improving the economic and environmental climate in rural communities.

To apply for a business and industrial loan, contact the Farmers Home Administration county offices. See also FmHA state offices (C1.2).

2.51 Consolidated Farm and Rural Development Act Loans and Grants

Financial assistance is available to businesses under the Consolidated Farm and Rural Development Act, administered by the Department of Agriculture. The types of assistance available include loans, grants, and loan guarantees; they can be used to establish or improve facilities.

Cooperative Extension Service (see C1.1).

2.52 Rural Housing Site Loans

The Farmers Home Administration (FmHA) makes loans to finance building sites which may be developed into desirable residential communities. The sites must be in rural areas and must be sold on a nonprofit basis.

Rural areas include open country and places with a population of 10,000 or less that are rural in character and not closely associated with urban areas. Loans may be made in towns with populations between 10,000 and 20,000 that are outside of standard metropolitan statistical areas if the Secretary of Agriculture and the Secretary of Housing and Urban Development find there is a serious lack of mortgage credit.

Loans may be made to public or private local nonprofit organizations with legal authority to buy, develop, and sell homesites to elibible applicants.

Applicants for loans are made at the local country offices of FmHA. See also FmHA state offices (C1.2).

2.53 Rural Electrification and Telephone Assistance

Rural telephone companies and rural electric utilities may obtain loans and loan guarantees through the Rural Electrification Administration (REA) of the Department of Agriculture. REA also has a staff of engineering, accounting, and management specialists located throughout the United States to offer technical assistance.

REA, Department of Agriculture, Washington, DC 20250; 202-447-5606.

2.54 Grants to Help Develop Private Business

The Farmers Home Administration (FmHA) makes grants to facilitate development of private business enterprises in rural areas or cities up to 50,000 population, with priority to applications for projects in open country, rural communities, and towns of 25,000 or smaller.

Eligibility is limited to public bodies, such as incorporated towns and villages, boroughs, townships, counties, states, authorities, and districts.

Funds may be used to finance industrial sites that will result in development of private business enterprises. Costs that may be paid from grant funds include the acquisition and development of land and the construction of buildings, plants, equipment, access streets and roads, parking areas, utility and service extensions, refinancing, and fees.

Grant funds may be used jointly with funds furnished by the applicant, including FmHA loan funds.

FmHA (see C1.2).

2.55 Loans for Rural Rental Housing

Loans for rental housing in rural areas are available from Farmers Home Administratipn (FmHA) to provide living units for persons with low and moderate income and for those age 62 or older. Loans may be made for housing in open country and communities up to 20,000 people, but applicants in towns of 10,000 to 20,000 should check with their local FmHA office to see whether the agency can serve them.

Loans are primarily made to build, purchase, or repair apartment-style housing, usually consisting of duplexes, garden-type, or similar multiunit dwellings. The housing must be modest in size, design, and cost, but adequate to meet the tenants' needs.

Funds may also be used to buy and improve the land on which the buildings are to be located; to provide streets and water and waste disposal systems; to supply appropriate recreation and service facilities; to install laundry facilities and equipment; and to landscape, including lawn seeding and shrubbery and tree planting.

Funds may not be used for nursing, special care, or other institutional types of housing.

Eligibility of applicants will be determined by FmHA. Borrowers should have the ability and experience to operate and manage a rental housing project successfully.

Rental housing loans can be made to individuals, trusts, associations, partnerships, limited partnerships, state or local public agencies, consumer cooperatives, and profit and nonprofit corporations. Nonprofit corporations may be organized on a regional or multicounty basis.

Applications for rental housing loans should be made at the FmHA county office.

See also FmHA state offices (C1.2).

2.56 Business Loans for Farmers

The Farmers Home Administration (FmHA) makes loans to family farmers and ranchers and gives technical and management assistance for development and operation of nonfarm enterprises to supplement farm income. If a real estate loan is to be made, the enterprise must be located on the borrower's farm. Each person applying for credit gets equal consideration without regard to race, creed, sex, or national origin. Applications of eligible veterans are given preference. Veterans and nonveterans must meet the same requirements and qualifications for loans.

Enterprises for which loans can be made include repair shops, service stations, restaurants, grocery stores, welding shops, roadside stands, boarding animals, cabinet shops, riding stables, sporting goods stores, beauty shops, custom services, camping sites, and barber shops.

Applications for business loans are made at the local county office of the FmHA. See also FmHA state offices (C1.2).

2.57 Soil and Water Loans

The Farmers Home Administration (FmHa) makes soil and water loans and provides technical management assistance to owners or operators of farms and ranches for developing, conserving, and making proper use of their land and water resources.

Loans may be used to drill wells and otherwise improve water supply systems for irrigation, home use, and livestock; to purchase pumps, sprinkler systems, and other irrigation equipment; to acquire a water supply or water right; to purchase water stock or membership in an incorporated water user's association; to construct and repair ponds and tanks, ditches, and canals for irrigation; to dig ditches and install tile to drain farmland; and to develop ponds and water control structures for the production of fish under controlled conditions.

These loans may also be used to level land; carry out basic land treatment practices including liming, fertilizing, and seeding; develop subsoil or sod land; establish permanent pastures and farm forests; establish approved forestry practices on a farm, such as pest control, thinning, and fire protection.

Funds may also be used to build dikes, terraces, waterways, and other erosion control structures.

In addition, loan funds may be used to obtain plans and pay fees for legal, engineering, and other technical services.

FmHa (see C1.2).

2.58 Farm Labor Housing Loans

The Farmers Home Administration (FmHA) makes loans and grants to finance low-rent housing for domestic farm laborers.

Funds may be used to build, buy, improve, or repair farm labor housing and to provide related facilities. They also may be used to buy building sites, purchase basic durable household furnishings, and to develop water, sewage disposal, and heating and lighting systems. Funds may not be used to refinance debts.

A *loan* may be made to an individual farm owner, association of farmers, state or political subdivision, broadly based public or private nonprofit organization, or a nonprofit organization of farmworkers. To be eligible, an applicant must (1) be unable to obtain funds from private lenders on terms and conditions the borrower can reasonably be expected to meet; (2) have authority to obtain, give security for, and raise revenue to repay the loan; (3) have sufficient income to make loan payments, pay insurance premiums, taxes, maintenance, and to otherwise carry out a sound operation.

A *grant* may be made to a state political subdivision, a broadly based nonprofit organization, or a nonprofit organization of farmworkers. To be eligible, an applicant must (1) be unable to provide necessary housing from his own resources, including an FmHA labor housing loan; (2) have adequate initial operating capital and, after the project is completed, have income needed for a sound operation; and (3) possess the legal capacity to contract for a grant.

To apply for a farm labor housing loan, contact the FmHA county office. See also FmHA state offices (C1.2).

2.59 Emergency Loans

Farmers Home Administration (FmHA) emergency loans may be made in counties where property damage or severe production losses have occurred as a result of a natural disaster and the area has been named eligible for assistance.

A presidential declaration will identify major disaster and emergency areas. The Secretary of Agriculture can make a designation whenever a natural disaster has substantially affected farming, ranching, or aquaculture operations in an area. For designation by the Secretary, a formal request must be made by the state governor, followed by an assessment of damage in each affected county.

In natural disaster situations involving no more than twenty-five farm, ranch, or aquaculture operators in any one county, emergency loans may be authorized by the state director of the FmHA at the request of the state governor or a local governing body, including an Indian tribal council.

Loans may be made to applicants to cover actual losses and expenses for damaged or destroyed farm property and production. Such loans are at five percent interest, and funds may be used to repair, restore, or replace damaged or destroyed farm property and supplies, to pay expenses incurred for crop production, and to pay farm debts owed to other creditors.

A borrower eligible for an emergency loan for actual losses may also be eligible for a loan at the prevailing market interest rates to construct or improve buildings (including a home) and facilities. Such loans may also be made to purchase livestock and to pay costs incident to reorganizing the farming system to make it a sound operation, equivalent to the operation prior to the disaster. These funds may be used to buy essential home equipment and furnishings and to refinance debts under certain conditions.

Subsequent emergency loans for operating purposes may be made at prevailing interest rates for each year up to five years to permit the borrower to return to usual credit sources.

Applications for emergency loans are made at the county offices of FmHA.

See also FmHA state offices (C1.2).

2.60 Farm Operating Loans

The Farmers Home Administration (FmHA) makes farm operating loans, accompanied by technical management assistance, to operators of family farms.

The loans are tailored to a borrower's needs. The FmHA county supervisor helps the borrower analyze his problems, determine his available resources, and plan how these resources, plus those obtained by the loan, may best be used.

Farm operating loans may be used to pay for items necessary to the success of the proposed operation, such as livestock, poultry, farm and home equipment, fencing, feed, seed, fuel, fertilizer, chemicals, hail and other crop insurance, food, clothing, medical care, personal insurance, and to hire labor. Certain debts may be refinanced.

Minor improvements to buildings and real estate may be made, and water systems developed for home use, livestock, and irrigation. Funds can finance the purchase and operation of equipment for producing and harvesting trees and other products, for producing fish under controlled conditions, and for nonfarm businesses and recreational enterprises such as fishing, horseback riding, camping, and hunting.

Pollution control and abatement and alteration of equipment, facilities, or methods of operation to comply with the Occupational Safety and Health Act of 1970 are permissible uses.

Applications for farm operating loans are made at county offices of the FmHA. See also FmHA state offices (C1.2).

Financial Management, Taxes, and Insurance (2.100-2.204)

Financial Management Assistance (2.100-2.115)

2.100 *Bank/SBA Loans*

Bank/SBA Loans, Partnership for Small Business Progress, A Handbook for Banks and Other Private Lending Institutions, #045-000-00122-9, 1973, 121 pp., $2.00; GPO (see C1.0).

2.101 *Measurement of Corporate Profits*

Some of the ratios commonly used to measure profits, as well as some of the measurement problems that arise in periods of inflation are explained in this booklet. Measurement problems peculiar to the extractive industries are also discussed.

#052-070-02292-2, 33 pp., 45¢; GPO (see C1.0).

2.102 *The Vital Majority, Small Business in the American Economy*

A wide range of subjects is covered in this book of essays marking the twentieth anniversary of the Small Business Administration. Typical topics are: finance, accounting, marketing, government assistance programs, information systems and computerization, research and development, management strategies, labor relations, taxation, and market structures.

#045-000-00124-5, 510 pp., $6.75; GPO (see C1.0).

2.103 *Financial Control by Time-Absorption Analysis*

A profit control technique that can be used by all kinds of business is described in this book. It includes a step-by-step approach which shows how to establish this method in a given business.

#SBA 1.12:37, 138 pp., $1.40; GPO (see C1.0).

2.104 *Cash Planning in Small Manufacturing Companies*

Designed for the owners of small firms and the specialists who study them, this book reports on research on cash planning for small manufacturers.

#SBA 1.20:1, 276 pp., $2.70; GPO (see C1.0).

2.105 *Cost Accounting for Small Manufacturers*

Designed for small manufacturers and their accountants, this book stresses the importance of determining and recording costs accurately. It includes diagrams, flow charts, and illustrations.

#SBA 1.12:9, 163 pp., $1.60; GPO (see C1.0).

2.106 *Financial Recordkeeping for Small Stores*

A basic recordkeeping system for small store owners whose business does not justify hiring a trained fulltime bookkeeper is described in this book. It discusses accounts receivable, depreciation, taxes, maintaining records of transactions, and more.

#045-000-00142, 135 pp., $1.55; GPO (see C1.0).

2.107 *Handbook of Small Business Finance*

Procedures for keeping accurate, well organized accounting records and for making regular financial reports are described in this handbook. Also, proper techniques to analyze the reports are explained. It discusses such topics as good bookkeeping methods, profit and loss statements, balance sheets, and techniques (such as ratio analysis) for measuring performance of a business.

#045-000-00139, 64 pp., 75¢; GPO (see C1.0).

2.108 Financial Assistance Necessitated by Rail Service Discontinuance

Quick identification of loan and technical assistance sources for businesses in general, as well as sources of help for businesses hurt by rail service interruption, can be made in this brochure entitled *Opportunities for Business Credit and Other Federal Assistance for Individuals, Small Businesses, and Communities Adversely Affected by Rail Service Discontinuance or Abandonment.*

Free; SBA (see C1.110).

2.109 *The Why and What of Bookkeeping*

Educators and businessmen who teach management courses will find this presentation useful. It includes a lesson plan, lecture, visual aids, case studies, study assignments, and selected bibliography and handout material.

#045-000-00092-3, 64 pp., 1974, $3.20; GPO (see C1.0).

2.110 *Financing New Technological Enterprise*

Problems associated with the acquisition of venture capital, particularly those relating to new technologically oriented businesses, are examined in this report. Steps to be taken to improve capital flow are recommended.

50¢; GPO (see C1.0).

2.111 Small Business Administration *Annual Report*

The *Annual Report* of the Small Business Administration (SBA) provides a description and performance analysis of each of the agency's financial and management assistance programs, demonstrating the breadth of activity of SBA.

$3.20; GPO (see C1.0).

2.112 Free Publications on Financial Management

The following publications are available, free, from SBA (see C1.110).

Order No.	Management Aids Series
170	*The ABC's of Borrowing*
174	*Is Your Cash Supply Adequate?*
176	*Financial Audits: A Tool for Better Management*
220	*Basic Budgets for Profit Planning*
222	*Business Life Insurance*
	Small Marketers Aids Series
110	*Controlling Cash in Small Retail and Service Firms*
126	*Accounting Services for Small Service Firms*
142	*Steps in Meeting Your Tax Obligations*
144	*Getting the Facts for Income Tax Reporting*
146	*Budgeting in a Small Service Firm*
147	*Sound Cash Management and Borrowing*
148	*Insurance Checklist for Small Business*
	Small Business Bibliographies
20	*Retail Credit and Collections*
87	*Financial Management*

2.113 Small Business Institute Program

The Small Business Institute program, a three-way cooperative between collegiate schools of business administration, members of the nation's small business community, and the Small Business Administration (SBA) is a new source of management assistance. Under the supervision of university faculty and SBA staff, senior and graduate students of business administration work directly with owners of small firms, providing vital management assistance to small businesses while undergoing meaningful learning experiences themselves.

The program began in the fall of 1972. In the

first year of its life, 1,100 small firms received counseling and 2,200 students were involved. In 1976, 385 schools participated, involving over 22,000 students and 8,800 small businesses. Satisfaction rate among clients was over 80 percent.

SBA (see C1.110).

2.114 University Business Development Centers

Growing out of the Small Business Institute concept (see 2.113), the University Business Development Center (UBDC) program is an experimental Small Business Administration concept being tested in eight universities. It is a university-based and administered program to interrelate the academic, professional, and technological resources of universities with all existing government programs designed to assist the business community. While each agency continues to administer its own programs, the university serves as a funnel or mixing device for them, so that the collection of programs will work as an integrated unit serving the whole community, rather than as an uncoordinated variety of programs.

A functioning UBDC can offer the following services to its business clients:

—Business and product evaluation and development
—Entrepreneur evaluation, recommendations, counseling, and training
—Analysis, correction, and followup of financial, marketing, technical, production, legal, and any other type of problem faced by small business owners
—Feasibility studies and development of business plans for present and future entrepreneurs
—Access to and application of technology, paid for by the taxpayers in over $350 billion worth of research and development projects since 1947
—Assistance not only in surviving (when 57 percent of new businesses fail in the first five years) but also in expanding on a solid basis

Universities currently involved are the Universities of Maine at Bangor, Missouri at St. Louis, Nebraska at Omaha, Georgia at Athens, and West Florida at Pensacola; and Rutgers University, New Brunswick, New Jersey; California State University at Chico; and California Polytechnic at Pomona.

2.115 Revolving Line of Credit

Under this program, the Small Business Administration (SBA) seeks to help small firms obtain a line of credit from a bank in order to fulfill construction or other contracts by guaranteeing the credit extended by the bank.

SBA (see C1.110).

Tax Credits and Tax Planning (2.150-2.157)

2.150 Tax Credit and Training Reimbursement: The Work Incentive Program

The Work Incentive Program (WIN) is a program intended to help recipients of Aid to Families with Dependent Children get and keep jobs. It provides a variety of supportive services to applicants to prepare them for work, and of incentives for employers to participate. WIN is jointly administered by the Department of Labor and the Department of Health, Education, and Welfare.

One incentive for employers to offer jobs is a sizable tax credit. It allows them to receive a credit, deducted from their federal income tax liability, amounting to 20 percent of the first year's wages paid to every WIN registrant they hire and keep on the job.

Another incentive arises from the "hire first, train later" concept. Here, WIN reimburses employers for the cost of on-the-job training provided for the WIN participants they employ. The employers get trained workers, compensation for the training, and a tax credit on their wages.

Contact the manager of the local State Employment Service or the headquarters of the State Employment Security Agency (see C1.73).

2.151 Investment Tax Credit

If a business acquires new or used depreciable property and places it in service during the tax year, it may qualify for an investment tax credit. The amount of the investment in qualifying property eligible for tax credit depends upon the useful life of the property and whether the property is new or used. The credit allowable is 10 percent of the eligible investment and is limited to the income tax liability in excess of $25,000, whichever is less.

The investment tax credit is described in the *Tax Guide for Small Business* (see 2.154).

IRS (see C1.95).

2.152 Employee Stock Ownership Plan Tax Credit

Under the Tax Reduction Act of 1975, certain tax incentives are offered businesses which participate in the relatively new means of employee compensation referred to as Employee Stock Ownership Plans (ESOP). An ESOP is an employee plan of the defined contribution type that is designed to invest primarily in employer securities. One of its basic purposes is to provide employees with some ownership in the companies for which they work.

IRS publishes a Technical Information Release (TIR-1413) which answers some basic questions about such a plan, including election of an eleven percent investment credit; funding requirements, requirements other than funding; and taxability and deductibility of ESOP funds. In addition, IRS will issue determination letters to employers who have specific questions or problems regarding whether or not a particular ESOP qualifies or meets the requirements of the Act with respect to the eleven percent investment credit.

IRS (see C1.95).

2.153 Business Tax Kit

The IRS will assemble a tax information and forms kit tailored to an individual business. It usually consists of selected publications from their publications list.

The kit can be obtained from the Public Affairs Division, Internal Revenue Service, Department of the Treasury, 1111 Constitution Avenue N.W., Washington, DC 20224; 202-964-4021. IRS area offices can also provide the proper guides and forms (see C1.95).

2.154 *Tax Guide for Small Business*

Tax Guide for Small Business contains information useful in starting, operating, or disposing of a business. It explains how the federal tax laws apply to sole proprietorships, partnerships, and small corporations. The latest edition reflects the provisions of the Tax Reform Act of 1976, which contains substantial changes in the tax law affecting business.

If the *Tax Guide* does not supply all the needed answers, an IRS area office may be contacted for assistance (see C1.95).

2.155 Free Publications on Taxes

The following publications are available, free, from IRS (see C1.95).

No.

225 *Farmer's Tax Guide*
349 *Federal Highway Use Tax*
463 *Travel, Entertainment, and Gift Expense*
505 *Tax Withholding and Declaration of Estimated Tax*
509 *Tax Calendar and Checklist for 1977*
510 *Information on Excise Taxes for 1977*
512 *Credit Sales by Dealers in Personal Property*
521 *Tax Information on Moving Expense*
522 *Tax Information on Disability Payments*
529 *Miscellaneous Deductions and Credits*
533 *Information on Self-Employment Tax*
534 *Tax Information on Depreciation*
535 *Tax Information on Business Expenses*
537 *Tax Information Installment and Deferred-Payment Sales*
538 *Tax Information on Accounting Periods and Methods*
539 *Withholding Taxes and Reporting Requirements*
541 *Tax Information on Partnership Income and Losses*
542 *Corporations and the Federal Income Tax*
544 *Sales and Other Dispositions of Assets*
545 *Income Tax Deduction for Interest Expense*
547 *Tax Information on Disasters, Casualty Losses, and Thefts*
548 *Tax Information on Deductions for Bad Debts*
549 *Condemnations of Private Property for Public Use*
550 *Tax Information on Investment Income and Expenses*
552 *Recordkeeping Requirements and a Guide to Tax Publications*
556 *Audit of Returns, Appeal Rights, and Claims for Refund*
557 *How to Apply for Recognition of Exemp-*

tion for an Organization

558 *Tax Information for Sponsors of Contests and Sporting Events*
564 *Tax Information on Mutual Fund Distributions*
572 *Tax Information on Investment Credit*
575 *Tax Information on Pension and Annuity Income*
578 *Tax Information for Private Foundations and Foundation Managers*
582 *Federal Use Tax on Civil Aircraft*
583 *Recordkeeping for a Small Business*
584 *Workbook for Determining Your Disaster Loss*
587 *Business Use of Your Home*
588 *Tax Information on Condominiums and Cooperative Apartments*
589 *Tax Information on Subchapter S Corporations*
590 *Tax Information on Individual Retirement Savings Programs*
595 *Tax Guide for Commercial Fishermen*
900 *Quick Index to Taxpayer Information Publications*

2.156 *Taxation, a Key Factor in Business Decisions*

Educators and others who teach management courses will find this presentation useful. It includes a lesson plan, lecture, visual aids, case studies, study assignments, and selected bibliography and handout material.

#045-000-00096-6, 74 pp., $4.00; GPO (See C1.0).

2.157 Tax Information and Education

Information and guidance on tax matters, including assistance in the preparation of returns, is available to individuals or groups interested in the tax system or having questions on his or their tax returns. Various types of tax courses can be arranged for groups of taxpayers, such as small business associations, and for taxpayers with unusual circumstances, such as those who have suffered property losses in natural disasters. Toll-free telephone services are available to any taxpayer in the nation.

IRS (see C1.95).

Insurance
(2.200-2.204)

2.200 *Insurance and Risk Management for Small Business*

The definition of insurance, the necessity of obtaining professional advice on buying insurance, and the main types of insurance a small business may need are all discussed in this book.

#SBA 1.12:30, 72 pp., 95¢; GPO (see C1.0).

2.201 Health Insurance Coverage for Alcoholism

The National Institute on Alcohol Abuse and Alcoholism (NIAAA) is working with the health insurance industry to find ways and means of providing coverage for alcoholism. Currently, outright exclusion of alcoholism from coverage is common; however, limiting of benefits is more often the case. NIAAA's efforts to encourage insurance coverage are aimed primarily at assisting the nation's facilities for the treatment of alcoholism to provide quality care.

Occupational Programs, NIAAA, 5600 Fishers Lane, Rockville, MD 20852.

2.202 Federal Crime Insurance Program

The Federal Crime Insurance Program (FCIP) offers low cost, easily obtainable, noncancellable burglary and robbery insurance to small businessmen and residential property owners and tenants in states which have been declared eligible. A state becomes eligible for the program when the administrator determines that affordable crime insurance is virtually impossible to get through normal channels, and when no steps have been taken to remedy that situation. FCIP is now available in the District of Columbia and the following twenty states:

Arkansas	Iowa	New York
Colorado	Kansas	Ohio
Connecticut	Maryland	Pennsylvania
Delaware	Massachusetts	Rhode Island
Florida	Minnesota	Tennessee
Georgia	Missouri	Virginia
Illinois	New Jersey	

State crime insurance programs similar to the

FCIP are available in California, Michigan, Indiana, and Wisconsin.

In the twenty states mentioned, FCIP policies can be written by any licensed property insurance broker or agent, or by the private insurance company designated under contract as the servicing company for a particular state. It is renewable regardless of losses and is available at uniform rates to everyone in the eligible state, regardless of their occupation or the crime rate in their neighborhood.

Commercial losses from burglary or robbery can be insured in amounts ranging from $1,000 to $15,000. Typical commercial premiums range from $35 for $1,000 coverage in a low-crime area for businesses with annual gross receipts under $100,000, to $748 for $15,000 coverage in a high-crime area.

To obtain FCIP insurance, an application from any licensed broker or agent or state servicing company must be filled out and half the year's premium paid. The applicant will be billed for the second half six months later.

Necessary inspections are made by the servicing insurance company and paid for by the federal government.

Federal Insurance Administration, Department of Housing and Urban Development, Washington, DC 20410. See also HUD field offices (C.140).

2.203 Riot Insurance

The purpose of riot insurance is to assure availability of essential coverage for urban property, particularly that located in areas possibly subject to riots or civil disturbance, by providing reinsurance to insurers against catastrophic loss from riot or civil disorder. Federal reinsurance of this nature is available only to property insurance companies that cooperate as risk-bearing members of a State Fair Access to Insurance Requirements (FAIR) plan. FAIR plans operate in 25 states, the District of Columbia, and Puerto Rico.

Administrator, Federal Insurance Administration, Department of Housing and Urban Development, Washington, DC 20410. See also HUD field offices (C1.40).

2.204 Flood Insurance

Flood insurance is offered to insure persons against physical damage or to loss of real or personal property caused by floods, mudslides, or flood-caused erosion, and to promote wise flood plain management practices in the nation's flood-prone areas. Property owners may buy flood insurance at a rate lower than a normal actuarial rate. The maximum amount available is $100,000 for residential nonfamily structures.

Administrator, Federal Insurance Administration, Department of Housing and Urban Development, Washington, DC 20410; 202-755-5581, or toll free: 800-424-8872, 8873. See also HUD field offices (C1.40).

Export Financing (2.250-2.260)

2.250 *Export Opportunities for American Business through the International Banks*

The role of international banks in assisting businesses seeking to develop trade overseas is explained in this brochure.

Office of International Development Banks, Department of the Treasury, Washington, DC 20220.

2.251 *A Guide to Financing Exports*

A Guide to Financing Exports reviews all major sources of financial assistance and insurance for exporting: the Export-Import Bank, Foreign Credit Insurance Association, Overseas Private Investment Corporation, and Community Credit Corporation.

Free; Department of Commerce (see C1.10).

2.252 Export-Import Bank of the United States (Eximbank)

Eximbank offers direct loan for large projects and equipment sales that usually require longer term financing. It cooperates with banks at home and abroad to provide a number of financial arrangements to help United States exporters offer credit guarantees to commercial banks that finance export sales; and, through the Foreign Credit Insurance Association, it provides insurance to United States exporters which enables them to extend credit terms to their foreign buyers. In all cases, the bank must find a reasonable assurance of repayment as a precondition of participation in a transaction.

Export-Import Bank, 811 Vermont Ave. N.W., Washington, DC 20571.

2.253 Foreign Credit Insurance Association

The export credit insurance offered by Foreign Credit Insurance Association (FCIA) provides an incentive to United States exporters to offer competitive terms to buyers. FCIA administers the United States export credit insurance program on behalf of its member insurance companies and the government-owned Eximbank. Eximbank assumes all liability for the political risks.

One of FCIA's major forms of coverage is a master policy which provides automatic coverage for all of an exporter's sales, both short and medium term, on credit terms ranging up to five years. In addition, FCIA offers service industries a services export program which extends to them the same credit insurance traditionally offered to commodity industries.

FCIA, One World Trade Center, Ninth Floor, New York, NY 10048.

2.254 Overseas Private Investment Corporation

The Overseas Private Investment Corporation (OPIC) offers investment guarantees comparable to those offered by FCIA (see 2.253) and Eximbank to United States manufacturers who wish to establish operations in less developed nations either by themselves or as a joint venture with local capital.

OPIC, 429 20th St. N.W., Washington, DC 20527.

2.255 Western Hemisphere Trading Corporation

If a company qualifies for Western Hemisphere Trading Corporation status, it receives a special deduction from taxable income, resulting in a substantial tax reduction. It is taxed at approximately 70 percent of its profits. The company pays 15.6 percent on its first $35,000 net profit and 34 percent on the balance, whereas the normal rate is 22 percent on the first $25,000 and 48 percent on the balance. In order to qualify, all business of the firm must be conducted in the western hemisphere and 95 percent of the firm's income must be derived from exporting.

Office of Export Development, Bureau of International Commerce, Department of Commerce, Washington, DC 20230.

2.256 Domestic International Sales Corporation

Domestic International Sales Corporation (DISC) is a new category of corporation, created in 1972, which entitles a company to defer tax on 50 percent of its export income until such income is distributed to shareholders. The tax-deferred earnings retained by the DISC may be invested in its own export business or loaned to domestic producers of export goods.

A DISC is a domestic company that limits its activities almost solely to export sales, lease or rental transactions, and related activities. It can operate as a principal, buying and selling for its own account, or as a commission agent. It can be an independent merchant or broker, or a subsidiary of another firm.

Office of Export Development, Bureau of International Commerce, Department of Commerce (see C1.10).

2.257 Private Export Funding Corporation

The Private Export Funding Corporation (PEFCO) is owned by 62 investors, mostly commercial banks. It lends only to finance the export of goods and services of United States manufacture and origin. Its loans generally have maturities in the medium term area and all are unconditionally guaranteed by Eximbank as to payment of interest and repayment of principal. PEFCO's funds supplement the financing of United States exports available through commercial banks and Eximbank.

PEFCO, 280 Park Ave., New York, NY 10007.

2.258 Carnets

Carnets are international customs documents which guarantee against customs duties. They are composed of a series of vouchers which list the goods covered and the countries to be visited. The carnet system is designed to permit duty-free temporary entry of commercial samples for the purpose of demonstration and promotion.

Foreign Business Practices Division, Bureau of International Commerce, Department of Commerce (see C1.10).

2.259 Export Management Companies

Under contract, Export Management Companies (EMC) can perform the following activities on behalf of an exporter: market research, location of distributors, exhibition and promotion of product, responsibility for shipping details (export declarations, customs, insurance, packing, marking), and general consultation. Some EMC's even communicate with overseas buyers on the client's letterhead with the designation "export department."

The EMC can also be of assistance in extending credit to foreign buyers and in determining if it would be profitable actually to produce the product in the country in question.

The EMC operates on either a commission basis or a direct buy-and-sell arrangement in which the EMC receives an overseas order, then purchases from the manufacturer and resells abroad. EMC's specialize in allied but not competitive products and know where the demand is and what its intensity and future are.

EMC's are particularly useful to the smaller firm, although they are utilized by firms of all sizes. There are about 1,000 of them in the United States.

A helpful book, *A Directory of U.S. Export Management Companies*, lists 668 EMC's, including addresses, telephone numbers, and a product index (75¢; GPO (see C1.0).

There are many sources of assistance for choosing an EMC: field offices of the Department of Commerce (see C1.10), foreign trade divisions of chambers of commerce, foreign trade bank executives, and industry trade associations.

2.260 The Export Credit Sales Program

The Export Credit Sales Program provides financing of export sales of United States agricultural commodities for a maximum of thirty-six months. An application for financing is submitted by the United States exporter and, if approved, it permits him to sell such agricultural commodities to a foreign importer on a deferred payment basis. Commodities eligible for financing under this program and the rate of interest to be charged are announced each month in a Department of Agriculture press release. Eligibility is usually limited to primary commodities.

Assistant Sales Manager, Commercial Export Program, Office of the General Sales Manager, Department of Agriculture, Washington, DC 20250; 202-447-4274.

Chapter 3

MARKET RESEARCH, MARKETING, GOVERNMENT PROCUREMENT

CHAPTER ABSTRACT

Market analysis information and opportunities to sell to the government are the focus of this chapter. The market analysis aspect examines primarily the wealth of statistical data available from the government. Such data provide extremely detailed information on population, housing, and business activity in forms which can be used to delineate areas of market potential and sales territories.(See also Appendix C2, "Understanding and Using Census Data.")

"Marketing and Sales Management Publications" (3.0-3.10) describes management development programs in marketing, marketing guides and commentaries, and publications which assist in interpreting government statistics for marketing purposes.

"Statistical Directories and Guides to Data Sources" (3.50-3.68) lists statistical source directories, guides to the Bureaus of Census and Labor Statistics, and guides to agricultural research and statistics.

"Data Bases for Market and Sales Analysis" (3.100-3.120) is the heart of the chapter. It describes publications, subscription services, and research sources which can supply detailed market analysis data by geographic area or kind of business or product.

"Technical Assistance in Market Research" (3.150-3.155) discusses consultative services available in interpreting government statistics, and other sources of marketing advice and special assistance.

"Postal Service Information" (3.200-3.202) describes a variety of programs useful to businesses which depend upon mail efficiency.

The balance of this chapter is designed to increase business awareness of opportunities to sell commodities, services, and research expertise to the government, the largest buyer of goods and services in the world.

"Government Procurement Guides and Directories" (3.250-3.259) lists information sources which can familiarize the businessman with the world of government procurement. (See also Business Service Centers, 3.450.)

"Research and Development Guides and Opportunities" (3.300-3.310) looks primarily at research and development possibilities in government, including possibilities with unsolicited proposals.

"Department of Defense Procurement" (3.351-3.356) is treated separately because the Department of Defense is the largest procurement agency in government and because it handles most of its buying activities independently.

"Special Assistance and Procurement Specifications" (3.450-3.459) describes sources for assistance in getting on bidder's lists for the government, and special lists of set-aside contracts for small business. It also lists publications providing detailed information on specifications.

Publications and Films on Marketing and Sales Management (3.0-3.10)

3.0 *Measuring Markets—A Guide to the Use of Federal and State Statistical Data*

Some of the measurable characteristics and dimensions of a market, and the principal statistical series of interest, are described in this booklet, along with a series of cases which illustrate how government statistics can aid in measuring markets. Some of these cases are presented in Appendix C2.

$1.35; GPO (see C1.0).

3.1 *Practical Business Use of Government Statistics*

Government statistics and marketing are discussed in this publication. It gives real examples which apply to the three basic market analysis questions: How big is the market, where is it, and what are its characteristics?

28 pp., 1975, 35¢; GPO (see C1.0).

3.2 Business Service Checklist

All new publications and information releases, services, and activities of the Department of Commerce, including both domestic and foreign trade developments and reports, are included in this weekly list.

$9.70 per year; GPO (see C1.0).

3.3 *Marketing and Low-Income Consumers*

Over 320 articles, reports, and studies on marketing and low-income consumers are listed in this reference source. Each concise summary tells how the source is particularly useful.

GPO (see C1.0).

3.4 Free Publications on Marketing and Sales

The following publications are available, free, from SBA (see C1.110).

Order No. Management Aids Series

85 *Analyzing Your Cost of Marketing*
178 *Effective Industrial Advertising for Small Plants*
187 *Using Census Data in Small Plant Marketing*
188 *Developing a List of Prospects*
190 *Measuring the Performance of Salesmen*
192 *Profile Your Customers to Expand Industrial Sales*
193 *What Is the Best Selling Price?*
194 *Marketing Planning Guidelines*
196 *Tips on Selecting Salesmen*
200 *Is the Independent Sales Agent for You?*
203 *Are Your Products and Channels Producing Sales?*
204 *Pointers on Negotiating DOD Contracts*
215 *How to Prepare for a Pre-Award Survey*

Small Marketers Aids Series

109 *Stimulating Impulse Buying for Increased Sales*
111 *Interior Displays: A Way to Increase Sales*
113 *Quality and Taste as Sales Appeals*
121 *Measuring the Results of Advertising*
128 *Building Customer Confidence in Your Service Shop*
156 *Marketing Checklist for Small Retailers*

Small Business Bibliographies

3 *Selling by Mail Order*
9 *Marketing Research Procedures*
12 *Statistics and Maps for National Market Analysis*
13 *National Directories for Use in Marketing*
20 *Advertising—Retail Stores*
29 *National Mailing-List Houses*
56 *Training Commercial Salesmen*
67 *Manufacturers Sales Representatives*

3.5 *Selecting Advertising Media—A Guide for Small Business*

Helping small businesses to decide which medium to use for making a product, a service, or a store known to potential customers and what is the best use of advertising money is the purpose of this book.

#SBA 1.12:35, 56 pp., 65¢; GPO (see C1.0).

3.6 *Training Salesmen to Serve Industrial Markets*

The role of sales in marketing programs of small manufacturers, suggestions for salesmen to use in servicing customers, and material useful in training programs are discussed in this book.

#SBA 1.12:36, 85 pp., $1.15; GPO (see C1.0).

3.7 Publications on Marketing and Sales

Educators and businessmen who teach management courses will find these presentations useful. They include a lesson plan, lecture, visual aids, case studies, study assignments, and selected bibliography and handout material.

As priced; GPO (see C1.0).

Managing to Sell, #045-000-00091-5, 74 pp., $4.00
Aspects of Sales Promotion, #045-000-00095-8, 64 pp., $3.20
Effective Advertising, #045-000-00084-2 (being reprinted)
Why Customers Buy (and Why They Don't), #045-000-00086-9, 52 pp., $3.40
Marketing Research, Instructor's Manual, #045-000-00087-7, 78 pp., $3.65

3.8 *The Vital Majority, Small Business in the American Economy*

A wide range of subjects is covered in this book of essays marking the twentieth anniversary of the Small Business Administration. Typical topics are: finance, accounting, marketing, government assistance programs, information systems and computerization, research and development, management strategies, labor relations, taxation, and market structures.

#045-000-00124-5, 510 pp., $6.75; GPO (see C1.0).

3.9 Data Sources for Specific Industry Marketing

Unless otherwise indicated, the following publications are available, as priced, from Consumer Goods and Services Division, Bureau of Domestic Commerce, Room 1104, Department of Commerce, Washington, DC 20230.

Food Industries Data Sources, 59 pp., free
Household Furniture and Appliances: Basic Information Sources, 22 pp., free
Retail Data Sources for Market Analysis, 18 pp., free
Wholesale Data Sources for Market Analysis, 12 pp., free
Business Machine Market Information Sources, 41 pp., 50¢; Publication Sales Branch, Room 1617, Department of Commerce, Washington, DC 20230
Service Industry Data Sources for Market Analysis, free; Publication Sales Branch, Room 1617, Department of Commerce, Washington, DC 20230
Data Communications Market Information Sources, 53 pp., 95¢; GPO (see C1.0).

3.10 Films on Advertising and Customer Relations

The films described in this section are available from National Audio-Visual Center, General Services Administration, Order Section NACDO, Washington, DC 20409; for sale or rent as priced, except no rental of 8 mm. films.

The Advertising Question

Some of the misconceptions and attitudes which many small businessmen display toward advertising are demonstrated and corrected in this film.

14 min., 16 mm., sound, color, #118520; sale 16 mm., $63.50, rental 16 mm., $10.00; sale 8 mm., $41.50 (#009082).

Variations on a Theme

Many of the factors involved in implementing a successful sales event are demonstrated in this film. Meetings with all store personnel illustrate step-by-step preparations for the sale.

13 min., 16 mm., sound, color, #780500; sale 16 mm., $59.00, rental 16 mm., $10.00; sale 8 mm., $40.50 (#009084).

The Calendar Game

The need for advertising, planning, and budgeting by small retail and service businesses is the main point of emphasis in this film. Timing, choice of media, and plans for specific promotions are discussed.

14 min., 16 mm., sound, color, #194215; sale 16 mm., $63.50, rental 16 mm., $10.00; sale 8

mm., $40.75 (#009079).

The Follow-Up

In this film, illustrations of following up on a radio commercial, soliciting customers' reactions to store layouts and point-of-sale ads, and getting business associates' opinions of ads used or planned bring out many of the factors to consider in advertising/sales promotion follow-up.

13 min., 16 mm., sound, color, #335459; sale 16 mm., $59.00, rental 16 mm., $10.00; sale 8 mm., $40.00 (#009072).

You and Your Customers

Situations which small retailers may encounter involving customer relations are presented in this film. Audience involvement is stimulated by providing opportunity to stop the film for discussion following some of the more detailed situations, then presenting possible solutions to the problems presented on the screen.

14 min., 16 mm., sound, color, #826720, sale 16 mm., $63.50, rental 16 mm., $10.00; sale 8 mm., $39.00 (#009076).

Statistical Directories and Guides to Data Sources (3.50-3.68)

3.50 *Directory of Federal Statistics for Local Areas*

Information available on standard metropolitan statistical areas, counties, and cities is given in this directory.

$1.00; GPO (see C1.0).

3.51 *Directory of Federal Statistics for States*

Statistics available in over 200 publications published by federal agencies and departments are listed in this directory. A detailed bibliography lists the publications and the government agencies issuing them.

$2.25; GPO (see C1.0).

3.52 *Directory of Non-Federal Statistics for States and Local Areas: A Guide to Sources*

Information available for individual states, the District of Columbia, Puerto Rico, Guam, and the Virgin Islands for specified substate areas in thirteen major subjects is given in this directory. Detailed bibliographic entries list the publications containing the statistics and the issuing agency.

$6.25; GPO (see C1.0).

3.53 *Data User News*

This basic subscription service of the Bureau of the Census provides information on applications of census data and on new computer programs, news on user-oriented programs and products, announcements of workshops and seminars, a reader's exchange, and more. Eight or more pages each month bring news of activities, products, and publications in the field of small-area census data. A special section highlights the applications readers around the country have found for census data. Articles by Bureau specialists explain technical points, methodology, and processing techniques of the Bureau of the Census.

$4.00 per year; Subscriber Services Section, Bureau of the Census, Department of Commerce, Washington, DC 20233.

3.54 *Bureau of the Census Catalog*

The publications, computer tapes and punchcards, and related nonstatistical materials and services made available from January of each year are described in this catalog. Part I, *Publications*, is a classified, annotated bibliography of all publications issued by the Bureau during the period covered. Geographical and subject indexes are provided. Part II, *Data Files and Special Publications*, initiated in 1964, provides a listing of those materials which became available at the Bureau during the catalog period. Included are basic data files (on computer tape or punchcards), special tabulations (tapes, cards, and printed data) prepared for sponsors, and nonstatistical materials such as maps and computer programs.

A monthly supplement to the catalog lists major special publications, reports issued in a series at irregular intervals, and regular publications issued less frequently than quarterly.

Four quarterly issues and 12 monthly supplements, $14.40 per year; quarterly prices vary but generally stay between $2.00 and $4.00; GPO (see C1.0).

3.55 *Bureau of the Census Guide to Programs and Publications: Subjects and Areas*

A comprehensive review of the statistical programs of the Bureau of the Census and of the reports issued by the Bureau in the 1960's and early 1970's appears in this guide. It shows the geographic areas and principal subjects for most of the publications. For reports issued periodically, the areas covered in the latest issues are shown. Almost all statistical and geographic reports, including maps, published between 1968 and 1972 are covered.

$2.40; GPO (see C1.0).

3.56 *1970 Census Users' Guide*

Most of the information that data users will need for effective access and use of 1970 census data products is furnished in this two-part publication. Part I covers the decennial census program and related services. Part II is concerned exclusively with computer tape products.

Part I, $2.35; Part II, $4.40; GPO (see C1.0).

3.57 *Factfinder for the Nation:U.S. Bureau of the Census*

Issued irregularly, the *Factfinder* is published as a series of topical brochures that may be used individually, in selected interest groupings, or as complete sets. Each brochure, usually four pages, describes the range of census materials available in a given subject and suggests some of their uses. The subjects include minority statistics, population, housing and construction, retail and wholesale trade, selected services, manufactures, minerals, foreign trade, transportation, agriculture, governments, geographic tools, and others. There is also a brochure on the Bureau's history and organization that traces the development of each of the subject areas.

Prices vary; Subscriber Services, Bureau of the Census, Washington, DC 20233.

3.58 A Visual Aid for Quick Reference to Basic Publications of the Bureau of the Census

This is a display poster highlighting selected guides and major report series.

10¢; Data User Section, Bureau of the Census, Department of Commerce, Washington, DC 20233.

3.59 *Mini-Guide to the 1972 Economic Census*

Nine economic census programs are described in this publication. The programs are: census of wholesale trade, retail trade, selected service industries, manufacturers, mineral industries, construction industries, transportation, enterprise statistics, and outlying areas. The publication provides useful information and references on data collected, publication programs, geographic areas, and Standard Industrial Classification Manual.

$1.00; GPO (see C1.0).

3.60 *Index to 1970 Census Summary Tapes*

All tabulations in all six counts of the 1970 census summary data, organized alphabetically and by subject available, and cross referenced, are covered in this index.

$2.60; GPO (see C1.0).

3.61 *Guide to Census Bureau Data Files and Special Tabulations*

Data users who need data from the Bureau of the Census not contained in printed reports will find this publication useful. It describes the data files and special tabulations originating during the period 1958-1968 and currently available; it also provides information on how these materials may be obtained.

$1.25; GPO (see C1.0).

3.62 *Major Programs 1976, Bureau of Labor Statistics*

All the major surveys, publications, and subscription services of the Bureau of Labor Statistics (BLS) are listed in this publication. At the end of each survey description, BLS suggests the major uses for the data. Each survey entry includes descriptions under the following headings: data available, coverage, source of data, reference period, publications, and uses (such as economic indicator, marketing, regional analysis, government funding analysis, and plant location).

Major categories of data described include current employment analysis, employment structure and trends, prices and living conditions, wages and industrial relations, productivity and technology, occupational safety and health statistics, economic growth, and subscription services.

A companion volume is *Publications of the Bureau of Labor Statistics, January-June 1975*, which lists publications by subject area and regional office.

BLS (see C1.70).

3.63 Microfiche and Computer Tapes from Bureau of Labor Statistics

A growing amount of data is available in microfiche form which can be reproduced at no cost or at nominal cost, depending on the size of the request.

Some data, including unpublished data, are available on computer tape. The amount, kind, and prices of the data available change constantly.

BLS (see C1.70).

3.64 *Business and Economics*

Domestic and international commerce, banking and finance, manufacturing and production, consumer affairs, and minority enterprises are among the subjects covered by the current awareness service entitled *Business and Economics.* This is one of a series of 26 newsletters known as *Weekly Government Abstracts.* (For an annotation of the entire series, see 9.11). Each newsletter contains summaries of government research performed by hundreds of organizations, including United States government agencies, private researchers, universities, and special technology groups. The research summaries are listed within two weeks of their receipt at the National Technical Information Service. The last issue of each year is a subject index containing up to ten cross references for each research summary indexed.

$45.00 per year; NTIS (see C1.17).

3.65 Agricultural Marketing Service Information Division

Areas of interest of this division include food distribution and marketing; market news; standardization and voluntary inspection and grading for quality of grain, cotton, fruits, tobacco, dairy products, vegetables, seeds, meat, poultry, and eggs; mandatory inspection of egg products for wholesomeness; marketing regulation; marketing agreements and orders; purchase of surplus commodities; plentiful foods information program; transportation of farm commodities; emergency preparedness; plant variety protection.

Agricultural Marketing Service, Department of Agriculture, 14th St. and Independence Ave. S.W., Washington, DC 20250; 202-447-6766.

3.66 Economic Research Service

The Economic Research Service (ERS) of the Department of Agriculture gathers and analyzes economic information needed to improve agriculture and rural living. ERS experts can answer questions about the current situation and outlook, as well as provide information on the more fundamental relationships between supply and demand. Analysts also examine international developments that have a potential impact on United States farm trade. The Economic Development Division of ERS collects, analyzes, and publishes data on rural population, employment, income, farm and nonfarm workers, job skills, and education levels. It also evaluates changes in the condition of rural communities; i.e., schools, housing, medical services, and public facilities.

ERS, Department of Agriculture, Washington, DC 20250; 202-447-8038.

3.67 Publications of the Economic Research Service

Analysts at the Economic Research Service (ERS) publish annually some 100 separate research studies. Subjects are as diverse as an in-depth analysis of the futures market, agricultural history, and a look at the inroads made by substitutes and synthetics into traditional farm markets.

An accurate appraisal of the current outlook and stiuation for all major commodities, plus topics of general interest to the food and fiber industry, can be found in 22 separate *Situation Reports* published on a scheduled basis throughout the year.

Brief highlights of the latest situation and outlook appear monthly in the *Agricultural*

Outlook Digest.

Another monthly, the *Farm Index*, allows readers to keep abreast of current ERS research in easy-to-read language.

The quarterly, *Agricultural Economics Research*, a more technical publication, reports on the latest findings, developments, and research methods in agricultural economics.

Each year, ERS teams with several other Department of Agriculture agencies to produce the *Handbook of Agricultural Charts*. This is the most comprehensive collection of charts on agriculture, depicting everything from farm income trends and commodity prices to rural housing conditions and the cost of a week's food.

The annual *Agricultural Statistics* is another product of joint cooperation with other agriculture agencies. The handbook is a reliable reference source on agricultural production, supplies, consumption, facilities, and costs and returns.

ERS joins with the Bureau of the Census to produce the *Census-ERS Series*, annual estimates of farm population by age, sex, labor force status, and other characteristics.

The Balance Sheet of the Farming Sector is one of several farm finance reports that ERS issues on an annual basis. It provides a full statement of debts and assets of the entire agricultural sector.

A number of other periodic reports provide yearly wrap-ups on topics like farm costs and returns, the hired farm working force, and changes in farm production and efficiency.

A monthly summary of the current status and outlook for farm exports appears in *Foreign Agricultural Trade of the United States*. Supplements are published for the calendar year and the fiscal year.

Research reports, handbooks, statistical supplements, technical bulletins, and speeches are listed in the monthly *Checklist of New Reports*.

For sample copies, write Economic Research Service Publications Unit, Room 0054, Department of Agriculture, Washington, DC 20250.

3.68 Summary Tape Processing Centers

Census data are analyzed by over 175 local organizations (private, public, governmental, and academic) known as Summary Tape Processing Centers. A business seeking information for, for example, marketing or market research, may obtain analyses from them which otherwise would be difficult or expensive to develop.

The Centers vary greatly in services performed and in the geographic coverage of the data they analyze. They determine their own prices for services, as they are not affiliated with or supported by the Bureau of the Census.

For a list of the Centers, see Bureau of the Census (C1.3).

Data Bases for Market and Sales Analysis (3.100-3.120)

3.100 *Statistical Abstract of the United States*

The Statistical Abstract of the United States constitutes a one-volume basic reference source. Issued annually since 1878, it is the standard summary of statistics on the social, political, and economic organization of the United States. It presents a comprehensive selection of statistics from the publications and records of governmental and private agencies.

The current (1976) edition contains more than 1,400 tables and charts and an extensive guide to sources of additional data, as well as a two-page presentation of metric weights and measures. Although emphasis is given primarily to national data, many tables present data for regions and a smaller number for cities. Sections 33 and 34 present comprehensive data for states and for 157 standard metropolitan statistical areas having 200,000 or more inhabitants in 1970. Additional information for cities, counties, metropolitan areas, congressional districts, and other small units, as well as more historical data, are available in various supplements to the abstract.

There are 78 entirely new tables in this edition, covering such topics as crime, health-related problems, environmental concerns, federal government benefits and taxes, earnings, income shares of poorest and wealthiest, cost of living, big business, and oil and gas.

$8.00 paperbound, $10.50 clothbound; GPO (see C1.0).

3.101 *County Business Patterns*

Social Security tax records and census data are source materials for this publication. It contains a series of separate reports for each state, and a United States summary with data on employment, number and employment size of reporting units, and taxable payrolls for various segments of the economy. It is especially useful for analyzing market potentials, establishing sales territories and sales quotas, and locating facilities.

$5.45; GPO (see C1.0).

3.102 Neighborhood Population and Housing Data

Census tract reports from the census of population and housing present information on both population and housing subjects for small areas within each of the standard metropolitan statistical areas in the country. Population subjects include household and family characteristics, voter participation, fertility, school enrollment, number of minorities, migration patterns, and others. Housing subjects include tenure, number of rooms, plumbing facilities, year built, property value, and more. The reports can be extremely useful in many areas of business management, including locating or relocating a business, market research, and sales territory layout and evaluation.

Areas covered by census data and examples of data use in business are described in Appendix C2.

Subscriber Services Section, Bureau of the Census, Washington, DC 20233; see also Bureau of the Census (C1.13, C1.14) and Department of Commerce regional offices (C1.10).

3.103 *County and City Data Book*

Demographic, social, and economic data for counties, cities, standard metropolitan statistical areas, and urbanized areas are presented from the most recent censuses as well as from other governmental and private sources. The topics include agriculture, bank deposits, births, marriages, climate, home equipment, hospitals, family income, migration, population characteristics, presidential vote, local government finances, retail trade, school enrollment, selected services, and manufacturing. The book also includes maps for each state, showing counties, standard metropolitan statistical areas, and large cities; explanatory notes and source citations; and appendixes that expand or explain the coverage of the tables. A unique feature of this book is the availability of its contents on compendia tape and punchcards.

$18.65; GPO (see C1.0).

3.104 County-Level Socioeconomic Data Base

Market forecasters, local governments, business planners, and demographers can use the National Technical Information Service (NTIS) county-level socioeconomic statistical data base to produce specialized reports. The data base, compiled by the Economic Development Administration (EDA), merges the first and fourth counts of the 1970 Census of Population and Housing with summary data from the 1960 census, *County and City Data Book, County Business Patterns,* and *Income Data Files.*

Help in formulation of a search request and an estimate of search costs is available through information specialists at NTIS.

NTIS (see C1.17).

3.105 IRS Taxpayer Data on Tape and Paper

The number of tax returns, exemptions, adjusted gross income, and total tax dollars for each of 39,000 Zip Code areas throughout the country may be obtained from an Internal Revenue Service summary on magnetic tape or on paper. The information does not reveal data for any individual and applies to a tax year about five years before the current year. It does include detailed definitions of the items, a description of the system, and an explanation of the sources and limitations of the data.

Tape: #PB-209 352/PTC, $157.50; paper: $3.00 in all states except California, New York, Pennsylvania, and Texas, which are $6.00; NTIS (see C1.17).

3.106 *Current Population Reports*

Eight series of reports, as listed below, are included in this subscription service. Taken together, they represent a comprehensive view of the population which is useful in determining the precise location of markets.

Population Characteristics. Current national and, in some cases, regional data on geographic residence and mobility, fertility, education, school enrollment, marital status, and numbers and characteristics of households and families are included.

Special Studies. Infrequent reports are given on methods, concepts, or specialized data.

Population Estimates and Projections. Monthly estimates of the total population of the United States; annual midyear estimates of the population of the states, by broad age groups, and of the United States by age, race, and sex; annual estimates of the components of population change; and projections of the future population of the United States are given.

Federal-State Cooperative Program for Population Estimates.

Farm Population (Census-ERS). These data on the size and selected characteristics of the farm population of the United States are issued jointly with the Economic Research Service of the Department of Agriculture.

Special Censuses. Results are reported of population censuses taken at the request and expense of city or other local governments.

Consumer Income. Information given includes the proportions of families and persons at various income levels, and data on the relationship of income to age, sex, race, family size, education, occupation, work experience, and other characteristics.

Consumer Buying Intentions. Information on the proportion of households reporting intention to purchase automobiles, houses, and household equipment within a particular period of time is given.

Entire series: #C56.128, $56.00 per year; single copies vary in price; GPO (see C1.0).

3.107 *Input-Output Structure of the United States Economy: 1967*

Recently published by the Bureau of Economic Analysis, this study depicts the interrelationships in the economy of 85 broad industrial categories. By using these tables, a manufacturer can estimate the direct market potential in the industry to which he is selling, as well as the indirect demands of the industries it serves. The input-output study furnishes the market analyst with more factual information about interindustry sales and purchases and is considered one of the more effective tools for measuring markets.

Vol. 1, *Transactions Data for Detailed Industries,* $3.85; Vol. 2, *Direct Requirements for Detailed Industries*, $3.75; Vol. 3, *Total Requirements for Detailed Industries*, $3.85; GPO (see C1.0).

3.108 *Annual Survey of Manufactures*

The Annual Survey program is designed to provide estimates of general statistics (employment, payroll, man-hours, value added by manufacture) for industry groups and industries; general statistics for geographic division, states, standard metropolitan statistical areas, and cities, cross-classified by major industry group and large industrial counties; value of shipments for classes of products; expenditures for new plant and equipment for industries and industry groups, and for states and large standard metropolitan statistical areas; value of manufacturers' inventories for industry groups and industries; fuels and electric energy data by industry groups and states; gross book value of fixed assets and rental payments; and labor costs.

Series of six reports, $12.75 per year; Subscriber Services Section, Bureau of the Census, Washington, DC 20233; see also Department of Commerce district offices (C1.10).

3.109 Current Retail Trade

The Current Retail Trade subscription service includes the *Weekly Retail Sales Report*, the *Advance Monthly Retail Trade Sales Report,* the *Monthly Retail Trade Report*, and the *Annual Retail Trade Report.*

In the *Monthly Retail Trade Report*, whose coverage is comparable to that of the others, data are given for the United States, current month, with comparisons for previous months on estimates of monthly retail sales by major kind-of-business groups and selected individual kinds of business; separate figures are shown, in more limited kind-of-business detail, for firms operating eleven or more retail stores. Summary sales data are presented for geographic regions and divisions, selected states, large standard metropolitan statistical areas, and cities. Also included are national estimates of end-of-month accounts receivable balances outstanding for all retail stores and, separately, for firms operating eleven or more retail stores. Separate data are shown for charge accounts and installment accounts. National sales and accounts receivable estimates are shown adjusted for seasonal variations and trading day differences, as well as in unadjusted form. This report also includes data on department store sales published separately in *Monthly Department Store Sales for Selected*

Areas.

The entire series, $30.10 per year; GPO (see C1.0), or Department of Commerce (see C1.10).

3.110 *Monthly Wholesale Trade: Sales and Inventories*

For the current month and the twelve preceding months, data are presented for the United States on estimated monthly sales of merchant wholesalers, by kind of business and estimated monthly sales, by geographic division, for merchant wholesalers in total, for durable goods, and for nondurable goods wholesalers; monthly inventories of merchant wholesalers, for selected kinds of business; and estimated monthly sales, inventories, and stock-sales ratios of merchant wholesalers, for selected kinds of business. The December report also includes the previous year's sales inventories and stock-sales ratios, by kind of business. It also shows annual sales, year-end inventories, and stock-sales ratios from 1964 to 1974.

Sales and inventory trends are shown for about 55 kinds of business at the national level and for fourteen kinds of business by geographic divisions. The December report includes percent changes in annual sales of merchant wholesalers by geographic groups. Measures of sampling variability of the data are also included.

$7.20 per year; GPO (see C1.0).

3.111 *Monthly Selected Services Receipts*

Data are shown for the United States on monthly receipts of six major kind-of-business groups and seven selected service categories. The statistics include receipts for services to businesses as well as to household consumers. Data are adjusted for seasonal and trading day variations. Comparable data for the previous month and for the same month in the previous year are also shown, in addition to the percent change from the periods listed. Services included in the monthly survey correspond to those covered by the quinquennial census of business with the exception of such services as legal services, architectural and engineering services, dental laboratories, and travel agencies.

$1.00 per year; Subscriber Services Section, Bureau of the Census, Washington, DC 20233.

3.112 Industry Data Reports

The following publications are available, as priced, from GPO (see C1.0).

Construction Review consolidates almost all current government and some nongovernment statistics pertaining to the construction industry, along with feature articles and a yearly construction outlook. Monthly, $14.50 per year.

Containers and Packaging offers an economic review and outlook and an analysis of local and national container trends and developments. Quarterly, $3.00 per year.

Copper presents comprehensive supply-demand analyses and projections, imports and exports, and shipments of producers and fabricators. Quarterly, $3.00 per year.

Printing and Publishing publishes domestic data on employment, earnings, production, and exports and imports, as well as detailed analyses of current industry conditions. Quarterly, $3.00 per year.

Pulp, Paper, and Board presents economic analyses, feature articles, and statistics on production trends, capacity, world markets, inventories, and prices. Quarterly, $3.00 per year.

3.113 *Survey of Current Business*

The official source of data on national home and product accounts, this publication covers all aspects of the economy, including employment and prices. The statistical section includes 2,500 series from 100 sources. Each issue has an article on business and the economic situation, and other articles.

Monthly with weekly supplements, $48.30 per year; GPO (see C1.0).

3.114 Census of Business

The following publications are available from the Department of Commerce district offices (see C1.10), or from GPO (see C1.0).

Retail Trade presents statistics by kinds of business for states, standard metropolitan statistical areas, counties, and cities of 2,500 or more. It includes data on the number of establishments, sales, payroll, and personnel.

Wholesale Trade gives data on number of

establishments, sales, payroll, and personnel for kinds of business for states, standard metropolitan statistical areas, and counties.

Selected Services presents data on hotels, motels, barber shops, beauty parlors, and other retail organizations, including number of establishments, receipts, and payrolls for states, standard metropolitan statistical areas, counties, and cities.

3.115 Census of Housing

Series HC(3) *Block Statistics.* A census of housing report was issued for each city of 59,000 or more. Data are included on average room, average contract rent, average value, and other subjects. A map is also included.

Prices vary; GPO (see C1.0), or Department of Commerce district offices (see C1.10).

3.116 *National Travel, 1972 Census of Transportation*

The volume and characteristics of travel by the civilian population of the United States are described in this publication. Included are such aspects of the subject as who went where, when, for how long, by what means of transport, and the primary reason for the trip, as well as related socioeconomic factors. The volume is in three sections: *Summer Travel*, *Spring Travel*, and the annual *Travel During (year).*

$2.45; GPO (see C1.0).

3.117 Labor Statistics Data Base

Labor force information is available for metropolitan areas, cities, counties, states, census tracts, and other regions, with breakouts such as industry, salary levels, age, education levels, and distance to work.

The data base was assembled by the Lawrence Berkeley Laboratories, under contract to the Department of Labor, from the Labor Censuses of 1970 and 1973.

Help in obtaining a relevant report is available from information specialists at National Technical Information Service (NTIS).

NTIS (see C1.17).

3.118 Census of Agriculture: *Area Reports*

In this series, which consists of a separate paperbound report for each state (two or more for larger states), data are presented by state and county on farms, land use, farm income and sales, machinery and equipment, and more.

Prices vary; GPO (see C1.0).

3.119 Federal Communications Commission Licensee Data

Marketing to holders of Federal Communications Commission (FCC) licenses, including citizens band licenses, is made possible by obtaining the official FCC list of names and addresses of licensees. They are available on magnetic tape and on microfiche. The cost of microfiche is $1.75 per fiche. For example, the amateur radio file, currently consisting of 52 sheets of 48X microfiche, would cost $91.00.

Citizens band licensee data may be obtained by custom searches, paperbound and on magnetic tape. The Citizens Band Master File contains data on applicants and licensees, including station and license identification, mailing address, radio frequency, issue and expiration dates of the license, and various codes. Portions of the file are available, selected by state, ZIP Code, or call sign.

NTIS (see C1.17).

3.120 National Technical Information Service

NTIS (National Technical Information Service) emphasizes that searching before researching can save much effort, time, and money. Whether the research is intended to develop new technology or to provide data with which business decisions can be made, the resources available through NTIS may be useful.

NTIS provides a diversity of services and information. It is the central source for the public sale of government sponsored research, development, and engineering reports and other analyses. Much of the material to which NTIS can give access is related to engineering and the hard sciences, but there is a growing array of data sources of potentially great value for business planners, market researchers, and others who may need statistics or other data about social, psychological, or demographic factors.

For a complete annotation of NTIS capability, including on-line computer searches, published searches, bibliographic searches, and more, see 9.0-9.13.

Technical Assistance in Market Research (3.150-3.155)

3.150 Technical Assistance in Interpreting Census and Labor Statistics

Both the national and regional offices of the Bureau of Labor Statistics (BLS) and the Bureau of the Census respond to public requests for assistance on the application, uses, and limitations of their data. They are also in a position to tell an inquirer if they have any unpublished data which may be useful. The agencies do not ordinarily charge for consultation with their staff.

BLS (see C1.70).

3.151 Small Business Institute Program

The Small Business Institute program, a three-way cooperative between collegiate schools of business administration, members of the nation's small business community, and the Small Business Administration (SBA) is a new source of management assistance. Under the supervision of university faculty and SBA staff, senior and graduate students of business administration work directly with owners of small firms, providing vital management assistance to small businesses while undergoing meaningful learning experiences themselves.

The program began in the fall of 1972. In the first year of its life, 1,100 small firms received counseling and 2,200 students were involved. In 1976, 385 schools participated, involving over 22,000 students and 8,800 small businesses. Satisfaction rate among clients was over 80 percent.

SBA (see C1.110).

3.152 University Business Development Centers

Growing out of the Small Business Institute concept (see 3.151), the University Business Development Center (UBDC) program is an experimental Small Business Administration concept being tested in eight universities. It is a university-based and administered program to interrelate the academic, professional, and technological resources of universities with all existing government programs designed to assist the business community. While each agency continues to administer its own programs, the university serves as a funnel or mixing device for them, so that the collection of programs will work as an integrated unit serving the whole community, rather than as an uncoordinated variety of programs.

A functioning UBDC can offer the following services to its business clients:

—Business and product evaluation and development
—Entrepreneur evaluation, recommendations, counseling, and training
—Analysis, correction, and followup of financial, marketing, technical, production, legal, and any other type of problem faced by small business owners
—Feasibility studies and development of business plans for present and future entrepreneurs
—Access to and application of technology, paid for by the taxpayers in over $350 billion worth of research and development projects since 1947
—Assistance not only in surviving (when 57 percent of new businesses fail in the first five years) but also in expanding on a solid basis

Universities currently involved are the Universities of Maine at Bangor, Missouri At St. Louis, Nebraska at Omaha, Georgia at Athens, and West Florida at Pensacola; and Rutgers University, New Bruswick, New Jersey; California State University at Chico; and California Polytechnic at Pomona.

3.153 Economic Development Administration Technical Assistance

The Office of Technical Assistance of the Economic Development Administration (EDA) can conduct feasibility studies for firms on a repayment basis if the results of such work will likely result in increased jobs and economic upgrading. The project need not take place in an EDA specially designated area, although it is more likely to be approved if it is.

EDA inquiries and applications for technical assistance should be directed to the EDA regional director (see C1.11).

3.154 Small Business Investment Company

A Small Business Investment Company (SBIC) is a privately owned and privately operated small business investment company which has been licensed by the Small Business Administration (SBA) to provide equity capital and long-term loans to small firms. Often, an SBIC also provides management assistance to the companies it finances.

Small businesses generally have difficulty obtaining long-term capital to finance their growth. Prior to 1958, there were few places a small company could turn to for money once it had exhausted its secured line of credit from banks or SBA. To help close this financing gap, Congress passed the Small Business Investment Act of 1958, which authorized SBA to license, regulate, and help finance privately organized and privately operated SBIC's.

Today there are SBIC's located in all parts of the country. As an industry, the SBIC's have total assets of millions of dollars, and additional funds are available to them through borrowings from SBA and private sources.

Many SBIC's are owned by relatively small groups of local investors. An SBIC finances small firms in two general ways—be straight loans and by venture capital or equity investments. In some cases, these investments give the SBIC actual or potential ownership of a minority of a small business' stock. However, SBIC's are generally prohibited from taking a control position in a small concern. Usually, financing must be for at least five years, except that a borrower may elect to have a prepayment clause included in the financing agreement.

There are three free brochures put out by SBA which together give an overview of the SBIC: *SBIC Financing for Small Business; SBIC, Starting a Small Business Investment Company;* and *Section 301(d) SBIC's.*

Local attorneys, accountants, bankers, investment bankers, and business associates or advisers who have had dealings with SBIC's may be helpful. Also, SBA field offices will offer help. An agency information specialist will provide a list of licensed SBIC's and, while he is not permitted to recommend a specific company, he may be able to point out the types of investments various SBIC's in the area have been making. Lists of licensed SBIC's may also be obtained from the SBA.

SBA (see C1.110).

3.155 Minority Vendor Data Base System

This is a system designed to provide corporate purchasing personnel immediate access to qualified minority suppliers.

National Minority Purchasing Council, Inc., 6 N. Michigan Ave., Room 1104, Chicago, IL 60602; 312-346-4511.

Information on the Postal Service (3.200-3.202)

3.200 *Domestic Postage Rates, Fees and Information*

Many free publications are distributed by Postal Service customer service representatives and postmasters. One of the most basic is *Domestic Postage Rates, Fees and Information.* Other free publications tell customers how to use express mail, what addressing procedures are correct, how to presort and label mail, and other topics of interest to volume mailers.

Customers may contact their local customer service representative or postmaster to check on the pamphlets available. Requests for guides cannot be filled from Washington, D.C.

3.201 Bibliography on Postal Service Publications

The following publications are available at indicated prices from GPO (see C1.0).

The *Postal Bulletin* is available to those who feel their needs require advance information. Issued Thursday of each week, with supplemental issues as required, it contains current orders, instructions, and information relating to the Postal Service, including philately, airmail, money orders, parcel post, and more. It also provides advance notice of important changes in regulations.

$25.75 per year, subscriptions accepted for 1, 2, or 3 years.

Instructions for Mailers contains excerpts from Chapter 1 of the *Postal Service Manual*. It is issued for the specific use of individuals, companies, or organizations who use the mailing services of the Postal Service more than the average person.

Sold on a subscription basis only, with changes issued as required, for an indefinite period, $7.70.

Postal Service Manual, Chapters 1 through 6 revises and replaces the *Postal Manual*. It includes information on post office services (domestic); organization and administration of the Postal Service; postal procedures; personnel policies; transportation of mail; maintenance and procurement. Postal Service Orders are included in the appendix. So that subscribers may have current information and changes as they occur, a looseleaf supplementary service for an indefinite period is sold on a subscription basis only.

$33.00.

International Mail, formerly entitled *Directory of International Mail,* contains regulations for public use and detailed information on postage rates, services available, prohibitions, import restrictions, and other conditions governing mail to other countries. Countries are listed alphabetically with the specific requirements applicable to mail addressed to each of them.

Sold on a subscription basis only, with changes issued as required, for an indefinite period, $4.25.

Postal Service Manual (Chapter 5) contains policy guidelines and regulations affecting the transportation of mail.

Basic material, and supplements issued irregularly, for an indefinite period, $1.50.

Postal Life keeps postal employees informed and abreast of developments in the Postal Service. It contains articles with illustrations about new methods, techniques, and programs.

Bimonthly, subscriptions accepted for one year only, $6.40.

National ZIP Code Directory enables the user to determine the ZIP Code for every mailing address in the nation. It is for use by all mailers, especially those maintaining large mailing lists, permitting them to gain all the advantages possible from the addition of ZIP Code to their lists. ZIP Code listings are arranged alphabetically by state. Within each state, a complete listing is given of all post offices, stations, and branches, with the appropriate five-digit ZIP Code for each delivery area. An appendix after each state gives the ZIP Code for each address in the larger cities. Also in this directory are a listing of two-letter state abbreviations, a listing of Sectional Center Facilities, ZIP Code prefixes by state, a numerical list of post offices by ZIP Code, a listing of discontinued postal units, and ZIP Codes for Army and Air Force installations and APO and FPO units.

$7.50.

The Directory of Post Offices is used daily by business and individual mailers throughout the United States. It includes a list of all post offices, branches, and stations arranged alphabetically by states with ZIP Codes as an aid in determining parcel post zones. Also included are an alphabetical list of all post offices, named stations, and branches; lists of sectional centers and major cities by states; a numerical list of post offices by ZIP Code; a list of post offices, named stations, and branches discontinued or with names changed during the past two years; and a list of Army posts, camps, and stations, as well as Air Force bases, fields, and installations. APO's and FPO's are also included.

$5.55.

3.202 Special Programs of the Postal Service

The Postal Service now provides many services of value to business. Any business may contact its local post office and ask for a visit from the customer service representative (CSR), who can provide details on all of the programs listed below and suggest cost-effective ways of doing business. CSR's can also provide a free evaluation of the operations of a business mailing room and suggest mailing procedures that are most effective.

The following are some of the postal programs relevant to business:

Bulk Mail. Postage costs can be drastically cut by use of third-class bulk mail. It is possible to prepay postage by use of a permit imprint.

Presorted First Class Mail. A special, reduced first-class postage rate is available when a mailing of 500 or more pieces is presorted by ZIP Code.

Express Mail. Guaranteeed overnight delivery

is available from and to many Postal Service facilities. A shipment delivered to a specific post office Express Mail window by 5:00 p.m. will be delivered to the addressee the next day by 3:00 p.m. (or may be picked up by 10:00 a.m.). If a business depends on quick, regularly scheduled intercity shipments, the Postal Service will custom-tailor a special Express Mail program.

Priority Mail. First class mail over 13 ounces still receives the fastest transportation and most expeditious handling if special Priority Mail rates are paid.

Mailgram. A Mailgram is a message sent electronically to the addressee's post office for delivery with the next day's mail.

Free Presorting Equipment and Materials. The Postal Services encourages mailers to separate mail categories and to sort mail by ZIP Code, as this will speed delivery. The Postal Service will provide rubber bands, labels, pressure-sensitive bands, tags, sacks, and letter trays.

Verifying Mailing Lists. A local postmaster can check the names and addresses on a mailing list for correctness.

Postage Meters. Mail with metered postage skips the cancellation stage, and can therefore be delivered sooner. In many cities, the Postal Service will send a representative to a firm's office to reset a postage meter.

Bar Coding. Preprinted reply envelopes with bar coding in the lower right-hand corner are processed through special equipment, providing the most accurage and speedy method for reply mail.

Business Reply Mail. For a few cents per piece in addition to the regular postage, it is possible to pay the postage on reply mail only on pieces actually received.

Computerized Sorting Equipment. For faster delivery, all address formats should comply with the requirements of the computerized sorting equipment. For example, nothing should appear below or to the right of the ZIP Code.

Memos for Mailers. This is a free monthly publication of advice and news.

Postal Customers Councils. These groups can provide training sessions for employees and allow feedback to the Postal Service from business mailers.

Pool Case. If a large number of items is being sent from one area to be delivered in another area, efficiency and speed of delivery can be improved, and risk of damage or loss reduced, by using the pool case system. The items will be packed together in a large package addressed to the postmaster of the main office in the addressee region, and upon arrival the package will be opened and the contents delivered.

ZIP Code Computer Tapes. All of the street addresses covered by the Postal Service are listed on magnetic tape with their correct ZIP Codes. The tape is available for loan.

Selling to the Government (3.250-3.459)

Government Procurement Guides and Directories [3.250-3.259]

3.250 *United States Government Purchasing and Sales Directory*

Produced by the Small Business Administration (SBA), this volume is of general interest to businesses which wish to sell to the government. It includes descriptions of how the government buys, how to get on bidders' lists, how to prepare bids and proposals, and how the SBA can help a business sell to the government. Listings of products purchased by military and civilian agencies and the location of purchasing offices are included, as well as a chapter on buying surplus property from the government. The book describes the government's system of federal and military product specifications and indexes those specifications. Finally, it provides sample forms and a list of field offices.

$2.00; GPO (see C1.0).

3.251 *Commerce Business Daily*

Every business day, this publication lists hundreds of new specific business proposals for products and services wanted or offered by the United States government. It lists current information received daily from military and civilian procurement offices. It is of particular value to firms interested in bidding on United States government purchases or seeking subcontract opportunities from prime contractors.

Daily, $105.00 per year first class, $80 second class; GPO (see C1.0).

3.252 *Government Business Opportunities*

Business Service Centers (BSC) and government procurement procedures are described in this booklet. It also contains answers to many of the typical questions potential sellers have.

Free; BSC (see C1.105).

3.253 *United States Government Procurement Offices*

All the agency procurement offices in the states of a given region are listed in regional directories.

Free; BSC (see C1.105).

3.254 *Selling to the U.S. Government*

Government buying methods, the process of locating purchasing agencies and learning what they buy and how to have an opportunity to bid on government contracts and orders, and preparation of bids and proposals are described in this publication.

Free; SBA (see C1.110).

3.255 *Federal Buying Directory*

Federal agencies and officials in the Washington area who either buy or have knowledge of the buying done by their agencies are listed in this publication.

Free; BSC (see C1.105).

3.256 *Manual on Business Opportunities for Small and Minority Businesses*

Business opportunities in programs related to the Department of Housing and Urban Development (HUD) demand familiarity with HUD administrative requirements and operating processes. The *Manual on Business Opportunities for Small and Minority Businesses* is designed to advise businesses and professional people how to participate fully and effectively in housing development activities, and explains in great detail the roles of the following within the housing delivery system: sponsor/developer, planner, consultant, real estate broker/appraiser, architect, mortgage banker, attorney, contractor, and housing manager.

#023-000-00336-8, 1974, $2.15; GPO (see C1.0).

3.257 *Selling to NASA*

Selling to NASA describes the National Aeronautical and Space Administration (NASA), the NASA procurement process, NASA aids to small business and to minority business, and the scientific and technical information available from NASA. It includes a bidder's mailing list application, which NASA uses to decide which firms are qualified to bid or to submit proposals.

Among the matters covered are the annual compilation of NASA research and technology programs, the *Research and Technology Operating Plan Summary* (RTOP); bidder's mailing list information; reliability and quality assurance; safety; equal employment opportunity requirements; labor relations; security clearances; bonding; patents; grants; procurement regulations sources; invitations for bids; negotiated procurement; architect-engineer contracting; NASA's bid rooms where all open solicitations may be reviewed; the NASA Minority Business Enterprise Program; the NASA small business specialists at each installation; subcontracting opportunities for small firms; NASA's technical and technology utilization publications and services; a description of the activities of each of NASA's twelve installations and their respective procurement offices; and a directory of the small business specialists and minority business specialists.

#NHB 5100.1B, 48 pp., free; National Aeronautics and Space Administration, Code HB, Washington, DC 20546; 202-755-2288.

3.258 *Selling to ERDA*

Procurement centers of the Energy Research and Development Administration (ERDA) around the country are listed, and the commodities and services they purchase and procurement procedures used are described in this volume.

Public Affairs Office, ERDA, Washington, DC 20545; see also field offices (C1.150).

3.259 Government Agencies with Substantial Procurement Activities

While the General Services Administration

(see 3.450) and the Department of Defense (see 3.350-3.356) are by far the largest buyers of goods and services, with offices nationwide, many other agencies engage in buying goods independently. These agencies and their central procurement offices are listed below.

Office of Operations
Department of Agriculture
Washington, DC 20250

Office of Administrative Service
Division of Procurement
Department of Commerce
Washington, DC 20230

National Bureau of Standards
Department of Commerce
Washington, DC 20234

Commissioner of Patents
Washington, DC 20231

Administrator's Office
Maritime Administration
Department of Commerce
Washington, DC 20230

Assistant Secretary for Research and Monitoring
Environmental Protection Agency
Waterside Mall, Room 3202
Washington, DC 20460

National Center for Health Services Research and Development
5600 Fishers Lane
Rockville, MD 20852

Contracts and Grants Division
Office of Education
Department of Health, Education, and Welfare
Federal Office Building No. 6
400 Maryland Avenue S.W.
Washington, DC 20202

Assistant Secretary for Research and Technology
Department of Housing and Urban Development
Room 4100
451 7th Street S.W.
Washington, DC 20410

Geological Survey
Department of the Interior
18th and F Streets N.W.
Washington, DC 20410

Research and Development Guides and Opportunities (3.300-3.310)

3.300 *Small Business and Government Research and Development*

Owners of small research and development firms seeking government contracts will find this introductory booklet useful. It includes a discussion of procedures necessary to locate and interest government markets.

#SBA 1.12:28, 41 pp., 75¢; GPO (see C1.0).

3.301 Research and Development Opportunities for Small Firms

SBA (Small Business Administration) publishes, on a regional basis, directories identifying the names and major capabilities of small R&D business firms. These are distributed to major procurement installations for use in locating small business sources for R&D procurements. SBA also makes direct-source referrals to procuring installations for specific R&D solicitations.

SBA (see C1.110).

3.302 *Guide for the Submission of Unsolicited Research and Development Proposals*

The Department of the Interior has the statutory authority to initiate and support, through its various bureaus and offices, scientific research and development programs related to its responsibilities as the nation's principal natural resource agency. This brochure is directed toward present and prospective grantees and contractors of the Department. It is intended to acquaint members of the engineering and scientific community with the various research and development programs, to define the technological and scientific areas of interest to each of the component agencies, and to describe the policies and procedures relating to the preparation and submission of unsolicited proposals.

Office of Research and Development, Assistant Secretary for Energy and Minerals, Department of the Interior, Washington, DC 20241.

3.303 Opportunities through Submission of Unsolicited Proposals

Many government agencies encourage the submission of unsolicited proposals for research and development activities in their areas of interest. A listing of the appropriate offices to contact in civilian and military agencies with major research and development activities can be found in *U·S· Government Purchasing and Sales Directory*, pages 89-123.

#4500-00118, $2.35; GPO (see C1.0).

3.304 Research and Development with ERDA

Information helpful to those interested in preparing unsolicited proposals for submission to the Energy Research and Development Administration (ERDA) is provided in *Guide for the Submission of Research and Development Proposals by Individuals and Organizations.* It is specifically for the benefit of individuals, commercial firms, not-for-profit research organizations, and all other prospective proposers except educational institutions and not-for-profit institutions that conduct education and training activities, or whose facilities are used in joint programs with universities for such purposes. These excepted organizations should refer to *Guide for the Submission of Research Proposals from Educational Institutions.*

Both publications free; ERDA (see C1.150).

3.305 *Employment and Training Research and Development Projects*

The sixth annual edition of this publication of the Employment and Training Administration (ETA) summarizes ETA-funded projects. The catalog is the principal means of informing the public of developments in the research and development field in employment and training. It may be particularly useful to potential grant and contract applicants and to industrial and personnel relations people. The appendix contains guidelines for submitting proposals.

Free; ETA (see C1.72).

3.306 Agricultural Research

The Cooperative State Research Service supports basic and applied research in high priority problems of regional or national scope. Areas currently considered are rural development, environmental quality, food and nutrition, beef and pork production, pest management, and soybean research. Grants may be made to private organizations and to individuals for research to further the programs of the Department of Agriculture.

Administrator, Cooperative State Research Service, Department of Agriculture national office (202-447-4423); see also state headquarters (C1.1).

3.307 National Science Foundation

Business can benefit directly and indirectly from federal government support of scientific research and education projects, through the National Science Foundation (NSF). Indirect benefits can arise from NSF support of basic research conducted at universities and nonprofit organizations. Direct benefits are possible through participation in NSF's RANN (Research Applied to National Needs) program. NSF also encourages collaboration between industry and university researchers, and may support broader efforts through industry associations, groups of companies, or professional societies.

The RANN program supports problem-oriented research. Joint proposals between industry and universities or governments are encouraged, and NSF devotes a significant amount of its RANN program budget to awards to small businesses.

At present, the RANN program emphasizes the areas of resources, environment, productivity, intergovernmental science and R&D incentives, and exploratory research and technology assessment. NSF encourages the submission of unsolicited proposals; *Guidelines for Preparation of Unsolicited Proposals* will clarify procedures. The range of research topics supported is displayed in the latest *Guide to Programs,* the latest list of *Grants and Awards*, and the latest *Annual Report.*

Current information about individual NSF programs appears in the monthly *NSF Bulletin,* available free from the Public Information Branch, National Science Foundation, Washington, DC 20550.

General inquiries and requests for publications may be addressed to the Office of Programs and Resources, National Science Foundation, Washington, DC 20550; or, if west of the Rocky Mountains, to the Western Projects Office, National Science Foundation, 831 Mitten Road, Burlingame, CA 94010.

Small business inquiries may be addressed to the Special Assistant for Small Business, Intergovernmental Science and Public Technology, Research Applications Directorate, NSF, Washington, DC 20550.

3.308 Science Information Activities

The National Science Foundation sponsors project grants research contracts whose purpose is to foster the interchange of scientific information among scientists in the United States and foreign countries, to provide or arrange for services leading to a more effective dissemination of scientific information, and to undertake programs to develop new or improved methods for making scientific information available.

Funds may be used for paying costs considered necessary to conduct research or studies, such as salaries and wages, expendable equipment and supplies, travel, publication costs, other direct costs, and indirect costs.

Eligible applicants include national scientific societies, colleges, universities, nonprofit organizations, and profit-making organizations.

Division of Science Information, NSF, 1800 G St. N.W., Washington, DC 20550; 202-632-5824.

3.309 *NASA Research and Technology Operating Plan Summary*

Small research firms may ascertain technical requirements of NASA (National Aeronautical and Space Administration), and technical personnel may learn about current research and technology programs, by consulting the Research and Technology Operating Plan Summary. (RTOP). The RTOP is an annual compilation of NASA's funded research and technology programs. It is in abstract form, and each abstract briefly describes the NASA research and development objectives, identifies the installation of primary interest, and provides a point of contact for technical information.

NTIS (see C1.17).

3.310 Air Force Office of Scientific Research

The Air Force Office of Scientific Research considers unsolicited proposals and awards grants and contracts for phenomena-oriented research throughout those sciences related to the needs of the operational Air Force, including chemistry, mathematics, electronics, aero-mechanics, energy conversion, general physics, solid state physics, and the behavioral, biological, and information sciences. Research efforts are directed toward scientific problems of the researcher's own choosing and involve the search for new knowledge and the expansion of specific principles, rather than their utilization for equipment development.

1400 Wilson Blvd. (CCC), Arlington, VA 22209; 202-694-4875.

Department of Defense Procurement (3.350-3.356)

3.350 Department of Defense Procurement

The Department of Defense (DOD) is the largest buyer of goods and services in the government. It has procurement and contract administration offices from coast to coast.

Area offices of the DOD are able and willing to provide counseling and technical guidance in matters pertaining to defense procurement, including assistance with problems connected with contracts and aid in reference to buying activities. The area offices also have displays of representative bid sets from the military services and procurement materials and information of all kinds.

DOD, like most government agencies, is emphasizing small and minority business involvement in procurement activities and, in many cases, priority treatment is given to such firms by set-aside clauses in contract requests. DOD also emphasizes the subcontracting possibilities for such firms.

DOD (see C1.21).

3.351 *How to Do Business with the Defense Supply Agency*

The possibilities and procedures for selling to the Department of Defense are explained in this 22-page booklet.

Free; DSA (see C1.21).

3.352 *Selling to the Military*

Selling to the Military is a comprehensive guide for anyone interested in the possibility of selling to the Department of Defense. It discusses Department policy and gives pertinent addresses and telephone numbers. It also describes commodities generally purchased by every major Defense procurement center, including the Army, the Navy, the Air Force, the Defense Supply Agency, and the General Services Administration. It guides the seller through the government system of specifications and explains research and development activities as well as the purchase of regular goods and services. It also has a chapter on buying from the government.

98 pp., $1.80; GPO (see C1.0).

3.353 Subcontracting Possibilities

The Defense Supply Agency (DSA) of the Department of Defense publishes for each of its regions a listing of the companies which either have a contract currently or did at one time, and the product or service provided by the company. There is a separate publication for each region. A business can use this as a guide for contacting government contractors with whom there may be subcontracting possibilities. Minority contractors are listed separately in the volume. Although the volumes vary in size from region to region, they are usually well over 100 pages in length and are organized alphabetically.

DSA (see C1.21).

3.354 Small Business Marketing to the Department of Defense

The law and the Department of Defense (DOD) regulations provide that entire procurements, or parts of procurements, may be set aside exclusively for the competition of small business. A major portion of Defense Supply Agency (DSA) contracts goes to small business firms, as defined by the Small Business Administration (see 1.700). There is a small business and economic utilization specialist at each DSA buying office whose job is to help small businesses participate in DSA procurements. In addition, there are specialists available for consultation in each of the eleven Defense Contract Administration Services regional offices and several of the district offices. These specialists can also assist in obtaining subcontracts under large Department of Defense prime contractors.

DOD (see C1.20, C1.21, C1.22).

3.355 Defense Contracting Emphasis in Labor Surplus Areas

It is the policy of the Department of Defense to aid firms in labor surplus (high unemployment) areas. In order to execute this policy, a part of a procurement may be set aside for negotiation with concerns which are certified to be eligible or which will perform a substantial portion of the contracts thus awarded. The small business and economic utilization specialist at each Buying Office and at each Defense Contract Administration Office can explain this preference program and help those who wish to participate in Defense Supply Agency (DSA) procurements.

DSA (see C1.22).

3.356 *Small Business and Labor Surplus Area Specialists*

Small Business and Labor Surplus Area Specialists Designated to Assist Small, Minority, and LSA Businessmen is a publication intended for potential small business suppliers to the Department of Defense. It lists the locations of military and Defense Supply Agency procurement offices and small business specialists throughout the United States.

#008-000-00223-1, 1976, 61 pp., $1.10; GPO (see C1.0).

Specific Procurement Opportunities (3.400-3.405)

3.400 *List of Procurement Commodities*

A uniform standard list, covering all articles of supply normally purchased by the General Services Administration, is provided primarily for use in connection with filing of mailing list applications.

Free; BSC (see C1.105).

3.401 *Leasing Space to the Government*

Free pamphlet; BSC (see C1.105).

3.402 *List of ADP Commodities for Procurement*

Free; BSC (see C1.105).

3.403 *Competitive Bidding for Construction Contracts with General Services Administration*

Free; BSC (see C1.105).

3.404 *Contract Opportunities for Maintenance and Repair of Equipment*

Free; BSC (see C1.105).

3.405 Food for Peace

The Agricultural Trade Development and Assistance Act of 1954, as amended, commonly referred to as Food for Peace, authorizes foreign sales and grants of agricultural commodities. About $25 billion worth of agricultural commodities has been shipped under this program.

Title I of Public Law 480 provides for the concessional sale of agricultural commodities to friendly countries. Since 1972, sales have been negotiated only for long-term credit repayable in dollars or currencies readily convertible to dollars.

Title II of P.L. 480 authorizes donations of agricultural commodities to needy persons abroad through friendly governments, United States nonprofit voluntary agencies, and multilateral organizations.

Assistant Sales Manager, P.L. 480 Programs, Office of the General Sales Manager, Department of Agriculture, Washington, DC 20240; 202-447-5693.

Special Assistance and Procurement Specifications (3.450-3.459)

3.450 Business Service Centers

The General Services Administration maintains Business Service Centers (BSC), located in major metropolitan areas, which furnish advice and assistance to businesses interested in government procurement. The centers provide information and guidance on all GSA programs and maintain information on other agency buying programs so that businesses can be properly referred.

The centers assist GSA procurement officers by identifying potential suppliers. To do this, they actively seek out business concerns who may be able to supply the government's needs.

BSC (see C1.105).

3.451 Office of the Ombudsman

Businesses can obtain information and advice on a wide variety of subjects by applying to the Office of the Ombudsman of the Department of Commerce. This office, part of the Bureau of Domestic Commerce of the Domestic and International Business Administration, will help with specific problems confronted by businesses by locating needed information or finding the proper official to contact. The Office also solicits business opinions on government programs.

Typical areas in which help may be obtained from the Ombudsman are federal procurement, domestic or world markets, federal regulations, financial assistance, technology transfer, occupational safety and health, and product safety.

The Ombudsman issues *Situation Reports* from time to time on current topics. Subjects covered have included productivity, new product warranties, proposed legislation of interest to small business, and individual materials shortages. The *U.S. Industrial Outlook* is published annually, with planning and marketing data and informed opinion on over 200 industries as compiled and written by analysts of the Bureau of Domestic Commerce. The Ombudsman also holds seminars, briefings, and conferences with businesses.

Office of the Ombudsman, Bureau of Domestic Commerce, Room 3800, Department of Commerce, Washington, DC 20230; 202-377-3176.

3.452 Certificates of Competency

Following the government procurement bidding process, a government contracting officer may have doubts as to whether a small, low bidder has the capacity or necessary financial means to perform the contract if awarded. The Certificates of Competency (COC) program provides the small firm with an appeal procedure. If the Small Business Administration (SBA) disagrees with the contracting officer, it is authorized to certify that the small firm has the necessary production and financial ability to perform the contract at issue. The decision is binding on the contracting officer.

SBA (see C1.110).

3.453 Office of Small Business Research and Development of the National Science Foundation

Information on grants and contracts awarded by the National Science Foundation (NSF) to small businesses, and information on programs, policies, and procedures of NSF which are of interest to small businesses, will be made available by NSF's Office of Small Business Research and Development. The office will work with the Small Business Administration and the White House Office of Science and Technology Policy to prepare a comprehensive report on the technical capabilities of the small business community.

NSF, 1800 G St. N.W., Washington, DC 20550.

3.454 Services to Small and Minority Businesses from National Aeronautics and Space Administration

Small businesses and minority businesses receive special attention at NASA (National Aeronautics and Space Administration). Under its Small Business Program and its Minority Business Enterprise Program, NASA attempts to ensure that small and minority businesses have an equitable opportunity to participate in NASA procurement, and that they receive a fair share of NASA prime and subcontract awards.

NASA has a small business advisor at its headquarters to represent the interests of small business before NASA and a small business specialist at each installation whose primary responsibility is to foster small business procurement opportunities. Where possible, specific procurements are set aside for small business competition.

As to minority businesses, NASA works with the Office of Minority Business Enterprise (OMBE) and with the Small Business Administration (SBA) in assisting small firms owned and controlled by socially or economically disadvantaged individuals or groups. NASA gives special emphasis to identifying procurement requirements for referral to SBA for matching with the capabilities and potentials of firms approved under Section 8(a) of the Small Business Act. (Under Section 8(a), SBA contracts with NASA for supplies and services, and then subcontracts noncompetively for these requirements with approved firms.) In addition, NASA's headquarters has a minority business officer, and several NASA installations have minority business specialists.

Addresses of small business specialists and minority business specialists at NASA installations follow.

National Aeronautics and
Space Administration
Washington, DC 20546
202-755-2288

Ames Research Center
Moffett Field, Ca 94035
514-965-5800

Flight Research Center
Edwards, CA 93523
805-258-3311, ext 796

Goddard Space Flight Center
Greenbelt, MD 20771
301-982-5416 small business
301-982-6871 minority

Kennedy Space Center
Kennedy Space Center, FL 32899
305-867-7353

Langley Research Center
Hampton, Va 23365
804-827-3959

Lewis Research Center
Cleveland, OH 44135
216-433-4000 ext 543

Johnson Space Center
Houston, TX 77058
713-483-4511 small business
713-483-5473 minority

Marshall Space Flight Center
Huntsville, AL 35812
205-453-2675 small business
205-453-4200 minority

National Space Technology Laboratories
Bay St. Louis, MS 39520
601-688-3680

Wallops Flight Center
Wallops Island, VA 23337
804-824-3411 ext 542

NASA Pasadena Office
Pasadena, CA 91103
213-354-6051

Jet Propulsion Laboratory
Pasadena, CA 91103
213-354-6941 small business
213-354-3130 minority

3.455 Register of Small Business Facilities

The Small Business Administration (SBA) maintains a register of small firms which are interested in supplying goods and services to the government purchasing agencies and their prime contractors. Firms which have registered will be called upon when requests are made for sources of supplies or services. If necessary, SBA will conduct an on-site survey of a firm's facilities. The register is nationwide in scope.

Forms for registration are available at SBA area offices (see C1.110). Small manufacturing firms need Form 166; construction firms, general contractors, and firms with service facilities need Form 166B; and research and development firms need Form 1019.

3.456 Free Publications on Government Procurement

The following publications are available, free, from SBA (see C1.110).

Order No. Management Aids Series

211 *Termination of DOD Contracts for the Government's Convenience*
215 *How to Prepare for a Pre-Award Survey*

Technical Aids Series

78 *Controlling Quality in Defense Production*
82 *Inspection on Defense Contracts in Small Firms*

3.457 *Federal Procurement Regulations*

This subscription service, in loose-leaf form, includes Federal Procurement Regulation (FPR) circulars for an indefinite period, and the 1975 reprint which incorporates FPR amendments 1 through 136. It transmits new or revised FPR material prescribed by the Administrator of General Services under the Federal Property and Administrative Services Act of 1949.

#GS 1.6/5:964/rep.-2; GPO (see C1.0).

3.458 *Guide to Specifications and Standards of the Federal Government*

The purpose of this guide is to help current and prospective buyers better understand the complex problems involved in the development and use of specifications and standards, and to clarify the importance and advantages of knowing exactly what the government proposes to buy and exactly which is expected of the supplier in the way of quality, performance, and delivery.

Free; BSC (see C1.105).

3.459 *Index of Federal Specifications and Standards*

Issued annually by the General Services Administration, this index lists federal specifications alphabetically and numerically and specifies the cost of copies available for sale. The index also includes information concerning federal standards, federal qualified products lists, and related information. Cumulative supplements to the index are issued each month.

Free for bidding purposes; BSC (see C1.105).

Chapter 4

BUSINESS ADMINISTRATION

CHAPTER ABSTRACT

Publications and information sources of interest to the business administrator/manager are listed in this chapter.

The first section, "Business Administration Guides" (4.0-4.16), lists publications covering a wide range of management concerns from general business planning to such specific areas as establishing an employee suggestion system.

The next section, "Training and Technical Assistance in Management Development" (4.50-4.62), lists training programs for managers and sources of personalized assistance in business planning.

The third section, "Current Awareness Services for Administrators" (4.100-4.102), is the heart of the chapter. It describes subscription services available from the government which will keep the administrator abreast of the latest developments in many fields relevant to business planning, and bring to his attention new publications and services in government that may be used to advantage. The last part describes several business commentaries that have grown out of high-level conferences about business and the economy.

"Data: Business and the Economy" (4.250-4.318) lists guides to data and information, and publications with actual data on business trends. The data are generally broad, except for several publications which show trends for counties and some smaller areas. (For more specific data sources useful in site selection and market research, see Chapters 1 and 3.)

"Regulations and Consumer Affairs" (4.350-4.366) lists some of the regulatory agencies whose authority has impact on a broad spectrum of the business community. No attempt was made to make this an exhaustive list, since such an effort is beyond the intent of the *Guide*.

"The Postal Service" (4.400-4.401) is intended to simplify the complexities of the post office for businesses which need to keep informed of cost-effective mailing systems and procedures.

"Crime and Business" (4.450-4.455) lists publications and services in this area.

The last section, "Audio-Visual Management Aids" (4.500-4.502) lists filmographies and films that can be used in management development programs.

Business Administration Guides (4.0-4.16)

4.0 *Business Packaging*

While designed and composed primarily for minority business development, a manual entitled *Business Packaging* is of general interest as well. It discusses business development as an ongoing process of planning, financing, marketing, and resource utilization. It begins with a discussion of the characteristics generally required of an entrepreneur, and how to evaluate a business idea. It then discusses developing the business package, which includes market research, sales planning, a technical and operational plan, and financial planning. It points out both private and public-sector resources available to the entrepreneur, with a complete discussion of the Small Business Administration. Finally, it presents two case studies in detail. Each section includes not only narrative, but also sample forms and charts that can be used both to organize and to evaluate efforts at each stage.

Office of Community Development, Department of Housing and Urban Development, Washington, DC 20410; see also HUD field offices (C1.40).

4.1 *Improving Material Handling in Small Business*

The basics of material handling, the method of laying out workplaces, and other factors in setting up an efficient system are discussed.

#SBA 1.12:4, 42 pp., 60¢; GPO (see C1.0).

4.2 *Ratio Analysis for Small Business*

Ratio analysis is the process of determining relationships among certain financial or operating data of a business to provide a basis for managerial control. The purpose of this booklet is to help the owner/manager to detect favorable or unfavorable trends in the business.

#SBA 1.12:20, 65pp., 90¢; GPO (see C1.0).

4.3 *Guides for Profit Planning*

Guides for computing and using the break-even point, the level of gross profit, and the rate of return on investment are contained in this booklet. It is designed for readers who have no specialized training in accounting or economics.

#SBA 1.12:25, 52 pp., 85¢; GPO (see C1.0).

4.4 *Profitable Community Relations for Small Business*

Practical information on how to build and maintain sound community relations by participation in community affairs is provided in this booklet.

#SBA 1.12:27, 36 pp., 70¢; GPO (see C1.0).

4.5 *Management Audit for Small Manufacturers*

A series of questions in this booklet will indicate whether the owner/manager is planning, organizing, directing, and coordinating business activities efficiently.

#SBA 1.12:29, 58 pp., 75¢; GPO (see C1.0).

4.6 *Management Audit for Small Retailers*

149 questions in this booklet guide the businessman in examining himself and his business.

#SBA 1.12:31, 72 pp., 80¢; GPO (see C1.0).

4.7 *Small Store Planning for Growth*

The nature of growth, the management skills needed, and some techniques for use in promoting growth are discussed in this booklet, as well as a consideration of merchandising, advertising and display, and checklists for increasing transactions and gross margins.

#SBA 1.12:33, 99 pp., $1.75; GPO (see C1.0).

4.8 *Managing for Profits*

Various aspects of small business management, such as marketing, management, and credit, are discussed in the ten chapters of this book.

#SBA 1.2:M31/11, 170 pp., $1.95; GPO (see C1.0).

4.9 *Strengthening Small Business Management*

This twenty-one chapter book reflects the experience which the author gained in a lifetime of work with the small business community.

#SBA 1.2:M31/14, 158 pp., $2.25; GPO (see C1.0).

4.10 *Profitable Small Plant Layout*

The small business owner whose costs on finished goods are rising may find that his decreasing net profits and his lowered production stem from lack of economical and orderly movement of production materials from one process to another throughout the shop.

#SBA 1.12:21, 48 pp., 80¢; GPO (see C1.0).

4.11 *Analysis for Manager of People and Things*

Systems analysis as it is used in high-level decisions in the Department of Defense is explained in this guide. Since the object of offering these directions is to stretch resources in times of inflation and budget cuts, businesses may benefit as well.

#008-040-00062-2, 100 pp., $1.45; GPO (see C1.0).

4.12 *Correspondence Management*

Managing business correspondence is a basic concern in any office. This book gives recommendations from the *Records Management Handbook of the National Archives* on establishing a correspondence management program, lowering correspondence costs, improving quality, and increasing productivity.

#022-003-00899-3, 35 pp., 85¢; GPO (see C1.0).

4.13 *Better Communications in Small Business*

Smaller manufacturers can help themselves to win cooperation by means of more skillful communication. This booklet shows how better communications within the firm can improve operating efficiency and competitive strength.

#SBA 1.12:7, 37 pp., 65¢; GPO (see C1.0).

4.14 *An Employee Suggestion System for Small Companies*

The basic principles for starting and operating a suggestion system are explained in this booklet. It also warns of various pitfalls and gives examples and suggestions submitted by employees.

#SBA 1.12:1, 18 pp., 40¢; GPO (see C1.0).

4.15 Free Publications on General Management

The following publications are available, free, from Small Business Administration (see C1.110).

Management Aids Series

179 *Breaking the Barriers to Small Business Planning*
181 *Numerical Control Manufacturer*
189 *Should You Make or Buy Components?*
195 *Setting Pay for Management Jobs*
206 *Keep Pointed toward Profit*
207 *Pointers on Scheduling Production*
208 *Problems in Managing a Family-Owned Business*
212 *The Equipment Replacement Decision*
214 *The Metric System for Small Business*
218 *Business Plan for Small Manufacturers*
221 *Business Plan for Small Construction Firms*
224 *Association Services for Small Business*

Technical Aids Series

73 *Pointers in In-Plant Trucking*
91 *A Tested System for Achieving Quality Control*

Small Marketers Aids Series

25 *Are You Kidding Yourself about Your Profits?*
105 *A Pricing Checklist for Managers*
114 *Pleasing Your Boss, the Customer*
116 *How to Select a Resident Buying Office*
118 *Legal Services for Small Retail and Service Firms*
123 *Stock Control for Small Stores*
124 *Knowing Your Image*
125 *Pointers on Display Lighting*
130 *Analyze Your Records to Reduce Costs*
132 *The Federal Wage-Hour Law in Small Firms*
133 *Can You Afford Delivery Service?*

135 *Arbitration: Peace-Maker in Small Business*
137 *Outwitting Bad Check Passers*
138 *Sweeping Profit Out the Back Door*
139 *Understanding Truth-in-Lending*
140 *Profit by Your Wholesalers' Services*
141 *Danger Signals in a Small Store*
145 *Personal Qualities Needed to Manage a Store*
149 *Computers for Small Business—Service Bureau or Time Sharing?*
150 *Business Plan for Retailers*
153 *Business Plan for Small Service Firms*
155 *Keeping Records in Small Business*
157 *Efficient Lighting in Small Stores*

Small Business Bibliographies

10 *Retailing*
15 *Recordkeeping Systems—Small Store and Service Trades*
18 *Basic Library Reference Sources*
58 *Automation for Small Offices*
75 *Inventory Management*
85 *Purchasing for Owners of Small Plants*
86 *Training for Small Business*

4.16 *Starting and Managing a Small Business of Your Own*

A prospective businessman thinking of starting a new business should ask himself certain questions about his ability, resources, and knowledge. These things, and others which should be considered in choosing what business he is to go into, are discussed in clear and graphic form in *Starting and Managing A Small Business of Your Own.*

The pros and cons of buying a going business or investing in a franchise are discussed, as well as how to start a business from scratch. The basic aspects of managing a business (buying, pricing, selling, personnel, recordkeeping, and more) are explained in detail. Also, taxes, insurance, and laws and regulations a businessman is subject to are dealt with in some detail.

The final pages of the booklet are devoted to a comprehensive checklist for starting a business. Also included is a list of the field offices of the Small Business Administration.

#045-000-00123-7, 95 pp., $1.35; GPO (see C1.0).

Training and Technical Assistance in Management Development (4.50-4.62)

4.50 *Publications on Management Development*

Educators and others who teach management courses will find these presentations useful. They include a lesson plan, lecture, visual aids, case studies, study assignments, and selected bibliography and handout material.

As priced; GPO (see C1.0).

Success and Failure Factors in Small Business, #045-000-00083-4, 88 pp., $3.65
Records and Credit in Profitable Management, #045-000-00090-7, 66 pp., $3.85
Managing to Sell, #045-000-00091-5, 74 pp., $4.00
The Why and What of Bookkeeping, #045-000-00092-3, 64 pp., $3.20
Personnel Management, Developing Good Employees, #045-000-00094-0, 87 pp., $3.95
Aspects of Sales Promotion, #045-000-00095-8, 64 pp., $3.20
Taxation, A Key Factor in Business Decisions, #045-000-00096-6, 74 pp., $4.00
Communication and Control, #045-000-00097-4, 64 pp., $3.80
Human Factors in Small Business, #045-000-00079-6, 82 pp., $4.10
Choosing a Form of Business Organization, #045-000-00080-0, 62 pp., 3.20
Safeguarding Your Business and Management Succession, #045-000-00081-8, 70 pp., $3.75
Small Business Location and Layout, #045-000-00082-6, 64 pp., $3.55
Sources of Assistance and Information, #045-000-00085-1, 68 pp., $3.60
Why Customers Buy (And Why They Don't), #045-000-00086-9, 52 pp., $3.40
Marketing Research, Instructor's Manual, #045-000-00087-7, 78 pp., $3.65
Franchising, #045-000-00088-5, 67 pp., $3.60
Pricing in a Services Business, #045-000-00089-3, 63 pp., $3.55
Merchandise Pricing, #045-000-00101-6, 56 pp., $3.55
Merchandise Control, #045-000-00110-5, 67 pp., $3.60
Management Introduction to Work Processing, #008-020-00548-7, 136 pp., $2.10
Managing for Profits, #045-000-00005-2, 180 pp., $1.95

4.51 Graduate School of the Department of Agriculture

Continuing education and training of managers, technicians, and employees can be accomplished at modest cost at the Graduate School of the Department of Agriculture, located in Washington, D.C. The Graduate School is open to the public and offers courses on a wide variety of subjects of value to business but does not grant degrees.

Correspondence courses are available in such subjects as executive development, management, and supervision; accounting; engineering; English usage and writing; mathematics and statistics; and computer sciences.

The Individual Learning Center offers individualized, programmed, and self-instructional courses, which allow students to advance in easy step-by-step procedures through difficult material. Subjects available include grammar, punctuation, spelling, vocabulary, reading, metric system, fractions, decimals, algebra, calculus, statistics, accounting, management and supervision, computer programming, and office skills such as filing, shorthand, and business letters.

Employers with affirmative action problems may wish to consult with the staff of the Career Planning and Development Programs. Upward mobility of employees can depend upon increased educational and skills training opportunities, and the staff can help employers with the following services: (1) planning and developing upward mobility career development programs; (2) assessment services for determining training needs of employers; (3) vocational testing and counseling services for individuals or groups; and (4) development of special seminars and courses to meet specific needs.

Career Planning and Development Programs/ Individual Learning Center, Room 6834, South Building, Department of Agriculture, Washington, DC 20250; 202-447-6693 or 6694.

For information on correspondence courses: Office of Independent Study Programs, Room 6847, South Building, Department of Agriculture, Washington, DC 20250; 202-447-7123.

For a copy of the current catalog of the Graduate School: Information Office, Room 6847, South Building, Department of Agriculture, Washington, DC 20250; 202-447-4419.

4.52 Consulting Services in Statistical Interpretation

Regional and national office staffs of the Bureau of Labor Statistics (BLS) are available for consultation on the application, uses, and limitations of BLS data. Examples of assistance include the limitations of price indexes in contract escalation clauses, information on the prevalence of a variety of special provisions in collective bargaining agreements, comparative wage rates in different parts of the country, and occupational employment information needed for estimates of future requirements. Consulting services are almost always free.

In addition, the district offices of the Department of Commerce offer assistance in gaining access to the kind of data a manager may need, and in helping with interpretation.

BLS (see C1.70); Department of Commerce (see C1.10).

4.53 Service Corps of Retired Executives and Active Corps of Executives

The Service Corps of Retires Executives (SCORE) is a group of public-spirited, knowledgeable, and experienced retired executives from every job sector. Many were owners of small businesses. SCORE has a present membership of 5,198, with 292 chapters.

The Active Corps of Executives (ACE) is an important auxiliary to SCORE. It augments SCORE and furnishes needed special talents which may not be represented among other volunteers.

Both SCORE and ACE members participate in conducting workshops and in offering a wide range of management and technical counseling to the small business community. The volunteers donate their time to present and potential small business owners. The Small Business Administration (SBA) reimburses them for out-of-pocket expenses.

A counselor will meet with a client at a SCORE office or at the client's place of business; usually that will resolve the problem. At other times, counseling continues for as long as necessary.

SBA (see C1.110).

4.54 Management Assistance through Professional and Trade Associations

The Small Business Administration (SBA) is entering into agreements with ten to fifteen trade and professional associations to provide specialized management and technical assistance to small businesses that are socially or economically disadvantaged.

SBA (see C1.110).

4.55 Technology Assistance Program

In order to make the technological advances resulting from federally financed R&D available to small business concerns, the Technology Assistance Program for small business provides educational and technical assistance through workshops, consultation, and technical publications which identify technological advances from the federal government's stockpile of information.

SBA (see C1.110).

4.56 Management Training, Seminars, and Workshops

Small Business Administration (SBA) field offices offer prebusiness workshops, conferences, and problem clinics on developing a business plan for small businesses or those thinking about starting a business. SBA makes special efforts to increase the number of minority and disadvantaged businesses included in such groups.

SBA (see C1.110).

4.57 Small Business Institute Program

The Small Business Institute program, a three-way cooperative between collegiate schools of business administration, members of the nation's small business community, and the Small Business Administration (SBA) is a new source of management assistance. Under the supervision of university faculty and SBA staff, senior and graduate students of business administration work directly with owners of small firms, providing vital management assistance to small businesses while undergoing meaningful learning experiences themselves.

The program began in the fall of 1972. In the first year of its life, 1,100 small firms received counseling and 2,200 students were involved. In 1976, 385 schools participated, involving over 22,000 students and 8,800 small businesses. Satisfaction rate among clients was over 80 percent.

SBA (see C1.110).

4.58 University Business Development Centers

Growing out of the Small Business Institute concept (see 4.57), the University Business Development Center (UBDC) program is an experimental Small Business Administration concept being tested in eight universities. It is a university-based and administered program to interrelate the academic, professional, and technological resources of universities with all existing government programs designed to assist the business community. While each agency continues to administer its own programs, the university serves as a funnel or mixing device for them, so that the collection of programs will work as an integrated unit serving the whole community, rather than as an uncoordinated variety of programs.

A functioning UBDC can offer the following services to its business clients:

—Business and product evaluation and development
—Entrepreneur evaluation, recommendations, counseling, and training
—Analysis, correction, and follow-up of financial, marketing, technical, production, legal, and any other type of problem faced by small business owners
—Feasibility studies and development of business plans for present and future entrepreneurs
—Access to and application of technology, paid for by the taxpayers in over $350 billion worth of research and development projects since 1947
—Assistance not only in surviving (when 57 percent of new businesses fail in the first five years), but in expanding on a solid basis

Universities currently involved are the Universities of Maine at Bangor, Missouri at St. Louis, Nebraska at Omaha, Georgia at Athens, and West Florida at Pensacola; and Rutgers University, New Brunswick, New Jersey; California State University at Chico; and California Polytechnic at Pomona.

4.59 Cooperative Extension Service

The Cooperative Extension Service has agents in virtually every county in the country. The job of the agent is to provide technical assistance to whomever requests it on the development of resources—natural, human, and social—with a general orientation toward agriculture and rural development.

The agent can provide information and assistance in the following areas: *economic development*—how to bring in new businesses, new payrolls, new jobs, community recreation; *community services*—how to obtain better schools, water and utility systems, housing, sanitation, transportation, how to prepare for civil defense and natural disasters; and *human development*—how to set up training programs to teach people new skills to do new jobs, and how to improve the quality of living and the future for youth who remain in the community.

Many businessmen turn to the Cooperative Extension Service for technical information and training. Specialists help farmers and professors study the economic effects of foreign markets and consumer preferences. Professional people who serve agriculture—veterinarians, vocational agriculture teachers, bankers—use Extension information.

See county offices of Cooperative Extension Service; also state headquarters (C1.1).

4.60 Research Associate Program of the National Bureau of Standards

Firms which share a mutual interest with a unit of the National Bureau of Standards (NBS) may benefit from participation in the Research Associate Program. Under this program, an employee of a firm may work at NBS under the supervision of NBS professionals, using the facilities, laboratories, information, and services of NBS.

Industrial Liaison Officer, Research Associate Program, Room A-402, Administration Building, NBS, Washington DC 20234; 301-921-3591.

4.61 Office of the Ombudsman

Businesses can obtain information and advice on such matters as federal procurement, domestic or world markets, federal regulations, financial assistance, technology transfer, occupational safety and health, and product safety from the Office of the Ombudsman. The Ombudsman will help with specific problems confronted by businessmen, by locating needed information, the proper official to contact, or the right program.

The Ombudsman, which is part of the Bureau of Domestic Commerce of the Domestic and International Business Administration, solicits business opinions on government programs.

The Ombudsman issues *Situation Reports* from time to time on current topics. Subjects covered have included productivity, new product warranties, proposed legislation of interest to small business, and individual materials shortages. The *U.S. Industrial Outlook* is published annually, with planning and marketing data and informed opinion on over 200 industries as compiled and written by analysts of the Bureau of Domestic Commerce. The Ombudsman also holds seminars, briefings, and conferences with businesses.

Office of the Ombudsman, Bureau of Domestic Commerce, Room 3800, Department of Commerce, Washington, DC 20230; 202-377-3176.

4.62 The Call Contracting Program

The Call Contracting Program authorizes the Small Business Administration (SBA) to place contracts with qualified individuals and businesses in order to provide management and technical aid to SBA clients who meet the eligibility requirements of Sections 7(i) and 7(j) of the Small Business Act, as amended in 1974. It also allows SBA to initiate, organize, and maintain this management counseling service for small firms as required.

Professional consulting firms must qualify as existing small firms at the time of proposal and must meet the standards set out in the Request for Proposal (RFP). Potential consultants must have been in business for at least one year before the closing date for receipt of proposals and have a staff capacity to perform at least fifty percent of the work.

Eligible recipients of call-contract counseling include socially or economically disadvantaged individuals or firms and individuals or firms located in areas of high unemployment. Detailed information on eligibility requirements is available at regional offices of SBA.

Forms of assistance available are: bookkeeping and accounting services; production, engineering, and technical advice; feasibility studies, marketing analyses, and advertising expertise; legal services and specialized management training. There is no charge for these services.

To be considered as a prime contractor, the individual or firm should request that its name be added to the bidder's list and that it receive an RFP. Write the Program Manager, Small Business Administration, 1441 L St. N.W., Washington, DC 20416, or call 202-382-8277.

To be considered for counseling, contact the Management Assistance Officer at a field office of SBA (see C1.110).

Current Awareness Services for Administrators (4.100-4.102)

4.100 *Weekly Government Abstracts* for Business Administrators

Each of the following is one of twenty-six subscription newsletters known as *Weekly Government Abstracts.* All twenty-six are annotated in 9.11. Each newsletter contains summaries of government research performed by hundreds of organizations, including government agencies, private researchers, universities, and special technology groups. The research summaries are listed within two weeks of their receipt at the National Technical Information Service. The last issue of each year is a subject index containing up to ten cross references for each research summary indexed.

As priced; National Technical Information Service, 5285 Port Royal Road, Springfield, VA 22161; 703-557-4642.

Administration

Administration, management, management information systems, personnel management, labor relations, manpower studies, program administration, and inventory are covered in this newsletter.

$45.00 per year.

Business and Economics

Domestic and international commerce, banking and finance, manufcturing and production, consumer affairs, and minority enterprises are among the subjects covered by this newsletter.

$45.00 per year.

Industrial and Mechanical Engineering

Production planning, quality control, plant design and maintenance, environmental engineering, and labor psychology and esthetics are among the subjects covered by this newsletter.

$45.00 per year.

Transportation

Transportation by air, pipeline, surface, and subsurface, as well as global navigation systems, are among the subjects covered by this newsletter.

$45.00 per year.

Communication

Communication theory, satellites, radio and television graphics, and communications policies, regulations and studies are among the subjects covered by this newsletter.

$45.00 per year.

Computers, Control and Information Theory

Computer hardware and software, control systems, information theory, pattern recognition, and data processing are among the subjects covered by this newsletter.

$45.00 per year.

Urban Technology

Problems of urban administration, housing, health, finance, environment, and planning are among the subjects covered by this newsletter.

$45.00 per year.

4.101 Current Awareness Subscription Service

Status: A Monthly Chartbook of Social and Economic Trends

Status, a magazine prepared by the Bureau of the Census for the Office of Management and Budget, is a graphic presentation of current statistical information, focusing on major social and economic conditions within the United States. Data are included from many federal sources. Also provided are listings of basic sources for the material presented and a variety of color maps and charts designed to improve the understandability of timely, important statistical data. In each edition of *Status,* major sections provide current statistical graphic information about the people, the community, the economy, and other areas such as science and the environment. A special map is included each month to identify geographic areas of special concern. Although the magazine is aimed at decision-makers in all fields, it is not intended for the exclusive use of the professional statistician or economist.

Monthly, $3.60; Subscriber Services Section, Bureau of the Census, Department of Commerce, Washington DC 20233.

Data User News

This is the basic subscription service of the Bureau of the Census. It provides information on applications of census data and on new computer programs, news on user-oriented programs and products, announcements of workshops and seminars, a reader's exchange, and more. Eight or more pages each month bring news of activities, products, and publications in the field of small-area census data. A special section highlights the applications readers around the country have found for census data. Articles by Bureau specialists explain technical points, methodology, and processing techniques of the Bureau of the Census.

$4.00 per year; Subscriber Services Section, Bureau of the Census, Department of Commerce, Washington, DC 20233.

Announcing BLS Publications

At least two of these flyers are released each month from the regional offices of the Bureau of Labor Statistics (BLS). They serve to keep the businessman abreast of new BLS issuances useful in analyzing the economy and in manpower planning.

Free; BLS (see C1.70).

The following publications are available, as priced, from GPO (see C1.0):

Business Service Checklist

New publications important to both domestic and international trade are listed in this weekly news bulletin from the Department of Commerce. The checklist is the best way to keep abreast of government publications relating to business and the economy.

$9.70 per year.

Commerce America Newsletter and *Magazine*

Newsletter: The newsletter is a free publication put out by the area offices of the Domestic and International Business Administration. It is usually two pages and contains items of interest on such topics as government procurement, exporting, area activities, and seminars.

Magazine: The magazine is the principal publication of the Department of Commerce. It is a biweekly publication which provides brief descriptions of items or events of interest to business, major articles on economic highlights, domestic business developments, international business reports, individual business opportunities overseas, programs and information being offered to business, and calendars of important events.

$29.80 per year.

Monthly Checklist of State Publications

The documents and publications issued by the various states and received in the Library of Congress are recorded in this service.

#LC30.9, $21.90 per year, $1.50 single copy.

DIMENSIONS/NBS

Persons in business, industry, science, engineering, education, and the general public can learn of the latest advances in science and technology, with primary emphasis on the work at the National Bureau of Standards (NBS), through a subscription to the monthly *DIMENSIONS/NBS* magazine (formerly *Technical News Bulletin).*

$9.45 per year.

Housing and Planning References

Publications and articles on housing and planning that were received in the Department of Housing and Urban Development during a two-month period are published in this bimonthly service.

#HH1.23/3, $18.90 per year, $3.15 single copy.

HUD Challenge

This magazine serves as a forum for the exchange of ideas and innovations between HUD (Housing and Urban Development) staff throughout the country, HUD-related agencies, institutions, businesses, and the concerned public. As a tool of management, the magazine provides a medium for discussing official HUD policies, programs, projects, and new directions. It seeks to stimulate nationwide thought and action toward solving the nation's housing and urban problems.

#HH1.36, monthly, $15.90 per year, $1.40 single copy.

Agricultural Research

Results of Department of Agriculture research projects in livestock management, crops, soils, fruits and vegetables, poultry, and related agricultural fields are presented in this publication.

#A77.12, monthly, $6.50 per year, 55¢ single copy.

Extension Service Review

Pertinent information on agriculture extension programs of the United States, 4-H Club work, conservation, home demonstration, community cooperation, and other subjects are included in this service.

#A43.7, bimonthly, $3.60 per year, 60¢ single copy.

Monthly Catalog of U.S. Government Publications

The catalog is a comprehensive listing of all publications listed by the various departments and agencies of the government each month. It can be used as a current awareness tool, to keep abreast of the range of government publications available and of the latest prices.

$27.00 per year.

Selected U.S. Government Publications

New or still popular publications in many areas that are of interest to business, such as energy and the environment, health, science and technology, education, and business and industry are highlighted in this subscription service.

Free.

4.102 Business commentaries

The following publications are available, as priced, from GPO (see C1.0).

A Look at Business in 1990

The White House Conference on the Industrial World Ahead, held in Washington in 1972, is summarized. It contains projections of the various aspects of business to the year 1990.

$5.25.

Survival and Growth, The Small R&D Firm

The proceedings of a conference dealing with the problems of small firms in the research and development industry are reported in this publication.

#045-000-00119-9, 216 pp., $2.60.

The Vital Majority, Small Business in the American Economy

A wide range of subjects is covered in this book of essays marking the twentieth anniversary of the Small Business Administration. Typical topics are: finance, accounting, marketing, government assistance programs, information systems and computerization, research and development, management strategies, labor relations, taxation, and market structures.

#045-000-00124-5, 510 pp., $6.75.

The Multinational Corporation: Studies on U.S. Foreign Investment

Vol. 1, 1972, 197 pp., $2.10; Vol. 2, 1973, 82 pp., $1.00.

Japan, The Government-Business Relationship

In this publication, the extraordinary growth of the Japanese economy is examined, as are the intricate interactions of government and business groups.

#003-009-00202-8, 158 pp., $1.80.

Small Business Administration *Annual Report*

The *Annual Report* of the Small Business Administration (SBA) provides a description and performance analysis of each of the agency's financial and management assistance programs, demonstrating the breadth of activity of SBA.

$3.20.

Data: Business and the Economy (4.250-4.318)

Guides to Information and Data (4.250-4.257)

4.250 *A Directory of Information Resources in the United States: Federal Government*

Over 1,200 agencies and federally-supported organizations are listed in this exhaustive volume published by the National Referral Center of the Library of Congress. Organized alphabetically by agency, the *Directory* describes the areas of interest of each organization, its holdings of documents, its publications, and the information services it provides. For each organization, the address and telephone number are provided.

Much of the information available from the

resources listed in the *Directory* is technical in nature. An extensive subject index and a description of government-sponsored Information Analysis Centers are included.

#3000-00067, revised edition, $4.00; GPO (see C1.0).

4.251 *Directory of Federal Technology Transfer*

Private industry may share more effectively in the results of federal programs aimed at the development of knowledge and technologies, using this report. It is designed as an easy-to-use directory of federal technology transfer activities across a wide spectrum of federal government departments, agencies, and commissions. Each section gives a description of an agency's program, including its research base, its technology transfer policy and objectives, areas of responsibility, methods of implementation, accomplishments, and user organizations. Contact points through which a user can find the most pertinent elements of the agency are provided. There is an index to help users find activities or applications related to their areas of interest and also to determine whether activity areas are common to more than one federal agency.

The report is a product of the Committee on Domestic Technology Transfer of the Federal Coordinating Council for Science, Engineering, and Technology.

$4.30; GPO (see C1.0).

4.252 *Department of Commerce Publications Catalog and Index*

Each year the Department of Commerce issues an annual supplement with this title, listing the publications issued that year, arranged by the issuing bureau or office. It covers the articles printed in *Commerce Today, Construction Review, Survey of Current Business, Journal of Research,* and *Fishery Bulletin,* and includes a subject index.

#003-000-00503-8, $1.15; GPO (see C1.0).

4.253 A Visual Aid for Quick Reference to Basic Census Bureau Publications

This is a display poster highlighting selected guides and major report series.

10¢; Data User Section, Bureau of the Census, Department of Commerce, Washington, DC 20233.

4.254 *Bureau of the Census Catalog*

This catalog describes the publications, computer tapes and punchcards, and related nonstatistical materials and services made available from January of each year. Part I, *Publications,* is a classified, annotated bibliography of all publications issued by the Bureau during the period covered. Geographical and subject indexes are provided. Part II, *Data Files and Special Publications,* initiated in 1964, provides a listing of those materials which became available at the Bureau during the catalog period. Included are basic data files (on computer tape or punchcards), special tabulations (tapes, cards, and printed data) prepared for sponsors, and nonstatistical materials such as maps and computer programs.

A monthly supplement to the catalog lists major special publications, reports issued in a series at irregular intervals, and regular publications issued less frequently than quarterly.

$14.40 per year for four quarterly issues and 12 monthly supplements; quarterly prices vary but usually stay between $2.00 and $4.00; GPO (see C1.0).

4.255 *Bureau of the Census Guide to Programs and Publications: Subjects and Areas*

A comprehensive review of the statistical programs of the Bureau of the Census and of the report issued by the Bureau in the 1960's and early 1970's appears in this guide. It shows the geographic areas and principal subjects for most of the publications. For reports issued periodically, the areas covered in the latest issues are shown. Almost all statistical and geographic reports, including maps, published between 1968 and 1972 are covered.

$2.40; GPO (see C1.0).

4.256 *Bibliography on Housing, Building, and Planning*

Approximately 400 recent books and periodicals available in the United States on housing, building, and planning are included in this bibliography. It is useful in establishing a basic technical collection for universities, financial institutions, architects, planners, builders, and others.

43 pp., 50¢; GPO (see C1.0).

4.257 *Congressional Directory*

The *Congressional Directory* contains bibliographies and information on the organization of Congress. It may be useful to businesses which wish to contact the proper source quickly to express a view or request an audience. It is published annually and includes committee memberships, individual seniority rankings, and Congressional staff listings.

$5.05 paperbound, $6.80 clothbound; GPO (see C1.0).

Specific Data for Business Planning (4.300-4.318)

4.300 *U.S. Industrial Outlook*

Narrative outlook analyses and an appendix of statistical tables project industrial activity in the current year and provide a review of the prior year, with forecasts for ten years. The analyses cover 200 industries and forecast trends in four major segments of industry: manufacturing, construction, services, and communications.

$5.45; GPO (see C1.0).

4.301 *Service Industries: Trends and Prospects*

Trends emerging in the service sector, and the impact of demographic and economic changes on that sector, are discussed in this publication.

$1.40; GPO (see C1.0).

4.302 Industry Reports

The following publications are available, as priced, from GPO (see C1.0).

Construction Review consolidates almost all current government and some nongovernment statistics pertaining to the construction industry, along with feature articles and yearly construction outlook.

Monthly, $14.50 per year.

Containers and Packaging offers economic review and outlook, analysis of local and national container trends and developments.

Quarterly, $3.00 per year.

Copper presents comprehensive supply-demand analysis and projections, imports and exports, and shipments of producers and fabricators.

Quarterly, $3.00 per year.

Printing and Publishing publishes domestic data on employment, earnings, production, and exports and imports as well as detailed analyses of current industry conditions.

Quarterly, $3.00 per year.

Pulp, Paper, and Board presents economic analyses, feature articles, and statistics on production trends, capacity, world markets, inventories, and prices.

Quarterly, $3.00 per year.

4.303 *Monthly Retail Trade*

In this publication series, data are given for the United States, current month, with comparisons for previous months on estimates of monthly retail sales by major kind-of-business groups and selected individual kinds of business. Separate figures are shown, in more limited detail, for firms operating eleven or more retail stores. Summary sales data are presented for geographic regions and divisions, selected states, large standard metropolitan statistical areas, and cities. Also included are national estimates of end-of-month accounts receivable balances outstanding for all retail stores and, separately, for firms operating eleven or more retail stores.

Separate data are shown for charge accounts and installment accounts. National sales and accounts receivable estimates are shown adjusted for seasonal variations and trading day differences, as well as in unadjusted form. The report also includes data on department store sales published separately in *Monthly Department Store Sales for Selected Areas.*

$30.10 per year, single copies 25¢; GPO (see C1.0).

4.304 *Monthly Wholesale Trade: Sales and Inventories*

For the current month and twelve preceding months, data are presented for the United States on estimated monthly sales of merchant wholesalers by kind of business, estimated monthly sales, by geographic division, for merchant wholesalers in total, for durable goods, and for nondurable goods wholesalers; monthly inventories of merchant wholesalers, for selected kinds of business; and estimated monthly sales, inventories, and stock-sales ratios of merchant wholesalers, for selected kinds of business. The December report also includes twelve months' sales inventories and sales-stock ratios, by kind of business. It also shows annual sales, year-end inventories, and stock-sales ratios for the preceding ten years.

Sales and inventory trends are shown for about 55 kinds of business at the national level and fourteen kinds of business by geographic divisions. The December report includes percent changes in annual sales of merchant wholesalers by geographic groups.

#C3.133, $7.20 per year; GPO (see C1.0).

4.305 *Monthly Selected Services Receipts*

Data for the United States on monthly receipts of six major kind-of-business groups and seven selected service categories are shown in this subscription service. The statistics include receipts for services to businesses as well as to household customers. Data are adjusted for seasonal and trading day variations. Comparable data for the previous month and for the same month in the previous year are shown, in addition to the percent change from the periods listed. Services included in the monthly survey correspond to those covered by the quinquennial census of business with the exception of such services as legal services, architectural and engineering services, dental laboratories, and travel agencies.

Monthly, $1.00 per year; Subscriber Services Section, Bureau of the Census, Washington, DC 20233. See also Department of Commerce district offices (C1.10).

4.306 *Current Population Reports*

In addition to the findings of the Census of Population conducted every ten years, the Bureau of the Census publishes a continuing and contemporary statistical series of reports of population. Data are issued in seven separate series of reports on family characteristics, mobility, income, education, population estimates and projections, and other subjects.

Annual compilation of continuous reports, $56.00 per year; GPO (see C1.0).

4.307 *Business Conditions Digest*

Designed for business cycle analysis, this publication contains tables and charts for 300 economic series, including composite indexes. Also included are cyclical comparison charts, historical data, series descriptions and data sources.

#C56.111, $55.25 per year, $4.35 single issue; GPO (see C1.0).

4.308 *Defense Indicators*

Charts and data for sixty series on defense activity are included, as are data on obligations, contracts, orders, shipments, inventories, expenditures, employment, and earnings.

#C56.110, $17.90 per year, $1.50 single issue; GPO (see C1.0).

4.309 *Survey of Current Business*

The official source of data on national income and product accounts, this publication covers all aspects of the economy, including employment and prices. The statistical section includes 2,500 series from 100 sources. Each issue has an article on business and the economic situation, as well as other articles.

Monthly with weekly supplements, $48.30 per year; GPO (see C1.0).

4.310 *International Economic Indicators and Competitive Trends*

Business analysts, economists, and others wishing to assess the relative competitive positions of the United States will find this a valuable reference. Attractively presented tables, charts, and text provide a clear, easily readable source of the latest statistical information. It may be used for an overall view of international trends, or as a basis for more detailed analysis of the economic situation in major industrial countries.

$12.65 per year: GPO (see C1.0).

4.311 *Economic Indicators*

The Council of Economic Advisors prepares this publication for the Joint Economic Committee. It contains data on total output of the economy, income and spending, employment, unemployment, wages, production and business activity, prices, money, credit, security, markets, and federal finance.

Monthly, $10.10 per year; GPO (see C1.0).

4.312 *County and City Data Book*

Demographic, social, and economic data for counties, cities, standard metropolitan statistical areas and urbanized areas are presented from the most recent censuses as well as from other governmental and private sources. The topics include: agriculture, bank deposits, births, marriages, climate, home equipment, hospitals, family income, migration, population characteristics, presidential vote, local government finances, retail trade, school enrollment, selected services, manufacturing, and more. The book also includes maps for each state, showing counties, standard metropolitan statistical areas, and large cities; explanatory notes and source citations; and appendixes that expand or explain the coverage of the tables. A unique feature of this book is the availability of its contents on compendia tape and punchcards.

$18.65; GPO (see C1.0).

4.313 *County Business Patterns*

Social Security tax records and census data are source material for this publication. It contains a series of separate reports for each state, and a United States summary with data on employment, number and employment size of reporting units, and taxable payrolls for various segments of the economy. It is especially useful for analyzing market potentials, establishing sales territories and sales quotas, and locating facilities.

$5.45; GPO (see C1.0).

4.314 *Social Indicators—1973*

Selected statistics on social conditions and trends in the United States dealing with health, public safety, education, employment, income, housing, leisure and recreation, and population are presented in this 250-page publication.

$7.80; GPO (see C1.0).

4.315 *Franchising in the Economy*

Summary data on franchising grants between 1974 and 1976, data on sales distribution by franchising, and various other franchising statistics, are given in this publication, which summarizes the results of a special survey of franchisors. The products and services distributed through franchising are classified on the basis of major activity designated by the franchisor.

$2.00; GPO (see C1.0).

4.316 Publications of the Economic Research Service

Analysts at Economic Research Service (ERS) publish annually some 100 separate research studies. Subjects are as diverse as an in-depth analysis of the futures market, agricultural history, and a look at the inroads made by substitutes and synthetics into traditional farm markets.

An accurate appraisal of the current outlook and situation for all major commodities, plus topics of general interest to the food and fiber industry, can be found in 22 separate *Situation Reports* published on a scheduled basis throughout the year.

Brief highlights of the latest situation and outlook appear monthly in the *Agricultural Outlook Digest.*

Another monthly, the *Farm Index,* allows readers to keep abreast of current ERS research in easy-to-read language.

The quarterly, *Agricultural Economics Research,* a more technical publication, reports on the latest findings, developments, and research methods in agricultural economics.

Each year, ERS joins with several other Department of Agriculture agencies to produce the *Handbook of Agricultural Charts.* This is the most comprehensive collection of charts on agriculture, depicting everything from farm income trends and commodity prices to rural housing conditions and the cost of a week's food.

The annual *Agricultural Statistics* is another poduct of joint cooperation with other agriculture agencies. This handbook is a reliable reference source on agricultural production, supplies, consumption, facilities, and costs and returns.

ERS joins with the Bureau of the Census to produce the *Census-ERS Series,* annual estimates of farm population by age, sex, labor force status, and other characteristics.

The *Balance Sheet of the Farming Sector* is one of several farm finance reports that ERS issues on an annual basis. It provides a full statement of debts and assets of the entire agriculture sector.

A number of other periodic reports provide yearly wrap-ups on topics like farm costs and returns, the hired farm working force, and changes in farm production and efficiency.

A monthly summary of the current status and outlook for farm exports appears in *Foreign Agricultural Trade of the United States.* Supplements are published for the calendar year and the fiscal year.

Research reports, handbooks, statistical supplements, technical bulletins, and speeches are listed in the monthly *Checklist of New Reports.*

For sample copies, write Economic Research Service Publications Unit, Room 0054, Department of Agriculture, Washington, DC 20250.

4.317 *Employment and Earnings*

Included in this publication are detailed household data on labor force, total employment and unemployment, employment status of Vietnam era veterans, and jobseeking methods used by the unemployed; establishment data on employment, hours, earnings, and turnover rates; output per hour, hourly compensation, and unit labor costs; insured unemployment, nationally and by state and area; special articles presenting data on various phases of labor force; charts; and technical notes on concepts and methods.

$24.00 per year, single copy $2.70; GPO (see C1.0).

4.318 *Standard Industrial Classification Manual*

Business establishments have been classified by type of activity. The classification covers the entire field of economic activities: agriculture, forestry, construction, manufacturing, transportation, retail trade, real estate, wholesale trade, and government. It is set forth in the *Standard Industrial Classification Manual,* which is arranged alphabetically by principal product, processes, and services, and lists four-digit codes for each classification.

$6.75; GPO (see C1.0).

Regulations and Consumer Affairs (4.350-4.366)

4.350 *Disclosure and Corporate Ownership*

Corporate reporting requirements of federal regulatory agencies regarding stock ownership, control, diversification, debts, and officers are described in this document. It presents information concerning concentration of stock holdings and makes recommendations for further inquiry and action.

#052-071-00393-2, 419 pp., $4.05; GPO (see C1.0).

4.351 Commission on Civil Rights

The Commission on Civil Rights is an independent, bipartisan, fact-finding agency which investigates violations of civil rights and serves as a clearinghouse for civil rights information. Its areas of interest include civil rights and related subjects, such as sociology, economics, education, and administration of justice, housing, and employment.

The Commission answers inquiries and makes referrals. Its library is available for on-site use and interlibrary loan.

Commission on Civil Rights, 1121 Vermont Ave. N.W., Washington, DC 20425; 202-254-6000 (information office) and 202-254-6636 (library).

4.352 Commodity Futures Trading Commission

The Commodity Futures Trading Commission protects users of the commodity futures markets against cheating, fraud, and manipulative practices and provides general information to the public regarding futures trading on contract markets. Persons who believe they have been cheated or defrauded in their trading transactions should advise the Commission.

Deputy Executive Director, Commodity Futures Trading Commission, Washington, DC 20036; 202-254-7556.

4.353 *Legal Compilation, Environmental Protection Agency*

The current edition of the EPA *Legal Compilation* is an update through the first session of the 93rd Congress.

#055-000-00127-8, 2,726 pp., $10.25 per set; GPO (see C1.0).

4.354 Publications of the Food and Drug Administration

FDA Consumer contains information written especially for consumers about Food and Drug Administration regulatory and scientific decisions, and about the safe use of products regulated by FDA.

#HE20.4010, $8.55 per year, $1.15 single copy; GPO (see C1.0).

In the *Drug Bulletin,* information is published on products regulated by the Food and Drug Administration, including warnings, precautionary statements, and prescription information.

Food and Drug Administration, Rockville, MD 20852.

4.355 Federal Power Commission

The areas of interest of the Federal Power Commission include electric power production and distribution; law; management; mineral resources, particularly petroleum and natural gas; public utility valuation, depreciation, and rate structures; water power; hydroelectric power projects; electric and gas engineering; atomic energy; economics; accounting; and air and water pollution.

The FPC library permits on-site reference by researchers by special permission of the librarian.

Federal Power Commission, 825 N. Capitol St. N.E., Room 8506, Washington, DC 20406; 202-385-5191.

4.356 Federal Trade Commission

To prevent and eliminate monopolistic practices and unfair methods of competition, and to investigate and proscribe acts and practices which are unfair and deceptive to the consuming public, the Federal Trade Commission (FTC) investigates and corrects restrictive monopolistic practices, including price-fixing conspiracies, boycotts, price discrimination, and illegal mergers and acquisitions.

Major emphasis is also placed on investigating and correcting unfair or deceptive acts and practices, including false and misleading advertising, that are injurious to the consumer as well as to competition. Particular attention is directed to consumer redress, as appropriate, and warranty disclosure for breach of warranty or service contract obligation. Other areas of emphasis include consumer credit and reporting, fair packaging and labeling, food and drug advertising, general advertising, representations made by salesmen and others in the sale of goods and services in interstate commerce, and mislabeled wool, fur, and textile products.

Funds for the representation of certain interest in trade regulation rulemaking proceedings when the expense of participation would otherwise make such representation impossible are available through the FTC. Reasonable attorney fees, expert witness fees, and other costs of participating in trade regulation rulemaking proceedings may be included in the compensation.

Compensation is restricted to persons who have or represent an interest which would not otherwise be adequately represented in the proceeding, representation of which is necessary for a fair determination of proceeding taken as a whole, and who cannot participate effectively because of inability to pay certain costs of participation.

FTC regional offices, Bureau of Consumer Protection, or Bureau of Competition (see C1.104).

4.357 Interstate Commerce Commission

The Interstate Commerce Commission (ICC) regulates common carriers engaged in interstate commerce. Its activities include decisions and actions concerning interstate commerce of railroads, trucks, buses, barge operations and coastal shipping, freight forwarders, oil pipelines, express companies, and transportation brokers.

The pamphlet entitled *Arranging Transportation for Small Shipments: Shipper Rights, Remedies and Alternatives* summarizes the services small shippers and receivers of freight may legally expect from motor common carriers.

#026-000-01036, 8 pp., 35¢; GPO (see C1.0).

ICC, 12th St. and Constitution Ave. N.W., Washington, DC 20423; 202-275-7252, toll free 800-421-9312.

4.358 Department of Justice: Antitrust Activities and Unfair Government Competition

The Antitrust Division of the Department of Justice is authorized to assist businesses contemplating a merger or other activity which may have antitrust implications, by offering the concerned business a business review letter. Such a letter is based on a request from the business which contains complete information on the proposed activity. Businesses may be able to avoid having to make such a request by following the publication, *Merger Guidelines,* published free by the Department of Justice.

The Antitrust Division is also charged with the responsibility for studying, reporting, and advising on the competitive considerations involved in the policies of government departments and agencies. Specific statutory responsibility to render such advice to other government bodies includes matters relative to Nuclear Regulatory Commission licensing of nuclear power reactors; activities connected with the nation's defense program, Interstate Oil Compact, development of nuclear energy, and disposal of government-owned surplus property; and the filing of reports on the competitive factors involved in proposed bank mergers with the appropriate bank regulatory agencies.

National and field offices of Antitrust Division (see C1.60).

4.359 Library of Congress: Copyrights

The Copyright Office of the Library of Congress examines claims to copyright in a wide variety of literary, artistic, and musical works; registers those claims that meet legal requirements; and catalogs all registrations. It conducts correspondence about claims and supplies general information concerning copyright law and registration procedures.

Register of Copyrights, Library of Congress, Washington, DC 20559.

4.360 Price Commission Fact Sheets

Information for business executives is contained in these brochures: for example, profit margin fact sheet, profit margin regulations, productivity data amendment, price commission forms, and price commission form instructions.

The following brochures are available, as priced, from GPO (see C1.0):

Information for Business Executives, June 1972, #041-001-00075-7, 31 pp., 65¢

Information for Business Executives, August, 1972, #041-000-00077-1, 24 pp., 60¢

Information for Firms with Retailing and Wholesale Interests, September 1972, #041-001-00083-6, 52 pp., 90¢

Information for Business Executives, October 1972, #041-001-00083-6, 29 pp., 65¢

Information for Business Executives, January 1973, #041-001-00084-4, 30 pp., 65¢

4.361 Securities and Exchange Commission

The Securities and Exchange Commission (SEC) administers several laws designed to protect investors. Its areas of interest include securities; disclosure of financial and other information about companies whose securities are offered for public sale, traded on exchanges, or over the counter; enforcement of prohibitions against fraudulent acts or practices in the purchase and sale of securities; regulation of stock exchanges, broker-dealer and investment-advertiser firms, investment companies, and companies comprising electric and gas public utility holding company systems.

Information about companies which have filed reports with the SEC is available from the Office of Reports and Information (ORIS). ORIS responds to public inquiries and complaints, provides public reference services, and handles Freedom of Information Act and Privacy Act matters, in addition to its internal responsibilities. All public information on file with the SEC can be examined in the ORIS Public Reference Room, and copies may be obtained at cost. The Public Reference telephone number is 202-523-5360.

SEC publishes *SEC News Digest* (daily summary of SEC activities), *SEC Docket* (weekly, containing full text of SEC releases), *SEC Statistical Bulletin* (weekly), and *Official Summary of Security Transactions and Holdings.*

SEC, 500 N. Capitol St. N.W., Washington, DC 20549; 202-755-4846.

4.362 *Social Security Rulings, Cumulative Bulletins 1975*

Official rulings relating to the federal old-age, survivors, disability, health insurance, supplemental security income, and miners' benefit programs are made available to the public in this booklet.

#017-070-00280-3, 178 pp., $1.90; GPO (see C1.0).

4.363 Department of the Treasury: Antidumping

Dumping is the practice of selling foreign merchandise in the United States at less than fair value within the meaning of the Antidumping Act of 1921. The Department of the Treasury (through the Commissioner of Customs) is responsible for ascertaining all necessary facts bearing on the issue of sales at less than fair value, or the likelihood of such sales. The International Trade Commission (ITC) is then responsible for determining whether such sales are injurious to United States industry. Investigations are usually initiated as a result of a complaint filed by an affected industry in the United States.

United States Customs Service, Department of the Treasury, 1301 Constitution Ave. N.W., Washington, DC 20229; 202-964-8195.

4.364 *Consumer News*

This first newsletter of its kind, designed to keep consumers informed about what the government is doing to protect them, highlights the consumer activities of all federal agencies and covers unsafe products, unfair sales practices, air and water pollution, and many other issues.

#HE1.509, semimonthly, $4.00 per year; GPO (see C1.0).

4.365 *Situation Reports—Consumerism*

Various aspects of consumer affairs, with an emphasis on improving business-consumer relations, are described in this ongoing series of reports. Subjects scrutinized include complaints and remedies, financing, advertising and promotion, and advertising substantiation.

Office of the Ombudsman for Business, Bureau of Domestic Commerce, Room 3800, Department of Commerce, Washington, DC 20230.

4.366 *Action Guidelines*

This volume contains advisory committee studies in consumer affairs and business in the following areas: packaging and labeling, advertising and promotion, advertising substantiation, safety in the marketplace, product performance and servicing, product warranties, financing the American consumer, and complaints and remedies.

328 pp., $3.00; Consumer Information Services, 20-N, Montgomery Ward & Company, 535 W. Chicago Ave., Chicago, IL 60607.

The Postal Service (4.400-4.401)

4.400 Special Programs of the Postal Service

The Postal Service provides many services of value to business. Any business may contact its local post office and ask for a visit from the Customer Service Representative (CSR), who can provide details on all the programs listed below and suggest cost-effective ways of doing business. CSR's can also provide a free evaluation of the operations of a business mailing room and mailing procedures that are most effective.

The following are some of the postal programs relevant to business:

Bulk Mail. Postage costs can be drastically cut by use of third-class bulk mail. It is possible to prepay postage by use of a permit imprint.

Presorted First Class Mail. A special, reduced first-class postage rate is available when a mailing of 500 or more pieces is presorted by ZIP Code.

Express Mail. Guaranteed overnight delivery is available from and to many Postal Service facilities. A shipment delivered to a specific post office Express Mail Window by 5:00 p.m. will be delivered to the addressee the next day by 3:00 p.m. (or may be picked up by 10:00 a.m.). If a business depends on quick, regularly scheduled intercity shipments, the Postal Service will custom-tailor a special Express Mail program.

Priority Mail. First class mail over 13 ounces receives the fastest transportation and most expeditious handling if the special Priority Mail rates are paid.

Mailgram. A mailgram is a message sent electronically to the addressee's post office for delivery with the next day's mail.

Free Presorting Equipment and Materials. The Postal Service encourages mailers to separate mail categories and to sort mail by ZIP Code, as this will speed delivery. The Postal Service will provide rubber bands, labels, pressure-sensitive bands, tags, sacks, and letter trays.

Verifying Mailing Lists. A local postmaster can check the names and addresses on a mailing list for correctness.

Postage Meters. Mail with metered postage skips the cancellation stage, and can therefore be delivered sooner. In many cities, the Postal Service will send a representative to a firm's office to reset a postage meter.

Bar Coding. Preprinted reply envelopes with bar coding in the lower right-hand corner are processed through special equipment and can provide the most accurate and speedy method for reply mail.

Business Reply Mail. For a few cents per piece in addition to the regular postage, it is possible to pay the postage on reply mail only on pieces actually received.

Computerized Sorting Equipment. For faster delivery, all address formats should comply with the requirements of the computerized sorting equipment. For example, nothing should appear below or to the right of the ZIP Code.

Memos for Mailers. This is a free monthly publication of advice and news.

Postal Customers Council. These groups can provide training sessions for employees and allow feedback to the Postal Service from business mailers.

Pool Case. If a large number of items is being sent from one area to be delivered in another area, efficiency and speed of delivery can be improved, and risk of damage or loss reduced, by using the pool case system. The items will be packed together in a large package addressed to the postmaster of the main office in the addressee region, and upon arrival the package will be opened and the contents delivered.

ZIP Code Computer Tapes. All of the street addresses covered by the Postal Service are listed on magnetic tape with their correct ZIP Codes. The tape is available for loan.

4.401 Bibliography of Postal Service Publications

The following publications are available, at indicated prices, from GPO (see C1.0):

The *Postal Bulletin* is available to those who feel their needs require advance information. Issued Thursday of each week, with supplemental issues as required, it contains current orders, instructions, and information relating to the Postal Service, including philately, airmail, money orders, parcel post, and more. It also provides advance notice of important changes in regulations.

$25.75 per year, subscriptions accepted for 1, 2, or 3 years.

Instructions for Mailers contains excerpts from Chapter 1 of the *Postal Service Manual.* It is issued for the specific use of individuals, companies, or organizations who use the mailing services of the Postal Service more than the average person.

Sold on a subscription basis only, with changes issued as required, for an indefinite period, $7.70.

Postal Service Manual, Chapters 1 through 6 revises and replaces the *Postal Manual.* It includes information on post office services (domestic);

organization and administration of the Postal Service; postal procedures; personnel policies; transportation of mail; maintenance and procurement. Postal Service Orders are included in the appendix. So that subscribers may have current information and changes as they occur, a loose-leaf supplementary service for an indefinite period is sold on a subscription basis only.

$33.00.

International Mail, formerly entitled *Directory of International Mail,* contains regulations for public use and detailed information on postage rates, services available, prohibitions, import restrictions, and other conditions governing mail to other countries. Countries are listed alphabetically with the specific requirements applicable to mail addressed to each of them.

Sold on a subscription basis only, with changes issued as required, for an indefinite period, $4.25.

Postal Service Manual (Chapter 5) contains policy guidelines and regulations affecting the transportation of mail.

Basic material, and supplements issued irregularly, for an indefinite period, $1.50.

Postal Life keeps postal employees informed and abreast of developments in the Postal Service. It contains articles with illustrations about new methods, techniques, and programs.

Bimonthly, subscriptions accepted for one year only, $6.40.

National ZIP Code Directory enables the user to determine the ZIP Code for every mailing address in the nation. It is for use by all mailers, expecially those maintaining large mailing lists, permitting them to gain all the advantages possible from the addition of ZIP Code to their lists. ZIP Code listings are arranged alphabetically by state. Within each state, a complete listing is given of all post offices, stations, and branches, with the appropriate five-digit ZIP Code for each delivery area. An appendix after each state gives the ZIP Code for each address in the larger cities. Also in this directory are a listing of two-letter state abbreviations, a listing of sectional center facilities, ZIP Code prefixes by state, a numerical list of post offices by ZIP Code, a listing of postal units discontinued, and ZIP Codes for Army and Air Force installations and APO and FPO units.

$7.50.

The *Directory of Post Offices* is used daily by business and individual mailers throughout the United States. It includes a list of all post offices, branches, and stations arranged alphabetically by states with ZIP Codes as an aid in determining parcel post zones. Also included are an alphabetical list of all post offices, named stations, and branches; lists of sectional centers and major cities by states; a numerical list of post offices by ZIP Code, a list of post offices, named stations, and branches discontinued or with names changed during the past two years; and a list of Army posts, camps, and stations, as well as Air Force bases, fields, and installations. APO's and FPO's are also included.

$5.55.

Crime and Business (4.450-4.455)

4.450 Free Publications on Crime in Business

The following publications are available, free, from SBA (see C1.110).

Order No.:	Management Aids Series
209	*Preventing Employee Pilferage*
	Small Marketers Aids Series
119	*Preventing Retail Theft*
129	*Reducing Shoplifting Losses*
134	*Preventing Burglary and Robbery Loss*
151	*Preventing Embezzlement*

4.451 *The Cost of Crimes against Business*

The national cost of crime to United States business was estimated to have been over 20 billion dollars in 1974. This book focuses on the current economic impact of crime against business property in the United States. Statistics are also given on the business effects of such crimes as burglary, robbery, shoplifting, employee theft, arson, and others.

#003-025-00035-7, 1974, 52 pp., $1.10; GPO (see C1.0).

4.452 Crime in Retailing

The results of an analysis of the effect of crime against retailers are reported in this book. It covers burglary, robbery, vandalism, shoplifting, employee theft, bad checks, credit card fraud, and arson. It also gives suggestions on how employers can reduce losses from crime.

#003-008-00159-9, 1975, 42 pp., $1.10; GPO (see C1.0).

4.453 *Federal Government Sources on Crimes against Business*

#003-025-00029-2, 14 pp., 30¢; GPO (see C1.0).

4.454 Federal Crime Insurance Program

The Federal Crime Insurance Program (FCIP) offers low cost, easily obtainable, noncancellable burglary and robbery insurance to small businessmen and residential property owners and tenants in states which have been declared eligible. A state becomes eligible for the program when the administrator determines that affordable crime insurance is virtually impossible to get through normal channels, and when no steps have been taken to remedy that situation. FCIP is now available in the District of Columbia and the following twenty states:

Arkansas	Iowa	New York
Colorado	Kansas	Ohio
Connecticut	Maryland	Pennsylvania
Delaware	Massachusetts	Rhode Island
Florida	Minnesota	Tennessee
Georgia	Missouri	Virginia
Illinois	New Jersey	

State crime insurance programs similar to the FCIP are available in California, Michigan, Indiana, and Wisconsin.

In the twenty states mentioned, FCIP policies can be written by any licensed property insurance broker or agent, or by the private insurance company designated under contract as the servicing company for a particular state. It is renewable regardless of losses and is available at uniform rates to everyone in an eligible state, regardless of their occupation or the crime rate in their neighborhood.

Commercial losses from burglary or robbery can be insured in amounts ranging from $1,000 to $15,000. Typical commercial premiums range from $35 for $1,000 coverage in a low-crime area for businesses with annual gross receipts under $100,000, to $748 for $15,000 coverage in a high-crime area.

To obtain FCIP insurance, an application from any licensed broker or agent or state servicing company must be filled out and half the year's premium paid. The applicant will be billed for the second half six months later.

Necessary inspections are made by the servicing insurance company and paid for by the federal government.

Federal Insurance Administration, Department of Housing and Urban Development, Washington, DC 20410. See also area offices of HUD (C1.40).

4.455 *Selection and Application Guide to Fixed Surveillance Cameras*

Owners of retail stores can decide whether to buy theft-prevention surveillance cameras, and how to use them for best results, by consulting this guide produced by the National Bureau of Standards (NBS) in cooperation with the Naval Surface Weapons Center.

NBS, Washington, DC 20234.

Audio-Visual Management Aids (4.500-4.503)

4.500 National Audio-Visual Center

The National Audio-Visual Center (NAC) was created in 1969 to serve the public by (1) making federal audio-visual materials available for use through distribution services and (2) serving as the central clearinghouse for all United States government audio-visual materials.

Through the Center's distribution programs —sales, rentals, and loan referrals— the public has access to audio-visual materials covering a variety of subjects. Major subject concentrations in the Center's collection include medicine, dentistry, and the allied health sciences; education; aviation and space technology; vocational and management training; safety; and the environmental sciences.

Many of the Center's audio-visual materials are designed for general use, while others are designed for specific training or instructional programs. Instructional materials are appropriate for classroom use or for self-instruction. To complement and increase the effectiveness of these audio-visual programs, many are accompanied by printed materials such as teacher manuals, student workbooks, or scripts.

To keep the public informed about the availability of federal audio-visual materials, NAC sponsors three information services: reference, printed materials, and a master data file.

Reference. For questions on federal audio-visual materials, telephone or write the Center. A trained reference staff will respond quickly to such requests. These responses may range from a direct answer to the compilation of filmographies by subject or by federal agency.

Printed Materials. Printed materials issued by the Center are the principal means of keeping the public informed of the availability of federal audio-visual materials. *A Catalog of United States Government Produced Audio-Visual Materials* (Washington, 1974) lists over 4,000 titles available for sale or rental from the Center. Also available are minicatalogs by subject area, brochures on single and multiple titles, and filmographies on specialized subjects and on materials produced by individual federal agencies.

Master Data File. The Center is responsible for developing and maintaining a master data file on all federal audio-visual material. This resource is used by the reference staff in title and subject searches.

Federal audio-visual materials are available through the following programs of the NAC:

Sales. Most major audio-visual formats are available for purchase through the Center. These include motion pictures, video formats, slide sets, audiotapes, and multimedia kits. Other audio-visual formats (e.g., video cassettes) for motion pictures also can be supplied. Preview prior to purchase is available for 16 mm. motion pictures.

Rental. Only 16 mm. motion pictures, representing 80 percent of the Center's collection, are available through the rental program.

Loan Referrals. Free loan distribution of 16 mm. motion pictures is available to the public from commercial distributors. The Center keeps informed of all federally sponsored free loan programs and refers the user to the nearest free loan distributor.

For the NAC catalog, write National Audio-Visual Center, Reference Section, General Services Administration, Washington DC 20409; 301-763-1896.

4.501 Filmographies on Business Management

The following filmographies may be ordered free, from National Audio-Visual Center, Reference Section, General Services Administration, Washington, DC 20409.

C004 Films on Business Management and Office Administration

H016 Films on Business Ownership and Management

H029 Films on the Economics of Inflation

H014 Films on Information and Communication

G030 Films on Office Mail Operations and the Mail System

H016 Films on Operating a Small Business, including Communicating with Customers and Employees

4.502 Filmography on Business Administration

The following films may be ordered or rented (except 8 mm.), from National Audio-Visual Center, General Services Administration, Attention Order Section NACDO, Washington DC 20409.

The Business Plan—for Small Businessmen. The need for and elements in a business plan as a management tool for successful business operation are dramatized. Reasons for planning, and a factual presentation of the main points in a business plan, are presented.

#003510, 15 min., 16mm., sound, color; sale 16 mm., $68.00, rental 16 mm., $10.00; sale 8 mm., $42.75 (#009088).

How to Run Mail Room. Designed to solve mail room problems for both large and small volume mailers, this film demonstrates mail room practices and identifies the most common problems in metered mail.

#409150, 15 min., 16 mm., sound, color; sale, $68.00.

The Seventh Chair. This film deals with credit and collection problems.

#001430, 13 min., 16 mm., sound, color; sale 16 mm., $59.00, rental 16 mm., $10.00; sale 8 mm., $39.00 (#009086).

A Step in the Right Direction. The importance of merchandise control in retail stores is dramatized and some control procedures and techniques are illustrated in this film.

#712725, 13 min., 16 mm., sound, color; sale 16 mm., $59.00, rental 16 mm., $10.00; sale 8 mm., $42.00 (#009078).

Three Times Three. Through dramatization and narration, this film illustrates nine important keys to small business success: personal ability of the owner; use of outside assistance and an informed understanding of insurance, regulations, and taxes; business opportunity; knowing sources of capital; maintenance and use of business records; understanding financial factors; effective organization and planning; using good management techniques.

#747425, 14 min., 16 mm., sound, color; sale 16 mm., $63.50, rental 16 mm., $10.00; sale 8 mm., $40.00 (#009080).

The Heartbeat of Business. The importance of financial management is emphasized in this film. Some examples of good and bad financial management show that good practices are critical to success.

#001428, 15 min., 16 mm., sound, color; sale 16 mm., $68.00, rental 16 mm., $10.00; sale 8 mm., $43.25 (#009087).

The Follow-Up. The value of following up on advertisements and promotions becomes clear in this dramatization. Illustrations of following up on a radio commercial, soliciting customers' reactions to store layouts and point-of-sale ads, and getting business associates' opinions of ads used or planned bring out many of the factors to consider in advertising/sales promotion follow-up.

#335459, 13 min., 16 mm., sound, color; sale 16 mm., $59.00, rental 16 mm., $10.00; sale 8 mm., $40.00 (#009072).

The Language of Business. The need for systematic recordkeeping is emphasized in this film. It dramatically illustrates procedures for proper management.

#002505, 15 min., 16 mm., sound, color; sale 16 mm., $68.00, rental 16 mm., $10.00; sale 8 mm., $43.25 (#009077).

The Calendar Game. The need for advertising, planning, and budgeting by small retail and service businesses is the main point of emphasis in this film.

#194215, 14 min., 16 mm., sound, color; sale 16 mm., $63.50, rental 16 mm., $10.00; sale 8 mm., $40.75 (#009079).

The Advertising Question. This film is designed to correct some of the misconceptions and change some of the attitudes which many small businessmen display toward advertising. Business examples are shown to emphasize pertinent points.

#118520, 14 min., 16 mm., sound, color; sale 16 mm., $63.50, rental 16 mm., $10.00; sale 8 mm., $41.50 (#009082).

4.503 Films on Crime in Business

The following films are available, as priced, from National Audio-Visual Center, General Services Administration, Attention Order Section NACDO, Washington, DC 20409.

The Inside Story. Steps which can be taken to limit or prevent pilferage by plant employees are dramatized in this film.

#427915, 15 min., 16 mm., sound, color; sale 16 mm., $68.00, rental 16 mm., $10.00; sale 8 mm., $43.50 (#009073).

It Can Happen to You. Situations and procedures which encourage pilferage are shown in this film. Suggestions are made as to how to correct the problems.

#439685, 15 min., 16 mm., sound, color; sale 16 mm., $68.00, rental 16 mm., $10.00; sale 8 mm., $43.25 (#009085).

Burglary Is Your Business. Security measures which retailers can take to prevent burglaries are pointed out in this film.

#192460, 15 min., 16 mm., sound, color; sale 16 mm., $68.00, rental 16 mm., $10.00; sale 8 mm., $38.00 (#009083).

They're Out to Get You. The film shows how shoplifters operate and, indirectly, points out preventive measures small businesses can take to limit shoplifting.

#743125, 13 min., 16 mm., sound, color; sale 16 mm., $59.00, rental 16 mm., $10.00; sale 8 mm., $39.25 (#009081).

Chapter 5

HUMAN RESOURCES MANAGEMENT

CHAPTER ABSTRACT

This chapter, along with Chapter 6 (on affirmative action, OSHA, and product safety), attempts to familiarize the human resources manager with the wide range of services and information available to him from the government.

The first section, "Personnel Management" (5.0-5.109), describes, first, current awareness services which can keep managers aware of both trends and research useful in planning; second, publications useful in developing sound personnel management policies, and advisory services that any small business can call on for assistance in any field; third, statistical sources and statistics useful in setting personnel management standards and upgrading criteria.

The second section, "Labor-Management Relations" (5.150-5.315), deals first with innovations in voluntary labor-management cooperation and then with the more technical areas of collective bargaining, reporting and disclosure, and arbitration.

"Compensation of Employees" (5.350-5.464) deals with the law, planning data, and pensions and benefits.

The section entitled "Equal Employment Opportunity Planning" (5.500-5.608) lists information sources on recruitment, testing and counseling, and training. (Chapter 6 adds specific information for affirmative action planning.)

"Productivity and Human Resources Management" (5.650-5.756) is the section which separates the traditional personnel manager from the human resources manager. In this section, the manager of people is invited to look at the issues which expand the challenge of the job and make it an integral part of long-term corporate planning.

"The Troubled Employee" (5.800-5.812) supplements the previous section on productivity. It is a relatively new concern of business, but an increasingly important one because of its impact on productivity. Many sources of assistance are suggested for managers facing problems due to alcoholism or drug abuse among employees.

"Films on Personnel Management" (5.850-5.855) lists a variety of filmographies and films useful to the human resource manager.

Personnel Management (5.0-5.109)

Current Awareness Subscription Services (5.0-5.5)

5.0 *Monthly Labor Review*

Each month, special articles on labor economics, working conditions, and industrial relations are published in this authoritative research journal of the Bureau of Labor Statistics (BLS) of the Department of Labor. It serves as a medium for a wide range of other material on labor conditions and developments in the United States and abroad. Departments in the *Review* are as follows: Anatomy of Price Change, Book Reviews and Notes, Communications, Current Labor Statistics, Developments in Industrial Relations, Foreign Labor Developments, Labor Month in Review, Major Agreements Expiring Next Month, Research Summaries, Significant Decisions in Labor Cases, and Union Conventions.

$20 per year, $2.40 single copy; BLS (see C1.70).

5.1 *Weekly Government Abstracts—Administration, Behavior and Society, Industrial and Mechanical Engineering*

Each of the following is one of 26 subscription newsletters known as *Weekly Government Abstracts*. All 26 are annotated in 9.11. Each newsletter contains summaries of government research performed by hundreds of organizations, including government agencies, private researchers, universities, and special technology groups. The research summaries are listed within two weeks of their receipt at the National Technical Information Service. The last issue of each year is a subject index containing up to ten cross references for each research summary indexed.

As priced; NTIS (see C1.17).

Administration

Administration, management, management information systems, personnel management, labor relations, manpower studies, program administration, and inventory are among the subjects covered in this weekly publication.

$45.00 per year.

Behavior and Society

Job training, career development, organizational psychology, and international relations are among the subjects covered in this weekly publication.

$45.00 per year.

Industrial and Mechanical Engineering

Production planning, quality control, plant design and maintenance, environmental engineering, and labor psychology and esthetics are among the subjects covered in this weekly publication.

$45.00 per year.

5.2 Free Publications on Labor Trends

The following publications are available, free, from Bureau of Labor Statistics (see C1.70).

Order No.	Subject
301	*Employment and Wages* (report) Quarterly
305	*Labor Turnover in Manufacturing* (press release) Monthly
308	*Special Labor Force Reports* Occasional
309	*Occupational Injuries and Illnesses* (press release) Annual
310	*Productivity and Costs* (press release) Quarterly
	Productivity and Costs in Nonfinancial Corporations (press release) Quarterly
313	*Work Stoppages* (press release) Monthly
	Work Stoppages (summary) Annual
314	*New Publications on Wages and Industrial Relations* (announcements) Occasional
317	*Major Collective Bargaining Settlements* (press release) Quarterly
318	*Union Wage Rates for Building Trades* (press release) Quarterly
321	*Publications of the Bureau of Labor Statistics* (catalog)

Semiannual
322 *Occupational Outlook* (announcements)
Occasional
325 *Real Earnings* (press release)
Monthly
329 *International Comparisons* (press release)
Occasional
365 *The Employment Situation* (press release)
Monthly
Labor Force Developments (press release)
Quarterly
380 *Automation and Technological Change (announcements)*
Occasional

5.3 *Personnel Literature*

Selected books, pamphlets, and other publications received in the library of the Civil Service Commission during the previous month are listed in this monthly and annual index. Periodical articles, unpublished dissertations, and microfilms are also listed.

#CS1.62, $12.25 per year, 85¢ single copy, $2.40 annual index; GPO (see C1.0).

5.4 *Worklife Magazine*

Formerly *Manpower*, this magazine is designed for officials in industry, labor, and government who need authoritative information on what is being done in the Department of Labor about employment, and where, how, and for whom it is being done.

$15.30 per year, $1.30 single copy; GPO (see C1.0).

5.5 *Announcing BLS Publications*

At least two of these free flyers are released each month from the regional offices of the Bureau of Labor Statistics (BLS). They serve to keep the businessman abreast of new BLS publications which might be useful in analyzing the economy and in manpower planning.

Free; BLS (see C1.70).

Information Sources and Publications on Personnel Management (5.50-5.67)

5.50 *How to Develop and Apply Work Plans—A Federal Supervisor's Guide*

Working-level supervisors who have a responsibility for planning the activities of their units may profit from a handbook entitled *How to Develop and Apply Work Plans—A Federal Supervisor's Guide*, written by Charles F. Wilson. It describes the planning process and the ingredients of a work plan, prediction of workloads, determination of work objectives, organization and staffing of the plan, and assembling the work plan package. It also describes how to apply the plan, how to review and appraise it, and how to make revisions and report results. The handbook is replete with examples and illustrations, and contains a list of recommended readings.

#008-000-00213-4, 242 pp., $2.80; GPO (see C1.0).

5.51 Publications on Personnel Management

Educators and others who teach management courses will find these presentations useful. They include lesson plans, lectures, visual aids, case studies, study assignments, and selected bibliography and handout material.

As priced; GPO (see C1.0).

Personnel Management, Developing Good Employees, #045-000-00094-0, 87 pp., $3.95
Communication and Control, #045-000-00097-4, 64 pp., $3.80
Human Factors in Small Business, #045-000-00079-4, 82 pp., $4.10

5.52 *Analysis for Managers of People and Things*

Systems analysis as it is used in high-level decision-making in the Department of Defense is explained in this guide. Since the object of offering these directions is to stretch resources in times of inflation and budget cuts, businesses may benefit as well.

#008-040-00062-2, 100 pp., $1.45; GPO (see C1.0).

5.53 *Personnel Management Guides for Small Business*

Various aspects of personnel management for small firms are discussed in this book.

#SBA 1.12:26, 79 pp., $1.10; GPO (see C1.0).

5.54 *Human Relations in Small Business*

Finding and selecting employees, developing them, and motivating them are discussed in this booklet.

#SBA 1.12:3, 68 pp., 60¢; GPO (see C1.0).

5.55 *Better Communications in Small Business*

Smaller manufacturers can help themselves to win cooperation by means of more skillful communication. This booklet shows how better communication within the firm can improve operating efficiency and competitive strength.

#SBA 1.12:7, 37 pp., 65¢; GPO (see C1.0).

5.56 Free Publications on Personnel Management

The following publications are available, free, from Small Business Administration (see C1.110).

Order No.	
	Management Aids Series
185	*Matching the Applicant to the Job*
186	*Checklist for Developing a Training Program*
191	*Delegating Work and Responsibility*
195	*Setting Pay for Management Jobs*
197	*Pointers on Preparing an Employee Handbook*
198	*How to Find a Likely Successor*
205	*Pointers on Using Temporary Help Services*
209	*Preventing Employee Pilferage*
	Small Marketers Aids Series
106	*Finding and Hiring the Right Employee*
132	*The Federal Wage-Hour Law in Small Firms*
135	*Arbitration: Peacemaker in Small Business*
136	*Hiring the Right Man*
	Small Business Bibliographies
72	*Personnel Management*

5.57 Publications on Manpower Planning

The following publications are available, as priced, from GPO (see C1.0).

Scientific and Engineering Manpower Management, #006-000-00763-5, 80 pp., $1.10

Decision Analysis Forecasting for Executive Manpower Planning, #006-000-00788-1, 36 pp., 85¢

Job Placement, Creation and Development, #029-000-00040-0, 36 pp., 85¢

American Manpower Today, #029-000-00222-3, 28 pp., 75¢

The purpose, scope, and funding of the Department of Labor's various programs under the Comprehensive Employment and Training Act are encapsulated in this publication.

5.58 *The Labor Supply for Lower Level Occupations*

How and why the sources of workers for lower level occupations have changed in recent years is explained in this book. It projects the availability of workers for these types of occupations to 1985.

#029-000-00266-5, 113 pp., $1.85; GPO (see C1.0).

5.59 *Occupational Outlook Handbook* and *Quarterly*

Described in the handbook are the employment outlook, nature of work, training, requirements for entry, line of advancement, job locations, earnings, and working conditions for over 800 occupations and 30 major industries, including farming.

Bulletin 1785, $6.85; GPO (see C1.0).

The handbook is supplemented and brought up to date by *Occupational Outlook Quarterly.*

$4.00 for four school year issues; single copy $1.30; GPO (see C1.0).

5.60 *Federal Labor Laws and Programs, A Layman's Guide*

Summaries of laws and descriptions of Equal Employment Opportunity programs are included in this publication.

#029-003-00122-6, 254 pp., $2.10; GPO (see C1.0).

5.61 *Research and Development Projects*

The sixth annual edition of this publication of the Employment and Training Administration (ETA) summarizes ETA-funded projects. The catalog is the principal means of informing the public of developments in the research and development field in employment and training. It may be particularly useful to potential grant and contract applicants, and industrial and personnel relations people. The appendix contains guidelines for submitting proposals.

Free; Inquiries Office, ETA (see C1.72).

5.62 Small Business Institute Program

The Small Business Institute program, a three-way cooperative between collegiate schools of business administration, members of the nation's small business community, and the Small Business Administration (SBA) is a new source of management assistance. Under the supervision of university faculty and SBA staff, senior and graduate students of business administration work directly with owners of small firms, providing vital management assistance to small businesses while undergoing meaningful learning experiences themselves.

The program began in the fall of 1972. In the first year of its life, 1,100 small firms received counseling and 2,200 students were involved. In 1976, 385 schools participated, involving over 22,000 students and 8,800 small businesses. Satisfaction rate among clients was over 80 percent.

SBA (see C1.110).

5.63 University Business Development Centers

Growing out of the Small Business Institute concept (see 5.62), the University Business Development Center (UBDC) program is an experimental Small Business Administration concept being tested in eight universities. It is a university-based and administered program to interrelate the academic, professional, and technological resources of universities with all existing government programs designed to assist the business community. While each agency continues to administer its own programs, the university serves as a funnel or mixing device for them, so that the collection of programs will work as an integrated unit serving the whole community, rather than as an uncoordinated variety of programs.

A functioning UBDC can offer the following services to its business clients:

—Business and product evaluation and development
—Entrepreneur evaluation, recommendations, counseling, and training
—Analysis, correction, and follow-up of financial, marketing, technical, production, legal, and any other type of problem faced by small business owners
—Feasibility studies and development of business plans for present and future entrepreneurs
—Access to and application of technology, paid for by the taxpayers in over $350 billion worth of research and development projects since 1947
—Assistance not only in surviving (when 57 percent of new businesses fail in the first five years) but also in expanding on a solid basis

Universities currently involved are the Universities of Maine at Bangor, Missouri at St. Louis, Nebraska at Omaha, Georgia at Athens, and West Florida at Pensacola; and Rutgers University at New Brunswick, New Jersey; California State University at Chico; and California Polytechnic at Pomona.

5.64 National Technical Information Service

NTIS (National Technical Information Service) emphasizes that searching before researching can save much effort, time, and money. Whether the research is intended to develop new technology or to provide data with which business decisions can be made, the resources available through NTIS may be useful.

NTIS provides a diversity of services and information. It is the central source for the public sale of government-sponsored research, development, and engineering reports and other analyses. Much of the material to which NTIS can give access is related to engineering and the hard sciences, but there is a growing array of data sources of potentially great value for business planners, market researchers, and others who may need statistics or other data about social, psychological, or demographic factors.

For a complete description of NTIS capability, including on-line searches, published searches, bibliographic services, and more, see 9.0-9.13.

5.65 *The Personnel Management Function-Organization, Staffing, and Evaluation*

This publication updates sections of Personnel Bibliography Number 67. It covers material received in the Civil Service Commission library during 1975.

Personnel Bibliography Series #75, #006-000-00950-6, 18 pp., 45¢; GPO (see C1.0).

5.66 *Personnel Policies and Practices*

This publication updates Personnel Bibliography Number 68. Materials in this bibliography were received in the Civil Service Commission library during 1975.

Personnel Bibliography Series Number 71, #006-000-00946-8, 53 pp., $1.10; GPO (see C1.0).

5.67 *Maintenance Managers Guide*

A management-by-objectives program for maintenance departments has been developed by the Energy Research and Development Administration (ERDA). This publication briefly covers such matters as material control, preventive maintenance, job planning, and cost control. Prepared for ERDA-related organizations, the *Maintenance Managers Guide* has broad applicability.

#ERHQ-0004; Division of Construction Planning and Support, ERDA (see C1.150).

National Labor Statistics (5.100-5.109)

5.100 Bureau of Labor Statistics

The Bureau of Labor Statistics (BLS) is the principal data-gathering agency of the federal government in the broad field of labor economics. BLS collects, processes, analyzes, and disseminates data relating to employment, unemployment, the labor force, productivity, prices, family expenditures, wages, industrial relations, and occupational safety and health. BLS strives to have its data meet a number of criteria, including relevance to current social and economic issues, timeliness in reflecting as closely as possible today's rapidly changing economic conditions, accuracy and consistently high statistical quality, and impartiality in both subject matter and presentation. A significant portion of the data collected by BLS is relevant to union-management issues, including collective bargaining agreements, arbitration, union wage studies, conventions, and union constitution characteristics.

BLS (see C1.70).

5.101 Manpower Planning Data of BLS

All the major surveys of the Bureau of Labor Statistics (BLS) and the publications that result from those surveys are described in the guide entitled *Major Programs 1976—Bureau of Labor Statistics*. Surveys useful in manpower planning include: annual average employment levels for detailed occupational groups, worker characteristics and worklife expectancy, earnings by demographic group, occupational mobility, job search methods, employment by industry for over 226 detailed areas, labor turnover in 215 manufacturing industries and 95 areas, insured unemployment statistics, state and area occupational projections, and much more. Uses of the data are suggested in the guide.

Free; BLS (see C1.70).

5.102 *Publications of the Bureau of Labor Statistics*

Studies, reports, subscription services, and free releases are included in this semiannual catalog of publications.

BLS (see C1.70).

5.103 *Status—A Monthly Chartbook of Social and Economic Trends*

Status, a magazine prepared by the Bureau of

the Census for the Office of Management and Budget, is a graphic presentation of current statistical information, focusing on major social and economic conditions within the United States. Data are included from many federal sources. Also provided are listings of basic sources for the material presented and a variety of color maps and charts designed to improve the understandability of timely, important statistical data. In each edition of *Status*, major sections provide current statistical graphic information about the people, the community, the economy, and other areas such as science and the environment. A special map is included each month to identify geographic areas of special concern. The magazine is aimed at decision-makers in all fields; it is not intended for exclusive use by the professional statistician or economist.

Monthly, $3.60 each; Subscriber Services Section, Bureau of the Census, Department of Commerce, Washington, DC 20233.

5.104 Technical Assistance from BLS

Regional and national office staffs of the Bureau of Labor Statistics (BLS) are available for consultation on the application, uses, and limitations of BLS data. Examples of assistance include the limitations of price indexes in contract escalation clauses, information on the prevalence of a variety of special provisions in collective bargaining agreements, comparative wage rates in different parts of the country, and occupational employment information needed for estimates of future requirements. Consulting services are almost always free.

BLS (see C1.70).

5.105 BLS Libraries

Each regional office of the Bureau of Labor Statistics maintains a library with samples of Bureau publications which are available for public inspection. Library assistance is also available.

BLS (see C1.70).

5.106 *BLS Handbook of Methods*

Measures of an employment cost index, international prices, and unemployment in states and local areas are explained in this handbook. In addition to these new series, many of the chapters in the older series have been updated to reflect the continuing improvements in the Bureau's methods and techniques. Each chapter provides a brief account of how the program came into being, what it attempts to do, where the basic data came from, definition of terms used, and outline of the concepts adopted.

Bulletin 910, $3.50; GPO (see C1.0).

5.107 BLS Microfiche and Computer Tape Data

A growing amount of data is available in microfiche form which can be reproduced at no cost or at nominal cost, depending on the size of the request.

Some data, including unpublished data, are available on computer tape. The amount, kind, and prices of the data change constantly.

BLS (see C1.70).

5.108 *BLS Data Bank Files and Statistical Routines*

The Bureau of Labor Statistics will duplicate for interested users any of its data base tapes that meet confidentiality requirements. *BLS Data Bank Files and Statistical Routines* (1971) contains detailed information on available data files.

Free; BLS (see C1.70).

5.109 Unpublished Data of BLS

The Bureau of Labor Statistics generates some data as by-products or intermediate stages of certain programs. Often there is not great enough public demand or use for these data to justify publication. However, the Bureau will release any such summary files to interested parties at cost of duplication when the data meet the confidentiality requirement of all government data.

All unpublished data furnished by the Bureau is accompanied, as far as possible, by descriptions tions of the data, appropriate statements of the limitations of the data, and other technical documentation.

BLS (see C1.70).

Labor-Management Relations (5.150-5.315)

Labor-Management Cooperation and Technical Assistance (5.150-5.156)

5.150 Labor-Management Committees

One of the most effective means of improving labor-management relations, and an important technical assistance role for mediators, is the labor-management committee. These committees constitute communication forums not connected to the bargaining table. They can take various forms: in-plant committees, industry committees, or area-wide committees made up of companies and unions.

5.151 *Directory of Labor-Management Committees*

Labor-management cooperation committees in the United States, which exist outside the bargaining table and for the purpose of productivity enhancement, are listed in this guide. Listings are by state, with indexes by type of committee (area-wide, industry-wide, division-wide, plant-wide, Scanlon Plans) and by unions and companies. Labor-management committees address problems which affect the quality of working life, such as services, morale, working conditions, job satisfaction, and motivation. By providing the means for better two-way communications, they create opportunities for workers and management to share their ideas for improving the success of the enterprise.

$2.15; GPO (see C1.0).

5.152 *A "How-To" Manual on Labor-Management Committees*

The formation and function of labor-management committees are described in this 22-page typed manuscipt. Topics include framework for labor-management committee activity; determination of need for an in-plant labor-management committee; obtaining labor and management agreement and commitment to a labor-management committee; organization, composition, and agenda of in-plant committees; problems inherent in joint committees; "do's"; "don'ts"; sample format of contract language establishing a joint committee; and sample format of bylaws for joint committees.

Free; Federal Mediation and Conciliation Service (see C1.103).

5.153 *Recent Initiatives in Labor-Management Cooperation*

During a series of conferences on recent initiatives, labor-management case histories were presented. Participants in the conferences presenting the reports included panels of workers and managers involved in cooperative activities. The 96-page publication, *Recent Initiatives in Labor Management Cooperation*, based on these first-hand case histories, focuses on practical day-to-day experiences in starting committees and on benefits and problems of cooperative efforts.

National Commission on Productivity and Quality of Working Life, Wahsington, DC 20036.

5.154 Federal Mediation and Conciliation Service

The Federal Mediation and Conciliation Service (FMCS) is an independent agency of the federal government, created by Congress with a director appointed by the President. Its primary function is to promote labor-management peace and better labor-management relations. FMCS services are utilized solely on a volunteer basis, without charge. It makes the experience of its some 300 professionals in 79 cities from coast to coast available to assist businesses in labor-management negotiations and in dealing with potential problems while still in developmental stages. Comparisons have shown that mediator-assisted negotiations move more quickly with less risk of break-off or job action than negotiations without mediation. In recent years, because of their policy of aggressive mediation, the mediators are acting more and more in the role of labor-management consultants to business, at no expense.

FMCS (see C1.103).

5.155 Technical Assistance from FMCS

Technical assistance services include training,

education, consultation, and problem-solving activities performed by mediators for representatives of labor and management, other neutrals in dispute resolution, professional associations, and academic institutions. Assistance of this nature has increased dramatically over the past several years and is a major preventative program of the Federal Mediation and Conciliation Service (FMCS).

The Office of Technical Services of FMCS works closely with employers and labor organizations to develop so-called model program formats which are implemented by professional staff mediators out of the regional office. This service is strengthened by the existence of a system of regional coordinators, one in each region, to assist and supervise technical assistance activities.

In addition, the service is addressing itself more and more to questions of productivity and its impact on collective bargaining. In seeking to promote greater understanding of the need to attain better productivity and how labor and management can work together toward this end, FMCS has cooperated with the national Commission on Productivity and Quality of Working Life (see 5.700) in conferences held around the country on this subject.

FMCS (see C1.103).

5.156 FMCS Relations by Objectives Program

Relations by Objectives (RBO) is an intensive program of the Federal Mediation and Conciliation Service (FMCS) designed for utilization in cases of extremely poor labor-management relationships. At the end of fiscal year 1975, ten RBO programs, involving twenty-four mediators, had been carried out. Many more are being planned. These programs involve tailoring long-term programs aimed at changing the basic relationships that exist between the various parties. This is done by creating a kind of "road map" for them to follow in their particular setting. Public response to the program has been very positive to date.

FMCS (see C1.103).

Trends in Collective Bargaining (5.200-5.204)

5.200 Collective Bargaining Agreements on File

The national office of the Bureau of Labor Statistics (BLS) maintains a public file of collective bargaining agreements that contains approximately 7,000 contracts in the private and the public sectors. Copies of specific agreements are available for the cost of copying, unless the parties have asked that their contract be held in confidence. The file of nonconfidential agreements is open to the public. It is located in the national headquarters of the BLS.

Office of Information, BLS, Room S1032, 200 Constitution Ave. N.W., Washington, DC 20210; 202-523-7304.

5.201 Clauses Used in Collective Bargaining Agreements

Based on an analysis of about 1,800 major agreements, fifteen bulletins dealing with key issues in collective bargaining show how negotiators in various industries handle specific problems. Complete with illustrative clauses identified by company and union signatures, with detailed tabulations on prevalence of clauses, this collection of bulletins forms a basic reference source.

BLS (see C1.70).

Grievance Procedures	$1.45
Severance Pay and Layoff Benefit Plans	1.80
Supplemental Unemployment Benefit Plans and Wage-Employment Guarantees	1.80
Deferred Wage Increase and Escalator Clauses	1.10
Management Rights and Union Management Cooperation	1.35
Arbitration Procedures	2.40
Training and Retraining Provisions	1.05
Subcontracting	1.10
Paid Vacation and Holiday Provisions	1.90
Plant Movement, Transfer and Relocation Allowances	1.55
Seniority in Promotion and Transfer Provisions	1.25
Administration of Negotiated Pension, Health, and Insurance Plans	1.00
Layoff, Recall, and Worksharing Procedures Procedures	1.75
Administration of Seniority	1.25
Hours, Overtime, and Weekend Work	1.45

5.202 *Current Wage Developments*

A monthly report on employee compensation, wage and benefit changes resulting from collective bargaining agreements and management decisions, statistical summaries, and wage trends, this publication also includes key Pay Board rulings on wage and benefit changes, strikes or lockouts involving at least six workers and one full day or shift, and major agreements expiring during the month.

$12.00 per year, $1.35 single copy; GPO (see C1.0).

5.203 *Directory of National Unions and Employee Associations*

Names of offices and professional employees, and number of members and number of locals of each union are included in this directory. It has sections on union membership, structure, and function, and includes state labor organizations. It is kept current by supplements, issued at irregular intervals.

1973 edition, $4.45; GPO (see C1.0).

5.204 *A Directory of BLS Studies in Industrial Relations, 1960-1974*

The Division of Industrial Relations of the Bureau of Labor Statistics (BLS) has prepared numerous collective bargaining studies, calendars of major contract expirations, directories of unions and membership statistics, union administration, convention reports, and analyses of work stoppages, which are indexed in this directory.

Free; BLS (see C1.70).

Labor-Management Reporting and Disclosing Act (LMRDA) (5.250-5.252)

5.250 Overview of LMRDA

The Labor-Management Reporting and Disclosing Act (LMRDA) of 1959 is administered by the Office of Labor-Management Services Administration (LMSA) of the Department of Labor, and applies primarily to union reporting. However, it outlines certain employer activites which also require reporting by law. Employers must complete Employer Report Form LM-10, to disclose the following:

(1) Payments or other financial arrangements (other than those permitted under Sec. 302(c) of the Labor Relations Act, 1947, as amended, and payments and loans by banks and similar institutions) which they made during the previous fiscal year to any union, its officers, or its employees

(2) Payments to any of their employees for the purpose of causing them to persuade other employees with respect to their bargaining and representation rights, unless the other employees are told about these payments before or at the same time they are made

(3) Arrangements (and payments made under these arrangements) with a labor relations consultant or any other person for the purpose of persuading employees with respect to their bargaining and representation rights, or for obtaining information concerning employee activity in a labor dispute involving their company

In addition, labor relations consulants are required to submit reports on activities along these lines. The Act also gives the government the right of investigation to see that unions and management are in compliance.

5.251 Basic Publications Relevant to LMRDA

The following publications are available, as priced, from GPO (see C1.0).

Rights and Responsibilities under the LMRDA

Major provisions of LMRDA are outlined in nontechnical terms in this 12-page pamphlet.

20¢.

Reports Required under LMRDA

All reports required of unions and employers, as well as activities not requiring a report by the employer, are described in this publication. It includes a table indicating required report timing, signatures, and form numbers.

$1.00.

Labor-Management Reporting and Disclosure Act of 1959, As Amended

This is the public law itself.

5.252 Technical Assistance from Labor-Management Services Administration

Regional offices of the Labor-Management Services Administration (LMSA) can provide technical assistance in helping unions and employers comply with LMRDA. Advice is frequently given to unions on-site, primarily in helping them complete forms properly. Employers may find that any questions they have can be answered on the telephone.

LMSA (see C1.71).

Mediation and Arbitration (5.300-5.315)

5.300 Text of the Labor-Management Relations Act, As Amended

#3100-00146-3, 45¢; GPO (see C1.0).

5.301 *Federal Labor Laws*

All federal laws affecting labor and labor-management relationships, including regulations and interpretations, administered by the Wage and Hour Division of the Labor Management Services Administration, are included in this comprehensive guide. It is a loose-leaf service.

$75.00; GPO (see C1.0).

5.302 *A Layman's Guide to Basic Law under the National Labor Relations Act*

Both management and unions will find their rights and duties, under the National Labor Relations Act (NLRA) as amended, detailed in this 60-page basic handbook. It includes a description of the rights of employees and unions, including the right to form or not to form a union, and to strike or picket; collective bargaining procedures; the employee representative and election process; unfair labor practices of employers and unions; enforcement of the Act; a chart showing the types of cases in which an employer or a union may be involved under the Act; and the addresses of the 43 field offices of the National Labor Relations Board (NLRB).

#031-000-00095-5, $1.15; GPO (see C1.0), or NLRB (see C1.109).

5.303 Mediation by the Federal Mediation and Conciliation Service

By far the largest activity of the Federal Mediation and Conciliation Service (FMCS) is dispute mediation. Federal mediators, known as commissioners, are stationed strategically throughout the country. If the parties to a labor-management agreement wish help in averting or solving problems, they must file a notice with FMCS thirty days prior to contract termination or reopening date. The mediator will generally confer first with one of the parties and then with the other, to get their versions of the pending difficulties, and then call joint conferences with employer and union representatives. The mediator functions informally, meeting separately and jointly with the parties to help them find some mutually acceptable solution. It is the job of the mediator to act as third-party facilitator to the bargaining process. Mediators are on call twenty-four hours a day in principal cities throughout the country.

The agency has been developing a policy of aggressive mediation over the past few years. Under this policy, mediators are informed well ahead of time what cases they will be handling. They are therefore able to contact the parties long before bargaining even begins. Aggressive mediation also includes bringing in outside assistance in difficult disputes and escalating local disputes to the regional and national levels if necessary to further a settlement. In short, this policy means that FMCS tries to avoid crises by dealing with situations as early as possible.

Examples of mediator technical assistance include: (1) a new labor-management committee structure for long-term labor peace and improved communications in the Texas construction industry; (2) a training program for a southern plant with a history of wildcat strikes, utilizing simulated case studies developed around not only their particular problems, but personalities as well; (3) a community-wide committee of labor, management, academic, and public representatives in western New York that has reversed the exodus of industrial plants and declining employment; and (4) a postnegotiation study committee in an Illinois school district that later formed superintendents' and teachers' advisory councils which in turn led to contract renewal a year early.

FMCS (see C1.103).

5.304 Free Publications on Mediation

The following publications are available, free, from FMCS (see C1.103).

Mediation in Public Sector Labor-Management Disputes
One-page foldout.

Securing Labor-Management Peace through Mediation
One-page foldout.

The Mediator
This subscription service lists the latest cases, conferences, and news items important to mediators. It also serves as an in-house news organ and contains information about individual mediators.

5.305 Arbitration by FMCS

While mediation employs the federal staff of the Federal Mediation and Conciliation Service (FMCS), arbitration involves private professionals in the field of labor dispute litigation and settlement. FMCS maintains a roster of qualified arbitrators. Upon request, FMCS will furnish a panel of these arbitrators from which the parties may select the one most mutually satisfactory to hear the dispute and provide a final decision. FMCS can usually respond to an arbitration request within a week. The request should be signed by both parties, although under some circumstances a single request will also receive a response.
FMCS (see C1.103).

5.306 *Arbitration*

This ten-page brochure outlines the arbitration program.
Free; FMCS (see C1.103).

5.307 FMCS *Annual Report*

The *Annual Report* summarizes all activities of the Federal Mediation and Conciliation Service (FMCS), both qualitatively and quantitatively, and describes the services available to business and labor. Individual cases mediated and arbitrated in the year covered are discussed.
80 pp.; FMCS (see C1.103).

5.308 National Labor Relations Board

In its statutory assignment, the National Labor Relations Board (NLRB) has two primary functions: (1) to determine and implement, through secret ballot elections, the free democratic choice by employees as to whether they wish to be represented by a union and, if so, by which one; and (2) to prevent and remedy unlawful acts, called unfair labor practices, by either employers or unions. The NLRB does not act on its own motion in either function. It processes only those charges of unfair labor practices and petitions for employee elections which may be filed with it at one of its 31 regional offices of 13 smaller field offices (see C1.109).

NLRB administers the National Labor Relations Act of 1935 as amended in 1947 by the Taft-Hartley Act (Labor-Management Relations Act), and in 1959 by the Landrum-Griffin Act (Labor-Management Reporting and Ddisclosure Act). NLRB, therefore, administers all of the nation's principal labor relations laws. It emphasizes voluntary disposition of cases at all stages and, as a result, only about five percent of the unfair labor practice charges filed with the regional offices are litigated all the way through to a decision by the Board. In fiscal year 1975, a record total of 44,923 cases was received by the NLRB, a six percent increase over the previous year.
NLRB (see C1.109).

5.309 *The NLRB . . . What It is, What It Does*

This single-page foldout brochure gives an overview of the National Labor Relations Board (NLRB).
#3100-00113, 25¢; GPO (see C1.0).

5.310 Free Publications of NLRB

The following publications are available, free, from NLRB (see C1.109).

To Protect the Rights of the Public (English and Spanish editions)
Your Government Conducts an Election for You on the Job (English and Spanish editions)
A Career in Labor-Management Relations as a Stenographer and Typist
Where the Action Is...Labor-Management Rela-

tions Examiner

National Labor Relations Act Jurisdiction over Health Care Institutions

5.311 Decisions and Orders of the NLRB

The following publications are available, as priced, from GPO (see C1.0).

Volume	*Price*	*Period Covered*
203	$16.80	04/19/1973-06/06/1973
204	16.05	06/06/1973-07/23/1973
205	13.50	07/18/1973-09/12/1973
206	14.10	10/13/1973-11/06/1973
207	15.15	11/07/1973-12/26/1973
208	14.70	12/28/1973-02/12/1974
209	16.10	02/13/1974-04/09/1974
210	15.40	04/09/1974-05/30/1974
211	15.25	05/31/1974-06/25/1974
212	17.00	06/26/1974-08/22/1974
213	16.00	08/23/1974-10/08/1974

Court Decisions Relating to the National Labor Relations Act

Volume XXI, #3100-00119, $11.25; Volume XXII, #3100-00135, $12.20.

Index of Court Decisions Relating to the National Labor Relations Act, January 1, 1956-December 31, 1973

#031-000-00149-7, $4.85.

Guide for Hearing Officers in NLRB Representation Proceedings

Procedures, checklists, and reference materials for NLRB professional personnel in representation case hearings are provided in this guide, compiled by the Office of the General Counsel.

#031-000-00156-1, $3.15.

Classification Outline for Decisions of the National Labor Relations Board and Related Court Decision

The outline provides a subject matter classification system for procedural and legal issues of NLRB and related court decisions, using the classification system of the Classified Index.

#LR 1.8/7: 1972, $2.35.

Litigation Manual Outline and Litigation Manual 1956-1971

This outline provides a subject matter classification system for procedural and substantive legal issues presented in court decisions involving the National Labor Relations Act, together with a manual containing the classifications and scope notes for such court decisions from July 1, 1956, to June 30, 1971. Court cases after June 30, 1971 are indexed in the Classified Index.

#LR 1.6/2: L 71 956-71, $9.60.

5.312 Subscription Publications of NLRB

The following publications are available, as priced, from GPO (see C1.0); see also NLRB regional offices (C1.109).

National Labor Relations Board Case Handling Manual

In three parts, this manual provides complete, up-dated, procedural and operational guidelines to NLRB regional offices in processing cases received under the Act. Part One, entitled *Unfair Labor Practice Proceedings*, and Part Two, *Representation Proceedings*, have been published. Part Three, covering compliance proceedings and settlement agreements, is being prepared for publication.

Three-part manual, $26.50.

Rules and Regulations and Statements of Procedure of the National Labor Relations Board, Series 8, as Amended (1973)

This subscription service in loose-leaf form includes supplements for an indefinite period.

#86/Ser. 8/173, $7.00.

Decisions and Related Court Decisions

This service consists of a basic volume cumulative from July 1, 1970 to June 30, 1973, and cumulative supplements issued at intervals during the subscription period. Court decisions from June 30, 1971 to date will be added to the supplements and cumulated into the basic volumes of subsequent subscriptions.

#LR1.8/6:973, $19.50 for subsctiption service to publications issued July, 1973 to June, 1974.

Classified Index of NLRB and Related Court Decisions

Part One, July 1, 1974-June 30, 1975; Part Two, July 1, 1975-December 31, 1975. Part One is now available; Part Two is in preparation for publication.

$21.00 for both parts.

An Outline of Law and Procedure in Representation Cases

Compiled by the Office of the General Counsel, this publication is intended as a ready reference to the more significant areas of law and administrative policy applicable to representation proceedings at various stages of processing by the NLRB.

#031-000-00145-5, 436 pp., $5.60.

5.313 *NLRB Election Report*

The outcome of secret ballot voting by employees in NLRB-conducted representation elections, as officially certified following resolution of postelection objections and/or challenges, is listed in this monthly report.

NLRB national or regional offices (see C1.109).

5.314 Legal Responsibilities of Unions

Legal responsibilities of unions, potential liability for acts of discrimination, suggested strategies for limiting liability, proposal for union equal employment opportunity programs, and examples of current union efforts are described in an article entitled "The Union Role in Title VII Enforcement: Liability and Opportunity," by Herbert Hammerman and Marvin Rogoff, published in *Civil Rights Digest*, Spring, 1975.

A revised, condensed version of the article, "Title VII: Threat and Opportunity for Labor," by the same authors, was published in the April, 1976 issue of *Monthly Labor Review.*

Free; Industrial Relations Unit, Office of Compliance Programs, Equal Employment Opportunity Commission, Washington, DC 20506.

5.315 NLRB *Annual Report*

This is a comprehensive review of activities of the National Labor Relations Board (NLRB), including a summary of operations and decisions; jurisdiction and procedure of the Board; representation proceedings; unfair labor practices by employers and unions; Supreme Court litigation; enforcement, injunction, and contempt litigation; an index to all cases discussed; and numerous tables and charts. It constitutes an in-depth analysis of the NLRB.

#031-000-00153-6, $2.55; GOP (see C1.0).

Compensation of Employees (5.350-5.464)

Wage and Hour Standards (5.350-5.354)

5.350 Administration of Wage and Hour Laws

The Wage and Hour Division of the Employment Standards Administration (ESA) in the Department of Labor administers the national laws relating to wage and hour regulations. The major act administered is the Fair Labor Standards Act of 1938, as amended, although the Division also administers a number of others: The Davis-Bacon Act, Walsh-Healy Public Contracts Act, Farm Labor Contractor Registration Act, Age Discrimination in Employment Act, Federal Wage Garnishment Law, and Contract Work Hours and Safety Standards Act. Regional offices of the Wage and Hour Division can furnish detailed technical bulletins and pamphlets that give a general explanation of each law.

ESA (see C1.74).

5.351 *Federal Labor Laws*

All laws administered by the Wage and Hour Division Employment Standards Administration, Department of Labor, together with regulations and interpretations, are included in this loose-leaf system.

$75.00 per year; GPO (see C1.0).

5.352 *Handy Reference Guide to the Fair Labor Standards Act*

The standard publication for assisting employers in the administration of the Fair Labor Standards Act, this booklet includes discussion of basic standards, previously and newly covered employment, extended minimum wage provisions and exemptions, overtime provisions and exemptions, special provisions, equal pay and child labor provisions, recordkeeping, investigations, computation of back pay, and more.

65¢; GPO (see C1.0).

5.353 Technical Assistance in Wage and Hour Compliance

Regional and field offices of the Wage and Hour Division of the Employment Standards Administration (ESA) are able to provide technical assistance as to the laws they administer. Usually, actual field visits to a business are made for investigative purposes only; most employers find they can receive answers to their questions by telephone.

Although there are over a hundred field offices of the Wage and Hour Division, a separate listing of them is unavailable. In some cities, a field office may be listed in the telephone book; in many cities, they are located in the same place as the field offices of the Labor-Management Services Administration.

ESA (see C1.74).

5.354 *Defining the Terms "Executive," "Administrative," "Professional," and "Outside Salesman"*

ESA (see C1.74).

Wage Information for Planning (5.400-5.409)

5.400 *Directory of Area Wage Surveys, January 1973-December 1974*

Publications which have resulted from the annual wage survey program of the Bureau of Labor Statistics are listed in this directory. Included are listings of individual area wage surveys, summary bulletins, and relevant *Monthly Labor Review* articles.

The area listing includes all standard metropolitan statistical areas in the United States. The bulletins contain earnings information for selected office clerical, professional and technical, maintenance and power plant, and custodial and material movement occupations, as well as information on supplementary wage benefits. Wage practices and supplementary benefits studied include minimum entrance salaries for inexperienced typists and clerks; shift differentials; paid holidays; paid vacations; and health, insurance, and pension plans. In addition to all-industry information, data are provided whenever possible for the six major divisions studied: manufacturing; transportation, communication, and other public utilities; wholesale trade; retail trade; finance, insurance, and real estate; and services.

Summary bulletins bring data from each of the metropolitan areas studied into one bulletin. A second kind of summary bulletin presents information which has been projected from individual metropolitan area data to represent regions and the United States as a whole.

Prices for most bulletins are under $1.00. The directory: 35 pp., free; BLS (see C1.70).

5.401 *Directory of Industry and Municipal Government Wage Surveys and Union Wages and Hours Studies, 1960-1975*

Industry wage surveys, the first part of the directory, cover approximately fifty manufacturing and twenty nonmanufacturing industries and are usually nationwide in scope. The studies usually provide separate earnings data for selected regions and localities of industry concentration. The earnings data in the reports relate to average straight-time earnings of workers. Premium pay for overtime and for work on weekends, holidays, and late shifts is excluded. Incentive payments, such as those resulting from piecework, production bonuses, and commission systems, are included as earnings, but nonproduction bonus payments (e.g., Christmas bonuses) are not. Cost-of-living bonuses are considered as part of the workers' regular pay.

19 pp., free; BLS (see C1.70).

5.402 *Current Wage Developments*

Wage and benefit changes resulting from collective bargaining settlements and unilateral management decisions are discussed in this monthly publication. It includes statistical summaries and special reports on wage trends.

$12.00 per year, $1.35 single copy; GPO (see C1.0).

5.403 *Employment and Earnings*

Included in this publication are detailed household data on labor force, total employment and enemployment, employment status of Vietnam era veterans, and jobseeking methods used by the unemployed; establishment data on employment, hours, earnings, and turnover rates;

output per hour, hourly compensation, and unit labor costs; insured unemployment, nationally and by state and area; special articles presenting data on various phases of labor force; charts; and technical notes on concepts and methods.

$24.00 per year, $2.70 single copy; GPO (see C1.0).

5.404 Free Publications on Current Wages

By request, one can be put on a mailing list to receive one or all of the following free publications.

BLS (see C1.70).

Order No.	*Title*
301	*Employment and Wages* (report) Quarterly
314	*New Publications on Wages and Industrial Relations* (announcements) Occasional
317	*Major Collective Bargaining Agreements* (press release) Quarterly
318	*Union Wage Rates for Building Trades* (press release) Quarterly
325	*Real Earnings* (press release) Monthly

5.405 Compensation Studies of the Bureau of Labor Statistics

A comprehensive guide to activities of the Bureau of Labor Statistics, the publication entitled *Major Programs 1976—Bureau of Labor Statistics* lists the following surveys in the area of compensation: (1) *wage studies*: area, industry, professional, administrative, technical, and clerical salary surveys, union wage rates and hours, and annual earnings and employment patterns; (2) *compensation studies*: compensation expenditures and payroll hours, and employee-benefit plans (analysis of health, insurance, pensions); and (3) *wage trend studies*: current wage developments, wage chronologies, wage indexes, and major research in progress.

The guide explains the data available in each survey, the coverage and sources of data, the publications which carry the results, and the potential uses of the surveys for business. It also charts the kind of data available for each standard metropolitan statistical area in the country.

BLS (see C1.70).

5.406 Statistical Studies in Wages and Industrial Relations

Four major types of employee earnings surveys are conducted in the Bureau of Labor Statistics' Office of Wages and Industrial Relations to provide information on straight-time earnings by occupation and on establishment practices and supplementary wage provisions: (1) area surveys in selected metropolitan and, on a more limited scope, nonmetropolitan areas relating to occupations common to a variety of manufacturing and nonmanufacturing industries; (2) industry surveys in selected manufacturing and nonmanufacturing industries covering occupations peculiar to the specific industry; (3) national salary surveys covering selected professional, administrative, technical, and clerical occupations in private employment; and (4) surveys of union wage rates and hours covering selected journeyman, helper, and laborer classifications in four highly unionized industries in cities of 100,000 population or more.

In addition to studies of straight-time earnings by occupation, a group of surveys is conducted to measure employers' total expenditures for employee compensation, including, individually, the major supplements to straight-time pay for hours worked.

Digests and detailed analyses are made of the provisions of major types of employee benefit plans; e.g., health, insurance, and pension plans that supplement straight-time pay in American industry. Information is developed on the nature and prevalence of the plans.

BLS (see C1.70).

5.407 *A Directory of BLS Studies in Employee Compensation 1960-1975.*

The directory includes publications in the following areas: employee compensation and payroll hours (cross-industry studies, manufacturing, and nonmanufacturing studies); annual earnings and employment patterns; nonoccupational earnings and hours (area studies, manufacturing, and nonmanufacturing studies); employee benefit plans (pension and retirement plans, health and insurance plans; health, insurance, and retirement plans; supplemental unemployment benefits and severance pay plans); special and technical studies. Each subsection is divided into two parts: (1) bulletins and reports, and (2) *Monthly Labor Review* articles.

16 pp., free; BLS (see C1.70).

5.408 Publications on Equal Pay

Equal Pay for Equal Work

Official interpretations of the meaning and application of equal pay provisions added to the Fair Labor Standards Act by the Equal Pay Act of 1963 are collected in this pamphlet.

#029-005-00023-1, 28 pp., 60¢; GPO (see C1.0).

Equal Pay

This informative pamphlet explains key provisions and outlines the background of the Equal Pay Act of 1963. The Act prohibits discrimination in wages on the basis of sex.

#029-016-00017-8, 16 pp., 45¢; GPO (see C1.0).

5.409 *Directory of Wage Chronologies, 1948-June 1975*

All wage chronologies issued through June, 1975 are listed in this directory. The wage chronology program was designed to present, in summary form, changes in wages and related compensation practices made by specific employers or groups of employers, usually through agreements reached as a result of collective bargaining. The chronologies are intended primarily as tools for research and analysis. As such, they deal only with selected features of the varied history of collective bargaining or wage administration in each case. References to job security, union security, grievance procedures, employment practices, and similar matters are omitted. The situations selected for study are believed to have significance for wage determination that extends beyond the specific settlements.

13 pp., free; BLS (see C1.70).

Pensions and Benefits (5.450-5.464)

5.450 Employee Retirement Income Security Act of 1974

The purpose of the Employee Retirement Income Security Act of 1974 (ERISA) is to protect the interests of workers and their beneficiaries who depend on benefits from employee pension and welfare plans. The law requires disclosure of plan provisions and financial information and establishes standards of conduct for trustees and administration of welfare and pension plans. It sets up funding, participation, and vesting requirements for pension plans, and makes termination insurance available for most of them.

It is the practice of the Office of Employee Benefit Security and the regional offices of the Labor-Management Services Administration (LMSA) to answer inquiries of individuals and organizations, whenever appropriate, as to their status under the Act and as to the effect of their acts or transactions. Many questions can be answered by a telephone call. However, the Department of Labor has devised two formal types of technical assistance: an informational letter and an advisory opinion.

An informational letter is a written statement issued either by the Office of Employee Benefits Security or the regional or area offices of LMSA that does no more than call attention to a well established interpretation or principle of the Act, without applying it to a specific factual situation. Such a letter may be issued to any individual or organization when the nature of the request does not meet the criteria needed for the issuance of an advisory opinion.

Title I of the Act deals with the protection of employees' benefit rights and is administered by the Office of Employee Benefit Security, LMSA, Department of Labor.

Title II is composed of amendments to the Internal Revenue Code regarding pension and welfare plans and is administered by the Internal Revenue Service (IRS).

Title III deals with the division of responsibility among the agencies administering the law.

Title IV deals with plan termination insurance provisions and is administered by the Pension Benefit Guaranty Corporation (PBGC), an organization established by the Act for this purpose. PBGC has no regional offices; information can be had at regional offices of LMSA.

Office of Communications, PBGC, 2020 K St. N.W., Washington, DC 20006; 202-254-4817.

5.451 *ERISA Guidelines*

This publication is published jointly by the Department of Labor and the Internal Revenue Service as a compendium of authoritative rules relating to ERISA (Employment Retirement Income Security Act) requirements. These rules were published in recognition of the need to provide an immediate and complete set of interim guidelines to facilitate (1) the adoption of new employee benefit pension plans, and (2) prompt amendment of existing plans. The rules govern the application of (1) the qualification requirements of the Internal Revenue Code of 1954 added to or amended by ERISA, and (2) the qualification requirements of the provisions of Parts 2 and 3 of Title I of ERISA.

LMSA (see C1.71).

5.452 Introductory Publications on ERISA

Unless otherwise indicated, the following publications are available from regional offices of LMSA (see C1.71).

Coverage under the Employee Retirement Income Security Act of 1974

Coverage and exemptions under ERISA are outlined in this 12-page pamphlet.

Often-Asked Questions about the Employee Retirement Income Security Act of 1974

This 29-page booklet briefly answers questions about plans covered, fiduciary standards, reporting and disclosure, participation, vesting and funding, termination insurance, widow-widowers' benefits, enforcement, and what the Act does not cover. A reporting and disclosure section describes reports that must be filed with each administrative agency (Labor-Management Services Administration, Internal Revenue Services, and Pension Benefit Guaranty Corporation).

Reporting and Disclosure Employee Retirement Income Security Act of 1974

Reports required of each administering federal agency are described in this 14-page pamphlet.

Fiduciary Standards Employee Retirement Income Security Act

Fiduciary obligations under ERISA are outlined in this 11-page booklet. Also, the major Department of Labor interpretive releases in the *Federal Register* and the *Interpretive Bulletins* of the Pension and Welfare Benefit Programs are listed.

Identification Numbers under ERISA

This 7-page brochure is put out jointly by the three administrative agencies (Labor-Management Services Administration (LMSA), Internal Revenue Service (IRS), and Pension Benefit Guaranty Corporation (PBGC) and explains the usage of identification numbers on certain reporting forms relating to employee benefit plans filed under ERISA. These forms include: the Form 5300 Series, Applications for Determinations (IRS); the Form 550 Series, Annual Return /Report of Employee Benefit Plan (IRS/Department of Labor (DOL); and the PBGC-1 Package, Premium Payment and Annual Report Forms (PBGC). This publication is actually a guideline for report submission.

Pension Benefit Guaranty Corporation Annual Report

An introduction to the responsibilities under law of the Pension Benefit Guaranty Corporation (PBGC) is given in this 36-page annual report. In effect, the report constitutes a summary of PBGC activities and, indirectly, an overview of pension plan activity nationally.

Office of Communications, PBGC, 2020 K St. N.W., Washington, DC 20006.

PBGC Fact Sheet

A single page flyer summarizes the Pension Benefit Guaranty Corporation plan's termination insurance program.

Individual Retirement Accounts, IRA's

Basic information regarding Individual Retirement Accounts (IRA) is provided in this 17-page brochure. The PBGC gives advice and assistance on the economic desirability of establishing an IRA.

5.453 ERISA Technical Information

The following documents are available from regional offices of LMSA (see C1.71).

Order
No. *Subject*

TIR 1334 - questions and answers relating to defined contribution plans subject to ERISA
40 F.R. 17576 - Notice of Proposed Rule Making: Qualification (and other aspects) of HR-10 plans
T.D. 7358 - Temporary Regulations: Notification of interested parties
T.D. 7367 - Temporary Regulations: Notice of determination of qualifications
40 F.R. 41654 - Department of Labor—Minimum standards for hours of service, years of service, and breaks in service relating to participation, vesting, and accrual of benefits
TIR 1403 - Questions and answers relating mainly to defined benefit plans subject to ERISA (addition to TIR 1334)
40 F.R. 43034 - Notice of Proposed Rule Making: Definitions of multiemployer plan and plan administrator
T.D. 7377 - Temporary Regulations: Certain retroactive amendments of employee plans
T.D. 7379 - Temporary Regulations: Qualified joint and survivor annuities
T.D. 7380 - Temporary Regulations: Minimum Participation Standards
T.D. 7381 - Temporary Regulations: Commencement of Benefits
T.D. 7382 - Temporary Regulations: Requirement that benefits under a qualified plan are not decreased on account of certain Social Security increases
T.D. 7383 - Temporary Regulations: Nonbank trustees of pension and profit-sharing trusts benefiting owner-employers
40 F.R. 48517 - Notice of Proposed Rule Making: Certain Custodial Accounts
TIR 1408 - Questions and answers relating to mergers, consolidations, etc.
Rev. Rul. 75-480, 1975-44 IRB - Updating of Rev. Rul. 71-446 to reflect changes mandated by ERISA
Rev. Rul. 75-481, 1975-44 IRB - Guidelines for determining whether contributions or benefits under plan satisfy the limitations of Section 415 of the Code
TIR 1411 Rev. Proc. 75-49, 1975-48 IRB - Vesting and Discrimination
TIR 1413 - Questions and Answers relating to Employee Stock Ownership Plans
T.D. 7387 - Temporary Regulations on Minimum Vesting Standards
T.D. 7388 - Controlled groups, business under common control
TIR - Nonforfeiture of employee-derived accrued benefit upon death
- Department of Labor—Interpretive Bulletin: Definition of Seasonal Industries
- Department of Labor—additional requirements applicable to definition of multiemployer plan
- Department of Labor—suspension of benefits upon reemployment of retiree
- Assignment of alienation of plan benefits
TIR Rev. Rul. - Appropriate conversion factor

5.454 ERISA Technical Releases and Interpretive Bulletins

Technical releases are put out by the Office of Pension and Welfare Benefit Programs as initial guidelines in the interpretation and application of ERISA (Employment Retirement Income Security Act) provisions. These are usually interim releases prior to finalizing guidelines published in the form of interpretive bulletins.

Interpretive bulletins are required by the Act itself and are the standard, official reference for interpreting ERISA provisions. It is these bulletins which are then published in the *Federal Register*.

Information Office, LMSA national office; see also LMSA regional offices (C1.71).

5.455 *A Directory of BLS Studies in Employee Compensation, 1960-1975*

The following are a few of the listings related to pensions and benefits in the Directory. There are others which are out of print but available through regional or national office libraries. In addition, there are numerous articles from the *Monthly Labor Review*.

BLS (see C1.70).

Digest of Selected Pension Plans, BLS Report #429, free
Coverage and Vesting of Full-Time Employees under Private Retirement Plans, BLS Report #423, free
Characteristics of Terminated Retirement Plans, BLS Report #369, free
Digest of Health and Insurance Plans, $14.00 for subscription covering 1974 edition and supplements

Major Collective Bargaining Agreements: Administration of Negotiated Pension, Health and Insurance Plans, BLS Bulletin #1425-12, $1.00

5.456 *Pensions and Pension Plans, Selected References 1971-1974*

Pensions and pension plans are partially annotated in this reference guide, used as a standard reference in the library of the Office of the Assistant Secretary for Administration and Management of the Department of Labor. It consists of books, pamphlets, and articles from public and private sources. Categories are as follows: general references for pensions and pension plans (books, pamphlets, Congressional documents, periodical articles); management of pension funds; Civil Service pensions; Social Security pensions; pension plans under collective bargaining; plan terminations and mergers, and plant closing; misuse of pension funds; women and pensions; miscellaneous brief articles; and bibliographies and periodicals.

73 pp., $1.20; GPO (see C1.0).

5.457 Publications on Pension Administration

The following publications are available, as priced, from GPO (see C1.0).

Pension Trust Procedures and Guides for Integration of Qualified Plans, #048-004-519, 49 pp., 95¢
Position Classification, Pay, and Employee Benefits, #006-000-00896-8, 87 pp., $1.55
Administration Expenses of Welfare and Pension Plans, #029-000-00202-9, 146 pp., $1.65
Legislative History of Employee Retirement Income Security Act of 1974, #052-070-03342-8, sold in 3-volume set only, $41.00

5.458 Employee Stock Ownership Plan

Under the Tax Reduction Act of 1975, certain tax incentives are offered businesses which participate in the relatively new means of employee compensation referred to as Employee Stock Ownership Plans (ESOP). An ESOP is an employee plan of the defined contribution type that is designed to invest primarily in employer securities. Generally, one of its basic purposes is to provide employees with some ownership in the companies for which they work.

IRS publishes a technical information release (TIR 1413) which answers some basic questions about such a plan, including election of an eleven percent investment credit, funding requirements and requirements other than funding, and taxability and deductibility of ESOP funds. In addition, IRS will issue determination letters to employers with specific questions or problems regarding whether a particular ESOP qualifies or meets the requirements of the Act with respect to the eleven percent investment credit.

Internal Revenue Service, Department of the Treasury, Washington, DC 20224; 202-964-4021. See also IRS area offices (C1.95).

5.459 *Broadening the Ownership of New Capital: ESOP's and Other Alternatives*

Four major alternative measures for broadening stock ownership among Americans, including employee stock ownership plans (ESOP's), are examined in this brochure.

#052-070-03477-7, 62 pp., 80¢; GPO (see C1.0).

5.460 Advisory Opinions on Pension and Welfare Benefit Programs

An advisory opinion is a written statement issued to an individual or organization by the Administrator of the Pension and Welfare Benefit Programs or his delegate, that interprets and applies the Act to a specific factual situation. Advisory opinions are issued only by the Administrator or his delegate. If an advisory opinion is desired, a description of information needed for it is available from: Advisory Opinion, Office of Regulatory Standards and Exceptions, Pension and Welfare Benefit Programs, Department of Labor, Washington, DC 20216.

Advisory opinions are open to public inspection at the Public Disclosure Room, Department of Labor, 200 Constitution Avenue, Washington, DC 20216. In addition, advisory opinions and background files, with proprietary information deleted, are available upon written request at the cost of the search and copying required.

5.461 *Benefit Series Service—Unemployment Insurance*

Recent decisions in cases arising out of unemployment insurance claims are reported in this monthly publication. It comes in loose-leaf form.

$16.35 per year, no single copies sold; GPO (See C1.0).

5.462 Technical Assistance in Unemployment Insurance

The first line of inquiry for technical assistance in the area of unemployment insurance is the manager of the local unemployment insurance office. He can offer assistance in understanding the nuances of the law in a given state, and appeal rights and procedures.

If a problem cannot be solved by a telephone call, an expert may call at a client's place of business for consultation.

See also state headquarters of the Employment Service (see C1.73).

5.463 *Comparison of State Unemployment Insurance Laws*

Issued in loose-leaf form, this publication includes the basic edition and the revised sheets. Revised sheets may also be purchased separately.

#029-013-00070-5, $12.45; GPO (see C1.0).

5.464 Publications on Retirement

Retirement: Patterns and Predictions, #017-024-00388-3, 156 pp., $1.75; GPO (see C1.0)

Transition, A Guide to Retirement, #044-000-01428-9, 50 pp., 55¢; GPO (see C1.0)

Equal Employment Opportunity Planning (5.500-5.608)

Recruitment (5.500-5.507)

5.500 A No-Fee Recruitment Source: The State Employment Service

Over 2,400 local State Employment Service offices (called Job Services in many states) provide free prescreening job referral services to employers seeking workers and workers seeking jobs. These offices are usually the largest single source of labor supply in the area. At the national level, the United States Employment Service (USES) is the federal partner of a federal-state system which operates the public employment service program in all states. However, the local offices are the service delivery centers.

The Employment service (ES) is currently moving into an on-line computer-based system of matching jobs to workers which is aimed at greatly increasing the efficiency of processing both job orders and applications for employment. When the system is fully operative, an employer will be able to find out over the phone, immediately, how many applicants are potentially available in the area for any specific occupation, and who they are. The system is being installed nationally in stages and is expected to be complete by about 1978. This will give employers access to workers in other labor markets as well, if a job cannot be filled locally.

Information on the status of the system in any local area can be determined by calling the local office of the State Employment Service, which will be listed in the telephone directory under state services or in the yellow pages under employment agencies.

See also state headquarters of ES (see C1.73).

5.501 Staffing Services for New Plants

The State Employment Service (Job Service) can set up a prescreening unit for staffing an entire new plant. Arrangements can be worked out well in advance by contacting the local office manager serving the area of the new facility.

See also state headquarters of ES (see C1.73).

5.502 Tax Credit and Training Reimbursement: The Work Incentive Program

The Work Incentive Program (WIN) is a program intended to help recipients of Aid to Families with Dependent Children get and keep jobs. It provides a variety of supportive services to applicants to prepare them for work, and of incentives for employers to participate. WIN is jointly administered by the Department of Labor and the Department of Health, Education, and Welfare.

One incentive for employers to offer jobs is a sizable tax credit. It allows them to receive a credit, deducted from their federal income tax liability, amounting to 20 percent of the first year's wages paid to every WIN registrant they hire and keep on the job.

Another incentive arises from the "hire first, train later" concept. Here, WIN reimburses employers for the cost of on-the-job training provided for the WIN participants they employ. The employers get trained workers, compensation for the training, and a tax credit on their wages.

Contact the manager of the local State Employment Service; see also state headquarters (C1.73).

5.503 *Directory for Reaching Minority Groups*

#029-006-00005-9, 214 pp., $2.85; GPO (see C1.0).

5.504 Recruitment of Veterans

The State Employment Service (Job Service) gives preference to veterans in referrals to employers. Most local offices have a veterans' employment representative whose responsibility is to find jobs for veterans who apply.

5.505 Assistance from the National Alliance of Businessmen

The National Alliance of Businessmen (NAB) was formed in 1968 as a cooperative effort between business and government to encourage private-sector hiring of the disadvantaged. The program operates in over 130 offices across the country and is administered by executives on loan from participating companies for six months to two years. NAB conducts a pledge campaign among businesses in which job openings are solicited from employers. NAB then acts as a catalytic agent between the appropriate referral source and the employer. The employee groups NAB promotes include the unemployed poor, Vietnam-era veterans, needy youth, and ex-offenders. Supportive services include:

Awareness training. In many of its offices, NAB conducts awareness training for first-line supervisors in business, dealing with the problems of the disadvantaged employee.

Co-op Programs. NAB can establish the procedures to allow young high school students to work on alternate weeks while continuing their studies.

Split days for veterans. NAB will assist employers to set up a split workday program for veterans attending school, thus giving two veterans sustenance from a single job.

State Employment Service (C1.73), or local NAB offices

5.506 Job Service Improvement Program

The Job Service Improvement Program, currently operating in 36 states, the District of Columbia, and hundreds of cities, is a national effort to involve formally the expertise of the private sector in improving local delivery of service from State Employment Service offices. This is done by creating a local representative employer committee, usually under the auspices of the Chamber of Commerce, which provides an in-depth critique of quality of services employers receive from the local agency. The local office, in turn, creates a special task force to respond constructively to each comment of the employer committee. Once the committee approves the action plan produced by the task force, it is implemented, within budgetary restrictions, to improve service delivery in that community. Many states have then proceeded to create state employer committees to deal with problems beyond the scope of the local office. Three national meetings have also been held.

Employer Services Staff, United States Employment Service, Department of Labor, Washington, DC 20210; or see State Employment Service (C1.73).

5.507 Demonstration Project to Create Jobs

Ten cities have been selected for a unique demonstration that combines $4.8 million from three cabinet departments with resources of local governments and business and community organization to generate jobs for disadvantaged and moderate income groups.

The cities are Albuquerque, Baltimore, Bridgeport (Connecticut), Buffalo, Chicago, Dayton (Ohio), Kansas City (Missouri), Oakland (California), Philadelphia, and Pittsburgh.

The cities were identified in a joint announcement by the three participating agencies: the Departments of Labor, Commerce, and Housing and Urban Development.

The successful cities, chosen from a total of thirty competitors, have outlined a variety of improvements such as creation of economic development commissions, loan and bond programs to raise capital, industrial parks, neighborhood commercial revitalization ideas, and better ways of training and placing local residents in jobs.

The program is basically a research and demonstration effort. The ten cities have agreed to document their experiences and make them available to others.

United States Employment Service, Department of Labor, Washington, DC 20210.

Testing and Counseling (5.550-5.555)

5.550 Testing Tools Used by Employment Service Counselors

Occupational tests used in vocational counseling and selecting of persons for jobs play a vital role in Employment Service (ES) activities, and their development and validation constitute a continuing responsibility of the United States Employment Service (USES).

Non-ES groups—such as prime sponsors, vocational schools, high school counselors—interested in using USES tests should contact local ES (Job Service) offices to discuss the possibilities. Under some circumstances, arrangements can be made for ES staff to administer the tests for the organization. In other cases, the local Job Service office may grant permission for qualified staff of the non-ES group to administer the USES tests.

To date, eight types of testing tools have been developed. They are:

General Aptitude Test Battery (GATB) measures the vocational aptitudes of individuals who have basic literacy skills but need help in choosing an occupation. It consists of twelve tests that indicate aptitude in nine vocational areas. It measures, for example, a counselee's spatial aptitude, manual dexterity, and verbal aptitude.

Non-Reading Aptitude Test Battery (NATB) measures the aptitude of individuals who do not have the literacy skills to take the GATB. It consists of fourteen tests for the same nine aptitudes as measured by the GATB. Clients given the NATB are often referred to a training program that includes an education component.

GATB-NATB Screening Device is a short test which helps a counselor determine whether a counselee should take the GATB or the NATB.

Specific Aptitude Test Batteries (SATB) measure the potential of individuals to acquire skills needed for a specific job or occupational training program. SATB's have been developed for more than 450 specific occupations.

Clerical Skills Tests measure proficiency in regular and statistical typing, dictation and spelling, including medical and legal terms, to determine qualifications for clerical jobs.

Basic Occupation Literacy Test (BOLT) measures basic skills in reading and math that are needed for a specific job or particular training program. It is used for educationally deficient individuals.

Pretesting Orientation Techniques help prepare individuals to take tests and alleviate related anxieties. A counselee may take booklets home to read, practice GATB exercises, or participate in group sessions on the purposes of testing.

Interest Checklist is used to obtain information on occupational interests of a counselee. It consists of 173 sample job tasks and is geared to the Worker Traits and Occupational Group classification systems contained in the third and current edition of the *Dictionary of Occupational Titles* (see 5.655).

State headquarters or local offices of ES (see C1.73).

5.551 Research in Employment Service Testing Program

Under the direction of a small staff of psychologists, several research efforts are currently underway in the United States Employment Service (USES) testing program. Usually, forty state employment services collect the data for processing by the test development centers in Raleigh, Detroit, and Salt Lake City, which conduct the actual research studies. Current work consists of:

Development of Alternate Forms C and D of the GATB. These new alternate forms are designed to encourage a policy of retesting by local offices. Tests have been constructed and are now being standardized.

Improvement of the NATB. Research is in process to develop new subtests that will cut down on administration time (now three and a half hours) and provide more valid measures of four of the aptitudes.

Design of a New Spanish Edition of the NATB. Research on Bateria de Examenes de Aptitud General (BEAG) is nearly complete. The new edition is for general use with Spanish-speaking applicants.

Revalidation of SATB's on Minorities. Since 1972, a concerted effort has been under way to revalidate SATB's separately for samples of minorities, as well as nonminorities. Twenty-four SATB's have already been revalidated separately and determined equitable for minority use. Another twenty-six have been revalidated with some minority group representation in the sample group. Revalidations for an additional 196 are in various stages of data collection and/or analysis.

Validation of BOLT. Studies are being conducted to validate BOLT scores against job and training success.

Development of a USES Interest Inventory. The new inventory, which will replace the current Interest Checklist, will be oreinted to the career areas included in Volume II of the fourth edition of the *Dictionary of Occupational Titles* (DOT) (see 5.655). It will provide a direct way of measuring interests in terms by which occupations are classified in the DOT.

State headquarters or local offices of ES (see C1.73).

5.552 *Preemployment Inquiries and Equal Employment Opportunity Law*

Guidelines for preemployment interviews and employment application forms are provided in this Equal Employment Opportunities Commission (EEOC) report. It includes definitions of "business necessity" and job relatedness and a discussion of the numerous items that are and are not allowed in interviews and applications.

Free; Educational Programs Branch, EEOC, Room 4295, 2401 E St. N.W., Washington, DC 20506. See also district offices of EEOC (C1.102).

5.553 Publications on Equal Employment Opportunity Testing

Personnel Testing and Equal Employment Opportunity, #052-015-00014-6, 48 pp., 95¢; GPO (see C1.0).

Employment Testing: Guide Signs, Not Stop Signs, #005-000-00021-1, 30 pp., 60¢; GPO (see C1.0).

5.554 *Questions and Answers on the OFCC Testing and Selection Order*

Some of the most common questions about testing and selection compliance raised by contractors and compliance officers are covered in this booklet from the Office of Federal Contract Compliance (OFCC). It defines such terms as test, validation, adverse effect, and disparate effect.

#029-016-00023, 40¢; GPO (see C1.0); see also regional offices of OFCC (C1.76).

5.555 Publications on Equal Employment Opportunity Counseling

Equal Employment Opportunity Counseling, A Guidebook, #006-000-00903-4, 32 pp., 55¢; GPO (see C1.0).

EEO Counseling

This manual, designed for training Equal Employment Opportunity counselors, covers interviewing techniques, basic legal issues, a discussion of typical problems, and a sample discrimination case from start to finish.

#006-000-00782-1, 50 pp., $1.40; GPO (see C1.0).

Training
(5.600-5.608)

5.600 Comprehensive Employment and Training Act of 1973

The Comprehensive Employment and Training Act of 1973 (CETA) makes funds available to local prime sponsors, usually mayors' offices, and to governors of states for balance-of-state areas outside of independent prime sponsor areas, for the development of locally tailored employment and training programs. Prime sponsors consist of areas with a population of 100,000 or more. Under some circumstances, various areas can be combined into a consortium and qualify as a prime sponsor.

No prime sponsor is obliged to use its funds in any one prescribed area according to a formula.

Rather, it must analyze area needs and develop a comprehensive employment and training plan for the area, using area educational institutions, vocational technical schools, and occupational and on-the-job training techniques permissible under law. It is, in short, an attempt to promote local control, accountability, and flexibility to tailor programs around local needs.

The following areas may be of relevance to employers:

Affirmative Action Recruitment. By law, CETA activities heavily emphasize services to the disadvantaged. Many prime sponsors have placement services themselves, and many subcontract with state employment services for job placement activities. CETA projects are important to employers attempting to meet labor force parities in their establishments.

Occupational Training. If a local CETA prime sponsor opts to invest in occupational training, such training shall be, according to Department of Labor regulations, "designed for occupations in which skills shortages exist and for which there is reasonable expectation of employment. In making such determinations, a prime sponsor shall utilize available community resources such as local employment service offices and the National Alliance of Businessmen." Businesses, therefore, which offer genuine occupational opportunities, and in which there is a documentable need, will benefit by making this known to the local CETA prime sponsor and to cooperating agencies such as vocational technical schools, the National Alliance of Businessmen, and the Employment Service (ES).

On-the-Job Training. CETA funds may be utilized to assist individuals at the entry level of employment or those needing additional skills for upgrading into higher skills. Prime sponsors may reimburse and provide inducements to private employers for the bona fide training and related costs of enrolling individuals in the program, provided that payments to employers organized for profit are made only for the costs of recruiting, training, and supportive services which are over and above those normally provided by the employer. The prime sponsor can reimburse the employer for extraordinary training costs for training on the job, up to a level not to exceed 50 percent of entry level wages.

For further information on CETA matters in a local area, contact the manpower division of the mayor's office or the local ES office.

5.601 National On-the-Job Training Program

The purpose of the National On-the-Job Training (OJT) program is to provide occupational training for unemployed and underemployed persons who cannot reasonably be expected to obtain appropriate full-time employment otherwise. National OJT contracts cross regional boundaries and may be national in scope. Project grants may be used to reimburse instructors; for administrative costs, supplies, education, and trainee allowances; and for supportive services. Eligible applicants are national organizations possessing the capacity, the ability, and the desire to carry out the program objectives.

Director, Office of National Programs, Employment and Training Administration, Department of Labor, Washington, DC 20213; 202-376-6093.

5.602 Vocational Education and On-the-Job Training

According to the Education Amendments Act of 1976, "Funds available to the states under Section 120 may be used for establishing or expanding cooperative vocational education programs through local educational agencies with the participation of public and private employers. Such programs shall include provisions that ... (c) provision is made, where necessary, for reimbursement of added costs to employers for on-the-job training of students enrolled in cooperative programs, provided such on-the-job training is related to existing career opportunities susceptible of promotion and advancement and which do not displace other workers who perform such work" (Public Law 94-482, Title II, subpart 2, section 122(c). States are required to develop long-term plans and they may or may not choose to allocate funds to this activity.

To determine whether cooperative on-the-job training possibilities exist for the private sector in a given state, contact the State Supervisor of Cooperative Education, Vocational Education Division, State Department of Education, in the state capitol.

5.603 Technical Assistance with Apprenticeship and Training

The national and regional offices of the Bureau of Apprenticeship and Training (Employment and Training Administration (ETA), Department of Labor) are authorized by the National Apprenticeship Act of 1937 to promote labor standards and safeguard the welfare of apprentices and guide, assist, and improve apprenticeship. Field staff, with offices in every state, work closely with employers, unions, and state apprenticeship agencies to develop programs and devise ways to give better training. The Bureau approves and registers programs, gives employers technical assistance on training programs, and looks for ways to expand apprenticeship opportunities.

Regional offices of ETA (see C1.72); or local ES offices.

5.604 *Model for Training the Disadvantaged: TAT (Training and Technology) at Oak Ridge, Tennessee*

#029-000-00192-8, 50 pp., 85¢; GPO (see C1.0).

5.605 Publications on Training

The following publications are available, as priced, from GPO (see C1.0).

Apprenticeship in the United States, A Bibliography, #029-000-00217-7, 64 pp., $1.05

Basic Education and Manpower Programs, #029-000-00230-4, 60 pp., $1.15

Directory of Postsecondary Schools with Occupational Programs, #017-080-01477-7, 456 pp., $5.80

Directory of Representative Work Education Programs, #017-080-01244-8, 338 pp., $2.95

Disincentives to Effective Employee Training and Development, #006-000-00938-7, 148 pp., $2.60

Occupational Manpower and Training Needs, Information for Planning Training Programs for the 1970's, #029-001-01347-7, 116 pp., $1.80

On the Job Training and Wage Hour Standards in Foreign Countries, #029-001-00139-8, 54 pp., $1.15

5.606 Work Experience at Facilities of Energy Research and Development Administration

Employees from private industry who are qualified by training and experience to take full advantage of the learning opportunity may receive on-the-job training and opportunity to become familiar with the energy processes applicable to specified uses by being assigned to work at an Energy Research and Development Administration (ERDA) facility. For assignments involving access to classified information, the private employer must obtain an access permit and the employee assigned must have appropriate access authorization. No charge is made to participate.

For further information, contact the ERDA field office responsible for the facility at which assignment is proposed, an ERDA field office (see C1.150), or Office of Industry, State, and Local Relations, ERDA, Washington, DC 20545; 202-376-4115.

5.607 Graduate School of the Department of Agriculture

Continuing education and training of managers, technicians, and employees can be accomplished at modest cost at the Graduate School of the Department of Agriculture, located in Washington, D.C. The Graduate School is open to the public and offers courses on a wide variety of subjects of value to business, but does not grant degrees.

Correspondence courses are available in such subjects as executive development, management, and supervision; accounting; engineering; English usage and writing; mathematics and statistics; and computer sciences.

The Individual Learning Center offers idividualized, programmed, and self-instructional courses which allow students to advance in easy step-by-step procedures through difficult material. Subjects available include grammar, punctuation, spelling, vocabulary, reading, metric system, fractions, decimals, algebra, calculus, statistics, accounting, management and supervision, computer programming, and office skills such as filing, shorthand, and business letters.

Employers with affirmative action problems may wish to consult with the staff of the Career Planning and Development Programs. Upward mobility of employees can depend upon increased educational and skills training opportunities, and the staff can help employers with the following services: (1) planning and developing upward mobility career development programs; (2) assessment services for determining training needs of employers; (3) vocational testing and counseling services for individuals or groups; and (4) development of special seminars and courses to meet specific needs.

Career Planning and Development Programs/Individual Learning Center, Room 6834, South Building, Department of Agriculture, Washington, DC 20250; 202-447-6693 or 6694.

For information on correspondence courses: Office of Independent Study Programs, Room 6847, South Building, Department of Agriculture, Washington, DC 20250; 202-447-7123.

For a copy of the current catalog of the Graduate School: Information Office, Room 6847, South Building, Department of Agriculture, Washington, DC 20250; 202-447-4419.

5.608 Cooperative Extension Service

The Cooperative Extension Service has agents in virtually every county in the country. The job of the agent is to provide technical assistance to whomever requests it on the development of resources—natural, human, and social—with a general orientation toward agricultural and rural development.

The agent can provide information and assistance in the following areas: *economic development*—how to bring in new businesses, new payrolls, new jobs, community recreation; *community services*—how to obtain better schools, water and utility systems, housing, sanitation, transportation, how to prepare for civil defense and natural disasters; and *human development*—how to set up training programs to teach people new skills to do new jobs, how to improve the quality of living and the future for youth who remain in the community.

Many businesses turn to the Cooperative Extension Service for technical information and training. Specialists help farmers and processors study the economic effects of foreign markets and consumer preferences. Professional people who serve agriculture—veterinarians, vocational agriculture teachers, bankers—use Extension information.

See county offices of Cooperative Extension Service; also state headquarters (C1.1).

Productivity and Human Resources Management (5.650-5.756)

Job Analysis and Restructuring (5.650-5.668)

5.650 Occupational Analysis Services

Most State Employment Services (ES) (Job Services) have an experienced occupational analyst on the staff who can assist employers in solving staffing and job description problems related to recruitment and retention. Such services involve assistance in developing more adequate and reliable job specifications or restructuring of jobs to eliminate labor supply bottlenecks and to limit turnover and absenteeism. Many of these specialists have been in the field for years. They perform this valuable function at no cost to the employer.

Local ES offices, or state headquarters (see C1.73).

5.651 *Job Analysis for Human Resource Management: A Review of Selected Research and Development*

Major job analysis techniques and methodologies are summarized in this monograph, and their applications to selected human resource management (HRM) activities are suggested. Several individual projects employing job analysis for HRM purposes are discussed in terms of goals and objectives, major methodological characteristics, and significant results. Four applications of job analysis data—job restructuring, education and training, qualifications examining, and performance evaluation—are discussed. Also covered are some of the critical, nontechnical aspects of a job analysis, such as staffing the study and gaining support for it. Various formats for writing task descriptions and scales for use in analyzing data are discussed. A list of names and addresses of experts in the field of job analysis is included, and a bibliography.

Manpower Monograph #36, #2900-00224, $1.50; GPO (see C1.0).

5.652 Publications on Job Analysis

The following publications are available, as priced, from GPO (see C1.0).

Job Analysis for Improved Job-Related Selection, #006-000-00917-4, 48 pp., $1.20
Job Demands and Worker Health, #017-033-0083-2, 342 pp., $3.25
How to Prepare and Conduct Job Element Examinations, #006-000-00893-3, 88 pp., $1.90
Improving Employee Performance, #006-000-00196-1, 116 pp., $1.50
Executive Management Bulletin, Analyzing Manpower Requirements Using Statistical Estimates, #041-001-00007-1, 19 pp., 35¢
Upward Mobility through Job Restructuring, #006-000-00916-6, 36 pp., 65¢
Position Classification, Pay and Employee Benefits, #006-000-00896-8, 87 pp., $1.55
Job Satisfaction, Is There a Trend? #029-000-00195-2, 57 pp., $1.20 (see 5.653)

5.653 *Job Satisfaction: Is There a Trend?*

Some of the major research on job satisfaction that has been conducted in the past forty years is reviewed in this report. The information is presented in five major sections: national trends in job satisfaction; demographic and occupational distribution of job satisfaction; motivational assumptions about what Americans look for in jobs; the implications of job satisfaction or dissatisfaction for workers, employers, and society at large; and experiments to improve working conditions. Appendixes and bibliography are included.

Manpower Research Monograph #30, #029-000-00195-2, $1.20; GPO (see C1.0).

5.654 *Developing Your Manpower*

Recruitment, training, personnel policies, and procedures are discussed in this book. It includes sample forms and form development aids: job specification form; checklists for designing an application form; application form; telephone checklist for applicants with work experience; selection and assignment practices checklist; checklist on induction of new workers; checklists on training needs, employee morale, absenteeism, turnover, and exit interviews; and analysis of training and upgrading programs. The book also includes bibliographies in personnel administration, interviewing, personnel records, employee induction and training, and turnover and absenteeism.

55 pp., 60¢; GPO (see C1.0).

5.655 *Dictionary of Occupational Titles*

The *Dictionary* provides a standard reference for job definitions and occupational classification.

Volume I, *Definition of Titles,* lists alphabetically over 35,000 different occupational titles, and defines and identifies by code number almost 22,000 separate occupations throughout the American economy.

Volume II, *Occupational Classification and Industry Index,* presents the occupational classification structure used by the United States Employment Service, consisting of two arrangements of jobs. The first arrangement groups jobs in numerical order according to some combination of work field, purpose, material, product, subject matter, generic term, and/or industry. The second arrangement groups jobs according to some combination of required general educational development, specific vocational preparation, aptitudes, interests, temperaments, and physical demands. It also lists all titles by industry.

Vol. I, 809 pp., $7.75; Vol. II, 656 pp., $6.75; GPO (see C1.0).

5.656 *Selected Characteristics of Occupations (Physical Demand, Working Conditions, Training Time), A Supplement to the Dictionary of Occupational Titles*

Individual physical demands, working conditions, and training time data for all jobs defined in the *Dictionary of Occupational Titles* are listed in this supplement. The information provides additional source material for determining job relationships in such activities as vocational counseling, personnel and manpower activities, training, rehabilitation, and placement.

280 pp., $2.85; GPO (see C1.0).

5.657 *Selected Characteristics of Occupations by Worker Traits and Physical Strength, Supplement to the Dictionary of Occupational Titles*

In a rearrangement of the data contained in

the first supplement, this supplement presents data by the worker trait groups contained in Volume II of the *Dictionary of Occupational Titles* (see 5.655). They are then subgrouped by level of strength required. The supplement will be useful in counseling and placement activities, and particularly useful in determining utilization, transfer, and placement possibilities for handicapped and aged workers.

156 pp., $1.50; GPO (see C1.0).

5.658 *Vocational Education and Occupations*

This document links occupations and their worker trait groups with vocational-technical education programs of state and local schools. It is published jointly by the Office of Education and the Employment and Training Administration.

307 pp., $2.25; GPO (see C1.0).

5.659 *Handbook for Job Restructuring*

A self-contained instructional and reference document, this brochure is designed to provide basic techniques and procedures for restructuring jobs and job systems. The methodology contained in this handbook is derived from a special adaptation of the job analysis concepts and techniques developed by the Employment Service over a 35-year period. Its application can assist in many programs and activities relating to better utilization of manpower resources and development of manpower potential.

46 pp., 55¢; GPO (see C1.0).

5.660 *Handbook for Analyzing Jobs*

A basic tool for the collection, classifying, and recording of job analysis data, this handbook is a self-contained instructional and reference textbook containing concepts, procedures, and illustrative situations for conducting a complete job analysis study. It incorporates a new approach and structured procedure for obtaining current and comprehensive job and worker requirements data necessary for bringing together people and jobs. The methodology can be adapted to meet specific objectives, such as job restructuring, job development, curriculum planning, and other career development programs and activities.

345 pp., $2.50; GPO (see C1.0).

5.661 *Relating General Educational Development to Career Planning*

While this guide is designed primarily for the use of Employment Service personnel and affiliated state agencies engaged in such activities as interviewing, counseling, and planning educational programs for applicants, it should also prove useful to persons involved in related activities in schools, vocational guidance or rehabilitation centers, industrial personnel offices, and other institutions or establishments. The data in this publication are intended to facilitate the process of career development by providing techniques for determining the general educational development level of an individual and relating it to the general educational development required for different jobs.

45 pp., 50¢; GPO (see C1.0).

5.662 *Occupations in Electronic Computing Systems*

Twenty-nine different occupations peculiar to electronic computing are described in this booklet. It gives the education, training, and characteristics required of the worker by the job and lists the physical activities and environmental conditions usually encountered. It also has a glossary of technical terms, a bibliography, and a listing of organizations, colleges, and universities where additional information about electronic computing systems may be obtained.

130 pp., 60¢; GPO (see C1.0).

5.663 *Occupations and Trends in the Dairy Products Industry*

Current occupations and processes in the dairy products industry, reflecting changes which have occurred and are occuring due to the introduction of automated equipment, are described in this brochure.

186 pp., 75¢; GPO (see C1.0).

5.664 *Job Descriptions and Organizational Analysis for Hospitals and Related Health Services*

A completely revised version of the 1952 edition, this 1971 publication contains introductory materials, department narratives, organizational charts, and 238 job descriptions, including hospital occupations which have emerged since 1952. It provides reliable occupational information for hospital administrators, for management at various levels, for high school and college guidance counselors in assiting young people to plan study courses and research projects, for librarians in supplementing other job information on library shelves, for vocational counselors in setting up training courses in health occupations, and for personnel of the employment service for use in their placement, counseling, and related activities.

732 pp., $4.25; GPO (see C1.0).

5.665 Health Impact of Psychological Job Stress

Investigations in the area of job stress are aimed at uncovering the elements of psychologically stressful work situations and their associated health consequences, as well as identifying techniques to alleviate such problems.

A study directed to these ends and completed in 1975 involved examination of the health records of workers from hospitals, mental health clinics, and insurance company files. Of the 130 different occupations for which data were tabulated, four rated high in the incidence of job-related stress. These were inspectors, sales managers, mechanics, and public relations specialists.

A report on the extent and distribution of shiftwork systems in American industry indicates that over 25 percent of the United States work force is engaged in some sort of shiftwork. Industries and occupations showing the highest percentage of workers on shiftwork include printing and publishing, automobile manufacturing, primary metals, transportation, and hospital services.

National or regional offices of NIOSH (see C1.31).

5.666 Human Elements in Work Accidents

Research on human elements in work accidents deals with psychosocial factors in the worker and the work situation that may influence accident risk. Such research also seeks to apply behavioral science principles to enhance job safety. The National Institute of Occupational Safety and Health (NIOSH) has done research in this area which has yielded a questionnaire for diagnosing job safety needs, and a set of guidelines, based on psychological principles, for improving safety performance.

National or regional offices of NIOSH (see C1.31).

5.667 *Suggestions for Control of Turnover and Absenteeism*

Labor turnover and absenteeism are analyzed and corrective procedures are presented in this book. A guide for analyzing the cost of turnover and examples of turnover cost analysis are presented, together with causes and types of turnover. Computing absenteeism rates and factors influencing absenteeism are discussed. Many of the same sample forms and checklists as found in *Developing Your Manpower* (see 5.654) are included, with the following additions: checklist on orientation practices, checklist on health and safety, time card for unauthorized absence, supervisor's daily report, daily personnel report, exit interview report, monthly analysis of turnover, and absenteeism.

#2900-00161, 55 pp., $1.00; GPO (see C1.0).

5.668 Publications on Flexitime

A Guide to Flexitime

In this handbook, flexitime is defined as a system which enables employees to determine their own hours of arrival and departure from the office. The pros and cons are discussed, and instructions for conducting an experimental program are presented.

#006-000-00809-7, 206 pp., 65¢; GPO (see C1.0).

Flexible Working Hours, Selected References

#029-000-00262-2, 28 pp., 65¢; GPO (see C1.0).

Productivity Guides and Information (5.700-5.714)

5.700 National Center for Productivity and Quality of Working Life

The National Center for Productivity and Quality of Working Life is composed of leading business, labor, government, and public representatives. It was initiated in 1970 in response to a growing concern about the importance of productivity to the nation and the comparative international position of the United States in this respect. Since its inception, the Center has sponsored and participated in a continuing national dialogue on the subject of productivity and has promoted a number of productivity-enhancing programs in many sectors of the economy. In 1975, the Center gained a three-year Congressional authorization.

The program of the Center is based on a national policy statement which states that the sources for improvement in productivity and work quality are to be found in the following human resource factors: job security, labor-management relations, quality of working life, and education and training. Additional determinates are technology, capital, and government regulatory practices.

The Center has undertaken and involved itself in many activities of great potential value to businesses everywhere. Examples of Center activity are:

Third Party Evaluations. The Center has sponsored third-party evaluations of innovative practices in industry in order to determine their relevance to productivity and exportability to other businesses. Such studies are undertaken with the cooperation of labor and management. An example is a longitudinal analysis of the controversial Scanlon Plan as it was installed in a plant in Texas.

Study Team Tours. The Center has organized special productivity/human resource management tours by study teams. For example, a labor-management group spent three weeks in Japan, examining some of the outstanding quality control practices of that country. Another brief tour was hosted by IBM at one of their office products plants. Participants were able to observe quality control systems run by workers and built into the production process itself, and small group total assembly methods whose job enrichment techniques are transferable to a variety of industries.

Labor-Management Conferences. The Center seeks to give publicity to best practices in labor-management relations. For example, six conferences have been held around the country in which labor-management teams that have participated in innovative practices have reported on their experiences. Smaller meetings have been held in which senior corporate officials have shared experiences with firms wishing to undertake specific productivity programs.

Publications. Some of the publications produced by the Center, and others produced by the Office of Productivity and Technology of the Bureau of Labor Statistics, are listed in this section, together with references to other related publications and programs.

Referral Service. The Center operates a small and growing referral service for queries about the wide range of productivity and human resources management innovations going on in the country. It hopes eventually to establish a formal national referral service and information clearinghouse.

The National Center for Productivity and Quality of Working Life, Washington, DC 20036; 202-254-9890.

5.701 Publications on Productivity and Quality of Working Life

The following publications are available, free, from the National Center for Productivity and Quality of Working Life, Washington, DC 20036.

A National Policy for Productivity Improvement

The policy and intentions of the National Center for Productivity and Quality of Working Life are set forth in a brochure entitled *A National Policy for Productivity Improvement.* It includes positions in the major areas of labor-management relations, job security, quality of working life, education and training, technology and capital investment, and government regulation.

Productivity and the Quality of Work: A Perspective on Job Reform

This is a speech given by the Assistant to the Executive Director of the National Center for Productivity and Quality of Working Life, Mr. Terence G. Jackson, to the Swedish Manufacturers Association. It provides an overview of the productivity problem facing most industrialized nations, with examples of successful attempts to deal with the problem. It briefly contrasts United States productivity rates with those of Japan and alludes to the variance in management styles which may be responsible for the discrepancy. Finally, it discusses the whole area of computer-aided design and manufacturing and what it may mean in the future.

Current Publications

Forty-three publications of the National Center for Productivity and Quality of Working Life are annotated in this 11-page brochure. Publication categories include public sector studies, private sector studies, human resource management projects (particularly labor-management committees), job security and the quality of working life, and general studies on productivity and the economy and the Center itself. A few of the listings are:

Improving Productivity through Industry and Company Measurement
Improving Productivity: A Description of Selected Company Programs
Proceedings: Conference on Productivity through Engineering
Measuring Productivity in the Construction Industry
Productivity in the Food Industry
Recent Initiatives in Labor-Management Cooperation
Pointers for Labor-Management Committees
Productivity and Job Security: Retraining to Adapt to Technological Change

5.702 *Productivity and Technological Innovation: Selected Information Sources*

Nongovernmental references are listed here, as well as reports on productivity and technological innovation related to business issued by the Department of Commerce, National Center for Productivity and Quality of Working Life, and the Department of Labor.

Free; Office of the Ombudsman for Business, Bureau of Domestic Commerce, Room 3800, Department of Commerce, Washington, DC 20230.

5.703 *Improving Productivity, A Description of Selected Company Programs, Series 1*

Programs currently in operation in five diverse companies within different industries throughout the country are described in this report. It focuses on how the productivity improvement efforts were organized, what was done, how it was done, and what was accomplished.

#052-003-00114-4, 31 pp., 85¢; GPO (see C1.0).

5.704 *A Plant-Wide Productivity Plan in Action; Three Years of Experience with the Scanlon Plan*

The Scanlon Plan is basically an incentive system made up of three basic elements: the philosophy of cooperation, a suggestion system designed to increase efficiency and reduce costs, and a formula to permit a monthly bonus based on increases in productivity.

This publication presents a description of the plan itself as it was installed in a major company in Texas, as well as information concerning the plan's impact on productivity. Those factors affecting workers' acceptance of the plan over time are cited, and sociopsychological outcomes are presented, based on workers' evaluations.

Issues concerning the construction and review of the bonus formula are discussed, and the suggestion system receives detailed analysis.

Productivity gains as high as 41 percent are shown over the three-year period, and high levels of job satisfaction were expressed by both management and staff. The report is noteworthy in that it provides a three-year audit of financial and behavioral outcomes, traces suggestion behavior through both high and low-production volume, contains new material for calculation of productivity bonuses, describes the successful installation and operation of the plan in a large corporation, and summarizes presently available knowledge for successfully installing the plan. Also included is an extensive bibliography of private sources of information on the subject.

Free; National Center for Productivity and Quality of Working Life, Washington, DC 20036.

5.705 *Guide to Productivity Improvement Projects*

Projects undertaken to improve productivity, primarily by cities and states, are described in this guide. The subject areas covered include most human resources management categories. Although referring only to the public sector, businesses may find some of the annotations interesting and valuable. Individual addresses and phone numbers are given for follow-up contacts.

By subscription only: Productivity Guide, International City Management Association, 1140 Connecticut Avenue N.W., Washington, DC 20036.

5.706 *BLS Publications on Productivity and Technology*

This bibliography compiled by the Office of Productivity and Technology of the Bureau of Labor Statistics (BLS) lists books, articles in the *Monthly Labor Review,* bulletins, and reports about productivity studies in numerous economic sectors. It also includes a short list of other bibliographies. The following categories are listed: (1) *productivity studies:* concepts and techniques of productivity measurement; productivity trends in the private economy; productivity trends in individual industries; productivity in the federal government; (2) *technology studies:* case studies; industry studies; innovation studies; general studies; (3) *international comparisons:* labor costs and productivity; wages, prices, and living costs; unemployment; and (4) *construction labor requirements and studies:* studies by construction type.

BLS (see C1.70).

5.707 BLS Bulletins on Productivity

Productivity—how to improve it, how it is changing and different ways it can be measured—is the subject of three bulletins published by the Bureau of Labor Statistics and available from GPO (see C1.0).

Improving Productivity: Labor and Management Approaches, BLS Bulletin 1715, 45¢

Productivity and the Economy, BLS Bulletin 1710, 50¢

The Meaning and Measurement of Productivity, BLS Bulletin 1714, 30¢

5.708 *Labor-Management Productivity Committees in American Industry*

The limited experience in the United States of joint labor-management committees in dealing with production and related problems is reviewed in this booklet. It begins with committees set up in the 20's and 30's; describes the joint committee effort during World War II and post-War experience with the Scanlon Plan and committees in government; and reviews recent initiatives in basic steel, retail food, trucking, railroads, and other areas.

National Commission on Productivity and Quality of Working Life, Washington, DC 20036.

5.709 *Employment Security and Plant Productivity Committees in the Steel Industry*

This is a presentation by I.W. Abel, President, United Steel Workers of America and Vice-Chairman of the National Commission on Productivity and Quality of Working Life. It describes labor and management experiences in the steel industry with the Employment Security and Productivity Committees, which have raised productivity levels and provided the foundation for the historic Experimental Negotiating Agreement of 1973.

National Commission on Productivity and Quality of Working Life, Washington, DC 20036.

5.710 *Employee Incentives to Improve State and Local Government Productivity*

In this report by the National Commission on Productivity and Quality of Working Life, existing employee incentive programs and guidelines for future programs are discussed.

#052-003-00090-3, 177 pp., $3.05; GPO (see C1.0).

5.711 *Situation Reports—Productivity Series*

Bulletins on human productivity, labor-management relations, and productivity through job enrichment form a complete set of bulletins dealing with productivity measurement and its usefulness in improving the overall productivity of business.

Office of the Ombudsman for Business, Bureau of Domestic Commerce, Room 3800, Department of Commerce, Washington, DC 20230.

5.712 Statistical Studies in Productivity and Technology

The Bureau of Labor Statistics (BLS) prepares indexes of output per hour (of all persons) both quarterly and annually for the private economy as well as for the farm, nonfarm, and manufacturing sectors, and for nonfinancial corporations. It also investigates productivity trends in individual industries. Currently it publishes annual indexes for about fifty industries and adds measures for several new ones each year. It also prepares unpublished indexes of output per employee-hour, covering 450 manufacturing industries. Technological changes and their implications for productivity are also studied, and international labor comparisons are made.

The following is a partial list of publications available, mostly free, from BLS (see C1.70).

Computer Manpower Manpower Outlook (Bulletin 1826)
Current Developments in Productivity
Labor and Material Requirements for Private Multifamily Housing Construction
Outlook for Technology and Manpower in Printing and Publishing
Productivity: A Selected, Annotated Bibliography (Bulletin 1776)
Productivity: An International Perspective (Bulletin 1811)
Productivity and Costs for Nonfinancial Corporations
Productivity and Costs in the Private Economy
Productivity and the Economy (Bulletin 1779)
Productivity Indexes for Selected Industries (Bulletin 1890)
Technological Change and Manpower Trends in Five Industries (Bulletin 1856) (see 5.713)
Technological Change and Manpower Trends in Six Industries (Bulletin 1817)
The Revised Worksheet: Results of a Pilot Study in 16 Firms (Bulletin 1846)

5.713 *Technological Change and Manpower Trends in Five Industries*

Some of the major technological changes emerging among selected American industries are appraised in this book, and the potential impact of these changes on productivity and occupations over the next five to ten years is discussed. The following five industries are examined: pulp and paper, hydraulic cement, aircraft and missiles, steel, and wholesale trade.

#029-001-01405-8, 64 pp., $1.20; GPO (see C1.0).

5.714 *Improving Employee Performance and Organizational Effectiveness*

This publication updates portions of Nos. 67 and 68 of the Personal Bibliography Series. It covers material received in the Civil Service Commission library during 1975. Topics covered are: job satisfaction, motivation, job enrichment and enlargement, productivity, and creativity.

Personal Bibliography Series No. 75, #006-000-00948-4, 64 pp., $1.25; GPO (see C1.0).

Services to Employees (5.750-5.756)

5.750 *An Employee Suggestion System for Small Companies*

The basic principles for starting and operating a suggestion system are explained in this booklet. It also warns of various pitfalls and gives examples and suggestions submitted by employees.

#SBA 1.12:1, 18 pp., 40¢; GPO (see C1.0).

5.751 Organizing a Credit Union

A federal credit union is a cooperative association organized to promote thrift among its members and to accumulate a fund from these savings to make needed loans to members for useful purposes at reasonable interest rates. It is a corporation chartered and supervised by the federal government through the National Credit Union Administration (NCUA). A credit union is not a government agency.

Credit unions encourage their members to use their share accounts to accumulate savings out of income as a means of building economic security for themselves and their families. In addition, credit unions provide loans for emergency and any other purposes which are worthwhile for their members, such as consolidation of debts, payment of medical bills, and financing of the purchase and repair of automobiles. In these ways, credit unions help their members to help themselves to a greater degree of financial stability.

Credit unions do not require outside financial support, and there is no necessary cost to any employer whose employees organize a credit union. Many employers, however, find them so beneficial in maintaining employee morale and efficiency that they are glad to provide desk space or a small room on the premises to serve as a credit union office. The Federal Credit Union Act authorizes the use of government space by federal employee credit unions.

When the employer is willing to permit payroll deductions for credit union payments, experience has shown that operations are simplified and that the credit union serves a larger number of members.

Many employers permit employees to spend some official time conducting credit union business, especially during the first few months of operation. The personnel office and the credit union can be mutually helpful in assisting employees to help themselves and in making the credit union generally effective as an employee service organization.

NCUA (see C1.108).

5.752 Layoff Job Placement Assistance

Most local offices of the State Employment Service (ES) (Job Service) and of Unemployment Compensation will cooperate with an employer forced into a layoff situation, by providing in-house registry for unemployment claims and for other employment. The employer can thereby provide employees with immediate access to the job market outside that business.

Local offices or state headquarters of ES (see C1.73).

5.753 Trade Adjustment Assistance for Employees

Increased imports can result in unemployment. To help American workers who become totally or partially unemployed as a result of increased imports, the Department of Labor provides trade readjustment allowances. These are weekly payments which are added to state unemployment insurance payments. Workers can also receive job search allowances, relocation allowances, and training.

Local State Employment Service office; or Office of Trade Adjustment Assistance, Bureau of International Labor Affairs, Department of Labor, Washington, DC 20210; 202-523-6225.

5.754 Reemployment Rights of Veterans

Reemployment rights of veterans after performance of military training or service are the province of the Office of Veterans' Reemployment Rights of the Department of Labor.

Labor-Management Services Administration (see C1.71).

5.755 *Federal Benefits for Veterans and Dependents*

The booklet, *Federal Benefits for Veterans and Dependents,* will be useful to employers interested in assisting their veteran employees by helping to see that they receive the benefits due them or their dependents.

95¢; GPO (see C1.0).

5.756 Social Security

The Social Security Administration maintains over 1,300 offices across the country, where trained representatives can answer questions about the Social Security Act and provide assistance to anyone who wishes to file a claim.

The booklet entitled *Your Social Security* describes the Social Security system and how it works, including the cash benefits, who is eligible, how much money is available, why payments may be stopped, and how the system is financed. It is available at local Social Security offices.

The Troubled Employee: Alcoholism and Drug Abuse in Business and Industry (5.800-5.812)

5.800 Current Awareness Service on Occupational Alcoholism

An employer considering a troubled-employee assistance program can benefit from the Current Awareness Service of the National Clearinghouse for Alcohol Information (NCAI). This service offers two types of selective and continuing notification of recent technical and scientific books, journal articles, and conference proceedings covering a variety of alcohol-related subjects; all publications related to occupational alcoholism programs are included.

First, a monthly service, by individualized interest cards, offers information on the new audio-visual materials. The cards provide complete bibliographic references and also explain how to obtain copies of the material. In some cases, document reprints are available from the Clearinghouse.

Second, bibliographic booklets containing references and annotations for recent documents which have been judged significant because of their valuable technical content will be distributed automatically every six months.

One-time registration for each of these services will ensure that materials continue to arrive.

The following interest card topics may be chosen: Economic Factors (Code 1110), Employee Alcoholism Programs (Code 1120), Vocational Training and Rehabilitation (Code 1130), Health Insurance (Code 1140), and Occupational Alcoholism Programs, a bibliographic booklet (Code GG2).

Free; NCIA, P.O. Box 2345, Rockville, MD 20852; 301-948-4450.

5.801 *Information and Feature Service* of National Institute of Alcohol Abuse and Alcoholism

Information and Feature Service is a newsletter service of the National Institute of Alcohol Abuse and Alcoholism (NIAAA). Articles are designed to assist readers in keeping abreast of developments in treatment of alcoholism and to help local publications with their coverage of the field.

Free; IFS Editor, NCAI, P.O. Box 2345, Rockville, MD 20852; 301-948-4450.

5.802 *Occupational Alcoholism, Some Problems and Some Solutions*

An historical perspective of industrial alcoholism program activity is given in this 14-page booklet. The roles of supervisors, management, and labor in establishing and operating an employee counseling service are described. It does not present a program itself.

Free; NIAAA, P.O. Box 2345, Rockville, MD 20852; 301-443-1273.

5.803 Publications on Occupational Alcoholism

Unless otherwise indicated, the following publications are available, free, from the National Clearinghouse for Alcohol Information (NCAI), P.O. Box 2345, Rockville, MD 20852; or call the National Institute on Alcohol Abuse and Alcoholism (NIAAA) at 301-443-1273).

Health Insurance Coverage for Alcoholism traces the development of health insurance mechanisms to cover the costs of treatment for alcoholism in the United States. It covers model health insurance benefit provisions, which, if employed, would assure adequate coverage for treatment of alcoholism.

Occupational Programming—Problems in Research and Evaluation addresses three problems: (1) the use of penetration rates, (2) the use of success rates, and (3) problems associated with the design of research and evaluation studies.

Simulation of an Occupational Alcoholism Program examines the potential of occupational programs using the system dynamics approach, exploring the effectiveness of dealing with reduced productivity and improving profit.

Effects of Treatment on Job Performance identifies existing alcoholism treatment modes and assesses the impact of these modes on the work performance of employed problem drinkers.

Influence of Alcohol on Work Performance provides insights related to the impact of alcohol use in various activities relevant to work. It also shows demographic characteristics which appear to influence the pattern of alcohol consumption and alcohol-related behavioral changes.

Occupational Programming Marketing Survey, Research Report Summary shows the characteristics and attitudes of business, industry, and labor in two Michigan areas. It provides data about the need for occupational programming services to help characterize the potential market for services, and to give insight as to the nature of services desired and the most effective way of selling them.

A Seminar on Marketing the Occupational Alcoholism Program, Appendix A, B, C reviews the history of occupational alcoholism program and the efforts of the NIAAA in this area. It also summarizes the seminar, covering areas from creating a need and demand for the product, to company benefits, to utilizing executive peer pressure, to methods of selling a program.

#PB248809/AS, 54 pp., $5.00; NTIS (see C1.17).

Occupational Programming—An Annotated Bibliography contains over 300 references in the field of occupational programming which appeared in a diversity of texts, journals, Congressional reports, and other types of publications.

An Approach to Supervisory Training for North Carolina Occupational Program's Employee Assistance Programs reflects in its curriculum the broad-based philosophy of the overall occupational programming effort in North Carolina.

Publications Order Form lists additional general materials available through the Clearinghouse.

5.804 *Occupational Programs Audio-Visual Directory*

The National Institute on Alcohol Abuse and Alcoholism (NIAAA) and the National Clearinghouse for Alcohol Information (NCAI) have compiled this guide to meet the growing number of requests for information on films dealing with alcoholism.

Free; NCAI, P.O. Box 2345, Rockville, MD 20852; 301-948-4450.

5.805 *Occupational Alcoholism, Problems, Programs, Progress*

The current status of occupational alcoholism, troubled-employee programs, the occupational programs branch of the National Institute on Alcohol Abuse and Alcoholism (NIAAA), a Navy program to fight alcoholism, several industry programs, and an interview with an AFL-CIO official are all discussed in this reprint from *Alcohol Health and Research World*.

Free; Occupational Programs Branch, NIAAA, P.O. Box 2345, Rockville, MD 20852; 301-443-1273.

5.806 *Alcohol Health and Research World*

Formerly an experimental publication available free to professionals or persons with a special interest in alcoholism, this NIAAA quarterly is now an established journal.

$6.40 per year; GPO (see C1.0).

5.807 Developing Language on Alcoholism in Labor-Management Contracts.

A demonstration research project at Johns Hopkins University was aimed at helping workers with drinking problems retain their employment. Another aim of the project was to gain insight which might be useful in stimulating the development of contract language among participating employers and unions. A report of the project appeared in *Monthly Labor Review*, June 1975.

The full report, *The Development of Language Pertaining to Alcoholism in Collective Bargaining Agreements*, Report #9, was published by the Johns Hopkins University School of Hygiene and Public Health, 615 N. Wolfe St., Baltimore, MD 21205.

5.808 *National Directory of Occupational Program Consultants*

Occupational program consultants are listed in this directory. They can provide help in identifying and assessing community treatment resources and in arranging meetings with treatment program directors; help in identifying appropriate personnel and materials for training of agency supervisors and educational programs for employees; sample materials (e.g., policy statements, training instruments, recordkeeping forms); support in efforts to gain acceptance of the program from the agency's management, personnel office, local organized labor, and medical staff.

The consultants listed are not directly associated with the NIAAA or any other federal agency. They are employed by the states they serve. However, they work closely with NIAA and other federal, state, local, and private agencies concerned with prevention and treatment of alcoholism in places where people work. In those states where a consultant is not listed, the address and telephone number of the state alcohol authority is indicated.

NIAAA, Rockville, MD 20852; 301-443-1273.

5.809 *Solving Job Performance Problems*

Productivity losses and costs to business in the state of Florida are cited as examples of the tremendous personnel problems that can occur when employees have behavioral difficulties. This booklet discusses the need for assistance to the troubled employee in terms of benefit to management, establishing policy and procedures, the role of supervisors, identifying the work problem, documenting the problem, referring the employee to treatment, and training supervisory personnel.

Free; NCAI, P.O. Box 2345, Rockville, MD 20852; 301-948-4450.

5.810 *Assessing the Impact of Occupational Programs*

The impact on business of occupational programs for the troubled employee is discussed in this paper. It includes a bibliography of other publications relevant to starting and managing a troubled-employee program.

16 pp., free; NCAI, P.O. Box 2345, Rockville, MD 20852.

5.811 *Drugs and Employment*

Research studies on drug abuse of all kinds, including alcohol abuse in industry and the general labor force, are compiled in this 107-page bibliography. Each study is annotated and summarized, with a narrative describing methodology, findings, conclusions, and recommendations. It also lists articles, conference proceedings, and guides for managers in dealing with drug abuse in the labor force. It can serve as a basic reference and guide.

#1724-00424, $1.80; GPO (see C1.0).

5.812 *Obstacles to Treatment for Blue Collar Workers*

This report from the Director of the National Institute of Mental Health investigates why blue collar workers shun psychiatrists and mental health centers. It focuses workers in the auto industry.

#017-024-00509-6, 9 pp., 35¢; GPO (see C1.0).

Films on Personnel Management (5.850-5.855)

5.850 National Audio-Visual Center: Information, Services, and Programs

The National Audio-Visual Center (NAC) was created in 1969 to serve the public by (1) making federal audio-visual materials available for use through distribution services and (2) serving as the central clearinghouse for all United States government audio-visual materials.

Through the Center's distribution programs—sales, rentals, and loan referrals—the public has access to audio-visual materials covering a variety of subjects. Major subject concentrations in the Center's collection include medicine, dentistry, and the allied health sciences; education; aviation and space technology; vocational and management training; safety; and the environmental sciences.

Many of the Center's audio-visual materials are designed for general use, while others are designed for specific training or instructional programs. Instructional materials are appropriate for classroom use or for self-instruction. To complement and increase the effectiveness of these audio-visual programs, many are accompanied by printed materials such as teacher manuals, student workbooks, and scripts.

To keep the public informed about the availability of federal audio-visual materials, NAC sponsors three information services: reference, printed materials, and a master data file.

Reference. A trained reference staff at the Center will respond quickly to questions on federal audio-visual materials. These responses may range from a direct answer to the compilation of filmographies by subject or by federal agency.

Printed Materials. Printed materials issued by the Center are the principal means of keeping the public informed of the availability of federal audio-visual materials. *A Catalog of United States Government Produced Audio-Visual Materials* (Washington, 1974) lists over 4,000 titles available for sale or rental from the Center. Also available are minicatalogs by subject area, brochures on single and multiple titles, and filmographies on specialized subjects and on materials produced by individual federal agencies.

Master Data File. The Center is responsible for developing and maintaining a master data file on all federal audio-visual material. This resource is used by the reference staff in title and subject searches.

Federal audio-visual materials are available through the following programs of the NAC:

Sales. Most major audio-visual formats are available for purchase through the Center. These include motion pictures, video formats, slide sets, audiotapes, and multimedia kits. Other audio-visual formats (e.g., video-cassettes) for motion pictures also can be supplied. Preview prior to purchase is available for 16 mm. motion pictures.

Rental. Only 16 mm. motion pictures, representing 80 percent of the Center's collection, are available through the rental program.

Loan Referrals. Free loan distribution of 16 mm. motion pictures is available to the public from commercial distributors. The Center keeps informed of all federally sponsored free loan programs and refers the user to the nearest free loan distributor.

For the NAC catalog, write National Audio-Visual Center, Reference Section, General Services Administration, Washington, DC 20409; 301-763-1896.

5.851 Filmographies on Personnel Management

The following filmographies on personnel management are available, free, from Reference Section—Code A, National Audio-Visual Center, General Services Administration, Washington, DC 20409.

G062 Films on Employer-Employee Relations
H023 Films on Supervision
G016 Films on Training in the Food and Drug Industries
H008 Films on Career Development and Upward Mobility
G063 Films on Careers and Career Education
F010 Films on Counseling
C001 Audio-Visual Materials on Professions and Careers

5.852 Filmographies on Business Management

The following filmographies on business management are available, free, from Reference Section—Code A, National Audio-Visual Center, General Services Administration, Washington, DC 20409.

C004 Films on Business Management and Office Administration
H016 Films on Business Ownership and Management
H029 Films on the Economics of Inflation
H014 Films on Information and Communication
G030 Films on Office Mail Operations and the Mail System
H016 Films on Operating a Small Business, Including Communicating with Customers and Employees

5.853 Films on Personnel Management

The following films on personnel management are available for sale or rental (except no rental of 8 mm. film), as priced, from National Audio-Visual Center, General Services Administration, Attention: Order Section NACDO, Washington, DC 20409.

Arbitration of a Grievance

A sequel to *Anatomy of a Grievance*, this film is designed for use in public sector labor-management relations training. It shows the arbitration of a grievance by an arbitrator and teaches persons handling arbitration cases the techniques of preparation and presentation.

#005153, 36 min., sound, color, sale $163.50, rental $15.00.

At the Table

The negotiation of two federal bargaining issues, subcontracting and work schedules, is shown, as well as tactics and techniques of negotiation as practiced at the bargaining table.

#005412, 46 min., 16 mm., sound, color, sale $204.25, rental $17.50.

Counting What Counts—Work Counts

The meaning, techniques, and uses of work count as a scoring system for the supervisor's evaluation of employees are illustrated through animation.

#003572, Agency #MF61-5721, 10 min., 16 mm., sound, color, sale $45.50.

Now That's Upward Mobility

The concept and program components of upward mobility for lower level employees is introduced. An instructor's guide with script, pre and post-tests, discussion questions, and reproducible handouts are included. Designed for the orientation and training of supervisors, managers, EEO specialists, employee representatives, and upward mobility planners, this film is suitable for federal agencies, state and local governments, and private industry.

#009095, 67 2x2 color slides, 15 min. audiocassette, sale $12.00.

Remember My Name

In this film, the frustrations of employees in lower level, dead-end job situations are illustrated. The need for management and supervisory actions is stressed, to bring about equality of opportunity in employment and upward mobility within the federal government. The series was designed for use in federal agency supervisory and management training courses.

#000449, 18 min., 16 mm., sound, color, sale $81.75.

Basic Principles of Supervision, Part 3

How people should be helped to improve themselves, working in a safe and healthful environment, is the subject of this film. It emphasizes that people must have opportunities to show that they can accept greater responsibilities.

#004540, 29 min., 16 mm., sound, black and white, sale $131.75.

A Good Place to Start

Young federal employees talk about their jobs and their futures, showing how these individuals relate to their supervisors, co-workers, and work situations.

#366050, 29 min., 16 mm., sound, color, sale $122.50, rental $12.50.

Anything is Possible—with Training

Examples of successful employee training in a telephone answering service, a boatyard, and a newspaper office convince a woman planning to open a restaurant that employee training is essential to business success.

#141045, 14 min., 16 mm., sound, color; sale 16 m., $63.50, rental 16 mm., $10.00; sale 8 mm., $41.75 (#009074).

The Man or Woman for the Job

The importance of effective employee recruitment and selection procedures is made clear through the experiences of a small print shop owner who learns the hard way that such procedures are necessary. Brief vignettes of other types of business reflect various sources of employees.

#002338, 15 min., 16 mm., sound, color; sale 16 mm., $68.00, rental 16 mm., $10.00; sale 8 mm., $42.00 (#009089).

Games

The "games people play," intentionally or not, that keep minority members from advancing as their abilities allow are graphically exposed here.

#004672, 32 min., 16 mm., sound, color; sale $145.25, rent $12.50.

5.854 Filmographies on Minorities and the Disadvantaged

The following filmographies are available, free, from Reference Section—Code A, National Audio-Visual Center, General Services Administration, Washington, DC 20409.

G029 Films on Minorities, EEO, and Civil Rights
H026 Films on Community Youth Development Programs
F010 Films on Group Behavior and Performance-Centered Counseling
H036 Films on Reality Orientation
H010 The "To Live Again Series" of Films, with Viewpoints of Mentally, Physically, and Socially Rehabilitated Individuals
H025 Films on Aging, with Viewpoints of the Elderly

5.855 Filmographies on Drug and Alcohol Abuse

The following filmographies are available, free, from Reference Section—Code A, National Audio-Visual Center, General Services Administration, Washington, DC 20409.

H033 Audio-Visual Materials on Alcohol and Alcohol Abuse
H009E Films on Drug Abuse Counseling
H009C "The Social Seminar Series" of Films on Drug Abuse, Addiction, and Drug Education
H009G "The Professional Drug Films Series" on Drug Addiction and Counseling

Chapter 6

AFFIRMATIVE ACTION, OSHA, AND PRODUCT SAFETY

CHAPTER ABSTRACT

Resources for affirmative action planning and implementation, and for occupational safety and health programs, are concentrated in this chapter.

"Affirmative Action Guides and Directories" (6.0-6.12) describes publications which cover all phases of affirmative action planning. The subsequent sections list information and services in specific areas; e.g., sex and age discrimination, recruitment, training, and testing and counseling.

"Sources for Planning Data and Technical Assistance" (6.50-6.64) focuses on sources of statistics for analysis of labor force composition and trends in small areas. It includes both guidebooks to data sources and publications, and services which actually contain data.

"Job Analysis" (6.100-6.111) speaks to the problem of creating jobs in which employee motivation and upward mobility are maximized. Information on job satisfaction, turnover, and absenteeism are included because of their frequent connection with the problem of job structuring.

Basic publications in the field of occupational safety and health are described in "Guides and Information" (6.350-6.364). This section includes industry guidelines, recordkeeping requirements, available loans, and bibliographies.

Services which can keep managers aware of developments in the field are described in "Current Awareness Services" (6.400-6.403).

Preventative consultation services which industry can call upon without threat of citation are listed in "On-Site Technical Assistance" (6.450-6.454).

"Training" (6.500-6.517) explains how to stay abreast of new Occupational Safety and Health Administration (OSHA) training programs and lists a wide variety of educational sources and materials for general industry and specific industries.

The two sections on data (6.550-6.613) list general data and information sources on OSHA applied research, and data sources on specific health hazards.

"Consumer Product Safety" (6.700-6.705) lists some of the publications, technical assistance, and technology sources available in the field.

Affirmative Action and Equal Employment Opportunity (6.0-6.301)

Affirmative Action Guides and Directories (6.0 - 6.12)

6.0 *Equal Employment Opportunity Compliance Officer's Handbook*

The Office of Investigation and Compliance of the Employment Training Administration (ETA) has published *An Equal Employment Opportunity Compliance Officer's Handbook,* which answers questions about compliance reviews and complaint investigations.

An updated version of the 1972 publication of the same title, the new guide was developed with the direct assistance of experienced regional officers of the Equal Employment Opportunity Commission.

Free; Office of Investigation and Compliance, ETA (see C1.72).

6.1 *Guide to Resources for Equal Employment Opportunity and Affirmative Action*

In addition to federal sources, the *Guide to Resources for Equal Employment Opportunity and Affirmative Action* also includes numerous privately published guides and data sources. Its entire table of contents is presented:

55 pp., single copies free; Publications Unit, EEOC (see C1.102).

6.2 *Affirmative Action and Equal Employment: A Guidebook for Employers*

The two volumes of this affirmative action manual constitute the major publication of the Equal Employment Opportunity Commission (EEOC) for employers.

Volume I leads the reader through the legal bases for affirmative action and explains exactly what is considered discriminatory under law and what remedies have been prescribed. It then moves into the actual construction of an affirmative action plan, describing the need for a corporate policy statement and for internal and external publicity, as well as the need for an analysis of the internal labor force structure, including levels of employment and areas of underutilization. Setting goals and timetables and developing specific action plans to meet those goals is discussed in terms of recruitment, selection standards, upward mobility, pay and benefits, training, layoff and recall, and more. It also discusses establishment of an internal audit and reporting system for monitoring and evaluation.

Volume II is a set of appendixes to Volume I which includes sample documents and internal reporting forms for various program phases, data sources for labor force utilization analysis, recruitment resources, guidelines and regulations, and EEOC publications.

Single set of guidebooks, free; Affirmative Action, Publications Unit, EEOC (see C1.102). Additional copies may be purchased from GPO (see C1.0), #052-015-00024-3, $2.45 per set.

6.3 *Developing Your Manpower*

Recruitment, training, personnel policies, and procedures are discussed in this book. It includes sample forms and form development aids; a job specification form; checklists for designing an application form; an application form; a telephone checklist for applicants with work experience; a selection and assignment practices checklist; a checklist on induction of new workers; checklists on training needs, employee morale, absenteeism, turnover, and exit interviews; and an analysis of training and upgrading programs. The book also includes bibliographies in personnel administration, interviewing, personnel records, employee induction and training, and turnover and absenteeism.

55 pp., 60¢; GPO (see C1.0).

6.4 Publications on Equal Employment

The following publications are available, as priced, from GPO (see C1.0).

Research Report No. 44: Minorities and Women in Referral Units in Building Trades Unions, #0-554-254, $1.10

Employment Profiles of Minorities and Women in 20 Large SMSA's, #Y3.EQ2, $2.25

Toward Fair Employment and the EEOC: A Study of Compliance Procedure under Title VII of the Civil Rights Act of 1964, #Y3.EQ2:EN7/3, $1.70

Legislative History of Titles VII and XI of the Civil Rights Act of 1964, #0-387-902, $2.50

Legislative History of the Equal Employment Opportunity Act of 1972 Amending Title VII of the Civil Rights Act of 1964, #74-699-0, $11.25

6.5 *Federal Labor Laws and Programs, A Layman's Guide*

Summaries of laws and descriptions of Equal Employment Opportunity programs are included in this book.

#029-003-00122-6, 254 pp., $2.10.

6.6 *Civil Rights Digest, A Quarterly of the United States Commission on Civil Rights*

Current issues concerning civil rights are presented in this publication.

No subscription; single copy prices 85¢-$1.65; GPO (see C1.0).

6.7 *Statement on Affirmative Action for Equal Employment Opportunities*

The legal background supporting affirmative remedial action is described.

Free; Commission on Civil Rights, Washington, DC 20425.

6.8 Brochure on Enforcement Programs

The enforcement programs of the Civil Service Commission, the Office of Federal Contract Compliance Programs of the Department of Labor, and the Equal Employment Opportunity Commission are analyzed and evaluated in a brochure entitled *The Federal Civil Rights Enforcement Effort—174, Volume V: "To Eliminate Employment Discrimination."*

Free; Commission on Civil Rights, Washington, DC 20405.

6.9 "Job Discrimination and Affirmative Action"

Civil Rights Digest, Vol. 7, No. 3, Spring 1975, free; Commission on Civil Rights, Washington, DC 20425.

6.10 Affirmative Action for Federal Contractors

Federal contractors or subcontractors are obliged to develop affirmative action plans for minorities, women, the handicapped, and Vietnam-era veterans in all their establishments. Overall responsibility for monitoring affirmative action activities rests with the Office of Federal Contract Compliance (OFCC), Employment Standards Administration (ETA), Department of Labor. However, contractors or subcontractors are immediately responsible to the affirmative action officers in their particular contracting agency. (The regional and area offices of OFCC are listed in C1.76).

Exact affirmative action requirements for federal contractors and subcontractors are published in the *Federal Register.* For free copies of all relevant issues, contact an area office of the OFCC or the compliance officer of the contracting agency (see C1.76 and C1.101).

Also of relevance are the following publications, available from OFCC (see C1.76).

Executive Order 11246 ((*as Amended by Executive Order 11375)*

Revised Order No. 4: Affirmative Action Guidelines (with amendments as of July 12, 1974

Revised Order No. 14: Contractor Evaluation Procedures (with amendments as of May 28, 1975)

Guidelines on Discrimination because of National Origin, Religion and Sex

Affirmative Action for Equal Employment Opportunity

6.11 Publications of the Equal Employment Opportunities Commission

The following publications are available from the Equal Employment Opportunity Commission (see C1.102).

Could You be Practicing Illegal Job Discrimination and Not Even Know It? (Quiz for employers)

EEOC at a Glance

Job Discrimination—Laws and Rules You Should Know
Guidelines on discrimination because of sex, religion, national origin, and employee selection procedures are contained in this brochure.

Questions and Answers Concerning the EEOC Guidelines on Discrimination because of Sex

Equal Employment Opportunity Report
Job patterns for minorities and women in private industry are described. Vols. 1-10.

Know Your Rights! What You Should Know about Equal Employment Opportunity (for employees)

What Employers, Unions and Employment Agencies Should Know about Equal Employment Opportunity

Employment Problems of Women: A Classic Example of Discrimination

6.12 *Affirmative Action Planning for State and Local Governments*

A three-day training session in affirmative action, aimed primarily at the public sector, is the subject of this guide. A great deal of information is included which may be useful to business in defining equal opportunity problems and designing and implementing an action plan; information is also included on the role of the change agent, conducting a skills survey, and sex discrimination guidelines.

#0600-00758, $2.80; GPO (see C1.0).

Sources for Planning Data and Technical Assistance (6.50-6.64)

6.50 *Directory of Data Sources on Racial and Ethnic Minorities*

Annotated references to demographic, social, and economic data sources for various racial and ethnic minorities are given in this report.

#029-001-01777-4, $1.50; GPO (see C1.0).

6.51 *A Guide to Sources of Data on Women and Women Workers for the United States and for Regions, States and Local Areas*

Major data sources on population, education,

civilian labor force, employment, unemployment, occupation, industry, and labor reserve are listed in this comprehensive guide. The sources are given by region, state, or standard metropolitan statistical area. It includes basic data sources on minorities as well as women. Cited are materials from the Bureau of the Census and from the Department of Health, Education and Welfare, as well as extensive materials from the Bureau of Labor Statistics and Employment Standards Administration.

Free; Women's Bureau (see C1.78).

6.52 Workforce Data Packages

Workforce Data Packages to assist employers in preparing utilization analysis and affirmative action plans are being prepared by state employment services to meet federal contract compliance requirements. Packages include information by race and sex on population, labor force, employment status, occupations of employed persons, last occupations of experienced unemployed persons, and other information.

Request information for specific labor areas from appropriate research directors of State Employment Services (see C1.73).

6.53 Publications on Data Sources for Development of Goals for Minorities and Women

United States Working Women, A Chartbook
#029-001-01780-4, 72 pp., $1.75; GPO (see C1.0).

Women Workers in Regional Areas and in Large States and Metropolitan Areas
1971, free; Women's Bureau (see C1.78).

Facts on Women Workers of Minority Races
1974, free; Women's Bureau (see C1.78).

Women Workers (by State), 1970
Free; Women's Bureau (see C1.78).

Job Patterns for Minorities and Women in Private Industry
Numbers employed in companies filing EEO-1 reports are given by industry, industry group, major occupation group, sex and minority group, for the nation, states, and standard metropolitan statistical areas. More recent data are available on microfilm. Data on minority and female participation in joint apprenticeship programs are also available.

10 volumes (United States summary and nine census regions), 1975, free; Office of Research, EEOC (see C1.102).

Minorities and Women in State and Local Government, 1973 U.S. Summary
Numbers of minorities and women (by ethnic group) employed by state and local governments filing EEO-4 report forms are given by job categories and functions. There are also statistical tables and narrative analysis. Future publications will contain more detailed data by regions.

#5203-00051, $2.90; GPO (see C1.0). or Publications Unit, EEOC (see C1.102).

1973 State and Local Government Functional Profile Series
Separate volumes present detailed employment data by race, sex, and job categories in specific functional areas of government. Volumes now available are: Part I: *Financial Aid;* Part II: *Streets and Highways;* Part II: *Public Welfare;* Part IV: *Police Protection.*

Free; Publications Unit, EEOC (see C1.102).

Minorities and Women in Referral Units in Building Trades
This report is based on statistics collected in 1972 from local unions' Report EEO-5.

#5203-00038, $1.10; GPO (see C1.0).

Employment Profiles of Minorities and Women in 20 Large SMSA's, 1972
#5203-30039, $2.25; GPO (see C1.0).

U.S. Working Women
National data are included on employment and unemployment, educational status, job tenure, work-life expectancy, transportation, selected indicators by race and Spanish origin, and other factors affecting women at work.

#029-001-01780-4, $1.75; GPO (see C1.0).

Geographic Profile of Employment and Unemployment
Data are given on labor force, employment, and unemployment, by race and sex, for the nation, states, and standard metropolitan statistical areas.

Annual, free; BLS (see C1.70).

Minorities and Women in the Health Fields

Selected data are given on racial/ethnic minority groups and women in the health fields. The report includes data on applicants, workers, and enrollment in health occupations schools.

DHEW Publication #HRA 75-22, free; Public Health Service, Bureau of Health Resources Development, Building 31, Room 5B63, Bethesda, MD 20014.

6.54 *Directory of Federal Statistics for Local Areas*

Information available on standard metropolitan statistical areas, counties, and cities is described in this directory.

$1.00; GPO (see C1.0).

6.55 *Directory of Non-Federal Statistics for States and Local Areas: A Guide to Sources*

Information available for individual states, the District of Columbia, Puerto Rico, Guam, and the Virgin Islands, for specified substate areas and for thirteen major subjects, is described in this directory. Detailed bibliographic entries list the publications containing the statistics and the issuing agency.

$6.25; GPO (see C1.0).

6.56 State and Local Data Sources for Affirmative Action Planning

State and Local Employment Services

Basic data and special studies on employment and unemployment are available in these offices. Many state services prepare employment and unemployment surveys and market studies for special skills.

Contact Employment Service offices of research, employer relations, or labor market staff at state level (see C1.73).

State and City Department of Human Resources, and Departments of Industry, Labor, or Commerce

Employment, unemployment, and skill surveys are conducted in these offices. A listing of major state (as well as federal) agencies concerned with manpower, employment, industrial relations, and fair employment practices that can provide data and information on training programs and recruitment sources is *Labor Offices in the United States and Canada,* Employment Standards Administration (see C1.74).

Local and State Chambers of Commerce

These can be located through the local telephone directory.

Regional Offices, Equal Employment Opportunity Commission

This commission offers assistance on data and recruitment sources (see C1.102).

Regional Offices, Women's Bureau, Department of Labor

See C1.78.

6.57 *County and City Data Book*

Demographic, social, and economic data for counties, cities, standard metropolitan statistical areas, and urbanized areas are presented from the most recent censuses as well as from other governmental and private sources. The topics include: agriculture, bank deposits, births, marriages, climate, home equipment, hospitals, family income, migration, population characteristics, presidential vote, local government finances, retail trade, school enrollment, selected services, manufacturing, and more. The book also includes maps for each state showing counties, standard metropolitan statistical areas, and large cities; explanatory notes and source citations; and appendixes that expand or explain the coverage of the tables. A unique feature of this book is the availability of its contents on compendia tape and punchcards.

$18.65; GPO (see C1.0).

6.58 Labor Statistics Data Base

Labor force information is available for metropolitan areas, cities, counties, states, census tracts, and other regions, with breakouts such as industry, salary levels, age, education levels, and distance to work.

The data base was assembled by the Lawrence Berkeley Laboratories, under contract to the Department of Labor, from the Labor Censuses of 1970 and 1973.

NTIS (see C1.17); or contact a NTIS information specialist for help in obtaining a suitable report: 703-321-8525.

6.59 1970 Census of Population

The following publications are available, as priced, from GPO (see C1.0) or Department of Commerce (see C1.10).

1970 Census of Population: General Social and Economic Characteristics PC (1) - C Series

Separate reports are included for each state, with data on age, race, sex, Spanish heritage, mother tongue, years of school completed, vocational training, employment status, occupation, industry, and other factors. Data are presented for counties, standard metropolitan statistical areas (SMSA), urban areas, and places of 2,500 inhabitants sor more.

53 reports, $121.75; prices vary for individual state reports.

1970 Census of Population, Detailed Characteristics PC (1) - D Series

More detailed breakdowns of education, training, and occupation are given, cross-classified by sex, age, and race. Information is available for the nation, states, SMSA's, and large urban areas.

U.S. Census of Population 1970, Final Report PC (2) 7 (C) Occupation by Industry

Breakdowns in this report are by race, national origin, and sex.

$7.25.

Maps—Number of Indians by Counties of the United States: 1970 (GE-50 No. 549); Number of Negro Persons by Counties of the United States: 1970 (GE-50 No. 47); and Negro Population as Percentage of Total Population by Counties of the United States: 1970 (GE-50 No. 48)

50¢ each.

Persons of Spanish Origin in the United States, March 1975

This publication reports data on age, sex, marital status, education, employment status, major occupation, family income, and low income status by region (SMSA and other).

Current Population Reports, Series P-20, No. 290, issued February 1976, $1.50.

U.S. Census of Population Final Report PC 2 8 (B), Earnings by Occupation and Education

Detailed breakdowns are by industry, race, sex, and national origin.

$4.50.

6.60 County Level Socioeconomic Data Base

Market forecasters, local governments, business planners, and demographers can use the National Technical Information Service (NTIS) county-level socioeconomic statistical data base to produce specialized reports. The data base, compiled by the Economic Development Administration, merges the first and fourth counts of the 1970 Census of Population and Housing with summary data from the 1960 census, ***County and City Data Book, County Business Patterns,*** and income data files.

Contact a NTIS information specialist for help in formulation of a search request and for an estimate of search costs and time.

NTIS (see C1.17).

6.61 Neighborhood Population and Housing Data

Census tract reports from the census of population and housing present information on both population and housing subjects for small areas within each of the standard metropolitan statistical areas in the country. Population subjects include household and family characteristics, voter participation, fertility, school enrollment, number of minorities, migration patterns, and many more population profile subjects. Housing subjects include tenure, number of rooms, plumbing facilities, year built, property value, and more. The reports can be extremely useful in many areas of business management, including locating or relocating a business, market research, and sales territory layout and evaluation.

Areas covered by census data and examples of data use in business are described in Appendix C2.

Department of Commerce District Offices (see C1.10); or Subscriber Services Section, Bureau of the Census, Washington, DC 20233; see also Bureau of the Census (C1.13, C1.14).

6.62 *Workforce Data Sources, by State, for Developing Affirmative Action Plans*

Office of Federal Contract Compliance (see C1.76).

6.63 Technical Assistance in Affirmative Action Compliance

The Equal Employment Opportunity Commission (EEOC) is directed by Section 705 of the Civil Rights Act of 1964, as amended by the Equal Employment Opportunity Act of 1972, "to furnish persons subject to this title such technical assistance as they may request to further their compliance with this title." The Division of Voluntary Compliance Programs is charged with this responsibility. This office was originally conceptualized as the agency's positive, nonadversary arm, coequal with the agency's office for enforcement activities.

The Voluntary Programs office is responsible for providing technical assistance to employers, unions, and others in the development of policies and procedures in compliance with requirements under Title VII. Assistance ranges from intensive, in-depth review of current employment statistics and systems, culminating in development of broad total affirmative action programs, to information on one or more specific parts of such programs, such as application forms, recruitment and selection practices, appropriate data sources, utilization analysis computation, and compensation and benefit systems. Also available are detailed guidance and assistance in developing and reviewing written plans.

EEOC (see C1.102).

6.64 Seminars and Educational Programs

The Voluntary Programs office of the Equal Employment Opportunity Commission (EEOC) works with professional and trade associations in developing and participating in affirmative action seminars, workshops, conferences, training programs, and other educational programs. It can also assist such associations in the preparation of articles and guidebooks.

EEOC (see C1.102).

Job Analysis (6.100-6.111)

6.100 Occupational Analysis Services

Most State Employment Services (ES) (Job Services) have an experienced occupational analyst on the staff who can assist employers in solving staffing and job description problems related to recruitment and retention. Such services involve assistance in developing more adequate and reliable job specifications or restructuring of jobs to eliminate labor supply bottlenecks and to limit turnover and absenteeism. Many of these specialists have been in the field for years. They perform this valuable function at no cost to the employer.

Local offices or state headquarters of ES (see C1.73).

6.101 Publications on Job Analysis

The following publications are available, as priced, from GPO (see C1.0).

Job Analysis for Human Resource Management: A Review of Selected Research and Development, #029-000-00224-0, 92 pp., $1.50 (see 6.102)

Job Analysis for Improved Job-Related Selection, #006-000-00917-4, 48 pp., $1.20

Job Demands and Worker Health, #017-033-00083-2, 342 pp., $3.25

How to Prepare and Conduct Job Element Examinations, #006-000-00893-3, 88 pp., $1.90

Improving Employee Performance, #006-000-00196-1, 116 pp., $1.50

Analyzing Manpower Requirements Using Statistical Estimates, Executive Management Bulletin, #041-001-00007-1, 19 pp., 35¢

Upward Mobility through Job Restructuring, #006-000-00916-6, 36 pp., 65¢

Position Classification, Pay and Employee Benefits, #006-000-00896-8, 87 pp., $1.55

Job Satisfaction, Is There a Trend? #029-000-00195-2, 57 pp., $1.20 (see 6.103)

6.102 *Job Analysis for Human Resource Management: A Review of Selected Research and Development*

Major job analysis techniques and methodologies are summarized in this monograph, and their application to selected human resource management (HRM) activities is suggested. Several individual projects employing job analysis for HRM purposes are discussed in terms of goals and objectives, major methodological characteristics, and significant results. Four applications of job analysis data—job restructuring, education and training, qualifications examining, and performance evaluation—are discussed. Also covered are some of the critical, nontechnical aspects of a job analysis, such as staffing the study and gaining support for it. Various formats for writing task descriptions, and scales for use in analyzing data, are discussed. A list of names and addresses of experts in the field of job analysis is included, and a bibliography.

Manpower Monograph #36, #2900-00224, $1.50; GPO (see C1.0).

6.103 *Job Satisfaction: Is There a Trend?*

Some of the major research on job satisfaction that has been conducted in the past forty years is reviewed in this report. The information is presented in five major sections: national trends in job satisfaction; demographic and occupational distribution of job satisfaction; motivational assumptions about what Americans look for in jobs; the implications of job satisfaction or dissatisfaction for workers, employers, and society at large; and experiments to improve working conditions. Appendixes and bibliography are included.

Manpower Research Monograph #30, #029-000-00195-2, $1.20; GPO (see C1.0).

6.104 *Suggestions for Control of Turnover and Absenteeism*

Labor turnover and absenteeism are analyzed and corrective procedures are presented in this book. A guide for analyzing the cost of turnover and examples of turnover cost analysis are presented, together with causes and types of turnover. Computation of absenteeism rates and factors influencing absenteeism are discussed. Many of the same sample forms and checklists as found in *Developing Your Manpower* (see 5.654) are included, with the following additions: checklist on orientation practices, checklist on health and safety, time card for unauthorized absence, supervisor's daily report, daily personnel report, exit interview report, monthly analysis of turnover, and absenteeism.

#2900-00161, 55 pp., $1.00; GPO (see C1.0).

6.105 *Handbook for Job Restructuring*

A self-contained instructional and reference document, this publication is designed to provide basic techniques and procedures for restructuring jobs and job systems. The methodology contained in the handbook is derived from a special adaptation of the job analysis concepts and techniques developed by the United States Employment Service over a 35-year period. Its application can assist in many programs and activities relating to better utilization of manpower resources and development of manpower potential.

46 pp., 55¢; GPO (see C1.0).

6.106 *Handbook for Analyzing Jobs*

A basic tool for the collection, classifying, and recording of job analysis data, this publication is a self-contained instructional and reference textbook containing concepts, procedures, and illustrative situations for conducting a complete job analysis study. It incorporates a new approach for obtaining current and comprehensive data necessary for bringing together people and jobs. The methodology can be adapted to meet specific objectives, such as job restructuring, job development, curriculum planning, and other career development programs and activities.

345 pp., $2.50; GPO (see C1.0).

6.107 *Dictionary of Occupational Titles* and Related Publications

The following publications may be ordered, as priced, from GPO (see C1.0).

Dictionary of Occupational Titles

The *Dictionary* provides a standard reference for job definitions and occupational classifications.

Volume I, *Definition of Titles,* lists alphabetically over 35,000 different occupational titles, and defines and identifies by code number almost 22,000 separate occupations throughout the American economy.

Volume II, *Occupational Classification and Industry Index,* presents the occupational classification structure used by the United States Employment Service, consisting of two arrangements of jobs. The first arrangement groups jobs in numerical order according to some combination of work field, purpose, material, product, subject matter, generic term, and/or industry. The second arrangement groups jobs according to some combination of required general educational development, specific vocational preparation, aptitudes, interests, temperaments, and physical demands. It also lists all titles by industry.

Vol. I, 809 pp., $7.75; Vol. II, 656 pp., $6.75.

Selected Characteristics of Occupations (Physical Demand, Working Conditions, Training Time), A Supplement to the Dictionary of Occupational Titles

Individual physical demands, working conditions, and training time data for all jobs defined in the *Dictionary of Occupational Titles* are listed in this supplement. The information provides additional source material for determining job relationships in such activities as vocational counseling, personnel and manpower activities, training, rehabilitation, and placement.

280 pp., $2.85.

Selected Characteristics of Occupations by Worker Traits and Physical Strength, Supplement to the Dictionary of Occupational Titles

In a rearrangement of the data contained in the first supplement, this supplement presents data by the worker trait groups contained in Volume II of the *Dictionary of Occupational Titles.* They are then subgrouped by level of strength required. The supplement will be useful in counseling and placement activities, and particularly useful in determining utilization, transfer, and placement possibilities for handicapped and aged workers.

156 pp., $1.50.

Suffix Codes for Jobs Defined in the Dictionary of Occupational Titles

A unique three-digit suffix code for each job title defined in the dictionary is provided, thereby giving a numerical identification to such job titles within each six-digit dictionary code number. They are intended for statistical reporting and other activities where job titles cannot be used and identification is dependent upon numerical identification.

264 pp., $2.00.

Training Manual for the Dictionary of Occupational Titles

Part A, *Instructor's Guide,* provides a guide to instructions for initiating and conducting the self-training program covering the dictionary. Part B, *Trainee's Workbook,* is a self-instructional text, presented in the form of a linear program covering the contents, structure, arrangement, and use of the dictionary.

323 pp., $3.00.

6.108 *Vocational Education and Occupations*

Published by the Office of Education and the Employment Training Administration, this document links occupations and their worker trait groups with vocational-technical education programs of state and local schools.

307 pp., $2.25; GPO (see C1.0).

6.109 *Occupations in Electronic Computing Systems*

Twenty-nine different occupations peculiar to electronic computing are described in this publication. It gives the education, training, and characteristics required of the worker by the job and lists the physical activities and environmental conditions usually encountered.

130 pp., 60¢; GPO (see C1.0).

6.110 *Occupations and Trends in the Dairy Products Industry*

Current occupations and processes in the dairy products industry, reflecting changes which have occurred and are occurring due to the introduction of automated equipment, are described in this brochure.

186 pp., 75¢; GPO (see C1.0).

6.111 *Job Descriptions and Organizational Analysis for Hospitals and Related Health Services*

A completely revised version of the 1952 edition, this 1971 publication contains introductory materials, department narratives, organizational charts, and 238 job descriptions, including hospital occupations which have emerged since 1952. It provides reliable occupational information for hospital administrators, for management at various levels, for high school and college guidance counselors in assisting young people to plan study courses and research projects, for librarians in supplementing other job information on library shelves, for vocational counselors in setting up training courses in health occupations, and for personnel of the employment service for use in their placement, counseling, and related activities.

732 pp., $4.25; GPO (see C1.0).

Information on Sex and Age Discrimination (6.150-6.159)

6.150 *A Guide to Federal Laws Prohibiting Sex Discrimination*

#005-000-00105-6, 113 pp., $1.40; GPO (see C1.0).

6.151 *Legislative History of the Equal Employment Opportunity Act of 1972, Amending Title VII of the Civil Rights Act of 1964*

#052-070-01629-9, 2,067 pp., $14.50; GPO (see C1.0).

6.152 *Working Woman's Guide to Her Job Rights*

Included in this summary of federal legislation concerning the legal protection of women's employment opportunities is a digest of laws affecting preemployment, postemployment, and on-the-job rights, as well as the location of various state and federal agencies that provide personal assistance.

#029-016-00031-3, 34 pp., $1.20; GPO (see C1.0).

6.153 *Equal Pay*

This informative pamphlet explains key provisions and outlines the background of the Equal Pay Act of 1963. The Act prohibits discrimination in wages on the basis of sex.

#029-016-00017-8, 16 pp., 45¢; GPO (see C1.0).

6.154 *Equal Pay for Equal Work*

Official interpretations of the meaning and application of equal pay provisions added to the Fair Labor Standards Act by the Equal Pay Act of 1963 are collected here.

#029-005-00023-1, 28 pp., 60¢; GPO (see C1.0).

6.155 Law Against Age Discrimination

The Law Against Age Discrimination in Employment

1974, free; Wage and Hour Division (see C1.75).

Age Discrimination in Employment Act of 1967, as Amended

1975, free; poster and Spanish translation also available; Wage and Hour Division (see C1.75).

6.156 Publications on Sex Discrimination and Affirmative Action

Women in Apprenticeship—Why Not?

Manpower Research Monograph No. 33, 1974, 75¢; GPO (see C1.0).

Dictionary of Occupational Titles

Nearly 3,500 job titles have been revised, bringing them into conformance with equal employment legislation (see 6.107).

3rd ed., 1975, $4.30; GPO (see C1.0).

Sex Discrimination

This is a summary of requirements under Executive Order 11246, Public Health Service Act, Title IX of Education Amendments of 1972, Title VII of Civil Rights Act, and Equal Pay Act.

Free; Office of Civil Rights, Department of Health, Education, and Welfare, Washington, DC 20210.

EEOC Guidelines on Discrimination because of Sex

Free; Publications Unit, EEOC (see C1.102).

Questions and Answers Concerning the EEOC Guidelines on Discrimination because of Sex

Free; Publications Unit, EEOC (see C1.102).

Affirmative Action Programs for Women: A Survey of Innovative Programs

Free; Office of Research, EEOC (see C1.102).

An Affirmative Action Packet, available on request from the Women's Bureau (see C1.78), includes the publications listed below, and others. A full publications list, including much other useful information on women and employment, may also be requested.

Steps to Advance EEO for Women
Brief Highlights of Major Federal Laws and Orders on Sex Discrimination
State Hours Laws for Women: Changes in Status Since the Civil Rights Act of 1964
Twenty Facts on Women Workers
The Myth and the Reality
Fact Sheet on the Earnings Gap
Women Workers Today
Fact Sheet on Minority Women
Women Workers by State
Facts on Women Workers of Minority Races
Recruiting Sources for Women
Steps to Opening the Skilled Trades to Women
A Working Woman's Guide to Her Job Rights

6.157 *State Labor Laws in Transition: From Protection to Equal Status for Women*

Laws of special interest to women and trends that have become evident in the past dozen years are summarized in this publication, including state minimum wage laws, state equal pay and fair employment practices legislation, and some of the state protective laws. Information is also provided on the federal counterparts of these laws to the extent needed to clarify any issue. The legal provisions prohibiting sex discrimination are included, together with federal guidelines.

#029-002-00049-5, 21 pp., 35¢; GPO (see C1.0).

6.158 *1975 Handbook on Women Workers*

A comprehensive description of the status of women is presented in this volume. Areas analyzed include: employment by occupation and industry; income and earnings; education, training, and employment of women; the outlook for women workers; federal labor laws of special interest; state labor laws of special interest; maternity standards; civil and political status; federal aid to women; women's commissions; and international activities.

#029-016-00037-2, 435 pp., $4.70; GPO (see C1.0).

6.159 Information from the Women's Bureau

The Legal Status of Women

The legal status of women is summarized in this 10-page reprint from *The Book of States.* The following subject areas are covered: Equal Rights Amendment, credit, housing, maiden name, homemakers, abortion, jury service, women in public service, International Women's Year, commissions on the status of women, education, marriage laws, divorce laws, and child support.

Free; national and regional offices of Women's Bureau (see C1.78).

Publications of the Women's Bureau

Publications about women and work, including career opportunities, education and training, child care services, the law, and conference reports are listed in this leaflet.

Regional offices of Women's Bureau (see C1.78).

The Federal Women's Program

This is a film explaining the Federal Women's Program, a special area under the Equal Employment Opportunity program designed to achieve equal employment opportunity for women. The status of women in the nation's workforce is discussed, and their employment compared with that of men in the federal government.

27 min., 16 mm., sound, black and white, #005693, sale $71.00; National Audio-Visual Center, General Services Administration, Attention: Order Section NACDO, Washington, DC 20409.

Recruitment and Training (6.200-6.205)

6.200 *A Directory of Resources for Affirmative Recruitment*

A companion volume of *Guide to Resources for Equal Employment Opportunity and Affirmative Action* (see 6.1), this directory can be of great assistance in determining recruitment sources in a local area. The entire table of contents is presented:

Introduction: The Need for Affirmative Recruitment

I. Directories and Professional Rosters
   A. Minority Recruitment Sources
   B. Female Recruitment Sources
   C. Minority and Women Professionals in the Physical and Social Sciences
   D. General Sources

II. Organization Referral Sources
   A. National Sources
      1. Index to Organizations and Type of Service Provided
      2. Alphabetical Descriptive Listing of Organizations
   B. Regional or Local Referral Sources
      1. Index to Organizations and Type of Service
      2. General Regional and Local Sources
      3. Alphabetical Descriptive Listing of Organizations

91 pp., single copies free; Educational Programs Division, Office of Voluntary Compliance, EEOC (see C1.102).

6.201 Recruitment and Training Assistance: CETA

The Comprehensive Employment and Training Act of 1973 (CETA) makes funds available to local prime sponsors, usually mayors' offices, and to governors of states for balance-of-state areas outside of independent prime sponsor areas, for the development, within broad guidelines, of locally tailored employment and training programs. Prime sponsors consist of areas with a population of 100,000 or more. Under some circumstances, various areas can be combined into a consortium and qualify as a prime sponsor.

No prime sponsor is obliged to use its funds in any one prescribed area according to a formula. Rather, it must analyze area needs and develop a comprehensive employment and training plan for the area, using area educational institutions, vocational technical schools, and occupational and on-the-job training techniques permissible under law. It is, in short, an attempt to promote local control, accountability, and flexibility to tailor programs around local needs.

The following areas may be of relevance to employers:

Affirmative Action Recruitment. By law, CETA activities heavily emphasize services to the disadvantaged. Many prime sponsors have placement services themselves, and many subcontract with state employment services for job placement activities. CETA projects are important to employers attempting to meet labor force parities in their establishments.

Occupational Training. If a local CETA prime sponsor opts to invest in occupational training, such training shall be, according to Department of Labor regulations, "designed for occupations in which skills shortages exist and for which there is reasonable expectation of employment. In making such determinations, a prime sponsor shall utilize available community resources such as local employment service offices, the national Alliance of Businessmen, etc." Businesses, therefore, which offer genuine occupational opportunities, and in which there is a documentable need, will benefit by making this known to the local CETA prime sponsor and to cooperating agencies such as vocational technical schools, the National Alliance of Businessmen, and the Employment Service.

On-the-Job Training. CETA funds may be utilized to assist individuals at the entry level of employment or those needing additional skills for upgrading into higher skills. Prime sponsors may reimburse and provide inducements to private employers for the bona fide training and related costs of enrolling individuals in the program, provided that payments to employers organized for profit are made only for the costs of recruiting, training, and supportive services which are over and above those normally provided by the employer. The prime sponsor can reimburse the employer for extraordinary training costs for training on the job, up to a level not to exceed 50 percent of entry level wages.

For further information on CETA matters in a local area, contact the manpower division of the mayor's office, or the State Employment Security Agency office (see C1.73).

6.202 Tax Credit and Training Reimbursement: The Work Incentive Program

The Work Incentive Program (WIN) is intended to help recipients of Aid to Families with Dependent Children get and keep jobs. It provides a variety of supportive services to applicants to prepare them for work and offers incentives to employers to participate. WIN is jointly administered by the Departments of Labor and of

Health, Education and Welfare.

One incentive for employers to offer jobs is a sizable tax credit. It allows them to receive a credit, deducted from their federal income tax liability, amounting to 20 percent of the first year's wages paid to every WIN registrant they hire and keep on the job.

Another incentive arises from the "hire first, train later" concept. Here, WIN reimburses employers for the cost of the on-the-job training provided the WIN participants they employ. The employers get trained workers, compensation for the training, and a tax credit on their wages.

Contact the manager of the local State Employment Service; see also state headquarters (C1.73).

6.203 Recruitment of veterans

The State Employment Service (ES) (Job Service) gives preference to veterans in referrals to employers. Most local offices have a veterans' employment representative whose responsibility is to find jobs for veterans.

Local office of ES.

6.204 Publications on Training

The following publications are available, as priced, from GPO (see C1.0).

Apprenticeship in the United States, A Bibliography, #029-000-00217-7, 64 pp., $1.05

Basic Education and Manpower Programs, #029-000-00230-4, 60 pp., $1.15

Directory of Postsecondary Schools with Occupational Programs, #017-080-01477-7, 456 pp., $5.80

Disincentives to Effective Employee Training and Development, #006-000-00938-7, 148 pp., $2.60

Occupational Manpower and Training Needs, Information for Planning Training Programs for the 1970's, #029-001-01347-7, 116 pp., $1.80

Directory of Representative Work Education Programs, #017-080-01244-8, 338 pp., $2.95

6.205 *Directory for Reaching Minority Groups*

#029-006-00005-9, 214 pp., $2.85; GPO (see C1.0).

Testing and Counseling (6.250-6.255)

6.250 *A Selected Bibliography on Selection and Testing Procedures in Relation to Fair Employment*

A comprehensive current bibliography, with emphasis on legal and technical aspects of selection procedures, this reference includes federal guidelines and standards; texts; professional journal articles; and case citations and other useful sources on testing, validation procedures and studies, job analysis, licensing, and certification.

Free; Publications Unit, EEOC (see C1.02).

6.251 Publications on Testing, Counseling, and Training

The following publications are available, as priced, from GPO (see C1.0).

EEO Counseling

Designed for training Equal Employment Opportunity counselors, this manual covers interviewing techniques, basic legal issues, a discussion of typical problems, and a sample discrimination case from start to finish.

#006-000-00782-1, 50 pp., $1.40.

Personnel Testing and Equal Employment Opportunity
#052-015-00014-6, 48 pp., 95¢

Issues of Sex Bias and Sex Fairness in Career Interest Measurement
#017-080-01465-3, 219 pp., $3.20

Equal Employment Opportunity Counseling, A Guidebook
#006-000-00903-4, 32 pp., 55¢.

Employment Testing: Guide Signs, Not Stop Signs
#005-000-00021-1, 30 pp., 60¢.

Model for Training the Disadvantaged: TAT Training and Technology) at Oak Ridge, Tennessee
#029-000-00192-8, 50 pp., 85¢.

6.252 Testing Tools Used by Employment Service Counselors

Occupational tests used in vocational counseling and selection of persons for jobs play a vital role in Employment Service (ES) activities, and their development and validation constitute a continuing responsibility of the United States Employment Service (USES).

Non-ES groups—such as prime sponsors, vocational schools, high school counselors—interested in using USES tests may discuss the possibilities with local ES (Job Service) officials. Under some circumstances, arrangements can be made for ES staff to administer the tests for the organization. In other cases, the local Job Service office may grant permission for qualified staff of the non-ES group to administer the USES tests.

To date, eight types of testing tools have been developed. They are:

General Aptitude Test Battery (GATB) measures the vocational aptitudes of individuals who have basic literacy skills but need help in choosing an occupation. It consists of twelve tests that indicate aptitude in nine vocational areas. It measures, for example, a counselee's spatial aptitude, manual dexterity, and verbal aptitude.

Non-Reading Aptitude Test Battery (NATB) measures the aptitude of individuals who do not have the literacy skills to take the GATB. It consists of fourteen tests for the same nine aptitudes as the GATB. Clients given the NATB are often referred to a training program that includes an education component.

GATB-NATB Screening Device is a short test which helps a counselor determine whether a counselee should take the GATB or the NATB.

Specific Aptitude Test Battery (SATB) measures the potential of individuals to acquire skills needed for a specific job or occupational training program. SATB's have been developed for more than 450 specific occupations.

Clerical Skills Tests measure proficiency in regular and statistical typing, dictation, and spelling, including medical and legal terms, to determine qualifications for clerical jobs.

Basic Occupational Literacy Test (BOLT) measures basic skills in reading and math that are needed for a specific job or particular training program. It is used for educationally deficient individuals.

Pretesting Orientation Techniques help prepare individuals to take tests and alleviate related anxieties. A counselee may take booklets home to read, preactive GATB exercises, or participate in group sessions on the purposes of testing.

Interest Checklist is used to obtain information on occupational interests of a counselee. It consists of 173 sample job tasks and is geared to the Worker Traits and Occupational Group classification systems contained in the third and current edition of the *Dictionary of Occupational Titles* (see 5.655).

State Headquarters of ES (see C1.73); or local ES office.

6.253 *Preemployment Inquiries and Equal Employment Opportunity Law*

Guidelines for preemployment interviews and employment application forms are provided in this Equal Employment Opportunities Commission (EEOC) report. It includes definitions of "business necessity" and job relatedness and a discussion of the numerous items that are and are not allowed in interviews and applications.

Free; Educational Programs Branch, EEOC (see C1.102).

6.254 *Questions and Answers on the OFCC Testing and Selection Order*

Some of the most common questions about testing and selection compliance raised by contractors and compliance officers are covered in this booklet from the Office of Federal Contract Compliance (OFCC). It defines such terms as test, validation, adverse effect, and disparate effect.

#029-016-00023, 40¢; GPO (see C1.0); see also regional offices of OFCC (C1.76).

6.255 *Employee Testing and Selection Procedures*

OFCC (see C1.76).

Films on Affirmative Action (6.300-6.301)

6.300 Filmographies on Minorities and the Disadvantaged

The following filmographies are available, free, from Reference Section—Code A, National

Audio-Visual Center, General Services Administration, Washington, DC 20409.

- G029 Films on Minorities, EEO, and Civil Rights
- H026 Films on Community Youth Development Programs
- F010 Films on Group Behavior and Performance Centered Counseling
- H036 Films on Reality Orientation
- H010 The "To Live Again Series" of Films, with Viewpoints of Mentally, Physically, and Socially Rehabilitated Individuals
- H025 Films on Aging, with Viewpoints of the Elderly

6.301 *Games*

The "games people play," intentionally or not, that keep minority members of society from advancing as their abilities allow are graphically exposed in this film.

32 min., 16 mm., sound, color, #004672, sale $145.25, rent $12.50; National Audio-Visual Center, Attention Order Section, NACDO, General Services Administration, Washington, DC 20409. Available for free loan from Audio-Visual Support Center, Military District of Washington, Fort Myer, VA 22211.

Occupational Safety and Health (6.350-6.651)

General Guides and Information (6.350-6.364)

6.350 Recordkeeping for the Occupational Safety and Health Administration (OSHA)

The following publications are available, free, from OSHA (see C1.79).

What Every Employer Needs to Know about OSHA Recordkeeping

Answers to employers' most frequently-asked questions about recordkeeping and reporting requirements for OSHA (Occupational Safety and Health Administration) are given in this 28-page publication. It was prepared by the Bureau of Labor Statistics of the Department of Labor, in the Office of Occupational Safety and Health Statistics.

Recordkeeping Requirements under the Occupational Safety and Health Act of 1970

Work-related injuries and illnesses usually must be recorded by employers, although some are exempt. A full description of the forms to be used for this purpose is contained in a free booklet, *Recordkeeping Requirements under the Occupational Safety and Health Act of 1970,* which is published by the Bureau of Labor Statistics.

6.351 *OSHA Handbook for Small Business*

Small businesses must comply with Occupational Safety and Health Administration (OSHA) regulations just as must large businesses. To help small businesses meet legal requirements, OSHA has published a free booklet, the *OSHA Handbook for Small Businesses.* It explains how employers may establish voluntary safety and health programs. It includes a seven-point plan applicable to small businesses, and a number of sample self-inspection checklists. It explains where to go for help and advice, and how to obtain an on-site consultation from a specialist. (The consultant will not notify OSHA's inspectors of violations unless they present an imminent danger, and are resolved on the spot. A reasonable time will be given to resolve conditions for which danger is serious but not imminent.) The handbook also describes the role of state occupational safety and health programs, and discusses the publication *Job Safety and Health Standards for General Industry, Construction, and Maritime Employment,* copies of which are available free from OSHA field offices (see C1.79). It also discusses how to obtain a Small Business Administration loan to meet OSHA standards, and contains a list of publications available free from OSHA.

6.352 *All About OSHA*

In a 23-page booklet, OSHA is described and discussed. Aspects covered are its mission, who is covered, employers' rights and responsibilities, employees' rights and responsibilities, how OSHA sets standards and conducts inspections, and the role of state laws.

OSHA 2056, free; OSHA (see C1.79).

6.353 *How OSHA Monitors State Plans*

This is a 6-page booklet intended as a general information aid to employers and employees in states which have implemented their own OSHA-approved job safety and health plans.

OSHA 2221, free: regional offices of OSHA (see C1.79). Or #029-015-00048, 40¢; GPO (see C1.0).

6.354 *OSHA Inspections*

A brief booklet describes OSHA inspections, their purposes, authority, priorities, conduct, and consequences.

OSHA 2098, free; OSHA (see C1.79).

6.355 Small Business Administration Loans for OSHA Compliance

Information about loans for the purpose of compliance with regulations of the Occupational Safety and Health Administration (OSHA) can be obtained at area offices of the Small Business Administration (see C1.110).

The short pamphlet, *SBA Loans for OSHA Compliance,* explains how to get and use a loan before and after an OSHA inspection.

OSHA 2005, 8 pp., free; OSHA (see C1.79).

6.356 Task Force to Assist Small Businesses and Industries, and *Health and Safety Guides*

The Task Force to Assist Small Businesses and Industries functions through on-site visits and the development of *Health and Safety Guides.*

One aim of this program is to help employers understand what is required, under the Occupational Safety and Health Act of 1970, by assisting in recognizing, evaluating, and controlling safety and health problems within their establishments. The most common problems are identified from information obtained from other state and federal agencies, trade associations, and insurance companies, and from in-plant visits by safety and health professionals from National Institute for Occupational Safety and Health (NIOSH). Preventive and corrective measures for the problems found are then published in *Health and Safety Guides.*

Material contained in the guides relates to the most commonly found violations of OSHA standards and includes guidelines to good practices to prevent or minimize injuries and illnesses in the workforce. Each guide is sent to the relevant businesses to assist them in voluntarily complying with the Act and thereby provide safer and more healthful workplaces for employees.

NIOSH (see C1.31).

A list of the *Health and Safety Guides* follows. Single copies can be obtained, as priced, from: Publications, DTS, NIOSH, 4676 Columbia Parkway, Cincinnati, OH 45226. Multiple copies must be obtained from GPO (see C1.0).

Auto Repair and Body Shops, #1733-00048, $1.40
Bulk Petroleum Plants, #1733-00114-6, $2.50
Bottled and Canned Soft Drink Facilities, #1733-00079, $2.45
Concrete Products Industry, #1733-00095, $1.60
Electroplating Shops, #1733-00069, $1.30
Farm and Garden Machinery and Equipment Manufacturers, #1733-00117-1, $2.60
Fluid Milk Processors, #1733-00082, $1.75
Food Processors, #1733-00078, $2.00
Foundries, #1733-00123-5, $2.35
Grain Mills, #1733-00056, $1.60
Grocery Stores, #1733-00052, $1.55
Hotels and Motels, #1733-00105, $1.95
Laundries and Dry Cleaners, #1733-00080, $1.70
Manufacturers of Paint and Allied Products, #1733-00092, $1.35
Metal Stamping Operations, #1733-00093, $1.40
Millwork shops, #1733-00116-2, $2.60
Paperboard-Container Industry, #1733-00094, $1.95
Plastic Fabricators, #1733-00064, $1.70
Retail Bakeries, #1733-00049, $1.10
Retail Lumber and Building Materials, #1733-00065, $1.55
Service Stations, #1733-00055, $1.85
Sporting Goods Stores, #1733-00053. $1.65
Wooden Furniture Manufacturers, #1733-00091, $1.50

6.357 *Occupational Safety and Health—A Bibliography*

Published sources dealing with both general and specific aspects of occupational safety and health are annotated in this publication.

#PB230-147, $11.00; NTIS (see C1.17). Also available on microfiche for $2.25.

6.358 Publications on OSHA and Employees

The following publications are available, free, from OSHA (see C1.79).

The Employee and OSHA

This pocket-sized pamphlet outlines, in question and answer form, employees' rights and responsibilities.

OSHA 2099, 12 pp.; also available in Spanish: OSHA 2210.

Organizing a Safety Committee

A discussion of the usefulness, organization, and activities of a safety and health committee in a business is included in this booklet.

OSHA 2231, 8 pp.

Workers' Rights under OSHA

The rights and responsibilities of employees regarding standards, variances, inspections, discrimination, and state plans are outlined in this booklet.

OSHA 2253, 12 pp.

6.359 *OSHA Publications and Training Materials*

In a 10-page pamplet, various booklets and audio-visual materials related to the Occupational Safety and Health Administration (OSHA) available from OSHA, Government Printing Office, and the National Audio-Visual Center are listed.

OSHA 2019, free; OSHA (see C1.79).

6.360 *General Industry* and Related Publications

General Industry

All job safety and health rules and regulations pertaining to industry in general are included in this comprehensive 649-page publication containing the Occupational Safety and Health Administration's general industry standards, Part 1910, Title 29 of the Code of Federal Regulations. It was reprinted from the issue of the Code of Regulations dated July 1, 1975. The information in this edition was current as of January 1, 1976.

$5.35; GPO (see C1.0).

General Industry: OSHA Safety and Health Standards Digest

Most of the construction industry standards are summarized in this pocket-sized 44-page publication.

OSHA 2202, free; OSHA (see C1.79).

Questions and Answers to Part 1910, the OSHA General Standards

Typical questions with their answers are given in this 30-page booklet.

OSHA 2095, free; OSHA (see C1.79)

Longshoring Industry: OSHA Safety and Health Standards

The longshoring industry standards are summarized in this pocket-sized, 138-page publication.

OSHA 2232, free; OSHA (see C1.79).

6.361 *NIOSH Publications*

Criteria document abstracts, descriptions of technical sampling and analytical methods for dozens of chemicals, leaflets on specific hazards (e.g., lead, asbestos, power tools), and numerous *Health and Safety Guides* for specific businesses are listed in this catalog of the publications of the National Institute for Occupational Safety and Health (NIOSH).

Publications Dissemination Office, NIOSH, 4676 Columbia Parkway, Cincinnati, OH 45226; 513-684-8323.

6.362 Statistical Studies in Occupational Safety and Health

The Office of Occupational Safety and Health Statistics of the Bureau of Labor Statistics (BLS) conducts an annual survey of occupational injuries and illnesses among about 600,000 sample units across the nation. It is the largest sample survey conducted by the Bureau. Survey data are solicited from employers in agriculture, forestry, and fisheries; oil and gas extraction; contract construction; manufacturing; transportation and public utilities; wholesale and retail trade; finance, insurance, and real estate; and service industries. The Office develops estimates and incidence rates by industry for all work-related deaths, seven categories of nonfatal illnesses, and many nonfatal injuries. Publications resulting from the survey include:

Occupational Injuries and Illnesses by Industry, Bulletin 1830; BLS (see C1.70)

Occupational Safety and Health Statistics: Concepts and Methods, Report 438; BLS (see C1.70)

An Audio Aid on OSHA Recordkeeping, $5.00; National Audio-Visual Center, Washington, DC 20409

Recordkeeping under the Occupational Safety and Health Act, OSHA (see C1.79)

Special Industry and Accident Cause Studies of BLS, 56 studies can be purchased as a unit or individually; prices vary; NTIS (see C1.17)

An OSHA Guide: Evaluating Your Firm's Injury and Illness Experience for the National Emphasis Program Industries, OSHA Guide Series

- Construction Industries
- Manufacturing Industries
- Transportation, Communications, and Electric, Gas, and the Sanitary Service Industries
- Wholesale and Retail Trade Industries
- Service Industries

6.363 Occupational Safety and Health Review Commission

The Occupational Safety and Health Review Commission (OSHRC) hears appeals from decisions made in OSHA enforcement proceedings.

Office of Information and Publications, OSHRC, 1825 K St. N.W., Washington, DC 20006.

6.364 *The Impact on Small Business Concerns of Government Regulations that Force Technological Change*

The effect of federal regulations on small companies' finances and operations was the subject of a study done for the Small Business Administration (SBA) and reported in this publication. It advocates SBA intervention in the federal regulatory process to alleviate the difficulties faced by small firms, and tells how that could be done.

#045-000-00144-0, 317 pp., $3.90; GPO (see C1.0).

Current Awareness Services (6.400-6.403)

6.400 *Occupational Safety and Health Subscription Service*

All of the OSHA standards, interpretations, regulations, and procedures are provided in an easy-to-use loose-leaf form in this five-volume service.

General Industry, Maritime, $6.00; *Construction,* $8.00; *Other Regulations and Procedures,* $5.50; *Field Operations Manual, $8.00. GPO (see C1.0).*

6.401 *Job Safety and Health*

Employers can get information and ideas to aid in compliance with Occupational Safety and Health Administration (OSHA) requirements by a magazine entitled *Job Safety and Health.* It reports on the development of new standards, recent health research, industry/union activities and efforts to control job safety and health problems, and current safety and health issues. It also summarizes news from OSHA's national office, including regulations, policy statements, and new programs. It covers current OSHA publications, lists new entries in the *Federal Register*, reports key legal decisions of the Occupational Safety and Health Review Commission, and summarizes new research from the National Institute for Occupational Safety and Health.

$13.60 per year, 25 percent discount for 100 or more to a single address; GPO (see C1.0).

6.402 *Weekly Government Abstracts: Industrial and Mechanical Engineering*

Production planning, quality control, plant design and maintenance, environmental engineering and labor psychology and esthetics are among the subjects covered by the current awareness service entitled *Industrial and Mechanical Engineering.* This is one of a series of twenty-six newsletters known as *Weekly Government Abstracts.* (For an annotation on the entire series, see 9.11.) Each newsletter contains summaries of government research performed by hundreds of organizations, including United

States government agencies, private researchers, universities, and special technology groups. The research summaries are listed within two weeks of their receipt at the National Technical Information Service. The last issue of each year is a subject index containing up to ten cross references for each research summary indexed.

$45.00 per year; NTIS (see C1.17).

6.403 *Fireview*

Fireview is a newsletter published from time to time for those who are concerned about fire science, fire control, and new developments in fire safety engineering. It is relevant to concerned businessmen in that it deals with facilities, products, and preventative tools and materials.

Center for Fire Research, Bldg. 225, B142, National Bureau of Standards, Washington, DC 20230; 301-921-3143.

On-Site Technical Assistance (6.450-6.454)

6.450 On-Site Technical Help from National Institute for Occupational Safety and Health

On request, the National Institute for Occupational Safety and Health (NIOSH) will supply employers with various forms of technical assistance: a free evaluation, on site, of the potential toxicity of substances in the workplace; a free in-plant safety and accident-prevention survey; free consultation for small and medium-sized businesses on provision of medical services as part of occupational safety and health programs; and a free industrial hygiene survey.

Technical information is available to employers through the NIOSH series of *Health and Safety Guides,* through the *Good Industrial Hygiene Practice* manuals, and through the services of the NIOSH technical information group. Furthermore, NIOSH can draw on its computerized data file, NIOSHTIC, which contains over 45,000 technical documents.

An 8-page booklet entitled *Health Hazard Evaluation Program* describes the Health Hazard Evaluation program of NIOSH. This program allows employers or employees to get a free evaluation of the potential toxicity of substances in the workplace.

Office of Technical Publications, Room 3-10, NIOSH, 5600 Fishers Lane, Rockville, MD 20852; or Division of Technical Services, NIOSH, 4676 Columbia Parkway, Cincinnati, OH 45226; 513-684-8322. See also NIOSH regional offices (C1.31).

6.451 Industrial Hygiene Consultation and Training Assistance for Small Business

Small businesses can obtain help in complying with regulations of the Occupational Safety and Health Administration (OSHA) under the Program for Industrial Hygiene Consultation and Training Assistance for Small Business. This program, which is sponsored by the American Industrial Hygiene Association under a contract with OSHA, provides a free, informal, on-site walk-through health hazard survey, free training, free educational materials, and free consultation in education and training.

According to its sponsors, there is no obligation to carry out any recommendations that may come from plant surveys or conferences, and the program is in no way related to enforcement or compliance under the Occupational Safety and Health Act. Also, the sponsors promise that every measure will be taken to protect the confidentiality of information or observations developed from plant surveys or other sources.

Any firm which qualifies under Small Business Administration criteria is eligible. Contact the Program for Industrial Hygiene Consultation at one of the following locations:

School of Public Health
University of North Carolina
Chapel Hill, NC 27514

Center for Environmental Studies
Temple University
Philadelphia, PA 19140

Kettering Laboratory
University of Cincinnati
Eden and Bethesda
Cincinnati, OH 45219

School of Public Health and Community Medicine
University of Washington
Seattle, WA 98195

Department of Industrial Engineering
Texas A & M University
College Station, TX 77840

6.452 On-Site Consultation Provided by State Agencies

On-site consultation may allow a business to discover and correct occupational safety and health problems without being subjected to OSHA enforcement citations. Federal law bars OSHA itself from conducting on-site consultations without issuing citations for any violations found; but in many states, employers may obtain advisory consultations from state agencies without receiving citations.

In about half of the states, OSHA-approved state programs are in effect under section 18(b) of the Act. These programs emphasize voluntary compliance, and provide on-site consultation to businesses. In a number of other states, OSHA has contracted with state agencies under section 7(c)(1) of the Act to provide on-site consultation programs.

For information regarding on-site consultation in individual states, contact the appropriate designated agency (see C1.111).

6.453 OSHA National Emphasis Program

The Occupational Safety and Health Administration (OSHA) offers on-site consultation and education programs to foundry and metal-casting operators as part of its National Emphasis Program. Top management, supervisory, and union personnel are offered free seminars. The National Emphasis Program also includes OSHA enforcement inspections. It focuses on those hazards causing the greatest number of employee injuries and illnesses.

National Emphasis Program, OSHA, Washington, DC 20210; or call Office of Information, 202-523-8151.

6.454 NIOSH Occupational Health Programs

A complete occupational health program would not only exercise environmental control but also provide medical services for employee protection and treatment when necessary. The medical and health services component is the essential part of the complete program that is not regulated by law and that small industries may feel they are unable to supply.

For this reason, the National Institute for Occupational Safety and Health (NIOSH) has assigned a high priority to showing small and medium-sized establishments how they can obtain occupational medical services. In some cases, this involves devising a mechanism for delivery of the services; in others, it involves going to the community to find the potential for supplying the need.

NIOSH (see C1.31).

Training
(6.500-6.517)

6.500 Information on Training Programs

The National Institute for Occupational Safety and Health (NIOSH) runs many technical short courses in the recognition, avoidance, and prevention of unsafe or unhealthful working conditions and the importance and proper use of safety and health equipment. These courses, scheduled throughout the country, are listed in *Announcement of Courses.*

Environmental Management Branch, NIOSH Division of Training, 550 Main St., Room 9503, Cincinnati, OH 45202; 513-684-3252.

6.501 *Training Requirements of OSHA Standards*

A booklet designed to assist employers in identifying Occupational Safety and Health Administration (OSHA) standards which require the training of employees, this publication contains a hazard index and covers the requirements for general industry, maritime employment, construction, and agriculture. It also includes references to sources of information and to training courses and materials.

OSHA 2254 (supersedes OSHA 2082), 63 pp., free; OSHA (see C1.79).

6.502 *Directory of Training and Education Resources in Occupational Safety and Health*

NIOSH (see C1.31).

6.503 *The Industrial Environment—Its Evaluation and Control*

This is a comprehensive technical training syllabus prepared by the National Institute for Occupational Safety and Health (NIOSH).

NIOSH (see C1.31).

6.504 *A Guide to Voluntary Compliance*

This is a course which provides guidelines for developing systematic self-inspection procedures to help employers correct workplace deficiencies. It includes a student manual, an instructor's guide, and a set of 174 slides.

$55.00; National Audio-Visual Center, General Services Administration, Washington, DC 20409.

An instructor's curriculum plan is available separately.

#029-015-00043-1, $1.10; GPO (see C1.0).

6.505 *Principles and Practices of Occupational Safety and Health*

First-line supervisors can learn to identify, correct, or eliminate hazards found in their workplaces, using this programmed instruction course. It consists of seven manuals.

GPO (see C1.0).

6.506 *Employer-Employee Rights and Responsibilities under the Occupational Safety and Health Act*

This comprehensive package of instructional materials is designed to bring about an understanding of OSHA and the rights and responsibilities of both employer and employee. It includes an instructor's guide and a set of 189 color slides.

$30.00; National Audio-Visual Center, General Services Administration, Washington, DC 20409.

6.507 *Safety and Health in Excavation and Trenching Operations*

The problems and hazards of excavation and trenching are covered in this instructional program prepared by OSHA. It includes an instructor's guide and 139 color slides.

$21.00; National Audio-Visual Center, General Services Administration, Washington, DC 20409.

6.508 *Construction Safety and Health Training*

Supervisors and employees can be trained in safe work practices for all phases of construction jobs, using this 30-hour course. It includes five manuals (also available separately) and 466 slides.

$75.00; National Audio-Visual Center, General Services Administration, Washington, DC 20409. Single manuals: $1.75 each; GPO (see C1.0).

A 10-hour version, with 10 one-hour cassettes, 290 slides, and the manuals, is also available; $90.00, National Audio-Visual Center.

6.509 *An Audio Aid on OSHA Recordkeeping*

This includes an audio-cassette, sample OSHA forms for recording and reporting occupational injuries and illnesses, a booklet on recordkeeping requirements and a copy of *What Every Employer Needs to Know about OSHA Recordkeeping*.

$5.00; National Audio-Visual Center, General Services Administration, Washington, DC 20409.

6.510 *Sloping, Shoring, and Shielding*

Construction shoring procedures and techniques are taught in this one-day training program consisting of a classroom session and a practical, "hands-on" workshop. It includes an instructor's manual, outline for the workshop, and 60 color slides.

$20.00; National Audio-Visual Center, General Services Administration, Washington, DC 20409.

6.511 *OSA Safety and Health Training Guidelines for General Industry*

Twenty-five general industry operations, ranging from use of such equipment as powered industrial trucks to storage of toxic substances, are covered in this publication.

#PB-239310/AS, $5.50; NTS (see C1.17).

6.512 *OSHA Safety and Health Training Guidelines for Construction*

A set of fifteen guidelines to help construction employers set up training in the safe use of equipment, tools, and machinery on the job is presented in this publication.

#PB-239312/AS, $4.50; NTIS (see C1.17).

6.513 *OSHA Safety and Health Training Guidelines for Maritime Operations*

Longshoring operations are covered in this publication.

#PB-239311/AS, $4.00; NTIS (see C1.17).

6.514 NIOSH Training for Small Business

Together with OSHA's Office of Training and Education, the National Institute for Occupational Safety and Health (NIOSH) sponsored a program to develop industrial hygiene centers to serve primarily the small business sector. Initiated in late 1974 and expected to continue through 1977, this program is being administered by the American Industrial Hygiene Association.

In a related development, NIOSH had a key part in the development of OSHA contracts with five universities to offer consultative services and short training programs focusing on the occupational safety and health problems faced by small business. NIOSH continues to function as the technical coordinator of this program.

NIOSH (see C1.31).

6.515 OSHA Training Institute Instructor's Courses

The OSHA Training Institute has developed two courses for persons who wish to become instructors in occupational safety and health. To prepare for teaching the General Industry Safety course (available from the National Audio-Visual Center), the Institute provides *A Guide to Voluntary Compliance: Instructor's Course*. To prepare for teaching the 10-hour and the 30-hour courses for construction workers and supervisors, the Institute provides *Safety and Health Training for the Construction Industry: Instructors' Course*.

Each course is free, on a first-come, first-served basis, and lasts one week. Classes are held at, and information about dates is available from, the OSHA Training Institute, Department of Labor, 10600 West Higgins Road, Rosemont, IL 60018; 312-297-4810.

6.516 NIOSH-Sponsored College and University Courses

Training of specialists in occupational safety and health is supported by grants from the National Institute for Occupational Safety and Health (NIOSH). The grantees are colleges and universities.

Programs have been supported at Auburn University (Alabama), California State University, Catonsville Community College (Maryland), Clemson University (South Carolina), Colorado State University, Ferris State College (Michigan), Harvard University (Massachusetts), Housatonic Community College (Connecticut), Kansas State University, Kirkwood Community College (Iowa), Marshall University (West Virginia), Montana College of Mineral Science and Technology, Mount Sinai School of Medicine of the City University of New York, New York University, North Carolina State University, Northern Virginia Community College, Ohio Department of Health, Oklahoma State University of Agriculture and Applied Science, Quinnipiac College (Connecticut), Saint Augustine's College (North Carolina), Temple University (Pennsylvania), Texas A&M University, University of Michigan, University of Arizona, University of California, University of Cincinnati, University of Miami, University of Minnesota, University of North Carolina, University of Pittsburgh, and Wichita State University.

For a list describing the program in a given area, contact the Office of Extramural Activities, NIOSH, Room 501, Post Office and Courthouse Building, Fifth and Walnut Sts., Cincinnati, OH 45202.

6.517 Job Safety and Health Training Programs

Training in occupational safety and health is

available in many places throughout the nation. Information about programs available locally can be found through certain state agencies which have been designated to carry out occupational safety and health responsibilities (see C1.81).

Short-term (8-12 hours) courses designed for employers and employees are provided under a program funded by the Occupational Safety and Health Administration under a contract with the American Association of Community and Junior Colleges (see C1.80).

Data Bases and Research Information Sources (6.550-6.560)

6.550 NIOSH Applied Research

The applied research program of the National Institute for Occupational Safety and Health (NIOSH) is a major effort directed primarily toward development of criteria for occupational health and safety standards. In 1975, this research was conducted in the following areas: toxicology and pathology; development of methods for analysis of physical and chemical agents; physiology and ergonomics; engineering, including development of new measurement methods; behavioral and motivational factors operating on the employee; and physical agents at the workplace.

NIOSH (see C1.31).

6.551 Current Intelligence System

The National Institute of Occupational Safety and Health (NIOSH) issues current intelligence reports to the occupational health community; i.e., to health professionals in government, industry, labor, and academe. The purpose of these reports is to alert these groups to new or previously unsuspected occupational hazards in a manner useful to both the scientist and the layman.

Key information in the reports is identification of the occupational groups at risk from exposure to the hazard, and the number of workers involved. Also included is background information on the potential hazard (its use, its toxicity in man and animals, and its carcinogenic potential), what NIOSH action (if any) is warranted or planned, and precautions recommended at the workplace.

The current intelligence reports were inaugurated in January, 1975, when NIOSH alerted the occupational health community to the hazards associated with exposure to vinyl chloride. Since then, this information dissemination method has been used seven times to spread alerts to the following specific hazards: chloroprene, trichloroethylene, ethylene dibromide, asbestos exposure of automotive brake and clutch workers, chromate pigments, hexamethylphosphoric triamide, and polychlorinated biphenyls.

All of the substances reported to date have a relationship with cancer, but it is not anticipated that this will be true in the future.

NIOSH (see C1.31).

6.552 Illness and Injury Surveillance

Data describing the types and incidence of occupational injury and disease are collected and analyzed in the NIOSH Illness and Injury Surveillance program. Of particular concern is identifying occupational groups with unusual patterns of disease. Occupational groups that are shown by analysis to be at unusual risk can be scheduled for further evaluation by application of appropriate epidemiological and industrial hygiene methods.

NIOSH (see C1.31).

6.553 Industry Hazard Trends

NIOSH (National Institute for Occupational Safety and Health) is continuing to develop three information systems to amass the statistics needed to describe exposures to potentially hazardous agents for the nonagricultural work force. These systems are the National Occupational Hazard Survey, the National Surveillance Network, and the Hazard Data Base.

National Occupational Hazard Survey NOHS) has the basic aim of obtaining data that will make it possible to enumerate for specific chemical and physical agents the number of workers potentially exposed, the industries in which they work, and the occupational groups to which they belong. The NOHS has identified 4,391 potential hazards, 66 types of industries by two-digit Standard Industrial Classification descriptors, and 456 occupational groups coded under the Bureau of the Census coding scheme, all collected from some 5,000 workplaces across the country.

National Surveillance Network (NSN) is a data-gathering program that is operated in conjunction with state occupational health programs. NIOSH supplies data sheets, printed for a standard recording format designed for direct input to a computer, to the participating states. State personnel fill out the data sheets during their walk-through visits as part of their surveillance, compliance, or consultative services. The information thus collected is supplied to NIOSH (minus any specific identification of the business involved), which in turn subsequently supplies the cooperating states with satistical summaries and related data. As with NOHS, the basic use of the data is to describe exposures to potentially hazardous agents.

Hazard Data Base (HDB) program has its objective collecting and presenting data showing the distribution of occupational hazards. At this time, manufacturing and use formulations of 200 chemicals await input into the HDB, as does information on an additional 150 chemicals. These data will be included in the NOHS data base management system along with the NOHS and NSN data and other chemical hazard information available to NIOSH.

The three systems—NOHS, NSN, and HDB—can be accessed together or individually to provide NIOSH with basic information for planning and priority-setting and for making available information on hazard trends within industries.

NIOSH (see C1.31).

6.554 NIOSH Technical Information Services

Through the operation of technical libraries and other information systems, the technical information service of the National Institute for Occupational Safety and Health (NIOSH) gathers and evaluates technical information for the benefit of the NIOSH staff, other government agencies, industrial management, labor unions, citizens, and foreign parties. In 1975, NIOSH responded to 1,500 formal requests for occupational safety and health technical information with specific information packets.

NIOSH maintains a central computer file for occupational safety and health technical document entries from a present data base of about 45,000 documents. Access to other national and international computer and information retrieval systems is also used.

A cross index was developed to fifteen published sources of commercial and industrial chemical products. This library file provides access to published information on 118,000 trade-named products.

NIOSH (see C1.31).

6.555 National Technical Information Service Published Searches

National Technical Information Service (NTIS) provides on-line computer searches, published searches, and bibliographic searches of thousands of governmental and nongovernmental research in numerous fields.

NTISearch Published Searches are the same high quality computer searches that NTIS sells daily for $100 each, when they are custom-made (see NTISearch, 9.1). The only difference is that Published Searches have been completed and published in response to previous demand and are therefore less costly to produce. If one were to order an on-line NTISearch today, it might include a few more research summaries completed since the Published Search was done, but it would cost at least $100; the Published Search is $25.00.

Each one of these 1,000 specially priced Published Searches consists of as many as 100 different thorough research summaries (abstracts) of advanced technology for businessmen, scientists, and specialists in urban, economic, and social affairs. If, however, any Published Search turns out to be inadequate for the user's needs, full credit is applied toward an on-line NTISearch.

Each summary includes the title of the full report, its author, corporate or government source, pages, price, and ordering instructions.

For a list of the most recent Published Searches in the area of occupational safety and health, write NTIS (see C1.17).

6.556 *NIOSH Reports Available from NTIS*

Hundreds of technical NIOSH publications sold through NTIS, including many reports on health hazard evaluations done at specific companies, are listed.

Free; Division of Technical Services, NIOSH, 4676 Columbia Parkway, Cincinnati, OH 45226.

6.557 OSHA Technical Data Center

Technical information and reference

materials regarding occupational safety and health and standards of the Occupational Safety and Health Administration (OSHA) are available for use or copying at the OSHA Technical Data Center. The Center also keeps records of proceedings in the formulation of OSHA standards, distributes some OSHA documents, and will respond to inquiries from businesses. Its holdings include several thousand volumes and over a hundred journals.

Technical Data Center, OSHA, Department of Labor, Room N-3620, 200 Constitute Ave., Washington, DC 20210; 202-523-8076.

6.558 Health Impact of Psychological Job Stress

Investigations in the area of job stress are aimed at uncovering the elements of psychologically stressful work situations and their associated health consequences, as well as identifying techniques to alleviate such problems.

A study directed to these ends and completed in 1975 involved examination of the health records of workers from hospitals, mental health clinics, and insurance company files. Of the 130 different occupations for which data were tabulated, four rated high in the incidence of job-related stress. These were inspectors, sales managers, mechanics, and public relations specialists.

A report on the extent and distribution of shiftwork systems in American industry indicates that over 25 percent of the United States work force is engaged in some sort of shiftwork. Industries and occupations showing the highest percentage of workers on shiftwork include printing and publishing, automobile manufacturing, primary metals, transportation, and hospital services.

National or regional offices of NIOSH (see C1.31).

6.559 Human Elements in Work Accidents

Research on human elements in work accidents deals with psychosocial factors in the worker and the work situation that may influence accident risk. Such research also seeks to apply behavioral science principles to enhance job safety. The National Institute of Occupational Safety and Health (NIOSH) has done research in this area which has yielded a questionnaire for diagnosing job safety needs, and a set of guidelines, based on psychological principles, for improving safety performance.

National or regional offices of NIOSH (see C1.31).

6.560 Center for Fire Research

The Center for Fire Research of the National Bureau of Standards conducts extensive applied research in fire science and engineering which may be of value to virtually all kinds of business. All of the research and tools generated by the Center are eagerly disseminated to the public, since its goal is to develop a technical base needed to reduce loss by fire by 50 percent in one generation. In the area of fire science, the Center has four areas of emphasis: information and hazard analysis, chemistry, toxicology of combustion products, and physics and dynamics of fire. The area of fire safety engineering has a five-point program: product safety, furnishings safety, construction safety, fire detection and control systems, and design concepts.

Center for Fire Research, National Bureau of Standards, Department of Commerce, Washington, DC 20230.

Data on Specific Hazards
(6.600-6.613)

6.600 Proficiency Analytical Testing Program of NIOSH

Laboratories across the country can maintain the quality of their chemical analysis techniques by participation in the Proficiency Analytical Testing (PAT) program of the National Institute for Occupational Safety and Health (NIOSH). Operated by NIOSH's Chemical Reference Laboratory (CRL) in Cincinnati, Ohio, the PAT program submits identical reference samples to over one hundred laboratories. Each laboratory conducts its analysis of the sample and is later informed of the actual content of the sample and the standard deviation of the results of the analyses by the other laboratories. The CRL also works with the National Bureau of Standards in the development of Standard Reference Materials.

Chemical Reference Laboratory, NIOSH, 4676 Columbia Parkway, Cincinnati, OH 45226.

6.601 Product Criteria Documents

NIOSH, in criteria documents, makes recommendations to the Department of Labor for standards to protect workers from hazardous chemical and physical agents. Each criteria document provides, when appropriate, an environmental workplace limit, recommendations for medical examinations and clinical tests, recordkeeping, engineering and control procedures, personal protective clothing and devices, and methods for informing the employee of the workplace hazard.

The following criteria documents are available from GPO (see C1.0).

Ammonia, #1733-00036, $1.55
Asbestos, #1733-00009, $2.10
Benzene, #1733-00038, $2.10
Beryllium, #1733-00011, $2.10
Carbon Monoxide, #1733-00006, $2.00
Carbon Tetrachloride
Chloroform, #1733-00045, $1.95
Chromic Acid, #1733-00020, $1.55
Chromium VI, #1733-00125-1, $2.75
Coke Oven Emissions, #1733-00015, $1.35
Cotton Dust, #1733-00044, $2.35
Crystalline Silica, #1733-00050, $1.95
Emergency Egress, #1733-00124-3, $1.25
Ethylene Dichloride
Hot Environments, #1733-00010, $1.80
Hydrogen Fluoride
Identification System, #1733-00046, $1.35
Inorganic Arsenic 1975, #1733-00098, $2.35
Inorganic Fluorides, #1733-00118-9, $2.65
Inorganic Lead, #1733-00013, $1.25
Inorganic Mercury, #1733-00022, $2.00
IIsopropyl Alcohol
Methylene Chlorida
Nitric Acid
Noise, #1733-00007, $2.15
Phosgene, #1733-00134-1, $2.00
Sodium Hydroxide, #1733-00110, $2.15
Sulfur Dioxide, #1733-00029,$1.55
Sulfuric Acid, #1733-00034, $1.40
Toluene, #1733-00019, $1.25
Toluene Diisocyanate, #1733-00021, $1.75
Trichloroethylene, #1733-00023, $1.75
Ultraviolet Radiation, #1733-00012, $1.75
Xylene, #1733-00075, $1.75
Zinc Oxide, #1733-00109, $2.10

6.602 *Protection for Workers in Imminent Danger*

Designed to guide employees in reporting to the Occupational Safety and Health Administration (OSHA) any suspected imminent dangers, this 6-page booklet also explains the rights of employees.

OSHA 2205, free; regional offices of OSHA (C1.79). Or: #029-015-00046, $.40; GPO (see C1.0).

6.603 *Carbon Monoxide, Lead,* and *Carcinogens*

These three pamplets summarize what employers and employees should know and do about workplaces where carbon monoxide, lead, or 14 carcinogens are present.

OSHA 2224, OSHA 2230, and OSHA 2204, free; regional offices of OSHA (1.79). Or: $.50; GPO (see C1.0).

6.604 *Mercury, Vinyl Chloride*

These booklets discuss the standards and the prevention of hazards from mercury and vinyl chloride.

OSHA 2243 and OSHA 2225, 8 pp. each, free; OSHA (see C1.79).

6.605 *Women Workers and Job Health Hazards*

A reprint of an article from *Job Safety and Health*, this pamphlet discusses special hazards for women and the issue of sex discrimination.

10 pp., free; OSHA (see C1.79).

6.606 *New Hazards for Firefighters*

This reprint of an article from *Job Safety and Health* discusses hazards from new industrial chemicals and the inadequacy of firefighting equipment.

6 pp., free; OSHA (see C1.79).

6.607 *Essentials of Machine Guarding*

A general discussion of OSHA standards

regarding saws, presses, lathes, shears, jointers, milling machines, woodworking machines, and other machines is given in this booklet.

OSHA 2227, 20 pp., free; OSHA (see C1.79).

6.608 MEDLINE, TOXLINE

Health professionals may find out quickly and easily what has been published recently in any specific biomedical or toxicological subject area, using the on-line computerized data bases MEDLINE and TOXLINE, to which access is available through National Technical Information Service (NTIS). These two services are maintained by the National Library of Medicine.

MEDLINE, updated monthly, contains the current year's citations plus two previous years, for a total of about half a million references to 3,000 medical journals. There are ancillary files covering the biomedical literature beginning in 1969.

TOXLINE contains more than 375,000 references to published human and animal toxicity studies, effects of environmental chemicals and pollutants, adverse drug reactions and analytical methodology, dating from 1965 to the current year.

MEDLINE: #NTIS-PR-107; TOXLINE: #NTIS-PR-256; NITIS (see C1.17).

6.609 *Toxicity Bibliography*

Designed to provide health professionals working in toxicology and related disciplines access to the world's relevant and significant journal literature in this field, this bibliography covers the adverse and toxic effects of drugs and chemicals reported in approximately 2,300 biomedical jorunals.

#HE20.3613, $32.50 per year, $8.15 single copy; GPO (see C1.0).

6.610 *Toxicology Research Projects Directory*

Manifestations of exposure of man and animals to toxic substances are dealt with in this directory. It includes 2,500 projects organized in seven broad chapters to provide the reader with a general overview of toxicology. Projects are classified according to toxic agent, research orientation, and environmental concern.

$50.00 per year; NTIS (see C1.17).

6.611 Toxicity Data Base and Carcinogens

Over 16,500 chemical substances and their toxic effects are listed by the National Institute for Occupational Safety and Health (NIOSH) in the *Registry of Toxic Effects of Chemical Substances.* The reference information contained in the registry is stored in a computer memory and can be searched for special purposes. The result of one such search, entitled *Suspected Carcinogens—1975,* gives the full registry entries for 1,545 tumorigens.

Office of Technical Publications, NIOSH, Room 3-10, 5600 Fishers Lane, Rockville, MD 20852.

6.612 *Standards on Noise Measurements, Rating Schemes, and Definitions: A Compilation*

Materials assembled from various industrial and trade organizations, and technical and scientific societies concerned with acoustics, are collected in this volume.

#003-003-01593-8, 84 pp., $1.90; GPO (see C1.0).

6.613 Checklist of Publications on Specific Hazards

The following publications are available, as priced, from GPO (see C1.0).

Abrasive Metal Finishing, #1733-00122-7, 45¢
Behavioral Effects of Occupational Exposure to Lead, #1733-00067, $3.15
Behavioral Analysis of Worker and Job Hazards in the Roofing Industry, #1733-00077, $2.50
Biologic Standards for the Industrial Worker by Breath Analysis: Trichloroethylene, #1733-00032, $1.80
Caution: Inorganic Metal Cleaners Can Be Dangerous to Your Health, #1733-00108, $1.20
Collaborative Testing of Activated Charcoal Sampling Tubes for Seven Organic Solvents, #1733-00072, $2.95
Comparative Cause-Specific Mortality Patterns by Work Area within the Steel Industry, #1933-00059, $2.70
Compendium of Materials for Noise Control, #1733-00088, $4.20
Design Specifications for Respiratory Breathing

Devices for Firefighters, #1733-00104, $1.40
Development of Criteria for Industrial and Firefighters Head Protective Devices, #1733-00047, $1.45
Development of Design Criteria for Exhaust Systems for Open Surface Tanks, #1733-00040, $1.30
Development and Evaluation of Methods for the Elimination of Waste Anesthetic Gases and Vapors in Hospitals, #1733-00071, $2.15
Dysbarism-Related Osteonecrosis, #1733-00061, $4.50
Electronic Refinements for Improved Operation of Portable Industrial Hygiene Air Sampling Systems, #1733-00070, 85¢
Environmental Conditions in U.S. Copper Smelters, #1733-00063, $1.00
Evaluation and Control of Radon Daughter Hazards in Uranium Mines, #1733-00039, $1.30
Evaluation of Portable Direct-Reading Ozone Meters, #1733-00113-8, $2.25
Evaluation of Spark Source Mass Spectrometry in the Analysis of Biological Samples, #1733-00076, $1.70
Exposure Measurement Action Level and Occupational Environmental Variability, #1733-00112-0, $1.10
Federal Coal Mine Health Programs 1973, #1733-00107, $1.10
Films and Filmstrips on Occupational Safety and Health, #1733-00054, $1.10
Good Work Practices for Tannery Workers, #1733-00132-4, 45¢
Handbook of Statistical Tests for Evaluation of Employee Exposure to Air Contaminants, #1733-00058, $3.85
Health Effects of Occupational Lead and Arsenic Exposure—A Symposium, #1733-00121-9, $3.90
Hospital Occupational Health Service Study, Volume I, #1733-00033, $1.75
Hospital Occupational Health Service Study, Volume II, #1733-00033, $1.75
Hospital Occupational Health Service Study, Volumes III and IV, #1733-00101, $1.40
Hospital Occupational Health Service Study, Volume V, #1733-00102, $1.00
Hospital Occupational Health Service Study, Volume VI, #1733-00103, $1.10
How to Get Along with Your Solvent, #1733-00097, $1.20
Industrial Face Shield Performance Tests, #1733-00129-4, 85¢
Influence of Dynamic Exercise on Fatiguing Isometric Exercise and the Assessment of Changing Levels of Isometric Component, #1733-00074, $1.15
The Industrial Environment: Its Evaluation and Control, #1733-00396, $13.75
Industrial Noise Control Manual, #1733-00073, $3.25
Job Demands and Worker Health, #1733-00083, $3.25
Lead Exposure and Design Consideration for Indoor Firing Ranges, #1733-00111-1, $1.00
List of Personal Hearing Protectors and Attenuation Data, #1733-00101, $1.00
Machine Guarding—Assessment of Need, #1733-00066, $2.80
NIOSH Manual of Analytical Methods, #1733-00041, $3.90
Occupational Exposure to Fibrous Glass—A Symposium, #1733-00133-2, $4.75
Occupational Exposure to Hot Environments—A Proceedings, #1733-00120-1, $2.80
Occupational Health and Safety Symposia: A Proceedings, #1733-00119-7, $3.10
Occupational Safety Research Symposium—Personal Protection, #1733-00089, $2.75
Occupational Medicine Symposia, #1733-00087, $2.15
Occupational Safety and Health Effects Associated with Reduced Levels of Illumination Proceedings of a Symposium, #1733-00057, $2.30
Pilot Study for Development of an Occupational Disease Surveillance Method, #1733-00060, $2.50
A Prescription for Battery Workers, #1733-00130-8, 50¢
Protecting the Health of Coal Miners—An Interagency Approach, #1733-00014, 45¢
Registry of Toxic Effects of Chemical Substances
Rendering Plants—Good Practices for Employees, #1733-00127, 45¢
Safety Program Practices in High Versus Low Accident Rate Companies, #1733-00090, $2.70
Statistical Methods for the Determination of Non-Compliance with Occupational Health Standards, #1733-00062, $1.30
Survey of Hearing Conservation Programs in Industry, #1733-00085, $2.00
Suspected Carcinogens: Subfile of the Toxic Substances List, #1733-00084, $4.85
Theoretical and Laboratory Evaluation of a Portable Direct-Reading Particulate Mass

Concentration Instrument, #1733-00099, 90¢
Trace Element Analysis of Normal Lung Tissue and Hilar Lymph Nodes by Spark Source Mass Spectrometry, #1733-00042, $1.15
Toxicology of Beryllium, #1733-00005, 80¢
Urethane Foams—Good Practices for Employees' Health and Safety, #1733-00131-6, 40¢
UV Transfer Standard Detectors and Evaluation and Calibration of NIOSH UV Hazard Monitor, #1733-00043, 70¢
Working Safety with Pesticides, #1733-00126-0, 55¢

Audio-Visual Aids on Occupational Safety and Health (6.650-6.651)

6.650 Filmographies on Occupational Safety and Health

The following filmographies are available, free, from Reference Section—Code A, National Audio-Visual Center, General Services Administration, Washington, DC 20409.

G054 Films on Accident Prevention
G056 Films on Fire Safety
H006 Films on Highway Design and Engineering
G057 Films on Industrial Safety
G027 Films on On-the-Job Safety
G055 Films on Traffic Safety and Safe Operation of Light and Heavy Vehicles
G039 Films on X-Ray Safety, Electronics in the
G060 Home, Toy Safety, and more
G058 Films on Water Safety
G054 Films on Accidents and Accident Prevention in Aircraft and Space Operations

6.651 Films on Occupational Safety and Health

The following films are available, as priced, from the National Audio-Visual Center, Order Section NACDO, General Services Administration, Washington, DC 20409.

Employer and Employee Rights and Responsibilities

The purpose of these slides is to bring about an understanding of OSHA and the rights and responsibilities of both employer and employee. Student's manual and instructor's manual are included.

168 2x2 color slides, #005127, sale $30,00; extra student's manual, $3.50; extra instructor's manual, $8.50; slides $18.50 per set.

Excavation and Trenching Operations

The problems and hazards found in excavation and trenching are stressed. The proper methods, including various types of shoring, are shown. Instructor's guide and resource supplement are included.

139 slides, 35 mm., color, #689601, sale $21.00; extra instructor's guide, $4.00; resource supplement, $3.50.

Guide to Voluntary Compliance

Guidelines for developing systematic self-inspection procedures for the correction of workplace deficiencies and compliance with Occupational Safety and Health standards are provided in this film. It includes student manual and instructor's manual.

186 2x2 color slide, #005130, sale $55.00; extra student manual, $15.00; extra instructor's manual, $21.00; slides $20.00 per set.

An Audio Aid on OSHA Recordkeeping (Revised Ed.)

The Occupational Safety and Health Act is discussed. Then, using the sample forms as a guide, a detailed explanation is given as to how to recognize and record work-related injuries and illnesses. The Bureau of Labor Statistics Report No. 412, *What Every Employer Needs to Know about OSHA Recordkeeping,* is included as a handy reference guide to answer additional questions. Recordkeeping requirements booklets and OSHA forms Nos. 100, 101, and 102 are included.

20 min. audio-cassette, #009489, sale $5.00.

Access America

The ease and universality of access a well-designed barrier-free environment can provide is illustrated in this film, which shows functional and accessible buildings and facilities throughout the United States. It shows good design solutions which provide access at minimal cost in private business, government, historic preservation, education, transportation, and recreation.

13 min., 16 mm., sound, color, #008625, sale $59.00.

"I Never Had an Accident in My . . ."

For retail meat workers, this film alerts employees to job hazards and makes them aware of safety and health provisions that can protect them from job-related hazards. The film was produced by OSHA in cooperation with Local 324 of Greater New York of the Amalgamated Meat Cutters and Retail Food Store Employees Union.

18 min., 16 mm., color, sound, sale $75.75, rent $10.00.

CONSUMER PRODUCT SAFETY (6.700-6.708)

6.700 Consumer Product Safety Laws

The texts of the laws administered by the Consumer Product Safety Commission (CPSC) are presented in a publication entitled *A Compilation of Laws Administered by the U.S. Consumer Product Safety Commission.* Laws included are the Flammable Fabrics Act, the Federal Hazardous Substances Act, the Poison Prevention Packaging Act, and the Refrigerator Safety Act.

Free; Bureau of Information, CPSC (see C1.100); 800-638-2666 (toll-free).

6.701 *Handbook and Standard for Manufacturing Safer Consumer Products*

The purpose of this handbook is to offer guidelines to executive industrial management for establishing systems to prevent and detect safety hazards in consumer products. It was developed for use by persons in industry who are implementing or planning to implement the Consumer Product Safety Commission standard entitled *A System Standard for Manufacturing Safer Consumer Products.* It is made available to industry to encourage self-regulation and to help achieve, with minimum government intervention, the objectives of the Consumer Product Safety Act of 1972.

Both publications free; Bureau of Information and Education, CPSC (see C1.100); 800-638-2666 (toll-free).

6.702 Technical Assistance for New Product Safety

Regional Offices of the Consumer Product Safety Commission (CPSC) will offer informal opinions, on request, to businesses developing new products who wish to take preventive measures in advance of marketing a product.

CPSC (see C1.100)

6.703 Open Meetings of the Consumer Product Safety Commission

All interested persons, including consumers and industry representatives, have the opportunity to learn about and participate in regulatory actions that concern consumer products by participating in the open meetings held by the Consumer Product Safety Commission (CPSC). Open meetings can include those to discuss regulations under development or already in effect, other matters pending before the Commission, administrative hearings, and petitions under consideration. A public calendar of meetings is published at least seven days before the meeting and usually includes a two-week schedule. It is published each Friday.

To receive the free weekly calendar, write the Office of the Secretary, CPSC, Washington, DC 20207; 202-634-7700.

6.704 *Publications, Films, Fact Shows, Radio and TV Spots*

Publications, slide shows and films, fact sheets, and radio and TV spots available from the Consumer Product Safety Commission (CPSC) are described in this pamphlet. These items are intended primarily for consumer education.

Free; CPSC (see C1.100).

6.705 Center for Consumer Product Technology of the National Bureau of Standards

Safety and performance of consumer products and law enforcement equipment, and the energy efficiency of household appliances, are the areas of interest of the Center for Consumer Product Technology. The Center develops recommended voluntary product standards for industry, and conducts studies on consumer product hazards.

Center for Consumer Product Technology, Institute for Applied Technology, National Bureau of Standards, Building 224, Room A-355, Washington, DC 20234; 301-921-3751.

6.706 National Electronic Injury Surveillance System

National Electronic Injury Surveillance System is a hospital emergency room data system, designed to develop national accidental injury data which can used to identify product safety problems. Data are collected through a network of 119 hospitals and are assembled into the Consumer Product Hazard Index, a comprehensive index of product categories which most frequently appear to be associated with injuries. The index is a guide for activities of the Consumer Product Safety Commission (CPSC).

Office of the Chairman, CPSC (see C1.100).

6.707 National Injury Information Clearinghouse

This information center disseminates data on product-related injuries, and offers a reading room for manufacturers, lawyers, consumer groups, doctors, students, and free-lancers to review in-depth investigations and raw surveillance data. The Clearinghouse maintains and makes available such information as hazard analysis injury reports by product; summaries of in-depth investigations; *National Electronic Injury Surveillance System News* (see 6.706), which presents summary analyses of surveillance data and in-depth investigations on the top ninety products of the Consumer Product Hazard Index; and statistical data on potentially hazardous product-related items.

Office of the Chairman, CPSC (see C1.100).

6.708 Product Safety Indexed Document Collection

This collection of 10,000 documents constitutes a primary source of both technical data and business information on highly diverse types of consumer products. It includes technical reports, articles from professional and trade journals, papers from conferences, government publications, and more. Approximately 300 publications are scanned daily for their relevance to the safety of conumer products.

Office of the Chairman, CPSC (see C1.100).

Chapter 7

EXPORTING

CHAPTER ABSTRACT

This chapter describes the extraordinary range of publications, services, and opportunities available to potential and current United States exporters.

Most of these services originate with the Bureau of International Commerce (BIC) (see 7.0), of the Department of Commerce. The job of BIC is to help expand exports so that the United States can maintain a favorable trade balance. To do this, BIC provides help to the American export business by providing commercial, economic, promotional, shipping, and legal information on general export opportunities and on specific, prospective customers.

Free counseling on these matters is offered by BIC through the nationwide network of Department of Commerce district offices (see C1.10); most businesses will find it profitable to check with these district BIC offices before contacting national headquarters.

The first two sections (7.07-7.54) describe publications and services available from the government which are informative both for the exporter new to the field and for the exporter who is experienced. (For information oriented toward specific countries and commodities, see 7.250-7.271 and 7.350-7.357.)

"Immediate Trade Opportunities" (7.100-7.109) describes a variety of services resulting from the continuously updated marketing computer file of the Department of Commerce. This section is distinguished from the others because the services described are tailored to the special product or service of the inquiring business.

"Overseas Promotional Assistance" (7.150-7.171) describes marketing services available to businesses in foreign locales. Services range from on-site market testing and sales, to overseas office space.

Sources of personal consultation tailored to an individual exporter are described in "Advisory and Technical Assistance" (7.200-7.210).

"Country and Commodity Intelligence" (7.250-7.271) lists sources of information on exporting trends for specific commodities and specific countries. They can also serve as current awareness services in specialized areas.

"Financing" (7.300-7.311) covers both sources of export financing and of loan guarantees. Several guides to financial sources and management are included.

Sources of information offering a broad view of international export-import trends for business planners are listed in "International Market Trend Information" (7.350-7.357).

The last two sections, "Exporting Procedures and Regulations" (7.400-7.410) and "Foreign Legal Requirements" (7.450-7.454) list sources of information on procedural details and domestic and foreign legalities and resources.

Exporting Guides, Bibliographies, and Information Sources (7.0-7.12)

7.0 Organization of the Bureau of International Commerce

There are essentially three major offices of the Bureau of International Commerce (BIC): The Office of International Marketing, the Office of Export Development, and the Office of Market Planning. While each of these has several divisions, their general functions are as follows:

The Office of International Marketing provides overseas marketing assistance to United States companies through a variety of informational and promotional techniques; plans and implements individual country programs to support the marketing needs of United States business on a targeted industry, product, and market basis, and maintains appropriate information services for all such activities; and directs the exhibitions program at commercial trade fairs and United States trade centers.

The Office of Export Development conducts activities in the United States designed to stimulate export marketing in all segments of the domestic economy which have the capability to export; develops promotional activities for increasing national awareness of export potentials and benefits; provides information on commercial participants in world trade and furnishes specific trade investment opportunities to United States businessmen; assists qualified United States firms in achieving maximum participation in major systems and development projects abroad; encourages foreign direct capital investments and licensing by foreign firms in the United States; and provides information and other services consistent with United States balance of payments policies and objectives, to United States firms undertaking investments overseas.

The Office of Market Planning provides principal planning and strategy development for the Bureau; identifies those sectors of United States industry with the greatest export growth potential and examines foreign markets offering the greatest export opportunities to United States industry; establishes intensive promotion cycles for BIC export expansion activities; measures and evaluates Bureau programs; is responsible for programs to represent the interests of the Department to other agencies with regard to the official representation of United States commercial interests abroad.

7.1 *A Basic Guide to Exporting*

Each step involved in exporting, from getting started in a market to pricing, financing, communicating, and shipping, is explained in this basic guide. Services of the Department of Commerce are also described.

63 pp., $1.25; GPO (see C1.0).

7.2 *Export Marketing for Smaller Firms*

How to enter the export business or expand overseas business is explained in this publication. Other publications from the government and private sector useful in planning and executing export trade are annotated.

$1.65; GPO (see C1.0).

7.3 *How to Develop Export Markets for U.S. Foods and Agricultural Products*

A concise set of guidelines for the businessman who is contemplating exporting is provided in this exporter's guide. There is also an instructor's handbook, which provides information for use in conducting meetings, seminars, and workshops on export marketing of agricultural and food products. A visual outline suitable for making transparencies is included.

Extension Service, Department of Agriculture (see C1.1).

7.4 *Services Available to HUD-Related Businesses in International Trade*

A publication entitled *Services Available to HUD-Related Businesses in International Trade* contains basic data about governmental and nongovernmental organizations and trade associations which can help business seek out, consider, and undertake international business transactions.

It summarizes the services available from the Department of State, Department of Commerce, Department of Housing and Urban Development, Export-Import Bank, Overseas Private Investment Corporation, and several other agencies, and also contains basic information on eighteen nongovernmental organizations and trade associations. It summarizes various international organizations and discusses the sources of specific information about individual countries available from the Departments of Commerce, Defense, Housing and Urban Development, and State. It also contains a discussion of how to test foreign markets and promote sales by use of exhibits, catalog shows, trade fairs, and conferences, all with the assistance of the United States government.

#023-000-00301, $1.10; GPO (see C1.0).

7.5 *Publications for American Business from the Domestic and International Business Administration*

An overview of information offered exporters by the government is offered in this publication. It contains minimal annotations and indexes periodicals, studies, reports, books, and brochures of the Domestic and International Business Administration.

Free; Department of Commerce district offices (see C1.10).

7.6 *Foreign Investment and Licensing Checklist*

A checklist of factors to consider prior to negotiation of a foreign direct investment or licensing agreement is a feature of this 13-page publication designed to assist businesses in development of their own checklists when exploring investment and licensing opportunities abroad. It covers problems associated with both developing and developed countries.

Free; Foreign Investment Services Staff, Office of International Investment, BIC, Department of Commerce national or district offices (see C1.10).

7.7 *Department of Commerce Publications Catalog and Index*

Each year, the Department of Commerce issues an annual supplement with this title, listing the publications issued that year, arranged by the issuing bureau or office. It covers the articles printed that year in *Commerce Today*, *Construction Review*, *Survey of Current Business*, *Journal of Research*, and *Fishery Bulletin*, and includes a subject index.

#003-000-00503-8, $1.15; GPO (see C1.0).

7.8 *Selected Publications Checklist*

All of the major publication series published by the Office of International Affairs of the Department of Housing and Urban Development are listed in this brochure. It is reproduced below.

Office of International Affairs, Department of Housing and Urban Development (see C1.40).

Basic Utilities

A Systematic Approach to Basic Utilities in Developing Countries
Sewage Lagoons for Developing Countries

Bibliographies

Bibliography on Mortgage Finance
Socio-Physical Technology
Selected Bibliography on Housing, Building, and Planning
Selected Bibliography on New Towns
Bibliography on Canadian New Towns

Country Profiles

Housing and Urban Development in Australia, 1975
Housing in Guatemala, 1960
Housing and Urban Development in Iran, 1971
Housing and Urban Development in Israel, 1971
Housing and Urban Development in Japan, 1971
Housing in Jordan, 1965
Housing in Liberia, 1967
Housing and Urban Development in Panama, 1971
Housing and Urban Development in Peru, 1971
Self-Help Housing in Puerto Rico, 1971
Housing and Urban Development in Sweden, 1972
Housing and Urban Development in the United Kingdom, 1972

Design

Design for Livability
Proposed Minimum Standards for Permanent Low-Cost Housing
The Thermal Insulating Value of Air Space
Condensation Control in Dwelling Construction

Physiological Objectives in Hot-Weather Housing

Earth Construction and other Basic Technology
Hand Transit (its use)
Use of Spirit Level
Half Lap Joint Construction
Mortar and Block Mix
Brick Laying

Environment
The Human Environment: A World View
Report on the US-USSR Working Group on the Enhancement of the Urban Environment

Homeownership and Housing Management
Saving for a Home
Publicly Provided and Assisted Housing in the U.S.
Condominiums—Their Development and Management
Cooperative Housing
Homeownership in the United States
Cooperative Housing in the United States
Tenant Involvement in Public Housing
An Insured Building Warranty Plan for Home Buyers—English Experience

Housing Finance, Market Analysis, and Insurance
Establishing Savings and Loan Associations in Less-Industrialized Countries
Mortgage Credit Risk Analysis and Servicing of Delinquent Mortgages
European Subsidy Systems—An American Perspective
Estimating Housing Assistance Requirements and Subsidy Costs
Foreign Experience in the Financing of Housing for the Elderly
Housing Market Analysis in Latin America
Housing Market Analysis in Latin America —Worksheet
Bibliography on Mortgage Finance
Selected Statistical Information Related to Housing and Urban Development
Windstorm Insurance in the U.S.
Earthquake Insurance in the U.S.

International Business
Services Available to HUD-Related Businesses in International Trade
Urban Institutions Abroad
Proposed Minimum Standards for Permanent Low-Cost Housing
Housing Market Analysis in Latin America
Housing Market Analysis in Latin America —Worksheet
Comparisons on Construction Costs in Latin American Countries

Industrialized Building and Building Industry
Industrialized Housing—The Opportunity and the Problem in Developing Areas
Building Prefabrication—The State of the Art in World Perspective
Prefabricated Concrete Components for Low-Cost Housing Construction
Colonia Managua (a concrete "tilt-up" system)
Seasonal Unemployment in the Construction Industry
Planned Industrial Parks

Materials
Plant Requirements for the Manufacture of Building Bricks
Plant Requirements for the Manufacture of Wallboard
Prolonging the Life of Wood in Houses
Properties of Experimental Wood-Base House Flooring Materials
Palms—Their Use in Building
Grasses—Their Use in Building
Bamboo—Its Use in Building
Coral and Sea Water in Concrete

New Towns
Financing New Communities—European and U.S. Experience
General Observations on British New Town Planning
New Communities in Selected European Countries
Selected Bibliography on New Towns
Bibliography on Canadian New Towns
Transportation Innovations in New Communities Abroad
HUD-Financed New Communities

Planning and Land Development
Squatter Settlements—The Problem and the Opportunity
Planning Sites and Services Programs
Guidelines for Establishing and Administering Land Development Agencies in the Developing Countries
Urban Renewal
Urban Densities in the U.S. and Japan

Vehicle-Free Zones in City Centers
Village Housing in the Tropics
Village Markets in Ghana
Urban Planning in Developing Countries
Tennessee River Valley
General Observations on British New Town Planning
Major Airports and Their Effects on Regional Planning

Policy and Institutions
Strengthening Urban Administration in Developing Countries
Guidelines for Establishing and Administering Land Development Agencies in the Developing Countries
Urban Growth Policies in Six European Countries
A Study of the Financial Practices of Government in Metropolitan Areas

Self-Help Housing
Aided Self-Help in Housing Improvement
Aided Self-Help Housing in Africa
Leadership Training for Aided Self-Help Housing
How to Build a House Using Self-Help Housing Techniques
Colonia Managua (self-help housing in Nicaragua)
Special Report on Techniques of Aided Self-Help Housing—Some Examples
The Development of an Urban Aided Self-Help Housing Program in Guatemala City
Prefabricated Concrete Components for Low-Cost Housing Construction
Squatter Settlements—The Problem and the Opportunity
Self-Help Housing in Puerto Rico

Transportation
Urban Transportation in the Renewal of American Cities
Transportation Innovations in New Communities Abroad
Major Airports and Their Effects on Regional Planning
Vehicle-Free Zones in City Centers

7.9 *Fifteen Ways the U.S. Department of Commerce Can Help Make Your Business More Profitable*

This is an introductory pamphlet to Bureau of International Commerce services.

Free; Department of Commerce district offices (see C1.0).

7.10 *The Multinational Corporation: Studies on U.S. Foreign Investment*

Vol. 1, 1972, 197 pp., $2.10; Vol. 2, 1973, 82 pp., $1.00; GPO (see C1.0).

7.11 Technology Applications for Less Developed Countries

The Agency for International Development (AID) assists in the creation and supply of new information and methods in the science and technology fields which can be used to promote economic and social advancement in the less-developed countries of the world. AID does this by selecting specific aspects of knowledge developed by and for advanced countries, then systematically adapting such knowledge to make it relevant and useful in the less-developed countries. Research projects are carried out, under contractual agreement, for development problems in areas such as agriculture, health, population and family planning, nutrition, urban and rural development, science and technology, education, economics, and other social sciences, in order to make foreign assistance programs of the agency more effective.

Universities, research foundations, or other organizations which have the capability to understand overseas development problems and to seek solutions through applied research techniques in the above fields are eligible to apply for such contracts.

Director, Interregional Research Staff (TA/RES), Bureau of Technical Assistance, Agency for International Development, Washington, DC 20523; 202-632-1916.

7.12 National Technical Information Service

NTIS (National Technical Information Service) emphasizes that searching before researching can save much effort, time, and money. Whether the research is intended to develop new technology or to provide data with which business decisions can be made, the resources available through NTIS may be useful.

NTIS provides a diversity of services and information. It is the central source for the public sale of government-sponsored research, development, engineering reports, and other analyses. Much of the material to which NTIS can give access is related to engineering and the hard sciences, but there is a growing array of data sources of potentially great value for business planners, market researchers, and others who may need statistics or other data about social, psychological, or demographic factors.

For a complete description of NTIS capability, including on-line searches, published searches, bibliographic services, and more, see 9.0-9.13.

Current Awareness Services (7.50-7.54)

7.50 *Business Service Checklist*

New publications important to both domestic and international trade are listed in this weekly news bulletin from the Department of Commerce.

$9.70 per year; GPO (see C1.0).

7.51 *Export Briefs*

Trade opportunities and foreign trade developments are listed in this weekly trade letter.

Export Trade Services Division, Foreign Agricultural Service, Room 5940-S, Department of Agriculture, Washington, DC 20250.

7.52 *International Marketing Newsmemo*

Information bulletins received directly fro United States Foreign Service, usually distributed unedited, cover a wide range of industries, products, and countries. They are prepared by United States businessmen or by Department of Commerce officess.

NTIS (see C1.17).

7.53 *Commerce America Newsletter* and *Magazine*

Commerce America Newsletter is put out by the area offices of the Domestic and International Business Administration. It is usually two pages and contains items of interest on such topics as government procurement, exporting, area activities, and seminars.

Free; GPO (see C1.0).

Commerce America Magazine is the principal publication of the Department of Commerce. It is a biweekly publication which provides brief descriptions of items or events of interest to business, major articles on economic highlights, domestic business developments, international business reports, individual business opportunities overseas, programs and information being offered by various federal departments and agencies of interest to business, and calendars of important events.

$29.80 per year; GPO (see C1.0).

7.54 *Weekly Government Abstracts: Business and Economics*

Domestic and international commerce, banking and finance, manufacturing and production, consumer affairs, and minority enterprises are among the subjects covered by the current awareness service entitled *Business and Economics.* This is one of a series of 26 newsletters known as *Weekly Government Abstracts.* (For an annotation of the entire series, see 9.11). Each newsletter contains summaries of government research performed by hundreds of organizations, including United States government agencies, private researchers, universities, and special technology groups. The research summaries are listed within two weeks of their receipt at the National Technical Information Service. The last issue of each year is a subject index containing up to ten cross references for each research summary indexed.

$45.00 per year; NTIS (see C1.17).

Immediate Trade Opportunities (7.100-7.109)

7.100 Trade Opportunities Program

Trade Opportunities Program (TOP) is a computer program designed to match automatically an exporter's product with overseas needs on an up-to-the-minute basis.

The exporter identifies the products and types of markets needed, and the nature of the lead; i.e., direct sale, agency distributorship, or calls of tender. This information is fed into the TOP computer. It is run against buyer information from over 200 embassies and consulates in 127 countries. As soon as the computer finds a match, it automatically prints out the information in a special mailer. It includes an envelope for overseas follow-up. Each notice should be in the exporter's hands about one week after the need has been registered overseas.

The basic fee for the creation of a TOP file for an exporter is $25.00, for which the exporter receives up to fifty notices or printouts. For each notice there is an additional charge of 75¢. Hence the total cost for fifty notices is $62.50. Prices on larger numbers of notices may be computed in the same way.

Department of Commerce district offices (see C1.10); or Trade Opportunities Program, Department of Commerce, Washington, DC 20230.

7.101 New Product Information Service

The New Product Information Service (NPIS) is a Bureau of International Commerce (BIC) service which disseminates information worldwide about new United States products and tests market interest in them. The emphasis is on energy-efficient products. Any manufacturer is eligible, and the service is free.

A product selected for NPIS must be genuinely new, not simply a modification with marginal improvements, and must be immediately available for export. When a product is selected, it is published in *Commercial News for the Foreign Service* (CNFS), which is a basic informational link between the Department of Commerce and the Department of State's Foreign Service Posts. The Foreign Service Posts, in turn, extract the information from CNFS and put it in a specially tailored commercial newsletter for distribution within the foreign country. On receipt of an inquiry, the United States manufacturer may contact a Department of Commerce regional office for advice and assistance.

The district office of the Department of Commerce can supply Application Form DIB-4063T (see C1.10). The completed form should be sent to Office of International Marketing, Room 4009, Bureau of International Commerce, Department of Commerce, Washington, DC 20230.

7.102 American International Traders Register

The purpose of this service is to identify United States firms in, or interested in, exporting for possible participation in United States overseas projects. The list contains over 30,000 firms interested in exporting. Information available includes complete name and address of the firm, telephone number, name of international executive officer, and appropriate two-digit product code by Standard Industrial Classification for that firm. The data are provided in a tabular printout form for a fixed fee of $350.00. An additional charge of 3¢ each is made for pressure-sensitive address labels, if requested.

American International Traders Section, Room 1033, Export Information Division, Department of Commerce, Washington, DC 20230; 202-377-2107 or 4225.

7.103 Foreign Traders Index

The Foreign traders Index (FTI) is a master computer file of over 140,000 importing firms in 130 countries. The file now contains records from 1969 through the present, and there is a constant effort to keep the file current. Manufacturers, service organizations, agent representatives, retailers, wholesalers, and cooperatives are listed. There is minimal information on financial institutions and government agencies. The purpose of FTI is to provide a broad data base from which the following export mailing lists can be retrieved:

a. *Data Tape Service*. Companies may purchase all or part (selected countries) of FTI in magnetic tape form to run on their own computers. The service cost is $177.50 per country, up to 15 countries, or $2,500 for the entire file.

b. *Business Firms Trade List*. All FTI data for 34 developing countries, as of December 1976, are contained in the Business Firms Trade Lists.

The price of the data is $3.00 per country.

c. *State Trading Organizations.* These trade lists describe state-owned or controlled trading organizations in countries where all trade is conducted through such agencies. The price of the data is $3.00 per country.

d. *East-West Trading Firms.* This list includes firms trading with specific Communist countries and describes their activities. The price of the data is $3.00 per country.

e. *Export Mailing List Service* (EMLS). The above lists (a-d) are automatically produced. EMLS, however, is a special computer run, tailored to specific exporter needs. There is a $10.00 set-up charge, plus 6¢ per retrieved name. It is not possible to limit a list to a particular number, but the purchaser will be contacted if it appears that the list will substantially exceed 500. Normal delivery time is 21 days from receipt of request.

For detailed information on submitting a request for retrieval, send or call for the pamphlet entitled *Export Contact List Services* and a form request from the district office of the Department of Commerce (see C1.10).

All five export lists are available from the Bureau of International Commerce, Room 1033-EID/FTI, Department of Commerce, Washington, DC 20230; 202-377-2988. Or see district offices of Department of Commerce (see C1.10).

7.104 Foreign Investment Services Staff

Through the Foreign Investment Services Staff (FISS), assistance is given United States businesses in locating potential overseas licensees and partners. FISS provides specific regional and country marketing data and guides business toward sources of capital. *Commerce Today* publishes foreign investment and licensing proposals which request United States participation and technology.

Department of Commerce district offices (see C1.10).

7.105 Index to Trade Lists

An index of all printed trade lists, including the new ones that may not be listed here or in Bureau of International Commerce literature, is available by request.

Export Information Division, Room 1033, Bureau of International Commerce, Department of Commerce, Washington, DC 20230; see also district offices of Department of Commerce (C1.10).

7.106 Major Projects Programs

Under Major Projects Programs, direct assistance is provided United States companies, from the first announcement of a project in the planning stage to an actual bid. Specialists match up projects with United States firm capabilities in each project phase. The companies are notified of the bidding opportunity and are offered help in contract competition. Also, a businessman may take advantage of the Foreign Projects Reference Room, located at 14th Street between Constitution Avenue and E Street N.W., Washington, D.C. where major projects being considered by international financial houses can be examined.

The service targets $5 million projects in export value. In less than three years, the project produced nearly $3 billion in export sales for United States companies.

Department of Commerce district offices (see C1.10).

7.107 Target Industry Program

In intensive research in target markets, yielding a *Global Market Survey* for about twenty countries, United States advanced industry is matched with potential overseas buyers. In addition, a tailored marketing plan is developed. Fifteen industries have now been identified for Target Industry status. $353 million in new export business was generated in the first six campaigns, introducing 238 countries to exporting.

Office of International Marketing, BIC, Department of Commerce national or regional offices (see C1.10).

7.108 Overseas Product Sales Group

Overseas Product Sales Group (OPS) provides personalized assistance to Trade Opportunities Program (TOP) subscribers (see 7.100) in bidding against foreign competitors for export sales possibilities with a potential value of $1 million or more. The OPS specialists collect, inventory, and disseminate early information on export sales opportunities from the TOP computer and many other sources.

Department of Commerce district offices (see C1.10).

7.109 Trade Contact Survey

At the request of the Bureau of International Commerce (BIC), a foreign service officer stationed in a target market will make surveys to locate specific firms which meet the particular requirements of the exporting firm. The foreign service officer reports at least three suitable companies.

$10.00, each survey; Department of Commerce district offices (see C1.10).

Overseas Promotional Assistance (7.150-7.171)

7.150 United States Trade Center Exhibitions

The United States operates trade centers in major marketing centers of the world: Frankfurt, London, Mexico City, Milan, Osaka, Paris, Seoul, Singapore, Sydney, Stockholm, Taipei, Tehran, Tokyo, Vienna, and Warsaw. About seven major product exhibitions are held annually at each site, with about thirty exhibitors at each one. Sometimes product seminars are held in conjunction with the exhibitions to explain products more fully.

Trade center staff promote the exhibition prior to its occurrence. Prospect lists usually contain 6,000 to 20,000 names, and they are all directly invited to attend. The Department of Commerce can provide exhibit space, design and construct the exhibit, set up the display, supply all utilities, and pay for returning unsold items. An exhibitor must provide products, supply handout information, ship materials to the site, assign a representative, and make a specified and variable participation contribution.

Department of Commerce district offices (see C1.10).

7.151 *U.S. Trade Promotion Facilities Abroad*

Technical data, market summaries, and reviews of trade center activities and programs around the world are described in this brochure.

Free; Office of Export Development, Room 4002, BIC, Department of Commerce national office; see also district offices. See C1.10.

7.152 *International Marketing Events*

International Marketing Events serves as a guide to all United States-sponsored overseas promotional events, such as trade missions, trade center exhibitions, technical sales seminars, catalog exhibitions, and in-store promotions.

Office of International Marketing, Room 4009, BIC, Department of Commerce national office; see also district offices. See C1.10.

7.153 International Trade Fairs

There are over 800 specialized and general trade fairs held each year all around the world. Their purpose is the first-hand display of products for examination by potential foreign buyers. The Department of Commerce assists with display and promotion.

Department of Commerce district offices (see C1.10).

7.154 *Overseas Trade Promotions Calendar*

A 12-month schedule of international trade fairs, exhibitions, and all other activities planned by the Department of Commerce is offered in this publication.

Free; Office of Export Development, Room 4002, BIC, Department of Commerce national office; see also district offices. See C1.10.

7.155 Commercial Exhibitions

The Department of Commerce will sponsor pavilions for United States business in international exhibitions and trade fairs occurring outside United States trade center auspices. In addition, solo exhibitions are sponsored where no trade fairs are available and where research shows excellent trade possibilities exist. An intensive promotional campaign is conducted prior to each of these exhibitions, as with a United States trade center exhibition.

Department of Commerce district offices (see C1.10).

7.156 Joint Export Establishment Promotion

Joint Export Establishment Promotions (JEEP) are product exhibitions, participated in by up to eight manufacturers of related products. They are generally held when a full-scale exhibition is not warranted but there is an existing market that can be tapped. A JEEP may be initiated by the Department of Commerce or by a company or group of companies that produce related products.

The Department of Commerce provides facilities and technical assistance on shipping, marketing, background information on local trade practices, and display design. It will also provide up to $300 per participant for preexhibit promotion and will unpack, install, and repack display materials at the exhibit, as well as pay for return of unsold freight up to three tons. Participants must match the $300, provide display products and literature, provide a representative, and pay for shipment of materials to the display center.

Department of Commerce district offices (see C1.10).

7.157 Catalog Exhibitions

Where trade show participation possibilities are limited, exhibitions of catalogs and literature and sales aids at United States foreign service posts is possible. Such exhibitions are usually held in developing markets and are aimed at testing market interest, developing sales leads, and locating agents and distributors.

Department of Commerce district offices (see C1.10).

7.158 In-Store Promotions

In-store promotions are special sales events in which United States products are featured in a foreign retail store. Usually about one week in duration, the promotion includes extensive local media use.

Department of Commerce district offices (see C1.10).

7.159 Between-Show Promotions

Any exporter may use trade fair facilities free of charge for between-show displays, promotions, and seminars. Hundreds of firms do this annually. Market counseling and target audience identification is done at a modest cost.

Department of Commerce district offices (see C1.10).

7.160 *How to Get the Most from Overseas Exhibitions*

This is a step-by-step description of the process for participating in an overseas exhibition, including time-saving merchandising suggestions.

Free; Office of Export Development, Room 4002, BIC, Department of Commerce national office; see also district offices. See C1.10.

7.161 Carnet: Customs Privileges for Promotional Purposes

Carnets are international customs documents which guarantee against customs duties. They are composed of a series of vouchers which list the goods covered and the countries to be visited. The carnet system is designed to permit duty-free, temporary entry of commercial samples for the purpose of demonstration and promotion.

Foreign Business Practices Division, BIC, Department of Commerce national office (see C1.10).

7.162 Foreign Buyer Program

The Foreign Buyer Program is designed to encourage foreign buyers to visti the United States and to assist them in purchasing United States goods and services. The program is divided into three parts:

a. *Specialized foreign buyer programs* sponsor special buying groups with specific itineraries with selected United States suppliers.

b. *United States trade shows* are special domestic shows geared toward products with high sales potential. International visitors are welcomed to the show by the Department of Commerce.

c. *Individual foreign buyers programs* offer assistance from the Department of Commerce project officer to individual foreign buyers.

Foreign Buyer Staff, Office of Export Development, BIC, Department of Commerce national office (see C1.10).

7.163 Product Marketing Service

Through this service, office space is made available to United States businessmen doing business overseas. Such space is available for up to five days in all United States foreign trade centers around the world. The offices are fully equipped and offer free local telephone service, audio-visual equipment, and help in gaining secretarial and interpreter services (at the client's expense). The foreign trade center can also provide a market briefing and a list of key prospects, as well as help in setting up appointments.

The cost is $25.00 per day. Anyone is eligible who is a corporate decisionmaker and who takes with him the appropriate sales materials. In addition, the product must have a United States identify and at least 50 percent of its component value must be made in the United States.

Department of Commerce district offices (see C1.10).

7.164 U.S. Technical Sales Seminar

These seminars are relatives of the trade mission. They are designed especially for rapidly developing, high technology markets. The purpose is to introduce or more widely distribute United States know-how. The seminar usually consists of seven United States representatives, who visit three regional countries for about eighteen days. Technical papers are presented, and opportunities for sales development are arranged. Department of Commerce officials do preparatory and coordination work, as they do with the trade missions.

Office of International Marketing, BIC, Department of Commerce national office (see C1.10).

7.165 Trade Missions

Trade missions are personal tours of businessmen in groups of from five to twelve to specific markets to accomplish specific market development objectives. There are two kinds of missions:

a. *Specialized Trade Missions.* This type of mission is originated, organized, and run by the Department of Commerce. The Department selects a product grouping based on intensive market research, and announces the mission through the subscription bulletin *Commerce Today*. The Department then recruits the participants from private industry executives in the affected or interested industry group.

Each mission member must pay most of his major expenses in the promotion of his products. The mission has a mission director from the Department of Commerce and an advance man who establishes a tight schedule of appointments, meetings, and press conferences for each individual on the mission.

In many cases, nonparticipants can have their products represented overseas by trade mission representatives. It can be a unique opportunity for firms to be represented overseas without cost.

b. *Industry-Organized, Government-Approved Trade Missions* (IOGA). As the name indicates, these missions are initiated by a firm or group of firms in the private sector, or trade associations, Chambers of Commerce, or state government agencies, and gain Department of Commerce sanction and support by meeting specified criteria. IOGA's, once approved, are assigned a project officer and an advance officer who perform most of the functions that are performed for regular missions.

Essentially, an IOGA will meet Department of Commerce criteria if it has a product to meet a specific need and if it cooperates with the Department of Commerce. Together, the effectiveness of the mission is maximized.

Department of Commerce district offices (see C1.10).

7.166 Trade Announcement Service

United States businessmen traveling abroad are helped to market their products through embassy and consulate briefings, introductions, and other means. The traveler must notify the Bureau of International Commerce of his intention to travel and arrange, through meetings or correspondence, for specific assistance.

Department of Commerce district offices (see C1.10).

7.167 World Traders Data Reports

World Traders Data Reports is a service which offers on request a trade profile of a specific foreign company. It is conducted on site by a foreign service official. A typical report includes background information, year organized, number of employees, sales area, type of operation, products handled, name of contact officer, reputation of company in trade finance circles, names of foreign firms the company represents, and the foreign service officer's comments.

To apply for the service, request Form DIB-431 from the district offices of Department of Commerce (see C1.10). This office also offers assistance in filling out the form. Send the completed form to Bureau of International Commerce, Room 1033-EID/FTI, Department of Commerce, Washington, DC 20230.

$15.00 per report.

7.168 *Key Officers in Foreign Posts, A Guide for Businessmen*

$3.00 per year, $1.00 single copy; Department of Commerce district offices (see C1.10).

7.169 Agricultural Attaches

The agricultural attache is the official representative of United States agriculture overseas. The attache supervises market activities in his assigned country, reports to the Foreign Agricultural Service, and apprises the United States of trade possibilities. The attache is in frequent contact with foreign buyers and overseas representatives of United States firms and associations. Over 100 countries are covered by the agricultural attaches in the posts listed below.

Foreign Agricultural Service, Department of Agriculture, Washington, DC 20250; 202-447-3448.

Australia, Canberra
Austria, Vienna
Bangladesh, Dacca
Belgium, Brussels
Brazil, Brasilia
Canada, Ottawa
Chile, Santiago
Colombia, Bogota
Costa Rica, San Jose
Dominican Republic, Santo Domingo
Ecuador, Quito
El Salvador, San Salvador
France, Paris
Germany, Bonn
Greece, Athens
Guatemala, Guatemala City
Hong Kong
India, New Delhi
Indonesia, Jakarta
Iran, Tehran
Ireland, Dublin
Israel, Tel Aviv
Italy, Rome
Japan, Tokyo
Kenya, Nairobi
Korea, Seoul
Lebanon, Beirut
Liberia, Monrovia
Malaysia, Kuala Lumpur
Mexico, Mexico City
Morocco, Rabat
Netherlands, The Hague
New Zealand, Wellington
Nigeria, Lagos
Pakistan, Islamabad
Peru, Lima
Philippines, Manila
Poland, Warsaw
Portugal, Lisbon
South Africa, Pretoria
Spain, Madrid
Sweden, Stockholm
Switzerland, Bern
Taiwan, Taipei
Thailand, Bangkok
Trinidad, Port-of-Spain
Turkey, Ankara
U.S.S.R., Moscow
Uraguay, Montevideo
Venezuela, Caracas
Yugoslavia, Belgrade
Zaire, Kinshasa

7.170 The Foreign Agricultural Service

The Foreign Agricultural Service (FAS) of the Department of Agriculture is a service organization for exporters of food and agriculture products. It has agricultural attaches stationed at the leading markets overseas, commodity and trade policy specialists to analyze and work on various problems in world trade, and a worldwide program to develop export opportunities. Some of its services are described below:

The Trade Opportunity Referral Service offers information on where one can sell specific products overseas. Foreign buyers contact the United States agricultural attaches and give them information on the food products they want to purchase. This is cabled to the Washington office and disseminated to participating United States firms through a computerized direct mail service and a weekly trade bulletin called *Export Briefs.*

The New Product Testing program is designed to help locate overseas markets for new entrants into the overseas food market. First, it is determined if the specific product will be admitted to the foreign market by a label clearance procedure, using the overseas attaches of the FAS. There is a charge of $5.00 per label per country. If the product meets the entry requirements, the FAS can arrange a taste test by a consumer or marketing panel. Taste testing is presently operating in the United Kingdom, Sweden, France, Switzerland, Japan, West Germany, Spain, Belgium, Norway, Denmark, and Austria. The cost of the service in the various countries ranges from $50 to $200 per product. The seller is furnished with results indicating the level of product acceptance.

Test Marketing and Point-of-Purchase Promotions. Once the product is taste tested, the Service can arrange to have it test marketed to find out how it will actually sell. The procedure will vary according to the product and markets, but in most cases the test will be a point-of-purchase promotion in a retail group of stores, using consumer advertising and demonstrations to introduce the product. The selected products will be placed on the store shelves for a minimum period of one week, after which an inventory will be taken to determine sales results. Point-of-purchase promotions are a standard procedure in leading foreign markets for drawing consumer attention to United States food products. They are conducted through foreign attaches of the Service.

Trade Exhibits. Hotel-Restaurant-Institutional Exhibits/Demonstrations are held in several countries each year for all segments of the foreign food service trade. From twenty-five to fifty United States firms exhibit institutional size packs of products. Professional demonstrators are used. The exhibits run for two to three days and are usually held in a hotel.

International Food Shows are held annually in some of the leading foreign markets. The ones in which FAS participates are generally consumer-trade-oriented food and beverage expositions attracting exhibitors and buyers from many foreign countries.

Agent Food Exhibits are organized and managed by the agricultural attache with cooperation of the foreign agents of United States food companies. The exhibits are usually held in hotels, with the agents displaying the complete line of food products of the company or companies represented.

Catalog Shows feature a display of catalogs of various United States food items supplied by firms and their agents. Key members of the local import trade are invited. Orders can be placed directly from the catalogs, or the firms can be contacted for more information.

Agricultural Attache Product Displays are designed as a showpiece of United States food products for key officials in controlled economies where the consumer is unable to influence imports.

Livestock Shows are held in a number of countries to promote the sale of United States breeding stock and feedstuffs.

There is an exhibit fee for participating companies which covers exhibit space, facilities, and various trade relation services, including inviting members of the foreign trade to the exhibit. The exhibitor provides the product and full-time representation at the exhibit, if the activity requires exhibitor presence.

Sales Teams. Personal visits with foreign buyers are arranged by the Foreign Agricultural Service sales team program. FAS selects a market with export potential and selects five or six United States firms handling food products with sales possibilities in that market to participate in a sales mission. The program is backed by market research to identify the products of best export opportunity, and is tailored to the individual needs of each member of the team. Companies pay a participation fee and their representatives' travel and living expenses, and provide a supply of product samples for distribution to the buyers. FAS makes all necessary arrangements, including preparation and printing of a sales team brochure, rental of sales room facilities, and scheduling appointments with potential foreign buyers.

Foreign Agricultural Service, Department of Agriculture, Washington, DC 20250; 202-447-3448.

7.171 East-West Trade Assistance

The Bureau of East-West Trade assists with the procedural problems and details of dealing with the U.S.S.R., China, and Eastern Europe. It helps with trade fairs, exhibitions, etc. It also conducts research to find out needs and what is most likely to sell in a given area; the possibilities are then ranked in order of best potential. It provides counseling, literature, and studies, as well as information concerning whom to contact and how.

Bureau of East-West Trade, Department of Commerce, Washington, DC 20230.

Advisory and Technical Assistance (7.200-7.210)

7.200 Business Counseling Service

Counseling services, including assistance with market research, product promotion, and financing, with primary emphasis on exporting, are offered by the Department of Commerce district offices and by the Business Counseling Section of the Bureau of International Commerce in Washington, D.C. Designed to give businesses a maximum amount of information in a minimum amount of time, the service helps the businessman analyze problems and determine answers. Offices are located nationwide; each office can mobilize the resources of the Department of Commerce on behalf of a business.

The Washington office also has country specialists (see C1.15), with whom an exporter can discuss specific marketing problems. Finally, the Department of State has country desk officers who can brief businessmen on the political climate in specific countries (Department of State, 2201 C St. N.W., Washington, DC 20520; 202-655-4000).

7.201 *Export Directory*

This annual publication is a major source of information produced by the Foreign Agricultural Service (FAS). It lists current export services of FAS, state organizations and export groups, state departments of agriculture and associated organizations, United States market development cooperators, other United States agricultural trade associations, and more. It includes names, addresses, and telephone numbers in all areas.

Information Services Staff, Foreign Agricultural Service, Room 5918 South, Department of Agriculture, Washington, DC 20250; 202-447-3448.

7.202 Domestic Seminars

The purpose of the Domestic Seminars is to educate and inform United States business concerning exporting in specific market areas. District offices sponsor general as well as specific seminars on an ad hoc basis. Many focus on specific global areas or countries; e.g., "Doing Business in Peru," or "Exporting to the Far East."

Department of Commerce district offices (see C1.10).

7.203 District Export Councils

There is one Export Council connected with each Department of Commerce field office. A council consists of groups of businessmen experienced in export whose expertise is wide enough both to assist the novice and to exchange ideas with the veteran in business. Councils assist in seminars and workshops set up at the field office with cooperation of Chambers of Commerce, trade associations, banks, schools, and the Small Business Administration.

Department of Commerce district offices (see C1.10).

7.204 Agent Distributor Service

The goal of Agent Distributor Service is to find overseas representation for United States companies. It is a cooperative program between the Bureau of International Commerce and the Foreign Service, as is the Trade Contact Survey (see 7.109). It is primarily for those firms that feel they need help with their foreign distribution beyond what can be offered by other programs of the Bureau of International Commerce. The service gives on-site, overseas assistance in locating up to three foreign firms that are willing to correspond with a businessman regarding a specific proposal.

$25.00; Department of Commerce district offices (see C1.10).

7.205 Market Development Cooperators

The agricultural export development program is carried out in cooperation with more than sixty agricultural trade and producer groups, called cooperators. These groups are utilized to the maximum extent practicable in carrying out foreign market development activities. Preference is given to trade groups which are industry-wide or nationwide in membership and scope. Jointly financed export promotional activities undertaken by the Foreign agricultural Service (FAS) and these private industry groups include advertising, merchandising, trade servicing, training and educational programs, seminars, demonstrations, international trade exhibits, and trade missions to and from the United States.

The United States associations and trade groups with continuing agreements with the FAS for overseas market development projects are listed below.

Foreign Agricultural Service, Department of Agriculture, Washington, DC 20250; 202-447-3448.

American Angus Association
American Brahman Breeders' Association
American Hereford Association
American International Charolais Association
American Polled Hereford Association
American Quarter Horse Association
American Seed Trade Association
American Soybean Association
Brown Swiss Cattle Breeders Association
Burley and Dark Leaf Tobacco Export Association, Inc.
California Cling Peach Advisory Board
California Prune Advisory Board
California Raisin Advisory Board
Cotton Council International
Dairy Society International
Emba Mink Breeders Association
Florida Department of Citrus
Great Plains Wheat, Inc.
Holstein-Friesian Association of America
International Brangus Breeders' Association, Inc.
International Institute for Cotton
Leaf Tobacco Exporters Association, Inc.
Millers' National Federation
Mohair Council of America
National Association of Animal Breeders
National Dry Bean Council, Inc.
  Michigan Bean Industry
  New York State Bean Shippers Association
National Peanut Council
National Potato Promotion Board
National Red Cherry Institute
National Renderers Association
North America Blueberry Council
Northwest Horticultural Council
Poultry and Egg Institute of America
Protein Grain Products International
Rice Council for Market Development
Santa Gertrudis Breeders International
Tanners Council of America, Inc.
Tobacco Associates, Inc.
USA Dry Pea and Lentil Council, Inc.
U.S. Feed Grains Council
Western Wheat Associates, U.S.A., INC.

7.206 State Departments of Agriculture and State Export Agencies

State departments of agriculture and related agencies cooperate with the Department of Agriculture in promoting and marketing abroad United States foods and other agricultural products. Many states now have full-time international marketing specialists.

The states solicit exporters and potential exporters for the Trade Opportunity Referral Service (see 7.170); they solicit exhibitors for exhibits and export sales teams sponsored by the Department of Agriculture; and they help commercial companies get into the export business or expand existing export business.

Through the National Association of State Departments of Agriculture (NASDA) and the NASDA Subcommittee on International Trade, the states recommend and supply marketing representatives to undertake special missions and studies for the Department of Agriculture, including the recently inaugurated product identification studies in several world areas.

The state export marketing programs have been given new impetus by the organization of five regional groups that work exclusively on export activity. Forty-one states are members of one or more groups. The groups and member states are as follows:

Mid-America International Agri-Trade Council (MIATCO)
Member states: Illinois, Indiana, Iowa, Kansas, Michigan, Minnesota, Missouri, Nebraska,

North Dakota, Ohio, South Dakota, Wisconsin

Headquarters: 300 West Washington St., Suite 710, Chicago, IL 60606; 312-268-4488

Atlantic International Marketing Association (AIM)

Member states: Georgia, Maryland, North Carolina, South Carolina, Virginia

President: Gene Carroll, Jr., North Carolina Department of Agriculture

Pacific Northwest International Trade Council (PNITC)

Member states: Idaho, Montana, Oregon, Washington

President: John George, Ore-Ida Foods, Inc., Boise, ID 83707

Eastern U.S. Agricultural and Food export Council, Inc. (EUSAFEC)

Member states: Connecticut, Delaware, Maine, Massachusetts, New Hampshire, New Jersey, New York, Pennsylvania, Rhode Island, Vermont

Headquarters: 2 World Trade Center, Room 5095, New York, NY 10047; 212-432-0020

Southern United States Trade Association (SUSTA)

Member states: Alabama, Arkansas, Florida, Georgia, Kentucky, Louisiana, Maryland, Mississippi, North Carolina, Oklahoma, South Carolina, Tennessee, Texas, Virginia, West Virginia

Headquarters: International Trade Mart, Suite 338, 2 Canal St., New Orleans, LA 70103; 504-523-6887

7.207 Briefings on Foreign Commerce Affairs

The Office of Public Programs of the Department of State can arrange group briefings for businessmen visiting Washington, D.C., on many subjects relevant to political and economic conditions in foreign countries, and other exporting matters. Several times a year, three-day seminars are held for officials of international corporations, business planners, and economists.

Officials of the Department of State who are experienced in international commercial and economic matters are available, also, as speakers for meetings, seminars, workshops, and dinners throughout the United States on a reimbursable basis. Regional foreign policy conferences concentrating on economic and business issues are held periodically in cooperation with local cosponsors in major cities.

Office of Public Programs, Department of State, Washington, DC 20520; 202-632-1433.

7.208 Office of the Ombudsman

Businesses can obtain information and advice on such matters as federal procurement, domestic or world markets, federal regulations, financial assistance, technology transfer, occupational safety and health, and product safety from the Office of the Ombudsman. The Ombudsman will help with specific problems confronted by businessmen, by locating needed information, the proper official to contact, or the right program.

The Ombudsman, which is part of the Bureau of Domestic Commerce of the Domestic and International Business Administration, solicits business opinions on government programs.

The Ombudsman issues *Situation Reports* from time to time on current topics. Subjects covered have included productivity, new product warranties, proposed legislation of interest to small business, and individual materials shortages. The *U.S. Industrial Outlook* is published annually, with planning and marketing data and informed opinion on over 200 industries as compiled and written by analysts of the Bureau of Domestic Commerce. The Ombudsman also holds seminars, briefings, and conferences with business.

Office of the Ombudsman, Bureau of Domestic Commerce, Room 3800, Department of Commerce, Washington, DC 20230; 202-377-3176.

7.209 Telephone Directory of Country Marketing Managers

The Department of Commerce maintains specialists in export marketing for every area and country of the world. Their job is to keep abreast of anything that may bear upon export opportunities and keep those involved in trade in their areas current on new developments. The Department of Commerce district offices frequently ask their assistance or refer prospective traders to them. It is their job to assist the private sector in maximizing its exporting potential within a given area of the world.

Department of Commerce district offices (see C1.10); also Country Marketing Managers (see C1.15).

7.210 Department of Agriculture Export Specialists

Export Trade Services Division
Director: 202-447-6343
Chief, State/Trade Coordination Branch: 202-447-2423
Chief, Program Operations Branch: Overseas exhibits and other events, 202-447-7777
Chief, Program Development Branch: 202-447-7787

Program Managers
TORS and Export Briefs: 202-447-7103
Transportation Coordinator: 202-447-7481
New Products Testing System Coordinator: 202-447-2423

International Marketing Directors
Cotton: 202-447-5635
Dairy and Poultry: 202-447-6233
Fruits and Vegetables: 202-447-7931
Grain and Feed: 202-447-5217
Livestock and Meat: 202-447-3899
Oilseeds and Products: 202-447-8809
Tobacco and Seeds: 202-447-6917

Country and Commodity Intelligence (7.250-7.272)

7.250 *Global Market Surveys*

These surveys are in-depth, worldwide marketing studies for a particular product, kind of product, or carefully defined group of products. The surveys are usually between 100 and 200 pages long; executive summaries of five or six pages are also available. The *Global Market Survey* presents a comprehensive picture of the current market and its potential in individual countries around the world. There are currently about ten surveys which are recent enough to be useful.

Prices vary from $1.00 to about $4.00; GPO (see C1.0). See also Department of Commerce district offices (C1.10).

7.251 *Foreign Economic Trends and their Implications for the United States*

Every country in which United States goods are sold or in which there is an export potential is covered in this series. The current economic situation and trends, and the impact or potential this holds for United States trade, are assessed.

Approximately 150 reports, issued semi-annually, $37.50 per year; GPO (see C1.0).

7.252 *Overseas Business Reports*

Overseas Business Reports (OBR) are basic publications of the Bureau of International Commerce on leading United States trading partners. Most are revised annually. There are six series of OBR's:

Basic Data on the Economy of (country)
Market Factors in (country)
Marketing in (country)
Selling in (country)
World Trade Outlook in (region)

There are also miscellaneous OBR's such as *United States Trade with Major World Areas* and *Regional Trade Profiles*. Countries covered are listed in *Publications for American Business from DIBA*.

$36.50 per year for 60 to 70 reports on a given country, or 50¢ per single report; GPO (see C1.0).

7.253 *Urban Institutions Abroad*

The major organizations, governmental and nongovernmental, which support housing and community development are identified by country, in this book.

Office of International Affairs, Department of Housing and Urban Development (HUD) (see C1.40).

7.254 *HUD International Country Profile, Housing and Urban Development in (country)*

This series of publications provides basic information on the government, industry trends, national development plans, urban and rural development programs, transportation and communication, availability of local capital, contacts for businesses, bibliographies, and more, on selected countries in the developing world. The purpose of the series is to provide basic information to the United States housing industry, as well as to American businesses interested in foreign business opportunities and investments.

Office of International Affairs, HUD (see C1.40).

7.255 *Country Report Series, Housing in (country)*

In this series of reports, individual country reports are designed to assist in the orientation of AID (Agency for International Development) technicians, and to provide basic information for consultants scheduled to undertake overseas assignments as well as for American businessmen interested in foreign investment. The series is issued by the Office of International Affairs of the Department of Housing and Urban Development, as a service to AID.

Office of International Affairs, HUD (see C1.40).

7.256 *Market Potential for U.S. Agricultural Commodities in Select Mideastern and North African Countries*

The United States exporter will find this publication useful in deciding which countries are likely to be good markets for American farm products. After presenting a general overview of recent developments in the Mideastern and North African area, the report gives information on the foreign market development program of the Foreign Agricultural Service. It also includes detailed studies of market conditions in fourteen nations, and tables giving basic economic, demographic, and geographic information for each country.

Foreign Agricultural Service, Room 5918 South, Department of Agriculture, Washington, DC 20250.

7.257 *Sources of Information on American Firms for International Buyers*

Local sources, business directories, mailing list houses, trade association directories, directories of directories, and trade journals are listed in this sourcebook.

34 pp., 45¢; GPO (see C1.0).

7.258 *Engineers' Overseas Handbook*

United States engineering firms interested in developing business overseas will find in this handbook a condensed source of information on market conditions in 114 countries of the free world. Included are current conditions and important requirements which affect the ability of the consulting engineers to work on overseas projects.

#003-008-00138-6, 250 pp., $2.80; GPO (see C1.0).

7.259 *Country Market Sectoral Surveys*

These in-depth surveys concentrate on single-country analyses of the most promising areas for export opportunities. About fifteen industrial sectors are analyzed.

Prices range from 25¢ to 50¢ each; Department of Commerce district offices (see C1.10).

7.260 *Producer Goods Research*

A series of in-depth reports describes the most promising export opportunities for a single United States producer goods industry or group of industries.

Prices range from 25¢ to 50¢; NTIS (see C1.17).

7.261 *Consumer Goods Research*

A series of in-depth reports describes the most promising export opportunities for a single United States consumer goods industry or group of industries.

Prices range from 25¢ to 50¢; NTIS (see C1.17).

7.262 *Investment Handbooks*

Designed to assist both exporters and investors in marketing abroad, this series describes basic conditions and the economic outlook for a particular country, giving comprehensive data on the country's natural resources, industry, power facilities, finance, taxation, business methods, trade, and the government's attitude toward private foreign investment.

Department of Commerce district offices (see C1.10).

7.263 *Markets Abroad for U.S. Consumer Goods*

The market potential for American consumer goods in twenty foreign countries is analyzed in this brief survey by the United States government.

#COM-74-10975/PTC, $5.75 paperbound, $2.25 microfiche: NTIS (see C1.17).

7.264 *Foreign Market Reports*

Distributed by request only, this series of specialized reports on business developments is of interest to exporters of specific items. Commodity reports in manufacturing, power, transportation, communication, and construction are included. It is particularly useful in determining comparative market potential. Hundreds of reports are prepared each month by foreign service posts and, are listed monthly with cumulative indexes. Reports and indexes are provided free in response to specific requests for business purposes.

Index $10.00 per year; single copies range from $3.25 to $10.00; NTIS (see C1.17).

7.265 *Special Report on Techniques of Aided Self-Help Housing, Some Examples of Overseas Experience*

Eight experiences of aided self-help housing around the world are described in this publication. Such housing projects have been considered a way in which many families could obtain decent housing through their own efforts at a relatively small capital expenditure. In some developing countries, these housing policies have remained long after the experts have departed. This book outlines the positive and the negative aspects of some of these projects.

Office of International Affairs, HUD (see C1.40).

7.266 *Industrialized Housing—Opportunities and Problems in the Developing Areas*

Office of International Affairs, HUD (see C1.40).

7.267 *Bibliography on Housing, Building, and Planning*

Approximately 400 recent books and periodicals available in the United States on housing, building, and planning are listed in this bibliography. It is useful in establishing a basic technical collection for universities, financial institutions, architects, planners, builders, and others.

43 pp., 50¢; GPO (see C1.0).

7.268 Bibliography on Agricultural Exporting

Foreign Agriculture

Emphasis in this weekly magazine reporting on and interpreting world agricultural developments for United States producers, processors, distributors, and users of farm products is on current and background information useful to export marketing. It includes news and statistics on world crops and markets.

$34.35 per year; GPO (see C1.0).

Foreign Agricultural Circulars

Production, trade, and other specialized reports of twenty-three major world commodity groups issued at irregular intervals during the year are published in these circulars, along with monthly world agricultural production and trade statistical summaries on commodities in world trade.

United States residents wishing to receive the circulars on a regular basis may obtain the checklist from the Information Services Staff, Foreign Agricultural Service, Room 5918-S, Department of Agriculture, Washington, DC 20250. Single copies are free.

Special Reports

Reports on foreign agricultural situations relating particularly to agricultural commodity and trade policy developments are published in this series.

For catalog and ordering instructions, write the Information Services Staff, Foreign Agricultural Service, Room 5918-S, Department of Agriculture, Washington, DC 20250.

Foreign Agricultural Trade of the United States

The current status and outlook for United States agricultural trade are emphasized in this statistical and analytical review. It includes exports under specified government-financed programs, commercial exports, price developments, and quantity indexes for selected commodity groups.

Division of Information, Economic Research Service, Department of Agriculture, Washington, DC 20250.

World Agricultural Situation

World agriculture for the current calendar year is appraised in this publication. Regional situation reports are issued in April for the western hemisphere, western Europe, the Communist areas, Far East and Oceania, and Africa and West Asia. Each report gives data by country on agricultural output, United States trade, trends, and policy developments.

Division of Information, Economic Research Service, Washington, DC 20250.

7.269 Daily Foreign Press and Radio Translations

Hundreds of radio news transmissions, newspaper editorials, and articles and magazine features are monitored daily by the expert United States analysts of the Foreign Boradcast Information Service. The best of these translations are grouped in eight geographical areas.

Subscription to one geographic area, translations mailed daily, $125.00; discount price for additional areas. Also available on microfiche, mailed weekly, at a discount. NTIS (see C1.17).

7.270 *Trading with the USSR and Eastern Europe*

This report provides basic information concerning trading practices, foreign contracts, and trade data of each country that may be useful in exploring markets in the U.S.S.R. and eastern European countries. It includes elements of the trading practices and institutions common to all countries; brief summaries of trading institutions, systems, and procedures for each country; organizations that provide services to foreign businesses, and the Foreign Trade Organizations and products over which they have jurisdiction, by country; and trade statistics by commodity for each country, which may provide some historical perspective.

Foreign Agricultural Service, Room 5918 South, Department of Agriculture, Washington, DC 20250.

7.271 *Japan, the Government-Business Relationship*

In this publication, the extraordinary growth of the Japanese economy is examined, as are the intricate interactions of government and business groups.

#003-009-00202-8, 158 pp., $1.80; GPO (see C1.0).

7.272 Foreign Area Studies of the American University

The Foreign Area Studies program of the American University publishes a series of hardbound handbooks designed to give basic facts about the social, economic, political, and military institutions and practices of various countries. The handbooks, compiled from other published materials, emphasize an objective description of the nation's present society and the possible or probable changes that might be expected in the future.

The size of the volumes varies but is generally several hundred pages. An extensive bibliography is provided in each handbook.

Prices vary; GPO (see C1.0).

Financing (7.300-7.311)

7.300 *Export Opportunities for American Business through the International Banks*

Office of International Development Banks, Department of the Treasury, Washington, DC 20220.

7.301 The Export Credit Sales Program

The Export Credit Sales program provides financing of export sales of United States agricultural commodities for a maximum of 36 months. An application for financing is submitted by the United States exporter and, if approved, it permits sales of agricultural commodities to a foreign importer on a deferred payment basis. Commodities eligible for financing under this program and the rate of interest to be charged are announced each month in a Department of Agriculture press release. Eligibility is generally limited to primary commodities.

Assistant Sales Manager, Commercial Export Programs, Office of the General Sales Manager, Department of Agriculture, Washington, DC 20250; 202-447-4274.

7.302 *A Guide to Financing Exports*

All major sources of financial assistance and insurance for exporting are reviewed in this publication; i.e., Export-Import Bank, Foreign Credit Insurance Association, Overseas Private Investment Corporation, Community Credit Corporation.

Free; Office of Export Development, Room 4002, Department of Commerce national office (see C1.10).

7.303 *Foreign Investment Organizations Assist U.S. Firms*

United States companies considering overseas investment and licensing will find this booklet useful. It lists United States-based organizations representing foreign countries. The individuals and organizations listed can provide a wide range of services to facilitate investment in their countries. Current information on the economy, sources of finance, taxes, and investment incentives is available from these offices. In addition, in some cases potential local participants can be identified and assistance given to businessmen planning visits to their countries by making referrals to appropriate government and industry officials.

9 pp., free; Overseas Business Opportunities Division, BIC, Department of Commerce national office (see C1.10).

7.304 Export Management Companies

Under contract, Export Management Companies (EMC) can perform the following activities on behalf of an exporter: market research, location of distributors, exhibition and promotion of products, responsibility for shipping details (export declarations, customs, insurance, packing, marking), and general consultation. Some EMC's even communicate with overseas buyers on the client's letterhead with the designation "export department."

The EMC can also be of assistance in extending credit to foreign buyers and in determining if it would be profitable actually to produce the product in the country in question.

The EMC operates on either a commission basis or a direct buy-and-sell arrangement in which the EMC receives an overseas order, then purchases from the manufacturer and resells abroad. EMC's specialize in allied but not competitive products and know where the demand is and what its intensity and future are. Some are small and handle only a few manufacturers; others handle forty to fifty companies.

EMC's are particularly useful to the smaller firm, although they are utilized by firms of all sizes. There are about 1,000 of them in the United States.

There are many sources of assistance for choosing an EMC: District Export Councils, the Agency for International Development, field offices of the Small Business Administration, foreign trade divisions of Chambers of Commerce, foreign trade bank executives, and industry trade associations. A helpful book would be *A Directory of U.S. Export Management Companies,* which lists 668 EMC's, including addresses, telephone numbers, and a product indes.

75¢; GPO (see C1.0).

7.305 Private Export Funding Corporation

The Private Export Funding Corporation (PEFCO) is owned by 62 investors, mostly commercial banks. It lends only to finance the export of goods and services of United States manufacture and origin. Its loans usually have maturities in the medium-term area and all are unconditionally guaranteed by Eximbank (see 7.309) as to payment of interest and repayment of principal. PEFCO's funds supplement the financing of United States exports available through commercial banks and Eximbank.

Private Export Funding Corporation, 280 Park Ave., New York, NY 10017.

7.306 Domestic International Sales Corporation

Domestic International Sales Corporation

(DISC) is a new category of corporation, created in 1972, which entitles a company to defer tax on 50 percent of its export income until such income is distributed to shareholders. The tax-deferred earnings retained by the DISC may be invested in its own export business or loaned to domestic producers of export goods.

A DISC is a domestic company that limits its activities almost solely to export sale, lease or rental transactions, and related activities. It can operate as a principal, buying and selling for its own account, or as a commission agent. It can be an independent merchant or broker, or a subsidiary of another firm.

Office of Export Development, BIC, Department of Commerce national office (see C1.10).

7.307 Western Hemisphere Trading Corporation

If a company qualifies for Western Hemisphere Trading Corporation status, it receives a special deduction from taxable income, resulting in substantial tax reduction. It is taxed at approximately 70 percent of its profits. The company pays 15.6 percent of its first $35,000 net profit and 34 percent on the balance, whereas the normal rate is 22 percent on the first $25,000 and 48 percent on the balance. In order to qualify, all business of the firm must be conducted in the western hemisphere and 95 percent of the firm's income must be derived from exporting.

Office of Export Development, BIC, Department of Commerce national office (see C1.10).

7.308 Overseas Private Investment Corporation

Overseas Private Investment Corporation offers investment guarantees comparable to those offered by the Federal Credit Insurance Association (see 7.310) and Eximbank (see 7.309) to United States manufacturers who wish to establish operations in less-developed nations either by themselves or as a joint venture with local capital.

Overseas Private Investment Corporation, 429 20th St. N.W., Washington, DC 20527.

7.309 Export-Import Bank of the United States

Export-Import Bank of the United States (Eximbank) offers direct loans for large projects and equipment sales that usually require longer-term financing. It cooperates with banks at home and abroad to provide a number of financial arrangements to help United States exporters offer credit guarantees to commercial banks that finance export sales; and, through the Foreign Credit Insurance Association, it provides insurance to United States exporters which enables them to extend credit terms to their foreign buyers. In all cases, the bank must find a reasonable assurance of repayment as a precondition of participation in a transaction.

Export-Import Bank, 811 Vermont Ave. N.W., Washington, DC 20571.

7.310 Foreign Credit Insurance Association

The export credit insurance offered by Foreign Credit Insurance Association (FCIA) provides an incentive to United States exporters to offer competitive terms to buyers. FCIA administers the United States export credit insurance program on behalf of its member insurance companies and the government-owned Eximbank (see 7.309). Eximbank assumes all liability for the political risks.

One of FCIA's major forms of coverage is a master policy which provides automatic coverage for all of an exporter's sales, both short and medium term, on credit terms ranging up to five years. In addition, FCIA offers service industries a services export program which extends to them the same credit insurance traditionally offered to commodity industries.

FCIA, One World Trade Center, Ninth Floor, New York, NY 10048.

7.311 *Official U.S. and International Financing Institutions: A Guide for Exporters and Investors*

Information is provided, in this publication, on sources of financing, insurance, and procurement for United States exports and investments. Program volume, current interest rates, resources, and contact points are all discussed.

#003-009-00226-5, 12 pp., 35¢; GPO (see C1.0).

International Market Trend Information (7.350-7.357)

7.350 *Guide to Foreign Trade Statistics*

A complete listing and full description of all unpublished reference tabulations for the current year and the locations where they can be examined are available in this publication. It contains a detailed explanation of the foreign trade statistical program, with examples of tables and charts.

$4.05; Foreign Trade Division, Bureau of the Census, Washington, DC 20233.

7.351 *International Economic Indicators and Competitive Trends*

Business analysts, economists, and others wishing to assess the relative competitive positions of the United States will find this a valuable reference. Attractively presented tables, charts, and text provide a clear, easily readable source of the latest statistical information. It may be used for an overall view of international trends, or as a basis for more detailed analysis of the economic situation in major industrial countries.

$12.65 per year; GPO (see C1.0).

7.352 Monthly Import and Export Data on World Commodities

Monthly information on current import and export shipments for every traffic commoditiy is available from National Technical Information Service. Compiled by the Bureau of the Census, the information covers imports of merchandise for consumption, general imports of merchandise, exports of foreign and domestic merchandise, United States Exports Schedule B, waterborne general exports, waterborne exports, and Department of Defense (DOD) and non-DOD controlled cargo exports.

NTIS (see C1.17).

7.353 *Market Share Reports*

A business executive can compare his own export performance in any specific market with that of his own industry as a whole or with that of manufacturers of the same product in other countries, by using *Market Share Reports*. This tool gives a statistical picture of international trade in manufactured products, covering more than three-quarters of the total exported output of all the free world's factories. The 73 country reports produced annually trace shifting trends in the movement of goods between countries. The five-year spread of data on the imports of more than 1,000 commodities by ninety countries reflects both changing levels of those countries' import demands and shifts in the relative competitive positions of exporting countries.

Country reports: $3.75 each; $185.00 complete set. Commodity reports: $2.75 each; $2,027 complete set. A free publication (#COM-73-90036/PTC) describes the uses of these reports.

NTIS (see C1.17).

7.354 *International Finance*

International economic and financial developments are covered in this publication, which is the annual report of the National Advisory Council on International Monetary and Fiscal Policies. Among other topics treated are international monetary affairs, multilateral economic development assistance, trade policy and finance, foreign investment policies, and foreign indebtedness policies. It includes a variety of statistical tables.

$3.75; GPO (see C1.0).

7.355 *Foreign Agricultural Trade of the United States*

A monthly summary of the current status and outlook for farm exports appears in *Foreign Agricultural Trade of the United States*. Supplements are published for the calendar year and the fiscal year.

Economic Research Service Publications Unit, Room 0054, Department of Agriculture, Washington, DC 20250.

7.356 Economic Research Service

The Economic Research Service (ERS) gathers and analyzes economic information needed to improve agriculture and rural living. ERS experts can answer questions about the current situation and outlook, as well as provide information on the more fundamental relationships between supply and demand. Analysts also examine international developments that have a potential impact on United States farm trade. The Economic Development Division of ERS collects, analyzes, and publishes data on rural population, employment, income, farm and nonfarm workers, job skills, and education levels. It also evaluates changes in the condition of rural communities; i.e., schools, housing, medical services, and public facilities.

Economic Research Service, Department of Agriculture, Washington, DC 20250; 202-447-8038.

7.357 *Foreign Trade Reports*

This subscription service, available from GPO (see C1.0), covers United States foreign trade in the following categories:

FT990 *U.S. Imports for Consumption and General Imports, Commodity by Country,* $71.85 per year

FT410 *U.S. Exports of Domestic and Foreign Foreign Merchandise, Commodity by Country of Destination,* $122.20 per year

FT800 *U.S. Trade with Puerto Rico and the United States Possessions,* $16.30 per year

FT990 *Highlights of U.S. Export and Import Trade*

Interrelated statistical tables are provided in this report, identifying important movements in trade by commodity, country, United States Customs District, and method of transportation. $37.50 per year.

Exporting Procedures and Regulations (7.400-7.410)

7.400 *Foreign Business Practices*

The basics of laws and procedures for exporting, licensing, and overseas investment for the beginner are described in this volume. It includes reviews of international treaties and conventions affecting industrial property rights, patent and trademark protection overseas, and foreign joint ventures. It also includes information on how to use the Domestic International Sales Corporations (see 7.306), export trade associations, and Western Hemisphere Trading Corporations (see 7.307).

95 pp., $1.70; GPO (see C1.0).

7.401 Technical Help to Exporters Service of the British Standards Institution

Worldwide sale of manufactured products is dependent upon knowledge of current multinational government regulations and codes of practice, of foreign approval, and of certification procedures of the enforcing organizations.

The Technical Help to Exporters (THE) service of the British Standards Institution provides this vital information through National Technical Information Service (NTIS). The information is gathered worldwide, on the spot, by THE specialist engineers and reported in technical digests, special investigation reports, information sheets, translations, and annual directories. A publication, *Technical Help to Exporters Catalog,* is available on request from NTIS, reflecting the scope of the information available.

#NTIS-PR-244, free; NTIS (see C1.17). Annual membership in THE, $25.00.

7.402 *Export Administration Regulations*

A compilation of official regulations and policies governing the export licensing of commodities and technical data, this subscription service includes supplementary material issued as *Export Control Bulletins.* It also contains a new Commodity Control List, which replaces the Positive List, the General License GHK Commodity List, and others.

#C57.409/2:976, $45.00; GPO (see C1.0).

7.403 Trade Complaint and Inquiry Service

If there is a dispute between United States and foreign traders concerning an international business contract involving more than $500, the Trade Complaint and Inquiry Service will offer its services to settle or eliminate the dispute. Either party to the dispute may request the service. Department of Commerce decisions or recommendations are not binding on either party.

Department of Commerce district offices (see C1.10).

7.404 Free Trade Zones and Free Ports

A free trade zone is the most important of customs-privileged facilities of limited area now in operation abroad. It is an enclosed, policed area in a seaport or at an airport or other inland point treated for customs purposes as lying outside the customs territory of the country. Goods of foreign origin may be brought in, pending transshipment, reexportation, and, in some cases, importation into the local market, without payment of customs duties. Domestic goods intended for export or for admixture with foreign goods may also be brought into the free trade zone.

A free port is an area, generally encompassing an entire port and its surrounding locality, into which goods of foreign origin may be brought without imposition of customs duties or subject to a minimal revenue tariff, whether such goods are intended for reexport or for local consumption.

For detailed description of these and other special trade zones, write for *Free Trade Zones and Related Facilities*, Office of International Marketing, Bureau of International Commerce, Department of Commerce, Washington, DC 20230.

7.405 *International Mail*

International Mail, formerly entitled *Directory of International Mail*, contains regulations for public use and detailed information on postage rates, services available, prohibitions, import restrictions, and other conditions governing mail to other countries. Countries are listed alphabetically with the specific requirements applicable to mail addressed to each of them.

Sold on a subscription basis only, with changes issued as required, for an indefinite period, $4.25; GPO (see C1.0).

7.406 Legal Assistance with East-West Trade

Trading with Communist nations remains complex, but policy and legal information is available from the Office of East-West Trade.

Department of Commerce district offices (see C1.0); 202-632-9064.

7.407 *Ocean Freight Rate Guidelines*

75¢; GPO (see C1.0).

7.408 *Preparing Shipments to (country)*

Most countries are now represented in this series, which is part of the International Marketing Information Series of the Bureau of International Commerce.

Department of Commerce district offices (see C1.10).

7.409 International Trade Commission

International Trade Commission consists of six members appointed by the President. Its primary mission is to investigate and report on tariff and foreign trade matters, as required by statute. Its areas of interest include tariffs, tariff schedules and classification, foreign trade, commercial and customs policy, trade agreements, and unfair practices in import trade.

It publishes general reports, reports on commodities, reports on countries or other geographic areas (a publication list is available), and news releases.

Requests for information are handled by the Secretary's Office or referred directly to professional staff members, generally commodity analysts, lawyers, or international economists.

International Trade Commission, E St. between 7th and 8th Sts. N.W., Washington, DC 20436; 202-628-3947 ext 2.

7.410 Special Representative for Trade Negotiations

The Special Representative for Trade Negotiations is responsible for supervising and coordinating the trade agreements program. He directs United States participation in trade negotiations with other countries. Individuals affected by such activities may make their views known by formal testimony through their trade or professional organization, or independently by writing to the Special Representative for Trade Negotiations, 1800 G St. N.W., Washington, DC 20506; 202-395-3395.

Foreign Legal Requirements (7.450-7.454)

7.450 Protection of Property Overseas

The Office of Business Practices of the Department of State is active in government-business dialogues concerning the protection of industrial property, the transfer of technology, and various restrictive business practices overseas.

Office of Business Practices, Department of State, 2201 C St. N.W., Washington, DC 20520; 202-632-0266.

The Office of Operations can alert businesses to the importance of adequate theft and damage insurance coverage while living and traveling overseas.

Office of Operations, Department of State; 202-632-1962.

7.451 Expropriation

Businesses concerned with the possibility of expropriation of goods or facilities in a foreign country may contact the Bureau of Economic and Business Affairs of the Department of State. The Bureau can assist in obtaining just compensation.

Bureau of Business and Economic Affairs, Department of State, 2201 C St. N.W., Washington, DC 20520.

7.452 Patent, Copyright, and Trademark Protection Overseas

Patent, trademark, and copyright protection, as well as problems relating to licensing agreements, fall under the Office of Business Practices.

Office of Business Practices, Department of State, 2201 C St. N.W., Washington, DC 20520; 202-632-0266.

7.453 Corporate Citizenship Overseas

The Office of Private Cooperation works with key business organizations to assist United States firms operating abroad to develop more effective corporate citizenship approaches. This is done through research, workshops, and management training programs.

Office of Private Cooperation, Department of State, 2201 C St. N.W., Washington, DC 20520; 703-235-1016.

7.454 Authenticating Certificates of Incorporation

Foreign governments sometimes require American businesses conducting business abroad to receive certification from the United States government that they represent business entities operating legally within the United States. This certification may be required to register for visa purposes, to obtain work permits, or to license a vehicle. Businesses must first obtain from the appropriate official in their state of residence a certificate of incorporation. The Foreign Affairs Document and Reference Service of the Department of State will then authenticate that document so that it may be presented to the foreign government.

Foreign Affairs Document and Reference Service, Department of State, 2201 C St. N.W., Washington, DC 20520; 202-632-0406.

Chapter 8

ENERGY AND THE ENVIRONMENT

CHAPTER ABSTRACT

Few businesses can escape concerns about energy or the environment. This chapter includes information of value both to firms implementing their own energy conservation or antipollution measures, and to firms seeking business opportunities in these fields.

In the first section (8.0-8.19), the problem of energy conservation in business is examined through a number of publications and other sources. Available advice and counseling on the same subject are detailed in the second section (8.50-8.57). Of especial note in this section is the National Energy Information Center (see 8.57), a referral service for inquiries of all kinds regarding energy. Energy-related business opportunities are listed in the third section (8.100-8.104).

In the current awareness section (8.150-8.167), numerous sources of information are listed which are available to those who wish to expand their knowledge of the field of energy or to keep up with new developments.

"Research and Information on Specific Energy Sources" (8.200-8.216) lists publications and information sources on fossil, geothermal, solar, and nuclear energy.

In the section on business and the environment (8.250-8.453), many sources of information and assistance are listed in the first two parts (8.250-8.310). Potential financial assistance is described in the section entitled "Pollution Control Loans" (8.350-8.353). Sources of current research on air, water, and other types of pollution, and resources for land use planning, are found in the next two sections (8.400-8.453).

The section entitled "Research Sources on Energy and the Environment" (8.500-8.510) lists basic research sources available to help the businessman further his own research or keep up with progress in the field.

Finally, educational films on energy and the environment are listed (8.550-8.551).

Department of Energy

The Department of Energy (DOE) began operations on October 1, 1977. Its purpose is to bring together the many fragmented energy programs and offices created over the years within the federal government. The principal functions transferred to DOE originated in the following agencies:

Federal Energy Administration (FEA)
Federal Power Commission (FPC)
Energy Research and Development Administration (ERDA)
Department of the Interior
Department of Defense (Navy)
Interstate Commerce Commission (ICC)
Department of Commerce
Department of Housing and Urban Development

Many of the resources annotated in this chapter have been transferred to DOE; however, these resources continue to be available under their new auspices. Readers interested in a given item should use the address or telephone number listed with the item, as, in most cases, these remain the same under DOE.

Information and other services of interest to business in the area of energy have undergone reorganization under DOE. Energy research projects are grouped by their stage in the development process, rather than by energy type (such as solar, fossil, or nuclear). Thus, basic research is coordinated by the Office for Energy Research, while applications projects are under the Assistant Secretary for Energy Technology. Projects ready for commercial demonstration are transferred to either the Assistant Secretary for Conservation and Solar Applications or the Assistant Secretary for Resources Application. This last stage should have particular relevance to businesses seeking information about useful or marketable technologies.

Small businesses and individual inventors are the focus of the Office of Small Scale Technology. Included under a unit for Intergovernmental and Institutional Relations are the Energy Extension Service, the Oak Ridge Technical Information Center, and the offices for business relations and consumer affairs. In addition, there are offices for energy technology education and transfer.

Rapid changes may be expected in the field of energy and in the organization and activities of DOE. One way to keep posted on developments is to subscribe to the *Energy Insider,* a publication covering news about energy research projects, internal DOE personnel changes and other events, new publications related to energy, and a calendar of upcoming speeches and conferences on energy. *Energy Insider* replaces the Energy Research and Development Administration's *ERDA News;* its expanded coverage includes programs transferred from the FEA, FPC, Department of Commerce, and the other agencies contributing to DOE.

Energy Insider, biweekly, free; C-460, Department of Energy, Washington, DC 20545; 301-353-3449.

Energy and Business (8.0-8.216)

Information and Guides to Energy Conservation (8.0-8.19)

8.0 *Energy Conservation Program Guide for Industry and Commerce* and *Supplement 1*

Energy conservation in intermediate to small firms is the subject of this publication. It suggests specific ways to reduce energy use in manufacturing and commercial businesses, contains a description of an energy conservation program based on information gathered from engineers and energy managers, and explains how to implement the program.

Collected from many sources, a checklist of energy conservation opportunities is demonstrated by case studies showing energy savings actually achieved by firms. The guide also includes technical engineering data and conversion factors; yardsticks for evaluating capital expenditures; a description of possible Occupational Safety and Health (OSHA) and Environmental Protection Agency (EPA) impact on conservation measures; techniques for energy flow measurements; techniques for developing employee participation in an energy conservation program; and listing of persons, organizations, and literature which may be of assistance.

#C13.11:115, 212 pp., $2.90; GPO (see C1.0).

Energy Conservation Program Guide for Industry and Commerce—Supplement 1

Revised explanations of how to implement an energy conservation program, an expanded checklist of energy conservation opportunities, additional case histories, and revisions to sections of the handbook specified above are included in this supplement.

#C13.11:115/1, 89 pp., $2.25; GPO (see C1.0).

8.1 *How to Start an Energy Management Program*

The reasons for business to be concerned with saving energy, and a simple four-step process to follow in setting up an energy management program, are outlined.

$2.25; GPO (see C1.0). Also available from Office of Energy Policy and Programs, Department of Commerce (see C1.10).

8.2 Free Publications on Energy Conservation for Business

The following publications are available, free, from GPO (see C1.0) or from Office of Energy Policy and Programs, Department of Commerce (see C1.10).

Marketing Priorities and Energy
Energy Management: Trade Associations and the Economics of Energy
U.S. Department of Commerce Energy Conservation Programs
Thirty-Three Money-Saving Ways to Conserve Energy in Your Business

Total Energy Management

Building owners and managers will find in this booklet a practical approach to implementing energy conservation procedures and to using energy wisely.

Energy Management: Economic Sense for Retailers

By the intelligent conservation of energy, retailers can derive important benefits, such as reducing likelihood of store-closing or restrictive legislation, minimizing employee and customer inconvenience, and cutting operating costs. This booklet discusses how a retailer can start an energy conservation program.

Energy Management in Health Care Institutions

How to institute an energy management program while cutting operating costs is described in this publication.

How to Profit by Conserving Energy

A sample energy audit that businesses can use to measure the cost of energy per unit output is provided in this publication.

SavEnergy Kit for Promoting Energy Conservation

A model public awareness kit offers sample promotional materials which would be suitable for incorporation into a public affairs program.

8.3 *Energy Conservation through Effective Energy Utilization*

Ways to utilize thermal energy more effectively was the subject of a 1973 conference held at New England College, Henniker, New Hampshire; proceedings of the conference are summarized in this report.

#003-003-01638-1, 261 pp., $3.30; GPO (see C1.0).

8.4 *Handling Fuel and Fuel Problems, An Energy Handbook for Small Businesses*

Alternatives open to the small business owner-manager for meeting energy needs in the event of a national fuel crisis are discussed in this booklet from the Federal Energy Administration.

#041-018-00072-1, 10 pp., 35¢; GPO (see C1.0).

8.5 *How Businesses in Los Angeles Cut Energy Use by 20 Percent*

Los Angeles' way of dealing with the short-term effects of the national energy shortages during the winter of 1973-1974 is discussed in this report. It describes how the plan worked and the benefits and hardships imposed on commercial firms.

#PB-249-347, 22 pp., $3.50; NTIS (see C1.17). Or, #041-018-00042, 65¢; GPO (see C1.0).

8.6 *Applications of Thermography for Energy Conservation in Industry*

The furnaces and heating systems of fifteen industrial plants are described in this survey. The purpose of this project was to detect, by infrared thermography, heat losses in unit process equipment and auxiliary systems.

#003-003-01679-9, 28 pp., 75¢; GPO (see C1.0).

8.7 Voluntary Industrial Energy Conservation Program

Designed by the Federal Energy Administration (FEA) to encourage industry to undertake energy conservation programs and to lead the nation in an energy conservation ethic, this program focuses on ten of the most energy-intensive industries: aluminum, baking, cement, chemicals, copper, glass, meat packing, paper, petroleum refining, and steel. The program objectives are: identification of conservation potential, removal of restraints on industry's ability to reduce energy demands, establishment of industry-wide goals, dissemination of program information to the public, development of government policy initiatives that will spur energy conservation efforts.

FEA (see C1.153).

A booklet entitled *Voluntary Industrial Energy Conservation Program Progress Reports* is available from Office of Energy Programs, Department of Commerce national office (see C1.10).

8.8 Lighting and Thermal Operations Conservation Program

Energy conservation through voluntary compliance with new lighting and thermal operations guidelines is encouraged by the Lighting and Thermal Operations Conservation Program.

Federal Energy Administration (FEA) regional offices have primary responsibility for implementing the support program. Regional representatives will meet with key decision-makers in major corporations and companies, architects and engineers, building owners and managers, state and local government officials, and consumer and public-interest organizations throughout the country to enlist their cooperation. The cooperation of the American people in accepting less, but adequate, lighting, heating, and cooling, in their places of work and in their homes will be sought through a major public education program. Many industry guidelines have already been established.

FEA (see C1.153).

8.9 *Energy Conservation in the Food System, A Publications List*

Books for food wholesalers, retailers, manufacturers, and even some for the cooking public are annotated in this publication on how to conserve energy in various sectors of the food system.

#041-018-00110-7, 73 pp., $1.40; GPO (see C1.0).

8.10 *Guide to Energy Conservation for Food Service*

How-to procedures for saving energy that food service operators can perform are described in this book. Areas covered include beginning an energy conservation program, food preparation and storage, lighting, heating, ventilating, air conditioning, and sanitation.

#041-018-00085-2, 74 pp., $2.15; GPO (see C1.0).

8.11 *A Study of Energy Conservation Potential in the Meat Packing Industry*

Energy audits that were conducted in five meat packing plants are discussed in this report. The findings and recommendations presented represent specific examples of how to conduct a plant energy audit, and resultant energy savings from taking energy conservation measures.

#041-018-00118-2, 283 pp., $3.40; GPO (see C1.0).

8.12 *A Study of Energy Conservation Potential in the Baking Industry*

Energy audits were conducted in five bakeries, varying in size and end product. The findings and recommendations, presented in this report, represent specific examples of how to conduct a plant energy audit in the industry, resultant energy savings from taking energy conservation measures, and how to continue tracking energy use and savings.

#041-018-00117-4, 269 pp., $3.30; GPO (see C1.0).

8.13 Publications on Energy Conservation in Buildings

Building Technology Project Summaries

Energy conservation through the use of improved and innovative building components and materials, and improvement of the usefulness, safety, and economy of buildings, are the goals of the Center for Building Technology, of the National Bureau of Standards. Current projects of the center are described in *Building Technology Project Summaries.*

#003-003-01641-1, $2.05; GPO (see C1.0). Center for Building Technology, Institute for Applied Technology, National Bureau of Standards, Building 225, Room B-112, Washington, DC 20234; 301-921-3434.

Energy Conservation in Buildings—A Human Factors/Systems Viewpoint

The interface between energy conservation and occupant comfort in building design is examined in this booklet; the necessity for compromise is recognized.

#003-003-01693-4, 14 pp., 65¢; GPO (see C1.0).

A Study of the Physical Characteristics, Energy Consumption, and Related Institutional Factors in the Commercial Sector

Specific areas addressed in the report are: physical characteristics of existing commercial buildings in Baltimore, Maryland and Denver, Colorado; energy consumption of existing buildings in Baltimore; institutional factors related to constructing and/or operating more energy-efficient commercial buildings; policy options and their feasibility for inducing energy conservation through retrofit.

#PB-249 470/6BA, 199 pp.; NTIS, (see C1.17).

Evaluation of Building Characteristics Relative to Energy Consumption in Office Buildings

In this report, data are surveyed on a limited sample of office buildings to identify those factors which have an impact on energy consumption. Such data can be used for the development of coefficients for monitoring energy consumption, or as the basis of future research.

#PB-248 774/2BA, 69 pp.; NTIS (see C1.17).

A Market Study of Energy-Related Equipments for the Commercial Buildings Sector: Decision-Makers, Buying Process, and Marketing Strategies

Detailed information is provided in this report about the market for conservation practices in the commercial buildings sector that may be stimulated or supported by federal government actions and initiatives. It describes the commercial building sector, both existing and projected through 1980, and lists levels of energy consumption in each segment of the commercial buildings sector. Key decision-makers involved in the buying and adoption process used for energy-related equipment, both new and retrofit, are discussed. Existing market approaches, decision processes, areas of concentration for energy conservation, and recommendations for federal strategies to encourage energy conservation practices are covered.

#PB-248 618/1BA, 155 pp.; NTIS (see C1.17).

The Potential for Energy Savings through Reductions in Hot Water Consumption

America's patterns of heated water use are examined in this report. It estimates the energy savings obtained from various methods of using hot water; it evaluates the economic, social, and institutional problems involved in using hot water, and makes recommendations for legislation concerning hot water consumption. The report sets forth some of the many possible techniques for conserving hot water. Implementation in some cases requires changes in building codes and/or new legislation. The report also estimates energy savings that would result from the more promising energy conservation measures proposed.

#PB-247 370/OBA, 49 pp.; NTIS (see C1.17).

Guidelines for Saving Energy in Existing Buildings

National energy usage in existing commercial buildings is examined in this report, which is intended for engineers, architects, and skilled building operators who are responsible for analyzing, devising, and implementing comprehensive energy conservation programs. It includes energy conservation measures which can result in further energy savings of 15 to 20 percent, with an investment cost that can be recovered within ten years through lower operating expenses.

#PB249 928/3BA (ECM-1), 282 pp., $9.25; #PB249 929/IBA (ECM-2), $10.00; NTIS (see C1.17).

8.14 *Energy Conservation in New Building Design: An Impact Assessment of ASHRAE Standard 90-75*

In 1975, the American Society of Heating, Refrigerating, and Air Conditioning Engineers (ASHRAE) established the first major voluntary standard for energy usage in new buildings. This book is an assessment by Arthur D. Little, Inc. of the economic impact of that standard on the United States construction industry and on ten related building trades.

#041-018-00098-4, 257 pp., $3.35; brief summary, #041-018-00099-2, 35¢; GPO (see C1.0).

8.15 *Energy Conservation Applied to Office Lighting*

The literature and findings upon which the past practice of lighting design has been based are reviewed in this report. It makes recommendations and suggestions for changes that can be instituted to make lighting design and installation in the future more responsive to the needs of energy conservation.

#PB-244-154, 288 pp., $9.25; NTIS (see C1.17).

8.16 Regional Building Workshops

The Federal Energy Administration (FEA) holds separate workshops for four types of establishments: office buildings, supermarkets, retail stores, and restaurants. Each workshop is limited to 25 participants to insure an atmosphere conducive to learning, problem-solving, and open discussion among participants. Each workshop is free except for luncheon.

The workshop opens with an overview of the energy problem. During the session, participants learn about the five-step development of energy management plans: (1) how to select an energy management team, (2) how to conduct a building survey, (3) how to find energy conservation opportunities and calculate potential savings, (4) how to set up a complete energy management plan, (5) how to implement the plan and follow up on the results.

Each registrant at a buildings workshop is given a workbook, including a technical reference section to be used at the workshop and retained.

FEA (see C1.153).

8.17 Energy Conservation in Household Appliances

Safety and performance of consumer products and the energy efficiency of household appliances are the areas of interest of the Center for Consumer Product Technology. The Center develops recommended voluntary product standards for industry and conducts studies on consumer product hazards.

Center for Consumer Product Technology, Institute for Applied Technology, National Bureau of Standards, Building 224, Room A-355, Washington, DC 20234; 301-921-3751.

8.18 *Conservation and Environment Publications*

This 52-page booklet is a catalog of publications produced by the Federal Energy Administration's (FEA's) Office of Energy Conservation and its contractors. It covers buildings, business and industry, education, resources and environment, transportation, and general interest publications, and has a key word index.

#FEA/D-77/068, free; Publishing Services, Office of Energy Conservation and Environment, FEA (see C1.153).

8.19 *Total Energy Management: A Practical Handbook on Energy Conservation and Management*

A practical approach for building owners and managers to implement energy conservation procedures and to use energy wisely, described in this handbook, allows businesses to conserve energy while maintaining optimum business activity. Total Energy Management (TEM) is an energy conservation approach based on the premise that to effect energy savings in buildings, one must make the building's systems as efficient as possible, so that they will consume the smallest amount of energy necessary to perform the functions required.

#PB-254-683-6BA; NTIS (see C1.17).

Technical and Financial Assistance (8.50-8.57)

8.50 Energy Utilization Assistance from Field Offices of Energy Research and Development Administration

Field installations of Energy Research and Development Administration (ERDA) have technicians who can assist businesses in a variety of ways. For example, they can advise about appropriate energy systems for new facilities, or energy conversion in existing facilities. They can also advise about environmental pollution and energy conservation. ERDA supports a variety of research centers with specialized and general focus.

The following are major field operations offices of ERDA. They can direct the caller further, to more specialized centers, if necessary.

Albuquerque Operations Office
Energy Research and Development Administration;
H St. at Pennsylvania
Kirtland Air Force Base
P.O. Box 5400
Albuquerque, NM 87115

Chicago Operations Office
Energy Research and Development Administration
9800 S. Cass Ave.
Argonne, IL 60439

Grand Junction Operations Office
Energy Research and Development Administration
Grand Junction, CO 81501

Idaho Operations Office
Energy Research and Development Administration
550 Second St.
Idaho Falls, ID 83401

Nevada Operations Office
Energy Research and Development Administration
2753 S. Highland Dr.
P.O. Box 14100
Las Vegas, NV 89114

Oak Ridge Operations Office
Energy Research and Development Administration
P.O. Box E
Oak Ridge, TN 37830

Pittsburgh Naval Reactors Office
Energy Research and Development Administration
P.O. Box 109
W. Mifflin, PA 15122

Richland Operations Office
Energy Research and Development Administration
P.O. Box 550
Richland, WA 99352

San Francisco Operations Office
Energy Research and Development Administration
1333 Broadway
Oakland, CA 94612

Savannah River Operations Office
Energy Research and Development
Administration
P.O. Box A
Aiken, SC 29801

Schenectady Naval Reactors Office
Energy Research and Development
Administration
P.O. Box 1069
Schenectady, NY 12301

8.51 Work Experience at ERDA Facilities

Employees from private industry who are qualified by training and experience to take full advantage of the learning opportunity may receive on-the-job training and opportunity to become familiar with energy processes applicable to specified uses by being assigned to work at an Energy Research and Development Administration (ERDA) facility. The experience and knowledge such an individual would gain would help to expand the capabilities of industry in the applications of energy. For assignments involving access to classified information, the private employer must obtain an access permit and the employee assigned must have appropriate access authorization. No charge is made to participate.

For further information, contact the ERDA field office responsible for the facility at which assignment is proposed, or any ERDA field office (see C1.150), or the Office of Industry, State, and Local Relations at the headquarters office (see C1.150).

8.52 Technical Information Center

The Technical Information Center (TIC) of the Energy Research and Development Administration (ERDA) is the centralized point for the collection, processing, and distribution of technical reports generated by ERDA programs, for the creation of a centralized computer data base of abstracts and citations to the world's literature on energy, for the publication of a number of abstract journals and bibliographies from this data base, and for the editing, composition, make-up, and publications in various energy field.

The Center publishes on a regular basis *Nuclear Science Abstracts, ERDA Research Abstracts, Energy Abstracts for Policy Analysis, Nuclear Safety, Nuclear Regulatory Commission Issuances, Power Reactor Docket Information*, and a number of specialized bibliographies, critical reviews, and proceedings in the ERDA Conference Series.

It also conducts literature searches of the ERDA computerized energy data base, either on-line (RECON) or in batch mode (RESPONSA). It distributes full-size copies of ERDA-originated reports to official users, arranges for all ERDA reports to be available in microfiche form, and makes ERDA reports available for sale to the public through National Technical Information Service. It responds on a routine basis to letters from students, educators, and the lay public requesting information on energy. It also coordinates ERDA's translation efforts.

A detailed description of TIC's functions and services is available in a publication entitled *ERDA Technical Information Center—Its Functions and Services;* #TID-4600-R1, free. *How to Obtain Research and Development Reports* is published by TIC for ERDA contractors; free. Both publications available through NTIS (see C1.17).

8.53 Energy Technology Utilization Programs

The Energy Research and Development Administration (ERDA) supports technology transfer programs in numerous energy-related areas, such as energy physics, accelerator design, basic biological processes in plants and people, new materials, environmental pollutants, new energy technologies, and more. Any business may contact the addresses listed below for advice and counseling in energy matters as they relate to product development and improvement, energy conservation in plants and commercial buildings, energy systems, and other energy topics. (See also 8.50).

University of California
Lawrence Berkeley Laboratory
Building 90, Room 1106
Berkeley, Ca 94720
415-843-2740 ext 5545

University of California
Lawrence Livermore Laboratory
P.O. Box 808
Livermore, CA 94550
415-447-1100 ext 7191

Sandia Laboratories—9623
Technology Utilization Program
Albuquerque, NM 87115
505-264-1947

Union Carbide Corporation
Oak Ridge National Laboratory
P.O. Box X
Oak Ridge, TN 37830
615-483-8611 ext 0121

8.54 Assistance in Using Energy-Related Inventions

To encourage innovation in developing non-nuclear energy technology, the Energy Research and Development Administration (ERDA) and the National Bureau of Standards (NBS) provide assistance to individual inventors and small business research and development companies. The assistance provided includes evaluation of energy-related inventions and ideas, advice concerning engineering, marketing, business planning, licensing and patents, and limited funding where appropriate.

Inventions to be evaluated should be submitted to the Office of Energy-Related Inventions, NBS, Washington, DC 20234. Ask for an Evaluation Request Form (NBS-1019).

For further information, write Office of Industry, State, and Local Relations, ERDA, Washington, DC 20545. See also field offices (C1.150).

8.55 *Geothermal Energy Program*

Twenty-eight current geothermal energy grants, under six research categories, are described in this publication. It identifies the grantees and the principal investigators.

#038-000-00283-0, 34 pp., 85¢; GPO (see C1.0).

8.56 Emergency Energy Shortage Economic Injury Loans

Small businesses which suffer economic injury caused by an energy shortage may apply to the small Business Administration (SBA) for an emergency loan.

SBA (see C1.110).

8.57 National Energy Information Center

The Federal Energy Administration (FEA) maintains the National Energy Information Center (NEIC) in Washington, D.C., as a central referral service for inquiries of all kinds regarding energy. NEIC responds both to letters and to telephone inquiries, and will assist businesses either by finding answers or by a referral to the source which has the answers.

NEIC is located in the FEA headquarters and maintains a reference library covering a broad range of energy subjects. In addition, NEIC has a computer terminal with access to the RECON data retrieval system of the Energy Research and Development Administration (ERDA).

NEIC maintains the Federal Energy Information Locator System (FEILS), which contains most of the sources of energy information in the federal government. FEILS allows a researcher to identify federal agencies collecting specific kinds of energy data and, therefore, to locate that data. The system itself does not contain the data; it is the directory for the data.

FEILS contains information on energy sources (e.g., coal, natural gas); major related functions (e.g., exploration, extraction); characteristics (e.g., location, bed thickness of coal reserves); description of 44 federal entities conducting 261 energy programs; and program summaries for 600 publications, 200 data collection forms, and 98 computerized data bases or major files. FEILS publishes a directory and index to its services entitled *Energy Information in the Federal Government.*

NEIC has also published the *Directory of State Government Energy-Related Agencies,* which includes: (1) primary energy agencies; (2) energy conservation; (3) energy facilities siting; (4) comprehensive land use planning; (5) coastal zone management; (6) environmental impact assessments; (7) public utility regulation; (8) legislative committees; and (9) legislative service agencies.

Contact NEIC at the Federal Energy Administration (see C1.153); 202-566-9820.

Information in the Federal Government, #PB-246-703, FEA/B-75/375; NTIS (see C1.17).

Directory of State Government Energy-Related Agencies, #PB-246-891/6BA, 235 pp.; NTIS (see C1.17).

Energy-Related Business Opportunities (8.100-8.104)

8.100 Granting of Energy Patent Licenses

Nonexclusive, royalty-free, revocable licenses are granted by the Energy Research and Development Administration (ERDA) upon request to United States citizens and corporations on over 4,600 ERDA-owned United States patents. Exclusive and limited-exclusive licenses may also be granted. Similar licenses on over 3,500 ERDA-owned foreign patents may be accorded to United States citizens and corporations, and to others under terms and conditions which depend upon particular facts. Copies of United States patents may be obtained from the Patent and Trademark Office, Department of Commerce, Washington, DC 20231 at 50¢ per copy.

Assistant General Counsel for Patents, ERDA national office; see also field offices (C1.150).

8.101 *Selling to ERDA*

Information about the types of products purchased by the Energy Research and Development Administration (ERDA) is provided to potential suppliers in this booklet. These products include material, equipment, and supplies; construction and architect-engineering services; management services; nuclear fuel processing services; basic research, and applied research and development. Also included are the names and addresses of people to contact in ERDA and at its major contractors' offices.

A Bidder's Mailing List Application, Form 129, and *Selling to ERDA* are available from Director of Procurement, or Office of Public Affairs, ERDA national or regional offices (see C1.150).

8.102 Assistance in Using Energy-Related Inventions

To encourage innovation in developing nonnuclear energy technology, the Energy Research and Development Administration (ERDA) and the National Bureau of Standards (NBS) provide assistance to individual inventors and small business research and development companies. The assistance provided includes evaluation of energy-related inventions and ideas, advice concerning engineering, marketing, business planning, licensing and patents, and limited funding where appropriate.

Inventions to be evaluated should be submitted to the Office of Energy-Related Inventions, NBS, Washington, DC 20234. Ask for an Evaluation Request Form (NBS-1019).

For further information, write Office of Industry, State, and Local Relations, ERDA, Washington, DC 20545. See also field offices (C1.150).

8.103 *Contracting for Construction and Architect/Engineering Services*

The Energy Research and Development Administration (ERDA) published this booklet for architects, engineers, and construction contractors who wish to be considered for ERDA contracts. It discusses general policies, advertising for contracts, modes of payment, selection procedures, and other matters.

Division of Construction Planning and Support, ERDA (see C1.150).

8.104 Guides for Submitting Research and Development Proposals to ERDA

Guide for the Submission of Research and Development Proposals by Individuals and Organizations

Information helpful to those interested in preparing unsolicited proposals for submission to the Energy Research and Development Administration (ERDA) is provided in this publication. It is specifically for the benefit of individuals, commercial firms, not-for-profit research organizations, and all other prospective proposers except educational institutions and not-for-profit institutions that conduct education and training activities, or whose facilities are used in joint programs with universities for such purposes. These excepted organizations should refer to *Guide for the Submission of Research Proposals from Educational Institutions.*

Both publications free; ERDA (see C1.150).

Guide for the Submission of Unsolicited Research and Development Proposals

The Department of the Interior has the statutory authority to initiate and support scientific research and development programs related to its responsibilities as the nation's principal natural resources agency. This brochure is directed toward present and prospective grantees and contractors of the Department. It is intended to acquaint members of the engineering and scientific community with various research and development programs, to define the technological and scientific areas of interest to each of the component agencies, and to describe the policies and procedures relating to the preparation and submission of unsolicited proposals.

Office of Research and Development, Assistant Secretary for Energy and Minerals, Department of the Interior, Washington, DC 20241.

Current Awareness: Energy Research and Development (8.150-8.167)

8.150 *ERDA Energy Research Abstracts*

Abstracts and indexes of all United States government-originated literature on energy-related research and development are contained in this publication prepared by the Technical Information Center of the Energy Research and Development Administration (ERDA). Information on energy sources, such as solar, wind, geothermal, fossil, and nuclear, is included, as well as information on such matters as energy conservation, storage, and conversion. Literature from foreign governments with which ERDA has agreements for technical cooperation is also included.

Literature covered includes scientific and technical reports, patents, journal articles, conference papers, theses, books, and monographs. Each issue contains personal and corporate author, subject, and report number indexes. Indexes are cumulated annually.

Semimonthly, $184.00 per year including indexes, $18.00 semiannual index, $33.00 annual index; GPO (see C1.0).

8.151 *Energy Abstracts for Policy Analysis*

Abstracting and indexing coverage of selected, publicly available, nontechnological literature contributing to energy-related analysis and evaluation is provided in this abstracts journal. Areas covered are: policy; conservation; research and development studies; economics and sociology; supply and demand; forecasting; systems studies; and environment, health, and safety. Specific fields of energy covered are conventional and unconventional energy sources; electric power; energy conversion and storage; and energy consumption, including residential, commercial, industrial, agricultural, and transportation sectors and intersectorial studies; and efficient energy utilization in these sectors. It covers pertinent material from Congressional committee prints, federal agency and department reports, regional and state government documents, news reports, books, and conference proceedings and papers.

Monthly, $20.00 per year, $5.00 annual cumulative index; GPO (see C1.0).

8.152 Standing Orders for Energy-Related Technical Reports

Energy SOS

Immediate shipment of every printed report published by National Technical Information Service (NTIS) in the field of energy is possible through *Energy SOS* (standing order service). The reports are received weeks earlier than if ordered separately, and they are sold by NTIS at a 20 percent discount from the single-order price.

As many as 2,000 reports annually are shipped through *Energy SOS*, but for specific needs they can be limited to one or more of the following subjects: energy sources; energy use, supply and demand; power and heat generation; energy conversion and storage; energy transmission; fuel conversion processes; policies, regulations, and studies; engines and fuels.

#NTIS-PR-258; NTIS (see C1.17).

NTIS Newsletters and Journals

ERDA's unclassified technical reports, critical reviews, conference papers, and symposium results are available on standing order from NTIS in paper copy and in microfiche. These reports are summariezed in NTIS newsletters (see *Weekly Government Abstracts*, 9.11) and journals (*Government Reports Announcements & Index*, 9.203).

The price is $3.50 per title, and an annual standing order requires a minimum of $100.00 in an NTIS Deposit Account (see A2.1). In all areas, there are about 1,300 reports annually, but it is possible to limit the standing order to one or more of the following categories, among others:

General, Miscellaneous, and Progress Reports
Chemistry
Chemical Separations Processes for Plutonium and Uranium
Environmental and Earth Sciences
Heat Rejection and Utilization
Nonnuclear Energy Sources and Energy Conversion Devices
Safeguards—Nuclear Materials Security
Nuclear Materials Management
Controlled Thermonuclear Processes
Isotope Separation
Radioisotope and Radiation Applications
Materials
Particle Accelerators and High-Voltage Machines
Mathematics and Computers
Nuclear Propulsion Systems and Aerospace Safety
Physics—General
Physics—Atomic and Molecular
Physics—Cosmic and Terrestrial
Physics—Nuclear
Physics—Particles and Fields
Peaceful Applications of Explosions
Instruments
Engineering and Equipment
Health and Safety
Chemical High Explosives
Criticality Studies
Technology—Feed Materials
Biology and Medicine
Nuclear Raw Materials
Waste Management
Transportation of Property and Nuclear Materials
Gas-Cooled Reactor Technology
Light-Water Reactor Technology
General Reactor Technology
Liquid Metal Fast Breeder Reactors
Commercial Nuclear Power Plants
Nuclear Power Sources for Biomedical Application

8.153 *Energy: A Continuing Bibliography with Indexes*

Energy systems, research and development, energy conversion, transport, transmission, distribution and storage, with special emphasis on the use of hydrogen and of solar energy, are covered by the National Aeronautics and Space Administration's *Energy: A Continuing Bibliography with Indexes*.

$25.00 per year; NTIS (see C1.17).

8.154 *Weekly Government Abstracts: Energy*

Many aspects of energy, including sources, uses, supply and demand, conversion, storage, and regulation, are covered in this current awareness service entitled *Energy*. This is one of a series of twenty-six newsletters known as *Weekly Government Abstracts*. (For an annotation of the entire series, see 9.11.) Each newsletter contains summaries of government research performed by hundreds of organizations, including United States government agencies, private researchers, universities, and special technology groups. The research summaries are listed within two weeks of their receipt at the National Technical Information Service (NTIS). The last issue of each year is a subject index containing up to ten cross references for each research summary indexed.

$40.00 per year; NTIS (see C1.17).

8.155 *Monthly Energy Review*

The voice of the Federal Energy Administration, the *Monthly Energy Review* summarizes current events and presents information on energy sources, utilities, resource development, and prices. It succeeds the *PIMS Monthly Petroleum Report,* its supplements, and *Monthly Energy Indicators.*

$36.00 per year; NTIS (see C1.17).

8.156 Energy Bulletins and Information from Energy Research and Development Administration

The Energy Research and Development Administration (ERDA) distributes certain issuances to the public without charge. To see what is available and get on the mailing list for items relevant to specific fields of work, write the Office of Public Affairs, Program Coordination Branch, A1-5107, ERDA national office (see C1.150).

8.157 *Inventory of Energy Research and Development: 1973-1975*

A compilation of 8,139 projects with expenditures of $5,000 or more, these volumes encompass a wide range of energy-related research and development. Individual citations, which were developed from responses to questionnaires, include information on the research performers, sponsors and investigators, locations, numbers of scientists and engineers utilized, and expenditures.

Volume 1, *Energy Citations Concerned with Energy Sources*, #052-070-03606-1, 900 pp., $8.60.

Volume 2, *Project Citations Concerned with Electric Power and Energy Uses and Conservation*, #052-070-03206-5, 1,345 pp., $12.00.

Volume 3, *Project Citations Concerned with Economic and Legal Aspects and Health and Environmental Studies,* #052-070-03208-1, 1,317 pp., $12.00.

Volume 4, *Indexes and Appendixes*, #052-070-03209-0, 416 pp., $13.00.

Volume 5, *Summary Tables and Appendixes*, #052-070-03210-3, 106 pp., $2.30.

All volumes available from GPO (see C1.0).

8.158 Publications on the History of Energy Use in the United States

So What's New? Energy History of the U.S. 1776-1976

This full color wall chart helps to visualize the way the United States has discovered, transformed, used, and abused energy during the two centuries since independence. Included with the chart itself is an explanatory booklet that describes the arrangement of the chart, its color keys, and its chronology.

#052-010-00459-0, 24 pp., $2.05 per set; GPO (see C1.0).

Energy: Critical Choices Ahead

The history and long-term implications of the United States energy supply are described.

Free; GPO (see C1.0); or Office of Energy Policy and Programs, Department of Commerce (see C1.10).

8.159 *A National Plan for Energy Research, Development and Demonstration: Creating Energy Choices for the Future*

Volume I: *The Plan.* The national energy problem and the variety of research needed and planned to deal with it are discussed in this publication of the Energy Research and Development Administration (ERDA). It presents a picture of ERDA's role and the role of the public and industry.

Volume II: *Program Implementation.* Programs now under way and supported by the federal government, technologies being investigated, and activities in federal energy research and development programs are assessed in this volume. ERDA's views are presented on the course of action that the federal government should take in assisting the private sector in finding solutions to the national energy problem.

Volume I, $2.00; Volume II, $3.45; GPO (see C1.0).

8.160 *Information on International Research and Development Activities in the Field of Energy*

Information on 1,766 ongoing or recently completed energy research projects in France, Italy, Canada, and more than 25 other countries is contained in this publication.

#038-000-00282-1, 365 pp., $4.30; GPO (see C1.0).

8.161 *ERDA News*

The Energy Research and Development Administration (ERDA) publishes a free, biweekly newspaper on energy news and ERDA projects.

Office of Public Affairs, ERDA national office (see C1.150).

8.162 *ERDA Headquarters Reports*

All reports issued each month from the headquarters of the Energy Research and Development Administration (ERDA) are listed in this bulletin. It includes a cumulative list of ERDA reports, lists them by issuing office, and includes an index to key words in report titles.

#ERDA 77-41; NTIS (see C1.17).

8.163 *Directory of ERDA Information Centers*

Brief descriptions of 27 technical information centers operated or sponsored by the Energy Research and Development Administration (ERDA) are provided in this 38-page booklet. The products and services of the technical information centers are usually available at cost.

ERDA Technical Information Center, P.O. Box 62, Oak Ridge, TN 37830; 615-483-8611 ext 3-4352.

8.164 *Technical Reports of the Federal Energy Administration*

Citations for approximately 400 reports of the Federal Energy Administration and its contractors are listed in this bibliography. The reports were entered into the National Technical Information Service (NTIS) collection by September 30, 1976.

#PB-263332, $5.00; NTIS (see C1.17).

8.165 *Technical Books and Monographs*

Subjects covered in this 150-page bibliography are general reference, biology and medicine, chemistry, computers, energy, engineering, environment, health, physics, isotope separation, metallurgy, physics, reactors, and vacuum technology. The reports are published by a variety of governmental and private organizations.

#TID-4582-R11, free; Energy Research and Development Administration, P.O. Box 62, Oak Ridge, TN 37830.

8.166 *Waste Management Technology and Resource and Energy Recovery*

The three major areas of solid waste management (harzardous wastes, land disposals, and resource recovery) and energy recovery were the subjects of papers presented at the Fourth National Congress on Waste Management Technology and Resource and Energy Recovery in Atlanta, Georgia, on November 2-14, 1975. The papers are reprinted in this publication.

#055-002-00149-1, 38 pp., $3.45; GPO (see C1.0).

8.167 Federal Energy Administration Mailing List

Federal Energy Administration (FEA) maintains a mailing list for the purpose of distributing press releases and other publications as they become available.

Office of Communications and Public Affairs, FEA (see C1.153).

Research and Information on Specific Energy Sources (8.200-8.219)

8.200 *Fossil Energy Update*

Fossil Energy Update provides monthly abstracting and indexing coverage of current scientific and technical reports, journal articles, conference papers and proceedings, books, patents, theses, and monographs from all sources on fossil energy. All information announced in this publication, plus additional back-up information, is included in the energy information data base of the Energy Research and Development Administration's Technical Information Center.

The subject matter covered by *Fossil Energy Update* includes coal, petroleum, natural gas, oil shale, hydrogen production, hycrocarbon and alcohol fuels, electric power engineering, and magnetohydrodynamic generators. Corporate author, personal author, subject, and report number indexes are included. Indexes are cumulated annually.

$27.50 per year, $3.25 per issue; NTIS (see C1.17).

8.201 *Coal Processing, Production and Properties*

To aid those individuals and organizations involved in coal utilization and conversion research, the Energy Research and Development Administration has published an updated fossil energy bibliography entitled *Coal Processing, Production and Properties*. Dated September, 1976, it supplements the 1974 *Coal Processing* bibliography.

The two-volume bibliography goes back to the early 1930's and is current through August 1976. References are arranged in broad subject categories, such as mining, reserves and exploration, environmental aspects, waste management, transport and handling, by-products, marketing and economics, health and safety, management and policy, regulations, properties, and processing, which includes solvent extraction, carbonization, gasification, liquefaction, hydrogenation, desulfurization, and purification.

$12.50 (citations), $13.50 (indexes); NTIS (see C1.17).

8.202 *Coal Processing: Gasification, Liquefaction, Desulfurization*

This bibliography contains 7,441 references to scientific and technical information on coal research to produce clean-burning solid, gaseous, and liquid fuels. References are arranged chronologically in subject categories, such as processing, by-products, and waste management. A glossary of various processes used in converting and purifying coal is included. Also included are personal author, subject, and report number indexes.

757 pp., $13.60; NTIS (see C1.17).

8.203 *Petroleum Statistics Report*

Petroleum production, refining, importing, and other industry operations, are the subject of detailed statistics and discussion in the monthly *Petroleum Statistics Report*, compiled by the Federal Energy Administration.

This report combines the former *Weekly Petroleum Statistics Report* and *Weekly Petroleum Situation Report*.

$30.00 per year; NTIS (see C1.17).

8.204 *Geothermal Energy Update*

Information on the exploration and development of geothermal resources is announced in this monthly current awareness service. The publication contains references to reports, journal articles, conference proceedings, patents, theses, and monographs entered into the Energy Research and Development Administration's computerized energy information base through the Technical Information Center (TIC). *Geothermal Energy Update* is intended ot be an ongoing supplement to the bibliography, *Geothermal Resources*, which contains references to information entered into the TIC energy information base through July 1976.

Citations and abstracts are grouped under subject categories. Each issue contains corporate author, personal author, subject, and report number indexes. Indexes are cumulated annually.

$27.50 per year, $3.25 per issue; NTIS (see C1.17).

8.205 Nuclear Industry Seminars

Two-day information sessions led by Energy Research and Development Administration (ERDA) staff members are held once a year at ERDA's Grand Junction office. The purpose of the seminars is to disseminate up-to-date information on domestic uranium exploration and development, economics, production capability, estimated national uranium resources and requirements, and foreign uranium resources to representative of the uranium mining and milling industry, the nuclear industry, financial institutions, universities, and government. Any person with an interest in the uranium and nuclear industries is eligible to attend.

ERDA, Grand Junction Office, Grand Junction, CO 81501; 303-242-8621. Or Director, Division of Nuclear Fuel Cycle and Production, Attention: Assistant Director for Raw Materials, ERDA, Washington, DC 20545; 301-353-5311.

8.206 Nuclear Safety Information Center

The Nuclear Safety Information Center (NSIC) maintains a computerized bibliographic data base with more than 110,000 entries. It produces state-of-the-art reports and a technical journal, *Nuclear Safety*. It also offers a technical inquiry service, retrospective searches of the data base, consultation with specialists, access to its documents, and a biweekly SDI (Selected Dissemination of Information) service. A list of NSIC publications is available.

#NTIS-PR-209, free; NTIS (see C1.17). *Nuclear Safety* is available from GPO (see C1.0).

NSIC is located at Oak Ridge National Laboratory; address P.O. Box Y, Oak Ridge, TN 37830; 615-483-8611 ext 3-7253.

8.207 Nuclear Regulatory Commission *Standard Review Plan*

The *Standard Review Plan*, published by the Nuclear Regulatory Commission's (NRC) Office of Nuclear Reactor Regulation, is a safety review of applications to build and operate light-water-cooled nuclear power reactors. The purpose of the plan, which is composed of 224 subsections, is to improve both the quality and uniformity of the NRC staff's review of applications to build new cuclear power facilities, as well as the quality and uniformity of information supplied by applicants as the basis for the staff's review.

The *Standard Review Plan* describes in detail

the various safety-related technical areas reviewed by the NRC staff, the basis for review, and the conclusions which are sought in each area.

Issued irregularly; *Plan* and quarterly supplements on standing order $60.00; supplements only, $30.00. The *Plan* can also be ordered by chapter, at $10.00 per chapter. NTIS (see C1.17).

8.208 Access to Restricted Nuclear Information

Authorized persons may receive restricted data relating to civilian uses of atomic energy, and use the information in business, trade, or profession. The information provided is for use in activities related to civilian applications of atomic energy, such as research and development, design and construction, studies or evaluations, activities under licenses issued by the Nuclear Regulatory Commission, or in work or services to be performed for other organizations.

Energy Research and Development Administration (ERDA) field offices in Albuquerque, Chicago, Oak Ridge, Richland, San Francisco, and Savannah River (see C1.150). Or Office of Industry, State, and Local Relations, ERDA national office (see C1.15).

8.209 *An Inexpensive Economical Solar Heating System for Homes*

Complete with diagrams and instructions, this how-to guide demonstrates a solar heating system for homes at an estimated cost of $2,000, including a solar collector, heat exchanger, water pump, tank, piping, and automatic controls. All components used are available at local lumber yards, hardware stores, and plumbing supply stores.

#N76-27671/TA, 58 pp., $4.50; NTIS (see C1.17).

8.210 Bibliography on Solar Energy

Solar Energy for Space Heating and Hot Water, #SE101, 14 pp.; ERDA (see C1.150)

Solar Energy for Agriculture and Industrial Process Heat, #76-88, 8 pp.; ERDA (see C1.150)

Nontechnical Summary of Distributed Solar Power Collector Concepts, #SE102, 19 pp.; ERDA (see C1.150)

Solar Energy and Your Home, #HUD-PDR-183(3), 20 pp.; National Solar Heating and Cooling Information Center, P.O. Box 1607, Rockville, MD 20850; 800-523-2929 (Pennsylvania, 800-462-4983)

Minimum Energy Dwelling, 14 pp.; ERDA (see C1.150)

Buying Solar, Federal Energy Administration and Department of Health, Education and Welfare, #041-018-00120-4, $1.85; GPO (see C1.0)

Usable Electricity from the Sun, #060-000-00039-5, 8 pp., 35¢; GPO (see C1.0)

Development of Proposed Standards for Testing Solar Collectors and Thermal Storage Devices, #003-003-01579-2, 268 pp., $3.10; GPO (see C1.0)

Systems Engineering for Power, ERDA #77-37, 107 pp., $5.50; NTIS (see C1.17)

8.211 *An ERDA Solar Bibliography*

To aid those individuals and organizations engaged in solar energy research, demonstration, and development, the Energy Research and Development Administration (ERDA) has published an updated solar energy bibliography, dated March 1976. Entitled *An ERDA Solar Bibliography*, it supersedes an earlier bibliography issued in December 1975.

Coverage in the two-volume bibliography goes as far back as useful references could be obtained, and is current through 1975. References are arranged in broad subject categories, such as solar energy conversion, photovoltaic power plants, solar thermal plants, ocean thermal gradient power plants, solar radiation use, solar collectors and concentrators, tidal power, and environmental aspects and economics.

$13.75 (citations), $10.75 (indexes); NTIS (see C1.17).

8.212 National Solar Heating and Cooling Information Center

Information on all aspects of solar heating and cooling is provided by this organization. Its purpose is to encourage the use of solar energy systems for homes and commercial buildings.

Services available include a categorized mailing list for current information; guidance to builders, architects, and manufacturers; bibliographies of technical and nontechnical publications; a speakers' bureau; exhibits for trade shows and information of new grant opportunities from the Energy Research and Development Administration and the Department of Housing and Urban Development.

Solar Heating, P.O. Box 1607, Rockville, MD 20850; toll-free: 800-523-2929 (in Pennsylvania, 800-462-4983).

8.213 *Solar Energy: A Bibliography* and *Solar Energy Update*

Most of the technical and scientific information published on solar energy research, demonstration, and development is cited in *Solar Energy: A Bibliography*. The coverage goes back as far as useful references could be obtained, and it is current through 1975. References are added on a continuing basis and are available through the Energy Research and Development's (ERDA) on-line computer retrieval system, RECON.

Solar Energy Update is an ongoing supplement to this bibliography. It is a current awareness announcement of research, development, and demonstration information from all sources, providing abstracting and indexing coverage of reports, journal articles, conference proceedings, patents, theses, and monographs. Corporate author, personal author, subject, and report number indexes are included. The index is cumulated annually.

All information announced in *Solar Energy Update* is included in the energy information data base of ERDA's Technical Information Center.

Solar Energy: A Bibliography, TID 3351-R1P1, R1P2 (two volumes), 1976, $13.75, microfiche $2.25; NTIS (see C1.17).

Solar Energy Update, $27.50 per year, $3.25 per issue; NTIS (see C1.17).

8.214 *National Program for Solar Heating and Cooling (Residential and Commercial Applications)*

Commercial interest in producing and distributing solar heating and cooling systems is the goal of this program. Chapters include working examples of and research in solar heating and cooling, plus discussion of the strategy and goals of the Energy Research and Development Administration.

#052-010-00475-1, 83 pp., $2.50; GPO (see C1.0).

8.215 *Solar Power from Satellites*

Concepts involving advanced aerospace technology that might help satisfy the need for future sources of energy are surveyed in this publication. Specifically considered are ways to collect solar energy in space with satellites and to beam that power to earth to supplement other sources of electricity. Included are many ways to construct the satellites.

#052-070-03319-3, 228 pp., $2.70; GPO (see C1.0).

8.216 Publications from Energy Research and Development Administration on Energy Sources

Oil Shale
Nuclear Power Plant Safety
Plutonium in the Environment
How Probable is a Nuclear Plant Accident?
Heated Water from Power Plants
Nuclear Energy
Energy Conversion, Storage, and Transmission
Energy Technology
Waste Heat Recovery: More Power from Fuels
Fuel Cells: A New Kind of Power Plant
Experimental Electric Vehicle
Energy Savings through Automatic Thermostat Controls
New Energy Saving Light Bulb
Tomorrow's Cars
Environment, Health, and Safety
Solar Energy
Annual Cycle Energy System (ACES)
Totally Integrated Energy System (TIES)
The Energy Crisis
I've Got a Question about Using Solar Energy
Fusion
Energy from the Winds
Geothermal Energy
Energy Storage (9 pp.)
Energy Storage (35 pp., by William W. Eaton)

8.217 *Solar Heating and Cooling: An Economic Assessment*

The important economic considerations that

are necessary for an assessment of the potential for solar heating and cooling in the United States are introduced in this publication. Considered are: an introduction to residential and commercial solar energy technology; a methodology for assessing the economic feasibility of solar heating and cooling, with the results of a study of material, labor, marketing, and engineering costs; and an application of this methodology to the heating and cooling situations in twenty United States cities.

#038-000-00300-3, 53 pp., $1.20; GPO (see C1.0).

8.218 *Solar Energy Projects of the Federal Government*

171 solar energy projects administered by fourteen different federal agencies between July, 1973 and January, 1975 are identified in this report. Solar categories included are: heating and cooling of buildings, wind energy conversion, solar thermal conversion, ocean thermal conversion, photovoltaic electric power systems, and bioconversion to fuels. An introductory chapter provides an overview and analysis of the federal effort in solar energy and categorizes projects by agency, the amount of funding, and the major program areas. Appendixes provide brief summaries of each of the 171 projects.

#PB-241 620/4BA, 151 pp.; NTIS (see C1.17).

8.219 *Directory of Federal Energy Data Sources, Computer Products and Recurring Publications*

Two major types of federally-sponsored energy-related information are announced in this directory: energy information on magnetic tape, and recurring publications which contain energy-related numerical data. The information on magnetic tape is primarily in the form of data files. However, there are also computer programs, data base reference services, and mathematical models. The items are listed under broad subject categories. The citations include title, responsible agency, dates of coverage, accession number, availability information, and abstract. Each entry is indexed by subject, originating agency, and accession number.

#PB-254 163/9BA, 84 pp.; NTIS (see C1.17).

Business and the Environment (8.250-8.453)

Current Awareness: Environmental Protection (8.250-8.256)

8.250 *EPA Journal*

Monthly, $8.75 per year; GPO (see C1.0).

8.251 *EPA Reports Bibliography Quarterly*

All EPA (Environmental Protection Agency) items in the collection of National Technical Information Service (NTIS) are published quarterly, on a continuing basis, in *EPA Reports Bibliography Quarterly*. Each issue includes summaries, author, corporate source, subject, contract number, and title indexes.

$45.00 per year; NTIS (see C1.17).

8.252 *Selected References on Environmental Quality as It Relates to Health*

Citations from journal articles covering aspects of environmental pollution that concern health are listed in this monthly journal.

$13.45; GPO (see C1.0).

8.253 Periodicals on Pesticides

Pesticides Abstracts

Representing a monthly review of more than 500 domestic and foreign journals, this publication fosters current awareness of the major worldwide literature pertaining to the effects of pesticides on human beings.

$18.25 per year; annual index $2.95; GPO (see C1.0).

Pesticides Monitoring Journal

A new federal journal devoted wholly to information on pesticide levels relative to man and his environment, this quarterly journal will report data gathered from air, earth, water, food, and life by the various monitoring programs operated by the federal government, states, universities, hospitals, and nongovernmental research institutions.

$7.90 per year; GPO (see C1.0).

8.254 *Environmental Health Perspectives*

Bimonthly, $30.50 per year; GPO (see C1.0).

8.255 *Summaries of Foreign Government Environmental Reports*

Environmental protection reports prepared in foreign countries are translated into English and summarized monthly by the Environmental Protection Agency in *Summaries of Foreign Government Environmental Reports.*

$35.00 per year; NTIS (see C1.17).

8.256 *Weekly Government Abstracts*: Four Newsletters

Weekly Government Abstracts (see 9.11 for full annotation) consists of a series of weekly newsletters containing summaries of government research performed by hundreds of organizations, including United States government agencies, private researchers, universities, and special technology groups. The newsletters directly relevant to the subject of environmental protection, with a sampling of subjects covered, are as follows:

(1) *Urban Technology*, covering problems of urban administration, housing, health, finance and planning, as well as the environment;

(2) *Environmental Pollution and Control,* covering environmental health and safety; resource recovery; solid waste disposal; and air, water, and noise pollution;

(3) *Ocean Technology and Engineering*, covering oceanography, marine navigation, underwater construction and habitats, and marine geology; and

(4) *Natural Resources*, covering remote sensing of earth resources, watershed management, water quality, soil sciences, hydrology and limnology, and natural resource surveys.

Nos. (1), (3), and (4), $40.00 per year; No. (2), $60.00 per year; NTIS (see C1.17).

Information and Assistance on Environmental Protection (8.300-8.310)

8.300 *Finding Your Way through EPA*

Clients who have questions in the field of environmental protection may use this directory to locate persons within the Environmental Protection Agency (EPA) who can help them.

Public Information Center Facilities and Support Services Division, EPA, Washington, Dc 20460; 202-755-0890.

8.301 *Disposing of Small Batches of Hazardous Wastes*

Whether or not a waste contains hazardous components and, if so, how it should be handled and disposed of in order to protect public health and the environment is discussed in this report written to assist holders of small batches of wastes. It discusses information sources on waste handling and disposal and describes methods for the disposal of small batches of hazardous wastes.

#SW-562, 20 pp., free; Solid Waste Information, EPA, Cincinnati, OH 45268.

8.302 *Waste Management Technology and Resource and Energy Recovery*

The three major areas of solid waste management (hazardous wastes, land disposals, and resource recovery) and energy handling and conservation were the subjects of papers presented at the Fourth National Congress on Waste Management Technology and Resource and Energy Recovery in Atlanta, Georgia, on November 2-14, 1975. The papers are reprinted in this publication.

#055-002-00149-1, 38 pp., $3.45; GPO (see C1.0).

8.303 *Environmental Impact Statements: A Handbook for Writers and Reviewers*

#PB-226 276/PTC, $7.25 paperbound, $2.25 microfiche; NTIS (see C1.17).

8.304 National Weather Service

The National Weather Service provides daily weather forecasts and warns the nation of impending natural disasters such as hurricanes and tornadoes. It provides information on weather patterns and tendencies in specific areas, which is useful to agriculturalists and environmentalists.

National Weather Service, 8060 13th St., Room 401, Silver Spring, MD 20910.

8.305 Publications on Environmental Protection

The Small Business Administration (SBA) Management Aids Series includes two publications related to environmental protection: *Reducing Air Pollution in Industry* (#217), and *Solid Waste Management in Industry* (#219).

Free; SBA (see C1.110).

8.306 *Interim Guide for Environment Assessment*

This irregularly-issued publication consists of a basic manual and supplements issued irregularly for an indefinite period.

$20.00 per year; GPO (see C1.0).

8.307 *Legal Compilation, Environmental Protection Agency*

#055-000-00127-8, 2,726 pp., $10.25 per set; GPO (see C1.0).

8.308 Environmental Research Grants

The Environmental Protection Agency (EPA) conducts research and development in a variety of fields which are described in *Office of Research and Development Program Guide*. Persons interested in obtaining research grants or contracts may obtain a copy of the *Guide* from Office of Financial and Administrative Services, Office of Research and Development, EPA, Washington, DC 20460.

8.309 Citizens' Advisory Committee on Environmental Quality

The Citizens' Advisory Committee on Environmental Quality was established to advise the President and the Council on Environmental Quality on matters affecting environmental quality. It is interested in all matters affecting environmental quality, including the correlation of such considerations with other factors in federal policies and programs; stimulation of public and private participation in programs to protect against pollution of the nation's air, water, land, and living resources; cooperation between federal government, state and local governments, and private organizations in environmental programs; the effects of new and changing technologies on the environment; and outdoor recreation and beautification of the cities and countryside.

Citizens' Advisory Committee on Environmental Quality, 1700 Pennsylvania Ave. N.W., Washington, DC 20006; 202-223-3040.

8.310 *The Challenge of the Environment: A Primer on EPA's Statutory Authority*

The scope of the Environmental Protection Agency's duties and responsiblities is delineated by providing a brief summary of its legal authority.

#055-000-00078-6, 43 pp., 70¢; GPO (see C1.0).

Pollution Control Loans (8.350-8.353)

8.350 Loans from Small Business Administration for Water Pollution Control

Small businesses having to comply with various water pollution controls may apply to the Small Business Administration (SBA) for a disaster loan.

SBA (see C1.110).

8.351 Loans from Environmental Protection Agency for Water Pollution Control

Direct loan funds are provided to qualified small businesses for use in purchasing and establishing such additions, alterations, or changes in method of operation as are necessary and adequate to comply with pollution control requirements established under the Federal Water Pollution Control Act, under a program sponsored by the Office of Water and Hazardous Materials, Environmental Protection Agency (EPA), and Small Business Administration.

Water Planning Division, Office of Water and Hazardous Materials, EPA, Washington, DC 20460; 202-755-6023; see also regional offices (C1.151).

8.352 Loans from Small Business Administration for Air Pollution Control

Small Business Administration (SBA) authorizes, under certain circumstances, loans for firms having to comply with the Clean Air Act of 1970.

SBA (see C1.110).

8.353 Business and Industrial Loans from Farmers Home Administration

The Farmers Home Administration (FmHA) is authorized to make loans to profit as well as nonprofit organizations for the purpose of improving, developing, or financing business, industry, and employment and improving the economic and environmental climate in rural communities, including pollution abatement and control.

FmHA (see C1.2).

Research on Pollution Control (8.400-8.414)

8.400 *Selected Water Resources Abstracts Journal and Index*

Water-related aspects of the life, physical, and social sciences, as well as conservation, control, use, management, engineering, and legal aspects of water, are covered semimonthly in *Selected Water Resources Abstracts Journal and Index*, compiled by the Department of the Interior.

This periodical includes abstracts of current reports and articles on water pollution, waste treatment, water law, water yield, watershed protection, water demand, ground water, lakes and estuaries, hydraulics, and soil mechanics. Each issue is indexed by subject, personal and corporate author, and order number.

$75.00 per year, $100.00 with annual index; NTIS (see C1.17).

8.401 Water Resources Scientific Information Center

The Water Resources Scientific Information Center is responsive to technical and scientific information needs and provides communication and coordination among all those engaged in federally sponsored water resources research. The Center provides current information on water resources research by means of a semimonthly research results abstract bulletin, an abstract catalog of ongoing research projects, state-of-the-art reviews, and topical bibliographies. Abstracts of ongoing research projects are available. The Center also operates a computerized retrieval program to supply basic research information in response to specific inquiries.

Although complete copies of research reports are not distributed by the Center, many are available for purchase from National Technical Information Service.

Office of Water Research and Technology, Department of the Interior, Washington, DC 20240.

8.402 Water Pollution Control Data Publication Services

The Office of Water and Hazardous Materials (OWHM) of the Environmental Protection Agency (EPA) collects, analyzes, and publishes pollution control data in order to show types, trends, and progress in pollution control and prevention and to make these data available for official, technical, and administrative use and to the general public. The data can be used in the planning, programming, and budgeting of water pollution control programs at all levels of government. They can also be used to measure the effectiveness of these programs, to show a market potential to equipment manufacturers and construction firms, and to give direction to new control efforts. There are no use restrictions.

Some initial automatic distribution of these publications is made from headquarters of OWHM to government agencies at all levels and to companies or organizations with interests in the manufacture of equipment for the construction of waste treatment facilities. Some additional copies are available through the regional offices of EPA (see C1.151). Any individual organization or other entity can obtain copies of these publications at a nominal cost on request to the Government Printing Office (see C1.0).

8.403 Water Resources Planning

Information regarding water availability, purity, and conservation can be obtained from the river basin commissions, associated with the Water Resources Council. Such information may be useful to industries in site location, environmental protection, and energy conservation. Helpful information may also be gained in these matters from state water agencies, many of which have information specifically for business.

River Basin Commissions, Water Resources Council (see C1.152).

8.404 *Wastewater Treatment Construction Grants Data Base*

Monthly awards for wastewater treatment facilities under Public Law 92-500, as compiled by the Environmental Protection Agency, are listed by state in *Wastewater Treatment Construction Grants Data Base.* This periodical covers applicant, grant number, grant title, award date, award amount, grant step, description of the facility, and other information.

#PB-231 300/PTC, $100.00 per year; NTIS (see C1.17).

8.405 Water Resource Studies

The Water Resources Division of the Geological Survey is responsible for appraising the quantity and quality of the nation's water resources and for research on hydrologic problems related to the occurrence and distribution of both surface and ground water. The Survey monitors and evaluates surface and ground-water resources through a nationwide network of water stations and series of resource investigations with the cooperation of state, federal, and public agencies. Each year, over 800 reports and maps are produced which help in the correlation of the available supply of water. To make the data more readily available, the Survey transferred to computer tape about 245,000 station-years of records, and information on more than 40,000 ground-water wells and 5,000 water-quality stations.

Water Resources Division, Geological Survey (see C1.50).

8.406 Air Pollution Technical Information Center

The areas of interest of the Air Pollution Technical Information Center include air pollution technical literature from throughout the world; basic data on chemical, physical, and biological effects of varying air quality; and other information pertaining to air pollution and its prevention and control.

The Center provides individual literature searches resulting in a print-out of abstracts, and responds to inquiries concerning the secondary distribution of federally-produced air pollution-related documents. Services are provided free to individuals and organizations.

Publications include *Air Pollution Abstracts*, numerous bibliographies, some with abstracts, on air pollution and such related topics as odors, mercury, petroleum refineries, iron and steel mills, boilers, hydrochloric acid, chlorine, electric power production, cement manufacturing, sulfuric acid manufacturing, nitric acid manufacturing, municipal incineration, photochemical oxidants, beryllium, asbestos, hydrocarbons, nitrogen oxides, and carbon monoxide. A list of current technical publications is available.

Air Pollution Abstracts: GPO (see C1.0).

Air Pollution Technical Information Center, Technical Center, Room A222, N.C. 54 and Alexander Drive, Research Triangle Park, NC 27711; 919-549-8411 ext 2141.

8.407 Technical Information Services for Air Pollution Control

Data collected, analyzed, and published by the Office of Air and Waste Management (OAWM) of the Environmental Protection Agency (EPA) can be used in planning, programming, and budgeting of air pollution control programs. They can also be used to measure the effectiveness of these programs, to show a market potential to equipment manufacturers and construction firms, and to give direction to new control efforts. There are no use restrictions.

Computer-generated abstracts are available to anyone on request, as the result of a retrospective literature search. Initial automatic distribution of these publications is made by OAWM to state and local agencies of government and to other valid nongovernmental requesters. Some additional copies are available through regional offices of EPA (see C1.151). Copies are available at nominal cost from GPO (see C1.0) or from NTIS (see C1.17).

8.408 Air Pollution Control—National Ambient Air and Source Emission Data.

A single, standardized system for acquisition, validation, editing, analysis, and retrieval of source data for emissions and air quality provides data processing and anlysis of raw air quality and source inventory data submitted by state and local air pollution control agencies or collected by the Environmental Protection Agency (EPA). The data base thus provided is available for use by concerned citizen groups, local and other government agencies, the EPA, individuals, and profit and nonprofit organizations.

EPA regional offices (see C1.151). Or headquarters office: National Air Data Branch, Monitoring and Data Analysis Division, Office of Air Quality Planning and Standards, Office of Air and Waste Management, EPA, Research Triangle Park, NC 27711; 919-688-8146 ext 491.

8.409 Air Pollution Laboratory

The Air Pollution Laboratory of the Agricultural Evironmental Quality Institute, Department of Agriculture, is concerned with the effects of gaseous air pollutants on plants; methods of reducing losses to vegetation from air pollutants; and, especially, identification and development of resistant plant cultivars.

Air Pollution Laboratory, Agricultural Environmental Quality Institute, USDA Agricultural Research Center, Beltsville, MD 20705; 301-344-3035.

8.410 Solid Waste Disposal Information Services

Private agencies and institutions, as well as individuals, may receive technical information which can be used for planning, programming, and budgeting of solid waste management programs. Such information may be used to show market potential to equipment manufacturers and construction firms, and to give direction to new solid waste management efforts. There are no use restrictions other than those of applicability to solid waste and judgement as to propriety by the Environmental Protection Agency (EPA). (Fees for certain services may be charged; fee schedule may be obtained from EPA Public Information Office, 202-755-2808.)

Initial automatic distribution of these publications may be made to companies or organizations with interests in the manufacture of equipment for construction of solid waste management facilities.

Deputy Assistant Administrator for Solid Waste Management, Office of Air and Waste Management, EPA, Washington, DC 20460; 202-254-7820; see also regional offices of EPA (C1.151).

8.411 Office of Solid Waste Management Programs

The Office of Solid Waste Management Programs is concerned with solid waste management; source reduction; collection, processing, disposal, recycling, and reclamation of solid wastes; composition and analysis of solid wastes; hazardous wastes; regulations related to solid wastes; economic incentives and disincentives; technical assistance; citizen education.

The Office answers inquiries; provides consulting, reference, and literature-searching services; makes referrals to other sources of information; lends films and exhibits; and makes interlibrary loans. It maintains a data bank containing approximately 20,000 abstracts, used to respond to requests for literature searches, and a patent collection relating to solid waste management dating back to 1875.

Publications include *Solid Waste Management: Available Information Materials* (1973), listing *Solid Waste Management; Abstracts from the Literature*, directories, conference proceeding, technology transfer reports, guidelines, films, exhibits, audio-visual materials, and publications for the concerned citizen; periodic *Accession Bulletins*, listing new entries into the data bank; *User's Guide to the Solid Waste Information Retrieval System Thesaurus* (1973); *Information Retrieval Services of EPA's Office of Solid Waste Management Programs* (1972).

Office of Solid Waste Management Programs, EPA (see C1.151).

8.412 Technical Information on Pesticides

Access to the latest information available concerning exposure to, and the toxic effects of, pesticide chemicals introduced into man's environment is available in a range of publications and specialized information services available free or for purchase.

Publications available for *Compendium of Registered Pesticides, Pesticides Monitoring Journal*, quarterly, and *Pesticides Abstracts* on a monthly basis. The latter provides abstracts and indexes to much of the world's literature on pesticides. In addition, a *Current Awareness Service* bulletin is published monthly which consists of an up-to-date listing of publications in the field of pesticides. Reprints of the articles listed are available on request.

Services available also include reprints of published articles, literature searches, preparation of bibliographies, and other information which is of interest to the scientific community and the general public. Reference cards indexed by author and subject are available on apprixímately 25,000 individual citations of published articles related to pesticides. Entire articles for approximately 10,000 of these citations are also available on microfiche and as hard copy.

Fees for certain services may be charged; fee schedule may be obtained from EPA Information Office; 202-755-2808.

Office of Pesticides Programs Technical Services Division, Office of Water and Hazardous Materials, EPA national office; see also regional offices (C1.151).

8.413 *Standards on Noise Measurements, Rating, Schemes, and Definitions: A Compilation*

Materials assembled from various industrial and trade organizations, and technical and scientific societies concerned with acoustics, are brought together in this volume.

#003-003-01593-8, 84 pp., $1.90; GPO (see C1.0).

8.414 National Environmental Research Center

The Technical Information Office of the National Environmental Research Center is involved with pollution control technology, with emphasis on analytical quality control, environmental toxicology (air), radiation, solid waste, advanced waste treatment, and water supply. The Office answers technical inquiries and distributes technical literature. A list of available literature is provided upon request.

Technical Information Office, National Environmental Research Center, EPA, Cincinnati, OH 45268; 513-684-8258.

Land Use Planning (8.450-8.453)

8.450 Publications of the Geological Survey

Results of research and investigation by the Geological Survey are made available to the public through professional papers, bulletins, water-supply papers, circulars, miscellaneous reports, and several map and atlas series. All books, maps other than topographic quadrangle maps, and related Survey publications, are listed in the catalogs, *Publications of the Geological Survey, 1869-1961,* and *Publications of the Geological Survey, 1962-1970.* Yearly supplements keep the catalogs up to date. (See also *New Publications of the Geological Survey*).

Catalogs and annual supplements are available free; Geological Survey Public Information Offices and Branch of Distribution Offices (see C1.50).

8.451 Land Information and Analysis Programs of the Geological Survey

The Land Information and Analysis Office manages five multidisciplinary programs:

(1) The *Earth Sciences Applications* program is responsible for integrating the earth-science information collected by the Survey for use in analyzing land resource problems. The products, mainly thematic maps and reports, provide insight into the environmental consequences of land use decisions. For example, the San Francisco Bay region study has produced more than 70 geologic, hydrologic, and topographic maps and technical reports, plus 15 interpretive reports relating the data to land use planning and management alternatives and possible environmental impact.

(2) The *Resource and Land Investigations* program encompasses the multidisciplinary, multibureau efforts of the Department of the Interior. The national problems addressed include, for example, the delineation of environmentally endangered areas, the development and application of land use inventory systems, and the siting of onshore facilities associated with outer continental shelf energy resource development.

(3) The *Geography* program calls for the application of geographic analysis techniques to land and resource problems. Land use data are systematically collected, revised, and analyzed on a nationwide basis, and basic geographic research

is conducted.

(4) The *Earth Resources Observation Systems* (EROS) program is the largest departmental program to be managed by this new office. Since 1966, numerous experiments have been conducted applying remotely sensed data, primarily photographs and telecommunicated images obtained from satellites and high-altitude aircraft, to a wide variety of resource and environmental problems. The key facility of this program is the EROS Data Center in Sioux Falls, South Dakota, where the data are stored, reproduced, and distributed. The program includes research as well as user training in the interpretation and application of remotely sensed data and also includes the development of improved sensor and data processing systems.

(5) The *Environmental Impact Analysis* program directs the preparation and review of the environmental impact statements required of the Survey by the National Environmental Policy Act of 1969.

In addition, the Land Information and Analysis Office enters into cooperative projects with state, local, and other federal agencies.

Land Information and Analysis Office, Geological Survey national or regional offices (see C1.50).

8.452 Soil Surveys

The Soil Conservation Service (SCS) gives technical assistance to individuals, groups, organizations, cities, and other units in reducing costly waste of land and water resources and in putting to good use these national assets. SCS's technical staff diagnoses resource problems and prescribes safe use and treatment. The technical staff includes soil scientists; economists; agricultural, irrigation, hydraulic, draining, and cartographic engineers; and specialists in agronomy, biology, forestry, plant materials, range management, geology, and sedimentation.

These services may be particularly valuable in selecting a site for a factory or other building. The soil surveys are utilized by land use planners, developers and builders, construction engineers, and others. Such surveys can help avoid unnecessary complications that attend failure of foundations, soil slippage, flooded basements, and other structural breakdowns caused by adverse soil properties.

SCS publishes soil surveys of counties throughout the United States. The boundaries of each kind of soil in the county surveyed, gradated by soil hazard, are shown on detailed maps. Soil surveys describe important soil properties, such as flood hazard, natural drainage, depth to bedrock, depth to seasonal water table, permeability, shrinking and swelling potential, bearing capacity, and content of silt, sand, and clay. Soil surveys also provide interpretations of soil suitability and limitations for foundations of commercial buildings, for sanitary landfills, sewage lagoons, and septic tank absorption fields; for installation of underground pipelines; and for development of parks and other recreation areas. Since the manner in which tracts are subdivided is a major consideration in pricing units and estimating costs, soil surveys can help in planning lot size and layout of buildings, streets, and utilities in accordance with soil suitability and limitations.

Soil maps and supporting data provide information about flood hazard, wetness, erodability, bearing capacity, shrink/swell slippage, organic layers, and ease of excavation.

Interested parties may call the local office of the SCS to determine whether a soil survey of the area in question is available. If the survey has not yet been published, arrangements can be made to examine maps in their preliminary form.

National and local offices of SCS (see C1.3).

8.453 Conservation and Land Use Programs Division, Department of Agriculture

The Conservation and Land Use Programs Division of the Department of Agriculture is concerned with the application of conservation practices, including related pollution abatement and wildlife measures with federal cost-sharing assistance; agricultural conservation; soil bank; water bank; and long-term acreage diversion.

Conservation and Land Use Programs Division, Agricultural Stabilization and Conservation Service, Department of Agriculture, Washington, DC 20250; 202-447-6221.

Research Sources on Energy and the Environment (8.500-8.510)

8.500 Information on Energy and the Environment from National Technical Information Service

A great variety of information sources related to energy and the environment is available through the National Technical Information Service (NTIS) (see 9.0-9.13).

For example, *Selected Research in Microfiche* (SRIM) offers regular and prompt reports on a variety of subjects which the client may choose. *Weekly Government Abstracts* publishes a series of newsletters containing reports of the latest research available in relevant fields. Specific questions may be answered by a Published Search of the NTIS Bibliographic Data File; or, if more information is needed, an on-line NTISearch may be carried out.

8.501 Industrial Applications Centers

Countless dollars and effort are wasted in research and design facilities because technicians are too busy to search the literature before instigating new programs. Obviously, searching before researching is vital to economical innovation.

The six regional Industrial Applications Centers (IAC) of National Aeronautics and Space Administration (NASA) help answer this need both by searching the literature and by helping to evaluate and apply the results. The Centers maintain computerized access to about three-quarters of a million space-related reports, as well as ten times that many reports and articles from private and nonspace governmental sources. The Centers' resources cover the contents of more than 15,000 scientific and technical journals throughout the world, plus thousands of specialized governmental and industrial research reports. NASA believes that it is the world's largest technical data bank.

Major information sources accessible through IAC's now include:

Air Pollution Technical Information Center
Chemical Abstracts Condensates
Education Resources Information Center
Engineering Index
Government Reports Announcements (including data from all government agencies)
NASA International Aerospace Abstracts
NASA Tech Briefs
NASA Scientific and Technical Aerospace Report
Nuclear Science Abstracts
Selected Water Resources Abstracts

The IAC's also utilize specialized data files dealing with food technology, textile technology, metallurgy, medicine, business, economics, social sciences, and physical sciences.

Services offered by the IAC's are as follows:

(1) *Retrospective Searches.* Pertinent technical literature that covers the desired research topic has probably already been published and filed somewhere among millions of documents; to find it, IAC will conduct a retrospective search. The IAC will assign a scientist or engineer familiar with the relevant area of technology. Highly specific questions will be asked in order to define as precisely as possible just what is to be searched for. The search will then be conducted and the results evaluated. A typical retrospective report is available in less than fourteen days and consists of 30 to 300 abstracts. Full-text reports are available from the IAC. The customer pays only the cost of retrieval.

(2) *Current-Awareness Searches.* Just as retrospective searches are used for solving known problems, current-awareness searches often generate new ideas. The service consists of abstracts relating to a specific topic tailored to meet the exact needs explained to the personally-assigned IAC engineer. Subscribers receive monthly or quarterly updates on new developments in the same abstract form as the retrospective searches.

(3) *Technical Assistance.* NASA comments that its clients are more interested in answers than in abstracts. The professional staff members a the IAC's hold advanced degrees in chemistry, physics, engineering, or other technical fields. They are in an excellent position to offer suggestions on how the information they have gathered may be applied to best advantage.

NASA Industrial Applications Centers (see C1.107).

8.502 *How to Obtain Information in Different Fields of Science and Technology: A User's Guide*

This booklet contains 122 pages on the present knowledge domain of scientists and technologists; generation, use, and transfer of information; international medical information systems; federal information systems; the National Aeronautics and Space Administration Regional Dissemination Center; international information systems for physical scientists; and environmental information systems.

#AD780 061, $5.50; NTIS (see C1.17).

8.503 Technology Application Center

A Special Technology Group (see 9.9) interested in energy and environmental matters is the Technology Application Center (TAC) at the University of New Mexico.

Sponsored by the National Aeronautics and Space Administration, TAC identifies and disseminates the results of existing research and new high-interest areas of technology. It provides a full range of personalized information-searching services in the physical and social sciences, a current-awareness service, bibliographies with abstracts, and in-depth analysis and applications service in the areas of energy, remote sensing, and land use inventory and planning.

TAC subject areas include heat pipe technology, hydrogen energy, solar thermal energy use, wind energy utilization, remote sensing of natural resources, noise pollution, waste glass utilization, and rolamite.

Technology Application Center, University of New Mexico, Albuquerque, NM 87131; 505-277-3622.

8.504 Standard Reference Data on Energy and the Environment

The National Standard Reference Data System comprises the set of data centers and other data evaluation projects administered or coordinated by the National Bureau of Standards (NBS). The primary aim of this program is to provide critically evaluated numerical data, in a convenient and accessible form, to the scientific and technical community of the United States. A second aim is to advance the level of experimental measurements by providing feedback on sources of error in various measurement techniques. Through both these means, the program strives to increase the effectiveness and productivity of research, development, and engineering design.

Current projects relevant to energy and the environment deal with data that have an important application in some aspect of energy R&D or environmental quality improvement. Projects in chemical kinetics, nuclear properties, spectroscopic data, and interaction of radiation with matter are currently incorporated in this program. The output of these projects is particularly important in R&D on new energy sources, environmental monitoring techniques, and prediction of the effects of pollutants introduced into air, water, or land.

Office of Standard Reference Data, NBS, Washington, DC 20234.

8.505 Dissemination of Technical Information by Energy Research and Development Administration

Scientific, technical, and practical information is available from the Energy Research and Development Administration (ERDA) in the form of publications, exhibits, and information and data centers.

(1) *Publications.* A wide range of energy-related technical and popular-level publications is available free or for purchase. These include abstract journals and a magnetic tape information data base which covers much of the world's energy literature; scientific and technical books, monographs, and journals; engineering drawings and specifications for energy facilities and equipment; and educational books and pamphlets. *Technical Books and Monographs* is an annotated catalog of agency-sponsored books published or in preparation.

(2) *Exhibits.* A limited number of exhibits, popular-level, technical, or semitechnical in nature, is available. They deal with such subjects as fossil fuels, fusion, solar energy, nuclear energy, geothermal energy, conservation, environment and safety, and national security.

(3) *Technical Information.* Technical information is available from ERDA's information and data centers, which collect, summarize, and critically evaluate information in specialized areas of science and technology. *The Directory of ERDA Information Centers* is a guide which includes addresses and describes subject scope and services of each center.

Both publications free; ERDA (see C1.150).

8.506 Environmental Protection Agency Bibliographic Data Bases

The international literature related to solid waste information is accessible to the public through the Solid Waste Information Retrieval System (SWIRS) of the Environmental Protection Agency (EPA). This and a variety of other computerized data bases are described in the *Environmental Information Systems Directory.*

Other data bases are operated under the Library Systems Branch of the Environmental Protection Agency. Among them are the Ecological Air Pollutant Literature Search System, which gathers bibliographic information on literature principally concerned with air pollutants and their effects on vegetation and animals. Computerized bibliographies are available on microfiche, and the referenced literature is available in the reprint library of the Environmental Research Laboratory of the EPA.

Information on multimedia training resources in the water quality area is available on computer-generated bibliographies produced by the Water Quality Instructional Resources Information System (IRIS).

Health aspects of pesticides are the subject of the Pesticides Information System, which generates computerized bibliographies. All articles reviewed since 1969 are available on microfiche.

All of the above, as well as additional resources, are described in *A Description of the Environmental Protection Agency's In-House Library Systems* (#EPA-LIB-76-03), available from the Library Systems Branch, Environmental Protection Agency, Washington, DC 20460. (See C1.154 for list of EPA libraries.)

Environment Information Systems Directory: Management Information and Data Systems Division, Office of the Deputy Assistant Administrator for Administration, Environmental Protection Agency, Washington, DC 20460.

SWIRS: Solid Waste Information Retrieval System, P. O. Box 2365, Rockville, MD 20852.

Reprint library: Environmental Research Laboratory, Environmental Protection Agency, 200 S.W. 35th Street, Corvallis, OR 97330; 503-752-4211.

IRIS: Water Quality Instructional Resources Information System, Municipal Operations and Training Division, Manpower Planning and Training Branch, National Training Center, Environmental Protection Agency, Cincinnati, OH 45268.

Pesticides: Publications and Technical Literature Research Section, Office of Pesticides Programs, EPA, Washington, DC 20460.

8.507 United States International Environmental Referral Center

Information and data about the environment are available from thousands of sources. To facilitate access to these sources, the Environmental Protection Agency (EPA) has been designated as the United States Focal Point for the United Nations Environmental Program; its main function, as such, is to operate the International Environmental Referral Center (IERC).

Over 1,100 information sources are registered with IERC. Upon submission of an inquiry, a user will be furnished a listing of sources that are likely to provide the information requested. Information supplied includes the address of the source, a summary of its functions and activities, languages in which services are provided, products available, restrictions (if any), and a subject index of terms.

There is no charge for the referral service. The source of the required substantive information may or may not charge for providing its information.

International Environmental Referral Center, EPA, Room 2902 WSM, 401 M Street S.W., Washington, DC 20460; 202-755-1836, 1837, 1838; cable address: EPAWSH; telex 89-2758.

8.508 Environmental Research Sourcebooks

A Description of the Environmental Protection Agency's In-House Library Systems

The holdings and services of the 28 libraries of the Environmental Protection Agency are described in this brochure.

#EPA-LIB-76-03, Library Systems Branch, EPA, Washington, DC 20460. Also available is the *Environmental Protection Agency Library System Book Catalog.*

Environmental/Biomedical Terminology Index

In an effort to provide a general guide to the environmental/biomedical sciences, this index was published by the Information Center Complex of the Oak Ridge National Laboratory, Oak Ridge, Tennessee.

#ORNL/EIS-98, $16.25; NTIS (see C1.17).

The Microthesaurus of Soil Mechanics Terms

Over 4,000 terms are listed, covering the subjects of soil mechanics, engineering geology, soil dynamics, rock mechanics, and pavements. It was prepared by the Soil Mechanics Information Analysis Center and the United States Army Engineer Waterways Experiment Station.

NTIS (see C1.17).

Solid Waste Management Available Information Materials

All reports published by the Office of Solid Waste Management Programs from January 1966 through June 1976 are listed in this bibliography.

#SW-58.26, 103 pp.; Office of Solid Waste Management Programs, EPA, Washington, DC 20460.

Industrial Environmental Research Laboratory Report Abstracts

Reports issued by the Environmental Protection Agency Industrial Environmental Research Laboratory are abstracted in this free monthly bulletin.

Technical Information Coordinator, Mail Drop 64, Office of Research and Development, Industrial Environmental Research Laboratory, EPA, Research Triangle Park, NC 27711.

8.509 Earth Resources Observation Systems Data Center

The Earth Resources Observation Systems Data Center operates applications assistance facilities which maintain microfilm copies of aerial photographs and space images stored at the Center. Scientific personnel are available to assist users in selecting the appropriate data to apply to a variety of resource and environmental problems and to assist users in ordering data through a computer inquiry system. A visit to the Center may be arranged by phone or mail.

Applications Assistance Facilities (see C1.50).

8.510 National Energy Information Center

The Federal Energy Administration maintains the National Energy Information Center (NEIC) in Washington, D.C., as a central referral service for inquiries of all kinds regarding energy.

For a description of the services of NEIC, including the Federal Energy Information Locator System, see 8.57.

Films on Energy and the Environment (8.550-8.551)

8.550 *Energy Films Catalog*

Approximately two hundred films on subjects related to energy and its uses are listed in this catalog from the Energy Research and Development Administration (ERDA). The purpose of the films is to increase public understanding of energy problems and the resource, conservation, and technology options which may be applied.

The films are available for educational, nonprofit, and noncommercial screenings, and are free.

Audio-Visual Branch, Office of Public Affairs, ERDA (see C1.150); 301-973-4239.

8.551 Filmography on Energy and Environmental Protection

The following films are available, as priced, from National Audio-Visual Center, General Services Administration, Washington, DC 20409.

It's Dollars and Sense

How steps taken for energy reduction in hospitals and health care institutions have resulted in substantial dollar savings without affecting the quality of patient care is explained in this film. It covers load-shedding, heating and ventilation, efficiency testing and equipment maintenance, lighting, and other measures which can be used to conserve energy.

#007893, 16 mm., 28 min., color, sale $127.00.

Pesticides in the Environment

The hazards to man's environment caused by the misuse of chemical pesticides are outlined in this series.

#008157, 80 2x2 color slides, 17 min. audiocassette, sale $20.00.

Pesticide Use Training

This series on pesticide use consists of eight programs. It outlines what a private applicator must know in order to be competent in the use and handling of restricted-use pesticides. It includes recognition of common pests, reading a pesticide label, proper storage, use handling, disposal, recognition of risks to the environment, poison symptoms, procedures to follow in case of an accident, and legal responsibilities.

#008154, 430 2x2 color slides, 53 min. audiocassette, sale $75.00.

Hazardous Wastes, The Gross National By-Product

Defining hazardous wastes and explaining how they are produced, treated, transported, and disposed are the subjects of this film. The impact of poor hazardous waste management and possible solutions to the problem are also discussed, as well as ways for concerned citizens and public interest groups to take constructive action.

#007790, 44 2x2 color slides, 18 min. audiocassette, sale $10.00.

The Park

The character of on-site nuclear industry, its effect on natural resources and living species, and the importance of continuing the research that began before the industry arrived are examined in this film. It shows Energy Research and Development's Savannah River plant in South Carolina, designated the first National Environmental Park in 1972, where 300 square miles have been the subject of extensive scientific study.

#007819, 28 min., 16 mm., sound, color, sale $124.25. May be acquired on loan from ERDA-TIC Film Library, P.O. Box 62, Oak Ridge, TN 37830.

Where Airports Begin

How two communities developed their airports is the subject of this film. It stresses that to have an airport that is environmentally sound and is an economic stimulus, it is important to plan and to have community interaction. The film is applicable to communities either building a new airport or upgrading an existing one.

#007824, 20 min., 16 mm., sound, color, sale $86.50. May be acquired on loan from Film Library AAC-44E, Federal Aviation Administration, P.O. Box 25082, Oklahoma City, OK 73125.

Chapter 9

TECHNICAL INFORMATION AND DATA BASES

CHAPTER ABSTRACT

Managers, scientists, engineers, and others who may have a need for technical information will find listed in this chapter a wide array of data bases and information sources within the federal government. Social sciences, economics, management, physical sciences, medical sciences, and engineering are among the many fields included.

Although much of the chapter deals with direct sources of technical information, it also describes several key organizations which offer the additional service of helping the client to define specific problems and find further sources of information. Foremost among these are the National Technical Information Service (see 9.0-9.13), the NASA Industrial Applications Centers (see 9.20), the Smithsonian Science Information Exchange, Inc. (see 9.30), and the Library of Congress' National Referral Center for Science and Technology (see 9.40).

Specialized technical information may be located by using the variety of directories, guides, and other publications annotated, beginning with 9.200.

Current awareness of developments in specific fields is a necessary but difficult accomplishment for the professional, due to the sheer volume of new knowledge. A variety of current-awareness services and publications is annotated in 9.300-9.318. The reader's attention is drawn particularly to the series, ***Weekly Government Abstracts***, which provides inexpensive access to all nonclassified government-sponsored research.

Government statistics are available on many matters of interest to business. Directories and guides to statistical programs are annotated beginning with 9.400, while statistical programs are annotated beginning with 9.450.

Sources of Technical Information (9.0-9.75)

National Technical Information Service (9.0-9.13)

9.0 Description of National Technical Information Service

Research—whether to develop new technology or to provide data for business decisions—should begin with searching before researching, according to the National Technical Information Service (NTIS). The information desired may well have already been researched by others and be available for only a few dollars.

NTIS, part of the Department of Commerce, provides a diversity of services and information. It is the central source for the public sale of government-sponsored research, development, and engineering reports and other analyses. Much of the material to which NTIS can give access is related to engineering and the hard sciences, but there is a growing array of data sources of potentially great value for business planners, market researchers, and others who may need statistics or other data about social, psychological, or demographic factors.

NTIS supports itself entirely from revenue derived from sales of its publications and services. A current catalog and a copy of the Price Code List are available upon request. For information on how to order from NTIS and a list of services available, with telephone numbers, see A2.1 or C1.17.

9.1 NTISearch

NTISearch (pronounced en-tee-search) is an on-line computer search of the entire NTIS collection of federally sponsored research reports, which number some 420,000 reports published since 1964. About 60,000 new summaries and reports are added annually, at the rate of about 200 daily.

(The total NTIS collection includes more than 900,000 titles. Also, summaries of unpublished research are included on magnetic tape in the NTIS Bibliographic Data File, which is available for lease. An additional 180,000 descriptions of ongoing and recently terminated research projects, compiled by the Smithsonian Science Information Exchange (see 9.30), also are computer retrievable.)

NTISearch research summaries are thorough, averaging 250 words of description, and most of them are not otherwise available. Upon request, NTIS will include, with each search, specially priced microfiches of the entire texts of the summarized reports. Michrofiche ordered to accompany searches are $1.00 each, a 56 percent discount from the standard $2.25 price for a single fiche.

The system is automated but flexible, fast but accurate. The entire collection is combed to find the specific information needed.

To start an NTISearch, telephone the NTISearch Hot Line (703-321-9040) and state the problem. NTIS information specialists will estimate the likelihood of success and the delivery time—usually about ten days.

Cost of an on-line NTISearch varies from $100 to $200, depending on the number of research summaries produced. Published searches (see 9.2) are $25.00.

9.2 NTISearch Published Searches

NTISearch Published Searches are the same high quality computer searches that NTIS sells daily for $100 each when custom-made. The only difference is that Published Searches have been completed and published in response to previous demand and hence are less costly for NTIS to produce. There is no other difference. An on-line NTISearch ordered today might include a few more research summaries completed since the Published Search, but it would cost at least $100.

Each one of these 1,000 specially priced Published Searches consists of as many as 100 different thorough research summaries (abstracts) of advanced technology for businessmen, scientists, and specialists in urban, economic, and social affairs. Most of the reports summarized are sold by NTIS.

Each research summary—as many as 100 in any one Search—includes the title of the full report, its author, corporate or government source, pages, price, and ordering instructions.

If any Published Search does not meet the client's needs, full credit is given toward an on-line NTISearch.

$25.00 per Published Search. For a list of Published Searches, write NTIS (see C1.17); 703-321-9040.

9.3 NTIS Bibliographic Data File

The heart of the NTIS information collection is the NTIS Bibliographic Data File. It contains all the research summaries and other data and analyses of all NTIS technical, scientific, and social fields. Most items have full bibliographic citations and they may be used to create a wide variety of information products.

The magnetic tape containing the data file may be leased annually, and tapes back to 1964 may be acquired. Current tapes are shipped biweekly to subscribers.

The file may be searched by research report title, personal or corporate author, accession number, or contract number, and by subject, using key words and descriptors.

Lease fees are negotiated, based on factors such as the number of citations displayed or searches performed, and the possibility of third-party use. The basic lease fee is $2,000 per year.

NTIS (see C1.17).

9.4 NTIS Key Word Title Index to NTIS Bibliographic Data File

If the title, author, or accession (item) number of an NTIS report is known, but the price, availability, report date, number of pages, report number, title, or author is not, the NTIS key word index to the NTIS Bibliographic Data File may be consulted.

This index to 420,000 NTIS reports, plus an additional 21,000 reports held by the Superintendent of Documents, is available on microfilm. It contains all reports announced by NTIS from July 1964 through December 1974.

The microfilm index is in three sections, on continuous reels. The first section is a title index (using the key-word-out-of-context method, in which superfluous words such as "an," "of," "the," and high occurrence words such as "annual," "report," "volume," are omitted). The second section lists by accession (item) number, and the third section is by author.

Information brochure, *Key Word Title Index*, #NTIS-PR-254; NTIS (see C1.17).

9.5 NTIS Information Analysis Assistance

The NTIS team of expert information analysts is available to help a business find all the information needed about almost any field of interest—either through an NTISearch produced for immediate use, or by referral to Department of Commerce industry specialists, other information sources, or analysis centers.

NTIS (see C1.17); 703-321-9040.

9.6 Selected Research in Microfiche

As government-sponsored reports are received at the National Technical Information Service (NTIS), they are immediately classified according to some 500 subject categories and 200,000 descriptive terms. Within two weeks thereafter, a subscriber to the Selected Research in Microfiche (SRIM) program receives the full text of each report in the subscriber's chosen category or categories. Reports are sent biweekly.

An order may include any combination of categories or subcategories, and may be limited to reports of specific agencies. Further information on the contents of the SRIM categories can be found in two publications available from NTIS: #NTIS-PR-270 and #NTIS-PR-271. Also, SRIM information specialists can assist in making the selection.

Microfiche can save money. Each microfiche contains up to 98 pages of text, and the price for each SRIM microfiche title is only 45¢, a saving of $1.80 over the regular NTIS price of $2.25, and far less than the cost of the same report in paper copy. A portable microfiche reader can be obtained for as little as $25.00. If a paper copy is needed, it can be ordered from NTIS or produced by microfiche reproduction equipment. (A free buyer's guide to microfiche equipment is available from a non-profit organization, the National Microfilm Association, 8728 Colesville Road, Silver Spring, MD 20910.)

The cost of SRIM varies according to the number of microfiche titles received. Here are two typical examples of costs of SRIM:

(1) *Energy/Energy Use, Supply and Demand:* 140 complete report texts were sent out over a 12-month period, costing the customer $63.00. The same order for paper copies would have cost more than $850.

(2) *Administration/Public Administration and Government:* 168 complete report tests were sent out over a 12-month period, costing the customer $75.00. The same order for paper copy would have cost more than $1,025.

The SRIM information specialists will estimate the cost and will help limit the scope of an order to the research actually desired.

If a research need is not satisfied by existing SRIM categories, it is possible, for an additional annual computer service charge of $100, to customize an SRIM subscription by using SRIM Profile. An SRIM information specialist will help develop a selection strategy based upon index key words which are assigned to all NTIS reports.

An NTIS Deposit Account is necessary for SRIM service. It will conveniently handle payments for SRIM, as well as record tax deductions, assist in budgeting, and cut unnecessary red tape. A Deposit Account may be set up with a minimum deposit of $25.00 ($125.00 for SRIM Profile).

NTIS (see C1.17); 703-321-8883 or 8507.

A listing of the main SRIM categories follows:

Administration
Aeronautics and Aerodynamics
Agriculture and Food
Astronomy and Astrophysics
Atmospheric Sciences
Behavior and Society
Biomedical Technology and Engineering
Building Technology
Business and Economics
Chemistry
Civil and Structural Engineering
Communication
Computers, Control, and Information Theory
Detection and Countermeasures
Earth Sciences
Electrotechnology
Energy
Environmental Pollution and Control
Government Inventions for Licensing
Health Planning
Industrial and Mechanical Engineering
Library and Information Sciences
Materials Sciences
Mathematical Sciences
Medicine and Biology
Military Sciences
Missile Technology
NASA's Earth Resources Survey Program
Natural Resources
Navigation, Guidance, and Control
Non-Destructive Testing
Nuclear Science and Technology
Ocean Technology and Engineering
Ordnance
Physics
Photography and Recording Devices
Problem-Solving Information for States and Local Governments
Propulsion and Fuels
Space Technology
Transportation
Urban Technology

9.7 Engineering Index, Inc. Published Searches

NTISearch Published Searches are augmented by published searches of the Engineering Index, Inc. (Ei) data base, which includes more than 85,000 new engineering documents annually. Ei covers worldwide professional and industrial journals and proceedings, transactions, and special publications of engineering societies, associations, universities, and research institutions.

Subject index entries are listed below.

$25.00 per search, either paper or microfiche; NTIS (see C1.17).

Acoustic holography
Acrylic resins
Activated carbon
Aeration of sewage lagoons
Aerodynamic forces on motor vehicles
Antenna arrays
Artificial kidneys
Automobile air pollution
Band pass filters
Beam lead microelectronics
Cable television
Cathodic protection
Charge transfer devices
Corrosion in desalination plants
Cryogenic properties of aluminum
Data base management
Electric power consumption
Electrodialysis desalination
Semiconductor devices
Fiber optics
Turbines
Geothermal energy
Heat pipes
Holography
Incineration
Interactive computer graphics
Ceramics
Mechanical hearts

Microcomputers
Microwave
Ultrasonic testing
Oil shale mining
Permafrost
Printed circuits
Photography
Septic tanks
Sewage sludge disposal
Shipboard containerization
Solar energy
Superalloys
Ultrasonics in medicine
Underground coal gasification
Waste heat utilization
Wind power

9.8 *Data Item* of Engineering Sciences Data Unit

Engineering design data from one of the world's largest and most authoritative collections is available through NTIS from the Engineering Sciences Data Unit (ESDU) in London, England.

The basic ESDU package is the *Data Item*, a set of loose-leaf sheets devoted to a single topic and containing graphical data, equations, and tables, together with definitions and terminology, explanatory matter, and worked examples.

#NTIS-PR-245; NTIS (see C1.17).

9.9 Special Technology Groups

Special Technology Groups are concerned with analysis and communication of current and authoritative government-sponsored and privately-generated research. They are a principal information resource for the NTIS Bibliographic Data File.

Services of Special Technology Groups usually include: *Inquiry Services*: the custom searching of an information collection relevant to specific queries, sometimes combined with analytical research and evaluation; *Data Books and Research Reports*: state-of-the-art reports, annotated bibliographies, technical guides, and directories of terms and processes; and *Newsletters*: brief reflections of the latest technical achievements, as they are observed and recorded for subsequent detailed evaluation, usually available on a subscription basis.

Services and information offered by each Special Technology Group are described in *Special Technology Group Catalog*, #NTIS-PR-209, free; NTIS (see C1.17).

Special Technology Groups of general interest include:

1. Technology Application Center (TAC)

Sponsored by NASA, TAC identifies and disseminates the results of existing research and new high-interest areas of technology. It provides a full range of personalized information-searching services in the physical and social sciences, a current-awareness service, bibliographies with abstracts, and in-depth analysis and applications service in the areas of energy, remote sensing, and land-use inventory and planning. TAC subject areas include heat pipe technology, hydrogen energy, solar thermal energy use, wind energy utilization, remote sensing of natural resources, noise pollution, waste glass utilization, and rolamite.

TAC, University of New Mexico, Albuquerque, NM 87131; 505-277-3622.

2. Technical Help to Exporters (THE)

THE is an agency of the British Standards Institution. It provides information on the standards and regulations that products must meet in worldwide export markets. THE will research specific problems for individual companies, will help with technical difficulties related to specific products, can help obtain certificates of approval, and can help arrange tests and inspections. It provides a variety of export-related publications.

Annual membership in THE is $25.00, and requires an NTIS Deposit Account (see 9.6).

Technical Help to Exporters Catalog, #NTIS-PR-244, free; NTIS (see C1.17).

3. Engineering Sciences Data Unit (ESDU)

ESDU, located in London, provides engineers with design data in four primary areas of engineering: aeronautical, mechanical, structural, and chemical. ESDU staff gathers and evaluates all available data, published and unpublished, on a given topic. For each subject studied, one package of data is issued, a Data Item, representing an agreed correlation tailored to the needs of speedy and reliable application in engineering design and analysis.

More than 650 Data Items of varying size are currently available. Each includes a set of loose-leaf sheets devoted to a single topic with graphical data, equations, tables, definitions and terminology, explanatory matter, and worked examples.

For current prices: Brochure #NTIS-PR-245, free; NTIS (see C1.17).

4. Office of Standard Reference Data, National Bureau of Standards

Many publications of the Office of Standard Reference Data are available through NTIS.

See *Special Technology Groups Catalog*, #NTIS-PR-209, free; NTIS (see C1.17).

5. Metals and Ceramics Information Center (MCIC)

MCIC provides a wide range of publications and services. Subjects covered by MCIC include aluminum, magnesium, berryllium, ceramics and composites, high-temperature oxidation-resistant coatings, stainless and high-strength steels, nickel and cobalt-base alloys, powder metals, refractory metals, and titanium and titanium alloys. MCIC also provides a technical inquiry service.

Publications available are listed in *Special Technology Groups Catalog*, #NTIS-PR-209, free; NTIS (see C1.17).

MCIC, Battelle Memorial Institute, 505 King Ave., Columbus, OH 43201; 614-424-6424 ext 2758.

6. Plastics Technical Evaluation Center (PLASTEC)

PLASTEC provides a custom search service, expert evaluation of search data, answers to research inquiries, custom state-of-the art reports, publications, and use of the 20,000-volume PLASTEC library. Subjects covered by PLASTEC include end-use data, electrical and electronic application, mechanical goods application, microbiological deterioration, structural composites, packaging, and adhesives.

Publications available are listed in *Special Technology Groups Catalog*, #NTIS-PR-209, free; NTIS (see C1.17).

PLASTEC, Picatinny Arsenal, Dover, NJ 07801; 201-328-2778.

7. Nuclear Safety Information Center (NSIC)

NSIC maintains a computerized bibliographic data base with more than 110,000 entries. NSIC produces state-of-the-art reports and a technical journal, *Nuclear Safety*. It also offers a technical inquiry service, retrospective searches of the data base, consultation with specialists, access to its documents, and a biweekly SDI (Selected Dissemination of Information) service.

List of available publications: *Special Technology Groups Catalog*, #NTIS-PR-209, free; NTIS (C1.17).

Nuclear Safety: GPO (see C1.0).

NSIC, Oak Ridge National Laboratory, P.O. Box Y, Oak Ridge, TN 37830; 615-483-8611 ext 3-7253.

8. Reliability Analysis Center

Microcircuit reliability data are available from the Reliability Analysis Center, in the form of custom data analysis, custom retrospective searches, reliability consultation, and a free quarterly newsletter.

List of available publications: Special Technology *Groups Catalog*, #NTIS-PR-209, free; NTIS (see C1.17).

Reliability Analysis Center, Rome Air Development Center, Griffis Air Force Base, Rome, NY 13441.

9. Thermophysical and Electronic Properties Information Analysis Center (TEPIAC)

TEPIAC maintains a computerized bibliographic data base of over 140,000 unclassified technical papers and will conduct literature searches, perform data analysis, and provide technical advisory and consulting services.

List of available publications: *Special Technology Groups Catalog*, #NTIS-PR-209, free; NTIS (see C1.17).

TEPIAC, Center for Information and Numerical Data Analysis and Synthesis, Purdue Industrial Research Park, 2595 Yeager Road, West Lafayette, IN 47906; 317-463-1581, or call toll-free 800-428-7675.

10. Explosives Division Laboratory, Feltman Research Laboratory

The Encyclopedia of Explosives and Related Items is published by Explosives Division Laboratory. It now has seven volumes.

$37.50 each volume; NTIS (see C1.17).

11. Mechanical Properties Data Center (MPDC)

MPDC, a unit of the Department of Defense, maintains a data base on mechanical properties of metals and metal alloys. It will retrieve test data, conduct literature searches, and provide publications.

MPDC: 616-947-4500.

12. Machinability Data Center (MDC)

The Machining Data Handbook, $35.00; NTIS (see C1.17).

MDC, Cincinnati, Ohio.

13. Nondestructive Testing Information Analysis Center (NTIAC)

United States Army qualified users may obtain literature searches and answers to inquiries from NTIAC.

NTIAC, Army Materials and Mechanics Research Center, Watertown, MA 02172; 617-923-3343 or 3352.

14. Infrared Information and Analysis Center (IRIA)

Qualified users may obtain various services and publications.

IRIA, Environmental Research Institute of Michigan, P.O. Box 618, Ann Arbor, MI 48107; 313-994-1200 ext 214.

15. Chemical Propulsion Information Agency (CPIA)

Qualified users may obtain various services and publications.

List of available publications: *Special Technology Groups Catalog*, #NTIS-PR-209, free; NTIS (see C1.17).

CPIA, Applied Physics Laboratory, the Johns Hopkins University, Johns Hopkins Road, Laurel, MD 20810; 301-953-7100 ext 7800.

16. Toxicology Information Response Center (TIRC)

Toxicology information on environmental pollutants, industrial chemicals, food additives, pesticides, pharmaceuticals, and other topics of toxicologic concern, is available from TIRC. The TIRC information resources include MEDLINE, TOXLINE, the Oak Ridge National Laboratory computerized data bases and library holdings, and the TIRC library. TIRC performs custom searches of data bases and produces bibliographies and state-of-the-art reviews.

List of available publications: *Special Technology Groups Catalog*, #NTIS-PR-209, free; NTIS (see C1.17).

TIRC, Information Center Complex, Information Division, Oak Ridge National Laboratory, P.O. Box X, Building 7509, Oak Ridge, TN 37830; 615-483-8611, ext 3-1433.

17. Electromagnetic Compatibility Analysis Center (ECAC)

ECAC is a Department of Defense center for the analysis of problems pertaining to electromagnetic interference.

ECAC, North and Severn, Annapolis, MD 21402; 301-267-2546.

9.10 Information Analysis Centers

Analysis and communication of specialized state-of-the-art information is performed by over a hundred Information Analysis Centers. NTIS is the national marketing coordinator for the following Information Analysis Centers, each of which is a Special Technology Group (see 9.9):

Chemical Propulsion Information Agency
Electromagnetic Compatibility Analysis Center
Explosives Laboratory, Feltman Research Laboratories
Infrared Information and Analysis Center
Machinability Data Center
Mechanical Properties Data Center
Metals and Ceramics Information Center
Nondestructive Testing Information Analysis Center
Nuclear Safety Information Analysis Center
Plastics Technical Evaluation Center
Reliability Analysis Center
Technology Application Center
Thermophysical and Electronic Properties Information Analysis Center
Toxicology Information Response Center

Directory of Federally Supported Information Analysis Centers: $4.25 paper copy, $2.25 microfiche; NTIS (see C1.17).

9.11 *Weekly Government Abstracts*

Research summaries in 26 areas of government research, performed by hundreds of organizations, including United States government agencies, private researchers, universities, and special technology groups are available within two weeks of their receipt by National Technical Information Service in the series of newsletters known as *Weekly Government Abstracts*. The last issue of each year is a subject index containing up to ten cross references for each research summary indexed.

NTIS (see C1.17).

Titles, with prices, are as follows:

Administration, $40.00
Agriculture and Food, $40.00
Behavior and Society, $40.00
Biomedical Technology and Engineering, $40.00
Building Technology, $40.00

Business and Economics, $40.00
Chemistry, $40.00
Civil and Structural Engineering, $40.00
Communication, $45.00
Computers, Control and Information Theory, $40.00
Electrotechnology, $40.00
Energy, $40.00
Environmental Pollution and Control, $60.00
Government Inventions for Licensing, $165.00
Health Planning, $40.00
Industrial and Mechanical Engineering, $40.00
Library and Information Sciences, $30.00
Materials Sciences, $40.00
Medicine and Biology, $45.00
NASA Earth Resources Survey Program, $40.00
National Resources, $40.00
Ocean Technology and Engineering, $40.00
Physics, $45.00
Problem-Solving Technology for State and Local Governments, $60.00
Transportation, $40.00
Urban Technology, $40.00

9.12 *Subject Guide to the NTIS Information Collection*

A search tool which may be used independently or with the NTIS Bibliographic Data File (on magnetic tape) (see 9.3), or with the *Government Reports Announcements and Index* (see 9.13), and with the *Annual Index*, is the *Subject Guide to the NTIS Information Collection.*

The *Subject Guide* is a composite of the subject-indexing vocabularies used to index research reports in the NTIS Bibliographic Data File. It is sometimes called the NTIS Master Frequency List of Subject Terms.

All unique subject index terms are listed alphanumerically with frequency postings for the various index files and for the master file. The frequency postings include the number of times each term is used as a controlled thesaurus descriptor or as a key word (descriptor, identifier, open-ended term).

Revisions of the *Subject Guide* will be published annually and merged with the master list every three to five years.

Available on paper in four volumes, and in microfiche and microfilm, all at the same price of $125.00; NTIS (see C1.17).

9.13 *Government Reports Announcements and Index*

New government research is summarized biweekly in the *Government Reports Announcements and Index* (GRA&I), which is composed from the NTIS Bibliographic Data File (see 9.3). The GRA&I contains about 60,000 new summaries annually, in more than 7,000 pages. It is indexed by subject, personal and corporate authors, government contract, and order numbers.

The GRA&I is designed for librarians and technical information specialists and for those used to working with technical information terms and sources.

$165.00 per year; NTIS (see C1.17).

The *Annual Index* is published as a six-volume hardbound set: $345.00 for years beginning 1973, less for years beginning 1968.

National Aeronautics and Space Administration (NASA) (9.20-9.21)

9.20 Industrial Applications Centers

Countless dollars and effort are wasted in research and design facilities because technicians are too busy to search the literature before instigating new programs. Obviously, searching before researching is vital to economical innovation.

The six regional Industrial Applications Centers (IAC) help answer this need both by searching the literature and by helping evaluate and apply the results. The Centers maintain computerized access to about three-quarters of a million space-related reports as well as to ten times that many reports and articles from private and nonspace governmental sources. The Centers' resources cover the contents of more than 15,000 scientific and technical journals throughout the world, plus thousands of specialized governmental and industrial research reports. NASA believes that it is the world's largest technical data bank.

Major information sources accessible through IAC's now include:

Air Pollution Technical Information Center
Chemical Abstracts Condensates
Education Resources Information Center
Engineering Index

Government Reports Announcements
(including data from all government agencies)
NASA International Aerospace Abstracts
NASA Tech Briefs
NASA Scientific and Technical Aerospace Reports
Nuclear Science Abstracts
Selected Water Resources Abstracts

The IAC's also utilize specialized data files dealing with food technology, textile technology, metallurgy, medicine, business, economics, social sciences, and physical sciences.

Services offered by the IAC's are as follows:

1. *Retrospective Searches*. Pertinent technical literature that covers the desired research topic has probably already been published and filed somewhere among millions of documents; to find it, IAC will conduct a retrospective search. The IAC will assign a scientist or engineer familiar with the relevant area of technology. Highly specific questions will be asked in order to define as precisely as possible just what is to be searched for. The search will then be conducted and the results evaluated. A typical retrospective report is available in less than fourteen days and consists of thirty to 300 abstracts. Full-text reports are available from the IAC. The customer pays only the cost of retrieval.

2. *Current-Awareness Searches*. Just as retrospective searches are used for solving known problems, current-awareness searches often generate ideas which perhaps would not otherwise be considered. The service consists of abstracts relating to a specific topic tailored to meet the exact needs explained to the personally-assigned IAC engineer. Subscribers receive monthly or quarterly updates on new developments in the same abstract form as the retrospective searches.

3. *Technical Assistance*. NASA comments, "If you are like most clients, you are more interested in answers than abstracts." The professional staff members at the IAC's hold advanced degrees in chemistry, physics, engineering, or other technical fields. They are in an excellent position to offer suggestions on how the information they have gathered may be applied to best advantage.

NASA promises that the IAC's will protect the confidentiality of proprietary information.

Some examples of industrial use of technology from NASA are as follows:

Rechargeable heart pacemaker
Improved brake linings
Better batteries
Aptitude testing using a psychomotor device
Electrical wiring using a flat conductor cable that can be hidden by wall paint
Restoration of obliterated serial numbers in police work, by a cavitation technique
Recycling of nonferrous metals by a ferrofluidic technique
Radar-reflective lifecraft
Shock-absorbing highway guard-rail system
Self-lubricating bearings
Side-scanning radar for petroleum exploration
Increased life expectancy of electric meter coils
Improved wear resistance of valve surfaces by plasma arc spraying
Thermometer printing using inexpensive ceramic ink
Reduction of chemical effluents
Blood plasma protection by use of crystals which change color permanently if thawed
Improved building construction design, using NASA's Structural Analysis computer program
Safer handling of liquified natural gas

NASA (see C1.107).

9.21 NASA Field Centers

NASA maintains ten Field Centers, and each has a technology utilization officer. These individuals act as back-up to the Information Analysis Centers in matching industry problems to appropriate NASA scientific and engineering expertise.

NASA also has established four Biomedical Application Teams and two Technology Application Teams, which work to identify significant problems that might be solved by adapting space technology.

NASA Field Centers (see C1.107).

Smithsonian Science Information Exchange, Inc. (SSIE) (9.30)

9.30 Smithsonian Science Information Exchange, Inc.

Access to research which has not yet been published is possible through the various services of the Smithsonian Science Information Exchange, Inc. (SSIE). SSIE is a major national source for information on research in progress in all areas of basic and applied research in the life and physical sciences.

SSIE covers some 1,300 government agencies and private organizations, and its current file contains records of more than 200,000 ongoing or recently completed research projects, each of which is described by a brief abstract. SSIE's indexing system is designed to serve both the individual researcher and the manager of research activities.

The SSIE data base may be searched in a variety of ways. SSIE regularly conducts searches on subjects of high current interest, the results of which are compiled into research information packages announced in the *SSIE Science Newsletter*. Custom searches may be conducted, on the basis of individual request. The NTIS data base may also be included in the custom search. Current-awareness searches are available either monthly or quarterly. Searches may also reveal all research associated with a specific investigator or with a grant, contract, or accession number. Tabulations for administrative purposes may be obtained in a number of standard formats.

The SSIE current file covers two federal government fiscal years. However, the historical file covers the last five years, and it may be custom-searched by subject, by investigator, or for administrative tabulations. Abstracts retrieved are on microfilm.

On-line access to the SSIE data base is available to anyone in the United States and in many foreign countries who has a telephone and the right computer terminal equipment. The cost of searches is then greatly reduced. Access is through the System Development Corporations's SDC Search Service, in Santa Monica, California. The average on-line search costs only about $30.00 in connect time.

System Development Corporation, 2500 Colorado Avenue, Santa Monica, CA 90406 (213-829-7511); 7929 Westpark Drive, McLean, VA 22101 (703-790-9850); or 401 Hackensack Avenue, Hackensack, NJ 07601 (201-487-0571).

SSIE Science Newsletter: $10.00 per year; SSIE, Room 300, 1730 M Street N.W., Washington, DC 20036.

Custom searches: minimum charge $60.00 per search; includes up to 50 abstracts.

Custom plus NTIS data base: minimum charge $85.00, additional 25¢ per abstract over 125.

Monthly current-awareness searches: $180.00 per year; no limit on number of abstracts.

Quarterly current-awareness searches: on a custom basis, $50.00 each, 25¢ for each abstract over 50.

Name searches: $2.00 per name, $10.00 minimum.

Grant, contract, or accession number searches: $1.00 per number, $10.00 minimum.

Administrative tabulations: $160.00 per report, plus 7¢ per project tabulated.

Subject and administrative searches: $200.00 per search, plus 50¢ per document copy; investigator searches: $6.50 per name, $10.00 minimum.

Library of Congress (9.40-9.41)

9.40 National Referral Center for Science and Technology

Advice on where to obtain information on specific topics in science and technology may be obtained from the National Referral Center for Science and Technology of the Library of Congress.

The data base of this free service is a subject-indexes inventory, continuously updated by a professional staff of analysts, that contains descriptions of some 9,000 organizations (called information resources by the Center) having specialized knowledge in the broad range of science and technology. Included in the descriptions are detailed data on each resource's areas of interest and the types of information services it provides.

The Center does not itself attempt to furnish technical answers to inquiries, or even references to literature that might contain such answers. Instead, it directs those who have a question concerning a particular subject to organizations or individuals with specialized knowledge of that subject.

The Center is concerned with all fields of science and technology: the physical, biological, social, and engineering sciences, and the many technical areas relating to them. Similarly, it is concerned with all kinds of information resources, wherever they exist: in government, in industry, and in the academic and professional world.

Science and Technology Division, National

Referral Center for Science and Technology, Library of Congress, 10 First Street S.E., Washington, DC 20540; for general inquiries: 202-426-5678; for referral service: 426-5670; to register as an information source: 426-5680.

9.41 Scientific and Technical Literature Searches

Trained personnel in the Division of Science and Technology of the Library of Congress can conduct literature searches and assemble bibliographies in scientific and technical fields. This can be done on a one-time or a continuing basis at $11.00 per hour and a minimum fee of $88.00. A cost estimate is provided in advance. Brief technical inquiries entailing a bibliographic response may be answered free of charge.

Assistant Chief for Reference and Referral Serivces, Science and Technology Division, Library of Congress, Washington, DC 20540; 202-426-5687.

National Bureau of Standards (NBS) (9.50-9.52)

9.50 Institutes of NBS

The *Institute for Basic Standards* provides the central basis within the United States of a complete and consistent system of physical measurement; coordinates that system with measurement systems of other nations; and furnishes essential services leading to accurate and uniform physical measurements throughout the nation's scientific community, industry, and commerce.

The *Institute for Materials Research* conducts materials research leading to improved methods of measurement, standards, and data on the properties of well-characterized materials needed by industry, commerce, educational institutions, and government; provides advisory and research services to other government agencies; and develops, produces, and distributes Standard Reference Materials. The Institute also conducts a Nondestructive Evaluation Program.

The *Institute for Applied Technology* provides technical services to promote the use of available technology and to facilitate technological innovation in industry and government; cooperates with public and private organizations to develop technological standards, codes, and test methods; and provides technical advice and services to government agencies. The Institute includes the Center for Fire Research, the Center for Building Technology, and the Center for Consumer Product Technology, as well as other divisions.

The *Institute for Computer Sciences and Technology* conducts research and provides technical services designed to aid government agencies in improving cost effectiveness in the conduct of their programs through the selection, acquisition, and effective utilization of automatic data-processing equipment; and serves as the principal focus within the executive branch for the development of federal standards for automatic data-processing equipment, techniques, and computer languages.

The *Office for Information Programs* promotes optimum dissemination and accessibility of scientific information generated within NBS and other agencies of the federal government; promotes the development of the National Standard Reference Data System and a system of information analysis centers dealing with the National Measurement System; and gives NBS staff access to scientific information.

National Bureau of Standards, Washington, DC 20234 (headquarters and laboratories are located in Gaithersburg, Maryland, a suburb of Washington).

9.51 National Standard Reference Data System.

Industrial technicians, scientists, and engineers can improve the reliability of physical measurements and the level of experimental techniques by use of the data and information available through the National Standard Reference Data System (NSRDS) of the National Bureau of Standards (NBS).

The NSRDS compiles and evaluates data, which are then available for public use in several ways:

(1) The *Journal of Physical and Chemical Reference Data*, a quarterly, disseminates data compilations.

(2) Inquiries may be answered by the NBS Office of Standard Reference DATA (OSRD).

(3) The OSRD maintains a broad, though selective, collection of reference data compilations and ancillary publications. The OSRD library is open to visitors, and a list of the latest annotated accessions is available on request.

(4) Data bases on magnetic tape are available

through National Technical Information Service at $250.00 each. A new data analysis and retrieval system named TODARS is being used to search various data files.

A full description of the various programs is found in *NBS Technical Note 881* (April, 1975), National Bureau of Standards, Washington, DC 20234; or, same title, #C13.46:881, $1.10, GPO (see C1.0).

Journal of Physical and Chemical Reference Data, American Chemical Society, 1155 Sixteenth Street N.W., Washington, DC 20036; $75.00 per year.

Office of Standard Reference Data, NBS, Washington, DC 20234.

9.52 Standard Reference Materials Program

Adequate and consistent measurements for science, technology, and industry are made possible under the Standard Reference Materials (SRM) program of the National Bureau of Standards (NBS). The formal definition of an SRM is: "well-characterized and certified materials, produced in quantity: (1) to help develop reference methods of analysis or test; i.e., methods proved to be accurate; and/or (2) to calibrate a measurement system in order to (a) facilitate the exchange of goods; (b) institute quality control; (c) determine performance characteristics; and (d) characterize at scientific frontiers; and/or (3) to assure the long-term adequacy and integrity of the quality control process."

Under the SRM program, NBS makes available samples of materials with known characteristics and compositions, with which other materials may be compared.

Office of Standard Reference Materials, NBS, Washington, DC 20234. A free publication, NBS Monograph 148, *The Role of Standard Reference Materials in Measurement Systems*, is available upon request.

National Science Foundation (NSF) (9.60)

9.60 Description of NSF Programs

Business can benefit directly and indirectly from federal government support of scientific research and education projects, through the National Science Foundation (NSF). Indirect benefits are possible through participation in NSF's RANN (Research Applied to National Needs) program. NSF also encourages collaboration between industry and university researchers, and may support broader efforts through industry associations, groups of companies, or professional societies.

The RANN program supports problem-oriented research. Joint proposals between industry and universities or governments are encouraged, and NSF devotes a significant amount of its RANN program budget to awards to small businesses.

At present, the RANN program emphasizes the areas of resources, environment, productivity, intergovernmental science and R&D incentives, and exploratory research and technology assessment. NSF encourages the submission of unsolicited proposals (see *Guidelines for Preparations of Unsolicited Proposals*). The range of research topics supported is described in *Guide to Programs, Grants and Awards* and the *Annual Report*.

Current information about individual NSF programs appears in the monthly *NSF Bulletin*, free from the Public Information Branch, national Science Foundation, Washington, DC 20550.

Guidelines for Preparation of Unsolicited Proposals, other publications, and general inquiries: Office of Programs and Resources, National Science Foundation, Washington, DC 20550; or, if west of the Rocky Mountains, to the Western Projects Office, National Science Foundation, 831 Mitten Road, Burlingame, CA 94010.

Small business inquiries may be addressed to the Special Assistant for Small Business, Intergovernmental Science and Public Technology, Research Applications Directorate, National Science Foundation, Washington, DC 20550.

Department of Agriculture (9.70-9.75)

9.70 Economic Research Service

The Economic Research Service (ERS) gathers and analyzes economic information needed to improve agriculture and rural living. ERS experts can answer questions about the current situation and outlook, as well as provide information on the more fundamental relationships between supply and demand. Analysts also examine international developments that have a potential impact on United States farm trade. The Economic Development Division of ERS collects, analyzes, and publishes data on rural population, employment, incomes, farm and nonfarm workers, job skills, and education levels. It also evaluates changes in the condition of rural communities; i.e., schools, housing, medical services, and public facilities.

ERS, Department of Agriculture, Washington, DC 20250, 202-447-8038.

9.71 Publications of the Economic Research Service

Analysts at Economic Research Service (ERS) publish annually some 100 separate research studies. Subjects are as diverse as an in-depth analysis of the futures market, and a look at the inroads made by substitutes and synthetics into traditional farm markets.

An accurate appraisal of the current outlook and situation for all major commodities, plus topics of general interest to the food and fiber industry, can be found in 22 separate *Situation Reports* published on a scheduled basis throughout the year.

Brief highlights of the latest situation and outlook appear monthly in the *Agricultural Outlook Digest.*

Another monthly, the *Farm Index*, allows readers to keep abreast of current ERS research in easy-to-read language.

The quarterly, *Agricultural Economics Research*, a more technical publication, reports on the latest findings, developments, and research methods in agricultural economics.

Each year, ERS teams with several other Department of Agriculture agencies to produce the *Handbook of Agricultural Charts*. This is the most comprehensive collection of charts on agriculture, depicting everything from farm income trends and commodity prices to rural housing conditions and the cost of a week's food.

The annual *Agricultural Statistics* is another product of joint cooperation with other agriculture agencies. The handbook is a reliable reference source on agricultural production, supplies, consumption, facilities, and costs and returns.

ERS joins with the Bureau of the Census to produce the *Census-ERS Series*, annual estimates of farm population by age, sex, labor force status, and other characteristics.

The *Balance Sheet of the Farming Sector* is one of several farm finance reports that ERS issues on an annual basis. It provides a full statement of debts and assets of the entire agriculture sector.

A number of other periodic reports provide yearly wrap-ups on topics like farm costs and returns, the hired farm working force, and changes in farm production and efficiency.

A monthly summary of the current status and outlook for farm exports appears in *Foreign Agricultural Trade of the United States.* Supplements are published for the calendar year and the fiscal year.

Research reports, handbooks, statistical supplements, technical bulletins, and speeches are listed in the monthly *Checklist of New Reports.*

For sample copies, write ERS Publications Unit, Room 0054, Department of Agriculture, Washington, DC 20250.

9.72 Cooperative State Research Service

The Cooperative State Research Service supports basic and applied research in high priority problems of regional or national scope. Areas currently considered are rural development, environmental quality, food and nutrition, beef and pork production, pest management, and soybean research. Grants may be made to private organizations and individuals for research to further the programs of the Department of Agriculture.

Administrator, Cooperative State Research Service, Department of Agriculture, Washington, DC 20250; 202-447-4423.

9.73 Agricultural Marketing Services

The Agricultural Marketing Services provides timely information on prices, demand, movement, volume, and quality on all major agricultural commodities. The information can be used as a basis for judging prevailing commodity values. Market news is disseminated by the news media, as well as by mimeographed reports, bulletin boards, telephone, and telegraph.

Associate Administrator, Agricultural Marketing Service, Department of Agriculture, Washington, DC 20250; 202-447-4276.

9.74 National Agricultural Library

The National Agricultural Library serves as the national resource for information on agriculture and related subjects, collecting material in over fifty different languages and organizing this material for maximum use by scientists, students, and others.

Office of the Director, National Agricultural Library, Beltsville, MD 20705; 301-344-3779.

9.75 Agricultural Research Information Data Base

A computer-based information storage and retrieval system, the Current Research Information System (CRIS) is designed to improve communications among agricultural research scientists, especially with regard to research work currently under way, and to provide research managers with up-to-date and coordinated information on the total research programs of the Department of Agriculture and the State Agricultural Experiment Stations.

The areas of interest of CRIS include current agricultural research activities of the Department of Agriculture, the State Agricultural Experiment Stations, and other cooperating institutions.

CRIS answers inquiries regarding research projects or refers inquirers to persons performing the research.

Cooperative State Research Service, Department of Agriculture, South Agriculture Building, Room 6818, 14th Street and Independence Avenue S.W., Washington, DC 20250; 202-447-7273.

Additional Sources of Technical Information (9.100-9.122)

9.100 The *Federal Register*

The *Federal Register*, published daily, is the medium for making available to the public federal agency regulations and other legal documents of the executive branch. These documents cover a wide range of government activities.

Government requirements are published in the *Register* which involve environmental protection, consumer product safety, food and drug standards, occupational health and safety, and many more areas of concern to the public.

Perhaps more importantly, proposed changes in regulated areas are included. Each proposed change published carries an invitation for any citizen or group to participate in the consideration of the proposed regulation through the submission of written data, views, or arguments, and sometimes through oral presentations. The opportunity afforded citizens, through the publication of proposed rules and notices of public meetings, to be informed of and participate in the workings of their government is significant.

The Office of the Federal Register conducts briefings on how to use the *Federal Register*. "The *Federal Register*—What It Is and How to Use It" is a learning opportunity open to the general public and federal agency personnel and is designed as an introduction for the individual who needs to use *Federal Register* publications to keep track and gain understanding of federal regulations.

These sessions cover the following areas: a brief history of the *Federal Register*; the difference between legislation and regulations; an introduction to the finding aids of the Office of the Federal Register; the relationship between the *Federal Register* and the *Code of Federal Regulations*; and the important elements of a typical *Federal Register* document.

The *Federal Register* briefings are scheduled on a regular basis in Washington, D.C. Under certain circumstances and by special arrangement, these briefings may be scheduled in other cities.

For further information on the Federal Register briefings, write to the Office of the Federal Register, National Archives and Records Service, Washington, DC 20408; 202-523-5240.

$50.00 per year, $5.00 per month, single copy 75¢; GPO (see C1.0). Monthly, quarterly, and annual indexes are available.

9.101 Government-Industry Data Exchange Program

The Government-Industry Data Exchange Program (GIDEP) is a cooperative activity of technical data exchange among government agencies and industry participant organizations. Government agencies participating in the program include the Army, Navy, Air Force, NASA, DSA, FAA, NRC, and SBA. At present, over 300 contractors and government groups interchange engineering technical information on parts, components, and materials; manufacturing techniques and processes; calibration procedure; metrology-related data; and other technical reports on techniques, procedures, and methods for testing and application of parts and materials.

GIDEP is concerned with laboratory and field test data on parts, components, and materials; manufacturing processes and related technical data on parts application or testing; calibration procedures and related metrology data. GIDEP information is of interest to groups concerned with reliability, maintainability, spares provisioning, logistics support, procurement, receiving inspection, quality assurance, design engineering, environmental test laboratory, specifications and standards, and metrology.

Information services include program data outputs in the form of hard copy summary cards, microfilm cartridges containing complete detailed data, and computer listings providing summary tape information. A computer on-line inquiry system is also available for participant use to search and retrieve data bank information. SETE (Secretariat for Electronic Test Equipment) program data and services are directly available for GIDEP use. SETE operates a data bank on electronic test and checkout equipment. In addition, two special communication-type functions assist participants: the ALERT system, which notifies participants of potential problem areas involving use of parts and materials; and the UDR system, which provides an inquiry service among participants when specific data cannot be located at a particular activity. GIDEP has also initiated a pilot program of reliability data exchange with the European EXACT (International Exchange of Authenticated Electronic Component Performance Test Data) program.

GIDEP Program Manager, Hq. Naval Material Command (MAT034), Washington, DC 20390; 202-325-8780. Also, Naval Fleet Missile Systems Analysis and Evaluation Group (Code 860), Corona, CA 91720; 714-736-4677.

9.102 Water Resources Scientific Information Center

The Water Resources Scientific Information Center is responsive to technical and scientific information needs, and provides communication and coordination among all those engaged in federally sponsored water resources research. The Center provides current information on water resources research by means of a semimonthly research results abstract bulletin, an abstract catalog of ongoing research projects, state-of-the-art reviews, and topical bibliographies. Abstracts of ongoing research projects are available. Although complete copies of research reports are not distributed by the Center, many are available for purchase from the National Technical Information Service. The Center also operates a computerized retrieval program to supply basic research information in response to specific inquiries.

Office of Water Research and Technology, Department of the Interior, Washington, DC 20240.

9.103 Geological Survey Land Information and Analysis Programs

The Land Information and Analysis Office manages five multidisciplinary programs:

The *Earth Sciences Applications* program is responsible for integrating the earth-science information collected by the Geological Survey for use in analyzing land resource problems. The products, mainly thematic maps and reports, provide insight into the environmental consequences of land use decision. For example, the San Francisco Bay region study has produced more than 70 geologic, hydrologic, and topographic maps and technical reports, plus 15 interpretive reports relating the data to land use planning and management alternatives and possible environmental impact.

The *Resource and Land Investigations* program encompasses the multidisciplinary, multibureau efforts of the Department of the Interior. The national problems addressed include, for example, the delineation of environmentally endangered areas, the development and application of land use inventory systems, and the siting of onshore facilities associated with outer continental shelf energy resource development.

The *Geography* program calls for the application of geographic analysis techniques to land and resource problems. Land use data are systematically collected, revised, and analyzed on a nationwide basis, and basic geographic research is conducted.

The *Earth Resources Observation Systems* (EROS) program is the largest Departmental program to be managed by this new office. Since 1966, numerous experiments have been conducted applying remotely sensed data, primarily photographs and telecommunicated images obtained from satellites and high-altitude aircraft, to a wide variety of resource and environmental problems. The key facility of this program is the EROS Data Center in Sioux Falls, South Dakota, where the data are stored, reproduced, and distributed. The program includes research as well as user training in the interpretation and application of remotely sensed data and also includes the development of improved sensor and data processing systems.

The *Environmental Impact Analysis* program directs the preparation and review of the environmental impact statements required of the Survey by the National Environmental Policy Act of 1969.

In addition to managing these five programs, the Land Information and Analysis Office enters into cooperative projects with state, local, and other federal agencies.

Land Information and Analysis Office, Geological Survey, Reston, VA 22092; 703-860-7444. See also field offices of Geological Survey (C1.50).

9.104 Publications of the Geological Survey

Results of research and investigations by the Geological Survey are made available to the public through professional papers, bulletins, water-supply papers, circulars, miscellaneous reports, and several map and atlas series. All books, maps other than topographic quadrangle maps, and related Survey publications are listed in the catalogs, *Publications of the Geological Survey, 1879-1971,* and *Publications of the Geological Survey, 1962-1970.* Yearly supplements keep these catalogs up-to-date (see also *New Publications of the Geological Survey*).

Catalogs and annual supplements, free; Public Information Offices and Branch of Distribution Offices, Geological Survey (see C1.50).

9.105 Topographic Surveys and Mapping

The National Mapping Program of the Geological Survey, Department of the Interior, makes graphic or digital cartographic data and services readily available for a multiplicity of uses. Cartographic products include:

Aerial Photographs: low to high-altitude photographs which provide basic information on the character of the land surface for mapping and other purposes.

Geodetic Data: positions, elevations, and descriptions of control points which are used in the preparation of the map base.

Standard Topographic Maps: the basic map series from which smaller scale and special maps are usually derived.

Orthophotoquads: rectified aerial photographs in standard quadrangle format and with map information superimposed.

Smaller Scale and Special Maps: standard series at scales ranging from 1:50,000 to 1:1,000,000, and National Park maps and special products such as slope maps at various scales.

Digital Map Data: a numerical representation of the information normally shown on multipurpose topographic maps, to be used in planning and management activites as well as in map production and revision.

The National Atlas: a bound collection of full-color maps and charts showing physical features such as landforms, geology, soil, vegetation, and climate. Economic, social, and cultural data are also presented. The volume may be purchased for $100 from the Geological Survey. Selected *National Atlas* maps have been published in separate sales editions and can be purchased individually.

The National Cartographic Information Center of the Geological Survey provides a focal point for information on United States maps and charts, aerial photographs and space imagery, geodetic control, and related cartographic data. The Center serves the user of cartographic data in three ways: It furnishes information on cartographic data available from federal, state, and private organizations; it furnishes information on the data-collection plans of these organizations; and it processes orders for cartographic data.

National Cartographic Information Center, Geological Survey (see C1.50).

To inquire about map and report availability in a given area, contact regional offices of the Geological Survey (see C1.50). Maps may then be ordered as follows: For maps of areas east of the Missippi, including Minnesota, Puerto Rico, and the Virgin Islands: Branch of Distribution, Geological Survey, 1200 South Eads Street, Arlington, VA 22202; 703-557-2751. Maps for areas west of the Mississippi, including Alaska, Hawaii, Louisiana, Guam, and American Samoa:

Branch of Distribution, Geological Survey, Box 25286, Denver Federal Center, Building 41, Denver, CO 80225; 303-234-3832.

9.106 National Archives and Records Service

Businesses which need to understand the origins of legislation, the evolution of regulatory agencies, the adoption of trade standards and policies, or other matters involving the history of the government, may consult the National Archives and Records Service. It is the depository for the permanently valuable noncurrent records of the federal government.

The holdings of the Archives are described in *Guide to the National Archives and Records Service*, an 800-page source found in most major research libraries. Among those holdings are the records of various agencies related to business, such as the Securities and Exchange Commission, Federal Trade Commission, Small Business Administration, and Food and Drug Administration. A summary of the available records appears in *List of Record Groups of the National Archives and Records Service*, which is updated periodically.

Recent additions to the Archives collection, and articles based on records in the Archives, appear in a quarterly journal entitled *Prologue*. Much of the Archives information is available on microfilm. A free copy of the *Catalog of National Archives Microfilm Publications* is available upon request. Other publications are described in the free *Select List of Publications of the National Archives and Records Service*.

For assistance, information, and consultation about individual research requests, contact the Central Reference Division, National Archives and Records Service, Washington, DC 20408; 202-523-3218.

Microfilm: $12.00 per roll.

Publications mentioned: Publications Sales Office, Room G6, National Archives Building, Washington, DC 20408.

9.107 Technology Clearinghouse to Aid Minority Business

The Office of Minority Business Enterprise (OMBE) of the Department of Commerce has developed a program to provide minority-owned business firms with improved access to technical innovations developed under federal government contracts and by private corporations without federal aid.

The first phase of this new technology utilization program involved gaining support among a broad base of federal agencies and private businesses which conduct technology utilization programs.

Under the second phase, the Booker T. Washington Foundation, of Washington, D.C., will design and test the operation of a clearinghouse which will offer access to information concerning (1) product identification, (2) feasibility analysis, (3) marketing, and (4) financing to minority firms in adapting new technology for the development of commercial products. The new center will begin providing services to minority firms nationally when the designs have been fully tested.

OMBE (see C1.12).

9.108 Experimental Technology Incentives Program

The Experimental Technology Incentives Program is a joint effort between the Small Business Administration (SBA) and the National Bureau of Standards to devise new means and methods of assisting the small business research and development community.

Regional offices of SBA (see C1.110) will be informed when the program becomes operational.

9.109 Technology Transfer by Bureau of Mines

The Bureau of Mines attempts to develop and transfer technology in cooperation with industry by cooperative research and demonstration programs utilizing cost-sharing agreements, technical assistance to mine operators, conferences and briefings held in mining areas around the country, and technology transfer seminars which introduce and promote the application of accomplishments in specific research areas. Technological packages and information transferred include noise control, mine electrical power distribution, illumination systems, roof and dust control, mineland reclamation, and productivity.

Bureau of Mines activities, including mining research, metallurgy research, environmental repair, and mineral supply/demand analysis, are described in a booklet entitled *The Bureau of*

Mines: Its Mission and Programs.

Free; Office of Mineral Information, Bureau of Mines, Department of the Interior, 2401 E Street N.W., Washington, DC 20241; 202-634-1004. Information is also available through the state liaison officer in the state capital, listed in the telephone book under United States Government, Department of the Interior, Bureau of Mines. In addition, Bureau of Mines field centers, listed below, may be contacted.

Tuscaloosa, Alabama: Metallurgy Research Laboratory
Juneau, Alaska: Field Operatons Center
Denver, Colorado: Mining Research Center
  Intermountain Field Operations Center
College Park, Maryland: Metallurgy Research Center
Twin Cities, Minnesota: Mining Research Center
  Metallurgy Research Center
Rolla, Missouri: Metallurgy Research Center
Boulder City, Nevada: Metallurgy Research Center
Reno, Nevada: Metallurgy Research Center
Albany, Oregon: Metallurgy Research Center
Pittsburgh, Pennsylvania: Mining and Safety Research
  Eastern Field Operations Center
  Coal Preparation and Analysis Group
Wilkes-Barre, Pennsylvania: Environmental Field Office
Amarillo, Texas: Helium Operations
Salt Lake City, Utah: Metallurgy Research Center
Spokane, Washington: Mining Research Center
  Western Field Operations Center

9.110 Mineralogical Services of Bureau of Mines

To help persons searching for new mineral deposits within the territorial limits of the United States, the Bureau of Mines makes macroscopic and petrographic examinations of mineral specimens to help in determining the mineralogical content of the specimen, its general characteristics, and the potential commercial importance of the minerals present. This service may be obtained by submitting samples, not to exceed one pound each, to any of the following locations either in person or by mail.

Research Director
Albany Metallurgy Research Center
Bureau of Mines
P.O. Box 70
Albany, OR 97321

Chief
Boulder City Metallurgy Research Laboratory
Bureau of Mines
500 Date Street
Boulder City, NV 89005

Research Director
College Park Metallurgy Research Center
Bureau of Mines
College Park, MD 20740

Research Director
Reno Metallurgy Research Center
Bureau of Mines
1605 Evans Avenue
Reno, NV 89505

Research Director
Rolla Metallurgy Research Center
Bureau of Mines
Box 280
Rolla, MO 65401

Research Director
Salt Lake City Metallurgy Research Center
Bureau of Mines
1600 East First South
Salt Lake City, UT 84112

Chief
Tuscaloosa Metallurgy Research Laboratory
Bureau of Mines
Box L
University, AL 35486

Research Director
Twin Cities Metallurgy Research Center
Bureau of Mines
P.O. Box 1660
Twin Cities Airport
Twin Cities, MN 55111

Assistant Director—Metallurgy
Bureau of Mines
2401 E Street N.W.
Washington, DC 20241

9.111 Federal Assistance Programs Retrieval System

The Federal Assistance Programs Retrieval System (FAPRS) is a computerized means of identifying federal programs that can be used to meet the development needs of any community. FAPRS is designed to identify only those programs funded during the current fiscal year and for which the community meets the basic eligibility requirements. The program is a valuable research tool for local officials, community developers, planners, state officials, and Congress. FAPRS is now available for use throughout the nation.

The FAPRS program works by asking a user a series of questions. The answers to these questions give the computer the information it needs to process an inquiry. The only facts that a user must know are the approximate population of his town or city, and the name of the county in which it is located. In addition, the user of FAPRS must be able to define the specific community need; for example, a water tower. The FAPRS data base can provide all of the other information. After processing this information, the computer prints out a listing of federally funded programs which can meet the community's needs.

In short, the FAPRS program has reduced the researcher's task to studying only eight to twelve programs, rather than the more than 1,000 federal programs available for domestic assistance.

Not every community needs to have a computer terminal to be able to access the FAPRS program. The most economical use of the program is made by having computer terminals at the multicounty or state level. However, cities or counties at present having access to computer terminals can inexpensively access the FAPRS program.

FAPRS, Rural Development Service, Department of Agriculture, Washington, DC 20250; 202-447-9296.

9.112 Office of Weights and Measures of the National Bureau of Standards

Uniformity and accuracy in commercial weights and measures are promoted by the Office of Weights and Measures (OWM) of the National Bureau of Standards (NBS). Manufacturers of commercial weighing and measuring equipment may obtain a free valuation of the equipment's accuracy under OWM's Prototype Examination Program. OWM also conducts a nationwide training program for industry service officials and for local weights and measures officials.

OWM's main role is to conduct research and provide technical information. Its laboratories produce standards, it conducts surveys of industry practices, and it holds conferences and training sessions, all with the goal of promoting a uniform weights and measures system.

Office of Weights and Measures, NBS, Washington, DC 20234; 301-921-2805.

9.113 Calibration and Test Services of NBS

Technical equipment of many types can be accurately calibrated with the assistance of the Office of Measurement Services of the National Bureau of Standards (NBS).

A detailed description of the services available is found in NBS Special Publication 250; Office of Measurement Services, NBS, Washington, DC 20234; 301-921-2805.

9.114 Center for Building Technology of NBS

Energy conservation through the use of improved and innovative building components and materials, and improvement of the usefulness, safety, and economy of buildings, are the goals of the Center for Building Technology of the National Bureau of Standards (NBS).

Current projects are listed in NBS Special Publication 446, *Building Technology Project Summaries*; Center for Building Technology, Institute for Applied Technology, NBS, Building 225, Room B-112, Washington, DC 20234; 301-921-3434.

9.115 Center for Consumer Product Technology of NBS

Safety and performance of consumer products and law enforcement equipment and the energy efficiency of household appliances are the areas of interest of the Center for Consumer Product Technology. The Center develops recommended voluntary product standards for industry and conducts studies on consumer product hazards.

Center for Consumer Product Technology, Institute for Applied Technology, NBS, Building

224, Room A-355, Washington, DC 20234; 301-921-3751.

9.116 Research Associate Program of NBS

Firms which share a mutual interest with a unit of the National Bureau of Standards (NBS) may benefit from participation in the Research Associate Program. Under this program, an employee of a firm may work at NBS, under the supervision of NBS professionals, using the facilities, laboratories, information, and services of NBS.

Industrial Liaison Officer, Research Associate program, Room A-402, Administration Building, NBS, Washington, DC 20234; 301-921-3591.

9.117 Standards Information Services of NBS

Up-to-date information on standards, specifications, test methods, codes, and recommended practices issued by government agencies, technical societies, government purchasing offices, and foreign national and international standardizing bodies may be obtained from the Standards Information Services of the National Bureau of Standards (NBS). Inquiries are answered by use of a computerized Key-Word-in-Context (KWIC) index, or by consulting the technical reference collection.

A list of publications is available upon request: Standards Information Services, Room B-162, Building 225, NBS, Washington, DC 20234; 301-921-2587. The reference collection is open Monday through Friday and is located in Room B-151, Technology Building, National Bureau of Standards, Gaithersburg, Maryland (about 25 miles from Washington, D.C.).

9.118 Educational Resources Information Center

Educational Resources Information Center (ERIC) is a nationwide, comprehensive information system dedicated to the progress of education by transmitting research results to teachers, administrators, education specialists and researchers, public officials, commercial and industrial organizations, and the public. The headquarters office is known as Central ERIC to distinguish it from its field activities, which are operated with National Institute of Education support by universities, professional societies, other nonprofit institutions, and commercial organizations. Central ERIC is responsible for the development and operation of the information network of clearinghouses, each of which deals with one or more specific subjects and provides specialized services.

National Institute of Education, 300 Seventh Street S.W., Washington, DC 20202; 202-755-7574.

9.119 Management Information Systems Service

The Scientific and Engineering Systems Division, Army Munitions Command, provides information on management systems, data automation, information management, scientific and technical information systems, engineering data storage and retrieval, data exchange, and computer-assisted design and manufacture.

The Division answers inquiries and makes referrals. Services are provided free to government and to industrial scientists and engineers.

Management Information Systems Directorate, Attention: AMSMU-MI-SE, Hq. U.S. Army Munitions Command, Dover, NJ 07801; 201-328-2284 or 2148.

9.120 Center for Fire Research

The Center for Fire Research of the National Bureau of Standards (NBS) conducts extensive applied research in fire science and engineering which may be of value to virtually all kinds of business. All of the research and tools generated by the Center are eagerly disseminated to the public, since its goal is to develop a technical base needed to reduce loss by fire by fifty percent in one generation. In the area of fire science, the Center has four areas of emphasis: information and hazard analysis, chemistry, toxicology of combustion products, and physics and the dynamics of fire. The area of fire safety engineering has a five-point program: product safety, furnishings safety, construction safety, fire detection and control systems, and design concepts.

Center for Fire Research, NBS, Washington, DC 20234.

9.121 Defense Documentation Center

Research and development reports produced by Department of Defense organizations and their contractors are available from the Defense Documentation Center (DDC). The services of DDC are available to contractors, subcontractors, and grantees of all federal government agencies.

Unclassified reports added to the DDC collection are announced in the National Technical Information Service's *Government Reports Announcements*. The DDC collection includes over a million titles, more than half of which are under computer control for quick retrieval. Classified reports are available only to registered users, and are announced semimonthly in *Technical Abstract Bulletin*, published by DDC.

Costly duplication of R&D effort may be prevented by consultation with the DDC Research and Technology Work Unit Information System, which maintains a computer data base on current research and development projects sponsored by the Department of Defense.

Administrator, DDC, Cameron Station, Alexandria, VA 22314.

9.122 Federal Information Center

Federal Information Centers (FIC) are clearinghouses for information about the federal government. If a citizen has a question of any sort about the government and does not know which of the hundreds of the offices has the answer, he may contact an FIC by phone, visit, or mail. The FIC will either provide the answer or refer the inquirer to the person or office that has the answer. Often, the center can also help with information about state and local government.

The centers are located nationwide. Many cities also have toll-free telephone tielines to other cities in which a center is actually located.

FIC (See C1.106).

Guides to Technical Information and Technology (9.200-9.318)

Directories to Sources of Information (9.200-9.207)

9.200 *How to Obtain Information in Different Fields of Science and Technology: A User's Guide*

National Technical Information Service (NTIS) describes this publication as "122 pages on the present knowledge domain of scientists and technologists; generation, use, and transfer of information; international medical information systems; federal information systems; the NASA Regional Dissemination Center; international information systems for physical scientists; environmental information systems."

#AD 780061, $5.50; NTIS (see C1.17).

9.201 *A Directory of Information Resources in the United States: Federal Government*

Over 1,200 agencies and federally supported organizations are listed, regardless of areas of interest, in this exhaustive volume published by the National Referral Center of the Library of Congress. Organized alphabetically by agency, the *Directory* describes the areas of interest of each organization, its holdings of documents, its publications, and the information services it provides. For each organization, the address and telephone number are provided.

Much of the information available from the resources listed in the *Directory* is technical in nature. It contains an extensive subject index and a description of government-sponsored Information Analysis Centers.

#3000-00067, revised edition 1974, $4.00; GPO (see C1.0).

9.202 Directories of Technical Information Resources Regarding Social, Physical, and Biological Sciences; Toxicology; and Water

Information resources in social sciences, biological sciences, physical sciences, engineering, toxicology, and regarding water are described in a series of directories published by the National

Referral Center of the Library of Congress.
GPO (see C1.0).

Social Sciences, Revised Edition, #3000-00065, 700 pp., $6.90
Biological Sciences, #3000-00060, 577 pp., $5.00
Physical Sciences, Engineering #3000-00040, 803 pp., $7.40
General Toxicology, 293 pp., $3.00
Water, 248 pp., $1.50

9.203 *Government Reports Announcements and Index*

New Government research is summarized weekly in the *Government Reports Announcements and Index* (GRA&I), which is composed from the NTIS Bibliographic Data File. The GRA&I contains about 60,000 new summaries annually, in more than 7,000 pages. It is indexed by subject, personal and corporate authors, government contract, and order numbers.

The GRA&I is designed for librarians and technical information specialists and for those used to working with technical information terms and sources.

$165.00 per year. The *Annual Index* is published as a six-volume hardbound set: $345.00 for years beginning 1973, less for years beginning 1968. NTIS (see C1.17).

9.204 *Directory of Federally Supported Information Analysis Centers*

More than 100 organizations which provide information analysis services in a variety of fields are listed in *Directory of Federally Supported Information Analysis Centers.*

#PB-233 582/PTC, $4.50; NTIS (see C1.17).

9.205 *Directory of Federal Technology Transfer*

An easy-to-use directory of federal technology transfer activities across a wide spectrum of federal government departments, agencies, and commissions, this report provides a tool for private industry to share more effectively the results of federal programs aimed at the development of knowledge and technologies. The report is a product of the Committee on Domestic Technology Transfer of the Federal Coordinating Council for Science, Engineering, and Technology.

Each section gives a description of an agency's program, including the agency's research base, its technology transfer policy and objectives, areas of responsibility, methods of implementation, accomplishments, and user organizations. Contact points through which a user can find the most pertinent elements of the agency are provided. There is an index to help users find activities or applications related to their areas of interest and also to determine whether activity areas are common to more than one federal agency.

$4.30; GPO (see C1.0).

9.206 *Federal Domestic Assistance Catalog*

The Federal Domestic Assistance Catalog is a comprehensive description of the hundreds of assistance programs of the federal government. It is maintained on magnetic tape by National Technical Information Service (NTIS), which can conduct on-line computer searches. It is also available in paper copy.

$16.00 paperbound; GPO (see C1.0). Also NTIS (see C1.17).

9.207 Federal Information Processing Standards Publications

Publications in this series collectively constitute the Federal Information Processing Standards Register. The purpose of the Register is to serve as the official source of information in the federal government regarding standards issued by National Bureau of Standards according to its legal mandate. The publications include approved federal information processing standards information of general interest, and a complete index of relevant standards publications.

GPO (see C1.0).

Guides to Specialized Information (9.250-9.257)

9.250 *Subject Guide to the NTIS Information Collection*

A search tool which may be used independently or with the NTIS Bibliographic Data File (on magnetic tape) (see 9.3), or with the *Government Reports Announcements and Index* (see 9.12), and with the *Annual Index*, is the *Subject Guide to the NTIS Information Collection.*

The *Subject Guide* is a composite of the subject-indexing vocabularies used to index research reports in the NTIS Bibliographic Data File. It is sometimes called the NTIS Master Frequency List of Subject Terms.

All unique subject index terms are listed alphanumerically with frequency postings for the various index files and for the master file. The frequency postings include the number of times each term is used as a controlled thesaurus descriptor or as a key word (descriptor, identifier, open-ended term).

Revisions of the *Subject Guide* will be published annually and merged with the master list every three to five years.

Available on paper in four volumes, and in microfiche and microfilm, all at the same price of $125.00; NTIS (see C1.17).

9.251 *NTIS Subject Classification*

Hundreds of subject groups are relevant to NTIS products and services. The *NTIS Subject Classification* contains the two subject classification systems used to classify the NTIS information collection.

69 pp., $5.00; NTIS (see C1.17).

9.252 *Energy: A Continuing Bibliography with Indexes*

Energy systems, research and development, energy conversion, transport, transmission, distribution and storage, with special emphasis on the use of hydrogen and of solar energy, are covered by the National Aeronautics and Space Administration quarterly, *Energy: A Continuing Bibliography with Indexes.*

$25.00 per year; NTIS (see C1.17).

9.253 NASA *Patent Abstracts Bibliography*

Patented inventions of the National Aeronautics and Space Administration are available for exclusive or nonexclusive licenses, under a NASA policy to promote fast commercial use of space technology. *Patent Abstracts Bibliography* documents all available NASA patents twice each year.

$9.00; NASA (see C1.107).

9.254 *Toxicology Research Projects Directory*

The *Toxicology Research Projects Directory* deals with manifestations of exposure of man and animals to toxic substances. It includes 2,500 projects, organized in seven broad chapters, to provide the reader with a general overview of toxicology. Projects are classified according to toxic agent, research orientation, and environmental concern.

$50.00 per year; NTIS (see C1.17).

9.255 Data Sources for Specific Businesses

Unless otherwise indicated, the following publications are available, as priced, from Consumer Goods and Services Division, Bureau of Domestic Commerce, Room 1104, Department of Commerce, Washington, DC 20230.

Business Machine Market Information Sources, 41 pp., 50¢; Publication Sales Branch, Room 1617, Department of Commerce, Washington, DC 20230

Data Communications Market Information Sources, 53 pp., 95¢

Food Industries Data Sources, 59 pp., free

Household Furniture and Appliances: Basic Information Sources, 22 pp., free

Retail Data Sources for Market Analysis, 18 pp., free

Wholesale Data Sources for Market Analysis, 12 pp., free

9.256 Satellite Image Catalogs

Images taken by satellites of the earth are identified in catalogs prepared by the NASA Image Processing Facility (IPF), located at the Goddard Space Flight Center. Each month, the *U.S. Standard Catalog* and the *Non-U.S. Standard Catalog* appear, and annually the IPF publishes a cumulative edition for each individual satellite.

United States coverage includes imagery of the continental United States, Alaska, and

Hawaii and adjacent areas.

United States coverage: $45.00 per year, with cumulative issue, $65.00; non-United States coverage: $60.00, with cumulative issue, $80.00; NTIS (see C1.17).

9.257 *Directory of U.S. Government Audio-Visual Personnel*

Federal agencies and their personnel involved in radio, television, motion pictures, still photography, sound recordings, and exhibits are listed in this reference publication. Telephone numbers and mailing addresses are included.

6th edition, 1977, $3.00; National Audio-Visual Center, General Services Administration, Washington, DC 20409.

Current Awareness in Technical Fields (9.300-9.318)

9.300 Selected Research in Microfiche

As government-sponsored reports are received at the National Technical Information Service (NTIS), they are immediately classified according to some 500 subject categories and 200,000 descriptive terms. Within two weeks thereafter, a subscriber to the Selected Research in Microfilm (SRIM) program receives the full text of each report in the subscriber's chosen category or categories. Reports are sent biweekly.

An order may include any combination of categories or subcategories, and may be limited to reports of specific agencies. Further information on the contents of the SRIM categories can be found in two publications available from NTIS: #NTIS-PR-270 and #NTIS-PR-271. Also, SRIM information specialists can assist in making the selection.

Microfiche can save money. Each microfiche contains up to 98 pages of text, and the price for each SRIM microfiche title is only 45¢, a saving of $1.80 over the regular NTIS price of $2.25, and far less than the cost of the same report in paper copy. A portable microfiche reader can be obtained for as little as $25.00. If a paper copy is needed, it can be ordered from NTIS or produced by microfiche reproduction equipment. (A free buyer's guide to microfiche equipment is available from a non-profit organization, the National Microfilm Association, 8728 Colesville Road, Silver Spring, MD 20910.)

The cost of SRIM varies according to the number of microfiche titles received. Here are two typical examples of costs of SRIM:

(1) *Energy/Energy Use, Supply and Demand*: 140 complete report texts were sent out over a 12-month period, costing the customer $63.00. The same order for paper copies would have cost more than $850.00.

(2) *Administration/Public Administration and Government*: 168 complete report texts were sent out over a 12-month period, costing the customer $75.00. The same order for paper copy would have cost more than $1,025.

The SRIM information specialists will estimate the cost and will help limit the scope of an order to the research actually desired.

If a research need is not satisfied by existing SRIM categories, it is possible, for an additional annual computer service charge of $100, to customize an SRM subscription by using SRIM Profile. An SRIM information specialist will help develop a selection strategy based upon index key words which are assigned to all NTIS reports.

An NTIS Deposit Account is necessary for SRIM service. It will conveniently handle payments for SRIM, as well as record tax deductions, assist in budgeting, and cut unnecessary red tape. A Deposit Account may be set up with a minimum deposit of $25.00 ($125.00 for SRIM Profile).

NTIS (see C1.17); 703-321-8883 or 8507.

9.301 *Weekly Government Abstracts*

Research summaries in 26 areas of government research, performed by hundreds of organizations, including United States government agencies, private researchers, universities, and special technology groups are available within two weeks of their receipt by National Technical Information Service in the series of newsletters known as *Weekly Government Abstracts*. The last issue of each year is a subject index containing up to ten cross references for each research summary indexed.

NTIS (see C1.17).

Titles, with prices, are as follows:

Administration, $40.00
Agriculture and Food, $40.00
Behavior and Society, $40.00
Biomedical Technology and Engineering, $40.00

Building Technology, $40.00
Business and Economics, $140.00
Chemistry, $40.00
Civil and Structural Engineering, $40.00
Communication, $45.00
Computers, Control and Information Theory, $40.00
Electrotechnology, $40.00
Energy, $40.00
Environmental Pollution and Control, $60.00
Government Inventions for Licensing, $165.00
Health Planning, $40.00
Industrial and Mechanical Engineering, $40.00
Library and Information Sciences, $30.00
Materials Sciences, $40.00
Medicine and Biology, $45.00
NASA Earth Resources Survey Program, $40.00
Natural Resources, $40.00
Ocean Technology and Engineering, $40.00
Physics, $45.00
Problem-Solving Technology for State and Local Governments, $60.00
Transportation, $40.00
Urban Technology, $40.00

9.302 Standing Orders for Energy-Related Reports

Energy SOS

Immediate shipment of every printed report published by NTIS in the field of energy is possible through *Energy SOS* (Standing Order Service). The reports are received weeks earlier than if ordered separately, and they are sold by NTIS at a 20 percent discount from the single-order price.

As many as 2,000 reports annually are shipped through *Energy SOS,* but for specific needs they can be limited to one or more of the following subjects:

Energy Sources
Energy Use, Supply, and Demand
Power and Heat Generation
Energy Conversion and Storage
Energy Transmission
Fuel Conversion Processes
Policies, Regulations, and Studies
Engines and Fuels

NTIS (see C1.17).

ERDA Reports

The unclassified technical reports of the Energy Research and Development Administration (ERDA), as well as their critical reviews, conference papers, and symposium results, are available on standing order from NTIS in paper copy and in microfiche. These reports are summarized in NTIS newsletters (see *Weekly Government Abstracts*) and journals (*Government Reports Announcements and Index*). Altogether, there are about 1,300 reports annually, but it is possible to limit the standing order to one or more categories.

The price is $3.50 per title, and an annual standing order requires a minimum of $100.00 in an NTIS Deposit Account (see A2.1). NTIS (see C1.17).

A partial list of categories follows:

General, Miscellaneous, and Progress Reports
Chemistry
Chemical Separations Processes for Plutonium and Uranium
Environmental and Earth Sciences
Heat Rejection and Utilization
Nonnuclear Energy Sources and Energy Conversion Devices
Safeguards—Nuclear Material Security
Nuclear Materials Management
Controlled Thermonuclear Processes
Isotope Separation
Radioisotope and Radiation Applications
Materials
Particle Accelerators and High-Voltage Machines
Mathematics and Computers
Nuclear Propulsion Systems and Aerospace Safety
Physics—General
Physics—Atomic and Molecular
Physics—Cosmic and Terrestrial
Physics—Nuclear
Physics—Particles and Fields
Peaceful Applications of Explosions
Instruments
Engineering and Equipment
Health and Safety
Chemical High Explosives
Criticality Studies
Technology—Feed Materials
Biology and Medicine
Nuclear Raw Materials
Waste Management
Transportation of Property and Nuclear Materials
Gas-Cooled Reactor Technology
Light-Water Reactor Technology
Liquid Metal Fast Breeder Reactors
General Reactor Technology

Commercial Nuclear Power Plants
Nuclear Power Sources for Biomedical Applications

9.303 *Government Reports Announcements and Index*

New government research is summarized biweekly in the *Government Reports Announcements and Index* (GRA&I), which is composed from the Bibliographic Data File (see 9.3). The GRA&I contains about 60,000 new summaries annually, in more than 7,000 pages. It is indexed by subject, personal and corporate authors, government contract, and order numbers.

The GRA&I is designed for librarians and technical information specialists and for those used to working with technical information terms and sources.

$165.00 per year. The *Annual Index* is published as a six-volume hardbound set; $345.00 for years beginning 1973, less for years beginning 1968; NTIS (see C1.17).

9.304 *Scientific and Technical Aerospace Reports*

Reports issued by the National Aeronautics and Space Administration (NASA), as well as by other government agencies, universities, industry, and research organizations both in the United States and abroad are announced, abstracted, and indexed in *Scientific and Technical Aerospace Reports* (STAR).

$66.90 per year; cumulative indexes $28.10 per year; GPO (see C1.0).

9.305 NASA Abstracts of Reports Announced in *STAR Journal*

Aeronautics and space research reports are announced in the NASA *STAR Journal*, distributed biweekly, and microfiche abstracts of the reports announced are available biweekly.

$45.00 per year; NTIS (see C1.17).

9.306 *NASA Tech Briefs*

NASA research results in many innovations with potential for commercial application, and the monthly *NASA Tech Briefs* are one or two-page reports on new products and devices, manufacturing processes and techniques, and materials. *Briefs* are issued in nine categories: electronic components and circuits, electronic systems, physical sciences, materials, life sciences, mechanics, machinery, fabrication technology, and mathematics and information sciences.

$40.00 for all nine categories, $25.00 single category, annual indexes under $10.00; NTIS (see C1.17).

Briefs are also collected and published quarterly by NASA, free to any United States citizen or organization. Director, Technology Utilization Office, P.O. Box 8757, Baltimore/Washington International Airport, MD 21240.

9.307 *Journal of Research*

Research on physics, mathematics, and chemistry, conducted by the National Bureau of Standards (NBS) is reported in the *Journal of Research*. It is published in two sections, *Physics and Chemistry* and *Mathematical Sciences.*

Physics and Chemistry: bimonthly, $17.00 per year; *Mathematical Sciences*, quarterly, $9.00 per year; GPO (see C1.0).

9.308 *DIMENSIONS/NBS*

Persons in business, industry, science, engineering, and education, and the general public, can learn of the latest advances in science and technology, with primary emphasis on the work at the National Bureau of Standards (NBS), through a subscription to the monthly *DIMENSIONS/NBS* magazine (formerly *Technical News Bulletin*).

$9.45 per year; GPO (see C1.0).

9.309 Technical Publications of the National Bureau of Standards

Technical information on a variety of subjects is published from time to time by the National Bureau of Standards (NBS). Engineering, industrial practice (including safety codes), mathematics, physics, chemistry, biology, computer programming, building materials, manufactured products, and information processing are among the subjects covered.

In addition to monographs, handbooks, and various special publications, NBS has a separate series of publications devoted to each of the following subjects: Applied Mathematics, National Standard Reference Data, Building Science, and Consumer Information. NBS also publishes specialized *Technical Notes*, and develops nationally recognized requirements for products, published as *Voluntary Product Standards*.

NBS issues standards for the Federal Information Processing Standards Register, and issues reports on its work for outside sponsors in its *NBS Interagency Reports*.

NBS, Washington, DC 20234.

9.310 Publications of the National Standards Reference Data System

The National Standard Reference Data System (NSRDS), under the National Bureau of Standards (NBS), is a means of coordinating on a national scale the production and dissemination of critically evaluated reference data in the physical sciences. The NBS Office of Standard Reference Data coordinates a complex of data evaluation centers located in university, industrial, and other government laboratories as well as within the NBS data on physical and chemical properties and retrieved from the world scientific literature.

NSRDS date compilations, critical reviews, and related publications are described in the *NSRDS Publication List*, published from time to time.

The table of contents of the October 1976 edition of the *NSRDS Publication List* included the following:

Journal of Physical and Chemical Reference Data
NSRDS-NBS Series
Other NSRDS Data Publications
Other NBS Compilations of Data
Compilations of the Berkeley Particle Data Group
Nondata Publications from NSRDS Related Projects
Indexes to Radiation Chemistry Literature
Computer Programs for Handling Technical Data
Translations from the Russian

Office of Standard Reference Data, NBS, Washington, DC 20234.

9.311 *Fireview*

Fireview is a newsletter published from time to time for those who are concerned about fire science, fire control, and new developments in fire safety engineering. It is relevant to concerned businessmen in that it deals with facilities, products, and preventative tools and materials.

Center for Fire Research, Building 225, Room B142, NBS, Washington, DC 20234; 301-921-3143.

9.312 *MOSAIC*

Significant work in research, education, and policy studies in the sciences is discussed in *MOSAIC*, a nontechnical bimonthly magazine published by the National Science Foundation.

$8.55 per year; GPO (see C1.0).

9.313 *Journal of Physical and Chemical Reference Data*

Quantitative data for engineering, physics, and chemistry, including recommended values, uncertainty limits, critical commentary on methods of measurement, and full references to the original literature, are available in the quarterly *Journal of Physical and Chemical Reference Data*. The major publication medium of the National Standard Reference Data System of the National Bureau of Standards, the *Journal* is published by the American Institute of Physics (AIP) and the American Chemical Society (ACS).

$75.00 per year, $25.00 for members of AIP, ACS, or an affiliated society; American Chemical Society, 1155 Sixteenth Street N.W., Washington, DC 20036; 202-872-4364.

9.314 NBS Bibliographic Subscription Periodicals

The National Bureau of Standards (NBS) issues current-awareness and literature-survey bibliographies in the following technical areas:

Cryogenics, biweekly, $20,00 per year; NTIS (see C1.17)
Liquified Natural Gas, quarterly, $20.00 per year; NTIS (see C1.17)
Superconducting Devices and Materials, quar-

terly, $20.00 per year; NTIS (see C1.17) *Electromagnetic metrology*, monthly, $100.00 per year; Electromagnetics Division, National Bureau of Standards, Boulder, CO 80302.

9.315 *Selected Water Resources Abstracts Journal and Index*

Water-related aspects of the life, physical, and social sciences, and conservation, control, use, management, engineering, and legal aspects of water are covered semimonthly in *Selected Water Resources Abstracts Journal and Index*, compiled by the Department of the Interior.

This periodical includes abstracts of current reports and articles on water pollution, waste treatment, water law, water yield, watershed protection, water demand, ground water, lakes and estuaries, hydraulics, and soil mechanics. Each issue is indexed by subject, personal and corporate author, and order number.

$75.00 per year, $100.00 with annual index; NTIS (see C1.17).

9.316 *Tech Progress Reports*

Naval research reports and inventions are covered in the United States Naval Research Laboratory *Tech Progress Reports*. Coverage includes chemistry, electricity, metallurgy, physics, ocean sciences and engineering, radar, and related fields.

Monthly, $40.00 per year; NTIS (see C1.17).

9.317 *Data User News*

This is the basic subscription service of the Bureau of the Census. It provides information on applications of census data and on new computer programs, news on user-oriented programs and products, announcements of workshops and seminars, and a reader's exchange. Eight or more pages each month bring news of activities, products, and publications in the field of small-area census data. A special section highlights the applications readers around the country have found for census data. Articles by Bureau specialists explain technical points, methodology, and processing techniques of the Bureau of the Census.

Monthly, 8-12 pp., $4.00 per year; Subscriber Services Section, Bureau of the Census, Department of Commerce, Washington, DC 20233.

9.318 *Fishery Bulletin*

Original research papers, and occasionally reviews of topical interest in the broad discipline of fishery science, are published in this bulletin. Among the research fields included are ecology, oceanography, and limnology; mariculture; ocean pollution; physiology, behavior, and taxonomy of marine organisms, particularly fishes; technology; gear development; and economics.

Quarterly, $11.80 per year; GPO (see C1.0).

Statistical Guides, Statistics, and Computers (9.400-9.507)

Guides to Statistical Sources and Statistics (9.400-9.410)

9.400 *Directory of Federal Statistics for Local Areas*

Information available on standard metropolitan statistical areas, counties, and cities is described in this directory. Other types of areas are also indicated, with reference to those publication programs that cover them.

$1.00; GPO (see C1.0).

9.401 *Directory of Non-Federal Statistics for States and Local Areas: A Guide to Sources*

Information available for individual states, the District of Columbia, Puerto Rico, Guam, and the Virgin Islands for specified substate areas for 13 major subjects is described in this directory. Detailed bibliographic entries list the publications containing the statistics and the issuing agency.

$6.25; GPO (see C1.0).

9.402 *1970 Census User's Guide*

Most of the information that data users will need for effective access and use of 1970 census data products is furnished in this two-part publication. Part I covers the decennial census program and related services. Part II is concerned exclusively with computer tape products.

Part I, $2.35; Part II, $4.40; GPO (see C1.0).

9.403 *Bureau of the Census Guide to Programs and Publications: Subjects and Areas*

A comprehensive review of the statistical programs of the Bureau of the Census and of the reports issued by the Bureau in the 1960's and the early 1970's appears in this guide. It shows the geographic areas and principal subjects for most of the publications. For reports issued periodically, the areas covered in the latest issues are shown. Almost all statistical and geographic reports, including maps, published between 1968 and 1972 are covered.

$2.40; GPO (see C1.0).

9.404 *Bureau of the Census Catalog*

Publications, computer tapes and punchcards, and related nonstatistical materials and services of the Bureau of the Census made avaliable from January of each year are described in this catalog. Part I, *Publications*, is a classified, annotated bibliography of all publications issued by the Bureau during the period covered. Geographical and subject indexes are provided. Part II, *Data Files and Special Publications*, provides a listing of those materials which became available at the Bureau during the catalog period. Included are basic data files (on computer tape or punchcards), special tabulations (tapes, cards, and printed data) prepared for sponsors, and nonstatistical materials such as maps and computer programs.

A monthly supplement to the catalog lists major special publications, reports issued in a series at irregular intervals, and regular publications issued less frequently than quarterly.

Four quarterly issues and 12 monthly supplements, $14.00 per year; quarterly prices vary but generally stay between $2.00 and $4.00; GPO (see C1.0).

9.405 *Index to 1970 Census Summary Tapes*

This index with cross reference guide covers all tabulations in all six counts of the 1970 census summary data, organized alphabetically by subject available. Counts 1-5 are indexed in Section A. Count 6 is indexed in Section B.

$2.60; GPO (see C1.0).

9.406 *Dictionary of Economic and Statistical Terms*

This publication includes definitions of the terms used in government reporting in such areas as gross national product, national income and product accounts, balance of payments accounts, and economic and statistical indicators, as well as demographic and social terms, plus tables for clarification of terms used.

$2.00; GPO (see C1.0).

9.407 *Review of Public Data Use*

Public data, statistics, data bases—how to gain access to them and how to interpret and benefit from them—are the subjects of the bimonthly *Review of Public Data Use*. The *Review* includes two formerly separate newsletters: *Access News* and *1970 Census Technical Bulletins*.

$60.00 per year, $15.00 single issue; NTIS (see C1.17).

9.408 Publications of the Bureau of Labor Statistics

Publications of the Bureau of Labor Statistics, January-June 1975

Although as of this writing, this bibliography has not been updated, it is an annotated guide to many publications of the Bureau of Labor Statistics (BLS) and gives the reader a general view of the range and capability of the BLS.

Free; BLS (see C1.70).

Major Programs 1976, Bureau of Labor Statistics

All the major surveys, publications, and subscription services of the BLS are listed in this publication. At the end of each survey description, BLS suggests the major uses of the data. Each survey entry includes descriptions under the following headings: data available, coverage, source of data, reference period, publications, and uses (such as economic indicator, marketing, regional analysis, government funding analysis, and plant location).

Major categories of data described include current employment analysis, employment structure and trends, wages and trends, wages and industrial relations, productivity and technology, occupational safety and health statistics, economic growth, and subscription services.

Most of the BLS data are derived from surveys or developed in cooperation with other state and federal agencies and may be in written form, on computer tape, or on microfiche.

Free; BLS (see C1.70).

9.409 Bureau of Labor Statistics *Handbook of Methods*

Measures of an employment cost index, international prices, and unemployment in states and local areas are explained in this handbook from the Bureau of Labor Statistics (BLS). In addition to these new series, many of the chapters in the older series have been updated to reflect the continuing improvements in the Bureau's methods and techniques. Each chapter provides a brief account of how the program came into being, plus what it attempts to do, where the basic data came from, definition of terms used, and outline of the concepts adopted.

Bulletin 910, $3.50; GPO (see C1.0).

9.410 *Statistical Services of the United States Government*

The statistical system of the federal government is explained in this book. It describes the principal statistical data and the principal available data and states the statistical responsibilities of each agency. It also incudes a list of major statistical publications.

234 pp., $3.40; GPO (see C1.0).

Statistical Sources (9.450-9.461)

9.450 *Statistical Abstract of the United States*

The *Statistical Abstract of the United States* constitutes a one-volume basic reference source. Issued annually since 1878, it is the standard summary of statistics on the social, political, and economic organization of the United States. It presents a comprehensive selection of statistics from the publications and records of governmental and private agencies.

This edition contains more than 1,400 tables and charts and an extensive guide to sources of additional data, as well as a two-page presentation of metric weights and measures. Although emphasis is given primarily to national data, many tables present data for regions and a smaller number for cities. Sections 33 and 34 present comprehensive data for states and for 157 standard metropolitan statistical areas having 200,000 or more inhabitants in 1970. Additional information for cities, counties, metropolitan areas, Congressional districts, and other small units, as well as more historical data, are available in various supplements to the abstract.

There are 78 entirely new tables in this edition, covering health-related problems, crime, environmental concerns, federal government benefits and taxes, earnings, income shares of poorest and wealthiest, cost of living, big business, oil and gas, etc.

1976 ed., $8.00; GPO (see C1.0).

9.451 *In-put-Output Structure of the United States Economy: 1967*

This study and its supporting statistics, published by the Bureau of Economic Analysis, depicts the interrelationships in the economy of 85 broad industrial categories. By using these tables, a manufacturer can estimate the direct market potential in the industry to which he is selling, as well as the indirect demands of the industries it serves. The input-output study furnishes the market analyst with factual information about interindustry sales and purchases and is considered one of the more effective tools for measuring markets.

Vol. 1, *Transactions Data for Detailed Industries*, $3.85; Vol. 2, *Direct Requirements for Detailed Industries*, $3.75; Vol. 3, *Total Requirements for Detailed Industries*, $3.85; all from GPO (see C1.0).

9.452 *County Business Patterns*

Social Security tax records and census data

are source materials for this publication. It contains a series of separate reports for each state, and a United States summary with data on employment, number and employment size of reporting units, and taxable payrolls for various segments of the economy. It is especially useful for analyzing market potentials, establishing sales territories and sales quotas, and locating facilities.

$5.45; GPO (see C1.0).

9.453 *County and City Data Book*

Demographic, social, and economic data for counties, cities, standard metropolitan statistical areas, and urbanized areas are presented from the most recent censuses as well as from other governmental and private sources. The topics include: agriculture, bank deposits, births, marriages, climate, home equipment, hospitals, family income, migration, population characteristics, presidential vote, local government finances, retail trade, school enrollment, selected services, and manufacturing, among others. The book also includes maps for each state showing counties, standard metropolitan statistical areas, and large cities; explanatory notes and source citations; and appendixes that expand or explain the coverage of the tables. A unique feature of this book is the availability of its contents on compendia tape and punchcards.

$18.65; GPO (see C1.0).

9.454 *Handbook of Labor Statistics*

Historical tables of all major series published by the Bureau of Labor Statistics, and related series from other government agencies and foreign countries, are available in this reference guide.

Bulletin 1865, $5.35; GPO (see C1.0).

9.455 Access to Unpublished Labor Statistics Data

The Bureau of Labor Statistics (BLS) generates some data as by-products or intermediate stages of certain programs. Often there is not great enough public demand or use for these data to justify publication. However, the Bureau will release any such summary files to interested parties at cost of duplication when the data meet the confidentiality requirement of all government data.

All unpublished data furnished by the Bureau will be accompanied, so far as possible, by descriptions of the data, appropriate statements of the limitations of the data, and other needed technical documentation.

BLS (see C1.70).

9.456 *BLS Data Bank Files and Statistical Routines*

The Bureau of Labor Statistics (BLS) will duplicate for interested users any of its data base tapes that meet confidentiality requirements. *BLS Data Bank Files and Statistical Routines* (1971) contains detailed information on available data files.

Free; BLS (see C1.70).

9.457 Labor Statistics on Microfiche and Computer Tapes

A growing amount of data is available in microfiche form which can be reproduced at no cost or at nominal cost, depending on the size of the request.

Some data, including unpublished data, are available on computer tape. The amount, kind, and prices of the data change constantly.

BLS (see C1.70).

9.458 Labor Statistics Data Base

Labor force information is available for metropolitan areas, cities, counties, states, census tracts, and other regions, with breakouts such as industry, salary levels, age, education levels, and distance to work.

The data base was assembled by the Lawrence Berkeley Laboratories, under contract to the Department of Labor, from the Labor Census of 1970 and 1973.

Contact a NTIS information specialist for help in obtaining a suitable report; see C1.17; 703-321-8525.

9.459 County-Level Socioeconomic Data Base

Market forecasters, local governments, business planners, and demographers can use the

NTIS county-level socioeconomic statistical data base to produce specialized reports. The data base, compiled by the Economic Development Administration, merges the first and fourth counts of the 1970 Census of Population and Housing with summary data from the 1960 census, *County and City Data Book*, *County Business Patterns*, and income data files.

A NTIS information specialist can help in formulation of a search request and in estimating search costs and time (see C1.17); 703-321-8525.

9.460 Internal Revenue Service Taxpayer Data

The number of tax returns, exemptions, adjusted gross income, and total tax dollars for each of 39,000 ZIP Code areas throughout the country may be obtained from an Internal Revenue Service summary on magnetic tape or on paper. The information does not reveal data for any individual and applies to a tax year about five years before the current year. The data are accompanied by detailed definitions of the items, a description of the system, and an explanation of the sources and limitations of the data.

Tape: #PB-209 352/PTC, $157.50; paper: $3.00 for each state, except California, New York, Pennsylvania, and Texas, which are $6.00 each; both paper and tape from NTIS (see C1.17).

9.461 Agricultural Commodity Data

A great deal of current information about American agriculture is available from the Crop Reporting Board of the Statistical Reporting Service of the Department of Agriculture. The Board estimates production, stocks, inventories, disposition, utilization, and prices of agricultural commodities. Estimates also cover other items concerning agriculture, such as fertilizer, labor, and population.

A limited amount of current agricultural data is available on magnetic tape. The Statistical Reporting Service maintains a file of publications from recent years, with some of these data also on magnetic tape.

The commodity and other estimates, with their respective dates of issuance, are listed in the *Crop Reporting Board Catalog*.

Free; Crop Reporting Board, Statistical Reporting Service, Room 0005, Department of Agriculture, Washington, DC 20250.

Other publications of interest are:

Weekly Weather and Crop Bulletin. This summarizes the weather and its effect on crops the previous week, for 43 states and the New England area.

Agricultural Climatology Service Office, Room 1137, Department of Agriculture, Washington, DC 20250.

Agricultural Situation. Current trends in agriculture, reviews of economic, marketing, and research developments affecting farmers, and a tabular summary of key agricultural statistics are given in this periodical.

11 issues annually; Statistical Reporting Service Information Staff, Room 5855, Department of Agriculture, Washington, DC 20250.

Agricultural Statistics. A comprehensive statistical report, this publication contains current and historical agricultural data.

Revised annually, c. 600 pp.; GPO (see C1.0).

Index of Estimates. This publication identifies the Crop Reporting Board publications which carry estimates of commodities and related items.

Crop Reporting Board, Statistical Reporting Service, Room 0005, Department of Agriculture, Washington, DC 20250.

Computers and Software (9.500-9.507)

9.500 Computer Software Management and Information Center

Many computer programs developed at taxpayer expense can be incorporated into existing commercial or industrial operations with minor or no modification. These programs can save an organization the high cost of development time. In scientific and engineering disciplines, such computer software is available from the Computer Software Management and Information Center (COSMIC) of the National Aeronautics and Space Administration (NASA).

Hundreds of programs are included in the COSMIC inventory. Each has been subjected to thorough evaluation of documentation, checking of completeness and compiler syntax correctness, and correction of any errors found. Information about new COSMIC software appears regularly in *NASA Tech Briefs* (see 9.306) and in NASA's quarterly *Computer Programs Abstracts* ($1.00 per year; GPO (see C1.0)).

COSMIC will search for useful programs if a customer can define his needs. If customer requirements are less definite, COSMIC can send descriptions of programs in the customer's area of interest. COSMIC also will help the customer to implement his programs. Sometimes a program's documentation alone can aid a customer in design and development of his own software.

COSMIC's services are available from:

COSMIC
Suite 112, Barrow Hall
University of Georgia
Athens, GA 30601
404-542-3265

NASA Industrial Applications Center
University of Connecticut
Storrs, CT 06268
203-486-4533
429-6421

NASA Industrial Applications Center
P.O. Box 12235
Research Triangle Park, NC 27709
919-549-8291

NASA Industrial Applications Center
University of Pittsburgh
Pittsburgh, PA 15260
412-624-5211
621-6877

NASA Industrial Applications Center
Indiana University
Bloomington, IN 47401
812-337-8884
337-7970

NASA Industrial Applications Center
University of New Mexico
Albuquerque, NM 87131
505-277-3622
277-3118

NASA Industrial Applications Center
University of Southern California
Los Angeles, CA 90007
213-746-6132
746-6133

9.501 *Directory of Computerized Data Files, Software and Related Technical Reports*

The National Technical Information Service (NTIS) *Directory of Computerized Data Files, Software and Related Technical Reports* is a unique guide to machine-readable data files, software, and related technical reports available to the public from more than 100 federal agencies. The information for the directory was gathered in cooperation with the Machine-Readable Data Branch of the National Archives and Records Service.

More than 800 data files and/or related software are listed and described in the directory. Additionally, more than 400 closely related technical reports are listed. The directory is a bibliographic reference offering direct mail-order service for items available from NTIS. Others may be ordered directly from the originating agencies.

#NTIS-SR-7502/PTC, 50¢; NTIS (see C1.17).

9.502 Statistical Software

The Bureau of Labor Statistics (BLS) has developed several statistical programs that are for sale to users who have machine-processing capabilities. Programs available include multiple regression programs, seasonal adjustment programs, and table-producing language. Summary descriptions are provided in *Major Programs 1976, Bureau of Labor Statistics* (see 9.408). All of these systems and programs operate in an IBM OS/360 environment at BLS.

BLS (see C1.70).

9.503 Software for Local Government Problem-Solving

Problem-solving computer software for local governments is available from National Technical Information Service (NTIS). Among the programs are Municipal Information Systems, Forecasting Municipal Water Requirements, Urban Simulation, and Health Care Delivery Concepts.

#NTIS-PR-257; NTIS (see C1.17).

9.504 Access to Urban Government Computer Software

Computer programs and magnetic tapes

generated by metropolitan areas participating in projects sponsored by the Urban Information Systems Interagency Committee (USAC) are available from National Technical Information Service (NTIS). These programs are developed by individual local governments.

USAC Product Manager, NTIS (see C1.17).

9.505 *Federal Information Processing Standards*

Federal Information Processing Standards (FIPS) are standards of data elements and codes in code systems as developed by the National Bureau of Standards. They are described in a series of publications which also announce the adoption of standards and give policy administration and general guidance. Eight to ten standards are issued at irregular intervals during a year and are sold only on an annual (standing order) basis on microfiche.

$50.00 per year, back issues $100.00 a set; NTIS (see C1.17).

9.506 *ADP Security Manual*

Directives in the field of automatic data processing security are listed in this manual from the Department of Defense. It covers such areas as personnel and communication security, equipment security, and security testing. Many of the procedures can be applied to the security needs of private industry.

#008-000-00186-3, 52 pp., $1.05; GPO (see C1.0).

9.507 *A Review of Network Access Techniques with a Case Study: The Network Access Machine*

A minicomputer system that acts as a network access point for overall computer operation is described in detail in this booklet.

#003-003-01640-3, 30 pp., 85¢; GPO (see C1.0).

Technical Information and Services (9.550-9.570)

9.550 Abstracts of Foreign Language Political, Economic, and Technical Reports

Scientists, engineers, technicians, researchers, and businessmen can gain access to current foreign thought in many political, economic, and technical areas through the reports of the Joint Publications Research Service (JPRS). Reports in 44 specific areas are available.

An index to JPRS translations entitled the *Bell and Howell TRANSDEX Index* is available from the MicroPhoto Division of Bell and Howell, Old Mansfield Road, Wooster, OH 44691.

NTIS (see C1.17); 703-321-8543. Call JPRS at 703-841-1050 for information on specific translation problems.

9.551 Daily Foreign Press and Radio Translations

Hundreds of radio news transmissions, newspaper editorials, and articles and magazine features are monitored daily by the expert United States analysts of the Foreign Broadcast Information Service. The best of these translations are grouped in eight geographical areas.

Subscription to one geographic area, translations mailed daily, $125.00; discount price for additional areas. Also available on microfiche, mailed weekly, at a discount. NTIS (see C1.17).

9.552 *Trends in Communist China*

Chinese, Soviet, and other Communist media discussions of key issues are available weekly in an analytical report, *Trends in Communist Media*. Prepared by the Foreign Broadcast Information Service, *Trends* describes communist media in the perspective of past conduct and behavior and identifies new elements or departures from a standard line. Material is six months old, as it is published only after being declassified.

$60.00 per year, also available in microfiche; NTIS (see C1.17).

9.553 *Translations of People's Republic of China Press*

Daily news on China, regarding local industry, agriculture, mining, sports, Communist Party ideology, political activity, foreign affairs, and the Chinese view of international events, is available through *Translations of People's Republic of China Press*. It includes three major series: (1) a daily survey of newspapers, covering five days of press activity, issued weekly, about 300 pages; (2) magazine selections from nontechnical publications, issued monthly, about 300 pages; and (3) background briefs compiled from varied sources, zeroing in on specific topical subjects in each edition.

Issued irregularly, $275.00 per year, including quarterly subject index; NTIS (see C1.17).

9.554 *Daily Report: People's Republic of China*

The *Daily Report: People's Republic of China*, issued by the Foreign Broadcast Information Service, is one of the most improtant information sources on China. The information, from the New China News Agency, Peking Radio, *People's Daily* (Jen-min Jih-pao), and *Red Flag* (Hung Chi), enables researchers to analyze Chinese current events, identify personalities and trends, and learn first-hand of crop damage and petroleum production, among much other information.

An *Index* to the *Daily Report* is issued quarterly and includes a subject index and a name index of important people, institutions, and organizations.

Daily Report: $125.00 per year, or $100.00 in microfiche; *Index*: $165.00 per year. When ordered with the *Index*, an annual microfiche subscription (issued weekly) to the *Daily Report* costs $32.00. NTIS (see C1.17).

9.555 Special Foreign Currency Science Information Program

Half of the world's scientific literature is published in non-English languages. The National Science Foundation administers the Special Foreign Currency Science Information Program, which produces more than 50,000 pages a year of foreign research and development results.

Newly completed translations are announced in *Weekly Government Abstracts* (see 9.301) and in *Government Reports Announcements and Index* (see 9.303). A list of translations in progress is available upon request from National Technical Information Service.

NTIS (see C1.17).

9.556 IRS-Docketed Civil Tax Cases

Every pending civil tax case docketed in the Tax Court, the United States District Courts, the Court of Claims, or in appellate courts, is listed on a microfilm available monthly from National Technical Information Service (NTIS). The listings include taxpayer's name, the court, the assigned Chief Counsel, field office or division, and the filing date of the petition or complaint. Cases are added each month as docketed and removed when closed. Multiple issue cases are listed under each issue.

A subscription includes the Uniform Issue List and an index used for broad identification of issues, which has eight-digit numbers and brief titles keyed to Internal Revenue Code sections.

$78.00 per year; NTIS (see C1.17).

9.557 Library of Congress Photoduplication Service

Materials from the collection of the Library of Congress may be reproduced in the form of electrostatic prints, positive photostats, or microfilm, for libraries or members of the public. Copies of manuscripts, prints, photographs, maps, and book material are made available upon request. Anyone may request photocopies, but copyrighted or otherwise restricted materials may not be reproduced without special permission. Fees vary according to the nature of the request (e.g., microfilm versus photostatic prints or limited versus detailed search) and number of pages reproduced.

Photoduplication Service, Library of Congress, Washington, DC 20540; 202-426-5654.

9.558 Aircraft Accident Reports

Reports are available on major aircraft accidents, giving facts, circumstances, the probable causes, air carrier, and date and place of accident, as compiled by the Department of Transportation.

All United States civil aviation accidents are similarly reported, but in brief format.

Both $35.00 per year; NTIS (see C1.17).

9.559 National Commission on New Technological Uses of Copyrighted Works

Rapid technological change in the fields of photocopying, computer software, and computer data bases has led to great uncertainty as to how to afford protection to works of authorship. The National Commission on New Technological Uses of Copyrighted Works began work in 1975 to explore the issues and make recommendations to Congress.

National Commission on New Technological Uses of Copyrighted Works, Washington, DC 20558; 202-557-0996.

9.560 *Parkinson's Disease and Related Disorders: Citations from the Literature*

Parkinson's disease and related matters are covered by the citations compiled monthly by the National Library of Medicine and published in *Parkinson's Disease and Related Disorders: Citations from the Literature.*

$25.00 per year; NTIS (see C1.17).

9.561 *Aerospace Medicine and Biology*

Aerospace research, emphasizing biological, physiological, and environmental effects on man during and after space flights, is reported monthly in *Aerospace Medicine and Biology*, compiled by National Aeronautics and Space Administration, the American Institute of Aeronautics and Astronautics, and the Library of Congress.

$18.75 per year; NTIS (see C1.17).

9.562 *Building Technology Project Summaries*

Research projects undertaken in 1975 by the Center for Building Technology are summariezed in this book. Research was undertaken in such areas as energy conservation, mobile homes, and building materials.

#003-003-01641-1, 102 pp., $2.05; GPO (see C1.0).

9.563 *Some References on Metric Information*

Included in this pamphlet is a list of publications on metric information produced by the National Bureau of Standards (NBS), another assembled by the National Council of Teachers of Mathematics, and a list of additional sources.

Free; Office of Information Acitivies, NBS, Washington, DC 20234.

9.564 Laboratory Testing Program of NIOSH

Laboratories across the country can maintain the quality of their chemical analysis techniques by participation in the Proficiency Analytical Testing (PAT) program of the National Institute for Occupational Safety and Health (NIOSH). Operated by NIOSH's Chemical Reference Laboratory (CRL) in Cincinnati, Ohio, the PAT program submits identical reference samples to over one hundred laboratories. Each laboratory conducts its analysis of the sample, and is later informed of the actual content of the sample and the standard deviation of the results of the analyses by the other laboratories. The CRL also works with the National Bureau of Standards in the development of Standard Reference Materials.

Chemical Reference Laboratory, NIOSH, 4676 Columbia Parkway, Cincinnati, OH 45226.

9.565 Railroad Design Data Base

Manufacturers of parts for railroad trucks and passenger cars may benefit from access to the Department of Transportation's data bank dealing with the most effective design parameters for railroad trucks and cars. The series of tests is contained on over 200 reels of magnetic tape, and these are available separately.

For price and ordering information, contact the Computer Products Manager, NTIS (see C1.17).

9.566 Publications on Mining Research

Research 75

An annual summary of significant results in mining, metallurgy, and mineral economics from the Bureau of Mines, this publication lists hundreds of projects and studies. Interested readers are invited to contact the researchers whose names appear with the articles. A directory is included at the end, as well as a listing of representative publications authored by personnel of the Bureau of Mines over the past three years.

$2.35; GPO (see C1.0).

Mining Research Review

Bureau of Mines research programs for 1975 in areas including technology improvement for mineral extraction, productivity, health and safety, and environmental protection are reviewed in this book. Most of the projects described were accomplished by contracting.

Free; Office of Mineral Information, Bureau of Mines, Department of the Interior, Washington, DC 20241; 202-634-1004.

9.567 *Engineering Design Handbooks*

Design engineers and others engaged in the design, development, and upgrading of Army equipment, materiel, components, and techniques may need the *Engineering Design Handbooks* published by the United States Army Materiel Command. They contain fundamental information and basic data, are paperbound, and vary in size from 200 to 600 pages. They may be ordered individually, as priced and abstracted in *Government Reports Announcements and Index* (see 9.303). They also may be ordered automatically as they become available.

Product Manager, NTIS (see C1.17); 703-557-4734.

9.568 NIOSH Toxicity Data Base and Related Publications

Over 16,500 chemical substances and their toxic effects are listed by the National Institute for Occupational Safety and Health (NIOSH) in the *Registry of Toxic Effects of Chemical Substances.* The reference information contained in the *Registry* is stored in a computer memory and can be searched for special purposes. The result of one such search, entitled *Suspected Carcinogens —1975*, gives the full *Registry* entries for 1,545 tumorigens.

Office of Technical Publications, NIOSH, Room 3-10, 5600 Fishers Lane, Rockville, MD 20852.

9.569 MEDLINE and TOXLINE

Health professionals may find out quickly and easily what has been published recently in any specific biomedical or toxicological subject area, using the on-line computerized data bases MEDLINE and TOXLINE, to which access is available through National Technical Information Service (NTIS). These two services are maintained by the National Library of Medicine.

MEDLINE, updated monthly, contains the current year's citations plus two previous years, for a total of about half a million references to 3,000 medical journals. There are ancillary files covering the biomedical literature beginning in 1969.

TOXLINE contains more than 375,000 references to published human and animal toxicity studies, effects of environmental chemicals and pollutants, adverse drug reactions and analytical methodology, dating from 1965 to the current year.

MEDLINE: #NTIS-PR-107; TOXLINE: #NTIS-PR-256; NTIS (see C1.17).

9.570 *Standard Industrial Classification Manual*

Business establishments have been classified by type of activity. The classification covers the entire field of economic activities: agriculture, forestry, construction, manufacturing, transportation, retail trade, real estate, wholesale trade, and government. It is set forth in the *Standard Industrial Classification Manual*, which is arranged alphabetically by principal product, processes, and services, and lists four-digit codes for each classification.

$6.75; GPO (see C1.0).

Chapter 10

MINORITIES AND THE DISADVANTAGED

CHAPTER ABSTRACT

There are a number of programs and opportunities within the federal government which are specifically oriented toward or particularly helpful to minorities and the disadvantaged. These programs are annotated in this chapter. In addition to these special programs, the items annotated in the other chapters of this *Guide* are also available to minority-owned business.

The list of publications in the first section (10.0-10.10) includes information on setting up a business, business opportunities, and business problems.

Vital sources of management assistance (10.50-10.102) are listed in the second section, along with information on programs set up to help small businesses benefit from various technological innovations.

"Marketing Assistance" (10.150-10.159) includes programs to help minority businesses locate and develop marketing opportunities.

In the final section, "Financial Assistance" (10.200-10.215), various loan programs are described. Also included in this section is the definition of a small business for Small Business Administration loan purposes.

Publications on Minority Business Concerns (10.0-10.10)

10.0 *Business Packaging*

While designed and composed primarily for minority business development, this manual is of general interest as well. It discusses business development as an ongoing process of planning, financing, marketing, and resource utilization. It begins with a discussion of the characteristics generally required of an entrepreneur, and how to evaluate a business idea. It then discusses developing the business package, which includes market research, sales planning, a technical and operational plan, and financial planning. It points out both private and public-sector resources available to the entrepreneur, with a complete discussion of the Small Business Administration. Finally, it presents two case studies in detail. Each section includes not only narrative, but also sample forms and charts that can be used both to organize and to evaluate efforts at each stage.

Office of Community Development, Department of Housing and Urban Development, Washington, DC 20410; see also regional offices of HUD (C1.40).

10.1 Publications of the Office of Minority Business Enterprise

The Office of Minority Business Enterprise (OMBE) produces the following publications, available from the field offices of OMBE (see C1.12):

The Business Resource Center
The Minority Business and Trade Associations
National Minority Purchasing Council
OMBE Funded Organizations
Report of the Task Force on Education and Training for Minority Business Enterprise
Banking for the Non-Banker
Organizing a Bank
Vendor Facts 1975
Progress Report 1976
Franchise Opportunity Handbook
Directory of Minority Media
National Directory of Minority Manufacturers
Urban Business Profiles
Small Business Reporter Publications Index
Businessman's Information Guide
Federal Procurement and Contracting Training Manual for Minority Entrepreneurs
Business Packaging
Minority Markets
Minority Suppliers Guide 1975
Women-Owned Businesses 1972 (MB-72)
Developing Marketing Plans as Part of the Loan Packaging Process
MB-72-1: Black
MB-72-2: Spanish Origin
MB-72-3: Asian Americans, American Indians, and Others
MB-72-4: Minority-Owned Businesses
Minority Business Enterprise—A Bibliography
Accounting System Survey and Audit Guide
Try Us 1976

10.2 *Access*

Information on the latest minority contract awards, programs and companies supporting minority business concerns, the growth of minority business overall and in specific industries, and publications of interest to the minority businessman can be found in *Access*, a 10-20 page bimonthly publication of the Office of Minority Business Enterprise (OMBE) of the Department of Commerce.

Free; OMBE (see C1.12).

10.3 *Minority-Owned Business: Black*

Data on businesses owned by blacks are featured in this survey. Statistics are given on the number of firms, gross receipts, and numbers of paid employees, distributed geographically by industry, size of firm, and legal form of firm organization. Maps and tables are included.

#003-024-00988-9, 161 pp., $3.45; GPO (see C1.0).

10.4 *Minority Ownership of Small Businesses, Thirty case Studies*

An account of the experiences of thirty minority individuals who started their own business ventures is presented in this publication. It reports the events and circumstances as perceived by the individual businessmen and others involved in managing, financing, or otherwise assisting the various ventures. It illustrates the particular problems confronting thirty minority members who found business ownership and management considerably different and more difficult and uncertain than they had expected or had been prepared to deal with. These thirty cases include a wide variety of businesses in retail sales, various areas of the service trade, manufacturing, and construction.

#017-080-00882-3, 87 pp., $1.30; GPO (see C1.0).

10.5 *Black Americans, A Decade of Occupational Change*

#029-001-00967-4, 26 pp., 65¢; GPO (see C1.0).

10.6 *The Vital Majority, Small Business in the American Economy*

A wide range of subjects is covered in this book of essays marking the twentieth anniversary of the Small Business Administration. Typical topics are: finance, accounting, marketing, government assistance programs, information systems and computerization, research and development, management strategies, labor relations, taxation, and market structures.

#045-000-00124-5, 510 pp., $6.75; GPO (see C1.0).

10.7 Publications on Crimes against Business

The following publications are available, as priced, from GPO (see C1.0).

The Cost of Crimes against Business, 52 pp., $1.10
Crime in Retailing, 42 pp., $1.10
Federal Government Sources on Crimes against Business, 14 pp., 30¢

10.8 *Minority Enterprise Progress Report*

This is the annual report of the Office of Minority Business Enterprise (OMBE). It presents an overview of national trends in minority business and the programs of OMBE designed to assist minority business in organization, development, marketing expansion, and other areas.

Free; regional or area offices of OMBE (see C1.12).

10.9 Small Business Administration *Annual Report*

The *Annual Report* of the Small Business Administration (SBA) provides a description and performance analysis of each of the agency's programs, demonstrating the breadth of activity of SBA.

$3.20; GPO (see C1.0).

10.10 *Manual of Business Opportunities for Small and Minority Businesses*

In this handbook, the roles of the housing development team are described: attorney, planner, architect, sponsor/developer, real estate appraiser/broker contractor, consultant, mortgage banker, and management.

Information within each of the chapters regarding increased opportunities for minority participation in housing production encourages greater minority participation within the housing delivery system.

The tools and methods described in the text point the direction for improved cooperation between private enterprise and government and acceleration of participation by minorities in developing the environment.

The booklet serves as a resource for paraprofessionals and persons with limited experience who are interested in participating in the housing development process. It will also help minority professionals to become more familiar with their job and help them to expand their participation in housing.

#023-000-00336-8, $2.15; GPO (see C1.0).

Technical Assistance (10.50-10.102)

Management Assistance (10.50-10.59)

10.50 Services for Minority Businesses

The Office of Minority Business Enterprise (OMBE) assists a number of organizations whose purpose is to help the minority entrepreneur. These organizations are described below, listed according to the category of program services they primarily provide.

Business Development Centers (BDC) provide all the services of a CCAC, BRC, and LBDO (see below) at a single, one-stop location.

Business Management Development (BMD) organizations conduct business management development programs and provide education and training to existing and potential minority entrepreneurs.

Business Resource Centers (BRC) identify and mobilize private sector resources, including volunteer services, and make them available to minority entrepreneurs through the the OMBE-funded Business Development Organizations (BDO). They also help develop local markets for the entrepreneur and seek new sources of capital.

City OMBE's (CO) mobilize and coordinate city resources to assist the development of minority-owned business.

Construction Contractor Assistance Centers (CCAC) provide management and technical assistance to and monitor the operations of minority contractors, to enable them to acquire bonding, financing, and other resources needed to compete effectively.

Contracted Support Services (CSS) provide management and technical assistance to other OMBE-funded business assistance organizations, special projects fostering development of minority-owned businesses, and qualified minority businesses whose needs cannot be served by other OMBE organizations.

Experiment and Demonstration (E&D) projects examine the feasibility of new program approaches or methods for developing minority-owned business.

Local Business Development Organizations (LBDO) provide information, counseling, and assistance in acquiring business opportunities, capital, management, and technical assistance in order to establish new businesses or expand existing businesses.

Minority Business and Trade Associations (MB&TA) provide cooperative services to enhance the competitive position of their members.

National Business Development Organizations (NBDO) provide, through their local chapters or affiliates, information, counseling, and assistance in acquiring business opportunities, capital, management, and technical assistance to expand existing or create new businesses.

Private Resources Program (PRP) stimulates business opportunities and provides management and technical assistance through national professional and trade organizations.

State OMBE's (SO) mobilize and coordinate state resources to assist the development of minority-owned business.

OMBE (see C1.12).

10.51 Service Corps of Retired Executives/ Active Corps of Executives

The Service Corps of Retired Executives (SCORE) is a group of public-spirited, knowledgeable, and experienced retired executives from every job sector. Many were owners of small businesses. SCORE has a present membership of 5,198, with 292 chapters.

The Active Corps of Executives (ACE) is an important auxiliary to SCORE. It augments SCORE and furnishes needed special talents which may not be represented among other volunteers.

Both SCORE and ACE members participate in conducting workshops and in offering a wide range of management and technical counseling to the small business community. The volunteers donate their time to present and potential small business owners; SBA reimburses them for out-of-pocket expenses.

A counselor will meet with a client at a SCORE office or at the client's place of business; usually that will resolve the problem. At other times, counseling continues as long as necessary.

SBA regional offices (see C1.110).

10.52 Small Business Institute Program

The Small Business Institute program, a three-way cooperative between collegiate schools of business administration, members of the nation's small business community, and the Small Business Administration (SBA) is a new source of management assistance. Under the supervision of university faculty and SBA staff, senior and graduate students of business administration work directly with owners of small firms, providing vital management assistance to small businesses while undergoing meaningful learning experiences themselves.

The program began in the fall of 1972. In the first year of its life, 1,100 small firms received counseling and 2,200 students were involved. In 1976, 385 schools participated, involving over 22,000 students and 8,800 small businesses. Satisfaction rate among clients was over 80 percent.

SBA (see C1.110).

10.53 University Business Development Centers

Growing out of the Small Business Institute (see 10.52) concept, the University Business Development Center (UBDC) program is an experimental Small Business Administration concept being tested in eight universities. It is a university-based and administered program to interrelate the academic, professional, and technological resources of universities with all existing government programs designed to assist the business community. While each agency continues to administer its own programs, the university serves as a funnel or mixing device for them, so that the collection of programs will work as an integrated unit serving the whole community, rather than as an uncoordinated variety of programs.

A functioning UBDC can offer the following services to its business clients:

—Business and product evaluation and development
—Entrepreneur evaluation, recommendations, counseling, and training
—Analysis, correction, and follow-up of financial, marketing, technical, production, legal, and any other type of problem faced by small business owners
—Feasibility studies and development of business plans for present and future entrepreneurs
—Access to and application of technology, paid for by the taxpayers in over $350 billion worth of research and development projects since 1947
—Assistance not only in surviving (when 57 percent of new businesses fail in the first five years), but in expanding on a solid basis

Universities currently involved are the Universities of Maine at Bangor; Missouri at St. Louis; Nebraska at Omaha; Georgia at Athens; and West Florida at Pensacola; and Rutgers University, New Brunswick, New Jersey; California State University at Chico; and California Polytechnic at Pomona.

10.54 Management Training and Workshops

Small Business Administration (SBA) field offices offer prebusiness workshops, conferences, and problem clinics on developing a business plan for small businesses or those thinking about starting a business. SBA makes special efforts to increase the number of minority and disadvantaged businesses included in such groups.

SBA (see C1.110).

10.55 Management Assistance through Professional and Trade Associations

The Small Business Association (SBA) is entering into agreements with ten to fifteen trade and professional associations to provide specialized management and technical assistance to small businesses in the socially or economically disadvantaged sector.

SBA (see C1.110).

10.56 Contracted Management Consultation

The Call Contracting Program (formerly the 406 Program) authorizes the Small Business Administration (SBA) to place contracts with qualified individuals and businesses in order to provide management and technical aid to SBA clients who meet the eligibility requirements of Sections 7(i) and 7(j) of of the Small Business Act, as amended in 1974. It also allows SBA to initiate, organize, and maintain this management counseling service for small firms as required.

Professional consulting firms must qualify as existing small firms at the time of proposal and must meet the standards set out in the Request for Proposal (RFP). Potential consultants must have been in business for at least one year before the closing date for receipt of proposals and have a staff capacity to perform at least 50 percent of the work.

Eligible recipients of call-contract counseling include socially or economically disadvantaged individuals or firms and individuals or firms located in areas of high unemployment. Detailed information on eligibility requirements is available at regional offices of SBA.

Forms of assistance available are: bookkeeping and accounting services; production, engineering, and technical advice; feasibility studies, marketing analyses, and advertising expertise; legal services and specialized management training. There is no charge for these services.

To be considered as a prime contractor, the individual or firm should request that its name be added to the bidders list and that it receive an RFP. Write the Program Manager, Small Business

Administration, 1441 L Street N.W., Washington, DC 20416, or call 202-382-8277.

To be considered for counseling, contact the Management Assistance Officer at regional offices of SBA (see C1.110).

10.57 Technical Assistance from the Economic Development Administration

The Office of Technical Assistance of the Economic Development Administration (EDA) can conduct feasibility, marketing, and other studies for firms on a repayment basis if the results of such work will be likely to result in increased jobs and economic upgrading. The project need not take place in an EDA specially-designated area, although it is more likely to be approved if it is.

EDA (see C1.11).

10.58 Management Assistance from Small Business Investment Companies

Since the ultimate success of a Small Business Investment Company (SBIC) is linked to the growth and profitability of its so-called portfolio companies (i.e., those it has helped to finance), many SBIC's offer management services as a supplement to financing. As a condition of financing, it may insist on certain improvements in the operations of a small business; for example, installation of better accounting methods or inventory controls. Similarly, as part of the financing agreement, the small business may be required to furnish the SBIC with regular financial statements or progress reports.

The extent of management services offered varies with the individual SBIC.

A large SBIC is usually staffed by an experienced and diversified management team. If desirable, a specialist from the SBIC may work with a portfolio company to iron out specific problems which arise during the company's growth. Other SBIC's have small staffs which divide their time between seeking new investments and working with portfolio companies. Many SBIC managers call in consultants to supplement their work with portfolio companies, while others draw on the talents of their own board members. Some SBIC's which concentrate on well-secured loans do not offer management assistance.

SBA (see C1.110).

10.59 Inter-Agency Council on Minority Enterprise

The Inter-Agency Council on Minority Enterprise coordinates the federal government's efforts to assist minority business people. Since the establishment of the Office of Minority Business Enterprise (OMBE), the Council has played a major role in bringing about a four-fold increase in federal loans, loan guarantees, and grants to minority business, and in government purchases from minority firms.

OMBE Information Service, OMBE (see C1.12).

Technology Transfer (10.100-10.102)

10.100 Technology Assistance Program for Small Business

In order to make the technological advances resulting from federally financed R&D available to small business concerns, the Technology Assistance Program for Small Business provides educational and technical assistance through workshops, consultation, and technical publications which identify technological advances from the federal government's stockpile of information.

SBA (see C1.110).

10.101 Experimental Technology Incentives Program

The Experimental Technology Incentives Program is a new program which is a joint effort between the Small Business Administration (SBA) and the National Bureau of Standards to devise new means and methods of assisting the small business research and development community.

SBA (see C1.110).

10.102 Technology Clearinghouse to Aid Minority Business

The Office of Minority Business Enterprise (OMBE) in the Department of Commerce has developed a program to provide minority-owned business firms with improved access to technical innovations developed under federal government contracts and by private corporations without federal aid.

The first phase of this new technology utilization program involved gaining support among federal agencies and private businesses who conduct technology utilization programs.

Under the second phase, the Booker T. Washington Foundation of Washington, D.C. will design and test the operation of a clearinghouse which will offer access to information concerning (1) product identification, (2) feasibility analysis, (3) marketing, and (4) financing to minority firms in adapting new technology for the development of commercial products. The new center will begin providing services to minority firms nationally when the designs have been fully tested.

OMBE (see C1.12).

Marketing Assistance (10.150-10.159)

10.150 Minority Business Associations and Purchasing Councils

The following are organizations in the private sector which the Office of Minority Business Enterprise (OMBE) may have had a hand in forming or providing technical support for, and with which it maintains close contact.

Minority Business Associations (MBA) are organized by minority businesses to promote sales on special days, events to draw customers to the community, neighborhood improvement projects, or anything else affecting the health of business. MBA's can receive financial support from OMBE, primarily for staff support.

Information Center, OMBE, Department of Commerce, Washington, DC 20230; 202-967-5542 or 5407.

The *National and Regional Minority Purchasing Council* was formed in 1972 to lead the way in opening doors in majority corporations to new or expanded purchases of goods and services from minority businesses. The Council grew to 825 members by the end of 1974, with 190 of these from the Fortune 500 companies. The Council maintains its headquarters in Chicago and is supported by 26 regional councils across the country. Members of the councils are top-level executives.

National Minority Purchasing Council, 6 North Michigan Avenue, Room 1104, Chicago, IL 60602; 312-346-4511.

10.151 Minority Vendor Data Base System

By using the Minority Vendor Data Base System, corporate purchasing personnel are afforded immediate access to qualified minority suppliers.

National Minority Purchasing Council, 6 North Michigan Avenue, Room 1004, Chicago, IL 60602; 312-346-4511.

10.152 *Small Business and Labor Surplus Area Specialists Designated to Assist Small, Minority, and LSA Businessmen*

Intended for potential small business suppliers to the Department of Defense, this publication lists the locations of military and Defense Supply Agency procurement offices and small business specialists throughout the United States.

#008-000-00223-1, 61 pp., $1.10; GPO (see C1.0).

10.153 Services to Small and Minority Businesses from National Aeronautics and Space Administration

Small businesses and minority businesses receive special attention at the National Aeronautics and Space Administration (NASA). Under its Small Business Program and its Minority Business Enterprise Program, NASA attempts to ensure that small and minority businesses have an equitable opportunity to participate in NASA procurement, and that they receive a fair share of NASA prime and subcontract awards.

NASA has a small business advisor at its headquarters to represent the interests of small business before NASA and a small business specialist at each installation with a primary responsibility for fostering small business procurement opportunities. Where possible, specific procurements are set aside for small business competition.

As to minority businesses, NASA works with the Office of Minority Business Enterprises (OMBE) and with the Small Business Administration (SBA) in assisting small firms owned and controlled by socially or economically disadvantaged individuals or groups. NASA gives special emphasis to identifying procurement requirements for referral to SBA for matching with the capabilities and potentials of firms approved under

Section 8(a) of the Small Business Act. (Under Section 8(a), SBA contacts with NASA for supplies and services, and then subcontracts non-competitively for these requirements with approved firms.)

In addition, NASA's headquarters has a minority business officer, and several NASA installations have minority business specialists. These people may be reached at the following addresses:

NASA Headquarters 202-755-2288
Washington, DC 20546

Ames Research Center 514-965-5800
Moffett Field, CA 94035

Flight Research Center 805-258-3311 x796
Edwards, CA 93523

Goddard Space Flight Center 301-982-5416 (small business)
Greenbelt, MD 20771 301-982-6871 (minority business)

Kennedy Space Center 305-867-7353
Kennedy Space Center, FL 32899

Langley Research Center 804-827-3959
Hampton, VA 23365

Lewis Research Center 216-433-4000 x543
Cleveland, OH 44135

Johnson Space Center 713-483-4511 (small business)
Houston, TX 77058 713-483-5473 (minority business)

Marshall Space Flight Center 205-453-2675 (small business)
Huntsville, AL 35812 205-453-4200 (minority business)

National Space Technology Laboratories 601-688-3680
Bay St. Louis, MS 39520

Wallops Flight Center 804-824-3411 x542
Wallops Island, VA 23337

NASA Pasadena Office 213-354-6051
Pasadena, CA 91103

Jet Propulsion Laboratory 213-354-6941
Pasadena, CA 91103 213-354-3130

10.154 Procurement by Department of Defense

The Department of Defense (DOD) is the largest buyer of goods and services in the government. It has procurement and contract administration offices from coast to coast.

Area offices of DOD can provide counseling and technical guidance in matters pertaining to defense procurement, including assistance with problems connected with contracts and aid in reference to buying activities. The area offices also have displays of representative bid sets from the military services and procurement materials and information of all kinds.

DOD, as do most government agencies, emphasizes small and minority business involvement in procurement activities and, in many cases, priority treatment is given to such firms by set-aside clauses in contract requests. DOD also emphasizes the subcontracting possibilities for such firms.

DOD (see C1.20).

10.155 Special Opportunities for Disadvantaged Contractors: The 8(a) Program

Under the 8(a) program, the Small Business Administration (SBA) serves as prime contractor for federal goods and services and then subcontracts only to socially or economically disadvantaged firms, most of which are minority-owned. Firms with 8(a) status will be in an excellent position for business opportunities in fiscal year 1977 and after. However, the number of firms being admitted to this status is diminishing because of the efforts necessary to assist the firms in the present portfolio.

Firms that are awarded 8(a) contracts are offered free management and technical aid in the planning and operating stages of the business.

SBA (see C1.110).

10.156 Research and Development Opportunities for Small Firms

The Small Business Administration (SBA) publishes, on a regional basis, directories identifying the names and major capabilities of small

R&D business firms. These are distributed to major procurement installations for use in locating small business sources for R&D procurements. SBA also makes direct-source referrals to procuring installations for specific R&D solicitations.

SBA (see C1.110).

10.157 Subcontracting Possibilities Published by Department of Defense

The Defense Supply Agency of the Department of Defense, the largest government procurer of goods and services, publishes for each of its regions a listing of the companies which either have a contract currently or did at one time, and the product or service provided by the company. There is a separate publication for each region. A business can use this as a guide for contacting government contractors with whom there may be subcontracting possibilities. Minority contractors are listed separately in the volume. Although the volumes vary in size from region to region, they are usually well over 100 pages in length and are organized alphabetically. A copy may be obtained from any Defense Supply Agency (see C1.21).

10.158 Certificates of Competency

Following the government procurement bidding process, a government contracting officer may have doubts as to whether a small, low bidder has the capacity or necessary financial means to perform the contracts if awarded. The Certificates of Competency program provides the small firm with an appeal procedure. If the Small Business Administration (SBA) disagrees with the contracting officer, it is authorized to certify that the small firm has the necessary production and financial ability to perform the contract at issue. The decision is binding on the contracting officer.

SBA (see C1.110).

10.159 Minority Business Resource Center, Federal Railroad Administration

Railroads purchase a variety of goods and services, ranging from locomotives to nuts and bolts, from office furniture to paper clips, from sophisticated consulting services to janitorial services, from engineering and architectural services to purchasing of drafting services, from complete meals to cups of coffee, from renovation of office space to the rebuilding of major rail lines. In addition to purchasing products manufactured specifically for the industry, railroads purchase many standard commercial products. The scope of railroad procurement and the amount of money involved are large enough to mean unprecedented new and ongoing business opportunities for minority-owned firms.

The Minority Business Resource Center (MBRC) of the Federal Railroad Administration, Department of Transportation, helps ensure that businesses owned by minorities (including women) have maximum opportunity to participate in the railroad markets funded by the federal government.

MBRC was created in 1976. Its programs now under development include: (1) a national clearinghouse for information on business opportunities, management assistance, technical assistance, and bonding assistance; (2) management and technical assistance; (3) financial assistance, including venture capital, debt financing, and surety bonding; and (4) business development activities, including educational programs and identification of opportunities.

For information about assistance currently available, contact MBRC, Federal Railroad Administration, Department of Transportation, 400 7th Street S.W., Room 5424, Washington, DC 20590; 202-426-2852.

Financial Assistance (10.200-10.215)

10.200 Definition of Small Business for Small Business Administration Loan Purposes

For loan eligibility purposes, a small business is defined as one that is (1) independently owned and operated, (2) not dominant in its field of operations, and (3) is within the pertinent Small Business Administration (SBA) size standards. A business may be considered small if it has 250 employees or less, and large if it employs 1,500 or more. A firm which falls in the range between 250 and 1,500 may be considered either small or large, depending on the SBA size standard worked out for that particular field of operations.

There is an alternative size standard. Regardless of the number of employees, a business, together with its affiliates, may qualify if its assets do not exceed $9 million; its net worth does not exceed $4 million; and its average net income for the preceding two years, after federal income taxes, did not exceed $400,000. Average net income must be computed without benefit of any carryover loss.

By this definition, 97 percent of United States businesses fall into the small business category, and they account for 48 percent of the gross national product.

10.201 Small Business Investment Company

A Small Business Investment Company (SBIC) is a privately owned and privately operated small business investment company which has been licensed by the Small Business Administration (SBA) to provide equity capital and long-term loans to small firms. Often, an SBIC also provides management assistance to the companies it finances.

Small businesses often have difficulty obtaining long-term capital fo finance their growth. Prior to 1958, there were few places a small company could turn for money once it had exhausted its secured line of credit from banks or SBA. To help close this financing gap, Congress passed the Small Business Investment Act of 1958, which authorized SBA to license, regulate, and help finance privately organized and privately operated SBIC's.

Today there are SBIC's located in all parts of the country. As an industry, the SBIC's have total assets of millions of dollars, and additional funds are available to them through borrowings from SBA and private sources.

Many SBIC's are owned by relatively small groups of local investors. An SBIC finances small firms in two general ways—by straight loans and by venture capital or equity investments. In some cases, these investments give the SBIC actual or potential ownership of a minority of a small business' stock. However, SBIC's are usually prohibited from taking a control position in a small concern. Financing must be for at least five years, except that a borrower may elect to have a prepayment clause included in the financing agreement.

There are three free brochures put out by SBA which together give an overview of the SBIC: *SBIC Financing for Small Business; SBIC, Starting a Small Business Investment Company;* and *Section 301(d) SBIC's.*

Local attorneys, accountants, bankers, investment bankers, and business associates or advisers who have had dealings with SBIC's may be helpful. Also, SBA field offices will offer help. An agency information specialist will provide a list of licensed SBIC's, and while he is not permitted to recommend a specific company, he may be able to point out the types of investments various SBIC's in the area have been making.

SBA (see C1.110).

10.202 Minority Enterprise Small Business Investment Company

Under Section 301(d) of the Small Business Investment Act of 1958, special small business investment companies called Minority Enterprise Small Business Investment Companies (MESBIC) can be and have been established which concentrate on providing equity funds, long-term loans, and management assistance to small business concerns owned by socially or economically disadvantaged persons. The Small Business Administration booklet entitled *Section 301(d) SBIC's* reviews the procedure for setting up and operating a MESBIC.

The booklet is available at area offices of Small Business Administration (see C1.110); or write Director, Office of Program Development, SBA, 1441 L Street N.W., 8th Floor, Washington, DC 20416.

10.203 Economic Opportunity Loan Program

The Economic Opportunity Loan Program (EOL) makes it possible for disadvantaged individuals who have the capability and desire to own their own businesses to borrow money for starting or expanding. It provides both financial and management assistance. The maximum amount of an EOL is $100,000 for up to fifteen years. There are procedures to follow for both new and existing firms desiring to participate.

SBA (see C1.110).

10.204 Pool Loans

Under Section 7(a)(5) of the Small Business Act, Small Business Administration (SBA) is authorized to make loans to pools formed by several small business concerns. Formation of such pools must be cleared by the Department of Justice and information furnished to the Federal Trade Commission. Loan proceeds must be used to obtain raw materials, equipment, inventories, supplies or benefits of research and development, or to construct facilities for such purposes.

SBA (see C1.110).

10.205 Loans for Assistance to the Handicapped

Under legislation passed in 1973, the Small Business Administration may make loans to small firms owned by handicapped persons as well as to nonprofit organizations where at least 75 percent of the manhours are performed by handicapped individuals.

SBA (see C1.110).

10.206 *SBA Business Loans*

The basics of Small Business Administration (SBA) loaning procedures and limitations are explained in this 16-page booklet, *SBA Business Loans*.

SBA can aid business directly or indirectly in a number of ways. When financing is not available otherwise on reasonable terms, SBA may guarantee up to 90 percent or $350,000, whichever is less, of a bank loan to a small firm. If an SBA-guaranteed loan is not available, SBA will then consider advancing funds on an immediate participation basis with a bank. SBA will consider making a direct loan only when these forms of financing are not obtainable. The agency's share of an immediate participation loan may not, at the present time, exceed $150,000. Direct loans may not exceed $100,000 and at times may not be available due to fiscal restraints.

SBA's specific lending objectives are to (1) stimulate small business in deprived areas, (2) promote minority enterprise opportunity, and (3) promote small business contribution to economic growth.

Loans may be for as long as ten years, except those portions of loans for new construction purposes, which may have a maturity of fifteen years. Working capital loans, however, are usually limited to six years. Interest rates on SBA's portion of immediate participations, as well as direct loans, may not exceed a rate set by a statutory formula relating to the cost of money to the government, usually between 6 and 7½ percent.

Ineligible applicants include nonprofit enterprises, newspapers, magazine and book publishers, and radio and TV broadcasting companies.

SBA (see C1.110).

10.207 Small Business Administration Disaster Loans

Small Business Administration (SBA) is authorized to make loans to small firms suffering from the effects of government actions and other situations not caused by the small firm:

Economic Injury Disaster Loans are made to small firms suffering economic injury as the result of physical disasters such as floods, hurricanes, and tornadoes. This is one of the largest SBA loan programs.

Product Disaster Loans may be approved for small firms suffering from the effects of diseased food products.

Coal Mine Health and Safety Loans are made to small coal mine operators to assist them in complying with the Federal Coal Mine and Safety Act of 1969.

Consumer Protection Loans are those offered to firms having to comply with standards set up under the Egg Products Act of 1970, the Wholesale Poultry and Poultry Products Act of 1968, or the Wholesale Meat Act of 1967.

Occupational Safety and Health Loans are made to small firms suffering injury as a result of having to comply with regulations of the Occupational Safety and Health Administration.

Base Closing Economic Injury Loans may be made to businesses which suffer from the effects of the closing of major military installations.

Air Pollution Control Loans are authorized for firms having to comply with requirements of the Clean Air Act of 1970.

Water Pollution Control Loans are those made to small businesses having to comply with various water pollution controls.

Emergency Energy Shortage Economic Injury Loans are available to small businesses suffering economic injury caused by an energy shortage.

Strategic Arms Economic Injury Loans are made to small businesses directly or seriously affected by the significant reduction of the scope or amount of federal support for any project as a result of any international agreement limiting the development of strategic arms facilities.

10.208 Economic Injury Loans

Any small business is eligible for this type of loan if it suffers substantial economic injury as a result of its displacement by, or location in, adjacent to, or near a federally-aided urban renewal, highway, or other construction project.

A Small Business Administration (SBA) loan can help reestablish the business, either in its existing location or in a satisfactory new location. The loan supplements funds the firm receives from the public agency involved as compensation for the taking of the property and other losses.

Therefore, SBA loans may be used to:

(1) remodel the firm's building in its existing location; or to purchase, and, if necessary, remodel a building at another location; or to purchase land and construct a new building; (2) provide working capital for any increased rental or other operating costs resulting from a new, rented location; (3) make leasehold improvements on rented property; (4) replace fixtures, machinery, and equipment, with reasonable upgrading permitted (but the trade-in value of the old equipment must be applied to the cost of the replacements); (5) purchase a larger or different type of inventory that may be better suited to a new location; and (6) pay moving expenses in excess of the amount provided by the public agency involved in the construction project.

SBA (see C1.110).

10.209 Loans to Local Development Companies

The Small Business Administration (SBA) is authorized to make loans to state and local development companies for use in assisting specific small businesses. SBA may lend up to $500,000 for each small business that is to be assisted. Thousands of loans have been made to such companies to enable them to start, expand, or modernize small businesses.

The loans may be used to finance construction, modernization, or conversion of plants, including purchase of land, and to purchase machinery and equipment. They may not be used for working capital or for debt repayment, except interim debt incurred for construction of the project involved.

A loan may not be made if the funds needed are available from banks or other private lenders. To the extent that private sources do have funds, they may, and frequently do, participate with SBA in helping to finance projects. A development company is usually required to provide from its own funds at least 20 percent of the cost of the project.

The SBA booklet, *Loans to Local Development Companies*, furnishes more information (SBA, see C1.110).

10.210 Minority-Owned Financial Institutions

The Office of Minority Business Enterprise (OMBE) provides assistance in the organization and development of minority banks, savings and loans organizations, and insurance companies.

OMBE (see C1.12).

10.211 Revolving Line of Credit

Under this program, the Small Business Administration (SBA) seeks to help small firms obtain a line of credit from a bank in order to fulfill construction or other contracts, by guaranteeing the credit extended by the bank.

SBA (see C1.110).

10.212 Lease Guarantee Program

This program is designed to provide small businesses with the credit required to compete on a more equal basis with large businesses for space on prime industrial and commercial property. Either through participating private insurance companies, or directly if no participation is available, the Small Business Administration will guarantee the payment of the rent under leases entered into by small businesses which qualify.

SBA (see C1.110).

10.213 Surety Bond Guarantee Program

Small contractors who would not ordinarily be capable of securing bid, performance, and payment bonds through the established surety bond industry channels are provided surety bond assistance through this program. The SBA (Small Business Administration) assistance for the required bonding consists of a 90 percent guarantee of the potential losses of private surety companies on a contract bond issued to the small contractor.

SBA (see C1.110).

10.214 Federal Crime Insurance Program

The Federal Crime Insurance Program (FCIP) offers low cost, easily obtainable, non-cancellable burglary and robbery insurance to small businesses and residential property owners and tenants in states which have been declared eligible. A state becomes eligible for the program when the administrator determines that affordable crime insurance is virtually impossible to get through normal channels, and when no steps have been taken to remedy that situation. FCIP is now available in the District of Columbia and the following twenty states:

Arkansas	Iowa	New York
Colorado	Kansas	Ohio
Connecticut	Maryland	Pennsylvania
Delaware	Massachusetts	Rhode Island
Florida	Minnesota	Tennessee
Georgia	Missouri	Virginia
Illinois	New Jersey	

State crime insurance programs similar to the FCIP are available in California, Michigan, Indiana, and Wisconsin.

In the twenty states mentioned, FCIP policies may be written by any licensed property insurance broker or agent, or by the private insurance company designated under contract as the servicing company for a particular state. It is renewable regardless of losses and is available at uniform rates to everyone in an eligible state, regardless of their occupation or the crime rate in their neighborhood.

Commercial losses from burglary or robbery can be insured in amounts ranging from $1,000 to $15,000. Typical commercial premiums range from $35 for $1,000 coverage in a low-crime area for businesses with annual gross receipts under $100,000, to $748 for $15,000 coverage in a high-crime area.

To obtain FCIP insurance, an application from any licensed broker or agent or state servicing company must be filled out and half the year's premium paid. The applicant will be billed for the second half six months later.

Necessary inspections are made by the servicing insurance company and paid for by the federal government.

Federal Insurance Administration, Department of Housing and Urban Development (see C1.40).

10.215 Riot Insurance

The purpose of this insurance is to assure availability of essential coverage for urban property, particularly that located in areas possibly subject to riots or civil disturbance, by providing reinsurance to insurers against catastrophic loss from riot or civil disorder. Federal reinsurance of this nature is available only to property insurance companies that cooperate as risk-bearing members of a state Fair Access to Insurance Requirements (FAIR) plan. FAIR plans operate in twenty-five states, the District of Columbia, and Puerto Rico.

Department of Housing and Urban Development regional offices (see C1.40); or write Administrator, Federal Insurance Administration, Department of Housing and Urban Development, Washington, DC 20410.

PART C

Appendix

Appendix C1

GUIDE TO DEPARTMENTS AND AGENCIES LISTED IN APPENDIX C1

C1.0 GOVERNMENT PRINTING OFFICE NATIONAL AND REGIONAL OFFICES

National Office

North Capitol and H St. N.W.
Washington, DC 20401
202-275-2051

Regional Offices

Atlanta Bookstore
Federal Bldg., Rm. 100
275 Peachtree St. N.E.
Atlanta, GA 30303
404-526-6947

Boston Bookstore
Rm. G 25, JFK Bldg.
Government Center
Boston, MA 02203
617-223-6071

Canton Ohio Bookstore
Federal Office Bldg.
201 Cleveland Ave. S.W.
Canton, OH 44702
216-455-8971

Chicago Bookstore
Rm. 1463
Everett McKinley Dirksen Bldg.
219 S. Dearborn St.
Chicago, IL 60604
312-353-5133

Dallas Bookstore
Rm. 1C46
Federal Bldg.-U.S. Courthouse
1100 Commerce St.
Dallas, TX 75202
214-749-1541

Detroit Bookstore
Rm. 229, Federal Bldg.
231 W. Lafayette Blvd.
Detroit, MI 48226

Denver Bookstore
Rm. 1421
Federal Bldg.-U.S. Courthouse
1961 Stout St.
Denver, CO 80202
303-837-3967

Kansas City Bookstore
Rm. 135, Federal Office Bldg.
601 E. 12th St.
Kansas City, MO 64106
816-374-2160

Los Angeles Bookstore
Rm. 1015, Federal Office Bldg.
300 N. Los Angeles St.
Los Angeles, CA 90012
213-688-5841

New York Bookstore
26 Federal Plaza, Rm. 110
New York, NY 10007
212-264-3826

Philadelphia Bookstore
Main Lobby
U.S. Post Office and Courthouse
9th and Chestnut Sts.
Philadelphia, PA 19107
215-597-0677

San Francisco Bookstore
Rm. 1023, Federal Office Bldg.
450 Golden Gate Ave.
San Francisco, CA 94102
415-556-6657

Cleveland Bookstore
1st Fl., Federal Office Bldg.
1240 E. 9th St.
Cleveland, OH 44114

Seattle Bookstore
Rm. 194, Federal Office Bldg.
915 First Ave.
Seattle, WA 98104

Milwaukee Bookstore
Rm. 190, Federal Bldg.
519 Wisconsin Ave.
Mailwaukee, WI 53202

Jacksonville Bookstore
Rm. 158, Federal Bldg.
400 W. Bay St.
Jacksonville, FL 32202

Department of Agriculture

C1.1 COOPERATIVE EXTENSION SERVICE NATIONAL AND STATE HEADQUARTERS

National Office

Department of Agriculture
Washington, DC 20250
202-447-6283

State Headquarters

Auburn University
Auburn, AL 36830

University of Alaska
College, AK 99701

University of Arizona
Tucson, AZ 85721

University of Arkansas
Little Rock, AR 72203

University of California
2200 University Ave.
Berkeley, CA 94720

Colorado State University
Ft. Collins, CO 80521

University of Connecticut
Storrs, CT 06268

University of Delaware
Newark, DE 19711

Federal City College and Washington Technical Institute
1424 K St. N.W.
Washington, DC 20005

University of Florida
Gainesville, FL 32601

University of Georgia
Athens, GA 30601

Guam Extension Office
Department of Agriculture
Government of Guam
Agana, GU 96910

University of Hawaii
Honolulu, HI 96822

University of Idaho
Moscow, ID 83843

University of Illinois
Urbana, IL 61801

Purdue University
Lafayette, IN 47907

Iowa State University
Ames, IA 50010

Kansas State University
Manhattan, KS 66502

University of Kentucky
Lexington, KY 40506

Louisiana State University
Baton Rouge, LA 70803

University of Maine
Orono, ME 04473

University of Maryland
College Park, MD 20742

University of Massachusetts
Amherst, MA 01002

Michigan State University
East Lansing, MI 48823

University of Minnesota
St. Paul, MN 55101

Mississippi State University
Mississippi State, MS 39762

University of Missouri
Columbia, MO 65201

Montana State University
Bozeman, MT 59715

University of Nebraska
Lincoln, NE 68503

University of Nevada
Reno, NV 89507

University of New Hampshire
Durham, NH 03824

Rutgers - The State University
New Brunswick, NJ 08903

New Mexico State University
Las Cruces, NM 88001

Cornell University
Ithaca, NY 14850

North Carolina State University
Raleigh, NC 27607

North Dakota State University
Fargo, ND 58102

Ohio State University
Columbus, OH 43210

Oklahoma State University
Stillwater, OK 74074

Oregon State University
Corvallis, OR 97331

The Pennsylvania State University
University Park, PA 16802

University of Puerto Rico
Rio Piedras, PR 00928

University of Rhode Island
Kingston, RI 02881

Clemson University
Clemson, SC 29631

South Dakota State University
Brookings, SD 57006

University of Tennessee
Knoxville, TN 37901

Texas A&M University
College Station, TX 77843

Utah State University
Logan, UT 84321

University of Vermont
Burlington, VT 05401

Virginia Polytechnic Institute
Blackburg, VA 24061

P.O. Box 166
Kingshill, St. Croix, VI 00850

Washington State University
Pullman, WA 99163

West Virginia University
Morgantown, WV 26506

University of Wisconsin
Madison, WI 53706

University of Wyoming
Laramie, WY 82070

C1.2 FARMERS HOME ADMINISTRATION NATIONAL AND STATE OFFICES

National Office

Department of Agriculture
Washington, DC 20250
202-447-4323

State Offices

Rm. 717, Aronov Bldg.
S. Court St.
Montgomery, AL 36104
205-832-7077

Rm. 6095, Federal Bldg.
230 N. First AVe.
Phoenix, AZ 85025
602-261-3191

P.O. Box 2778
Little Rock, AR 72203
501-378-6282

459 Cleveland St.
Woodland, CA 95695
916-440-3223

Rm. 231, Bldg. A
Diamond Hill Complex
2490 W. 26th Ave.
Denver, CO 80211
303-837-4347

Suite 2
151 E. Chestnut Hill Rd.
Newark, DE 19713
302-731-8310

P.O. Box 1088
Gainesville, FL 32602
904-376-3218

355 E. Hancock Ave.
Athens, GA 30601
404-546-2162

Rm. 429, Federal Bldg.
304 N. 8th St.
Boise, ID 83702
208-342-2711 ext 664

2106 W. Springfield Ave.
Champaign, IL 61820
217-356-1127

Suite 1700
5610 Crawfordsville Road
Indianapolis, IN 46224
317-269-6414

Rm. 873, Federal Bldg.
210 Walnut St.
Des Moines, IA 50309
515-284-4121

536 Jefferson St.
Topeka, KS 66607
913-234-8661 ext 375

333 Waller Ave.
Lexington, KY 40504
606-252-3212 ext 2733

3727 Government St.
Alexandria, LA 71301
318-448-3421

USDA Office Bldg.
Orono, ME 04473
207-942-8385

Rm. 209
1405 S. Harrison Rd.
East Lnasing, MI 48823
517-372-1910 ext 272

Rm. 252
U.S. Courthouse - Federal Bldg.
316 N. Robert St.
St. Paul, MN 55101
612-725-5842

Rm. 830, Milner Bldg.
Jackson, MS 39201
601-969-4316

Parkade Plaza, Terrace Level
Columbia, MO 65201
314-442-2271 ext 3241

Federal Bldg.
P.O. Box 850
Bozeman, MT 59715
406-587-3211

Rm. 308, Federal Bldg.
100 Centennial Mall N.
Lincoln, NE 68508
402-471-5551

Rm. 3414, Federal Bldg.
517 Gold Ave. S.W.
Albuquerque, NM 87102
505-766-2462

Rm. 871, Federal Plaza
100 S. Clinton St.
Syracuse, NY 13202
315-473-3458

Rm. 525, Federal Bldg.
310 New Bern Ave.
Raleigh, NC 27601
919-755-4640

P.O. Box 1737
Bismark, ND 58501
701-225-4011 ext 4237

Rm. 448, Old Post Office Bldg.
121 E. State St.
Columbus, OH 43215
614-469-5606

Agricultural Center Office Bldg.
Stillwater, OK 74074
405-372-7111 ext 239

Rm. 1590, Federal Bldg.
1220 S.W. 3rd Ave.
Portland, OR 47204
503-221-3731

Rm. 728, Federal Bldg.
3rd and Walnut Sts.
P.O. Box 905
Harrisburg, PA 17108
717-782-4476

G.P.O. Box 6106G
San Juan, PR 00936
809-722-3508

P.O. Box 21607
Columbia, SC 29221
803-765-5876

P.O. Box 821
Huron, SD 57350
605-352-8651 ext 355

538 U.S. Court House Bldg.
801 Broadway
Nashville, TN 37203
615-749-5501

3910 South General Bruce Dr.
Temple, TX 76501
817-773-1711 ext 301

Rm. 5311, Federal Bldg.
125 S. State St.
Salt Lake City, UT 84138
801-524-5027

141 Main St.
P.O. Box 588
Montpelier, VT 05602
802-223-2371

P.O. Box 10106
Richmond, VA 23240
804-782-2451

Rm. 319, Federal Office Bldg.
301 Yakima St.
Wenatchee, WA 98801
509-663-0031

Federal Bldg.
P.O. Box 678
Morgantown, WV 26505
304-559-7791

P.O. Box 639
First Financial Plaza
1305 Main St.
Stevens Point, WI 54481
715-341-5900

P.O. Box 820
Casper, WY 82601
307-265-5550 ext 5271

C1.3 SOIL CONSERVATION SERVICE, STATE CONSERVATIONISTS—NATIONAL AND STATE OFFICES

National Office

Department of Agriculture
Washington, D.C. 20250
202-447-4543

Field Offices

Wright Bldg.
138 S. Gay St.
P.O. Box 311
Auburn, AL 36830
205-821-8070

Suite 129, Professional Bldg.
2221 E. Northern Lights Blvd.
Anchorage, AK 99504
907-276-4246

230 N. First Ave.
3008 Federal Bldg.
Phoenix, AZ 85025
602-261-6711

Federal Bldg., Rm. 5029
700 W. Capitol St.
P.O. Box 2323
Little Rock, AR 72203
501-378-5445

2828 Chiles Road
Davis, CA 95616
916-758-2200 ext 210

Rm. 313
2490 W. 26th Ave.
P.O. Box 17107
Denver, CO 80217
303-837-4275

Mansfield Professional Park
Route 44A
Storrs, CT 06268
203-429-9361, 9362

Treadway Towers, Suite 2-4
9 E. Lookerman St.
Dover, DE 19901
302-678-0750

Federal Bldg.
P.O. Box 1208
Gainesville, FL 32601
904-377-8732

Federal Bldg.
355 E. Hancock Ave.
P.O. Box 832
Athens, GA 30601
404-546-2273

Alexander Young Bldg., Rm. 440
Honolulu, HI 96813
808-546-3165

Rm. 345
304 N. 8th St.
Boise, ID 83702
208-384-1601 ext 1601

Federal Bldg.
200 W. Church St.
P.O. Box 678
Champaign, IL 61820
217-356-3785

Atkinson Square-West
Suite 2200
5610 Crawfordsville Rd.
Indianapolis, IN 46224
317-269-6515

823 Federal Bldg.
210 Walnut St.
Des Moines, IA 50309
515-862-4260

760 S. Broadway
P.O. Box 600
Salina, KS 67401
913-825-9535

333 Waller Ave.
Lexington, KY 40504
606-252-2312 ext 2749

3737 Government St.
P.O. Box 1630
Alexandria, LA 71301
318-448-3421

USDA Bldg.
University of Maine
Orono, ME 04473
207-866-2132, 2133

Rm. 522, Hartwick Bldg.
4321 Hartwick Rd.
College Pakr, MD 20740
301-344-4180

29 Cottage St.
Amherst, MA 01002
413-549-0650

1405 S. Harrison Rd.
East Lansing, MI 48823
517-372-1910 ext 242

200 Federal Bldg. and U.S. Courthouse
316 N. Robert St.
St. Paul, MN 55101
612-725-7675

Milner Bldg., Rm. 590
210 S. Lamar St.
P.O. Box 610
Jackson, MS 39205
601-969-4330

Parkade Plaza Shopping Center
(Terrace Level)
P.O. Box 459
Columbia, MO 65201
314-442-2271 ext 3155

Federal Bldg.
P.O. Box 970
Bozeman, MT 59715
406-587-5271 ext 4322

Federal Bldg.
U.S. Courthouse, Rm. 345
Lincoln, NE 68508
402-471-5301

U.S. Post Office Bldg.
P.O. Box 4850
Reno, NV 89505
702-784-5304

Federal Bldg.
Durham, NH 03824
603-868-7581

1370 Hamilton St.
P.O. Box 219
Somerset, NJ 08873
201-246-1205 ext 20

517 Gold Ave. S.W.
P.O. Box 2007
Albuqueque, NM 87103
505-766-2173

U.S. Courthouse and Federal Bldg.
100 S. Clinton St., Rm. 771
Syracuse, NY 13202
315-473-3530

Federal Bldg., Fifth Fl.
310 New Bern Ave.
P.O. Box 27307
Raleigh, NC 27611
919-755-4165

Federal Bldg.
Rosser Ave. and Third St.
P.O. Box 1458
Bismarck, ND 58501
701-255-4011 ext 421

311 Old Federal Bldg.
Third and State Sts.
Columbus, OH 43215
614-469-6785

Agriculture Bldg.
Farm Rd. and Brumley St.
Stillwater, OK 74074
405-372-7111 ext 204

Federal Office Bldg.
1220 S.W. 3rd Ave.
Portland, OR 97209
503-221-2751

Federal Bldg. & Courthouse
Box 985, Federal Square Sta.
Harrisburg, PA 17108
717-782-4403

Federal Office Bldg., Rm. 633
Chardon Ave.
Hato Rey, PR 00918
Mailing Address: GPO Box 4868
Hato Rey, PR 00936
809-753-4206

222 Quaker Lane
West Warwick, RI 02893
401-828-1300

240 Stoneridge Drive
Columbia, SC 29210
803-765-5681

239 Wisconsin Ave. S.W.
P.O. Box 1357
Huron, SD 57350
605-352-8651

561 U.S. Courthouse
Nashville, TN 37203
615-749-5471

Federal Bldg.
101 S. Main St.
P.O. Box 648
Temple, TX 76501
817-773-1711 ext 331

4012 Federal Bldg.
125 S. State St.
Salt Lake City, UT 84138
801-524-5051

Suite 205
Burlington Square
Burlington, VT 05401
802-862-6501 ext 6261

Rm. 9201, Federal Bldg.
400 N. 8th St.
P.O. Box 10026
Richmond, VA 23240
804-782-2457

360 U.S. Courthouse
W. 920 Riverside Ave.
Spokane, WA 99201
509-456-3711

75 High St.
P.O. Box 865
Morgantown, WV 26505
304-599-7151

4601 Hammersley Road
Madison, WI 53711
608-252-5351

Federal Office Bldg.
P.O. Box 2440
Casper, WY 82601
307-265-5550 ext 3217

Department of Commerce

C1.10 DEPARTMENT OF COMMERCE NATIONAL, REGIONAL, AND DISTRICT OFFICES

National Office:

Department of Commerce
Washington, D.C. 20230
202-377-2000

Regional Secretarial Representatives

Region 1
(Maine, Vermont, New Hampshire, Connecticut, Rhode Island, Massachusetts)

John F. Kennedy Federal Bldg.
Rm. E429
Boston, MA 02203
617-223-0695

Region 2
(New York, New Jersey, Virgin Is., Puerto Rico)

Federal Bldg., Rm. 1311
26 Federal Plaza
New York, NY 10007
212-264-5647

Region 3
(Pennsylvania, Delaware, Maryland, West Virginia, District of Columbia, Virginia)

Wm. J. Green Federal Bldg.
Rm. 10424
600 Arch St.
Philadelphia, PA 19106
215-597-7527

Region 4
(Kentucky, Tennessee, Mississippi, Alabama, Florida, Georgia, North Carolina, South Carolina)

Suite 300
1365 Peachtree St.
Atlanta, GA 30309
404-881-3165

Region 5
(Ohio, Indiana, Illinois, Michigan, Wisconsin, Minnesota)

CNA Bldg., Rm. 1402
55 E. Jackson Blvd.
Chicago, IL 60604
312-353-0340

Region 6
(Louisiana, Arkansas, Oklahoma, New Mexico, Texas)

Federal Bldg., Rm. 9C37
1100 Commerce St.
Dallas, TX 75242
214-749-2891

Region 7
(Missouri, Iowa, Nebraska, Kansas)

Federal Bldg., Rm. 1844
601 E. 12th St.
Kansas City, MO 64106
816-374-3961

Region 8
(Colorado, Utah, Wyoming, Montana, North Dakota, South Dakota)

Title Bldg., Rm. 515
909 17th St.
Denver, CO 80202
303-327-4285

Region 9
(Arizona, Nevada, California, Hawaii)

Federal Bldg., Box 36165
450 Golden Gate Ave.
San Francisco, CA 94102
415-556-5145

Region 10
(Idaho, Washington, Oregon, Alaska)

Federal Bldg., Rm. 958
915 Second Ave.
Seattle, WA 98174
206-442-5780

District Offices of the Domestic and International Business Administration

Alabama

Suite 200-201
908 S. 20th St.
Birmingham, AL 35205
205-254-1331

Alaska

412 Hill Bldg.
632 Sixth Ave.
Anchorage, AK 99501
907-265-5307

Arizona

508 Greater Arizona Savings Bldg.
112 N. Central Ave.
Phoenix, AZ 85004
602-261-3285

Arkansas

1100 N. University, Suite 109
Little Rock, AR 72207
501-378-5157

California

Rm. 800
11777 San Vicente Blvd.
Los Angeles, CA 90049
213-824-7591

233 A St., Suite 310
San Diego, CA 92101
714-293-5395

Federal Bldg., Box 36103
450 Golden Gate Ave.
San Francisco, CA 94102
415-556-5860

Colorado

Rm. 165, New Customhouse
19th & Stout St.
Denver, CO 80202
303-837-3246

Connecticut

Rm. 610-B, Federal Office Bldg.
450 Main St.
Hartford, CT 06103
203-244-3530

Florida

Rm. 821
City National Bank Bldg.
25 W. Flagler St.
Miami, FL 33130
305-350-5267

128 N. Osceola Ave.
Clearwater, FL 33515
813-446-4081

604 N. Hogan St.
Jacksonville, FL 32202
904-791-2796

Collins Bldg., Rm. G-20
Tallahassee, FL 32304
904-488-6469

Georgia

Suite 600
1365 Peachtree St. N.E.
Atlanta, GA 30309
404-526-6000

235 U.S. Courthouse and P.O. Bldg.
125-29 Bull St.
Savannah, GA 31402
912-232-4321 ext 204

Hawaii

286 Alexander Young Bldg.
1015 Bishop St.
Honolulu, HI 96813
808-546-8694

Idaho

P.O. Box 9366
Boise, ID 83707
208-342-2711

Illinois

1406 Mid Continental Plaza Bldg.
55 E. Monroe St.
Chicago, IL 60603
312-353-4450

Indiana

357 U.S. Courthouse &
Federal Office Bldg.
46 E. Ohio St.
Indianapolis, IN 46204
317-269-6214

Iowa

609 Federal Bldg.
210 Walnut St.
Des Moines, IA 50309
515-284-4222

Kansas

Rm. 341, Clinton Hall
Wichita State University
Wichita, KS 67208
316-267-6160

Kentucky

Rm. 2332
Capitol Plaza Office Tower
Frankfort, KY 40601
502-875-4421

Louisiana

432 International Trade Mart
No. 2 Canal St.
New Orleans, LA 70130
504-589-6546

Maine

Maine State Pier
40 Commercial St.
Portland, ME 04111
207-775-3131

Maryland

415 U.S. Customhouse
Gay and Lombard Sts.
Baltimore, MD 21202
301-962-3560

Massachusetts

10th Fl.
441 Stuart St.
Boston, MA 02116
617-233-2312

Michigan

445 Federal Bldg.
231 W. Lafayette
Detroit, MI 48226
313-226-3650

Rm. 288
Graduate School of Business
Administration
University of Michigan
Ann Arbor, MI 48104
313-994-3297

17 Fountain St. N.W.
Grand Rapids, MI 49503
616-456-2411

Minnesota

218 Federal Bldg.
110 S. Fourth St.
Minneapolis, MI 55401
612-725-2133

Mississippi

P.O. Box 849
2003 Walter Sillers Bldg.
Jackson, MS 39205
601-969-4388

Missouri

120 S. Central Ave.
St. Louis, MO 63105
314-425-3302, 3304

Rm. 1840
601 E. 12th St.
Kansas City, MO 64106
816-374-3142

Montana

210 Miners Bank Bldg.
Park St.
Butte, MT 59701
406-723-6561 ext 2317

Nebraska

Suite 703A, Capitol Plaza
1815 Capitol Ave.
Omaha, NE 68102
402-221-3665

Nevada

2028 Federal Bldg.
300 Booth St.
Reno, NV 89502
702-784-5203

New Jersey

Gateway Bldg., 4th Fl.
Market St. & Penn Plaza
Newark, NJ 07102
201-645-6214

New Mexico

Suite 1015
505 Marquette Ave. N.W.
Albuquerque, NM 87102
505-766-2386

New York

1312 Federal Bldg.
111 W. Huron St.
Buffalo, NY 14202
716-842-3208

Federal Office Bldg., 37th Fl.
26 Federal Plaza
Foley Square
New Yoirk, NY 10007
212-264-0634

North Carolina

203 Federal Bldg.
W. Market St.
P.O. Box 1950
Greensboro, NC 27402
919-378-5345

151 Haywood St.
Asheville, NC 28802
704-254-1981

Ohio

10504 Federal Office Bldg.
550 Main St.
Cincinnati, OH 45202
513-684-2944

Rm. 600
666 Euclid Ave.
Cleveland, OH 44114
216-522-4750

Oklahoma

4020 Lincoln Blvd.
Oklahoma City, OK 73105
405-231-5302

Oregon

Rm. 618
1220 S.W. 3rd Ave.
Portland, OR 97204
503-221-3001

Pennsylvania

9448 Federal Bldg.
600 Arch St.
Philadelphia, PA 19106
215-597-2850

2002 Federal Bldg.
1000 Liberty Ave.
Pittsburgh, PA 15222
412-644-2850

Puerto Rico

Rm. 659, Federal Bldg.
San Juan, PR 00918
890-763-6363 ext 555

Rhode Island

1 Weybosset Hill
Providence, RI 02903
401-277-2605 ext 22

South Carolina

2611 Forest Drive
Forest Center
Columbia, SC 29204
803-765-5345

Suite 631, Federal Bldg.
334 Meeting Place
Charleston, SC 29403
803-577-4361

Tennessee

Rm. 710
147 Jefferson Ave.
Memphis, TN 38103
901-521-3213

Rm. 1004
Andrew Jackson Office Bldg.
Nashville, TN 37219
615-749-5161

Texas

Rm. 7A5
1100 Commerce St.
Dallas, TX 75202
214-749-1515

1017 Old Federal Bldg.
201 Fannin St.
Houston, TX 77002
713-226-4231

37 N. Durango St.
San Antonio, TX 78285
512-227-9147

Utah

1203 Federal Bldg.
125 S. State St.
Salt Lake City, UT 84138
801-524-5116

Virginia

8010 Federal Bldg.
400 N. 8th St.
Richmond, VA 23240
804-782-2246

Washington

Rm. 706, Lake Union Bldg.
1700 Westlake Ave. N.
Seattle, WA 98109
206-442-5615

West Virginia

3000 New Federal Office Bldg.
500 Quarrier St.
Charleston, WV 25301
304-343-6181 ext 375

Wisconsin

Federal Bldg./U.S. Courthouse
517 E. Wisconsin Ave.
Milwaukee, WI 53202
414-224-3473

Wyoming

6022 O'Mahoney Federal Center
2120 Capitol Ave.
Cheyenne, WY 82001
307-778-2220 ext 2151

C1.11 ECONOMIC DEVELOPMENT ADMINISTRATION NATIONAL, REGIONAL, AND FIELD OFFICES

National Office

Department of Commerce
Washington, DC 20230
202-377-5113

Area Offices

Alabama

Rm. 732, Aronov Bldg.
474 S. Court St.
Montgomery, AL 36104
205-832-7125

Alaska

Suite 455
632 Sixth Ave.
Anchorage, AK 99501
907-265-5317, 5318

Arizona

Suite 512
112 N. Central Ave.
Phoenix, AZ 85004
602-261-3818

Arkansas

Rm. 312, Federal Bldg.
700 W. Capitol
Little Rock, AR 72201
501-378-5637

California

Suite 900
11777 San Vicente Blvd.
Los Angeles, CA 90049
213-824-7521

Rm. W-1146, New Federal Bldg.
2800 Cottage Way
Sacramento, CA 95825
916-484-4314

Suite 101
2502 Merced St.
Fresno, CA 93721
209-487-5356

Suite K
77 Jack London Square
Pakland, CA 94607
415-273-7081

Colorado

Suite 505
909 17th St.
Denver, CO 80202
303-837-3057

Connecticut

Sixth Fl.
60 Washington St.
Hartford, CT 06106
203-244-2336, 2686

Florida

Suite 203
547 N. Monroe St.
Tallahassee, FL 32304
904-224-8525

Georgia

Suite 700
1365 Peachtree St. N.E.
Atlanta, GA 30309
404-526-2857

Idaho

Suite 304
American Reserve Bldg.
2404 Bank Drive
Boise, ID 83075
208-342-2711 ext 2521

Illinois

Suite D
606 E. Main St.
Carbondale, IL 62901
618-549-0765

Indiana

Rm. 336, Federal Courts Bldg.
46 E. Ohio
Indianapolis, IN 46204
317-269-6210

Kentucky

Rm. 204
333 Waller Ave.
Lexington, KY 40507
606-252-2312 ext 2596

P.O. Box 241
Fountainbleu Motel, Office Annex
210 E. 9th St.
Hopkinsville, KY 42240
502-885-5311

Louisiana

Rm. 301-302
707 Florida
Baton Rouge, LA 70801
504-348-0181 ext 227

Maine

Rm. 607, Federal Bldg.
40 Western Ave.
Augusta, ME 04330
207-622-6171 ext 272

Maryland

Rm. 103
1419 Forest Drive
Annapolis, MD 20401
301-269-0177

Massachusetts

441 Stuart St.
Boston, MA 02116
617-223-6468

Michigan

Rm. 306
Capital Savings & Loan Bldg.
112 E. Allegan St.
Lansing, MI 48933
517-372-1910

Minnesota

Rm. 415, Federal Bldg.
Bemidji, MN 56601
218-751-4415

Rm. 407, Federal Bldg.
515 W. First St.
Duluth, MN 55802
218-783-9692 ext 326

Mississippi

Rm. 630, Milner Bldg.
210 Lamar St.
Jackson, MS 39201
601-969-4342

Missouri

Rm. 201, Crestwood Bank Bldg.
9705 U.S. Highway 66
St. Louis MO 63126
314-425-3309

Montana

Rm. 339, Federal Bldg.
N. Main St.
Butte, MT 59701
406-723-6561 ext 2381

New Hampshire

204 FOB
55 Pleasant St.
Concord, NH 03301
603-225-6450

New Jersey

Rm. 501, Federal Bldg.
402 E. State St.
Trenton, NJ 08608
609-599-3511 ext 244

New Mexico

Rm. 205
121 Sandoval St.
First Northern Plaza
Santa Fe, NM 87501
505-988-6557

New York

Rm. 939
100 State St.
Albany, NY 12207
518-472-3688

North Carolina

Rm. 314, Federal Bldg.
310 New Bern Ave.
Raleigh, NC 27611
919-755-4570

North Dakota

P.O. Box 1911
Bismarck, ND 58501
701-255-4011

Ohio

Rm. 405, Security Bank Bldg.
Athens, OH 45701
614-593-8146

Oklahoma

Rm. 815, Old Post Office Bldg.
N.W. Third and Harvey Sts.
Oklahoma City, OK 73102
405-736-4011 ext 4197

Oregon

Rm. 584, Pittock Bldg.
921 S.W. Washington St.
Portland, OR 97205
503-221-3078

Pennsylvania

Rm. 10424
William J. Green Jr. Federal Bldg.
600 Arch St.
Philadelphia, PA 19106
215-597-9523

Puerto Rico

Rm. 407, Pan American Bldg.
255 Avenida Ponce de Leon
Hato Rey, San Juan, PR 00917
809-763-6363 ext 436, 439

South Carolina

Rm. 204
2611 Forest Drive
Columbia, SC 29204
803-765-5676

South Dakota

Rm. 321, Federal Office Bldg.
Pierre, SD 57501
605-244-8280

Tennessee

Suite A-903
Federal Bldg. - U.S. Courthouse
Nashville, TN 37203
615-749-5911

Texas

Suite 600, American Bank Tower
221 W. Sixth St.
Austin, TX 78701
512-397-5317

1205 Texas Ave.
Rm. 416, Federal Bldg.
Lubbock, TX 79408
807-762-7661

Utah

Rm. 1205, Federal Bldg.
125 S. State St.
Salt Lake City, UT 84111
801-524-5119

Virginia

Rm. 8002, Federal Office Bldg.
400 N. 8th St.
Richmond, VA 23240
804-782-2567

Washington

4327 Rucker Ave.
Everett, WA 98203
206-258-2667

Suite 224, Lake Union Bldg.
1700 Westlake Ave. N.
Seattle, WA 98109
206-442-7556

West Virginia

B-020, Federal Bldg.
Beckley, WV 25801
304-253-2723

Rm. 304, New P.O. Bldg.
West Pike St.
Clarksburg, WV 26301
304-623-3461 ext 272, 273

Suite 319, The Prichard Bldg.
601 Ninth St.
Huntington, WV 25701
304-529-2311 ext 2591

Wisconsin

510 S. Barstow
Eau Claire, WI 54701
715-834-9508

C1.12 OFFICE OF MINORITY BUSINESS ENTERPRISE NATIONAL, REGIONAL, AND FIELD OFFICES

National Office

Department of Commerce
Washington, D.C. 20230
202-377-3024

Regional Offices

Suite 505
1371 Peachtree St. N.E.
Atlanta, GA 30309
404-526-5091

55 E. Monroe St.
Suite 1438
Chicago, IL 60603
312-353-8375

Suite 1702
1412 Main St.
Dallas, TX 75202
214-749-7581

Rm. 3714
26 Federal Plaza
New York, NY 10007
212-264-3262

Rm. 15043, Federal Bldg.
P.O. Box 36114
450 Golden Gate Ave.
San Francisco, CA 94102
415-556-7234

Suite 420
1730 K St. N.W.
Washington, DC 20006
202-634-7897

Field Offices

Suite 714
First American Bank Bldg.
Memphis, TN 38103
901-534-3216

Rm. 1100
Ainsley Bldg.
14 N.E. First Ave.
Miami, FL 33132
305-350-4721

908 S. 20th St.
Birmingham, AL 35205

100 Lincoln Bldg.
1367 E. 6th St.
Cleveland, OH 44114
216-522-3354

Suite 535
2 Gateway Center
4th and State
Kansas City, KS 66101
816-374-4561

Rm. 479, 4th Fl.
210 N. 12th St.
St. Louis, MO 63101
314-622-4311

Suite 1401
Western Bank Bldg.
505 Marquette Ave.
Albuquerque, NM 87101
505-766-3379

Rm. 616
Federal Bldg.
600 South St.
New Orleans, LA 70130
504-527-2935

Rm. B-412
Federal Bldg.
727 E. Durango
San Antonio, TX 78206
512-225-4416

441 Stuart St.
10th Fl.
Boston, MA 02116
617-223-5375

Suite 908
2500 Wilshire Blvd.
Los Angeles, CA 90057
213-688-7157

112 N. Central Ave.
Suite 515
Phoenix, AZ 85004
602-261-3503

Rm. 9436
600 Arch St.
Philadelphia, PA 19106
215-597-9236

C1.13 SUMMARY TAPE PROCESSING CENTERS, BUREAU OF THE CENSUS

Alabama

Department of Community Development
Rm. 1000, City Hall
Birmingham, AL 35205
205-254-2730

Graduate Program in Hospital and Health Administration
School of Community and Allied Health Resources
University of Alabama in Birmingham
Rm. 205 SCAHR
Birmingham, AL 35294
205-934-5661

University Computer Center
University of South Alabama
Mobila, AL 36608
205-460-6161

Center for Bus. and Econ. Research
University of Alabama
Box AK
University, AL 35486
205-348-6191

Alaska

Institute of Social and Economic Research
University of Alaska
Anchorage, AK 99504
907-276-5575

Fairbanks, AK 99701
907-479-7436

Arizona

Resource Consultants, Inc.
505 N. Alvernon Way
Tucson, AZ 85711
602-326-2449

Arkansas

Industrial Research and Extension Center
University of Arkansas
P.O. Box 3017
Little Rock, AR 72203
501-371-1971

California

Lawrence Berkeley Laboratory
Computer Science and Applied Mathematics Department
Berkeley, CA 94720
415-843-2740 ext 5063

Alfred Gobar Associates, Inc.
207 S. Brea Blvd.
Brea, CA 92621
714-529-9411

Urban Decision Systems, Inc.
P.O. Box 25953
2032 Armacost Ave.
Los Angeles, CA 90025
213-826-6596

Research Systems, Inc.
365 S. Meadows Ave.
Manhattan Beach, CA 90266
213-372-8838

Allstate Research Center
Allstate Insurance Co.
321 Middlefield Rd.
Menlo Park, CA 94025
415-324-2721

David Bradwell and Associates
Pier 3, The Embarcadero
San Francisco, CA 94111
415-433-7550

Wilbur Smith and Associates, Inc.
Rm. 1500
111 Pine St.
San Francisco, CA 94104
405-433-3840

Decision Making Information
Suite 800
2700 N. Main St.
Santa Ana, CA 92701
714-558-1321

Demographic Research Company
3104 Fourth St.
Santa Monica, CA 90405
213-392-4840

Speron, Inc.
14760 Oxnard St.
Van Nuys, CA 91401
213-873-4114

Colorado

Business Research Division
Graduate School of Business Administration
University of Colorado
Boulder, CO 80309
303-492-8227

Bureau of Business and Public Research
School of Business
University of Northern Colorado
Greeley, CO 80631
303-351-2080

Connecticut

ADVo-System, Inc.
239 Service Road W.
Hartford, CT 06101
203-525-9101

Social Science Data Center
University of Connecticut
Storrs, CT 06268
203-486-4440

District of Columbia

Applied Urbanetics, Inc.
Third Floor
1701 K St. N.W.
Washington, DC 20006
202-331-1800

Metropolitan Washington Council of Governments
1225 Connecticut Ave. N.W.
Washington, DC 20036
202-223-6800

Florida

Census Access Program
University of Florida Libraries
Library West 148
Gainsville, FL 32611
904-392-0361, 0359

Regional Information Coordinating Center
Tampa Bay Planning Council
Suite 540
St. Petersburg, FL 33713
813-898-0891

Applications Group
Computing Center
Florida State University
Tallahassee, FL 32306
904-599-4770

Electronic Data Processing Division
Department of General Services
State of Florida
Larson Bldg.
Tallahassee, FL 32304
904-488-4571

Georgia

Demographic Research and Training
Social Science Research Institute
University of Georgia
221 Baldwin Hall
Athens, GA 30601
404-542-5942

Office of Planning and Budget
State of Georgia
270 Washington St. S.W.
Atlanta, GA 30334
404-656-3868

Computer Center
Georgia State University
University Plaza
Atlanta, GA 30303
404-658-2639

Hawaii

Department of Budget and Finance
Electronic Data Processing Division
P.O. Box 150
Honolulu, HI 96810
808-548-5910

Idaho

Center for Research Grants and Contracts
Boise State University
1910 College Blvd.
Boise, ID 83725
208-385-1571

Illinois

Department of Sociology-Anthropology
Illinois State University
Normal, IL 61761
309-438-2387
or 436-7667

Indiana

Computer Center
University of Evansville
P.O. Box 329
Evansville, IN 47701
812-479-2451

Research Associates, Inc.
P.O. Box 44640
Indianapolis, IN 46244
317-263-6926

Iowa

Department of Sociology & Anthropology
Iowa State University
103 East Hall
Ames, IA 50011
515-294-8369

Institute of Urban and Regional Research
University of Iowa
102 Church St.
Iowa City, IA 52242
319-353-3862

Kansas

Institute for Social and Environmental Studies
University of Kansas
607 Blake Hall
Lawrence, KS 66045
913-864-3701

Louisiana

State Planning Office
4528 Bennington Drive
Baton Rouge, LA 70804
504-389-7041

Louisiana Computing Corporation
3444 Olympic Drive
Metairie, LA 70002
504-455-5500

Bureau of Business Research
College of Business Administration
Northeast Louisiana University
Monroe, LA 71201
318-372-2123

Research Division
College of Administration & Business
P.O. Box 5796
Ruston, LA 71270
318-257-3701

Maine

Public Affairs Research Center
Bowdoin College
Brunswick, ME 04011
207-725-8731

Maryland

BRC Associates, Inc.
Suite 211
7979 Old Georgetown Road
Bethesda, MD 20014
301-656-2996

System Sciences, Inc.
4720 Montgomery Lane
Bethesda, MD 20014
301-654-0300

Data Services Div.
Westat, Inc.
11600 Nevel St.
Rockville, MD 20852
301-881-5310

Massachusetts

Urban Data Processing, Inc.
20 South Ave.
Burlington, MA 01775
617-273-0900

Laboratory for Computer Graphics and Spatial Analysis
Harvard University
520 Gund Hall
48 Quincy St.
Cambridge, MA 02138
617-495-2526

Information Processing Services
Massachusetts Institute of Technology
Rm. 39-469
Cambridge, MA 02139
617-253-7044, 7769

Michigan

Inter-University Consortium for Political and Social Research
P.O. Box 1248
Ann Arbor, MI 48106
313-764-8508
or 763-5010

Information Services Office
SE Michigan Council of Governments
8th Fl., Book Bldg.
Detroit, MI 48226
313-961-4266

NE Michigan Council of Governments
P.O. Box 457
131 Shipp St.
Gaylord, MI 49735
517-732-3551

Tri-County Regional Planning Commission
2722 E. Michigan Ave.
P.O. Box 21217
Lansing, MI 48505
517-487-9424

Oakland County Planning Division
1200 N. Telegraph Rd.
Pontiac, MI 48053
313-858-0720

Minnesota

Minnesota Analysis and Planning System
415 Coffey Hall
Agricultural Extension Service
University of Minnesota
St. Paul, MN 55108
612-373-1225

Mississippi

Department of Sociology
Mississippi State University
P.O. Box Drawer C
State College, MS 39762
601-325-5024

Missouri

Public Affairs Information Service
University of Missouri-Columbia
311 Middlebush Hall
Columbia, MO 65201
314-882-8256

Office of Administration
Division of Budget and Planning
P.O. Box 809
Room B-9, Capitol Bldg.
Jefferson City, MO 65101
314-751-2073

Mid-America Regional Council
Third Fl.
20 W. Ninth St. Bldg.
Kansas City, MO 64105
816-474-4240

NLT Computer Services Corporation
P.O. Box 1432
Kansas City, MO 64141
816-471-5535

University of Missouri-St. Louis
Computer Center
8001 Natural Bridge Rd.
St. Louis, MO 63121
314-453-5131

Montana

Research Information Systems Division
Department of Community Affairs
Capital Station
Helena, MT 59601
406-449-2896

Nebraska

Academic Computing Services
University of Nebraska
Rm. 225, Nebraska Hall
Lincoln, NE 68508
402-472-3175

Metromail
Division of Metromedia
P.O. Box 81637
Lincoln, NE 68501
402-475-4591

Douglas County Systems and Data Processing Center
1910 Harney St.
Omaha, NE 68102
402-444-7265

Nevada

Central Data Processing Division
Department of General Services
Carson City, NV 89710
702-885-4091

New Jersey

Princeton-Rutgers Census Data Project
Princeton University Computer Center
87 Prospect Ave.
Princeton, NJ 08540
609-452-6052

New Mexico

Bureau of Business and Economics Research
Institute for Social Research and Development
Institute Building
University of New Mexico
Albuquerque, NM 87106
505-277-2216

New York

New York State Department of Commerce
99 Washington St.
Albany, NY 12245
518-474-6100

Community Health Information Profiles
Department of Soc. and Prevention Medicine
State University of New York at Buffalo
2211 Main St.
Buffalo, NY 14214
716-831-5521

National Planning Data Corp.
20 Terrace Hill, P.O. Box 610
Ithaca, NY 14850
607-273-8208

Market Statistics
633 Third Ave.
New York, NY 10017
212-986-4800

Tri-State Regional Planning Commission
World Trade Center
New York, NY 10048
212-938-3323

Technical Assistance Center
State University of New York
Plattsburgh, NY 12901
518-564-2214

Genesee Computer Center, Inc.
20 University Ave.
Rochester, NY 14605
716-232-7050

North Carolina

Social Science Data Library
Institute for Research in Social Science/UNC Computation Center
University of North Carolina at Chapel Hill
Chapel Hill, NC 27514
919-933-3061

System Sciences, Inc.
Box 2345
Chapel Hill, NC 27514
919-929-7116

Department of Cultural Resources
Division of State Library
109 E. Jones St.
Raleigh, NC 27611
919-829-3683

Ohio

Northeast Ohio Areawide Coordinating Agency
439 The Arcade
Cleveland, OH 44114
216-241-2414

Office of Population Statistics
Ohio Department of Economics and Community Development
24th Fl.
30 E. Broad St.
Box 100
Columbus, OH 43216
614-466-6963

Census Processing Center
Battelle-Columbus Laboratories
505 King Ave.
Columbus, OH 43201
614-424-6424 ext 2081

Oklahoma

University Computer Center
Oklahoma State University
Mathematical Sciences Bldg.
Stillwater, OK 74074
405-624-6301

Oregon

Bureau of Governmental Research and Service
P.O. Box 3177
Eugene, OR 97403
503-686-5234

Center for Population Research & Census
Portland State University
P.O. Box 751
Portland, OR 97207
503-229-3922

Pennsylvania

Robinson Associates, Inc.
Bryn Mawr Hall
15 Morris Ave.
Bryn Mawr, PA 19010
215-527-3100

Central Management Information Center
State of Pennsylvania
Bldg. #33, Bomb Rd.
Harrisburg International Airport
Middletown, PA 17057
717-787-7783

Delaware Valley Regional Planning Commission
Penn Towers Bldg.
1819 John F. Kennedy Blvd.
Philadelphia, PA 19103
215-568-3211

K. H. Thomas Associates
P.O. Box 1707
1009 Western Savings Bank Bldg.
Philadelphia, PA 19105
215-574-0463

ECCO Consulting, Inc.
607 Washington Rd.
Pittsburgh, PA 15228
412-561-5509

Innovative Systems, Inc.
341 Fourth Ave.
Pittsburg, PA 15222
412-391-2364

Southwestern Pennsylvania Regional Planning Commission
564 Forbes Ave.
Pittsburgh, PA 15219
412-391-4120

Data Access and Technical Assistance Program (EDCNP/King's College)
King's College
133 N. River St.
Wilkes-Barre, PA 18711
717-824-9931

York County Planning Commission
220 S. Duke St.
York, PA 17403
717-843-9954

Rhode Island

Social Science Data Center
Department of Sociology
Brown University
Maxey Hall
Providence, RI 02912
401-863-2550

South Carolina

Wilbur Smith & Associates, Inc.
4500 Jackson Blvd.
Columbia, SC 29202
803-771-8844

Tennessee

Bureau of Business and Economic Research
Memphis State University
Memphis, TN 31852
901-231-1281

Reg. and Urban Studies Information Center
Oak Ridge National Laboratory
P.O. Box X
Oak Ridge, TN 37830
615-483-8611 ext 30311 or 30353

Texas

Institute of Urban Studies
University of Texas at Arlington
P.O. Box 19069
Arlington, TX 76010
817-273-3071

Texas Natural Resources Informational System
P.O. Box 13087
Austin, TX 78711
512-475-3321

Houston-Galveston Area Council
Suite 200
3701 W. Alabama
P.O. Box 22777
Houston, TX 77027
713-627-3200

Urban Systems Laboratory
University of Houston
Houston, TX 77024
713-748-6600

Computer Services
University of Texas at Dallas
P.O. Box 688
Richardson, TX 75080
214-690-2252

Alamo Area Council of Governments
400 Three Americas Bldg.
San Antonio, TX 78205
512-225-5201

Utah

Population Research Laboratory
Utah State University
Logan, UT 84321
801-752-4100 ext 291

Bureau of Economic and Business Research
University of Utah
Rm. 404, College of Business Bldg.
Salt Lake City, UT 84112
801-322-7274

Virginia

Consolidated Analysis Centers, Inc.
1815 N. Ft. Myer Dr.
Arlington, VA 22209
703-841-7800

Tayloe Murphy Institute
University of Virginia
P.O. Box 6550
Charlottesville, VA 22906
804-924-7451

Division of Planning and Budget
Commonwealth of Virginia
Ninth Street Office Bldg.
Richmond, VA 23219
804-786-7771

Claritas Corporation
Suite 903
1911 N. Ft. Meyer Dr.
Rosslyn, VA 22209
703-841-9200

Data Use and Access Laboratories, Inc. (DUALabs)
Suite 900
1601 N. Kent St.
Rosslyn, VA 22209
703-525-1480

Washington

Population Studies Division
Office of Program Planning and Fiscal Management
State of Washington
House Office Bldg.
Olympia, WA 98504
206-753-5617

Social Data Processing Center
Department of Sociology
Washington State University
Todd Hall, Room 145
Pullman, WA 99163
509-335-8927

Urban Data Center
University of Washington
121 More Hall FX 10
Seattle, WA 98195
206-543-7625

West Virginia

Grants Information Division
Governor's Office of Federal-State Relations
State Capitol
Charleston, WV 25305
304-348-3878

Wisconsin

Management Information Systems Section
Bureau of Program Management
Department of Administration
Rm. B-140
1 West Wilson St.
Madison, WI 53702
608-266-1067

Wyoming

Division of Business and Economic Research
University of Wyoming
P.O. Box 3925
University Station
Laramie, WY 82070
307-766-5141

C1.14 TELEPHONE CONTACTS FOR DATA USERS, BUREAU OF THE CENSUS

(Area Code 301)

Acting Director	763-5192
Program and Policy Development Office (PPDO)	-2758
Congressional Liaison	-5360
Public Information Office (PIO)	-7273

Demographic Fields

Associate Director for Demographic Fields	-5167
Demographic Surveys Division (DSD)	-2777
Housing Division (HOUS)	-2863
International Statistical Programs Center (IPSC)	-2832
Office of Demographic Analysis (ODA)	-1774
Population Division (POP)	-7646
Statistical Methods Division (SMD)	-2672
Assistant Director for Demographic Censuses, and Chief, Demographic Census Staff (DCS)	-7670

Demographic Subject Matter Contacts

Age and Sex: United States	POP	-5368
States (age only)	POP	-5072
Aliens	POP	-7571
Americans Overseas	POP	-7890
Annexation Population Counts	POP	-5716
Apportionment	POP	-5161
Armed Forces	POP	-5368
Births and Birth Expectations: Fertility Statistics	POP	-5303
Census Tract Population	POP	-5161
Citizenship: Foreign Born Persons, Country of Birth; Foreign Stock Persons, Mother Tongue	POP	-7571
Commuting (Journey to Work): Means of Transportation; Place of Work	POP	-5226
Consumer Expenditure Survey	DSD	-2380
Consumer Purchases and Ownership of Durables	POP	-5032
Crime Victimization Survey	DSD	-1735
Crime, National Survey	ODA	-1765
Current Population Survey	DSD	-2773
Decennial Census: General Plans	DSD	-2748
Content and Tabulations	DSD	-7325
Minority Statistics Program	DSD	-5169
Disabled	POP	-5032
Education; School Enrollment	POP	-5050
Employment; Unemployment; Labor Force	POP	-2825
Families: Size; Number; Marital Status	POP	-5189
Farm Population	POP	-5161
Health Surveys	DSD	-5508
Housing: Housing Information, Decennial Census	HOUS	-2873
Annual Housing Survey	HOUS	-2881
Housing Vacancy Data	HOUS	-2880
Residential Finance	HOUS	-2866
Income Statistics: Decennial Census	POP	-5682
Current Surveys; Revenue Sharing	POP	-5060
Incorporated/Unincorporated Places	POP	-5161
Industry and Occupation Statistics (see also Economic Fields)	POP	-5144
Institutional Population	POP	-5189
International Population	ISPC	-2870
Land Area	POP	-5161
Longitudinal Surveys	DSD	-2764
Migration: Mobility	POP	-5255
Mortality and/or Death	POP	-5303
Population Count Complaints	POP	-5716
Population: General Information; Census data; Characteristics; Survey Data	POP	-5002/5020
Population Estimates and Projections: Estimates		
Counties and Local Areas; Revenue Sharing	POP	-7722
Congressional Districts	POP	-5072
Individual States; SMSA's	POP	-5313
United States (National)	POP	-5368
Estimates Research	POP	-7883
Federal-State Cooperative Program for Local Population Estimates	POP	-7722
Projections of the Population	POP	-5300
Poverty Statistics; Low Income Areas	POP	-5790
Prisoner Surveys' National Prisoner Statistics	DSD	-1832
National Prisoner Statistics	ODA	-1778
Race and Ethnic Statistics: Black, American Indians, and Other Races	POP	-7890
Spanish Population	POP	-5219
Religion	POP	-7571
Revenue Sharing	POP	-5179
Sampling Methods	SMD	-2672
Social Stratification	POP	-5050
Special Censuses	DCS	-5806
SMSA's: Area Definition and Total Population	POP	-5161
Special Surveys	DSD	-5507
Travel Surveys	DSD	-1798
Urban/Rural Residence	POP	-5161
Veteran Status	POP	-5050
Voting Registration	POP	-5050
Voting Rights	POP	-5072

Economic Fields

	(Area Code 301)
Associate Director for Economic Fields	763-5274
Business Division (BUS)	-7564
Construction Statistics Division (CSD)	-7163
Foreign Trade Division (FTD)	-5342
Governments Division (GOVS)	-7366
Industry Division (IND)	-5850
Assistant Director for Economic and Agriculture Censuses, and Chief, Economic Census Staff (ECS)	-7356
Agriculture Division (AGR)	-5230
Economic Surveys Division (ESD)	-7735

Economic Subject Matter Contacts

Agriculture:		
General Information	AGR	-5170
Crop Statistics	AGR	-1939
Farm Economics	AGR	-5819
Livestock Statistics	AGR	-1974
Special Surveys	AGR	-5914
Construction Statistics:		
Census/Industries Surveys	CSD	-5435
Special Trades: Contractors; General Contractor-Builder	CSD	-7547
Current Programs		
Construction Authorized by Building Permits (C40 Series); and Residential Demolitions (C45 Series)	CSD	-7244
Expenditures on Residential Additions, Alterations, Maintenance and Repairs, and Replacements (C50 Series)	CSD	-5717
Housing Starts (C20 Series); Housing Completions (C22 Series); and New Residential Construction in Selected SMSA's (C21 Series)	CSD	-7314
Price Indexes for New One-Family Homes Sold (C27 Series)	CSD	-7842
Sales of New One-Family Homes (C25 Series)	CSD	-7314
Value of New Construction Put in Place	CSD	-5717
County Business Patterns	ESD	-7642
Energy-Related Statistics	DIRS	-7184
Enterprise Statistics	ESD	-7086
Environmental Surveys	IND	-5616
Exports, Origin of	IND	-5616
Foreign Trade Information	FTD	-5140
Governments:		
Criminal Justice Statistics	GOVS	-2842
Eastern States Government Sector	GOVS	-7783
Western States Government Sector	GOVS	-5344
Employment	GOVS	-5086
Finance	GOVS	-5847
Governmental Organization	GOVS	-5308
Revenue Sharing	GOVS	-5272
Taxation	GOVS	-5302
Industry and Commodities Classification	ESD	-5449
Manufactures:		
Census/Annual Survey of Manufactures	IND	-7666
Subject Reports	INC	-5872
Durables	IND	-7304
Nondurables	IND	-2510
Current Programs	IND	-7800
Shipments, Inventories, and Orders	IND	-2502
Durables	IND	-2518
Nondurables	IND	-5911
Fuels/Electric Energy Consumed by Manufacturers	IND	-5938
Mineral Industries	IND	-5938
Minority Businesses	ESD	-7690
Puerto Rico:		
Censuses of Retail Trade, Wholesale Trade, and Selected Services Industries	BUS	-5282
Retail Trade:		
Census:	BUS	-7038
Monthly Retail Trade Report; Accounts Receivable; and Monthly Department Store Sales	BUS	-7128
Weekly Retail Sales Report; Advance Monthly Retail Sales; and Retail Inventories Survey	BUS	-7660
Selected Services Industries:		
Census	BUS	-7039
Current Services Reports	BUS	-7077
Transportation:		
Commodity Transportation Survey; Truck Inventory and Use; Domestic Movement of Foreign Trade Data	ESD	-5430
Wholesale Trade:		
Census	BUS	-5281
Current Wholesale Sales and Inventories; Green Coffee Survey; Canned Food Survey	BUS	-5294

User Services, Geographic Matters, Publications, and Field Operations

	(Area Code 301)
Associate Director for Administration and Field Operations	763-5238
Administrative Services Division (ASD)	-5400
Data User Services Division (DUSD)	-7720
Geography Division (GEO)	-5636
Assistant Director for Field Operations, and Chief, Field Division (FLD)	-5000
Data Preparation Division (DPD)	812-335-1344

User Services

		(Area Code 301)
Age Search	DUSD	763-7662
Bureau of the Census Catalog	DUSD	-5574
Census Procedures, History of	DUSD	-7337
Central City Profiles	DUSD	-2400
College Curriculum Support Project	DUSD	-7368
Computer Tapes; Computer Programs	DUSD	-2400
Data User News, Monthly Newsletter	DUSD	-7454
Data User Training:		
Seminars, Workshops, Training Courses, Conferences, and Exhibits	DUSD	-5293
National Services Program—Exhibits for Minority Organizations	DUSD	-1978
Indexes to 1970 Census Summary Tapes and to Selected 1970 Census Printed Reports	DUSD	-7368
Map Orders	DUSD	-2400
Microfilm	DUSD	-2400
Public Use Samples	DUSD	-7368
Special Tabulations	DUSD	-2400
Statistical Compendia:		
Congressional District Data Reports; County and City Data Book; Historical Statistics of the United States	DUSD	-5475
Statistical Abstract; Pocket Data Book	DUSD	-7024
Summary Tape Processing Centers	DUSD	-7454
Unpublished Census Tables	DUSD	-2400

Geographic Matters

Area Measurement and Centers of Population	GEO	-5707
Boundaries and Annexations	GEO	-5437
1970/1980 Census Geography	GEO	-2668
Computer Graphics and Computer Mapping	GEO	-7442
GBF/DIME System	GEO	-7315
Geographical Statistical Areas	GEO	-7291
Geographic Uses of Earth Resources Satellite Technology:		
United States	GEO	-5720
International	GEO	-5720
GE-50 Series Maps	GEO	-5035
Revenue Sharing Geography	GEO	-5437
Urban Atlas	GEO	-2668

Publications

Library	ASD	-5040
Publications Microfiche	ASD	-5042
Subscriber Services (Publications)	ASD	-7472

Field Operations

Census Bureau Regional Offices

Regional Directors	Data User Services Officer
Atlanta, GA 404-881-2271	404-881-2271
Boston, MA 617-223-2327	617-223-0668
Charlotte, NC 704-372-0711 ext. 351	704-372-0711 ext 351
Chicago, IL 312-353-6251	312-353-0980
Dallas, TX 214-749-2814	214-749-2394
Denver, CO 303-234-3924	303-234-3924
Detroit, MI 313-226-7742	—
Kansas City, KS 816-374-4601	816-374-4601
Los Angeles, CA 213-824-7317	213-824-7291
New York, NY 212-264-3860	—
Philadelphia, PA 215-597-4920	—
Seattle, WA 206-442-7800	206-442-7080

Statistical and Survey Methodology

(Area Code 301)

Associate Director for Statistical Standards and Methodology		763-7247
Center for Census Use Studies (CCUS)		-7490
Research Center for Measurement Methods (RCMM)		-7028
Assistant Director for Statistical Standards and Methodology, and Chief, Statistical Research Division (SRD)		-2562
Chief Census Research and Technical Advisor		-7650

Subject Matter Contacts

(Area Code 301)

Census Use Study Publications	CCUS	763-2428
Computer Graphics and Computer Mapping—Specific User Applications	CCUS	-2650
GBF/DIME System—Specific User Applications	CCUS	-2650
GBF/DIME Workshops	CCUS	-2428
Survey Methodology Information System	SRD	-7600

C1.15 COUNTRY MARKETING MANAGERS, BUREAU OF INTERNATIONAL COMMERCE

Country Marketing Managers

Africa (sub. Sahara)	202-377-4927
Europe	
France and Benelux Countries	-4504
Germany and Austria	-5228
Italy, Greece, and Turkey	-3944
Nordic Countries	-3848
Spain, Portugal, Switzerland, and Yugoslavia	-2795
United Kingdom and Canada	-4421
Far East	
Australia and New Zealand	-3646
East Asia and the Pacific	-5401
Japan	-2425
South Asia	-2522
Latin America	
Brazil, Argentina Paraguay, and Uruguay	-5427
Mexico, Central America, and Panama	-2314
Remainder of South America and Caribbean Countries	-2995

Commerce Action Group for the Near East

North Africa	-5737
Near East	
Bahrain, Iraq, Jordan, Kuwait, Lebanon, Oman, Peoples Democratic Republic of Yemen, Quatar, Saudi Arabia, Syria, United Arab Emirates, Yemen Arab Republic	-5767
Iran, Israel, Egypt	-3752

Bureau of East West Trade

Eastern Europe	-2645
USSR	-4655
People's Republic of China	-3583

C1.16 MINORITY ENTERPRISE SMALL BUSINESS INVESTMENT COMPANY FIELD OFFICES

Alabama

Commercial Investment Resources
19 W. Oxmoor Rd.
Birmingham, AL 35209

Alaska

Alyeska Investment Company
1815 S. Bragaw St.
Anchorage, AK 99504

Arizona

Associated Southwest Investors, Inc.
114 W. Adams
Phoenix, AZ 85003

Arkansas

Venture Capital, Inc.
975 Tower Bldg.
P.O. Box 1343
Little Rock, AR 72203

California

Fong Venture Capital Corp.
2245 Parktown Circle
Sacramento, CA 95825

Business Equity and Development Corp.
1411 W. Olympic Blvd.
Los Angeles, CA 90015

Opportunity Capital Corp. of California
680 Beach St.
San Francisco, CA 94109

Risk Capital Funding, Inc.
16055 Venture Blvd.
Encino, CA 91316

Southern California Minority Capital Corp.
2651 S. Western Ave.
Los Angeles, CA 90018

The Chinese Investment Co. of California
1017 Wilshire Blvd.
Los Angeles, CA 90017

Space Ventures, Inc.
500 E. Carson Plaza Dr.
Carson, CA 90745

Telacu Investment Co., Inc.
1330 S. Atlantic Blvd.
E. Los Angeles, CA 90722

MCA New Ventures, Inc.
100 Universal City Plaza
Universal City, CA 91608

Connecticut

Business Ventures, Inc.
226 Dixwell Ave.
New Haven, CT 06511

Cominvest of Hartford, Inc.
18 Asylum St.
Hartford, CT 06103

Hartford Community Capital Corp.
70 Farmington Ave.
Hartford, CT 06101

Florida

Allied Investment Developers Inc.
1200 Biscayne Blvd.
Miami, FL 33132

Burger King MESBIC, Inc.
7360 N. Kendall Dr.
Miami, FL 33156

Florida Crown MESBIC
604 Hogan St.
Jacksonville, FL 32202

Urban Ventures, Inc.
4680 N.W. 7th Ave.
Miami, FL 33127

Georgia

ECCO MESBIC, Inc.
Central Administration Bldg.
Mayfield, GA 31509

Enterprises Now, Inc.
2001 Martin Luther King Jr. Dr.
Atlanta, GA 30310

Hawaii

Pacific Venture Capital, Ltd.
1427 Dillingham Blvd.
Honolulu, HI 96817

Illinois

NIA Corp.
2400 S. Michigan Ave.
Chicago, IL 60601

Amoco Venture Capital Co.
200 E. Randolph Dr.
Chicago, IL 60601

Chicago Community Ventures Inc.
19 S. LaSalle St.
Chicago, IL 60603

Combined Opportunities, Inc.
5050 N. Broadway
Chicago, IL 60640

The Urban Fund, Inc.
300 N. State St.
Chicago, IL 60610

CEDCO Capital Corp.
162 N. State St.
Chicago, IL 60601

Tower Ventures, Inc.
Sears Tower
Chicago, IL 60684

Indiana

Indianapolis Business Investment Company
5750 N. Michigan Rd. N.W.
Indianapolis, IN 46208

Minority Venture Co. Inc.
Knute Rockne Memorial Bldg.
Notre Dame, IN 46556

Kentucky

Equal Opportunity Finance, Inc.
P.O. Box 1915
Louisville, KY 40201

Financial Opportunities, Inc.
981 S. Third St.
Louisville, KY 40203

Louisiana

Gulf South Venture Corp.
821 Gravier St.
New Orleans, LA 70112

SCDF Investment Corp.
P.O. Box 3885
Lafayette, LA 70501

Louisiana Venture Capital Corp.
315 North St.
Natchitoches, LA 71457

Edict Investment Company
7887 Walmsley Ave.
New Orleans, LA 70125

Business Capital Corp.
1732 Canal St.
New Orleans, LA 70112

Maryland

Baltimore Community Investment Company
1925 Eutaw Place
Baltimore, MD 21217

Massachusetts

Greater Springfield Investment Corp.
121 Chestnut St.
Springfield, MA 01103

Massachusetts Venture Capital Corp.
141 Milk St.
Boston, MA 02109

W.C.C.I. Capital Corp.
791 Main St.
Worcester, MA 01610

Michigan

Independence Capital Formation, Inc.
3049 Grand Blvd.
Detroit, MI 48202

Motor Enterprises, Inc.
3044 W. Grand Blvd.
Detroit, MI 48202

Pooled Resources Investing in Minority Enterprises, Inc.
1845 David Whitney Bldg.
Detroit, MI 48226

Minnesota

Paulucci Venture Capital Corp.
P.O. Box 6509
duluth, MN 55806

Mississippi

INVESAT Capital Corp.
1414 Deposit Guarantee Bldg.
Jackson, MS 39201

New Jersey

Broad Arrow Investment Corp.
P.O. Box 2231R
Morristown, NJ 07960

Rutgers Minority Investment Co.
92 New St.
Newark, NJ 07102

New York

BanCap Corp.
420 Lexington Ave.
New York, NY 10017

Capital Formation MESBIC, Inc.
5 Beekman St.
New York, NY 10038

CEDC MESBIC, Inc.
106 Main St.
Hempstead, NY 11550

Coalition SBIC
1270 Avenue of the Americas
New York, NY 10017

ODA Capital Corp.
125 Heyward St.
Brooklyn, NY 11206

Minority Equity Capital Co.
470 Park Ave. S.
New York, NY 10016

North Street Capital Corp.
250 North St.
White Plaines, NY 10625

Pioneer Capital Corp.
1440 Broadway
New York, NY 10018

Equitable Life Community Enterprise Corp.
1285 Avenue of the Americas
New York, NY 10019

North Carolina

Forsyth County Investment Corp.
Fourth and Liberty Sts.
Winston-Salem, NC 27101

Ohio

Dayton MESBIC, Inc.
40 W. 4th St.
Dayton, OH 45402

Glenco Enterprises, Inc.
1464 E. 105 St.
Cleveland, OH 44106

Oklahoma

American Indian Investment Opportunities, Inc.
555 Constitution St.
Norman, OK 73069

Pennsylvania

Cottman Capital Corp.
575 Virginia Ave.
Ft. Washington, PA 19034

Alliance Enterprise Corp.
1616 Walnut St.
Philadelphia, PA 19103

Greater Philadelphia Venture Capital Corporation, Inc.
225 S. 15th St.
Philadelphia, PA 19102

Progress Venture Capital Corp.
1501 N. Broad St.
Philadelphia, PA 19122

Puerto Rico

North American Investment Corp.
Banco de Ponce Bldg.
Hato Rey, PR 00918

Texas

MESBIC Financial Corp. of Dallas
7701 Stemmons Freeway
Dallas, TX 75247

Utah

First Venture Capital Corp.
47 E. 7200 S.
Midvale, UT 84047

Virginia

East West United Investment Company
1340 Old Chain Bridge Rd.
McLean, VA 22101

Norfolk Investment Co. Inc.
203 Granby St.
Norfolk, VA 23510

Washington

Model Capital Corp.
105 - 14th Ave.
Seattle, WA 98122

MESBIC of Washington, Inc.
120 - 23rd Ave. E.
Seattle, WA 98112

Washington, D.C.

Minority Investment Co., Inc.
1019 - 19th St. N.W.
Washington, DC 20036

MODECO Investment Co.
1120 Connecticut Ave. N.W.
Washington, DC 20036

Wisconsin

REC Business Opportunities Corp.
316 Fifth St.
Racine, WI 53403

SC Opportunities, Inc.
1112 7th Ave.
Monroe, WI 53566

C1.17 NATIONAL TECHNICAL INFORMATION SERVICE NATIONAL OFFICE AND TELEPHONE NUMBERS

National Office

Department of Commerce
5285 Port Royal Road
Springfield, VA 22161
703-321-8525

Special Telephone Numbers

Rush Handling
703-557-4700

Telex
89-9405

Telecopier or 3-M Facsimile Service
703-321-8547
202-724-3378

Pick-Up Service
703-557-4650

Information
202-724-3382
-3383
-3509

Order Follow-Up
703-557-4660

Telephone Orders for Documents and Reports
703-557-4650

Subscriptions
703-557-4630

Selected Research in Microfiche SRIM)
703-557-4630

NTISearches and On-Line Searches
703-557-4642

Customer Accounts
703-557-4770

Computer Products
703-557-4763

Department of Defense

C1.20 DEFENSE CONTRACT ADMINISTRATION REGIONAL AND DISTRICT OFFICES

Regional Offices

805 Walker St.
Marietta, GA 30060
404-424-6000 ext 231

666 Summer St.
Boston, MA 02210
617-542-6000 ext 886

O'Hare International Airport
P.O. Box 66475
Chicago, IL 60666
312-694-6390, 6391

Federal Office Bldg., Rm. 1821
1240 E. 9th St.
Cleveland, OH 44199
216-522-5122, 5150

500 S. Ervay St.
Dallas, TX 75201
214-744-4581 ext 205

11099 S. LaCienega Blvd.
Los Angeles, CA 90045
213-643-0620, 0621

60 Hudson St.
New York, NY 10013
212-264-0833, 0834

2800 S. 20th St.
P.O. Box 7478
Philadelphia, PA 19101
215-271-4006, 4007

1136 Washington Ave.
St. Louis, MO 63101
314-268-6223

District Offices

908 S. 20th St.
Birmingham, AL 35205
205-254-1460

3555 Maguire Blvd.
Orlando, FL 32803
305-894-7711 ext 281

96 Murphy Rd.
Hartford, CT 06114
203-244-3336

U.S. Courthouse and Federal Office Bldg.
100 State St.
Rochester, NY 14614
716-263-6419

Finance Center, Bldg. 1
United States Army
Fort Benjamin Harrison, IN 46249
317-546-9211 ext 3155

744 N. 4th St.
Milwaukee, WI 53203
414-272-8180 ext 207

McNamara Federal Office Bldg.
477 Michigan Ave.
Detroit, MI 48226
313-226-5180

3800 N. Central Ave.
Phoenix, AZ 85012
602-261-4467

866 Malcolm Rd.
Burlingame, CA 94010
415-692-0300 ext 523

Bldg. 5D
U.S. Naval Support Activity
Seattle, WA 98115
206-527-3451

605 Stewart Ave.
Garden City, L.I., NY 11533
516-741-8000 ext 379

240 Route 22
Springfield, NJ 07081
201-379-7950

300 E. Joppa Rd.
Towson, MD 21204
301-828-1545

Federal Bldg.
Fort Snelling
Twin Cities, MN 55111
612-725-3808

C1.21 DEFENSE SUPPLY AGENCY NATIONAL AND REGIONAL PROCUREMENT OFFICES

National Office

Defense Supply Agency Headquarters
Cameron Station
5010 Duke St.
Alexandria, VA 22314
202-274-6471

Defense Supply Centers

Defense Construction Supply Center
3990 E. Broad St.
Columbus, OH 43215
614-236-3541, 3735

Defense Electronics Supply Center
1507 Wilmington Pike
Dayton, OH 45444
513-296-5231, 5232

Defense Fuel Supply Center
Cameron Station
5010 Duke St.
Alexandria, VA 22314
202-274-7428

Defense General Supply Center
Bellwood, Petersburg Pike
Richmond, VA 23297
804-275-3617, 3287

Defense Industrial Supply Center
700 Robbins Ave.
Philadelphia, PA 19111
215-697-2747, 2748

Defense Personnel Support Center
2800 S. 20th St.
Philadelphia, PA 19101
215-271-2321

Defense Subsistence Regions

Defense Subsistence Region
Alameda, DPSC
2155 Mariner Square Loop
Alameda, CA 94501
415-869-2051, 2052

Defense Subsistence Region
Pacific, DPSC
Bldg. 476, Naval Supply Center
Pearl Harbor, HI 96813

Defense Subsistence Office
Fort Worth, DPSC
Federal Center, Bldg. 23, Rm. 7
P.O. Box 6838
Fort Worth, TX 76115
817-924-3228

Defense Subsistence Office
Cheatam, DPSC
Cheatam Annex
Williamsburg, VA 23185
804-887-7246

Defense Subsistence Office
Kansas City, DPSC
Rm. 1908
911 Walnut St.
Kansas City, MO 64108
816-374-5271

Defense Subsistence Office
Chicago, DPSC
14th Fl.
55 E. Jackson Blvd.
Chicago, IL 60605
312-353-5067

Defense Subsistence Office
New Orleans, DPSC
4400 Dauphine St.
New Orleans, LA 74140
504-948-5272

Depots

Defense Depot Memphia
Memphis, TN 38114
901-744-5652

Defense Depot Ogden
Odgen, UT 84407
801-399-7347

Defense Depot Tracy
Tracy, CA 95376
209-835-0800 ext 205

Defense Industrial Plant Equipment Center
Memphis, TN 38114
901-744-5671

Department of Health, Education, and Welfare

C1.30 SOCIAL SECURITY REGIONAL OFFICES AND PROGRAM SERVICE CENTERS

Regional Offices

Rm. 1100-A
JFK Federal Bldg.
Boston, MA 02203
617-223-6810

Rm. 2719
300 S. Wacker Dr.
Chicago, IL 60606
312-353-4247

Rm. 240
50 Seventh St. N.E.
Atlanta, GA 30323
404-257-5961

3521-35 Market St.
P.O. Box 8788
Philadelphia, PA 19101
215-596-6941

Rm. 4033, Federal Bldg.
26 Federal Plaza
New York, NY 10007
212-264-3915

Rm. 431-A, Federal Bldg.
601 E. 12th St.
Kansas City, MO 64106
816-758-3701

Rm. 2535
1200 Main Tower Bldg.
1200 Commerce St.
Dallas, TX 75202
214-729-4210

Rm. 8005, Federal Bldg.
1961 Stout St.
Denver, CO 80294
303-327-2388

26th Fl.
100 Van Ness Ave.
San Francisco, CA 94102
415-556-4910

Rm. 2068
Arcade Plaza Bldg., MS-201
1321 Second Ave.
Seattle, WA 98101
206-399-0417

Program Service Centers

Northeastern Program Service Center
96-05 Horace Harding Expressway
Flushing, NY 11368

Mid-Atlantic Program Service Center
300 Spring Garden St.
Philadelphia, PA 19123

Southeastern Program Service Center
2001 Twelfth Ave. N.
Birmingham, AL 35285

Great Lakes Program Service Center
600 W. Madison St.
Chicago, IL 60606

Mid-America Program Service Center
601 E. Twelfth St.
Kansas City, MO 64106

Western Program Service Center
P.O. Box 2000
Richmond, CA 94801

C1.31 NATIONAL INSTITUTE OF OCCUPATIONAL SAFETY AND HEALTH NATIONAL AND REGIONAL OFFICES

National Office

5600 Fishers Lane
Rockville, MD 20852
301-443-2140

Regional Offices

Region 1

JFK Federal Bldg.
Government Center
Boston, MA 02203
617-223-6668

Region 2

Federal Bldg.
26 Federal Plaza
New York, NY 10007
212-264-2485

Region 3

P.O. Box 13716
Philadelphia, PA 19101
215-596-6716

Region 4

50 Seventh St. N.E.
Atlanta, GA 30323
404-526-5474

Region 5

300 S. Wacker Dr.
Chicago, IL 60607
312-353-1710

Region 6

Rm. 1700-A
1200 Main Tower Bldg.
Dallas, TX 75202
214-655-3081

Region 7

601 E. 12th St.
Kansas City, MO 64106
816-374-5332

Region 8

9017 Federal Bldg.
19th & Stout Sts.
Denver, CO 80202
303-837-3979

Region 9

50 Fulton St. (223 FOB)
San Francisco, CA 94102
415-556-3781

Region 10

Arcade Bldg.
1321 Second Ave.
Seattle, WA 98101
206-442-0530

Department of Housing and Urban Development

C1.40 DEPARTMENT OF HOUSING AND URBAN DEVELOPMENT NATIONAL, REGIONAL, AND AREA OFFICES

National Office

451 Seventh St. S.W.
Washington, DC 20410
202-655-4000

Regional and Area Offices

Region 1
(Connecticut, Maine, Massachusetts, New Hampshire, Rhode Island, Vermont)

JFK Federal Bldg.
Boston, MA 02203

Area Offices: Manchester, N.H.; Boston, Mass.; Hartford, Conn.

Region 2
(New Jersey, New York, Puerto Rico, Virgin Islands)

26 Federal Plaza
New York, NY 10007

Area Offices: New York, N.Y.; Newark, N.J.; Camden, N.J.; Buffalo, N.Y.; San Juan, P.R.

Region 3
(Delaware, District of Columbia, Maryland, Pennsylvania, Virginia, West Virginia)

Curtis Bldg.
6th and Walnut Sts.
Philadelphia, PA 19106

Area Offices: Pittsburgh, Pa.; Philadelphia, Pa.; District of Columbia; Baltimore, Md.; Richmond, Va.

Region 4
(Alabama, Florida, Georgia, Kentucky, Mississippi, North Carolina, South Carolina, Tennessee)

Peachtree—Seventh Bldg.
50 Seventh St. N.E.
Atlanta, GA 30323

Area Offices: Birmingham, Ala.; Jacksonville, Fla.; Atlanta, Ga.; Louisville, Ky.; Jackson, Miss.; Greensboro, N.C.; Columbia, S.C.; Knoxville, Tenn.

Region 5
(Illinois, Indiana, Minnesota, Michigan, Ohio, Wisconsin)

300 S. Wacker Dr.
Chicago, IL 60606

Area Offices: Detroit, Mich.; Chicago, Ill.; Indianapolis, Ind.; Minneapolis, Minn.; Columbus, Ohio; Milwaukee, Wisc.

Region 6
(Arkansas, Louisiana, New Mexico, Oklahoma, Texas)

New Dallas Federal Bldg.
1100 Commerce St.
Dallas, TX 75202

Area Offices: Dallas, Tex.; Oklahoma City, Okla.; San Antonio, Tex.; New Orleans, La.; Little Rock, Ark.

Region 7
(Iowa, Kansas, Missouri, Nebraska)

Federal Office Building
911 Walnut St.
Kansas City, MO 64106

Area Offices: Kansas City, Kans.; St. Louis, Mo.; Omaha, Nebr.

Region 8
(Colorado, Montana, North Dakota, South Dakota, Utah, Wyoming)

Federal Bldg.
19tha and Stout Sts.
Denver, CO 80202

No Area Offices
Insuring Offices: Casper, Wyo.; Helena, Mont.; Fargo, N.D.; Sioux Falls, S.D.; Salt Lake City, Utah

Region 9
(Arizona, California, Hawaii, Nevada,, Guam, American Samoa)

450 Golden Gate Ave.
P.O. Box 36003
San Francisco, CA 94102

Area Offices: San Francisco, Calif.; Los Angeles, Calif.

Region 10
(Alaska, Idaho, Oregon, Washington)

Arcade Plaza Bldg.
1321 Second Ave.
Seattle, WA 98101

Area Offices: Seattle, Wash.; Portland, Ore.

C1.41 FEDERAL DISASTER ASSISTANCE ADMINISTRATION NATIONAL AND REGIONAL OFFICES

National Office

451 Seventh St. S.W.
Washington, DC 20410
202-655-4000

Regional Offices

Region 1
(Connecticut, Maine, Massachusetts, New Hampshire, Rhode Island, Vermont)

Rm. 710
150 Causeway St.
Boston, MA 02114
617-223-4271

Region 2
(New Jersey, New York, Puerto Rico, Virgin Islands)

Rm. 1349
26 Federal Plaza
New York, NY 10007
212-264-8980

Region 3
(Delaware, District of Columbia, Maryland, Pennsylvania, Virginia, West Virginia)

Suite 1426, Curtis Bldg.
625 Walnut St.
Philadelphia, PA 19106
215-597-9416

Region 4
(Alabama, Canal Zone, Florida, Georgia Kentucky, Mississippi, North Carolina, South Carolina, Tennessee)

Suite 750
1375 Peachtree St. N.E.
Atlanta, GA 30309
404-285-3641

Region 5
(Illinois, Indiana, Michigan, Minnesota, Ohio, Wisconsin)

Rm. 520
300 S. Wacker Dr.
Chicago, IL 60606
312-353-1500

Region 6
(Arkansas, Louisiana, New Mexico, Oklahoma, Texas)

Rm. 13C28, Federal Bldg.
1100 Commerce St.
Dallas, TX 75202
214-749-1411

Region 7
(Iowa, Kansas, Missouri, Nebraska)

Old Federal Office Bldg.
911 Walnut St.
Kansas City, MO 64106
816-758-5912

Region 8
(Colorado, Montana, North Dakota, South Dakota, Utah, Wyoming)

Rm. 1140, Lincoln Tower Bldg.
1860 Lincoln St.
Denver, CO 80203
303-327-2891

Region 9
(American Samoa, Arizona, California, Guam, Hawaii, Nevada, Trust Territory of the Pacific Islands)

Mezzanine
120 Montgomery St.
San Francisco, CA 94104
415-556-8794

Region 10
(Alaska, Idaho, Oregon, Washington)

Rm. M-16, Arcade Bldg.
1319 2nd Ave.
Seattle, WA 98101
206-399-1310
206-442-1310

Department of the Interior

C1.50 GEOLOGICAL SURVEY NATIONAL AND FIELD OFFICES AND EROS APPLICATIONS ASSISTANCE FACILITIES

National Office

National Center
12201 Sunrise Valley Dr.
Reston, VA 22092
703-860-7444

Field Offices

Alaska

108 Skyline Bldg.
508 Second Ave.
Anchorage, AK 99501
907-277-0577

California

7638 Federal Bldg.
300 N. Los Angeles St.
Los Angeles, CA 90012
213-688-2850

504 Custom House
555 Battery St.
San Francisco, CA 94111
415-556-5627

Colorado

1012 Federal Bldg.
1961 Stout St.
Denver, CO 80202
303-837-4169

District of Columbia

1028 GSA Bldg.
19th and F Sts. N.W.
Washington, DC 20244
202-343-8073

Texas

1C45 Federal Bldg.
1100 Commerce St.
Dallas, TX 75202
214-749-3230

Utah

8102 Federal Bldg.
125 S. State St.
Salt Lake City, UT 84138
801-524-5652

Virginia

1C402 National Center, STOP 302
12201 Sunrise Valley Dr.
Reston, VA 22092
703-860-6167

Washington

678 U.S. Courthouse
W. 920 Riverside Ave.
Spokane, WA 99201
509-456-2524

EROS Applications Assistance Facilities

Alaska

University of Alaska
Geophysical Institute
College, AK 99701
907-479-7558

Arizona

Suite 1880, Valley Center Bldg.
Phoenix, AZ 85073
602-261-3188

California

122 Building 3
345 Middlefield Rd.
Menlo Park, CA 94025
415-323-8111 ext 2157

Canal Zone

HQ Inter American Geodetic Survey
Headquarters Bldg.
Drawer 934
Fort Clayton, Canal Zone
202-697-1201 ext 83-3897

Colorado

Box 25046, STOP 504
Denver Federal Center
Denver, CO 80225
303-234-4879

Missouri

National Space Technological Laboratories
Bay St. Louis, MO 39520
601-688-3451

South Dakota

EROS Data Center
Geological Survey
Sioux Falls, SD 57198
605-594-6111

Virginia

National Center, STOP 730
1925 Newton Square E.
Reston, VA 22090
703-860-7868

Department of Justice

C1.60 ANTITRUST DIVISION NATIONAL AND FIELD OFFICES

National Office

Constitution Ave. and 10th St. N.W.
Washington, DC 20530
202-737-8200

Field Offices

California

Box 36046
450 Golden Gate Ave.
San Francisco, CA 94102

U.S. Courthouse
Los Angeles, CA 90012

Georgia

1776 Peachtree St. N.W.
Atlanta, GA 30309

Illinois

219 S. Dearborn St.
Chicago, IL 60604

New York

26 Federal Plaza
New York, NY 10007

Ohio

New Federal Bldg.
Cleveland, OH 44199

Pennsylvania

501 U.S. Customs House
Philadelphia, PA 19106

Department of Labor

C1.70 BUREAU OF LABOR STATISTICS NATIONAL AND REGIONAL OFFICES

National Office

Department of Labor
200 Constitution Ave. N.W.
Washington, DC 20210
202-523-8165

Regional Offices

Region 1
(Connecticut, Maine, Massachusetts, New Hampshire, Rhode Island, Vermont)

Rm. 1603-B, JFK Government Center
Boston, MA 02203
617-223-6727

Region 2
(New Jersey, New York, Puerto Rico, Virgin Islands, Canal Zone)

1515 Broadway
New York, NY 10036
212-971-5401

Region 3
(Delaware, District of Columbia, Maryland, Pennsylvania, Virginia, West Virginia)

3535 Market St.
Philadelphia, PA 19104
215-506-1154

Region 4
(Alabama, Florida, Georgia, Kentucky, Mississippi, North Carolina, South Carolina, Tennessee)

Rm. 540
1371 Peachtree St. N.E.
Atlanta, GA 30309
404-526-5416

Region 5
(Illinois, Indiana, Michigan, Minnesota, Ohio, Wisconsin)

9th Fl., Federal Office Bldg.
230 S. Dearborn St.
Chicago, IL 60604
312-353-7226

Region 6

(Arkansas, Louisiana, New Mexico, Oklahoma, Texas)

2nd Fl., 555 Griffin Square Bldg.
Dallas, TX 75202
214-749-3641

Regions 7 and 8

(Colorado, Iowa, Kansas, Missouri, Montana, Nebraska, North Dakota, South Dakota, Utah, Wyoming)

Rm. 1500, Federal Office Bldg.
911 Walnut St.
Kansas City, MO 64106
816-374-2378

Regions 9 and 10

(Alaska, Arizona, California, Hawaii, Idaho, Nevada, Oregon, Washington)

450 Golden Gate Ave.
P.O. Box 36017
San Francisco, CA 94102
415-556-3178

C1.71 LABOR-MANAGEMENT SERVICES ADMINISTRATION NATIONAL, REGIONAL, AND AREA OFFICES

National Office

Department of Labor
200 Constitution Ave. N.W.
Washington, DC 20210
202-523-8165

Regional Offices

Regions 1 and 2

(Connecticut, Maine, Massachusetts, New Hampshire, Rhode Island, Vermont, New York, New Jersey, Puerto Rico, Virgin Islands, Canal Zone)

Rm. 3515
1515 Broadway
New York, NY 10036
212-971-7031

Region 3

(Delaware, District of Columbia, Maryland, Pennsylvania, Virginia, West Virginia)

14120 Gateway Bldg.
3535 Market St.
Philadelphia, PA 19104
215-596-1134

Region 4

(Alabama, Florida, Georgia, Kentucky, North Carolina, Mississippi, South Carolina, Tennessee)

Rm. 300
1371 Peachtree St. N.E.
Atlanta, GA 30309
404-526-5237

Region 5

(Illinois, Indiana, Michigan, Minnesota, Ohio, Wisconsin)

Rm. 1060, Federal Office Bldg.
230 S. Dearborn St.
Chicago, IL 60604
312-353-1920

Regions 6, 7, and 8

(Arkansas, Louisiana, New Mexico, Oklahoma, Texas, Colorado, Iowa, Kansas, Missouri, Montana, Nebraska, North Dakota, South Dakota, Utah, Wyoming)

Rm. 2200, Federal Office Bldg.
911 Walnut St.
Kansas City, MO 64106
816-374-5131

Regions 9 and 10

(Alaska, Arizona, California, Hawaii, Idaho, Nevada, Oregon, Washington)

Rm. 9061, Federal Office Bldg.
450 Golden Gate Ave.
San Francisco, CA 94102
415-556-5915

Area Offices

California

Rm. 7731, Federal Bldg.
300 N. Los Angeles St.
Los Angeles, CA 90012
213-688-4975

Colorado

Rm. 15415, Federal Bldg.
1961 Stout St.
Denver, CO 80202
303-837-3203

District of Columbia

Rm. 509, Vanguard Bldg.
1111 20th St. N.W.
P.O. Box 19257
Washington, DC 20036
202-254-6510

Florida

18350 N.W. 2nd Ave.
Miami, FL 33169
305-350-4611

Hawaii

Rm. 601
1833 Kalakaua Ave.
Honolulu, HI 96815
808-955-0259

Louisiana

Rm. 940, Federal Office Bldg.
600 South St.
New Orleans, LA 70130
504-589-6173

Massachusetts

Rm. 211, New Studio Bldg.
110 Tremont St.
Boston, MA 02108
617-223-6736

Michigan

Rm. 1906, Washington Blvd. Bldg.
234 State St.
Detroit, MI 48226
313-226-6200

Minnesota

Rm. 110, Federal Courts Bldg.
110 S. Fourth St.
Minneapolis, MN 55401
612-725-2292

Missouri

Rm. 570
210 N. 12th Blvd.
St. Louis, MO 63101
314-425-4691

New Jersey

Rm. 305
9 Clinton St.
Newark, NJ 07102
201-645-3006

New York

Rm. 1310, Federal Bldg.
111 W. Huron St.
Buffalo, NY 14202
716-842-3260

Ohio

Rm. 821, Federal Office Bldg.
1240 E. Ninth St.
Cleveland, OH 44199
216-522-3855

Pennsylvania

Rm. 1436, Federal Office Bldg.
1000 Liberty Ave.
Pittsburgh, PA 15222
412-644-2925

Puerto Rico

Rm. 650, Federal Office Bldg.
Carlos Chardon St.
Hato, Rey, PR 00918
809-759-8745

Tennessee

Rm. 716
1808 W. End Bldg.
Nashville, TN 37203
615-749-5906

Texas

Rm. 707, 555 Griffin Square Bldg.
Griffin and Young Sts.
Dallas, TX 75202
214-749-2886

Washington

Rm. 3135, Federal Bldg.
909 First Ave.
Seattle, WA 98174
206-442-5216

C1.72 EMPLOYMENT AND TRAINING ADMINISTRATION NATIONAL AND REGIONAL OFFICES

National Office

Department of Labor
200 Constitution Ave. N.W.
Washington, DC 20210
202-523-8165

Regional Offices

Region 1
(Connecticut, Maine, Massachusetts, New Hampshire, Rhode Island, Vermont)

Rm. 1707, JFK Bldg.
Government Center
Boston, MA 02203
617-223-6439

Region 2
(New York, New Jersey, Puerto Rico, Virgin Islands)

Rm. 3713
1515 Broadway
New York, NY 10036
212-399-5445

Region 3
(Delaware, District of Columbia, Maryland, Pennsylvania, Virginia, West Virginia)

P.O. Box 8796
Philadelphia, PA 19101
215-596-6346

Region 4
(Alabama, Florida, Georgia, Kentucky, Mississippi, North Carolina, South Carolina, Tennessee)

Rm. 405
1371 Peachtree St. N.E.
Atlanta, GA 30309
404-526-3267

Region 5
(Illinois, Indiana, Minnesota, Michigan, Ohio, Wisconsin)

230 S. Dearborn St.
Chicago, IL 60604
312-353-0648

Region 6
(Arkansas, Louisiana, New Mexico, Oklahoma, Texas)

Rm. 317, 555 Griffin Square Bldg.
Griffin and Young Sts.
Dallas, TX 75202
214-749-2721

Region 7
(Iowa, Kansas, Missouri, Nebraska)

Rm. 1000, Federal Bldg.
911 Walnut St.
Kansas City, MO 64106
816-374-3796

Region 8
(Colorado, Montana, North Dakota, South Dakota, Utah, Wyoming)

1961 Stout St.
Denver, CO 80202
303-837-3031

Region 9
(Arizona, California, Guam, Hawaii, Nevada)

Federal Bldg.
450 Golden Gate Ave.
P.O. Box 36084
San Francisco, CA 94102
415-556-7414

Region 10
(Alaska, Idaho, Oregon, Washington)

Rm. 1145, Federal Bldg.
909 First Ave.
Seattle, WA 98174
206-442-5570

Dept. of Labor and Industrial Relations
825 Mililani St.
Honolulu, HI 96813
808-548-3150

C1.73 STATE EMPLOYMENT SECURITY AGENCIES

Alabama

Dept. of Industrial Relations
Industrial Relations Bldg.
619 Monroe St.
Montgomery, AL 36104
205-263-7671

Alaska

Employment Security Division
Department of Labor
P.O. Box 3-7000
Juneau, AK 99811
907-465-2714

Arizona

Dept. of Economic Security
1717 W. Jefferson St.
P.O. Box 6339
Phoenix, AZ 85005
602-271-5678

Arkansas

Employment Security Division
Box 2981
Little Rock, AR 72203
501-371-2121

California

Dept. of Employment Development
800 Capitol Mall
Sacramento, CA 95814
916-445-8008

Colorado

Dept. of Employment
1210 Sherman St.
Denver, CO 80203
303-893-2400

Connecticut

Employment Security Division
Hartford, CT 06115
203-566-4280

Delaware

Dept. of Labor
801 West St.
Wilmington, DE 19899
302-571-2710

District of Columbia

Dept. of Manpower
Employment Security Bldg.
500 C St. N.W.
Washington, DC 20001
202-393-6151

Florida

Dept. of Commerce
201 Caldwell Bldg.
Tallahassee, FL 32304
904-488-7821

Georgia

Dept. of Labor
Rm. 290, State Labor Bldg.
Atlanta, GA 30334
404-656-3014

Guam

Dept. of Labor
Agana, GU 96910

Hawaii

Dept. of Labor and Industrial Relations
825 Mililani St.
Honolulu, HI 96813
808-548-3150

Idaho

Dept. of Employment
317 Main St.
P.O. Box 35
Boise, ID 83707
208-964-2611

Illinois

Dept. of Labor
Bureau of Employment Security
910 S. Michigan Ave.
Chicago, IL 60605
312-793-3500

Indiana

Employment Security Division
10 N. Senate Ave.
Indianapolis, IN 46204
317-633-4103

Iowa

Dept. of Job Service
1000 E. Grand Ave.
Des Moines, IA 50319
515-863-5135

Kansas

Dept. of Human Resources
401 Topeka Blvd.
Topeka, KS 66603
913-232-4161

Kentucky

Dept. of Human Resources
Bureau of Manpower Services
New Capitol Annex Bldg.
Frankfort, KY 40601
502-564-3703

Louisiana

Dept. of Employment Security
Employment Security Bldg.
1001 N. 23rd St.
P.O. Box 44094, Capitol Station
Baton Rouge, LA 70804
504-387-2192 ext 205

Maine

Employment Security Commission
20 Union St.
Augusta, ME 04332
207-289-3814

Maryland

Dept. of Employment and Social Services
Employment Security Administration
1100 N. Eutaw St.
Baltimore, MD 21201
301-383-5070

Massachusetts

Charles F. Hurley Employment Security Bldg.
Government Center
Boston, MA 02114
617-727-6600

Michigan

Dept. of Labor
michigan Employment Security Commission
510 Boulevard Bldg.
7310 Woodward Ave.
Detroit, MI 48202
313-872-4900

Minnesota

Dept. of Employment Service
390 N. Robert St.
St. Paul, MN 55101
612-296-2536

Mississippi

Employment Security Commission
1520 W. Capitol St.
P.O. Box 1699
Jackson, MS 39205
601-354-8711

Missouri

Dept. of Labor and Industrial Relations
Division of Employment Security
432 E. Dunkin St.
P.O. Box 59
Jefferson City, MO 65101
314-751-3215

Montana

Employment Security Division
P.O. Box 1728
Helena, MT 59601
406-449-3662

Nebraska

Dept. of Labor
Division of Employment
P.O. Box 94600, State House Station
Lincoln, NE 68509
402-475-8451

Nevada

Dept. of Employment Security
500 E. Third St.
Carson City, NV 89701
702-882-7206

New Hampshire

Dept. of Employment Security
Rm. 204
32 S. Main St.
Concord, NH 03301
603-224-3311

New Jersey

Dept. of Labor and Industry
John Fitch Plaza
P.O. Box V
Trenton, NJ 08625
609-292-2405

New Mexico

Employment Security Commission
The National Bldg.
P.O. Box 1928
Albuquerque, NM 87103
505-842-3239

New York

Dept. of Labor
State Office Bldg. Campus
Albany, NY 12226
518-457-6330

North Carolina

Employment Security Commission
903 Jones and N. McDowell Sts.
P.O. Box 25
Raleigh, NC 27611
919-929-7546

North Dakota

Employment Security Bureau
201 E. Broadway
P.O. Box 1537
Bismarck, ND 58501
701-244-2837

Ohio

Bureau of Employment Services
145 S. Front St.
P.O. Box 1618
Columbus, OH 43216
614-469-4636

Oklahoma

Oklahoma Employment Security Commission
Will Rogers Memorial Office Bldg.
Oklahoma City, OK 73105
405-521-3794

Oregon

Employment Division
875 Union St. N.E.
Salem, OR 97311
503-378-3211

Pennsylvania

Dept. of Labor and Industry
Bureau of Employment Security
7th and Forester Sts.
Harrisburg, PA 17121
717-787-6223

Puerto Rico

Bureau of Employment Security
414 Barbosa Ave.
Hato Rey, PR 00917
809-765-3030

Rhode Island

Dept. of Employment Security
24 Mason St.
Providence, RI 02903
401-861-6200

South Carolina

Employment Security Commission
1225 Laurel St.
P.O. Box 995
Columbia, SC 29202
803-758-2583

South Dakota

Dept. of Labor
Employment Services Division
607 N. Fourth St.
Aberdeen, SD 57401
605-622-2686

Tennessee

Dept. of Employment Security
Cordell Hull State Office Bldg.
Nashville, TN 37219
615-741-2131

Texas

Texas Employment Commission
TEC Bldg.
Austin, TX 78778
512-472-6251 ext 418

Utah

Dept. of Employment Security
Industrial Commission
174 Social Hall Ave.
p.o. box 11249
Salt Lake City, UT 84111
801-588-5500

Vermont

Dept. of Employment Service
Green Mountain Drive
P.O. Box 488
Montpelier, VT 05602
802-229-0311

Virginia

Virginia Employment Commission
703 E. Main St.
P.O. Box 1358
Richmond, VA 23211
703-770-3001

Virgin Islands

Employment Security Agency
P.O. Box 1092
Charlotte Amalie, St. Thomas, VI 00801
809-774-1440

Washington

Employment Security Department
Employment Security Bldg.
Olympia, WA 98504
206-753-5114

West Virginia

Dept. of Employment Security
State Office Bldg.
Charleston, WV 25305
304-348-2630

Wisconsin

Dept. of Industry
Labor and Human Relations
Employment Security Division
201 E. Washington Ave.
P.O. Box 1607
Madison, WI 53701
608-266-0049

Wyoming

Employment Security Commission
ESC Bldg.
Center and Midwest Sts.
P.O. Box 2760
Casper, WY 82601
307-237-3701

C1.74 EMPLOYMENT STANDARDS ADMINISTRATION NATIONAL AND REGIONAL OFFICES

National Office

Department of Labor
200 Constitution Ave. N.W.
Washington, DC 20210
202-523-8165

Regional Offices

Region 1
(Connecticut, Maine, Massachusetts, New Hampshire, Rhode Island, Vermont)

Rm. 1612C, JFK Federal Bldg.
Boston, MA 02203
617-223-4305

Region 2
(Canal Zone, New Jersey, New York, Puerto Rico, Virgin Islands)

Rm. 3300
1515 Broadway
New York, NY 10036
212-399-5551

Region 3
(Delaware, District of Columbia, Maryland, Pennsylvania, Virginia, West Virginia)

15th Fl., Gateway Bldg.
3535 Market St.
Philadelphia, PA 19104
215-596-1185

Region 4
(Alabama, Florida, Georgia, Kentucky, Mississippi, North Carolina, South Carolina, Tennessee)

Rm. 305
1371 Peachtree St. N.E.
Atlanta, GA 30309
404-526-2818

Region 5
(Illinois, Indiana, Michigan, Minnesota, Ohio, Wisconsin)

8th Fl.
U.S. Courthouse & Federal Office Bldg.
230 S. Dearborn St.
Chicago, IL 60604
312-353-7280

Region 6
(Arkansas, Louisiana, New Mexico, Oklahoma, Texas)

555 Griffin Square Bldg.
Young and Griffin Sts.
Dallas, TX 75202
214-749-2037

Region 7
(Iowa, Kansas, Missouri, Nebraska)

Rm. 2000
911 Walnut St.
Kansas City, MO 64106
816-374-5381

Region 8
(Colorado, Montana, North Dakota, South Dakota, Utah, Wyoming)

15412 Federal Bldg.
1961 Stout St.
Denver, CO 80202
303-837-4613

Region 9
(Arizona, California, Hawaii, Nevada)

Rm. 10353
450 Golden Gate Ave.
San Francisco, CA 94102
415-556-1318

Region 10
(Alaska, Idaho, Oregon, Washington)

Rm. 4141
909 First Ave.
Seattle, WA 98104
206-442-1536

C1.75 WAGE AND HOUR DIVISION NATIONAL AND AREA OFFICES

National Office

Department of Labor
200 Constitution Ave. N.W.
Washington, DC 20210
202-523-8165

Area Offices

Alabama

1931 Ninth Ave. S.
Birmingham, AL 35205
205-254-1305

Rm. 417, 951 Government St. Bldg.
P.O. Box 4396
Mobile, Al 36604
205-690-2311

421 S. McDonough St.
P.O. Box 2269
Montgomery, AL 36104
205-832-7450

Alaska

(Seattle, WA area office)

Arizona

Park Plaza Bldg.
1306 N. First St.
Phoenix, AZ 85004
602-261-4224

Arkansas

Rm. 3527, Federal Office Bldg.
700 W. Capitol Ave.
Little Rock, AR 72201
501-378-5292

California

7717 Federal Bldg.
300 N. Los Angeles St.
Los Angeles, CA 90012
213-688-4957, 4958

Rm. 1603-E
2800 Cottage Way
Sacramento, CA 95825
916-484-4447

Suite 440
1600 N. Broadway
Santa Ana, CA 92706
714-836-2156

Colorado

228 U.S. Custom House
721 - 19th St.
Denver, CO 80202
303-837-4405

Connecticut

305 Post Office Bldg.
135 High St.
Hartford, CT 06101
203-244-2660

Delaware

(Baltimore, MD area office)

District of Columbia

(Hyattsville, MD area office)

Florida

Rm. 215, Romark Bldg.
3521 W. Broward Blvd.
Fort Lauderdale, FL 33312
305-792-5310 ext 251

Suite 121
3947 Boulevard Center Drive
Jacksonville, FL 32207
904-791-2489

Rm. 202
1150 S.W. 1st St.
Miami, FL 33130
305-350-5767

Rm. 309, Orlando Professional Center
22 W. Lake Beauty Dr.
P.O. Box 8024A
Orlando, FL 32806
305-841-1026

Suite 110, Mills Bldg.
5410 Mariner St.
Tampa, FL 33609
813-228-2154

Georgia

Rm. 1100, Citizenship Trust Bldg.
75 Piedmont Ave. N.E.
Atlanta, GA 30303
405-526-6396

202 Internal Revenue Bldg.
15th St. and Third AVe.
Columbus, GA 31902
404-324-2137

Rm. 210, U.S. Post Office Bldg.
127 Bull St.
Savannah, GA 31401
912-232-4321 ext 222

Hawaii

Rm. 614
1833 Kalakaua Ave.
Honolulu, HI 96815
808-588-0264, 0265

Idaho

(Portland, OR and Seattle, WA area offices)

Illinois

16th Fl., Dirksen Federal Bldg.
219 S. Dearborn St.
Chicago, IL 60604
312-353-8302

Rm. 207
7111 W. Foster Ave.
Chicago, IL 60656
312-775-5733

2222 W. 95th St.
Chicago, IL 60643
312-238-8832

Rm. 25, Federal Bldg.
600 E. Monroe St.
Springfield, IL 62701
217-525-4060, 4061

Indiana

465 Federal Bldg.
Ohio and Pennsylvania Sts.
Indianapolis, IN 46204
317-269-7168

307 Commerce Bldg.
103 W. Wayne St.
South Bend, IN 46601
219-234-4045

Iowa

Rm. 643, Federal Bldg.
210 Walnut St.
Des Moines, IA 50309
515-284-4625

Kansas

745 R. H. Garvey Bldg.
300 W. Douglas
Wichita, KS 67202
316-267-6311 ext 466

(also Kansas City, MO area office)

Kentucky

Suite C, Concord Square
1460 Newton Rd.
Lexington, KY 40505
606-252-2312 ext 2791

187-E Federal Bldg.
600 Federal Plaza
Louisville, KY 40202
502-582-5226

Louisiana

Rm. 216-B, Hoover Bldg.
8312 Florida Blvd.
Baton Rouge, LA 70806
504-924-5160

632 Federal Bldg.
600 South St.
New Orleans, LA 70130
504-589-6171

Maine

76 Pearl St.
P.O. Box 211
Portland, ME 04112
207-775-3131 ext 344

Maryland

1022 Federal Office Bldg.
Charles Center
31 Hopkins Plaza
Baltimore, MD 21201
301-962-2265

Suite 904, Presidential Bldg.
6525 Belcrest Rd.
Hyattsville, MD 20782
301-436-6767

Massachusetts

Rm. 1522
100 Summer St.
Boston, MA 02111
617-223-6751, 5541, 5345

Rm. 804
1200 Main St.
Springfield, MA 01103
413-781-9353

Michigan

16641 E. Warren Ave.
Detroit, MI 48224
313-226-6935, 6936, 6937

14740 Plymouth Rd.
Detroit, MI 48227
313-226-7447, 7448, 7449

Rm. 134, Federal Bldg. & U.S. Courthouse
110 Michigan St.
Grand Rapids, MI 49502
616-456-2338

Minnesota

224 Federal Bldg.
110 S. Fourth St.
Minneapolis, MN 55401
612-725-2594

Mississippi

675 Milner Bldg.
210 S. Lamar St.
Jackson, MS 39201
601-969-4347

Missouri

2900 Federal Office Bldg.
911 Walnut St.
Kansas City, MO 64106
816-374-5721

Rm. 563
210 N. 12th St.
St. Louis, mO 63101
314-425-4706

Montana

(Salt Lake City, UT area office)

Nebraska

2118 Federal Bldg.
215 N. 17th St.
Omaha, N.E. 68102
402-221-4682

Nevada

(Phoenix, AZ area office)

New Hampshire

(Portland, ME area office)

New Jersey

Rm. 836
970 Broad St.
Newark NJ 07102
201-645-2279

145 E. State St.
Trenton, NJ 08608
609-599-3511

New Mexico

307 Federal Bldg.
421 Gold S.W.
P.O. Box 1869
Albuquerque, NM 87103
505-766-2477

New York

Rm. 631
271 Cadman Plaza E.
Brooklyn, NY 11201
212-596-3160

Rm. 303
E. Fordham Rd.
Bronx, NY 10452
212-298-4472

617 Federal Bldg.
117 W. Huron St.
Buffalo, NY 14202
716-842-3210

159 N. Franklin St.
Hempstead, Long Island, NY 11550
516-481-0582

Rm. 2946
26 Federal Plaza
New York, NY 10007
212-264-8185

Rm. 264
Leo W. O'Brien Federal Bldg.
Albany, NY 12207
518-472-3596

North Carolina

401 BSR Bldg.
316 E. Morehead St.
Charlotte, NC 28202
704-372-0711 ext 431

239 Federal Bldg.
324 Market St.
P.O. Box 2220
Greensboro, NC 27402
919-275-9111 ext 494

Rm. 408, Federal Bldg.
310 New Bern Ave.
P.O. Box 27486
Raleigh, NC 27611
919-755-4190

North Dakota

(Denver, CO area office)

Ohio

1010 Federal Office Bldg.
550 Main St.
Cincinnati, OH 45202
513-684-2942, 2943

Rm. 817, Federal Bldg.
1240 E. Ninth St.
Cleveland, OH 44199
216-522-3892

213 Bryson Bldg.
700 Bryden Rd.
Columbus, OH 43215
614-943-5677

Oklahoma

Rm. 210, Post Office Bldg.
Third and Robinson Sts.
Oklahoma City, OK 73102
405-231-4545

Rm. 4562, Federal Bldg.
333 W. Fourth St.
Tulsa, OK 74103
918-581-7695

Oregon

528 Pittock Block
921 S.W. Washington St.
Portland, OR 97205
503-221-3057

Pennsylvania

Rm. 774, Federal Bldg.
228 Walnut St.
Harrisburg, PA 17108
717-782-4539

Rm. 4244
600 Arch St.
Philadelphia, PA 19106
215-597-4950

702 Federal Bldg.
1000 Liberty Ave.
Pittsburgh, PA 15222
412-644-2996

Rm. 3329, Penn Place
20 N. Pennsylvania Ave.
Wilkes-Barre, PA 18701
717-825-6811 ext 312

Puerto Rico

Rm. 403, New Federal Bldg.
Carlos Chardon St.
Hato Rey, PR 00918
809-759-8895

Americo Marin Bldg.
105 E. Mendez Vigo
Mayaguez, PR 00708
809-832-3495

Rhode Island

210-212 John E. Fogarty Federal Bldg.
24 Weybosset St.
Providence, RI 02903
401-528-4378

South Carolina

Rm. 105-C, Liberty House
2001 Assembly St.
Columbia, SC 29201
803-765-5981

South Dakota

(Denver, CO area office)

Tennessee

Rm. 202
608 S. Gay St.
Knoxville, TN 37902
615-637-9300

486 Federal Office Bldg.
167 N. Main St.
Memphis, TN 38103
901-534-3418

Rm. 610
1720 W. End Ave.
Nashville, TN 37203
615-749-5452

Texas

Rm. 503, 555 Griffin Square Bldg.
Griffin and Young Sts.
Dallas, TX 75202
214-749-3324

Rm. 2
1515 Airway Blvd.
El Paso, TX 79925
925-543-7634

Rm. 7A12
819 Taylor St.
Fort Worth, TX 76102
817-334-2678

Suite 1025, The Six Hundred Bldg.
600 Leopard St.
Corpus Christi, TX 78401
512-888-3156

Rm. 2103
2320 LaBranch St.
Houston, TX 77004
713-226-4304

Rm. 311, Federal Bldg.
727 E. Durango
San Antonio, TX 78206
512-225-4304

621 Citizen's Tower
Fifth and Franklin Sts.
Waco, TX 76701
817-756-6511 ext 296

Utah

3207 Federal Office Bldg.
125 S. State St.
Salt Lake City, UT 84138
801-524-5706

Vermont

(Springfield, MA area office)

Virginia

7000 Federal Bldg.
400 N. Eighth St.
Richmond, VA 23240
804-782-2995

457 Poff Federal Bldg.
210 Franklin Rd. S.W.
Roanoke, VA 24011
703-982-6331

Washington

2008 Smith Tower Bldg.
506 Second Ave.
Seattle, WA 98104
206-442-4482

West Virginia

Suite 100
22 Capitol St.
Charleston, WV 25301
304-343-6181 ext 448

Wisconsin

114 Lincoln Bldg.
303 Price Pl.
Madison, WI 53705
608-252-5221

Rm. 601, Federal Bldg.
1517 E. Wisconsin Ave.
Milwaukee, WI 53202
414-224-3585

Wyoming

(Salt Lake City, UT or Denver, CO area offices)

C1.76 OFFICE OF FEDERAL CONTRACT COMPLIANCE PROGRAMS NATIONAL, REGIONAL, AND AREA OFFICES

National Office

Department of Labor
200 Constitution Ave. N.E.
Washington, DC 20210
202-523-8165

Regional Offices

Region 1
(Connecticut, Maine, Massachusetts, New Hampshire, Rhode Island, Vermont)

Rm. 1612, JFK Federal Bldg.
Government Center
Boston, MA 02203
617-223-5565

Region 2
(New York, New Jersey, Puerto Rico, Virgin Islands)

1515 Broadway
New York, NY 10036
212-399-5563

Region 3
(Pennsylvania, Maryland, Delaware, District of Columbia, West Virginia, Virginia)

Rm. 1543, Gateway Bldg.
3535 Market St.
Philadelphia, PA 19104
215-596-1213

Region 4
(Mississippi, Tennessee, Alabama, Florida, South Carolina, North Carolina, Georgia, Kentucky)

Rm. 720
1371 Peachtree St. N.E.
Atlanta, GA 30309
404-526-4211

Region 5
(Wisconsin, Illinois, Indiana, Minnesota, Ohio, Michigan)

Rm. 854
230 S. Dearborn St.
Chicago, IL 60604
312-353-8887

Region 6
(Arkansas, Louisiana, New Mexico, Oklahoma, Texas)

555 Griffin Square Bldg.
Young and Griffin Sts.
Dallas, TX 75202
214-749-1134

Region 7
(Nebraska, Kansas, Iowa, Missouri)

Rm. 2000, Federal Office Bldg.
911 Walnut St.
Kansas City, MO 64106
816-374-5384

Region 8
(Colorado, Montana, North Dakota, South Dakota, Utah, Wyoming)

Rm. 230, New Custom House
19th and Stout Sts.
Denver, CO 80202
303-837-4978

Region 9
(Arizona, California, Hawaii, Nevada, the Pacific)

Rm. 10353
450 Golden Gate Ave.
San Francisco, CA 94102
415-556-3597

Region 10
(Alaska, Washington, Oregon, Iadho)

1911 Smith-Towers Bldg.
506 Second Ave.
Seattle, WA 98104
206-442-4508

Area Offices

California

Rm. 3251, Federal Bldg.
300 N. Los Angeles St.
Los Angeles, CA 90012
213-688-4961

Rm. 341
211 Main St.
415-556-6017

Ohio

803 Federal Bldg.
1240 E. Ninth St.
Cleveland, OH 44199
216-293-3882

C1.77 OFFICE OF WORKER'S COMPENSATION PROGRAMS NATIONAL AND DISTRICT OFFICES

National Office

Department of Labor
200 Constitution Ave. N.W.
Washington, DC 20210
202-523-8165

District Offices

District 1
(Maine, New Hampshire, Vermont, Massachusetts, Rhode Island, Connecticut)

Rm. 1612C, JFK Federal Bldg.
Government Center
Boston, MA 02203
617-223-6755

District 2
(New York, New Jersey)

Rm. 3306
1515 Broadway
New York, NY 10036
212-971-5501

District 3
(Pennsylvania, West Virginia)

Rm. 2100, Gateway Bldg.
3535 Market St.
Philadelphia, PA 19104
215-597-1180, 1181, 1182

District 4
(Maryland, District of Columbia)

Rm. 1026, Federal Bldg.
Charles Center
Baltimore, MD 21201
301-962-3677

District 5
(Virginia)

Rm. 101, Stanwick Bldg.
3661 Virginia Beach Blvd. E.
Norfolk, VA 23502
703-441-6585

District 6
(North Carolina, Kentucky, Tennessee, South Carolina, Georgia, Florida, Alabama, Mississippi, except Gulf Coast of Mississippi)

400 W. Bay St.
P.O. Box 332a
Jacksonville, FL 32202
904-791-3428

District 7
(Arkansas, Louisiana, lower part of Mississippi and Gulf Coast of Mississippi)

Rm. 1048, Federal Office Bldg.
600 South St.
New Orleans, LA 70130
504-527-6135

District 8
(Texas, Oklahoma, New Mexico)

Rm. 2108
2320 La Branch
Houston, TX 77004
713-527-5801

Rm. 212, U.S. Post Office Bldg.
601 Rosenberg
Galveston, TX 77550
713-527-6172

District 9
(Ohio, Indiana, Michigan)

Rm. 879
1240 E. Ninth St.
Cleveland, OH 44199
216-522-3803

District 10
(Illinois, Minnesota, Wisconsin)

8th Fl.
230 S. Dearborn St.
Chicago, IL 60604
312-353-5650

District 11
(Missouri, Kansas, Iowa, Nebraska)

Rm. 2000, Federal Office Bldg.
911 Walnut St.
Kansas City, MO 64106
816-374-2723

District 12
(Montana, Wyoming, Utah, Colorado, North Dakota, South Dakota)

Rm. 15412, Federal Office Bldg.
1961 Stout St.
Denver, CO 80202
303-837-2611

District 13
(California, Arizona, Nevada)

Rm. 10301
450 Golden Gate Ave.
Box 36066
San Francisco, CA 94102
415-556-5757

4th Fl.
400 Ocean Gate
Long Beach, CA 90802
213-432-6940

District 14
(Washington, Oregon, Alaska, Idaho, Hawaii)

Rm. M-17, Arcade Bldg.
1319 Second Ave.
Seattle, WA 98101
206-442-5521

Rm. 610
1833 Kalakaua Ave.
Honolulu, HI 96815
808-588-0266

District 40
(District of Columbia)

Rm. 405
666 11th St. N.W.
Washington, DC 20211
202-382-3831

C1.78 WOMEN'S BUREAU NATIONAL AND REGIONAL OFFICES

National Office

Department of Labor
200 Constitution Ave. N.W.
Washington, DC 20210
202-523-8165

Regional Offices

Region 1
(Connecticut, Maine, Massachusetts, New Hampshire, New Jersey)

Rm. 1612C, JFK Federal Bldg.
Boston, MA 02203

Region 2
(Canal Zone, New Jersey, New York, Puerto Rico, Virgin Islands)

Rm. 3310
1515 Broadway
New York, NY 10036
212-399-5452

Region 3
(Delaware, District of Columbia, Maryland, Pennsylvania, Virginia, West Virginia)

Rm. 15460, Gateway Bldg.
3535 Market St.
Philadelphia, PA 19104
215-596-1183

Region 4
(Alabama, Florida, Georgia, Kentucky, North Carolina, South Carolina, Mississippi, Tennessee)

Rm. 315
1371 Peachtree St. N.E.
Atlanta, GA 30309
404-516-5461

Region 5
(Illinois, Indiana, Michigan, Minnesota, Ohio, Wisconsin)

230 S. Dearborn St.
Chicago, IL 60604
312-353-6985

Region 6
(Arkansas, Lousiana, New Mexico, Oklahoma, Texas)

555 Griffin Square Bldg.
Young and Griffin Sts.
Dallas, TX 75202
214-749-2568

Region 7
(Iowa, Kansas, Missouri, Nebraska)

2000 Federal Office Bldg.
911 Walnut St.
Kansas City, MO 64106
816-374-5363

Region 8
(Colorado, Montana, North Dakota, South Dakota, Utah, Wyoming)

15412 Federal Bldg.
1961 Stout St.
Denver, CO 80202
303-837-4613

Region 9
(Arizona, California, Hawaii, Nevada)

Rm. 10341
450 Golden Gate Ave.
P.O. Box 36017
San Francisco, CA 94102
415-556-2377

Region 10
(Alaska, Idaho, Oregon, Washington)

Rm. 4141
909 First Ave.
Seattle, WA 98104
206-442-1534

C1.79 OCCUPATIONAL SAFETY AND HEALTH ADMINISTRATION (OSHA) NATIONAL, REGIONAL, AND AREA OFFICES

National Office

Department of Labor
200 Constitution Ave. N.W.
Washington, DC 20210
202-523-1865

Regional Offices

Region 1
(Connecticut, Maine, Massachusetts, New Hampshire, Rhode Island, Vermont)

Rm. 1804, JFK Federal Bldg.
Government Center
Boston, MA 02203
617-223-6712, 6713

Region 2
(Canal Zone, New York, New Jersey, Puerto Rico, Virgin Islands)

Rm. 3445
1515 Broadway
New York, NY 10036
212-399-5941

Region 3
(Delaware, District of Columbia, Maryland, Pennsylvania, Virginia, West Virginia)

Suite 15220, Gateway Bldg.
3535 Market St.
Philadelphia, PA 19104
215-596-1201

Region 4
(Alabama, Florida, Georgia, Kentucky, North Carolina, South Carolina, Mississippi, Tennessee)

Suite 587
1375 Peachtree St. N.E.
Atlanta, GA 30309
404-881-3575

Region 5
(Illinois, Indiana, Minnesota, Michigan, Ohio, Wisconsin)

32nd Fl., Rm. 3263
230 S. Dearborn St.
Chicago, IL 60604
312-353-4716, 4717

Region 6
(Arkansas, Louisiana, New Mexico, Oklahoma, Texas)

Rm. 602
555 Griffin Square Bldg.
Dallas, TX 75202
214-749-2477

Region 7
(Iowa, Kansas, Missouri, Nebraska)

Rm. 3000
911 Walnut St.
Kansas City, MO 64106
816-374-5861

Region 8
(Colorado, Montana, North Dakota, South Dakota, Utah, Wyoming)

Rm. 15010, Federal Bldg.
1961 Stout St.
Denver, CO 80202
303-837-3883

Region 9
(Arizona, California, Hawaii, Nevada, Guam, American Samoa, Trust Territory of the Pacific Islands)

9470 Federal Bldg.
450 Golden Gate Ave.
P.O. Box 36017
San Francisco, CA 94102
415-556-0586

Region 10
(Alaska, Idaho, Oregon, Washington)

Rm. 6048, Federal Office Bldg.
909 First Ave.
Seattle, WA 98174
206-442-5930

Area Offices

Alabama

Todd Mall
2047 Canyon Rd.
Birmingham, AL 35216
205-822-7100

Rm. M104
1129 Noble St.
P.O. Box 1788
Anniston, AL 36201
205-237-4212

Rm. 204, U. S. Post Office Bldg.
Sheffield, AL 35660
205-383-0010

Rm. 329, Aronov Bldg.
474 S. Court St.
Montgomery, AL 36103
205-832-7159

Rm. 600, Commerce Bldg.
118 N. Royal St.
Mobile, AL 36602
205-690-2131

Rm. 1750, Safeguard Bldg.
106 Wynn Dr.
Huntsville, AL 35807
205-895-5268

Alaska

Rm. 227, Federal Bldg.
605 W. 5th Ave.
Anchorage, AK 99501
907-272-5561 ext 851

Arizona

Suite 318, Amerco Towers
2721 N. Central Ave.
Phoenix, AZ 85004
602-261-4858

Rm. 3-I
301 W. Congress St.
Tucson, AZ 85701
602-792-6286

Arkansas

Suite 212, West Mark Bldg.
4120 W. Markham
Little Rock, AR 72205
501-378-6291

California

Suite 530
400 Oceangate
Long Beach, CA 90802
213-432-3434

Rm. 1706
100 McAllister St.
San Francisco, CA 94102
415-556-7260

Rm. 1409
2800 Cattage Way
Sacramento, CA 95825
916-484-4363

Rm. 202
2110 Merced St.
Fresno, CA 93721
209-487-5454

Colorado

Squire Plaza Bldg.
8527 W. Colfax Ave.
Lakewood, CO 80215
303-234-4471

Connecticut

Rm. 617B, Federal Bldg.
450 Main St.
Hartford, CT 06103
203-244-2294

Delaware

Rm. 3007, Federal Office Bldg.
844 King St.
Wilmington, DE 19801
302-571-6115

District of Columbia

Rm. 602, Railway Labor Bldg.
400 First St. N.W.
Washington, DC 20215
202-523-5224, 5225

Florida

Rm. 204, Bridge Bldg.
3200 E. Oakland Park Blvd.
Fort Lauderdale, FL 33308
305-566-6547

Suite 4, Art Museum Plaza
2809 Art Museum Dr.
Jacksonville, FL 32207
904-791-2895

Rm. B-16
100 N. Palafax St.
P.O. Box 12212
Pensacola, FL 32581
904-438-2543

Kozerama Bldg.
1300 Executive Center Dr.
Tallahassee, FL 32301
904-877-3215

Rm. 918, Barnett Bank Bldg.
1000 N. Ashley Dr.
Tampa, FL 33602
813-228-2821

Georgia

Suite 33, Bldg. 10
LaVista Perimeter Office Park
Tucker, GA 30084
404-939-8987

Suite 310A, Enterprise Bldg.
6605 Abercorn St.
Savannah, GA 31405
912-354-0733

Riverside Plaza Shopping Center
2720 Riverside Dr.
Macon, GA 31204
912-746-5143

Hawaii

Suite 505
333 Queen St.
Honolulu, HI 96813
808-546-3157

Idaho

1315 W. Idaho St.
Boise, ID 83707
208-342-2711 ext 2867, 2868, 2869

Suite B, Yellowstone Plaza Bldg.
475 Yellowstone Ave.
P.O. Box 2072
Pocatello, ID 83201
208-233-6374

Illinois

16th Fl.
230 S. Dearborn St.
Chicago, IL 60604
312-353-1390

3rd Fl.
228 N.E. Jefferson
Peoria, IL 61603
306-673-9515

305 S. Illinois St.
Belleville, IL 62220
618-277-5300

Indiana

Rm. 423, U.S. Post Office & Courthouse
46 E. Ohio St.
Indianapolis, IN 46204
317-269-7290

Iowa

Rm. 638
210 Walnut St.
Des Moines, IA 50309
515-284-4794

Kansas

Rm. 512, Petroleum Bldg.
221 S. Broadway
Wichita, KS 67202
316-267-6311 ext 644

Kentucky

Suite 554E
600 Federal Place
Louisville, KY 40202
502-582-6111, 6112

Louisiana

Rm. 202
546 Carondelet St.
New Orlenas, LA 70130
504-589-2451, 2452

Suite 200, Hoover Annex
2156 Wooddale Blvd.
Baton Rouge, LA 70806
504-387-0181 ext 474

Rm. 8A09, New Federal Office Bldg.
500 Fannin St.
Shreveport, LA 71101
318-226-5360

Maine

Rm. 617B, Federal Bldg.
450 Main St.
Hartford, CT 06103
203-244-2294

Maryland

Rm. 1110A, Federal Bldg.
Charles Center
31 Hopkins Plaza
Baltimore, MD 21201
301-962-2840

Massachusetts

400-2 Totten Pond Rd.
Waltham, MA 02154
617-894-2400

Suite 513
1300 Main St.
Springfield, MA 01103
413-781-2420 ext 312

Michigan

Rm. 628
231 W. Lafayette
Detroit, MI 48226
313-226-6720

Minnesota

Rm. 437
110 S. Fourth St.
Minneapolis, MN 55401
612-725-2571

Mississippi

5760 I-55 N.
Frontage Rd. E.
Jackson, MS 39211
601-969-4606

Missouri

Rm. 1100
1627 Main St.
Kansas City, MO 64108
816-374-2756

Rm. 520
210 N. 12th Blvd.
St. Louis, MO 63101
314-279-5461

Montana

Suite 525, Petroleum Bldg.
2812 1st Ave. N.
Billings, MT 59101
406-245-6711 ext 6640, 6649

Nebraska

Rm. 100, Overland-Wolf Bldg.
6910 Pacific St.
Omaha, NE 68106
402-221-9341

113 W. 6th St.
North Platte, NE 69101
308-534-9450

Nevada

Suite 222
1100 E. William St.
Carson City, NV 89701
702-883-1226

Rm. I-606
300 Las Vegas Blvd. S.
Las Vegas, NV 89101
702-385-6570

New Hampshire

Rm. 426, Federal Bldg.
55 Pleasant St.
Concord, NH 03301
603-224-1995

New Jersey

Rm. 1435C
970 Board St.
Newark, NJ 07102
201-645-5930

Bldg. T3, Belle Mead GSA Depot
Belle Mead, NJ 08502
201-359-2777

Rm. 206
Teterboro Airport Professional Bldg.
377 Rt. 17
Hasbrouck Heights, NJ 07604
201-288-1700

Rm. 408
519 Federal St.
Camden, NJ 08101
609-757-5181

2E Blackwell St.
Dover, NJ 07801
201-361-4050

New Mexico

Rm. 3114, Federal Bldg.
500 Gold Ave. S.W.
P.O. Box 1428
Albuquerque, NM 87103
505-766-3411

New York

Rm. 1405
90 Church St.
New York, NY 10007
212-264-9840

Rm. 203, Midtown Plaza
700 E. Water St.
Syracuse, NY 13210
315-473-2700

185 Montague St.
Brooklyn, NY 11201
212-330-7667

136-21 Roosevelt Ave.
Flushing, NY 11354
212-445-5005

Rm. 132, Leo W. O'Brien Federal Bldg.
Clinton Ave. & North Pearl St.
Albany, NY 12207
518-472-6085

Rm. 600, Federal Office Bldg.
100 State St.
Rochester, NY 14614
716-263-6755

Rm. 302
200 Mamaroneck Ave.
White Plains, NY 10601
914-761-4250 ext 721

Rm. 1002
111 W. Huron St.
Buffalo, NY 14202
716-842-3333

370 Old Country Rd.
Garden City, Long Island, NY 11530
516-294-0400

North Carolina

Rm. 406, Federal Office Bldg.
310 New Bern Ave.
Raleigh, NC 27601
919-755-4770

North Dakota

Russel Bldg.
Highway 83 N., Rt. 1
Bismarck, ND 58501
701-255-4011 ext 521

Ohio

Rm. 847, Federal Office Bldg.
1240 E. Ninth St.
Cleveland, OH 44199
216-522-3818

Rm. 4028, Federal Office Bldg.
550 Main St.
Cincinnati, OH 45202
513-684-2354

Rm. 109
360 S. Third St.
Columbus, OH 43215
614-469-5582

Rm. 734, Federal Office Bldg.
234 N. Summit St.
Toledo, OH 43604
419-259-7542

Oklahoma

Rm. 514, Petroleum Bldg.
420 S. Boulder
Tulsa, OK 74103
918-589-2451

Suite 408
50 Penn Place
Oklahoma City, OK 73118
405-231-5351

Oregon

Rm. 640
1200 S.W. Third St.
Portland, OR 97204
503-221-2251

Pennsylvania

Rm. 4256, Federal Bldg.
600 Arch St.
Philadelphia, PA 19106
215-597-4955

Rm. 436, Swank Bldg.
Main and Bedford Sts.
Johnstown, PA 15907
814-535-3504

Burneson Bldg.
933 Park Avenue
Meadville, PA 16335
814-724-8031

Rm. B, Central Plaza
E. King St.
Lancaster, PA 17602
717-394-0681 ext 73, 74

Suite No. 470, Armenara Office Center
444 E. College Ave.
State College, PA 16801
814-234-6695

Rm. 22, U.S. Post Office Bldg.
5th and Hamilton Sts.
Allentown, PA 18101
215-434-0181 ext 266

Rm. 802, Jonnet Bldg.
4099 William Penn Highway
Monroeville, PA 15146
412-644-2905

Rm. 3107, Penn Place
20 N. Pennsylvania Ave.
Wilkes Barre, PA 18701
717-825-6811 ext 538, 539

Progress Plaza
49 N. Progress Ave.
Harrisburg, PA 17109
717-657-0100

Puerto Rico

Condominium San Alberto Bldg.
San Juan, PR 00936

Rm. 328
605 Condado Ave.
Santurce, PR 00907
809-753-4457

Rhode Island

Rm. 503A, Federal Bldg. & U.S. Courthouse
Providence, RI 02903
401-528-4466

South Carolina

Suite 102, Kittrell Center
2711 Middleburg Dr.
Columbia, SC 29204
803-765-5904

Rm. 627, Federal Bldg.
334 Meeting St.
Charleston, SC 29403
803-577-2423

South Dakota

Rm. 408, Court House Plaza Bldg.
300 N. Dakota Ave.
Sioux Falls, SD 57102
605-336-2980 ext 425

Tennessee

Suite 302
1600 Hayes St.
Nashville, TN 37203
615-749-5313

Rm. 207, Federal Bldg.
167 N. Main
Memphis, TN 38103
901-534-4179

Texas

Rm. 421, Federal Bldg.
1205 Texas Ave.
Lubbock, TX 79401
806-762-7681

Rm. 2118
2320 LaBranch St.
Houston, TX 77004
713-226-5431

Suite 310, American Bank Tower
221 W. 6th St.
Austin, TX 78701
512-397-5783

Suite 300, Professional Bldg.
2900 North St.
Beaumont, TX 77702
713-838-0271 ext 258, 259

Rm. 3
1515 Airway Blvd.
El Paso, TX 79925
915-543-7828

Rm. 215
1015 Jackson Keller Rd.
San Antonio, TX 78213
512-225-4569

Suite 9
Riverview Professional Blvd.
S. 77 Sunshine Strip
Harlingen, TX 78550
512-425-6811, 6812

Suite 1322
600 Leopard St.
Corpus Christi, TX 78401
512-888-3257

1425 W. Pioneer Dr.
Irving, TX 75061
214-749-7555

Utah

Rm. 452, U.S. Post Office Bldg.
350 S. Main St.
Salt Lake City, UT 84101
801-524-5080

Vermont

Rm. 426, Federal Bldg.
55 Pleasant St.
Concord, NH 03301
603-224-1995

Virginia

Rm. 111, Stanwick Bldg.
3661 Virginia Beach Blvd.
Norfolk, VA 23502
804-441-6381

400 N. 8th St.
P.O. Box 10186
Richmond, VA 23240
804-782-2864, 2865

Rm. 107, Falls Church Office Bldg.
900 S. Washington St.
Falls Church, VA 22046
703-557-1330

210 Franklin Rd. S.W.
P.O. Box 2828
Roanoke, VA 24011
703-982-6342

Washington

121 107th St. N.E.
Bellevue, WA 98004
206-442-7520

Rm. 410
904 Riverside Ave.
P.O. Box 2132
Spokane, WA 99210
509-624-5235

West Virginia

Suite 1726, Charleston National Plaza
700 Virginia St.
Charleston, WV 25301
304-343-6181 ext 420, 429

Rm. 411, U.S. Courthouse & Federal Bldg.
Chapline and 12th Sts.
Wheeling, WV 26003
304-232-1062

Rms. 401-403, U.S. Post Office
401 Davis Ave.
Elkins, WV 26241
304-636-6224

Wisconsin

Rm. 400, Clark Bldg.
633 W. Wisconsin Ave.
Milwaukee, WI 53203
414-224-3315

2326 S. Park St.
Madison, WI 53713

Rm. 204, U.S. Postal Service Bldg.
219 Washington Ave.
Oshkosh, WI 54901
414-231-1406, 1408

Rm. B-9
Federal Bldg. and U.S. Courthouse
500 Barstow St.
Eau Claire, WI 54701
715-832-9019

Wyoming

Squire Plaza Bldg.
8527 W. Colfax Ave.
Lakewood, CO 80215
303-234-4471

C1.80 OSHA/COMMUNITY COLLEGE TRAINING PROGRAM PARTICIPANTS

American Association of Community and Junior Colleges
1 Dupont Circle N.W.
Washington, DC 20036

Alvin Community College
Occupational Safety and Health Project
3110 Mustang Rd.
Alvin, TX 77511

Community College of Allegheny County
Occupational Safety and Health Project
1130 Perry Highway—111 Pines Plaza
Pittsburgh, PA 15237

Delgado College
Occupational Safety and Health Project
615 City Park Ave.
New Orleans, LA 70019

Garland County Community College
Occupational Safety and Health Project
Hot Springs National Park, AR 71901

Greenville Technical College
Occupational Safety and Health Project
P.O. Box 5616, Station B
Greenville, SC 28606

Inver Hills Community College
Occupational Safety and Health Project
8445 College Trail
Inver Grove Heights, MN 55075

Middlesex County College
Occupational Safety and Health Project
Woodbridge Ave.
Edison, NJ 08817

Pioneer Community College
Occupational Safety and Health Project
560 Westport Rd.
Kansas City, MO 64111

San Diego Community College District
Occupational Safety and Health Project
3375 Camino Del Rio S.
San Diego, CA 92108

South Oklahoma City Junior College
Occupational Safety & Health Project
7777 South May Ave.
Oklahoma City, OK 73149

Springfield Technical Community College
Occupational Safety & Health Project
One Armory Square
Springfield, MA 01105

Stark Technical College
Occupational Safety & Health Project
6200 Frank Ave. N.W.
Canton, OH 44720

Triton College
Occupational Safety and Health Project
2000 Fifth Ave.
River Grove, IL 60171

Utah Technical College at Provo
Occupational Safety and Health Project
1395 N. 150 E.
Provo, UT 84601

Valencia Community College
Occupational Safety and Health Project
P.O. Box 3028
Orlando, FL 32802

Waukesha County Technical Institute
Occupational Safety and Health Project
800 Main St.
Pewaukee, WI 53072

West Virginia Northern Community College
Occupational Safety and Health Project
87 Fifteenth St.
Wheeling, WV 26003

Department of the Treasury

C1.95 INTERNAL REVENUE SERVICE NATIONAL AND REGIONAL OFFICES, AND TOLL-FREE TELEPHONE NUMBERS

National Offices

Department of the Treasury
1111 Constitution Ave. N.W.
Washington, DC 20224
202-964-4021

Director, Training Division
Internal Revenue Service
Washington, DC 20224
202-964-3197

Director, Taxpayer Service Division
Internal Revenue Service
Washington, DC 20224
202-964-6352

Regional Offices

Central Region
(Michigan, Indiana, Ohio, Kentucky, West Virginia)

550 Main St.
Cincinnati, OH 45202

Mid-Atlantic Region
(Pennsylvania, New Jersey, Delaware, Maryland, Virginia)

2 Penn Center Plaza
Philadelphia, PA 19102

Midwest Region
(North Dakota, South Dakota, Iowa, Nebraska, Minnesota, Missouri, Wisconsin, Illinois)

1 N. Wacker Dr.
Chicago, IL 60601

North Atlantic Region
(Maine, Vermont, New Hampshire, New York, Massachusetts, Connecticut, Rhode Island)

90 Church St.
New York, NY 10007

Southeast Region
(Tennessee, North Carolina, Mississippi, Alabama, Georgia, Florida, South Carolina)

275 Peachtree St. N.E.
Atlanta, GA 30303

Southwest Region
(Wyoming, Colorado, Kansas, New Mexico, Oklahoma, Texas, Arkansas, Louisiana)

7839 Churchill Way
Dallas, TX 75230

Western Region
(Washington, Idaho, Montana, Oregon, California, Nevada, Utah, Arizona, Hawaii, Alaska)

525 Market St.
San Francisco, CA 94105

Toll-Free Telephone Numbers

Alabama

Birmingham	252-1155
Decatur	355-1855
Huntsville	539-2751
Mobile	433-5532
Montgomery	264-8441
Muscle Shoals Area	767-0301
Tuscaloosa	758-4434
Elsewhere in Alabama	800-292-6300

Alaska

Anchorage	276-1040
Elsewhere in Alaska, call operator and ask for	Zenith 3700

Arizona

Phoenix	257-1233
Tucson	624-8751
Elsewhere in Arizona	800-352-6911

Arkansas

Little Rock	376-4401
Elsewhere in Arkansas	800-482-9350

California

Please call your toll-free telephone number shown in the white pages of your local telephone directory under U.S. Government, Internal Revenue Service, Federal Tax Assistance.

Colorado

Denver	825-7041
Elsewhere in Colorado	800-332-2060

Connecticut

Bridgeport	576-1433
Hartford	249-8251
Stamford	348-6235
Elsewhere in Connecticut	1-800-842-1120

Delaware

Wilmington	571-6400
Elsewhere in Delaware	800-292-9575

District of Columbia

Call	488-3100

Florida

Fort Lauderdale	491-3311
Jacksonville	354-1760
Miami	358-5072
Orlando	422-2550
Pensacola	434-5215
St. Petersburg	576-7400
Tampa	223-9741
West Palm Beach	655-7250
Elsewhere in Florida	1-800-342-8300

Georgia

Atlanta	522-0050
Augusta	724-9946
Columbus	327-7491
Macon	746-4993
Savannah	355-1045
Elsewhere in Georgia	1-800-222-1040

Hawaii

Hilo	935-4895
Honolulu	546-8660
Kauai	245-2731
Lanai, call operator and ask for	Enterprise 8036
Maui	244-0685
Molokai, call operator and ask for	Enterprise 8034

Idaho

Boise	336-1040
Elsewhere in Idaho	800-632-5990

Illinois

Chicago	435-1040
Elsewhere in area code 312 (except city of Chicago) and residents in Joliet Region Telephone Directory	800-972-5400
Springfield	789-4220
Elsewhere in all other locations in Illinois	800-252-2921

Indiana

Evansville	424-6481
Fort Wayne	423-2331
Gary	938-0560
Hammond	938-0560
Indianapolis	635-2275
Muncie	288-4594
South Bend	232-3981
Terre Haute	232-9421
Elsewhere in Indiana	800-382-9740

Iowa

Cedar Rapids	366-8771
Des Moines	284-4850
Elsewhere in Iowa	800-362-2600

Kansas

Kansas City	722-2910
Topeka	357-5311
Wichita	263-2161
Elsewhere in Kansas	800-362-2190

Kentucky

Lexington	255-2333
Louisville	584-1361
Northern Kentucky (Cincinnati local dialing area)	621-6281
Elsewhere in Kentucky	800-292-6570

Louisiana

Baton Rouge	387-2206
New Orleans	581-2440
Shreveport	424-6301
Elsewhere in Louisiana	800-362-6900

Maine

Augusta	622-7101
Portland	775-7401
Elsewhere in Maine	1-800-4522-8750

Maryland

Baltimore	962-2590
Prince Georges County	488-3100
Montgomery County	488-3100
Elsewhere in Maryland	800-492-0460

Massachusetts

Boston	523-1040
Brockton	580-1770
Fitchburg	345-1031
Lawrence	682-4344
Lowell	957-4470
New Bedford	996-3111
Springfield	785-1201
Worcester	757-2712
Elsewhere in Massachusetts	1-800-392-6288

Michigan

Ann Arbor	769-9850
Detroit	237-0800
Flint	767-8830
Grand Rapids	774-8300
Lansing	394-1550
Mount Clemens	469-4200
Muskegon	726-4971
Pontiac	858-2530
Elsewhere in area code 313, call	800-462-0830
Elsewhere in area codes 517, 616, and 906, call	800-482-0670

Minnesota

Minneapolis	291-1422
St. Paul	291-1422
Elsewhere in Minnesota	800-652-9062

Mississippi

Biloxi	868-2122
Gulfport	868-2122
Jackgon	948-4500
Elsewhere in Mississippi	1-800-222-8070

Missouri

Columbia	443-2491
Jefferson City	635-9141
Joplin	781-8500
Kansas City	474-0350
St. Joseph	364-3111
St. Louis	342-1040
Springfield	887-5000
Elsewhere in Missouri	800-392-4200

Montana

Helena	443-2320
Elsewhere in Montana	800-332-2275

Nebraska

Lincoln	475-3611
Omaha	422-1500
Elsewhere in Nebraska	800-642-9960

Nevada

Las Vegas	385-6291
Reno	784-5521
Elsewhere in Nevada	800-492-6552

New Hampshire

Manchester	668-2100
Portsmouth	436-8810
Elsewhere in New Hampshire	1-800-582-7200

New Jersey

Camden	966-7333
Hackensack	487-8981
Jersey City	622-0600
Newark	622-0600
Paterson	279-9400
Trenton	394-7113
Elsewhere in New Jersey	800-242-6750

New Mexico

Albuquerque	766-3401
Elsewhere in New Mexico	800-432-6880

New York

Albany District (*Eastern Upstate New York*)	
Albany	449-3120
Poughkeepsie	452-7800
Elsewhere in Eastern Upstate New York	1-800-342-3700
Brooklyn District	
Brooklyn	596-3770
Nassau	248-3620
Queens	596-3770
Suffolk	724-5000
Buffalo District (*Western Upstate New York*)	
Binghamton	772-1540
Buffalo	855-3955
Niagara Falls	285-9361
Rochester	263-6770
Syracuse	425-8111
Utica	797-2550
Elsewhere in Western Upstate New York	1-800-462-1560
Manhattan District	
Bronx	732-0100
Manhattan	732-0100
Rockland County	352-8900
Staten Island	732-0100
Westchester County: North (Peekskill Area)	739-9191
South (Mt. Vernon, New Rochelle, White Plains—Yonkers Area)	212-732-0100

North Carolina

Charlotte	372-7750
Greensboro	274-3711
Raleigh	828-6278
Elsewhere in North Carolina	800-822-8800

North Dakota

Fargo	293-0650
Elsewhere in North Dakota	800-342-4710

Ohio

Akron	253-1141
Canton	455-6781
Cincinnati	621-6281
Cleveland	522-3000
Columbus	228-0520
Dayton	228-0557
Elyria	323-8090
Lima	228-6037
Lorain	933-9591
Mansfield	524-2095
Toledo	255-3730
Youngstown	746-1811
Elsewhere in Northern Ohio	800-362-9050
Elsewhere in Southern Ohio	800-582-1700

Oklahoma

Oklahoma City	231-5121
Tulsa	583-5121
Elsewhere in Oklahoma	800-962-3456

Oregon

Eugene	485-8285
Medford	779-3375
Portland	221-3960
Salem	581-8720
Elsewhere in Oregon	800-452-1980

Pennsylvania

Allentown	437-6966
Bethlehem	437-6966
Erie	456-8831
Harrisburg	783-8700
Philadelphia	574-9900
Pittsburgh	281-0112
Elsewhere in area codes 215 and 717, call	800-462-4000
Elsewhere in area codes 412 and 814, call	800-242-0250

Rhode Island

Block Island, call operator and ask for	Enterprise 1040
Burrillville—Gloucester	568-3100
Hope Valley—South County	539-2361
Newport	847-2463
Providence	274-1040
Tiverton—Little Compton	624-6647
Woonsocket	722-9245

South Carolina

Charleston	722-1601
Columbia	799-1040
Greenville	242-5434
Elsewhere in South Carolina	1-800-922-8810

South Dakota

Aberdeen	225-9112
Rapid City	348-9400
Sioux Falls	334-6600
Elsewhere in South Dakota	800-592-1870

Tennessee

Chattanooga	892-3010
Johnson City	929-0181
Knoxville	637-0190
Memphis	522-1250
Nashville	259-4601
Elsewhere in Tennessee	800-342-8420

Texas

Amarillo	376-2184
Austin	472-1974
Beaumont	835-5076

Dallas	742-2440
El Paso	543-7572
Ft. Worth	334-3811
Houston	965-0440
Lubbock	747-4361
San Antonio	229-5211
Waco	752-6535
Wichita Falls	723-6702
Elsewhere in Texas	800-492-4830

Utah

Salt Lake City	524-4060
Elsewhere in Utah	1-800-662-5370

Vermont

Burlington	658-1870
Elsewhere in Vermont	1-800-642-3110

Virginia

Baileys Crossroads (Northern Virginia)	557-9230
Chesapeake	461-3770
Norfolk	461-3770
Portsmouth	461-3770
Richmond	649-2361
Virginia Beach	461-3770
Elsewhere in Virginia	800-552-9500

Washington

Everett	259-0861
Seattle	442-1040
Spokane	456-8350
Tacoma	383-2021
Vancouver	695-9252
Yakima	248-6891
Elsewhere in Washington	800-732-1040

West Virginia

Parkersburg	485-1601
Elsewhere in West Virginia	800-642-1931

Wisconsin

Milwaukee	271-3780
Elsewhere in Wisconsin	800-452-9100

Wyoming

Cheyenne	635-4124
Elsewhere in Wyoming	800-525-6060

Agencies

C1.100 CONSUMER PRODUCT SAFETY COMMISSION NATIONAL AND AREA OFFICES

National Office

1750 K St. N.W.
Washington, DC 20207
202-634-7700

Area Offices

Atlanta Area
(Alabama, Florida, Georgia, Kentucky, Mississippi, North Carolina, South Carolina, Tennessee)

1330 W. Peachtree St. N.W.
Atlanta, GA 30309
404-526-2231

Boston Area
(Connecticut, Massachusetts, Maine, New Hampshire, Rhode Island, Vermont)

Rm. 1607
100 Summer St.
Boston, MA 02110
617-223-5576

Chicago Area
(Illinois, Indiana)

Rm. 2945
230 S. Dearborn St.
Chicago, IL 60604
312-353-8260

Cleveland Area
(Ohio, Michigan)

Rm. 520, Plaza Nine Bldg.
55 Erieview Plaza
Cleveland, OH 44114
216-522-3886

Dallas Area
(Oklahoma, New Mexico, Texas)

Rm. 410-C
500 S. Ervay
Dallas, TX 75201
214-749-3871

Denver Area
(Colorado, Montana, North Dakota, South Dakota, Utah, Wyoming)

Suite 938, Guaranty Bank Bldg.
817 17th St.
Denver, CO 80202
303-837-2904

Kansas City Area
(Iowa, Kansas, Missouri, Nebraska)

Suite 1500
Traders National Bank Bldg.
1125 Grand Ave.
Kansas City, MO 64106
816-374-2034

Los Angeles Area
(Southern California, Arizona)

Suite 1100
3600 Wilshire
Los Angeles, CA 90010
213-688-7272

Minneapolis Area
(Minnesota, Wisconsin)

Rm. 650, Federal Bldg.
Fort Snelling
Twin Cities, MN 55111
612-725-3424

New York Area
(New Jersey, New York, Puerto Rico, Virgin Islands)

6th Fl.
6 World Trade Center
Vesey St.
New York, NY 10048
212-264-1125

Philadelphia Area
(Delaware, District of Columbia, Maryland, Pennsylvania, Virginia, West Virginia)

10th Fl.
400 Market St.
Philadelphia, PA 19106
215-597-9105

San Francisco Area
(Northern California, Hawaii, Nevada)

Suite 500
100 Pine St.
San Francisco, CA 94111
415-556-1816

Seattle Area
(Alaska, Idaho, Oregon, Washington)

3240 Federal Bldg.
915 Second Ave.
Seattle, WA 98174
206-442-5276

C1.101 OFFICE OF CONTRACT COMPLIANCE BY DEPARTMENT AND BY AGENCY

Note: Telephone area codes are 202 unless specifically indicated otherwise.

Department of Agriculture

Office of Equal Opportunity
Department of Agriculture
Administration Bldg., Rm. 242-E
14th & Independence Ave. S.W.
Washington, DC 20250
447-4256

Contract Compliance Division
Department of Agriculture
Rm. 2405, Auditor's Bldg.
201 14th St. S.W.
Washington, DC 20250
447-3679

Department of Commerce

Special Assistant for Civil Rights
Department of Commerce
Rm. 4065
14th & Constitution Ave. N.W.
Washington, DC 20230
377-3940

Office of Civil Rights
Maritime Administration
Department of Commerce
Rm. 1608
14th & Constitution Ave. N.W.
Washington, DC 20230
377-3886

Office of Civil Rights
Economic Development Administration
Department of Commerce
Rm. 6022
14th & Constitution Ave. N.W.
Washington, DC 20230
377-5575

Department of Defense

Deputy Assistant Secretary of Defense (Equal Opportunity)
Rm. 3-E-318, The Pentagon
Washington, DC 20301
697-6381

Director for Equal Opportunity (Civilian)
OASD (M & RA)
Rm. 3-E-314, The Pentagon
Washington, DC 20301
695-0105

Contract Administration Services
Defense Logistics Agency
Cameron Station
Alexandria, VA 22314
274-7271

Energy Research and Development Administration

Office of Equal Opportunity
Energy Research and Development Administration
Rm. 6238
20 Massachusetts Ave. N.W.
Washington, DC 20545
353-5161, 4663

Environmental Protection Agency

Office of Civil Rights (A-105)
Environmental Protection Agency
Rm. 735, West Tower, Waterside Mall
Fourth and M Sts. S.W.
Washington, DC 20460
755-0555

General Services Administration

Rm. 5002
Office of Civil Rights
General Services Administration
18th and F Sts. N.W.
Washington, DC 20405
566-0450

Rm. 5022A
Construction Branch
General Services Administration
18th and F Sts. N.W.
Washington, DC 20405
566-0044

Department of Health, Education and Welfare

Office for Civil Rights
Department of Health, Education and Welfare
Rm. 5027, North Bldg.
330 Independence Ave. S.W.
Washington, DC 20201
245-6404

Contract Compliance Division
Office for Civil Rights
Department of Health, Education and Welfare
330 Independence Ave. S.W.
Washington, DC 20201
245-1848

Insurance Compliance Staff
Social Security Administration
Annex Bldg., Rm. 4414
6401 Security Blvd.
Baltimore, MD 21235
301-594-3500

Department of Housing and Urban Development

Office of Fair Housing and Equal Opportunity
Department of Housing and Urban Development
Rm. 5100
451 Seventh St. S.W.
Washington, DC 20410
755-7252

Office of Civil Rights Compliance and Enforcement
Department of Housing and Urban Development
Rm. 5216
451 Seventh St. S.W.
Washington, DC 20410
755-5518

Department of the Interior

Office for Equal Opportunity
Department of the Interior
Rm. 1324
18th and C Sts. N.W.
Washington, DC 20240
343-5693, 7494

Department of Justice

Office of Civil Rights Compliance
Law Enforcement Assistance Administration
Department of Justice
Rm. 1100
633 Indiana Ave. N.W.
Washington, DC 20530
376-3597

Civil Rights Division
Department of Justice
Rm. 5643
10th & Pennsylvania Ave. N.W.
Washington, DC 20530
739-2151

Office of Management and Budget

Office of Management and Budget
New Executive Office Bldg., Rm. 7001
726 Jackson Place N.W.
Washington, DC 20503
395-3262

National Aeronautics and Space Administration

Office of Equal Employment Opportunity Programs
NASA-Code U
Rm. 168, FOB-10B
610 Independence Ave. S.W.
Washington, DC 20546
755-2220

Small Business Administration

Compliance Division
Small Business Administration
Rm. 326
1441 L St. N.W.
Washington, DC 20416
653-6589

Tennessee Valley Authority

Equal Employment Opportunity
Tennessee Valley Authority
400 Commerce Ave., EPB21C
Knoxville, TN 37902
615-637-2621

Contract Compliance Office
Equal Employment Opportunity Staff
Tennessee Valley Authority
500 Commerce Union Bank Bldg.
Chattanooga, TN 37402
615-755-2743

Department of Transportation

Director of Civil Rights
Department of Transportation
Rm. 10217
400 Seventh St. S.W.
Washington, DC 20590
426-4648

Public Programs Division
Office of Civil Rights
Department of Transportation
Rm. 9128
400 Seventh St. S.W.
Washington, DC 20590
426-4754

Department of the Treasury

Equal Opportunity Program
Department of the Treasury
Rm. 1000
1612 K St. N.W.
Washington, DC 20220
634-5589

Veterans Administration

Contract Compliance Service
Veterans Administration
Washington, DC 20420
389-2907
148-2907

C1.102 EQUAL EMPLOYMENT OPPORTUNITY COMMISSION NATIONAL, REGIONAL, AND DISTRICT OFFICES, AND REGIONAL OFFICES OF GENERAL COUNSEL

National Office

2401 E St. N.W.
Washington, DC 20506
202-634-7040

Regional Offices

Suite 1150
Citizens Trust Bldg.
75 Piedmont Ave. N.E.
Atlanta, GA 30303
404-526-6991

Rm. 2643
230 S. Dearborn St.
Chicago, IL 60604
312-353-1488

Rm. 7B11
1100 Commerce St.
Dallas, TX 75242
214-749-1841

Rm. 113
601 E. 12th St.
Kansas City, MO 64106
816-374-2781

Rm. 1615
26 Federal Plaza
New York, NY 10007
212-264-3640

3rd Fl.
127 N. 4th St.
Philadelphia, PA 19106
215-597-7784

Suite 740
300 Montgomery St.
San Francisco, CA 94104
415-556-1775

District Offices

Suite 1515
Western Bank Bldg.
505 Marquette N.W.
Albuquerque, NM 87101
505-766-2061

10th Fl., Citizens Trust Bldg.
75 Piedmont Ave. N.E.
Atlanta, GA 30303
404-526-4566

Suite 210, Rotunda Bldg.
711 W. 40th St.
Baltimore, MD 21211
301-962-3932

2121 Eighth Ave. N.
Birmingham, AL 35203
205-254-1166

Suite 1000
150 Causeway St.
Boston, MA 02114
617-223-4535

Rm. 320
One W. Genesee St.
Buffalo, NY 14202
716-842-5170

2nd Fl.
403 N. Tryon St.
Charlotte, NC 28202
704-372-0711

Rm. 234, Federal Bldg.
536 S. Clark St.
Chicago, IL 60605
312-353-2687

Rm. 7019, Federal Bldg.
550 Main St.
Cincinnati, OH 45202
513-684-2379

Rm. 402, Engineers Building
1365 Ontario St.
Cleveland, OH 44114
216-522-4794

6th Fl., Corrigan Tower
212 N. St. Paul
Dallas, TX 75201
214-749-1751

2nd Fl., Columbine Bldg.
1845 Sherman St.
Denver, CO 80203
303-837-3668

Rm. 461
Federal Bldg. and Old Courthouse
231 W. Lafayette St.
Detroit, MI 48226
313-226-7636

Rm. 330, First National Bldg.
109 S. Oregon
El Paso, TX 79901
915-543-7596

Rm. 1101, Federal Bldg.
2320 LaBranch
Houston, TX 77004
713-527-5611

Rm. 456, Federal Bldg. & U.S. Courthouse
46 E. Ohio St.
Indianapolis, IN 46204
317-331-7212

5th Fl., Petroleum Bldg.
200 E. Pascagoula St.
Jackson, MS 39201
704-372-0711

1st Fl.
1150 Grand
Kansas City, MO 64106
816-374-5773

9th Fl.
3255 Wilshire Blvd.
Los Angeles, CA 90010
213-798-3400

Suite 1004, Dermon Bldg.
46 N. Third St.
Memphis, TN 38103
901-521-3591

Suite 414, Dupont Plaza Center
300 Biscayne Boulevard Way
Miami, FL 33131
305-350-4491

Rm. 612
342 N. Water St.
Milwaukee, WI 53202
414-362-1185

Rm. 502
744 Broad St.
Newark, NJ 07102
201-645-5967

Rm. 1007, Hale Boggs Federal Bldg.
500 Camp St.
New Orleans, LA 70130
504-589-2721

Rm. 1301
90 Church St.
New York, NY 10007
212-264-7161

Rm. 2411
Federal Office Bldg. & U.S. Courthouse
200 N.W. 4th St.
Oklahoma City, OK 73101
405-231-4912

2nd Fl.
219 N. Broad St.
Philadelphia, PA 19107
215-597-9350

Suite 1450
201 N. Central Ave.
Phoenix AZ 85073
602-261-3882

Rm. 3028A, Federal Bldg.
1000 Liberty Ave.
Pittsburgh, PA 15222
412-644-3444

Rm. 6213
400 N. 8th St.
Richmond, VA 23219
804-782-2911

Suite B-601
727 E. Durango
San Antonio, TX 78206
512-229-6051

Suite 325
1390 Market St.
San Francisco, CA 94102
415-556-0260

4th Fl.
414 Olive Way
Seattle, WA 98101
206-399-0968

1601 Olive St.
St. Louis, MO 63103
314-425-5571

Suite 402
1717 H St. N.W.
Washington, DC 20006
202-653-6197

Regional Offices of General Counsel

Suite 201
1389 Peachtree St. N.E.
Atlanta, GA 30309
404-526-2171

Rm. 1401
55 E. Jackson Blvd.
Chicago, IL 60604
312-353-8086

6th Fl.
1513 Stout St.
Denver, CO 80202
303-327-2771

Suite 200
127 N. 4th St.
Philadelphia, PA 19106
215-597-0881

Suite 1010
1390 Market St.
San Francisco, CA 94102
415-556-0833

C1.103 FEDERAL MEDIATION AND CONCILIATION SERVICE NATIONAL, REGIONAL, AND FIELD OFFICES

National Office

2100 K St. N.W. 202-653-
Washington, DC 20427

Office of National Director	-5300
Office of Mediation Services	-5240
Office of the General Counsel	-5305
Office of Arbitration Services	-5280
Office of Technical Services	-5320
Office of Information	-5290
Office of Administration	-5333

Regional Offices

Region 1

2937 Federal Bldg.
26 Federal Plaza
New York, NY 10007
212-264-1000

Region 2

401 Mall Bldg.
4th and Chestnut Sts.
Philadelphia, PA 19106
215-597-7676

Region 3

Suite 400
1422 W. Peachtree St. N.W.
Atlanta, GA 30309
404-526-2473

Region 4

1525 Superior Bldg.
815 Superior Ave. N.E.
Cleveland, OH 44114
216-522-4800

Region 5

1402 Dirksen Bldg.
219 S. Dearborn St.
Chicago, IL 60604
312-353-7350

Region 6

Chromalloy Plaza, Fifth Fl.
120 S. Central
St. Louis, MO 63105
314-425-3291

Region 7

Box 36007
450 Golden Gate Ave.
San Francisco, CA 94102
415-556-4670

Region 8

Rm. 440
Fourth and Vine Bldg.
2615 Fourth Ave.
Seattle, WA 98121
206-442-5800

Field Offices

Region 1

703 Federal Office Bldg.
405 Main St.
Hartford, CT 06103

2011 U.S. Post Office and Federal Bldg.
151 Forrest Ave.
P.O. Box 3587
Portland, ME 04101
207-772-4424

100 Summer St.
Suite 1540
Boston, MA 02110

320 Federal Bldg. and Courthouse
595 Main St.
Worcester, MA 01601

20 Evergreen
East Orange, NJ 07018
201-645-2200

306 U.S. Post Office and Courthouse
P.O. Box 870
Albany, NY 12201

1105 New Federal Bldg.
111 W. Huron St.
Buffalo, NY 14202

404 Imperial Square Bldg.
175 Fulton Ave.
Hempstead, L.I., NY 11550
516-538-3232

U.S. Courthouse and Federal Bldg.
100 S. Clinton St.
Syracuse, N.Y. 13202

Room 1
100 Jenckes Hill Rd.
Lincoln, RI 02865

Region 2

2100 K St. N.W.
Washington, DC 20427
202-653-7680

1011 Federal Office Bldg.
Charles Center
31 Hopkins Plaza
Baltimore, MD 20201
301-837-2429

518 U.S. Post Office and Courthouse
402 E. State St.
Trenton, NJ 08608
609-394-7195

301 Farr Bldg.
739 Hamilton St.
Allentown, PA 18101
215-433-1927

420 Commerce Bldg.
12th and State Sts.
Erie, PA 16501
814-455-4914

504 Federal Office Bldg.
228 Walnut St.
Harrisburg, PA 17108
717-782-2220

2017 Federal Bldg.
1000 Liberty Ave.
Pittsburgh, PA 15222

8225 Federal Office Bldg.
400 N. 8th St.
P.O. Box 10027
Richmond, VA 23240
804-648-6785

2040 Federal Bldg.
425 Juliana St.
P.O. Box 1945
Parkersburg, WV 26101
304-485-6329

Region 3

428 S. Twentieth Bldg.
908 S. 20th St.
Birmingham, AL 35205
205-254-1445

433 Federal Bldg. and
U.S. Courthouse
113 St. Joseph St.
Mobile, AL 36602
205-690-2141

Box 35052
400 W. Bay St.
Jacksonville, FL 32202
904-791-2630

1301 Federal Office Bldg.
51 S.W. First Ave.
Miami, FL 33130
305-350-5520

731 Federal Office Bldg.
500 Zack St.
Tampa, FL 33602
813-228-2591

924 F. Edward Hebert Bldg.
600 South St.
New Orleans, LA 70130
504-589-6112

1115 Jefferson First Union Bldg.
S. Tryon at Third St.
Charlotte, NC 28282
704-372-0711 ext 401

1019 First Tennessee Bldg.
7th and Market St.
Chattanooga, TN 37402
615-266-4470

Suite 300, Bldg. 2
1111 N. Shore Dr.
Knoxville, TN 37919
615-637-9300 ext 1248

471 Clifford David Federal Bldg.
167 N. Main St.
Memphis, TN 38103
901-534-3276

Suite 1203
1808 West End Bldg.
Nashville, TN 37203
615-749-5935

Region 4

Executive Park, Suite 222
Building Two
Louisville, KY 40207
502-582-5204

402 Federal Bldg. and U.S. Courthouse
231 W. Lafayette
Detroit, MI 48226
313-226-7765

250 Federal Bldg. and U.S. Courthouse
110 Michigan N.W.
Grand Rapids, MI 49502
616-456-2401

The Bell Bldg.
500 W. Crosstown Pkwy.
Kalamazoo, MI 49001
616-345-2409

201 U.S. Post Office and Federal Bldg.
500 Federal St.
Saginaw, MI 48607
517-793-2340 ext 428

428 Federal Bldg. and U.S. Courthouse
2 S. Main St.
Akron, OH 44308
216-375-5720

5106 Federal Office Bldg.
Cincinnati, OH 45202
513-684-2951

Rm. 102, Office Bldg. One
6600 Busch Blvd.
Columbus, OH 43229
614-469-5575

603 Federal Bldg.
200 W. Second St.
Dayton, OH 45402
513-225-2891

709 Federal Bldg.
234 Summit St.
Toledo, OH 43604
419-259-6400

Region 5

3024 W. Lake Ave.
Nucli Bldg.
Peoria, IL 61614

Rm. 300
3600 E. State St.
Rockford, IL 61108
815-399-4412

240 Federal Bldg. and U.S. Courthouse
101 N.W. Seventh St.
Evansville, IN 47708
812-423-4271

Suite B-105
2346 S. Lynhurst Dr.
Indianapolis, IN 46241
317-269-7233

Suite 328, JMS Bldg.
108 N. Main St.
South Bend, IN 46601
219-232-9961

214 Federal Bldg.
325 E. Walnut St.
Green Bay, WI 54301
414-465-3933

350 Federal Bldg.
517 E. Wisconsin Ave.
Milwaukee, WI 53202
414-224-3296

North Bldg., Suite 250
17 Washington Ave.
Minneapolis, MN 55401
612-725-2581

Region 6

5411 Federal Office Bldg.
700 W. Capitol St.
Little Rock, AR 72201
501-378-5460

510 American Bldg.
1st Ave. and 2nd St. S.E.
Cedar Rapids, IA 52401
319-366-2411

722 Federal Bldg.
210 Walnut St.
Des Moines, IA 50309
515-284-4110

612 Century Plaza
111 W. Douglas
Wichita, KS 67202
316-267-6311 ext 173

1768 Federal Bldg.
601 E. 12th St.
Kansas City, MO 64106
816-374-3026

245 Landmark Bldg.
309 N. Jefferson St.
Springfield, MO 65806
417-865-3793

Rm. 303
6818 Grover
Omaha, NE 68106
402-221-9401

513 U.S. Post Office and Courthouse
3rd and Robinson Sts.
Oklahoma City, OK 73102
405-231-4984

Rm. 1235
1200 Main-Tower Bldg.
Dallas, TX 75202
214-749-2917

6016 Federal Bldg. and U.S. Courthouse
515 Rusk Ave.
Houston, TX 77002
713-226-4257

Region 7

Valley Bank Center
Suite 2980
Phoenix, AZ 85025
602-261-3648

Suite 700
3660 Wilshire Bldg.
Los Angeles, CA 90010
213-688-7180

Rm. 2330
New Federal Bldg.
2800 Cottage Way
Sacramento, CA 95825
916-468-4534

936 San Diego Trust and Savings Bldg.
530 Broadway
San Diego, CA 92101
714-895-6260

Rm. 604, Hawaiian Life Bldg.
1311 Kapiolani Blvd.
Honolulu, HI 96814
808-546-5663

3002 Federal Bldg.
517 Gold S.W.
Albuquerque, NM 87101
505-766-2459

Region 8

Rm. 165
Federal Bldg. and U.S. Courthouse
4th and F Sts.
Anchorage, AK 99510

Rm. 17539
Federal Bldg. and U.S. Courthouse
1961 Stout St.
Denver, CO 80202
303-837-3186

Central Plaza, Suite 310
600 Central Ave.
Great Falls, MT 59401
406-452-0180

Rm. 795, U.S. Courthouse
920 W. Riverside Ave.
Spokane, WA 99201
509-456-2516

320 U.S. Courthouse
620 S.W. Main
Portland, OR 97205
503-221-2176

Rm. 4221, New Federal Bldg.
125 S. State St.
Salt Lake City, UT 84138
801-524-5250

C1.104 FEDERAL TRADE COMMISSION REGIONAL AND LOCAL OFFICES; CONSUMER PROTECTION AND RESTRAINT OF TRADE MATTERS

Regional or Local Offices

Rm. 13209, Federal Bldg.
11000 Wilshire Blvd.
Los Angeles, CA 90024
213-824-7575

450 Golden Gate Ave.
Box 36005
San Francisco, CA 94102
415-556-1270

6th Fl., Gelman Bldg.
2120 L St.
Washington, DC 20037
202-254-7700

Rm. 800
730 Peachtree St. N.E.
Atlanta, GA 30308
404-526-5836

Suite 1437
55 E. Monroe St.
Chicago, IL 60603
312-353-4423

Rm. 1301
150 Causeway St.
Boston, MA 02114
617-223-6621

22nd Fl., Federal Bldg.
26 Federal Plaza
New York, NY 10007
212-264-1207

Rm. 1339, Federal Office Bldg.
1240 E. Ninth St.
Cleveland, OH 44199
216-522-4207

Rm. 452-B
500 S. Ervay St.
Dallas, TX 75201
214-749-3056

28th Fl., Federal Bldg.
915 Second Ave.
Seattle, WA 98174
206-442-4655

Suite 2900
1405 Curtis St.
Denver, CO 80202
303-837-2871

Headquarters for Consumer Protection Matters

Bureau of Consumer Protection
Federal Trade Commission Bldg.
6th and Pennsylvania Ave. N.W.
Washington, DC 20580
202-523-3727

Headquarters for Restraint of Trade Matters

Bureau of Competition
Federal Trade Commission Bldg.
6th and Pennsylvania Ave. N.W.
Washington, DC 20580
202-523-3601

C1.105 NATIONAL AND REGIONAL BUSINESS SERVICE CENTERS,, GENERAL SERVICES ADMINISTRATION

National Office

General Services Administration
General Services Bldg.
18th and F Sts. N.W.
Washington, DC 20405
202-655-4000

Regional Offices

Region 1
(Connecticut, Maine, Massachusetts, New Hampshire, Rhode Island, Vermont)

Regional Director of Public Services (1FI)
General Services Administration
John W. McCormack Bldg.
Boston, MA 02109
617-223-2868

Region 2
(New Jersey, New York, Puerto Rico, Virgin Islands)

Regional Director of Public Services (2FI)
General Services Administration
26 Federal Plaza
New York, NY 10007
212-264-1234

Region 3
(District of Columbia, Maryland, Virginia, West Virginia)

Regional Director of Public Services (3FI)
General Services Administration
7th & D Sts. S.W.
Washington, DC 20407
202-472-1804

(Pennsylvania and Delaware)

Manager, Business Service Center
General Services Administration
600 Arch St.
Philadelphia, PA 19106
215-597-9613

Region 4
(Alabama, Florida, Georgia, Kentucky, Mississippi, North Carolina, South Carolina, Tennessee)

Regional Director of Public Services (4FI)
General Services Administration
1776 Peachtree St.
Atlanta, GA 30309
404-526-5661

Region 5
(Illinois, Indiana, Michigan, Minnesota, Ohio, Wisconsin)

Regional Director of Public Services (5FI)
General Services Administration
230 S. Dearborn St.
Chicago, IL 60604
312-353-5383

Region 6
(Iowa, Kansas, Missouri, Nebraska)

Regional Director of Public Services (6FI)
General Services Administration
1500 E. Bannister Rd.
Kansas City, MO 64131
816-926-7203

Region 7
(Arkansas, Louisiana, New Mexico, Oklahoma, and Texas (except below)

Regional Director of Public Services (7FI)
General Services Administration
819 Taylor St.
Fort Worth, TX 76102
817-334-3284

(Gulf Coast Area from Brownsville, Texas, to New Orleans, Louisiana)

Manager, Business Service Center
General Services Administration
FOB Courthouse
515 Rusk St.
Houston, TX 77002
713-226-5787

Region 8
(Colorado, North Dakota, South Dakota, Montana, Utah, Wyoming)

Regional Director of Public Services (8FI)
General Services Administration
Bldg. 41, Denver Federal Center
Denver, CO 80225
303-234-2216

Region 9
(Northern California, Hawaii, and Nevada (except Clark County)

Regional Director of Public Services (9FI)
General Services Administration
525 Market St.
San Francisco, CA 94105
415-556-2122

(Los Angeles, Southern California, Clark County, Nevada, and Arizona)

Manager, Business Service Center
General Services Administration
300 N. Los Angeles
Los Angeles, CA 90012
213-688-9012

Region 10
(Alaska, Idaho, Oregon, Washington)

Regional Director of Public Services (10FI)
General Services Administration
440 Federal Bldg.
915 Second Ave.
Seattle, WA 98174
206-442-5556

C1.106 FEDERAL INFORMATION CENTERS, GENERAL SERVICES ADMINISTRATION

Arizona

Federal Bldg.
230 N. First Ave.
Phoenix, AZ 85025

(From Tucson, call toll-free: 622-1511)

California

Federal Bldg.
300 N. Los Angeles St.
Los Angeles, CA 90012
213-688-3800

Federal Bldg. & U.S. Courthouse
650 Capitol Mall
Sacramento, CA 95814
916-449-3344

202 C St.
San Diego, CA 92101
714-293-6030

Federal Bldg. & U.S. Courthouse
450 Golden Gate Ave.
San Francisco, CA 94102
415-556-6600

(From San Jose, call toll free: 275-7422)

Colorado

Federal Bldg. & U.S. Courthouse
1961 Stout St.
Denver, CO 80202
303-837-3602

(From Colorado Springs, call toll free: 471-9491)

(From Pueblo, call toll free: 544-9523)

District of Columbia

7th and D Sts. S.W.
Washington, DC 20407
202-755-8660

Florida

Federal Bldg.
51 S.W. First Ave.
Miami, FL 33130
305-350-4155

(From Fort Lauderdale, call toll free: 522-8531)
(From West Palm Beach, call toll free: 833-7566)

William C. Cramer Federal Bldg.
144 First Ave. S.
St. Petersburg, FL 33701
813-893-3495

(From Jacksonville, call toll free: 354-4756
(From Tampa, call toll free: 229-7911)

Georgia

Federal Bldg.
275 Peachtree St. N.E.
Atlanta, GA 30303
404-526-6891

(From Birmingham, Ala., call toll free: 322-8591)
(From Charlotte, N.C., call toll free: 376-3600)

Hawaii

U.S. Post Office, Courthouse, and Customhouse
335 Merchant St.
Honolulu, HI 96813
808-546-8620

Illinois

Everett McKinley Dirksen Bldg.
219 S. Dearborn St.
Chicago, IL 60604
312-353-4242

(From Milwaukee, Wisc., call toll free: 271-2273)

Indiana

Federal Bldg. & U.S. Courthouse
46 E. Ohio St.
Indianapolis, IN 46204
317-633-8484

Kentucky

Federal Bldg.
600 Federal Pl.
Louisville, KY 40202
502-282-6261

Louisiana

Federal Bldg.
701 Loyola Ave.
New Orleans, LA 70113
504-527-6696

(From Mobile, Ala., call toll free: 438-1421)

Maryland

Federal Bldg.
31 Hopkins Plaza
Baltimore, MD 21201
301-962-4980

Massachusetts

John F. Kennedy Federal Bldg.
Government Center
Boston, MA 02203
617-223-7121

(From Providence, R.I., call toll free: 331-5565

Michigan

Federal Bldg. & U.S. Courthouse
231 W. Lafayette St.
Detroit, MI 48226
313-226-7016

Minnesota

Federal Bldg. & U.S. Courthouse
110 S. 4th St.
Minneapolis, MN 55401
612-725-2073

Missouri

Federal Bldg.
601 E. 12th St.
Kansas City, MO 64106
816-374-2466

(From St. Joseph, call toll free: 233-8206)
(From Topeka, Kans., call toll free: 232-7229)
(From Wichita, Kans., call toll free: 263-6931)

Federal Bldg.
1520 Market St.
St. Louis, MO 63103
314-622-4106

Nebraska

Federal Bldg., U.S. Post Office & Courthouse
215 N. 17th St.
Omaha, NE 68102
402-221-3353

(From Des Moines, Iowa, call toll free: 282-9091)

New Jersey

Federal Bldg.
970 Broad St.
Newark, NJ 07102
201-645-3600

(From Trenton, call toll free: 396-4400)

New Mexico

Federal Bldg. & U.S. Courthouse
500 Gold Ave. S.W.
Albuquerque, NM 87101
505-766-3091

(From Santa Fe, call toll free: 983-7743)

New York

Federal Bldg.
111 W. Huron St.
Buffalo, NY 14202
716-842-5770

(From Rochester, call toll free: 546-5075)
(From Syracuse, call toll free: 476-8545)

Federal Office Bldg.
26 Federal Plaza
New York, NY 10007
212-264-4464

(From Albany, call toll free: 463-4421)
(From Hartford, Conn., call toll free: 527-2617
(From New Haven, Conn., call toll free: 624-4720)

Ohio

Federal Bldg.
550 Main St.
Cincinnati,. OH 45202
513-684-2801

(From Columbus, call toll free: 221-1014)
(From Dayton, call toll free: 223-7377)

Federal Bldg.
1240 E. 9th St.
Cleveland, OH 44199
216-522-4040

(From Akron, call toll free: 375-5475)
(From Toledo, call toll free: 244-8625)

Oklahoma

U.S. Post Office & Federal Bldg.
201 N.W. 3rd St.
Oklahoma City, OK 73102
405-231-4868

(From Tulsa, call toll free: 854-4193)

Oregon

208 U.S. Courthouse
620 S.W. Main St.
Portland, OR 97205
503-221-2222

Pennsylvania

William J. Green, Jr. Federal Bldg.
600 Arch St.
Philadelphia, PA 19106
215-597-7042

(From Scranton, call toll free: 346-7081)

Federal Bldg.
1000 Liberty Ave.
Pittsburgh, PA 15222
412-644-3456

Tennessee

Clifford Davis Federal Bldg.
167 N. Main St.
Memphia, TN 38103
901-534-3285

(From Chattanooga, call toll free: 265-8231)
(From Little Rock, Ark., call toll free: 378-6177)

Texas

Fritz Garland Lanham Federal Bldg.
819 Taylor St.
Fort Worth, TX 76102
817-334-3624

(From Dallas, call toll free: 749-2131)

Federal Bldg. & U.S. Courthouse
515 Rusk Ave.
Houston, TX 77002
713-226-5711

(From Austin, call toll free: 472-5494
(From San Antonio, call toll free: 224-4471)

Utah

Federal Bldg., U.S. Post Office & Courthouse
125 S. State St.
Salt Lake City, UT 84138
801-524-5353

(From Ogden, call toll free: 399-1347)

Washington

Arcade Plaza
1321 2nd Ave.
Seattle, WA 98101
206-442-0570

(From Tacoma, call toll free: 383-5230)

C1.107 NATIONAL AERONAUTICS AND SPACE ADMINISTRATION FIELD CENTERS, TECHNOLOGY APPLICATION TEAMS, AND INDUSTRIAL APPLICATIONS CENTERS

National Office

400 Maryland Ave. S.W.
Washington, DC 20546
202-755-2320

Field Centers

Ames Research Center
Code AU: 230-2
Moffett Field, CA 94035
415-965-5554

Hugh L. Dryden Flight Research Center
P.O. Box 273
Edwards, CA 93523
805-258-3311 ext 568

Goddard Space Flight Center
Code 704.1
Greenbelt, MD 20771
301-982-6242

Johnson Space Center
Code AT3
Houston, TX 77058
713-483-3809

John F. Kennedy Space Center
Code SA-RTP
Kennedy Space Center, FL 32899
305-867-2780

Langley Research Center
Mail Stop 139A
Hampton, VA 23665
804-827-3281

Lewis Research Center
21000 Brookpark Rd.
Cleveland, OH 44135
216-433-4000 ext 6832

Marshall Space Flight Center
Code AT01
Marshall Space Flight Center, AL 35812
205-453-2224

NASA Resident Legal Office-JPL
4800 Oak Grove Dr.
Pasedena, CA 91103
213-354-6420

Wallops Flight Center
Wallops Island, VA 23337
804-824-3411 ext 201

Technology Utilization Office
Code KT
NASA Headquarters
Washington, DC 20546
202-755-3103

Technology Application Teams

Technology Applications Group
Informatics Information Systems Co.
P.O. Box 8756
Baltimore/Washington International Airport, MD 21240
301-796-5300 ext 252

Biomedical

Mail Code DE5
Lyndon B. Johnson Space Center
Houston, TX 77058
713-483-3753

Research Triangle Institute
P.O. Box 12194
Research Triangle Park, NC 27709

Stanford University School of Medicine
Cardiology Division
Biomedical Technology Transfer
Suite 3303
701 Welch Rd.
Palo Alto, CA 94303
415-497-5935

Advisory Center for Medical Technology and Systems
University of Wisconsin
1500 Johnson Dr.
Madison, WI 53706
608-263-1550

Technological

Public Technology, Inc.
Suite 1100
1140 Connecticut Ave. N.W.
Washington, DC 20036
202-452-7700

Stanford Research Institute
333 Ravenswood Ave.
Menlo Park, CA 94026
415-326-6200 ext 2864

Industrial Applications Centers

Aerospace Research Applications Center
Indiana University
400 E. 7th St.
Bloomington, IN 47401
812-337-7833

Knowledge Availability Systems Center
University of Pittsburgh
Pittsburgh, PA 15260
412-624-5211

New England Research Application Center
Mansfield Professional Park
Storrs, CT 06268
203-486-4533

North Carolina Science and Technology Research Center
P.O. Box 12235
Research Triangle Park, NC 27709
919-549-0671

Technology Application Center
University of New Mexico
Albuquerque, NM 87131
505-277-4000

Western Research Application Center
University of Southern California
University Park
Los Angeles, CA 90007
213-746-6132

C1.108 NATIONAL CREDIT UNION ADMINISTRATION NATIONAL AND REGIONAL OFFICES

National Office

2025 M St. N.W.
Washington, DC 20456
202-254-9800

Regional Offices

Region 1
(Connecticut, Maine, Massachusetts, New Hampshire, New York, Puerto Rico, Rhode Island, Vermont, Virgin Islands)

Rm. 3E
State Street South Bldg.
1776 Heritage Dr.
Boston, MA 02171
617-223-6807

Region 2
(Delaware, District of Columbia, Maryland, New Jersey, Pennsylvania)

Federal Bldg.
228 Walnut St.
Box 926
Harrisburg, PA 17108
717-782-4595

Region 3
(Alabama, Canal Zone, Florida, Georgia, Kentucky, Mississippi, North Carolina, South Carolina, Tennessee, Virginia, West Virginia)

Suite 500
1365 Peachtree St.
Atlanta, GA 30309
404-526-3127

Region 4
(Illinois, Indiana, Iowa, Michigan, Minnesota, North Dakota, Ohio, South Dakota, Wisconsin)

New Federal Bldg.
234 N. Summit St.
Toledo, OH 43604
419-259-7511

Region 5
(Arkansas, Colorado, Kansas, Louisiana, Missouri, Nebraska, New Mexico, Oklahoma, Texas, Utah, Wyoming)

Suite 1400
515 Congress Ave.
Austin, TX 78701
512-397-5131

Region 6
(Alaska, Arizona, California, Guam, Hawaii, Idaho, Montana, Nevada, Oregon, Washington)

Suite 1830
Two Embarcadero Center
San Francisco, CA 94111
415-556-6277

C1.109 NATIONAL LABOR RELATIONS BOARD NATIONAL AND FIELD OFFICES

National Office

Office of Information
1717 Pennsylvania Ave. N.W.
Washington, DC 20570
202-655-4000

Field Offices

New Federal Bldg.
Clinton Ave. at N. Pearl St.
Albany, NY 12207
518-472-2215

Patio Plaza Bldg., Upper Level
5000 Marble Ave. N.E.
Albuquerque, NM 87110
505-766-2582

409 Hill Bldg.
632 W. 6th Ave.
Anchorage, AK 99501
907-265-5271

Peachtree Bldg., Suite 701
730 Peachtree St. N.E.
Atlanta, GA 30308
404-526-5364

Federal Bldg., Rm. 1019
Hopkins Plaza
Baltimore, MD 21201
301-962-2737

2102 City Federal Bldg.
2026 Second Ave. N.
Birmingham, AL 35203
205-254-1492

12th Fl., Keystone Bldg.
99 High St.
Boston, MA 02110
617-223-3330

16 Court St., 4th Fl.
Brooklyn, NY 11241
212-596-3750

Federal Bldg., 9th Fl.
111 W. Huron St.
Buffalo, NY 14202
716-842-3106

Everett McKinley Dirksen Bldg., Rm. 881
219 S. Dearborn St.
Chicago, IL 60604
312-353-7574

Federal Office Bldg., Rm. 3003
550 Main St.
Cincinnati, OH 45202
513-684-3621

Suite 1965
Anthony J. Celebrezze Federal Bldg.
1240 E. 9th St.
Cleveland, OH 44199
216-522-3725

Suite 410
1570 Madruga Ave.
Coral Gables, FL 33146
305-350-5391

U.S. Custom House, Rm. 260
721 19th St.
Denver, CO 80202
303-837-3551

Rm. 300
Patrick V. McNamara Federal Bldg.
477 Michigan Ave.
Detroit, MI 48226
313-226-3210

Pershing Bldg., Suite 307
4100 Rio Bravo St.
El Paso, TX 79902
915-543-7737

Federal Office Bldg., Rm. 8A-24
819 Taylor St.
Fort Worth, TX 76102
817-334-2938

Pan Am Bldg., 7th Fl.
255 Ponce de Leon Ave.
Hato Rey, PR 00917
809-763-6363

Suite 308
1311 Kapiolani Blvd.
Honolulu, HI 96814
808-546-5100

One Allen Center
500 Dallas Ave.
Houston, TX 77002
713-226-4271

Federal Office Bldg., Rm. 232
575 N. Pennsylvania St.
Indianapolis, IN 46204
317-269-7401

Federal Bldg.
400 W. Bay St.
Jacksonville, FL 32202
904-946-3768

616 Two Gateway Center
Fourth at State
Kansas City, MO 66101
816-374-4434

Rm. 4-503
300 Las Vegas Blvd.
Las Vegas, NE 89101
702-385-6416

3511 Federal Bldg.
700 W. Capitol St.
Little Rock AR 72201
501-378-5512

Federal Bldg., Rm. 12100
11000 Wilshire Blvd.
Los Angeles, CA 90024
213-824-7371

Rm. 746
Clifford Davis Federal Bldg.
167 N. Main St.
Memphia, TN 38103
901-534-3171

Commerce Bldg., 2nd Fl.
744 N. 4th St.
Milwaukee, WI 53203
414-224-3870

316 Federal Bldg.
110 S. 4th St.
Minneapolis, MN 55401
612-725-2601

Federal Bldg., U.S. Courthouse
Room A-702
Nashville, TN 37203
615-749-5922

Plaza Tower, Suite 2700
1001 Howard Ave.
New Orleans, LA 70113
504-589-6396

Federal Bldg., 16th Fl.
970 Broad St.
Newark, NJ 07102
201-645-3240

Federal Bldg., 36th Fl.
Federal Plaza
New York, NY 10007
212-264-0330

Savings Center Tower, 10th Fl.
Peoria, IL 61602
309-671-7083

Suite 4400
William J. Green Jr. Federal Bldg.
600 Arch St.
Philadelphia, PA 19106
215-597-7608

La Torre Bldg.
6107 N. 7th St.
Phoenix, AZ 85014
602-261-6080

Porter Bldg., 10th Fl.
601 Grant St.
Pittsburgh, PA 15222
412-664-2944

310 Six Ten Broadway Bldg.
610 S.W. Broadway
Portland, OR 97205
503-221-3085

Puerto Rico (see Hato Rey)

Rm. 448
210 N. 12th St.
St. Louis, MO 63101
314-425-4142

13018 Federal Bldg., Box 36047
450 Golden Gate Ave.
San Francisco, CA 94102
415-556-6721

Federal Bldg., 29th Fl.
915 Second Ave.
Seattle, WA 98174
206-442-7542

Federal Office Bldg., Rm. 706
P.O. Box 3322
500 Zack St.
Tampa, FL 33602
813-228-2646

Gelman Bldg., Suite 100
2120 L St. N.W.
Washington, DC 20037
202-254-7612

1624 Wachovia Bldg.
301 N. Main St.
Winston-Salem, NC 27101
919-723-3382

C1.110 SMALL BUSINESS ADMINISTRATION NATIONAL, REGIONAL, AND FIELD OFFICES

National Office

1441 L St. N.W.
Washington, DC 20416
202-382-1891

Regional Offices

Region 1

10th Fl.
150 Causeway St.
Boston, MA 02114
617-223-2100

Region 2

Rm. 3214
26 Federal Plaza
New York, NY 10007
212-264-1468

Region 3

Suite 646, West Lobby
1 Bala Cynwyd Plaza
231 St. Asaph's Rd.
Philadelphia, Bala Cynwyd, PA 19004
215-597-3311

Region 4

Rm. 470
1401 Peachtree St. N.E.
Atlanta, GA 30309
404-526-0111

Region 5

Rm. 838, Federal Bldg.
219 S. Dearborn St.
Chicago, IL 60604
312-353-4400

Region 6

Suite 230
Regal Park Office Bldg.
1720 Regal Row
Dallas, TX 75235
214-749-1011

Region 7

23rd Fl.
911 Walnut St.
Kansas City, MO 64106
816-374-3318

Region 8

Executive Tower Bldg.
1405 Curtis St.
Denver, CO 80202
303-327-0111

Region 9

Box 36044
Federal Bldg.
450 Golden Gate Ave.
San Francisco, CA 94102
415-556-9000

Region 10

5th Fl., Dexter Horton Bldg.
710 2nd Ave.
Seattle, WA 98104
206-442-4343

Field Offices

Region 1

10th Fl.
150 Cuaseway St.
Boston, MA 02114
617-223-2100

4th Fl.
302 High St.
Holyoke, MA 01040
413-536-8770

Rm. 512, Federal Bldg.
40 Western Ave.
Augusta, ME 04330
207-622-6171

Rm. 213
55 Pleasant St.
Concord, NH 03301
603-224-4041

Rm. 710, Federal Bldg.
450 Main St.
Hartford, CT 06103
203-244-2000

Rm. 210, Federal Bldg.
87 State St.
Montpelier, VT 05602
802-223-7472

Rm. 710
57 Eddy St.
Providence, RI 02903
401-528-1000

Region 2

Rm. 3100
26 Federal Plaza
New York, NY 10007
212-264-4355

131 Jericho Turnpike
Jericho, L.I., NY 11753
516-997-7760

P.O. Box 1915
Chardon and Bolivia Sts.
Hato Rey, PR 00919
809-763-6363

Franklin Bldg.
St. Thomas, VI 00801
809-774-1331

Rm. 1635
970 Broad St.
Newark, NJ 07102
201-645-3581

1800 E. Davis St.
Camden, NJ 08104
609-757-5183

Rm. 1073, Federal Bldg.
100 S. Clinton St.
Syracuse, NY 13202
315-473-3350

Rm. 1311, Federal Bldg.
111 W. Huron St.
Buffalo, NY 14202
716-842-3240

Rm. 412
180 State St.
Elmira, NY 14904
607-734-1571

Rm. 922, Twin Towers Bldg.
99 Washington Ave.
Albany, NY 12210
518-472-4411

Federal Bldg.
100 State St.
Rochester, NY 14604
716-263-5700

Region 3

Suite 400, East Lobby
1 Bala Cynwyd Plaza
231 St. Asaph's Rd.
Philadelphia, Bala Cynwyd, PA 19004
215-597-3311

1500 N. 2nd St.
Harrisburg, PA 17108
717-782-2200

Penn Place
20 N. Pennsylvania Ave.
Wilkes Barre, PA 18702
717-825-6811

Rm. 5207, Lockbox 16
Federal Bldg.
844 King St.
Wilmington, DE 19801
302-571-6294

7800 York Rd.
Baltimore, Towson, MD 21204
301-962-2150

Rm. 301, Lowndes Bldg.
109 N. 3rd St.
Clarksburg, WV 26301
304-623-3461

Suite 628
Charleston National Plaza
Charleston, WV 25301
304-343-6181

Rm. 1401, Federal Bldg.
1000 Liberty Ave.
Pittsburgh, PA 15222
412-644-2780

Rm. 3015, Federal Bldg.
400 N. 8th St.
Richmond, VA 23240
804-782-2617

Suite 250
1030 15th St. N.W.
Washington, DC 20417
202-655-4000

Region 4

6th Fl.
1720 Peachtree St. N.E.
Atlanta, GA 30309
404-526-0111

Rm. 202
908 S. 20th St.
Birmingham, AL 35205
205-254-1000

230 S. Tryon St.
Charlotte, NC 28202
704-372-0711

215 S. Evans St.
Greenville, NC 27834
919-752-3798

Rm. 117
1801 Assembly St.
Columbia, SC 29201
803-765-5376

Suite 690, Petroleum Bldg.
200 E. Pascagoula St.
Jackson, MS 39201
601-969-4371

2nd Fl.
Gulf National Life Insurance Bldg.
111 Fred Halse Blvd.
Biloxi, MS 39530
601-863-1972

Rm. 261, Federal Bldg.
400 W. Bay St.
P.O. Box 3507
Jacksonville, FL 32202
904-791-2011

Rm. 188, Federal Bldg.
600 Federal Pl.
Louisville, KY 40202
502-582-5971

5th Fl.
2222 Ponce De Leon Blvd.
Miami, Coral Gables, FL 33184
305-350-5011

Suite 203
1802 N. Trask St.
Tampa, FL 33607
813-228-2594

Suite 1012
404 James Robertson Pkwy.
Nashville, TN 37219
615-749-5022

Rm. 307, Fidelity Bankers Bldg.
502 S. Gay St.
Knoxville, TN 37902
615-637-9300

Rm. 211, Federal Bldg.
167 N. Main St.
Memphis, TN 38103
901-521-3588

Rm. 229, Federal Bldg.
701 Clematis St.
W. Palm Beach, FL 33402
305-659-7533

Region 5

Rm. 437, Federal Bldg.
219 S. Dearborn St.
Chicago, IL 60604
312-353-4528

One North, Old State Capital Plaza
Springfield, IL 62701
217-525-4416

Rm. 317
1240 E. 9th St.
Cleveland, OH 44199
216-522-4180

Tonti Bldg.
34 N. High St.
Columbus, OH 43215
614-469-6860

Federal Bldg.
550 Main St.
Cincinnati, OH 45202
513-684-2814

McNamara Bldg.
477 Michigan Ave.
Detroit, MI 48226
313-226-6075

Don H. Bottum University Center
540 W. Kaye Ave.
Marquette, MI 49855
906-225-1108

5th Fl., Century Bldg.
575 N. Pennsylvania St.
Indianapolis, IN 46204
317-269-7272

Rm. 713
122 W. Washington Ave.
Madison, WI 53703
608-252-5261

Rm. 905
Continental Bank and Trust Co.
735 W. Wisconsin Ave.
Milwaukee, WI 53233
414-224-3941

Rm. 16, Federal Office Bldg. and U.S. Courthouse
500 S. Barstow St.
Eau Claire, WI 54701
715-834-9012

Plymouth Bldg.
12 S. 6th St.
Minneapolis, MN 55402
612-725-2362

Region 6

Rm. 300
1100 Commerce St.
Dallas, TX 75202
214-749-1011

Federal Bldg.
100 S. Washington St.
Marshall, TX 75670
214-935-5257

Patio Plaza Bldg.
5000 Marble Ave. N.E.
Albuquerque, NM 87110
505-766-5111

One Allen Center
500 Dallas
Houston, TX 77002
713-226-4011

Suite 900
611 Gaines St.
Little Rock, AR 72201
501-378-5011

712 Federal Office Bldg. and U.S. Courthouse
1205 Texas Ave.
Lubbock, TX 79408
806-762-7011

Suite 300
4100 Rio Bravo
El Paso, TX 79901
915-543-7200

222 E. Van Buren St.
Lower Rio Grande Valley
Harlingen, TX 78550
512-423-3011

3105 Leopard St.
Corpus Christi, TX 78408
512-888-3011

17th Fl., Plaza Tower
1001 Howard Ave.
New Orleans, LA 70113
504-589-2611

U.S. Post Office and Courthouse Bldg.
Fannin St.
Shreveport, LA 71163
318-226-5196

Suite 840
50 Penn Place
Oklahoma City, OK 73118
405-736-4011

Rm. A-513
727 E. Durango
San Antonio, TX 78206
512-229-5511

Region 7

5th Fl.
1150 Grande Ave.
Kansas City, MO 64106
816-374-5557

Rm. 749, New Federal Bldg.
210 Walnut St.
Des Moines, IA 50309
515-284-4422

Empire State Bldg.
Nineteen and Farnam Sts.
Omaha, NE 68102
402-221-4691

Suite 2500, Mercantile Tower
One Mercantile Center
St. Louis, MO 63101
314-425-4191

One Mercantile Tower
St. Louis, MO 63101
314-279-4110

Bldg. 107
4300 Goodfellow Blvd.
St. Louis, MO 63101
314-273-2222

Main Place Bldg.
110 E. Waterman St.
Wichita, KS 67202
316-267-6566

Region 8

Rm. 426A
721 19th St.
Denver, CO 80202
303-327-0111

Rm. 4001, Federal Bldg.
100 E. B St.
Casper, WY 82601
307-328-5330

Rm. 218, Federal Bldg.
653 2nd Ave.
Fargo, ND 58102
701-783-5771

618 Helena Ave.
Helena, MT 59601
406-588-6011

Rm. 2237, Federal Bldg.
125 S. State St.
Salt Lake City, UT 84111
801-588-5500

Rm. 402, National Bank Bldg.
8th and Main Ave.
Sioux Falls, SD 57102
605-782-4980

Federal Bldg.
515 9th St.
Rapid City, SD 57701
605-782-7000

Region 9

211 Main St.
San Francisco, CA 94102
415-556-9000

Rm. 4015, Federal Bldg.
1130 O St.
Fresno, CA 93721
209-487-5000

2800 Cottage Way
Sacramento, CA 95825
916-484-4200

301 E. Stewart
Las Vegas, NV 89121
702-385-6011

300 Booth St.
Reno, NV 89504
702-784-5234

Rm. 402
1149 Bethel St.
Honolulu, HI 96813
808-546-8950

ADA Plaza Center Bldg.
Agana, Guam 96910
**-777-8420

6th Fl.
350 S. Figueroa St.
Los Angeles, CA 90071
213-688-2000

112 N. Central Ave.
Phoenix, AZ 85004
602-261-3900

Rm. 4-S-33, Federal Bldg.
880 Front St.
San Diego, CA 92188
714-293-5444

Region 10

Rm. 1744, Federal Bldg.
915 Second Ave.
Seattle, WA 98174
206-442-4343

Suite 200, Anchorage Legal Center
1016 W. 6th Ave.
Anchorage, AK 99501
907-272-5561

501½ Second Ave.
Fairbanks, AK 99701
**907-452-1951

Rm. 408
216 N. 8th St.
Boise, ID 83701
208-554-1096

Federal Bldg.
1220 S.W. Third Ave.
Portland, OR 97205
503-221-2000

Rm. 651, Courthouse Bldg.
Spokane, WA 99210
509-452-2100

C1.111 STATE AGENCIES DESIGNATED BY OCCUPATIONAL SAFETY AND HEALTH ADMINISTRATION

Alabama

Alabama State Department of Labor
600 Administration Bldg.
64 N. Union St.
Montgomery, AL 36104
205-269-6211

Alaska

Alaska Department of Labor
P.O. Box 1149
Juneau, AK 99801
907-586-3005

American Samoa

Department of Manpower Resources
Pago Pago, American Samoa 96920

Arizona

Occupational Safety and Health Division
Industrial Commission of Arizona
P.O. Box 19070
Phoenix, AZ 85005
602-271-5795

Arkansas

Department of Labor
Capitol Hill Bldg.
Little Rock, AR 72201
501-317-1401

California

Agriculture and Services Agency
Rm. 409
1220 N St.
Sacramento, CA 95814
916-445-1935

Colorado

Department of Labor and Employment
200 E. Ninth Ave.
Denver, CO 80203
303-573-6440

Connecticut

Connecticut Department of Labor
200 Folly Brook Blvd.
Wethersfield, CT 06109
203-566-5123

Connecticut Department of Health
79 Elm St.
Hartford, CT 06115

Delaware

Department of Labor
801 West St.
Wilmington, DE 19899
302-571-2710

District of Columbia

Director of Industrial Safety
Government of the District of Columbia
Minimum Wage and Industrial Safety Board
2900 Newton St. N.E.
Washington, DC 20018
202-832-1230

Florida

Director, Division of Labor
Ashley Bldg., Rm. 201
1321 Executive Center Dr. E.
Tallahassee, FL 32301
904-599-8211

Georgia

See the Governor's Office.

Guam

Director of Labor
Occupational Safety and Health
Government of Guam
P.O. Box 2950
Agana, GU 96910
-772-6291

Hawaii

Director of Labor and Industrial Relations
825 Mililani St.
Honolulu, HI 96813
808-548-3150

Idaho

Department of Labor
Industrial Administration Bldg.
317 Main St.
Boise, ID 83702
208-384-2327

Illinois

Department of Labor
910 S. Michigan Ave.
Chicago, IL 60605
312-793-2800

Illinois Industrial Commission
160 N. LaSalle St.
Chicago, IL 60601
312-793-3333

Indiana

Indiana Division of Labor
1013 State Office Bldg.
Indianapolis, IN 46204
317-633-4473

Iowa

Bureau of Labor, State House
E. 7th and Court Ave.
Des Moines, IA 50319
515-281-3606

Kansas

Kansas Bureau of Labor
401 Topeka Ave.
Topeka, KS 66603
913-296-7474

Kentucky

Kentucky Department of Labor
Capital Plaza Towers, 12th Fl.
Frankfort, KY 40601

Louisiana

Louisiana Health and Human Resources Admin.
Division of Health
c/o Charity Hospital, Advisory Board Office
1532 Tulane Ave.
New Orleans, LA 70112

Department of Labor
P.O. Box 44063
Baton Rouge, LA 70804
504-389-5314

Maine

Commissioner of Manpower Affairs
20 Union St.
Augusta, ME 04330
207-289-3814

Maryland

Department of Licensing and Regulation
Division of Labor and Industry
203 E. Baltimore St.
Baltimore, MD 21202
301-383-2251

**Dial Operator for assistance.

Massachusetts

Department of Labor and Industries
Leverett Saltonstall Bldg.
100 Cambridge St.
Boston, MA 02202
617-727-3454

Michigan

Michigan Department of Labor
309 W. Washington
Box 30015
Lansing, MI 48909
517-373-9600

Michigan Department of Public Health
3500 N. Logan St.
Lansing, MI 48914
517-373-1320

Minnesota

Department of Labor and Industry
Space Center Bldg., 5th Fl.
444 Lafayette Rd.
St. Paul, MN 55101
612-296-2342

Mississippi

State Health Officer
State Board of Health
P.O. Box 1700
Jackson, MS 39205
601-354-6635

Missouri

Division of Labor Standards
P.O. Box 449
Jefferson City, MO 65101
314-751-2461

Montana

Bureau of Safety and Health
Division of Worker's Compensation
Department of Labor and Industry
815 Front St.
Helena, MT 59601
406-449-2047

Nebraska

Department of Labor
State Capitol
Lincoln, NE 63509
402-477-5211

Nevada

Department of Occupational Safety and Health
Nevada Industrial Commission
515 E. Musser St.
Carson City, NV 89701
702-885-5240

New Hampshire

Department of Labor
1 Pillsbury St.
Concord, NH 03301
603-271-3171

Occupational Health Service
Bureau of Occupational Health
Hazen Drive
Concord, NH 03301
603-271-2281

New Jersey

Department of Labor and Industry
P.O. Box V
Trenton, NJ 08625
609-292-2323

New Mexico

Environmental Improvement Agency
P.O. Box 2348
Santa Fe, NM 87501
505-827-5273

New York

Industrial Commissioner
Department of Labor
State Campus
Albany, NY 12226
518-457-3427

North Carolina

North Carolina Department of Labor
P.O. Box 27407
11 West Edenton St.
Raleigh, NC 27611
919-829-7166

OSHA Director
P.O. Box 27407
Raleigh, NC 27611

Puerto Rico

Secretary of Labor
Commonwealth of Puerto Rico
414 Barbosa Ave.
San Juan, PR 00917
809-765-3030

Rhode Island

Division of Occupational Safety
Department of Labor
235 Promenade St.
Providence, RI 02903
401-277-2500

South Carolina

South Carolina Department of Labor
3600 Forest Dr.
P.O. Box 11329
Columbia, SC 29211
803-758-2851

South Dakota

Secretary of Health
State Department of Health
Office Bldg. No. 2
Pierre, SD 57501
605-224-3361

Tennessee

Tennessee Department of Labor
501 Union Bldg., 2nd Fl.
Nashville, TN 37219

Tennessee Department of Public Health
344 Cordell Hull Bldg.
Nashville, TN 37219
615-741-2134

Texas

Division of Occupational Safety and State Safety Engineer
Texas Department of Health Resources
1100 W. 49th St.
Austin, TX 78756
512-397-5721 ext 275

Trust Territory of the Pacific

Division of Labor
Department of Resources and Development
Office of the High Commissioner
Saipan, Mariana Islands 96950

Utah

Utah Industrial Commission
350 E. 5th St.
Salt Lake City, UT 84111
801-328-6411

Vermont

Department of Labor and Industry
Montpelier, VT 05602
802-826-2286

Virgin Islands

Division of Occupational Safety and Health
Department of Labor
Government Complex Bldg. 2, Rm. 207
Lagoon St.
Frederiksted
St. Croix, VI 00840
809-772-1315

Virginia

Department of Labor and Industry
Ninth St. Office Bldg.
P.O. Box 1814
Richmond, VA 23214
804-786-2376

State Department of Health
James Madison Bldg.
109 Governor St.
Richmond, VA 23219
804-770-3561

Washington

Department of Labor and Industries
General Administration Bldg., Rm. 344
Olympia, WA 98504
206-753-6307

West Virginia

West Virginia Department of Health
State Capitol
Charleston, WV 25305
304-348-2971

West Virginia Department of Labor
State Capitol
Charleston, WV 25305
304-345-2195

West Virginia Insurance Commission
State Capitol
Charleston, WV 25305

Wisconsin

Department of Industry, Labor and Human Relations
201 E. Washington Ave.
P.O. Box 2209
Madison, WI 53701
608-266-7552

Wyoming

Occupational Health and Safety
Department
200 E. Eighth Ave.
P.O. Box 2186
Cheyenne, WY 82002
307-777-7786

Energy and the Environment

C1.150 ENERGY RESEARCH AND DEVELOPMENT ADMINISTRATION NATIONAL AND FIELD OFFICES

National Office

20 Massachusetts Ave. N.W.
Washington, DC 20545
301-353-3000

Field Offices

California

San Francisco Operations Office
1333 Broadway
Oakland, CA 94612
415-273-4237

Colorado

Grand Junction Office
P.O. Box 2567
Denver, CO 81501

Idaho

Idaho Operations Office
P.O. Box 2108
Idaho Falls, ID 83401
208-522-6640

Illinois

Chicago Operations Office
9800 S. Cass Ave.
Argonne, IL 60439
312-739-7711

New Mexico

Albuquerque Operations Office
P.O. Box 5400
Albuquerque, NM 87115
505-264-8211

Nevada

Nevada Operations Office
P.O. Box 14100
Las Vegas, NV 89114
702-734-3011

New York

Schenectady Naval Reactors Office
P.O. Box 1069
Schenectady, NY 12301
518-393-6611

Pennsylvania

Pittsburgh Naval Reactors Office
P.O. Box 109
West Mifflin, PA 15122
412-462-5000

South Carolina

Savannah River Operations Office
P.O. Box A
Aiken, SC 29801
803-824-6331

Tennessee

Oak Ridge Operations Office
P.O. Box E
Oak Ridge, TN 37830
615-483-8611

Washington

Richland Operations Office
P.O. Box 550
Richland, WA 99352
509-942-7411

C1.151 ENVIRONMENTAL PROTECTION AGENCY NATIONAL AND REGIONAL OFFICES

National Office

401 M St. S.W.
Washington, DC 20460
202-755-0707

Regional Offices

Region 1
(Connecticut, Maine, Massachusetts, New Hampshire, Rhode Island, Vermont)

Rm. 2203, JFK Federal Bldg.
Government Center
Boston, MA 02203
617-223-7210

Region 2
(New Jersey, New York, Puerto Rico, Virgin Islands)

Rm. 1009, Federal Plaza
New York, NY 10007
212-264-2525

Region 3
(Delaware, District of Columbia, Maryland, Pennsylvania, Virginia, West Virginia)

Curtis Bldg.
6th and Walnut Sts.
Philadelphia, PA 19106
215-597-9814

Region 4
(Alabama, Florida, Georgia, Kentucky, Mississippi, North Carolina, South Carolina, Tennessee)

Suite 300
1421 Peachtree St. N.E.
Atlanta, GA 30309
404-526-5727

Region 5
(Illinois, Indiana, Michigan, Minnesota, Ohio, Wisconsin)

12th Fl.
230 S. Dearborn
Chicago, IL 60604
312-353-5250

Region 6
(Arkansas, Louisiana, New Mexico, Oklahoma, Texas)

1600 Patterson St.
Dallas, TX 75201
214-749-1962

Region 7
(Iowa, Kansas, Missouri, Nebraska)

Rm. 249
1735 Baltimore Ave.
Kansas City, MO 64108
816-374-5493

Region 8
(Colorado, Montana, North Dakota, South Dakota, Utah, Wyoming)

Lincoln Tower Bldg.
1860 Lincoln St.
Denver, CO 80203
303-837-3895

Region 9
(Arizona, California, Hawaii, Nevada, American Samoa, Guam, Trust Territories of Pacific Islands, Wake Island)

100 California St.
San Francisco, CA 94111
415-556-2320

Region 10
(Alaska, Idaho, Oregon, Washington)

1200 6th Ave.
Seattle, WA 98101
206-442-1200

C1.152 RIVER BASIN COMMISSIONS, WATER RESOURCES COUNCIL

National Office

Water Resources Council
2120 L St. N.W.
Washington, DC 20037
202-254-6303

River Basin Commissions

Great Lakes Basin Commission
P.O. Box 999
Ann Arbor, MI 48106
313-769-7431

Missouri River Basin Commission
Suite 403
10050 Regency Circle
Omaha, NE 68114
402-221-9351

New England River Basin Commission
55 Court St.
Boston, MA 02108
617-223-6244

Ohio River Basin Commission
Suite 208-220
36 E. 4th St.
Cincinnati, OH 45202
513-684-3831

Pacific Northwest River Basin
Commission
P.O. Box 908
Vancouver, WA 98660
206-696-3601

Upper Mississippi River Basin Commission
Rm. 510, Federal Office Bldg.
Fort Snelling
Twin Cities, MN 55111
612-725-4690
Delaware River Basin Commission
Department of the Interior
Rm. 2347
18th and C St. N.W.
Washington, DC 20240
202-343-6412

Susquehanna River Basin Commission
Department of the Interior
Rm. 2353
18th and C St. N.W.
Washington, DC 20240
202-343-6412

C1.153 FEDERAL ENERGY ADMINISTRATION NATIONAL AND REGIONAL OFFICES

National Office

12th St. & Pennsylvania Ave. N.W.
Washington, DC 20461
202-961-6061

Regional Offices

Region 1

150 Causeway St.
Boston, MA 02114
617-223-3701

Region 2

26 Federal Plaza
New York, NY 10007
212-264-1021

Region 3

1421 Cherry St.
Philadelphia, PA 19102
215-597-3890

Region 4

1655 Peachtree St. N.E.
Atlanta, GA 30309
404-257-2837

Region 5

Federal Office Bldg.
175 W. Jackson Blvd.
Chicago, IL 60604
312-353-0540

Region 6

P.O. Box 35228
Dallas, TX 75235
214-749-7345

Region 7

112 E. 12th St.
P.O. Box 2208
Kansas City, MO 64142
816-758-2061

Region 8

P.O. Box 2647, Belmar Branch
Lakewood, CO 80226
303-234-2420

Region 9

111 Pine St.
San Francisco, CA 94101
415-556-7216

Region 10

915 2nd Ave.
Seattle, WA 98174
206-399-7280

C1.154 ENVIRONMENTAL PROTECTION AGENCY LIBRARIES

California

Region 9
100 California St.
San Francisco, CA 94111
415-556-1841

Los Angeles Public Contact Office
300 N. Los Angeles St.
Los Angeles, CA 90012
213-688-3232

Colorado

Region 8
1860 Lincoln St.
Denver, CO 80203
303-837-2560

National Enforcement Investigation Center
Rm. 2204, Bldg. 53
Denver Federal Center
Denver, CO 80225
303-234-2122

District of Columbia

Headquarters Library
Rm. 2404, PM-213
401 M St. S.W.
Washington, DC 20460
202-755-0308

Law Library
5th Fl. W., A-130
401 M St. S.W.
Washington, DC 20460
202-755-0766

Office of Pesticides Programs
Rm. 42-EB, WH-569
401 M St. S.W.
Washington, DC 20460
202-426-2432

Solid Waste Management Programs
Rm. 2439, AW-462
401 M. St. S.W.
Washington, DC 20460
202-755-9153

Water Planning Division Library
Rm. 813E, WH-554
401 M St. S.W.
Washington, DC 20460
202-755-6993

Florida

Gulf Breeze Sabine Island Lab
Gulf Breeze, FL 32561
904-932-5311 ext 218

Georgia

Region 4
345 Courtland St. N.E.
Atlanta, GA 30308
404-526-5216

Southeast Environmental Research Lab.
College Station Rd.
Athens, GA 30601
404-546-3103

Hawaii

Pacific Islands Contact Office
Rm. 601, Bishop Trust Bldg.
1000 Bishop St.
Honolulu, HI 96813
808-546-8910

Illinois

Region 5
Rm. 1455-A
230 S. Dearborn St.
Chicago, IL 60604
312-353-2022

Maryland

Annapolis Field Office, Region 3
Annapolis Science Center
Annapolis, MD 21401
301-224-2740

Massachusetts

Region 1
Rm. 2211-B, JFK Federal Bldg.
Boston, MA 02203
617-223-5791

Michigan

Motor Vehicle Emission Lab
2565 Plymouth Rd.
Ann Arbor, MI 48105
313-761-5230

Minnesota

National Water Quality Lab
6201 Congdon Blvd.
Duluth, MN 55804
218-727-6692 ext 538

Missouri

Region 7
Rm. 249
1735 Baltimore Ave.
Kansas City, MO 64108
816-374-5828

Nevada

Environmental Research Center
P.O. Box 15027
Las Vegas, NV 89114
702-736-2969

New Jersey

Region 2 Field Office
Edison, NJ 08817
201-548-3347 ext 520

New York

Region 2
26 Federal Plaza
New York, NY 10007
212-264-2881

North Carolina

Library Services, MD-35
Research Triangle Park, NC 27711
919-549-8411

Office of Air Quality Planning and Standards
826 Mutual Plaza
Research Triangle Park, NC 27711
919-688-8146

Ohio

Central Technical Library
26 W. St. Clair
Cincinnati, OH 45268
513-684-7701

Oklahoma

Robert S. Kerr Environmental Research Lab
P.O. Box 1198
Ada, OK 74820
405-332-8800

Oregon

Environmental Research Center
200 S.W. 35th St.
Corvallis, OR 97330
503-757-4731

Pennsylvania

Region 3
Curtis Bldg.
6th and Walnut Sts.
Philadelphia, PA 19106
215-597-0580

Rhode Island

Environmental Research Lab
P.O. Box 277
West Kingston, RI 02892
401-789-1071 ext 245

South Carolina

Bears Bluff Field Station
P.O. Box 368
Johns Island, SC 29455
803-559-0371

Texas

Region 6
First International Bldg.
1201 Elm St.
Dallas TX 75270
214-749-1171

Washington

Region 10
1200 Sixth Ave.
Seattle, WA 98101
206-442-1289

Field Studies Section
P.O. Box 219
Wenatchee, WA 98801
509-663-0031 ext 243

Appendix C2

UNDERSTANDING AND USING CENSUS DATA

C2.1 Orientation to the Bureau of the Census

While there are many agencies which publish statistics, almost all federal data are gathered and initially organized by the Bureau of the Census, a branch of the Department of Commerce.

The Bureau of the Census produces a never-ending stream of data in various forms and cross tabulations which have almost unlimited uses in both consumer and commercial markets. Detailed information is available to the public on numerous aspects of the buying population and business, from nationwide overviews to areas as small as city blocks.

Census data can be utilized in siting or expanding a plant and in manpower planning and utilization. They are also particularly useful in marketing activities, such as gauging potential markets, forecasting economic conditions and market potential, analyzing sales performance, laying out sales territories, and allocating advertising budgets. Census data can be a basic market research tool of any business (see Chapter 3).

In the larger Department of Commerce district offices, the Bureau of the Census is separately staffed; however, the Census staff works together with the staff of the district office and they are usually housed together.

A visit to a Department of Commerce district office may be particularly useful to a client, as many of these offices have an expert in governmental statistics and usage who can quickly answer questions or make the proper reference. Such a visit can save much time and energy and quickly orient a client both to government statistics and government services.

The Bureau of the Census, Department of Commerce district offices, and Business Service Centers (General Services Administration) cooperate on counseling, seminars, and publications available in their libraries. Although each agency has its specialty, each can refer a client to the proper source of expertise if it does not itself possess it.

C2.2 Censuses, Surveys, and Subject Areas

The Bureau of the Census engages in two major areas of activity: censuses and surveys. A census represents a 100 percent sampling of the target universe; a survey is a carefully constructed partial sampling of the target universe.

Censuses. Censuses of total population and housing are conducted every ten years in years ending in 0. Censuses of agriculture, business, construction industries, governments, manufactures, mineral industries, and transportation are conducted every five years in years ending in 2 and 7. The five-year censuses are referred to as *economic censuses*. In addition, *special censuses* are conducted from time to time for local governments. Because of the size of the sample, data from these censuses provide the most exhaustive geographic detail and cross tabulations. However, such data are not as current as data resulting from surveys.

Surveys. Annually, the Bureau conducts hundreds of surveys, entitled *Current Reports*, dealing with population, manufacturing activity and commodity production, retail and wholesale trade, distributive trades and services, state and local government finances, and housing. These are issued at various intervals—annually, quarterly, or monthly. One report, on retail trade, is issued weekly (see 3.109). Most of the statistics are national totals, but some apply to states and smaller areas. Surveys can be either on a recurring or nonrecurring basis, although most are recurring. They are particularly valuable as updates of census data.

One of the most important tasks of the Bureau of the Census is mapmaking. Before a census, the boundaries of each area to be studied must be decided upon and then mapped. For the 1970 census, some 135,000 maps were prepared, so that each census-taker could have his own. Another 150,000 maps were prepared for supervisors and other census officials. Other maps prepared by the Bureau are multicolored statistical maps, which provide information more vividly than do statistical tables.

Census Data Subject Areas. Both census and survey data are provided in the typical census data subject areas which follow. They are not all-inclusive and are enumerated only to indicate the breadth of data available.

Agriculture: number of farms, use of land, size of farm, type of operation, equipment and facilities, chemicals, crops harvested, irrigation and drainage, farm labor, farm expenditures, fertilizer and lime, nursery and greenhouse products, forest products, livestock, value of farm products, farm finance, ranking counties.

Construction: number of establishments, kind of business, number of employees, expenditures, receipts, location, type of construction, ownership, new or maintenance.

Housing: mortgages, form of debt, outstanding debt, interest rates, term, servicing costs, taxes, property location, number of rental units, year built, purchase price, value, rental receipts, owner's characteristics.

Manufacturing: number of establishments, quantity and value of products shipped, quantity and cost of materials consumed, costs of fuels and electric energy, capital expenditures, value of fixed assets, rental payments for facilities and machinery, inventories, employment, payrolls, man-hours and wages of production workers, value added by manufacturing, water use in manufacturing.

Mineral Industries: value of shipments, cost of supplies, quantity and cost of energy consumed and produced, value added, employment, payrolls, man-hours, capital expenditures, number and size of companies, cost of contract work, water use.

Commercial Fisheries: number of operators, number of vessels operated, employees, payrolls, operating costs excluding payroll, gross receipts, primary catch, fishing regions, vessel characteristics.

Population: characteristics, special studies, estimates and projections, farm population, consumer income, consumer buying indicators, employment, training.

Retail Trade, Wholesale Trade in Selected Service Industries: (1) *all industries:* kind of business, location, legal form of organization, number of proprietors of unincorporated businesses, size (number of establishments), size (number of employees), sales, payroll; (2) *retail trade:* sales by merchandise lines,

Fig. 1. Standard Metropolitan Statistical Areas: 1973

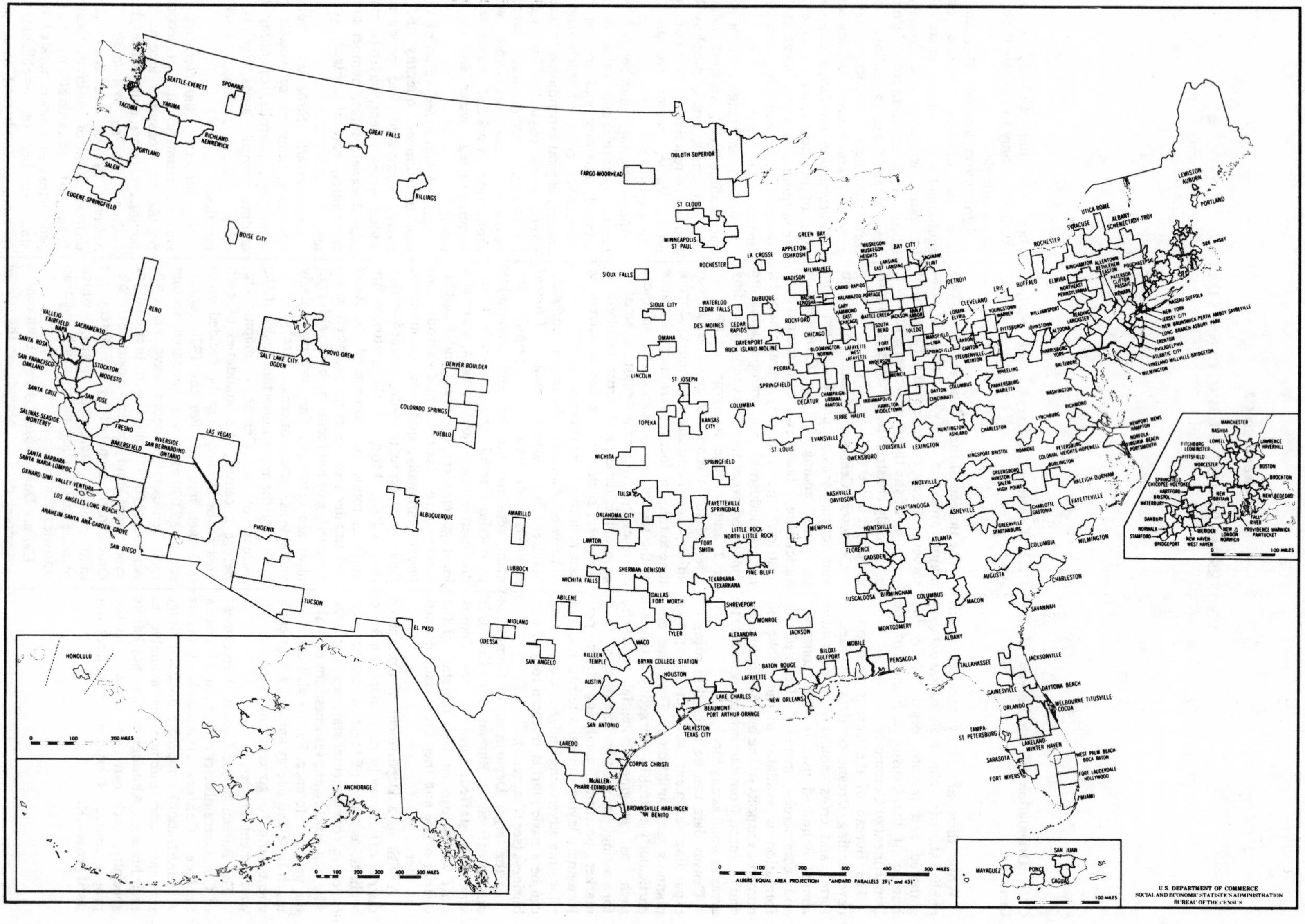

U.S. DEPARTMENT OF COMMERCE
SOCIAL AND ECONOMIC STATISTICS ADMINISTRATION
BUREAU OF THE CENSUS

eating and drinking places, vending machine number, storage capacity, prescriptions filled, number of pharmacists, gallons of gasoline sold; (3) *wholesale trade:* inventories, operating expenses, brokerage fees or commissions, receivables and bad-debt losses, value added by each, receipts by source, facilities, and equipment.

Transportation: personal: number and types of trips taken, origin and destination of trips taken, means of transport, purpose of trip, vacation travel, duration of travel, distance, size of party, type of lodging, occupation, education, family income, age; *commercial:* number of trucks and truck trailers, truck miles, average miles per truck, major use, body type and size, vehicle class size, year model, type fuel, range of operation, axle arrangement, products carried, maintenance.

There are also commodity reports, general economic studies and reports, geographic breakouts and cross references, foreign trade statistics, and population and manpower studies on many foreign countries. Also, the Bureau of the Census conducts major surveys for other government agencies: Current Population Surveys and Consumer Expenditure Surveys are conducted for the Bureau of Labor Statistics; a National Crime Survey and a Commercial Victimization Survey are conducted for the Law Enforcement Assistance Administration; Hospital Interview Surveys, Health Examination Surveys, and Hospital Discharge Surveys are conducted for the National Center for Health Statistics of the Department of Health, Education and Welfare; lastly, the Current Medicare Survey, Supplemental Income Survey, and Retirement History Survey are conducted for the Social Security Administration.

C2.3 Geographical Areas Covered

Many marketing, sales, and site location decisions can be more carefully made if two aspects of census data are considered together: the subject areas and their precise geographical location. In the following paragraphs, geographical areas covered by censuses and surveys are listed and defined.

Areas: United States, regions and divisions, states, Puerto Rico and outlying areas, Congressional districts, counties, county subdivisions (minor civil divisions, census county divisions, unorganized territories), places (incorporated, unincorporated, boundaries), municipalities, townships and school districts, wards, economic subregions, state economic areas, standard metropolitan statistical areas (standard consolidated areas, relationship to urbanized areas), urbanized areas (urban-rural areas, extended cities), census tracts, central business districts, major retail centers, enumeration districts, block

Fig. 2. City and Major Retail Centers: 1967
Denver, Colorado

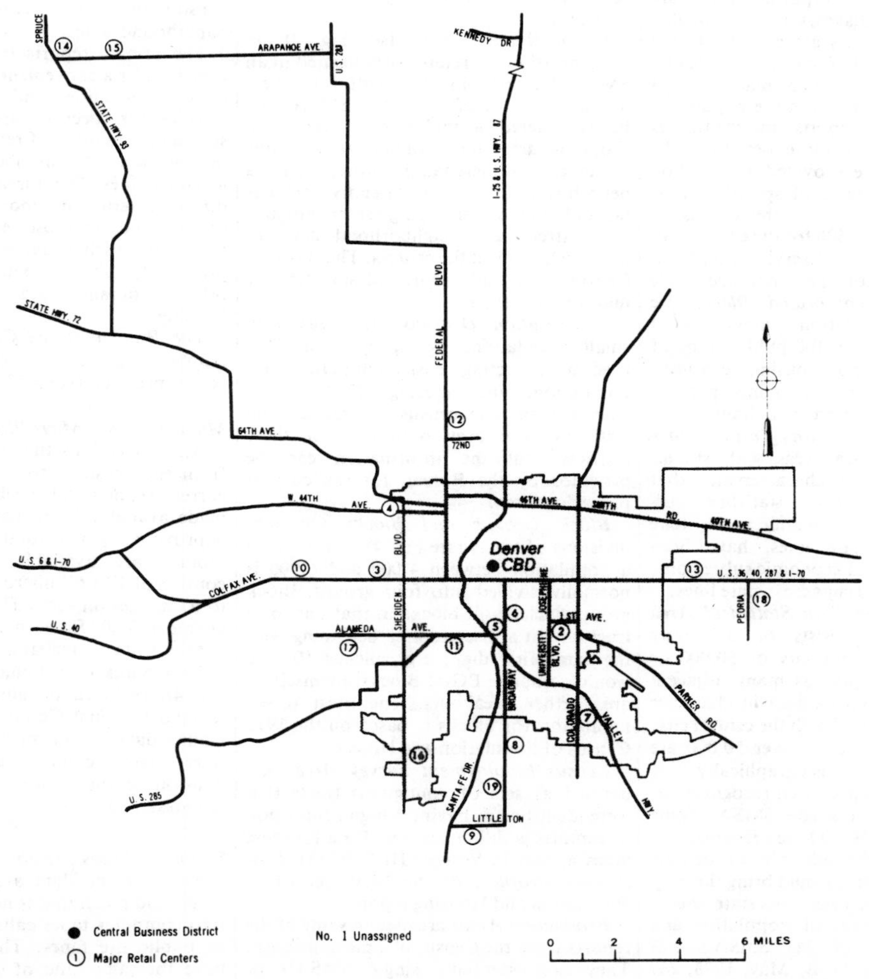

groups, census blocks, foreign trade statistical areas, international areas, other special purpose districts.

Regions and Divisions are groups of contiguous states.

County Subdivisions are of three types: *(1) Minor Civil Divisions* are the primary political or administrative subdivisions into which counties are divided by state law or county ordinance; e.g., townships or precincts. (2) *Census County Divisions* represent community areas which have been defined in recent decades by the Bureau of the Census with the cooperation of state and local officials. In many cases, they have replaced minor civil divisions. (3) *Unorganized Territories* may comprise two or more noncontiguous, unorganized areas. In the states of Maine, Minnesota, and South Dakota, there are a number of counties which contain territories of this type. Small isolated units of unorganized territories are also found in a few counties in other states, but they are not given special treatment.

Places refers to a concentration of population. Although the existence of legally prescribed boundaries, powers, and functions is not a criterion for this classification, most incorporated places are cities, towns, villages, or boroughs. Unincorporated places are also delineated in census reports. (1) *Incorporated Places:* Statistics for incorporated places of all types and sizes are given in the population and housing census reports, and the figures for larger cities are quite detailed. The other censuses have provided information for incorporated places of specified sizes, such as: over 10,000 for the census of governments, over 2,500 for the censuses of retail trade and selected service industries, and over 5,000 for the wholesale trade census. (2) *Unincorporated Places* are closely settled population centers without corporation limits. In the publications of the population and housing censuses, statistics are shown for unincorporated places with 1,000 or more inhabitants.

Economic Subregions and State Economic Areas are areas with similar social and economic characteristics that have been combined for statistical purposes. The 510 state economic areas, none of which cross state lines, have been consolidated into 121 economic subregions, which frequently do cut across state lines.

Standard Metropolitan Statistical Area (SMSA) usually consists of a county containing at least one city of 50,000 or more inhabitants, plus as many adjacent counties as are metropolitan in character and socially integrated with the central city. When two or more cities over 50,000 are closely associated geographically or economically, they are often recognized as central cities of a single SMSA. Some cities of less than 50,000 are recognized as central cities if the addition of densely settled adjacent places would bring them up to that total. SMSA's can cross state lines.

In the 1970 Census of Population and Housing, a total of 247 SmSA's was recognized (see Fig. 1). By May, 1973, 267 had been delineated. For detailed criteria and an up-to-date list of SMSA's and their constituent areas, see the National Bureau of Standard's publication, *U.S. Federal Information Processing Standards, Publication 8: Standard Metropolitan Statistical Areas,* available from GPO (see C1.0).

Census Tracts are small areas, homogeneous in population characteristics, economic status, and living conditions, into which large cities and adjacent areas have been divided for the purpose of showing small-area statistics. The average tract has about 4,000 residents. All 1970 SMSA's are completely tracted. Population and housing data from these censuses have been published in a series of reports. A great many more statistics have been tabulated but not published and are available at nominal cost. A great deal of information about the census tract program is available in the *Census Tract Manual*, published by the Bureau of the Census. (See district offices of the Department of Commerce, C1.10.)

The *Central Business District* (see Fig. 2) is usually the downtown retail trade area. The purpose of defining this is to provide a basis for comparing changes in business activity in this area with changes in the remainder of the metropolitan area or central city.

Major Retail Centers (see Fig. 3) are concentrations of retail stores located in an SMSA but not in the central business district of the chief city of the SMSA . To be considered a major retail center, a shopping area must contain at least one major general merchandise store, usually a department store. The category includes not only planned shopping centers but also older street and neighborhood developments which meet the criteria. The Business Census is the only source of statistics for major retail centers.

Enumeration Districts are areas with small population, averaging about 700, used in conducting censuses in agriculture, population, and housing. The districts change from one census to another. No statistics have been published for these districts, but the information can be provided by the Bureau for the cost of preparing them.

Block Groups and Blocks are subdivisions of tracts (see Fig. 4). A tract with a population between 4,000 and 6,000 is normally divided into four groups. Block groups include all blocks in that part of a tract within a discrete area beginning with the same first digit; e.g., blocks 101-110 would comprise BG-1. Blocks, themselves, are further breakouts. The most recent tabulation for blocks is based on the 1970 Census of Population and Housing.

Census Employment Survey Areas are defined as sets of contiguous tracts that were identified as having a high proportion of families with low income. Data for these areas appear in Volume III PHC (3), *Low Income Profiles,* of the 1970 Census of Population and Housing reports.

Production Areas are used in some of the reports from the Census of Transportation. They are essentially single SMSA's or clusters of SMSA's selected to represent relatively large but geographically compact concentrations of industrial activity.

C2.4 Data Availability and Technical Assistance

The Bureau of the Census is careful not to violate the confidentiality of any individual, household, or firm, or to provide any firm with an unfair competitive advantage. These qualifications, however, do not affect the ease of access to the data, and census data are available in a variety of forms. Those listed below represent a continually supplemented source of useful data.

Printed Reports

All Bureau activities, including censuses, recurring surveys, and special surveys, are available as printed reports. The publication program for the five-year recurring economic census, for example, usually consists of press releases of preliminary data, final reports consisting of numerous area and subject series, and, finally, a series of major volumes which consolidate and augment the previous paperbound series.

The printed reports from the decennial census offer a convenient source of general data. Population and housing characteristics for specified areas are reported, such as the number of rented housing units in a block and the number of families with given incomes. The Bureau released several different series of reports from the 1970 census, and, in most series, there is one report for each state. Some contain data principally about people and families; others contain data primarily about housing.

The Bureau of the Census publishes a number of guides, compendia, and specific census products (see 3.50-3.61).

Microfiche and Microfilm

All publications that provide final data from the censuses and surveys, including current reports and special reports, will be made available in microfiche form within approximately two months after the printed reports are available. The microfiche consists of 4" x 6" microfilm cards with up to 97 images on each. There is a minimum charge of $1.00 for each microfiche order.

Microfilm is available for the First and Fifth Counts of summary tape data (see Fig. 4). Technical documentation is needed to read the First Count data. While Fifth Count data are in an easy-to-read form, only state, county, and minor civil division/census county division summaries are presented.

Summary Tapes or *Public Use Tapes*

Most of the data available in printed form, and much that is not, has been made into computer tapes called summary tapes or public use tapes. The summary tapes have the same kind of data found in the printed reports; there is just more of it.

Fig. 3. Common Census Geographic Areas

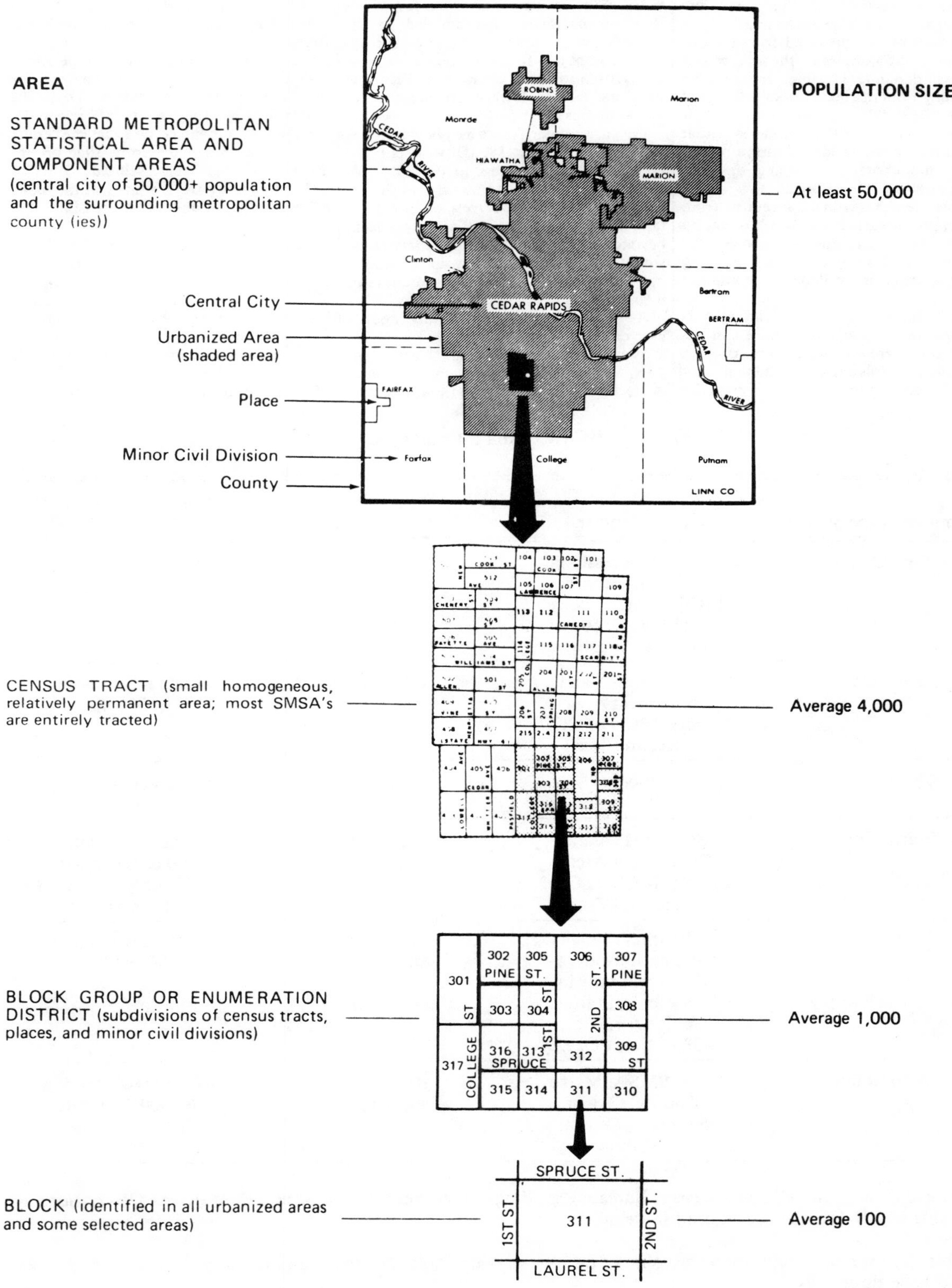
AREA
STANDARD METROPOLITAN STATISTICAL AREA AND COMPONENT AREAS (central city of 50,000+ population and the surrounding metropolitan county (ies))
Central City
Urbanized Area (shaded area)
Place
Minor Civil Division
County
POPULATION SIZE
At least 50,000
ROBINS
Marion
Monroe
CEDAR RIVER
HIAWATHA
MARION
Clinton
CEDAR RAPIDS
Bertram
BERTRAM
FAIRFAX
Fairfax
College
Putnam
LINN CO
CENSUS TRACT (small homogeneous, relatively permanent area; most SMSA's are entirely tracted)
Average 4,000
BLOCK GROUP OR ENUMERATION DISTRICT (subdivisions of census tracts, places, and minor civil divisions)
Average 1,000
301
302
PINE
305
ST.
306
307
PINE
303
304
308
309
ST
1ST
2ND
ST
316
313
SPRUCE
312
317
COLLEGE
315
314
311
310
BLOCK (identified in all urbanized areas and some selected areas)
Average 100
SPRUCE ST.
1ST ST.
311
2ND ST.
LAUREL ST.

There is practically no limit to the number of combinations or cross tabulations which may be prepared for an area. Summary tapes are particularly useful when heavy use is planned, because of the speed and convenience of machine processing.

The Bureau has prepared for sale tape files containing samples of the total census of population and housing, and samples containing 1 out of 100, 1 out of 1,000, and 1 out of 10,000 of all cases in the complete census. All information that might make possible identification of any person, household, or housing unit has been removed. The Bureau also makes available the nonconfidential returns from some of the public agencies which report on their activities for Bureau surveys; for example, information from each building permit issuance is available on computer tape.

The data on these tapes can also be obtained as print-outs of the tape content. Such displays are accompanied by technical memoranda explaining the content and organization of the display and supplying identification for the totals. Computer punchcards of the data are also available.

The majority of magnetic tapes were produced on the Bureau's Univac computers. The increase in demand for census data on magnetic tape has led to the preparation of data tapes for some surveys and censuses in a form that is acceptable or convertible to other computers. Technical personnel at the Bureau are prepared to advise on this question.

Census summary tapes may be purchased from the Bureau at $80.00 per reel if the user wants direct access to the data. Six series of computer tapes are available, involving about 2,000 reels of computer tape (see Fig. 4). Costs of this approach, beyond the cost of the tapes themselves, would include programming and computer operation, and in some cases purchase of maps.

As an alternative to purchasing tapes, a user might save time and money by visiting a Summary Tape Processing Center (see 3.68), where statistical data and assistance in accessing it and using it are readily available. Summary Tape Processing Centers are found nationwide (see C1.13).

Special Tabulations

If the data required are not available in either printed form or computer tape, the Bureau can conduct special tabulations and make them available in either tape form, computer print-outs, typewritten copy, or hand-posted statistical tables. Data file tabulations are subject to staff review by the Bureau to make certain that the results are in such summary form that no individual information is disclosed.

The following are examples of the kinds of special tabulations that are possible:

Wholesale Trade Data for New York State data for cities of 2,500 to 4,999

Grocery Store Sales by Size of Firm for stores with over one million dollars gross, stratified by eleven categories based on size of firm

Nonrubber Footwear by size of producing company for 1974

Manufacturing in the Oachita River Basin

Fig. 4. 1970 Census Summary Tapes

Summary Tape Series*	Areas Reported	Type of Data	No. of Tables and Data Cells for Each Area**
First Count	State, Congressional District, County, MCD or CCD, Place, and Block Group or Enumeration District	100 percent	54 tables containing 400 cells
Second Count	State, SMSA and Component Areas, County, MCD or CCD, Place, and Tract	100 percent	93 tables containing 3,500 cells
Third Count	Block	100 percent	36 tables containing 250 cells
Fourth Count	State, SMSA and Component Areas, County, MCD or CCD, Place, and Tract	100 percent and sample	327 tables containing 13,700 cells (more for State, County, and SMSA and Components)
Fifth Count	ZIP areas (3-digit areas nationwide; 5-digit areas only in SMSA's, State Cong. Dist., Co., MCD/CCD, BG/ED.	100 percent and sample	53 tables containing 900 cells
Sixth Count	State, SMSA, Metro. County, City of 50,000+, Central City	100 percent and sample	440 tables containing 260,000 data cells

*Referred to as "counts" by the Census Bureau, e.g., First Count, Second Count, etc. *Data Access Descriptions* are available which describe each Count in detail.

**A table, for example, might show the count of persons who are white, Negro, and other races. In this case, the table would have three cells.

Special tabulations are furnished by the Bureau at cost, including planning, running, and overhead. Costs, therefore, vary widely, depending upon the quantity of data requested, the amount of work required to obtain the data, the complexity of the specifications, processing costs, and other factors.

Technical Assistance

The Bureau of the Census utilizes its staff expertise and special machinery to provide technical assistance to customers, at cost, in designing sample surveys, collecting data by mail or field enumeration, tabulating tapes and punchcards provided by the customer, and providing population estimates and projections.

Due to staff limitations, the Bureau sets priorities in the delivery of special services. Work for other government agencies—federal, state, and local—is given first priority.

Seminars and Workshops

From time to time, when a need is identified, the Bureau conducts workshops and seminars for local and state governments, in conjunction with the district offices of the Department of Commerce. The seminars are announced in *Data User News* (see 3.53).

C2.5 Examples of the Use of Census Data

The following are ways in which businesses have found data produced by the government useful in market research, sales, and site location. The examples quoted are from *Measuring Markets* (see 3.0), and are intended primarily to illustrate the wide range of potential data application in business planning.

1. Ready Made Containers, Inc.

Problem: The sales manager for a manufacturer of corrugated and solid fibre boxes in one of the mountain states decided that he wanted to intensify the company's efforts in Arizona, one of the states which the firm served. In the Phoenix standard metropolitan statistical area (coextensive with Maricopa County), for example, the firm's sales totaled $850,000 in 1971—$680,000, or 80 percent, to firms within the food and kindred products industry, and the remaining $170,000, or 20 percent, to firms manufacturing electrical equipment and supplies. The sales manager felt this was a very poor sales record, considering the diversity of industry in the Phoenix area.

In view of this preliminary analysis, he decided to determine the market potential for fibre boxes in the Phoenix area as the first step in establishing the firm's sales potential (or market share) and setting a realistic sales quota for the area.

Source of Data: (1) *County Business Patterns, 1972;* (2) *1973 U.S. Industrial Outlook,* and (3) *Fibre Box Statistics 1972.*

Procedure: In order to estimate the total market potential for corrugated and solid-fibre boxes on an industry-by-industry basis, it was concluded that the initial analysis should be based on "end use" or consumption statistics as a means of determining the extent to which various industry groups use such products. Consumption per employee was determined by applying national employment data of each 2-digit Standard Industrial Classification (SIC) industry to the level of corrugated and solid fibre boxes used by each industry. The potential for Maricopa County was then determined by applying county employment data to arrive at the market potential for each using industry in the county. The 5-step procedure is shown below. The results appear in Table A.

(1) Value of the fibre container shipments by industry was arrived at by applying end-use percentage data from Source (1) to total United States shipments of the fibre box industry from Source (3). The resulting dollar values appear in Column 1 of Table A.

(2) Total United States and Maricopa County employment in each of the using industries was determined from Source (2). Columns 2 and 4 of Table A show these data.

(3) Consumption per employee in each of the using industries was calculated by dividing data in Column 1 by data in Column 2. The results appear in Column 3.

(4) An estimate of the value of fibre box use by each industry in Maricopa County was then obtained by multiplying the consumption per employee data in Column 3 by county employment in Column 4. The resulting dollar estimate for each 2-digit industry in Maricopa County appears in Column 5.

(5) Total market potential in Maricopa County was obtained by adding the potential for individual industries.

Conclusion: With a market potential for corrugated and solid fibre boxes totaling $14,098,000 in the Phoenix, Arizona area, the sales manager concluded that his company sales of $850,000 in Phoenix constituted 6.0 percent of the total market potential and was considerably less than he had originally imagined.

More importantly, he learned that the firm had no sales in a number of 2-digit industries which used a considerable quantity of corrugated and solid fibre boxes. The lumber and wood products industry (SIC 24), for example, was consuming approximately $1,259,000 of such boxes, yet the firm had no sales in this industry group. The stone, clay, and glass products industry (SIC 32) was an even larger untapped market, with a corrugated shipping container consumption of $1,407,000.

In light of these and other findings, the sales manager decided that his sales potential for the Phoenix area should be based upon the company's sales accomplishment in the food and kindred products industry, where its market share was 17.9 percent ($68,000 ÷ $3,793,000). Thus, the initial sales quota for the Phoenix area was set at $2,523,542 ($14,098,000 x 17.9 percent) or about triple the sales of the preceding year. Each industry group in turn was assigned a sales quota equal to 17.9 percent of its market potential; e.g., the apparel group (SIC 23) was assigned a sales quota of $22,554 ($126,000 x 17.9 percent).

2. The King Corporation

Problem: For years, the King Corporation, manufacturer of industrial lubricants, had no way of knowing whether or not it was obtaining a satisfactory volume of sales in any sales territory. Its only measure of sales performance was past sales in the same territory. Management decided to find a better measurement of the company's sales effectiveness.

Source of Data: County Business Patterns, 1972.

Procedure: (1) The company first analyzed its sales accounts, which were coded by the Standard Industrial Classification Code (SIC), to ascertain which industries now bought its products. This analysis revealed that the bulk of company sales was concentrated in three industries: apparel products (SIC 23), chemicals (SIC 28), and fabricated metals (SIC 34).

(2) The average annual volume of industrial lubricants used per employee was determined by mailing questionnaires to a sample of plants in these industries. The results indicated that the apparel industry used 30 pounds, the chemicals industry 50 pounds, and the metals industry 65 pounds per employee per year.

(3) Using these as market indexes, market potential was calculated for each industry, using employment data tabulated in *County Business Patterns* (see Table B). The market potential for industrial lubricants for Cook County, Illinois was computed as follows:

First, the total number of employees in each of the three industries was determined. Each total was then multiplied by the corresponding pounds of lubricant used per employee as determined by the questionnaires. The resulting figures, added together, represented the total estimated pounds of lubricant used in Cook County in these industries.

Conclusion: It was estimated that these three industries consumed 7.8 million pounds of industrial lubricants per year in Cook County, Illinois. Since the King Corporation accounted for slightly over 7 percent of total sales to the three industries, management decided to raise the sales quotas. They also decided to make field observations to determine why they were not getting a larger share of the market.

Furthermore, salesmen were furnished with a listing of other major manufacturers in the county who were non-users of the company's product and who might be potential customers. A year later, the results showed that total sales in the county had increased substantially, that products were sold to companies which had

Table A. Estimated Market for Corrugated and Solid Fibre Box by Industry Groups, Phoenix, Arizona, Standard Metropolitan Statistical Area, 1972

SIC major group code	Consuming industries	Value of box shinments by end use[1] ($1,000)	Employment by industry group[2]	Consumption per employee by industry group (1 ÷ 2) (dollars)	Maricopa County	
					Employment by industry group[2]	Estimated share of the market (3 x 4) ($1,000)
		1	2	3	4	5
20	Food and kindred products	1,171,800	1,536,307	763	4,971	3,793
21	Tobacco manufactures	29,400	63,919	460	–	–
22	Textile mill products	121,800	935,925	130	–	–
23	Apparel and other textile products	54,600	1,349,000	40	3,158	126
24	Lumber and wood products	42,000	579,037	725	1,736	1,259
25	Furniture and fixtures	147,000	468,311	314	1,383	434
26	Paper and allied products	567,000	631,588	898	284	255
27	Printing and publishing	58,800	1,056,336	56	4,346	243
28	Chemicals and allied products	260,400	849,969	306	1,133	347
29	Petroleum and coal products	33,600	139,228	241	–	–
30	Rubber and miscellaenous plastics products	163,800	555,539	295	779	230
31	Leather and leather products	21,000	277,371	76	–	–
32	Stone, clay and glass products	365,400	588,897	620	2,270	1,407
33	Primary metal industries	42,000	1,144,327	37	2,036	75
34	Fabricated metal products	184,800	1,312,595	141	3,271	461
35	Machinery, except electrical	105,000	1,769,738	59	14,691	867
36	Electrical equipment and supplies	256,200	1,698,725	151	23,788	3,592
37	Transportation equipment	109,200	1,700,723	64	2,484	159
38	Instruments and related products	29,400	383,585	77	D	–
39	Miscellaneous manufacturing industries	403,200	411,967	979	868	850
90	Government	33,600	–	–	–	–
	Total	[3] 4,200,000	–	–	–	14,098

D Data withheld to avoid disclosure of individual reporting units.
1 Based on data reported in *Fibre Box Industry Annual Report 1972*, Fibre Box Association.
2 *County Business Patterns, 1972.* U.S. Department of Commerce, Bureau of the Census.
3 *U.S. Industrial Outlook 1973– With Projections to 1980.* Bureau of Dmosetic Commerce, U.S. Department of Commerce.

Table B. Employment Data for Selected Industry Classifications in Cook County, Illinois, 1972

SIC code	Industry	Number of employees mid-March pay period	Taxable payrolls Jan.-Mar. ($1,000)	Total reporting units	Number of reporting units, by employment-size class							
					1 to 3	4 to 7	8 to 19	20 to 49	50 to 99	100 to 249	250 to 499	500 or more
28	Chemicals and allied products	32,661	82,459	534	92	86	99	126	53	54	13	11
281	Industrial chemicals	3,736	10,233	67	11	15	8	14	6	11	1	1
2813	Industrial gases	507	1,724	16	1	2	5	6	1	1	-	-
282	Plastics materials and synthetics	1,280	3,097	26	2	1	7	7	5	3	1	-
283	Drugs	4,319	11,833	46	12	11	6	10	2	2	1	2
2834	Pharmaceutical preparations	4,248	11,696	39	11	6	6	9	2	2	1	2
284	Soap, cleaners, and toilet goods	9,934	23,293	131	24	18	27	28	14	11	4	5
2841	Soap and other detergents	3,274	9,714	32	1	5	6	7	7	3	1	2
287	Agricultural chemicals	366	684	12	3	1	1	5	1	1	-	-
29	Petroleum and coal products	2,342	6,109	54	10	10	13	6	8	5	2	-
295	Paving and roofing material	1,296	3,027	27	6	7	5	1	3	4	1	-
2951	Paving mixtures and blocks	266	723	14	3	6	3	1	-	1	-	-
2952	Asphalt felts and coatings	1,030	2,303	13	3	1	2	-	3	3	1	-
30	Rubber and plastics	18,895	36,524	349	42	45	73	87	50	41	9	2
301	Tires and inner tubes	(D)	(D)	3	-	-	2	-	-	1	-	-
306	Fabricated rubber products, n.e.c.	(D)	(D)	49	2	7	12	9	10	8	-	1
307	Miscellaneous plastics products	15,765	30,138	296	39	38	59	78	40	32	9	1
31	Leather and leather products	4,206	8,075	81	14	13	19	11	12	10	1	1
311	Leather tanning and finishing	1,143	2,733	13	2	-	3	-	3	4	1	-
314	Footwear, except rubber	(D)	(D)	7	3	-	-	2	1	-	-	1
3141	Shoes, except rubber	(D)	(D)	5	2	-	-	1	1	-	-	1
22	Textile mill products	2,630	5,990	47	10	7	7	10	6	5	1	1
224	Narrow fabric mills	(D)	(D)	3	-	1	1	-	-	1	-	-
225	Knitting mills	247	346	7	2	1	1	2	-	1	-	-
2253	Knit outerwear mills	(D)	(D)	6	2	1	1	1	-	1	-	-
226	Textile finishing, except wool	183	365	12	3	3	2	4	-	-	-	-
23	Apparel and other textile products	18,066	29,037	450	97	79	118	82	40	22	8	4
231	Men's and boys' suits and coats	5,259	9,467	21	5	2	4	2	1	2	3	2
232	Men's and boys' furnishings	1,599	2,767	38	7	6	12	5	4	3	-	1
233	Women's and misses' outerwear	2,543	4,316	72	9	6	20	25	7	4	1	-
2331	Women's and misses' blouses and waists	230	365	5	-	-	2	2	-	1	-	-
34	Fabricated metal products	87,101	210,868	1,542	208	220	410	351	178	115	28	32
341	Metal cans	7,191	18,086	18	-	1	1	1	2	5	1	7
342	Cutlery, hand tools and hardware	5,845	12,687	92	17	17	14	13	16	9	4	2
343	Plumbing and heating, except electric	2,590	6,493	36	6	6	5	9	2	6	-	2
3431	Metal sanitary ware	(D)	(D)	4	-	-	-	2	-	1	-	1
344	Fabricated structural metal products	11,277	27,685	310	47	46	87	70	38	17	3	2

(D)–Denotes figures withheld to avoid disclosure of individual reporting units.

n.e.c.–Not elsewhere classified.

Source: *County Business Patterns, 1972.* Bureau of the Census, U.S. Department of Commerce.

previously bought none, and that the new sales quota was within 95 percent of actual sales results.

3. Ward Manufacturing Company

Problem: The Ward Manufacturing Company, a manufacturer of highly crafted household furniture, was introducing a new line and desired to construct a simplified model for allocating a total introductory advertising budget, by state, so as to reach the customers they assumed would be the prime buyers for their products.

Source of Data: Statistics of Income 1971: Individual Income Tax Returns.

Assumption: (1) The company decided to direct its advertising to families or individuals with an adjusted gross income of $15,000 or more, based on studies of other companies marketing similar furniture. (2) An introductory advertising budget of $150,000 was established.

Procedure: (See Table C for calculations.)

(1) The company first determined the number of income tax returns with $15,000 or more adjusted gross income for the nine states in the South Atlantic region, Column 1.

(2) The next step was to establish a market index for each state. This shown in Column 2 and is expressed as a percentage of the total number of returns in the region.

(3) The company allocated advertising appropriations for each state by multiplying the market index shown in Column 2 by the introductory advertising budget of $150,000; e.g., Delaware 2.6 x $150,000 = $3,900.

Conclusion: Using the procedures described in Table C, Ward allocated its introductory advertising budget by state. If so desired, the budget could be further allocated by major cities in the same manner as the state appropriations, by using census tract data which are available in the *1970 Census of Housing and Population.*

4. Freemans' Supermarket, Inc.

Problem: Freemans', a firm operating a chain of local supermarkets, wished to explore the possibility of expanding their operations into the Syracuse metropolitan area. The company had experienced rapid growth in the area in which they operated, and felt that the area was saturated with supermarkets. In selecting an area in the Syracuse, New York standard metropolitan statistical area, the firm wanted to choose the county which had experienced the greatest economic growth and which appeared to have future development characteristics.

Source of Data: (1) *Census of Housing; 1960 and 1970—Detailed Housing Characteristics;* (2) *Census of Population; 1960 and 1970—General Population Characteristics;* (3) *Census of Population; 1960 and 1970—General Social and Economic Characteristics;* and (4) *Census of Business; Retail Trade—1963 and 1972.*

Assumption: Freeman's marketing department held preliminary discussions with the firm's management to determine which economic growth factors would most affect grocery store sales. Based upon its knowledge and that of management, the marketing department assumed that greatest growth market indicators are population, income, housing units, car ownership, and grocery store sales. Since the *Census of Business, Retail Sales* shows sales of establishments with and without payroll, the marketing department chose those with payroll, because those without accounted for only 6.2 percent of sales in the metropolitan area.

Procedure: (See calculations in Table D.)

(1) Oswego County showed greater growth in population and number of families (Columns 1 and 2) in 1970 over 1960, than either Madison or Onandaga Counties.

(2) An examination of median family income (Column 3) showed that Oswego County had grown 3.3 percent more rapidly than either of the other counties.

(3) Oswego County had the greatest percentage increase in housing units (Column 4) and continued to maintain the largest share of units occupied by owners (Column 5). While median rent in Oswego and Onondaga Counties increased by the same percentage (Column 6), it was felt that Oswego had a better growth potential due to its land development possibilities.

(4) Column 7 shows that Oswego County had the greatest decline in number of housing units without automobiles, which is also an indication of economic growth.

(5) Oswego County also displayed the greatest growth in grocery store sales. Based on percentage increase (Column 8), it grew 10 percent more than its nearest rival, Madison County.

Conclusion: The market factors analyzed showed that Oswego County had the greatest growth and should continue to offer future development potential. Selection of an exact site for each supermarket within the county would be determined by an analysis of data in *Census Tract Reports* and *Major Retail Center Reports* (both published by the Bureau of the Census), the usual on-site survey, and other sources and methods determined by management.

Table C. Number of Individual Income Tax Returns with an Adjusted Gross Income of $15,000 or More in 1971, and Advertising Expenditures Estimated by State, 1974

South Atlantic Census Region	Number of Returns (1)	Market Index (2)	Distribution of Advertising Expenditures (3)
Delaware	39,406	2.6	$ 3,900
Maryland	323,217	21.1	31,650
District of Columbia	44,123	2.9	4,350
Virginia	276,550	18.1	27,150
West Virginia	54,446	3.7	5,550
North Carolina	176,698	11.5	17,250
South Carolina	79,038	5.2	7,800
Georgia	195,907	12.8	19,200
Florida	337,954	22.1	33,150
Total	1,527,339	100.0	$150,000

Source: *Statistics of Income 1971: Individual Income Tax Returns,* Internal Revenue Service, Department of the Treasury.

Table D. Market Factors for Evaluating Location Factors of a Food Store in Syracuse, New York, Standard Metropolitan Statistica Area

County	Population [1] (number)	Families [1] (number)	Family median income [2] (dollars)	Occupied housing units [3] (number)	Percent owner occupied [3]	Median rent [3] (dollars)	Housing units without automobiles (number) [3]	Grocery store sales* [4] ($1,000)
	(1)	(2)	(3)	(4)	(5)	(6)	(7)	(8)
Madison								
1960 ------	54,635	13,282	5,451	15,236	74.4	70	11.5	
1970 ------	62,864	14,660	7,123	17,741	74.6	108	11.3	
Percent change	15.1	10.4	30.7	16.4	0.2	54.3	1.7	
1963 ------								17,694
1972 ------								28,116
Percent change								58.9
Onondaga								
1960 ------	423,028	06,065	6,691	124,090	64.5	81	18.4	
1970 ------	472,746	14,707	8,208	145,322	62.6	121	16.7	
Percentage change	11.8	8.1	22.7	17.1	2.9	49.3	9.2	
1963								137,345
1972								190,158
Percentage change								38.4
Oswego								
1960 ------	86,118	21,063	5,580	24,323	76.0	69	17.9	
1970 ------	100,897	24,057	7,479	29,179	76.1	103	12.6	
Percentage change	17.2	14.2	34.0	20.0	0.1	49.3	29.6	
1963 ------								28,548
1972 ------								48,152
Percentage change								68.7

*1972 data are not absolute they are indicative of type statistics which will appear in the 1972 Census of Business.
[1] *Census of Population, 1960 and 1970– General Population Characteristics.* U.S. Department of Commerce.
[2] *Census of Population, 1960 and 1970–General and Social Economic Characteristics.* U.S. Department of Commerce.
[3] *Census of Housing, 1960 and 1970–Detailed Housing Characteristics.* U.S. Department of Commerce.
[4] Census of Business, 1963 and 1972–Retail Trade. U.S. Department of Commerce.

PART D

Index

Editor's Note: References whose numbers are preceded by A will be found in the Introduction. Those preceded by C are located in the Appendix. All others are in Part B.